SOCIOLINGUISTIC PERSPECTIVES ON REGISTER

OXFORD STUDIES IN SOCIOLINGUISTICS
Edward Finegan, *General Editor*

Locating Dialect in Discourse
The Language of Honest Men and Bonnie Lassies in Ayr
Ronald K. S. Macaulay

English in Its Social Contexts
Essays in Historical Sociolinguistics
Edited by Tim W. Machan and Charles T. Scott

Coherence in Psychotic Discourse
Branca Telles Ribeiro

Gender and Conversational Interaction
Edited by Deborah Tannen

Sociolinguistic Perspectives on Register
Edited by Douglas Biber and Edward Finegan

SOCIOLINGUISTIC
PERSPECTIVES
ON REGISTER

Edited by

DOUGLAS BIBER

EDWARD FINEGAN

New York   Oxford

OXFORD UNIVERSITY PRESS

1994

Oxford University Press

Oxford   New York   Toronto
Delhi   Bombay   Calcutta   Madras   Karachi
Kuala Lumpur   Singapore   Hong Kong   Tokyo
Nairobi   Dar es Salaam   Cape Town
Melbourne   Auckland   Madrid

and associated companies in
Berlin   Ibadan

Published by Oxford University Press, Inc.
198 Madison Avenue, New York, New York 10016-4314

Oxford is a registered trademark of Oxford University Press, Inc.

Library of Congress Cataloging-in-Publication Data
Sociolinguistic perspectives on register / edited by Douglas Biber
and Edward Finegan.
p. cm.   Includes bibliographical references.
ISBN 0-19-508364-4
1. Register (Linguistics)   2. Sociolinguistics.
I. Biber, Douglas.   II. Finegan, Edward, 1940–
P302.815.S65   1994
306.4'4—dc20   92-44536

3 5 7 9   8 6 4 2

Printed in the United States of America
on acid-free paper

Series Foreword

Sociolinguistics is the study of language in use. Its special focus is on the relationships between language and society, and its principal concerns address linguistic variation across social groups and across the range of communicative situations in which women and men deploy their verbal repertoires. In short, sociolinguists examine language as it is constructed and co-constructed, shaped and reshaped, in the discourse of everyday life, and as it reflects and creates the social realities of that life.

While some linguists study the structure of sentences independent of their context (independent of who is speaking or writing and to whom, independent of what has preceded and what will follow, and independent of the setting, topic, and purposes of the discourse), sociolinguists investigate language as it is embedded in its social and situational contexts. Not surprisingly, among people who are *not* professional linguists virtually all linguistic interest likewise focuses on language in use, for it is there that linguistic patterns reflect the intricacies of social structure and mirror the situational and strategic influences that shape discourse.

In offering a platform for studies of language use in communities around the globe, Oxford Studies in Sociolinguistics invites significant treatments of discourse and of social dialects and registers, whether oral, written, or signed, whether treated synchronically or diachronically. The series hosts studies that are descriptive or theoretical, interpretive or analytical. While most volumes will report original research, a few will synthesize or interpret existing knowledge. All volumes aim for a style accessible not only to linguists but to other social scientists and humanists interested in language use. Occasionally, a volume may appeal beyond scholars to students and to educated readers keenly interested in the everyday discourse of human affairs—for example, the discourse of doctors or lawyers trying to engage clients with their specialist registers, or of women and men striving to grasp the sometimes baffling character of their shared interactions.

By providing a forum for innovative and important studies of language in use, Oxford Studies in Sociolinguistics aims to influence the agenda for linguistic research in the twenty-first century and, in the meantime, to provide an array of insightful and provocative analyses to help launch that agenda.

For the present volume in the series, Douglas Biber and I have solicited essays designed to highlight some of the important issues surrounding the still nascent study of register and register variation. The word *register* appears in the titles of very few books now listed in library catalogues, but it is my hope that *Sociolinguistic Perspectives on Register,* besides adding a title to that list, will encourage further inquiry into this critical arena of sociolinguistics.

Edward Finegan

Preface

Functional linguists, sociolinguists, and anthropological linguists have long argued that language by nature is communicative, social, and interactional. Many thus advocate a socially constituted linguistics, one that takes the language repertoire of a community to be an elemental observation about language.

Although the linguistic repertoire of a community has not always been central to sociolinguistic analyses, important observations about repertoire form part of almost every sociolinguistic report. For more than three decades now, the linguistic repertoire of speech communities—the inventory of their registers—has won increasing attention from linguists, and quite a few have put it at the center of their research programs, some attempting to sort out the relationship between social dialect variation and register variation.

We have commissioned the essays in this book with the hope that this collection will help stimulate several kinds of linguistic research: (1) the description of situated varieties of language around the world, with respect both to other varieties in a community's repertoire and to related varieties in other communities; (2) the design of suitable frameworks for register analysis and description, including the relationship among *registers, styles, genres, text types,* and *dialects;* and (3) the formulating of theories that integrate the significant aspects of language variation, both social and situational. We note too that debate about language standards—for English and many other languages—raises critically important social questions, which have too often been addressed as matters of dialect, as matters having to do with who speaks what. Adopting the view that standard varieties are better viewed as registers, as is increasingly done, requires analysis of registers and register variation as a critically important social matter, and we hope that this book makes a contribution there as well.

The present volume includes theoretical frameworks and empirical analyses, linguistic descriptions and explanations for existing patterns of variation. It offers several of the most complete studies of registers published to date—sports reportage and coaching language, dinner table narratives, personal ads. It treats languages in obsolescence and in their youth. It examines registers from languages around the globe: Tok Pisin, Somali, Korean, Gaelic, and English, among others. It contains both synchronic and diachronic perspectives, and it presents detailed analyses of both register variation and individual registers.

In 1964 Erving Goffman wrote about "the neglected situation." Today, in linguistics, the social situation is no longer neglected, but its critical influence on the shape of language, and on the patterns of language use by different groups of complex speech communities, remains too little understood. In the 1990s social situation and its influence on language form will be under scrutiny, and *Sociolinguistic Perspectives on Register* is intended to be a useful and provocative contribution to that discussion.

Flagstaff, AZ   D. B.
Los Angeles, CA   E. F.
January 1993

Contents

Contributors

Dwight Atkinson
  Department of Linguistics, University of Southern California
Douglas Biber
  Department of English, Northern Arizona University
Paul Bruthiaux
  Department of English, City Polytechnic of Hong Kong
Courtney B. Cazden
  Graduate School of Education, Harvard University
Charles A. Ferguson
  Department of Linguistics, Stanford University
Nancy C. Dorian
  Departments of German and Anthropology, Bryn Mawr College
Edward Finegan
  Department of Linguistics, University of Southern California
Mohamed Hared
  Ottawa, Ontario
Shirley Brice Heath
  Department of Linguistics, Stanford University
Alan Hudson
  Department of Linguistics, University of New Mexico
Yong-Jin Kim
  Department of English, Soong Sil University
Juliet N. A. Langman
  Charlottesville, Virginia
Faye McNair-Knox
  Division of Teacher Education, Virginia Commonwealth University
Elinor Ochs
  Department of TESL and Applied Linguistics, University of California, Los Angeles
John R. Rickford
  Department of Linguistics, Stanford University
Suzanne Romaine
  Merton College, University of Oxford

Sociolinguistic Perspectives on Register

Introduction

Situating Register in Sociolinguistics

DOUGLAS BIBER AND EDWARD FINEGAN

Sociolinguists range widely in their interests, and the term *sociolinguistics* has very broad application. Some observers draw a distinction between "the sociology of language," with a focus on sociological matters, and "sociolinguistics," with a focus on language. In many instances the same inquiry and the same analysis may be viewed by some as sociological and by others as linguistic. The definition of sociolinguistics offered in the standard linguistics lexicon (Crystal 1991) is broad: "A branch of linguistics which studies all aspects of language and society." In the definition, the word *and* portrays sociolinguistics at its broadest. Only the initial position of the word *language* suggests any priority, while *all* suggests the potential scope of inquiry. Preferring the preposition *in* to the conjunction *and*, one leading sociolinguistics journal bears the title *Language in Society,* suggesting a preference for studies whose principal focus rests on *language* rather than *society.* Another journal, more interested in larger questions of language use, calls itself the *International Journal of the Sociology of Language.*

It isn't our goal even to attempt to define sociolinguistics once and for all.[1] Any definition we might offer would risk overlooking important research, while no benefit would accrue to studies definitionally included. Nor does the attempt to characterize sociolinguistics definitively make much sense in a time of inter-disciplinary studies, when researchers trained in one field successfully practice in another, often producing work that is of value to both. Among scholars of our acquaintance whose work is generally regarded as sociolinguistic we count mostly linguists, but also sociologists, anthropologists, philologists, and a communications theorist, as well as persons trained in literary analysis and in particular languages. What links these investigators and unites their work is a shared focus on *language in use,* language as it functions in the everyday social and vocational lives of speakers and writers. It is this focus on *language in use* that we take to be central to any definition of sociolinguistics, and it includes written and signed language as well as speech.

Many areas of exploration have a footing in sociolinguistics (or are otherwise closely related to it), including cross-cultural and interethnic communication; conversation analysis; discourse analysis; speech act theory and pragmatics; diglossia, code switching, and other macroscopic aspects of the sociology of language; language planning; institutional linguistics (especially in education, law, and medicine); corpus linguistics; pidgins and creoles; language birth and language death; historical linguistics; language standardization; social relations (especially of power and solidarity). For a wide array of references to these various facets of language study in a social context, readers can consult Fasold (1984, 1990), Wardhaugh (1992), and Wolfson (1989).

If *sociolinguistics* is a wide-ranging term, *register* is equally tough to corral. Broadly conceived, a register is a language variety viewed with respect to its context of use. Invoking the dictionary again, *register* "refers to a variety of language defined according to its use in social situations" (Crystal 1991). There are many motivations for examining language varieties in their situations of use and many aspects of the social situation that might be the focus of particular register studies. Indeed, linguists interested in register may discover valuable analyses carried out by (and for) people who most definitely are not linguists. To cite a notable example, *The Language of the Law* (Mellinkoff 1963) was written by a practicing attorney principally for readers whose familiarity with legalese derived from daily use at the bar. *The Language of the Law* is not a law book, and the lenses through which it views language are decidedly not those of a linguist. Yet no linguist discussing registers of legal language will want to overlook it. Linguists currently doing register analysis may find useful descriptions of particular language varieties in several arenas, by no means limited to linguistics journals or to papers authored by linguists. As the references appended to the chapters of this volume amply document, linguists writing about registers have cause to cite a wide range of journals from a variety of fields, and scores of books that no one would regard as linguistic treatises.

In addition to the term *register*, the terms *genre, text type,* and *style* have been used to refer to language varieties associated with situational *uses*. All these terms are distinguished from *dialect*, which is used to refer to language varieties associated with groups of *users* (as determined by geographic region, education, social class, sex, and so on). In Britain and North America, there are relatively long research traditions focusing on registers and on dialects alike.

Interest in register variation grew from the merging of situational, social, and descriptive analyses by anthropological linguists such as Boas, Sapir, Malinowski, Whorf, Bloomfield, and Firth during the first half of the twentieth century. These observers typically focused on non-Western languages and cultures and occasionally examined language in different social contexts. Two important early studies focusing on situational variation are Malinowski's (1923) discussion of the "context of situation" and Firth's (1935) elaboration of that concept. Early in the century Boas had established the value of collecting and analyzing natural texts, and that practice became the norm for linguists such as Sapir, Kroeber, and Bloomfield. Predating the early studies of social dialect variation in the mid-1960s, researchers such as Ferguson, Gumperz, Halliday, and Hymes examined linguistic variation across social situations and communicative uses, as well as across speaker groups. In the late 1950s and the 1960s a number of papers and books appeared describing particular registers of various languages and the ways in which linguistic form is influenced by communicative purpose and the context of situation. These include studies by Ferguson on High and Low diglossic varieties and on baby talk, by Gumperz on the range of "argots" used in rural South Asian villages, by Brown and Gilman on the role of second-person pronouns in relationships of "power" and "solidarity," by Brown and Ford on American English address terms, by Leech on press advertising and on the language of poetry, and by Crystal and Davy on conversation, unscripted commentary, newspaper reporting, legal documents, and the language of religion. Hymes (1964), Pride and Holmes (1972), and Giglioli (1972) have collected many valuable papers from this period.

Numerous dialect studies were carried out over this same period. Early in this century, dialect studies focused on regional variation, with the goal of mapping the geographical distribution of pronunciations and lexical variants. Researchers concentrated on the speech of rural communities, disregarding urban centers on the ground that they involved "too much mobility and flux" (Chambers and Trudgill 1980:35). By the mid-1960s, Labov and other researchers had established that patterns of variation in urban dialects are also highly systematic and that linguistic variants can be correlated with socioeconomic status and other demographic characteristics. Since that time, studies of social dialect variation in urban centers have multiplied, overshadowing the earlier focus on regional variation. For an overview of dialect research, see Chambers and Trudgill (1980).

Although social dialectologists are interested primarily in the nature of linguistic variation across social groups, they have also sometimes examined data representing a type of register variation, referred to as *styles,* collected as part of the sociolinguistic interview (e.g., Labov 1972, Trudgill 1974).[2] Other social dialect studies have incorporated different types of register variation. For example, Fischer (1958) distinguished among three levels of formality in his interviews, while Wald and Shopen (1981) distinguished between joking style and arguing style at Thanksgiving dinners. Bell (1984) distinguished among styles according to aspects of "audience design."

Regrettably, sociolinguistics textbooks have tended to overlook the rich tradition of register studies. The main register-related studies described in most sociolinguistics textbooks deal with *style* in the context of sociolinguistic interviews; address terms (in relation to power and solidarity); and conversation analysis.[3] According to Rickford and McNair-Knox (this volume), a similar trend is characteristic of many quantitative sociolinguists, who "came to ignore the casual/careful distinction—and to attend less and less to stylistic variation in general."

We attribute the neglect of register to a combination of several factors:

1. The development of anthropological linguistics, descriptive linguistics, functional linguistics, and sociolinguistics as distinct subfields, resulting in less cross-fertilization of ideas.

2. The prevailing view among linguists, strengthened by a diminished interest in historical linguistics, that spoken language is the basic or "true" form of language (e.g., Aronoff 1985:28).

This view has been slightly modified by many sociolinguists to the position that conversation is the basic form of language. Both views overlook written and signed varieties, as well as other spoken varieties, assuming that they are derivative from the "basic" spoken language.

    3. The related notion that analysis of written varieties is a literary concern rather than a linguistic one (historical linguistics excepted).

Thus the analysis of *genre, register,* and *stylistics* is seen as relating to written varieties and as based on literary and rhetorical interests rather than linguistic ones.

    4. The discounting within sociolinguistics of the significance of register differences in a speech community, and the extent and social importance of the linguistic differences associated with those register ranges.

One hallmark of this disregard is the neglect of the topic in sociolinguistic textbooks, mentioned previously. Another is the claim that "style" variation derives from "social dialect" variation, held by some because the range of variability associated with "style" is believed to be "always smaller than that along the dimension associated with social status" (Preston 1991:33, based on Bell 1984). This conclusion rests largely on consideration of "attention to speech" differences as manifested in sociolinguistic interviews, and some researchers regard it as dubious when judged relative to the full range of spoken and written registers in a community. Coupland (1988:55) captures the point when he says about the interview situation that it is "clearly able to capture only a tiny part of that variation in language that may be labelled 'stylistic' or 'contextual'."

    5. A preoccupation, among some sociolinguists, with the *linguistic variable* as the primary analytical construct, a preoccupation that has restricted the scope of much analysis to semantically neutral phonological variants.

As registers differ from social dialects precisely in that they serve different purposes, topics, and situations, they naturally vary in content as well as in form. Speakers do not typically "say the same thing" in conversation as in lectures, reports, academic papers, and congratulatory telegrams. Thus variation across registers involves *different* linguistic features, rather than semantically neutral variants of a single feature.

    6. The lack of a paradigmatic, or even dominant, methodological and theoretical framework for the analysis of registers.

As a result, even register analysts can fail to recognize the importance of individual studies in contributing to an overarching view of register variation.

    Despite neglect in sociolinguistics textbooks, register studies have clearly not been ignored. In addition to the long history of studies mentioned above, registers have continued to be analyzed by distinguished linguists, including Ferguson, Gumperz, and Hymes. Romaine (1980, 1982) has developed a sociohistorical approach, which combines analysis of register variation and dialect patterns in order to understand historical change. Labov has addressed register in his analyses of narrative structures (Labov and Waletsky 1967) and therapeutic discourse (Labov and Fanshel 1977). Numerous other linguists have explored register, and the chapter by Atkinson and Biber (this volume) surveys the extensive research on the subject.

What unites the work of linguists working on register is the centrality of text viewed in its context of social situation. Register *entails* text and implies a relationship between text and context. Register analysts explore the link between linguistic expression and social situation, with a view toward explanation. Hence neither sentences independent of their text nor texts independent of their social context will suffice; word lists will not suffice; intuitions will not suffice. Only a text suffices as an object of register analysis, and knowledge of the context in which it was created and the purpose for which it was intended is likewise crucial. There are no sentences in register analysis unless they form part of a text embedded in a social context. For spoken registers, the text is typically a transcript. For written registers, the text is given. In register analysis, different kinds of transcripts serve different purposes, as the chapters in this volume demonstrate.

Recently, Hymes (1984) argued that the analysis of register variation—"verbal repertoire" in his terms—should become the major focus of research within sociolinguistics. Hymes (1984:44) underscores the basic fact of sociolinguistic variation—that "no human being talks the same way all the time. . . . At the very least, a variety of registers and styles is used and encountered"—and he further argues that the "sociolinguistic perspective . . . has the possibility of taking the lead in transforming the study of language, through developing and consolidating the systematic study of verbal repertoire." Ure (1982:5) also remarks about the ubiquity of register variation, "each language community has its own system of registers . . . corresponding to the range of activities in which its members normally engage."

Given the central place of linguistic repertoire in human language, register variation should occupy a central place in (socio)linguistic research and theory. As Hymes (1984:44) has written:

> The abilities of individuals and the composite abilities of communities cannot be understood except by making "verbal repertoire," not "language," the central scientific notion. To do so requires a mode of description in linguistics which can address the organization of linguistic features in styles, that is, in ways which cut across the standard levels of linguistic structure. And it requires a mode of social description which can connect features of role, status, activity, setting, and the like with relevant features of voice and discourse.

The present book represents a step toward these research goals. It offers several sociolinguistic perspectives on registers and register variation, as well as efforts to integrate register analyses and social dialect analyses into a coherent theoretical framework. The book is organized into five parts: I. General Issues; II. Individual Registers; III. Register Variation; IV. Registers, Social Dialects, and Sociolinguistic Theory; and V. A Survey of Empirical Register Studies.

Part I deals with general descriptive, methodological, and theoretical issues relating to the analysis of register. In his chapter, Charles Ferguson identifies and describes working assumptions about conventionalization in relation to the analysis of dialects, registers, genres, varieties, and conversational interaction. He discusses issues of multiple determination (single linguistic features can simultaneously mark all kinds of language variation), attitudes, and the importance of diachronic analyses. Douglas Biber's chapter sketches a comprehensive analytical framework for register studies. It identifies several requirements of such a framework, surveys previous frameworks, and proposes a more explicit framework capable of characterizing the differing levels of generality among registers and the continuous relations among situational and linguistic parameters.

Part II offers exemplary studies of particular registers, relating them to various theoretical issues. The chapters in this section present analyses of registers in both developing languages and well-established languages, including some of the most complete descriptions of individual registers published to date. Suzanne Romaine, in her chapter on the language of sports reportage, describes the early development of a single register of Tok Pisin, a language itself in the relatively early stages of development. In addition to providing a detailed analysis of sports reportage as it emerged in the Tok Pisin newspaper *Wantok*, Romaine's study is notable in that it adopts an explicitly historical perspective, describing possible universal characteristics of sports reporting that may result from the shared cross-linguistic purposes of the register. The chapter by Shirley Brice Heath and Judith Langman describes another sports-related register: coaching language in English, specifically the language of baseball, softball, and basketball coaches. Heath and Langman locate the register situationally and then describe several characteristic linguistic features; their study is distinctive in that it includes analysis of characteristic discourse-level features in addition to syntactic features. They also address the implications of the observed patterns for recent coaching activities in education and business.

The chapter by Elinor Ochs challenges the stereotype that narratives of personal experience present recapitulations of past experience. She shows instead that narratives often deal with possible future experiences and, through a detailed analysis of dinner table conversations, analyzes various ways in which past, present, and future time experiences are interwoven into coherent discourse patterns in personal narratives. In the next chapter, Paul Bruthiaux provides an in-depth analysis of the simplified register of personal ads. Following in the tradition of Ferguson's analyses of baby talk and foreigner talk, Bruthiaux describes several linguistic characteristics of the personal ads register and relates his findings to those of other simplified registers.

Part III presents studies on register variation, presenting both synchronic and diachronic perspectives, and describing the patterns of variation in developing, mature, and dying languages. Two of the chapters in this section illustrate the multidimensional approach to register variation as applied to Korean and Somali. The chapter by Yong-Jin Kim and Douglas Biber analyzes the patterns of variation among spoken and written registers in Korean. This chapter shows that while several Korean dimensions of variation are similar to those in English, other dimensions relating to the presentation of self reflect the particular cultural priorities of

Korean. The chapter by Douglas Biber and Mohamed Hared on Somali is one of the few studies to date that analyzes register variation from a diachronic perspective. It presents three dimensions that distinguish among spoken and written registers in Somali and uses those dimensions to trace the initial creation and evolution of press registers, describing the radical influence of the addition of written registers on a developing language. When added to previously published studies on English and Tuvaluan, the analysis of the dimensions of variation in Korean and Somali provides a foundation for cross-linguistic generalizations concerning the patterns of register variation among spoken and written registers.

As a complement to Romaine's analysis of the birth of a register in Tok Pisin, and Biber and Hared's study on the initial evolution of written registers in Somali, Nancy Dorian's chapter takes up the subject of register variation in a dying language. Dorian examines the patterns of register variation in East Sutherland Gaelic, an isolated, minority-language community with essentially no socioeconomic differentiation among speakers. She asks whether the kinds and extent of register variation in a dying language differ markedly from those found in vital, urban vernaculars.

Part IV addresses broader issues concerning the relation of register variation to other kinds of linguistic variation, and the place of register variation in a comprehensive theory of sociolinguistics. The first two chapters deal with the influence of participants on the observed patterns of variation. Under the rubric *style shifting,* John Rickford and Faye McNair-Knox examine addressee-influenced and topic-influenced register variation. After their description of the general neglect of style within American variationist studies, the authors present a detailed analysis of the patterns of variation observed in four sociolinguistic interviews of the same person. In this study, Rickford and McNair-Knox convincingly argue for the importance of "audience design" and topic as sources of linguistic variation.

Courtney Cazden, in her chapter, examines similar conditioning factors from a different perspective. She returns to the theme developed in her earlier paper on the "neglected situation" in analyses of children's language use in educational circumstances, claiming that analysis of situational factors must complement generalizations made on the basis of cultural background and social class. On the basis of a survey of recent studies, she posits a fundamental distinction in the ways that children from different social groups respond to register variation associated with different task formats and participant structures.

In his chapter, Alan Hudson deals with the place of register variation in the sociology of language, tackling the issue of the extent to which diglossia is a special case of register variation or a distinct linguistic phenomenon. He surveys the literature on diglossia and other types of functionally conditioned variation, showing that in many respects the patterns of variation across registers are closely related to the differences between high and low diglossic varieties. The chapter by Edward Finegan and Douglas Biber argues that sociolinguistics must broaden the scope of its inquiry to include the full range of social and situational variation within communities. The authors rehearse the findings of previous sociolinguistic studies to show that certain patterns of variation are widespread, having the same systematic distributions across dialects, speech styles, and registers. To account for these patterns,

Finegan and Biber demonstrate that register variation inheres in communicative situations, and they argue that certain patterns of dialect variation are derivable from these more basic patterns of register variation.

Part V concludes the volume with a survey of register studies. Dwight Atkinson and Douglas Biber provide an extensive overview of empirical register studies, classifying each according to its chief research goals. Studies are grouped in four main classes—synchronic and diachronic analyses of individual registers and of register variation—and are also distinguished as to the nature of their data (whether relying on natural or elicited discourse), the character of the analysis (whether quantitative or qualitative), and the level of linguistic analysis.

Taken together, the chapters of this volume illustrate the wide scope of register analysis. Included are descriptions and explanations, theoretical and practical approaches, programmatic and unusually detailed visions. The chapters treat languages belonging to several language families: English, Tok Pisin, Korean, Somali, and Gaelic are directly examined, while Arabic, French, Portuguese, Spanish, Nukulaelae Tuvaluan, and others are discussed. Both written and spoken registers are represented, and a wide range of situations is analyzed—from personal ads in newspapers to family dinner table conversation, from written sports reportage to the language of coaches on the field. Some chapters take a diachronic approach, while most treat their registers synchronically; some chapters analyze the patterns of register variation, while others present detailed analyses of individual registers. Languages are examined in the earliest stages of development and in obsolescence. The communities studied differ widely, from a fishing village in Scotland to urban Papua New Guinea, from Mogadishu to Seoul to Port Moresby to Los Angeles. Finally, the contexts in which the texts are situated differ greatly as well, from relatively decontextualized newspaper articles to the intimacy of family talk at the dinnertable.

It is our hope that the sociolinguistic perspectives on register and register variation that are represented in this book, though only a few of many possible ones, will help stimulate further research into register and register variation and into the ways in which various aspects of sociolinguistic variation are related.

Notes

1. A stumbling block with the word *sociolinguistics* that has troubled some researchers is its suggestion that investigations of the relationship between language and society are "marked" in some way, *a kind of* linguistics that is less than central to the field. To some, the word *sociolinguistics* suggests that there can exist linguistic analyses that are asocial, and many sociolinguists regard asocial views of language as oxymoronic. Thus Hymes (1974) foresees a day when the prefix *socio-* in *socio*linguistics will be redundant. Labov (1972:xiii) resisted the word *sociolinguistics* "because it implies that there can be a successful linguistic theory or practice which is not social." He had earlier (Labov 1966:v) approved of the word in those instances when it "refers to the use of data from the speech community to solve problems of linguistic theory," but, he said, it is "more frequently used to suggest a new interdisciplinary field—the comprehensive description of the relations of language and society," and this he thought "an unfortunate notion, foreshadowing a long series of purely

descriptive studies with little bearing on the central theoretical problems of linguistics or of sociology." (Cf. Andresen 1990 and Newmeyer 1986 for discussion of autonomous and social orientations in linguistics.)

2. Studies that include analysis of both social dialects and styles are important in that they allow analysis of the parallel patterns of variation across social groups and situations, but they are limited in that these styles are all part of the sociolinguistic interview, differing principally with respect to topic and the amount of attention paid to speech (and they are typically analyzed with respect to a single linguistic feature).

3. In the revised edition of Trudgill's (1983) *Sociolinguistics: An Introduction to Language and Society,* one chapter is given over to "Language in Context," while the relationships among language and sex, social class, and ethnic group have a chapter each. In the index, *register* and *style* each have two pages referenced. Hudson (1980) gives a few pages to register, principally so as to distinguish it from dialect, the central focus of his book *Sociolinguistics.* In Wardhaugh's *An Introduction to Sociolinguistics* (1992), the index cites two pages under *register* and ten under *styles.* There is a small section on styles and registers in the chapter covering "Language, Dialects and Varieties," although elsewhere separate treatment is indeed given to other influences of situation on language form. The index in Fasold's *Sociolinguistics of Language* (1990) cites three pages for *style stratification* but does not have an entry for *register* or *style.*

References

Andresen, Julie Tetel. 1990. *Linguistics in America 1769–1924: A Critical History.* London: Routledge.

Aronoff, Mark. 1985. "Orthography and Linguistic Theory." *Language* 61:28–72.

Bell, Allan. 1984. "Language Style as Audience Design." *Language in Society* 13:145–204.

Chambers, J. K., and Peter Trudgill. 1980. *Dialectology.* Cambridge: Cambridge University Press.

Crystal, David. 1991. *A Dictionary of Linguistics and Phonetics,* 3rd ed. Oxford: Basil Blackwell.

Coupland, Nikolas. 1988. *Dialect in Use: Sociolinguistic Variation in Cardiff English.* Cardiff: University of Wales Press.

Fasold, Ralph. 1984. *The Sociolinguistics of Society.* Oxford: Basil Blackwell.

———. 1990. *The Sociolinguistics of Language.* Oxford: Basil Blackwell.

Firth, J. R. 1935. "The Technique of Semantics." *Transactions of the Philological Society.* Pp. 36–72.

Fischer, John L. 1958. "Social Influences in the Choice of a Linguistic Variant." *Word* 14:47–56.

Giglioli, Pier Paolo, ed. 1972. *Language and Social Context.* New York: Penguin.

Hudson, R. A. 1980. *Sociolinguistics.* Cambridge: Cambridge University Press.

Hymes, Dell, ed. 1964. *Language in Culture and Society.* New York: Harper and Row.

———. 1984. "Sociolinguistics: Stability and Consolidation." *International Journal of the Sociology of Language* 45:39–45.

Labov, William. 1966. *The Social Stratification of English in New York City.* Washington, DC: Center for Applied Linguistics.

———. 1969. "The Logic of Nonstandard English." *Georgetown Monographs on Language and Linguistics* 22:1–31. Excerpted in Giglioli, ed. Pp. 179–215.

———. 1972. *Sociolinguistic Patterns.* Philadelphia: University of Pennsylvania Press.

Labov, William, and Joshua Waletsky. 1967. "Narrative Analysis." In June Helm, ed.,

Essays on the Verbal and Visual Arts. Seattle: University of Washington Press. Pp. 12–44.

Labov, William, and David Fanshel. 1977. *Therapeutic Discourse*. New York: Academic Press.

Malinowski, Bronislaw. 1923. "The Problem of Meaning in Primitive Languages." Supplementary essay in C. K. Ogden and I. A. Richards, *The Meaning of Meaning*. New York: Harcourt, Brace. Pp. 296–336.

Mellinkoff, David. 1963. *The Language of the Law*. Boston: Little, Brown.

Newmeyer, Frederick J. 1986. *Linguistic Theory in America*, 2nd ed. San Diego: Academic Press.

Preston, Dennis R. 1991. "Sorting Out the Variables in Sociolinguistic Theory." *American Speech* 66:33–56.

Pride, J. B., and Janet Holmes, eds. 1972. *Sociolinguistics*. New York: Penguin.

Romaine, Suzanne. 1980. "The Relative Clause Marker in Scots English: Diffusion, Complexity, and Style as Dimensions of Syntactic Change." *Language in Society* 9:221–47.

———. 1982. *Socio-Historical Linguistics: Its Status and Methodology*. Cambridge: Cambridge University Press.

Trudgill, Peter. 1974. *The Social Differentiation of English in Norwich*. Cambridge: Cambridge University Press.

———. 1983. *Sociolinguistics: An Introduction to Language and Society,* rev. ed. New York: Penguin. [1st ed. 1974 under the title *Sociolinguistics: An Introduction*].

Ure, Jean. 1982. "Introduction: Approaches to the Study of Register Range." *International Journal of the Sociology of Language* 35:5–23.

Wald, Benji, and Timothy Shopen. 1981. "A Researcher's Guide to the Sociolinguistic Variable (ING)." In Timothy Shopen and Joseph M. Williams, eds., *Style and Variables in English*. Cambridge, MA: Winthrop. Pp. 219–49.

Wardhaugh, Ronald. 1992. *An Introduction to Sociolinguistics*, 2nd ed. Oxford: Basil Blackwell. [1st ed. 1986]

Wolfson, Nessa. 1989. *Perspectives: Sociolinguistics and TESOL*. Cambridge, MA: Newbury House.

I

GENERAL ISSUES

1

Dialect, Register, and Genre: Working Assumptions About Conventionalization

Charles A. Ferguson

1. Introduction

In this chapter I attempt to make explicit a number of working assumptions about conventionalization that seem to be implicit in sociolinguistic research touching on dialect variation, register variation, genre identification, and verbal interaction. In doing so I hope also to clarify some of the basic concepts of sociolinguistic research for students of human language phenomena. In recent years researchers and theorists operating from a number of different perspectives have come to make use of such terms as *dialect, register, genre,* and *conversation* in ways that sometimes cause confusion. The sociolinguistic perspective has, of course, no monopoly on correctness or truth or insight into the human condition. Also, conceptual confusion may sometimes signal the emergence of new and useful ways of thinking. Nevertheless, I am inclined to think that clarification of this one perspective may be of help in reducing some of the unnecessary and unhelpful confusion that appears in cross-disciplinary studies dealing with conventionalization in language.

Of the various fundamental and mysterious processes involved in the use of human language, one of the most fundamental and most mysterious is the process of conventionalization, that is, the process by which members of a community somehow come to share the sound-meaning pairings that constitute their means of verbal communication, in spite of the fact that no two speakers speak exactly the same way and the shared language keeps changing. Human language, although based on a species-specific innate ability to develop and use this special form of communication, is nevertheless largely a matter of convention, that is, an implicit contract among a community of users of a language variety that certain expressions will mean certain things when used in certain combinations under certain social conditions. Just how this 'contract' is constantly being achieved, maintained, and

This paper is essentially the content of the opening lectures of the course "Register, Genre, and Style" offered at the Linguistic Institute held at Stanford University in summer 1987.

changed is the problem of conventionalization.[1] One method of attack on the problem is to examine types of variation and change that occur. Four kinds of variation that have been identified and studied will be examined here in the attempt to clarify sociolinguistic working assumptions.

One of the kinds of variation noticed very early in human history is the way that people differ in their speech (and writing) depending on where they come from or where they belong in their society: dialect variation. The term *dialect* itself comes from ancient Greek, and insightful observations and comments about dialect variation have appeared in many societies and languages over the centuries. The systematic study of dialect variation and its historical development probably began, however, with eighteenth-century Chinese linguistic analyses of much earlier rhyming dictionaries, and then again, independently, with the construction of dialect atlases in late nineteenth-century Germany and France. Studies of English dialect variation in the form of descriptions of particular dialects and dictionaries of dialect words began at the turn of the twentieth century, but dialect atlases of English in the Continental style began only in 1930 in North America and 1948 in Great Britain. Introductory textbooks in English devoted to the general field of dialectology, as opposed to studies of English dialect variation, did not appear until the 1980s (Chambers and Trudgill 1980, Petyt 1984). International professional journals in the field are well established (e.g., *Zeitschrift für Dialektologie und Linguistik*). An example of a paper on dialect analysis from my own work is Ferguson (1973). There I characterized the variation in the pronunciation of earlier 'short *a*' in Philadelphia English in order (1) to show how in this particular respect the phonology of the English of Philadelphia differs from that of other varieties of English, (2) to attempt an explanation of how this characteristic of Philadelphia English arose, and (3) to begin to fit this bit of dialect variation into the larger picture of dialect variation and language change in the whole English-speaking world and to learn about the processes of variation and change in human language in general.

Another kind of variation is the linguistic difference that correlates with different occasions of use. People speak differently depending on whether they are addressing someone older or younger, of the same sex or opposite sex, of the same or higher or lower status, and so on; whether they are speaking on a formal occasion or casually; whether they are participating in a religious ritual, a sports event, or a courtroom scene. The first systematic analysis of this kind of variation, which came to be called register variation, began in Great Britain in the 1960s and is still active (cf. Ellis and Ure 1969, Ghadessy 1988). No general textbook has appeared[2] and no professional journal has been established, but the extensive publications in German on *Fachsprachen* 'occupational languages' and in English on 'Language for Special Purposes' (mostly on commercial and scientific registers of English) are close to register analysis. An example of a paper on register analysis from my own work is Ferguson (1983), in which I characterized syntactic aspects of the register of sports announcer talk in American English, in order (1) to show how in this particular respect this variety differs from other kinds of talk in American English, (2) to call for further research on this register and other kinds of register variation in English, and (3) to begin to fit this bit of register variation into the larger picture of register variation, including the processes by which structural features of language are adjusted in response to different occasions of use and different communicative functions, both in English and more generally.

The analysis of different kinds of literary texts, including their structures and uses, goes back to Aristotle's *Poetics,* and the study of genres, as these 'kinds' came to be called, has been active from ancient times to the present. In the decades after World War II many scholars tended to deemphasize, neglect, or deny the usefulness or even the possibility of genre analysis. In the 1970s, however, for various reasons genre analysis and genre theory became the focus of much literary research. Along with this resurgence of interest came a general recognition that genres in the sense of discourse types or message-forms (Hymes 1972:59–60) exist just as much in nonliterary spoken or written 'texts' as in literary texts, and some of the most insightful studies of genres and the principles behind the emergence and persistence of genres have come from folklorists, linguists, and discourse analysts of various approaches as well as literary scholars (cf. Bakhtin 1986, Fowler 1982, Todorov 1990). The literature on genre analysis is extensive, and at least one professional journal (*Genre*) is devoted primarily to this field. An example of a paper on genre analysis from my own work is Ferguson (1976), in which I characterized the form and content of the traditional Latin prayer in the mass of the Western church as well as some of its translations into other languages at the time of the Reformation and more recently. The purpose was to raise the issue of genre formation and the linguistic locus of genre descriptions.

These first three types of variation assume change over time in individual behavior (including processes of acquisition) and in processes of conventionalization in the community, that is, changes in shared patterns of language structure and use. They are, however, relatively global and static in conceptualization in that they do not focus on changes as they take place in the course of episodes of interaction such as conversations. This more local kind of variability is studied in conversational analysis of various kinds. In the course of a conversation, two participants may, for example, change the forms of address they use to each other, code switch from one language variety to another, or shift various structural features in accordance with their reactions to each other's messages and their own conversational strategies.

Conversation analysis, which studies such phenomena along with other language behavior such as the principles of turn-taking and the expression of deference, is of relatively recent origin, not really getting started until adequate means of recording became available. Chapter 6 of Levinson (1983) offers a convenient summary of this kind of research, and several readers and introductory textbooks have appeared (e.g., Goodwin 1981, Schenkein 1978). An example of a work of my own that includes conversation analysis done by others is Ferguson (1991), in which I examined mismatches in politeness agreement in conversational exchange in modern Persian and in Brazilian Portuguese, which have been studied through analysis of recorded conversations as well as analysis of attempts at realistic representations of conversation in literary works. The purpose of my study was (1) to show how microanalysis of ongoing conversations is a necessary complement to macroanalysis of sociolinguistic phenomena and (2) to suggest that pragmatically conditioned 'exceptions' to syntactic rules may coincide with long-term syntactic changes in progress.

An important aspect of any analysis of variation as part of the conventionalization process is the identification of attitudes held by speakers with regard to variant forms. All users of language in all speech communities apparently hold evaluative attitudes toward variant forms: some variants are regarded as 'better' or 'more beautiful' or 'more appropriate' or 'more correct' than others, either in an absolute sense or for use by certain people under certain conditions. Language change, that is, that aspect of conventionalization by which certain variants spread at the expense of others, is intimately connected with speakers' evaluative attitudes, and the analysis of language attitudes in relation to change is correspondingly important. An example of a work of my own that examines evaluative attitudes toward language is Ferguson (1977), in which I compared Indonesia, Israel, North India, and to a lesser extent Sweden on a set of factors that were likely to affect outcomes of official efforts at language planning in the area of lexicon. Factors discussed included grammatical and lexical structure, communicative functions of different variants, and language users' evaluative attitudes toward various languages and features of word formation in newly created lexical items. The goal was to understand the factors that make some neologisms succeed and others fail.

Finally, it is not possible to talk about conventionalization in a meaningful way without including a diachronic dimension. In one instance, this diachronic dimension refers to the way a child gradually comes to share many features of the ambient language, and in another instance it refers to the way a speaker of one variety comes to share features of a different variety (even a different language) with which he or she comes in contact. Perhaps the most challenging instance, however, is in what is usually called language change, that is, the way shared features of a speech community change more or less together so that communicative continuity is maintained in spite of the changes. Since the early work in modern linguistics was diachronic in focus there is an enormous literature on the diachrony of Indo-European languages and other language families as well as standard textbooks on the general field (e.g., Bynon 1977, Hock 1986). Although there are several journals devoted to the general field (e.g., *Diachronica*), there is only one, recently established, that focuses specifically on variation in relation to diachrony (*Language Variation and Change*). An example of my own work that explicitly analyzes diachrony is Ferguson (1990), in which I investigated sound changes from [s] to [h], and vice versa, in a number of speech communities of different languages and different times and places; the purpose was to discover favored patterns of change in terms of the phonetic features involved and the pathways of language change through the community.

Let us turn now to the specific working assumptions underlying sociolinguistic research on types of variation as manifestations of conventionalization.

2. Dialect

The basic working assumption implicit in sociolinguistic study of dialect variation is A.

A. *A group that operates regularly in a society as a functional element* (e.g., in terms of physical location, marriage patterns, or economic, religious, or other interactional behavior) *will tend to develop identifying markers of language structure and language use, different from the language of other social groups.*

The word *tend* here is intended to indicate that individual speakers will from time to time accommodate their speech in various ways to the speech of those with whom they interact frequently, those they see as belonging to a social group that they see themselves as belonging to, and those whom they see for one reason or another as appropriate models of behavior. This assumption does not entail any notion of exact parallelism between sociocultural phenomena and language phenomena; even less does it entail the notion that sociocultural phenomena 'cause' or are directly 'reflected in' language phenomena. After all, language phenomena are themselves sociocultural phenomena and are in part constitutive of the very social groups recognized by the participants or identified by analysts.[3]

For me the classical paper on this kind of analysis is still Gumperz (1958), in which a linguist studied the linguistic variation (phonological, morphological, and lexical) in the Hindi of a village in North India and attempted to relate the variation to various kinds of social groupings in that village. After eliminating the occasional use of regional standard and national standard forms of Hindi as out of his purview, Gumperz found six clusters of features (i.e., six different *dialects*) of vernacular Hindi used in a village of five thousand inhabitants, belonging to some thirty-one caste groups in the village. The linguistic stratification correlated in a very rough way with the caste stratification in that three of the dialects were used by the members of the 'touchable' castes and the other three were used each by one of the three 'untouchable' castes. One of the 'touchable' dialects was used only by certain Rajputs (dominant caste in numbers and landowning) who lived in two of the seven residential districts into which the village was divided. Another of the 'touchable' dialects was used by villagers of various castes regarded by their fellow villagers as 'old-fashioned'. The remaining 'touchable' dialect was the majority variety in the village.

Gumperz discussed children's play groups, adult intercaste friendships, details of ritual hierarchization, and settlement history as relevant factors in understanding the validity of the social groups and the origins of the linguistic differences. He found that the villagers were aware of some of the linguistic differences and unaware of others; some they attributed to particular characteristics of the speakers and others not. In short, the analysis showed typical complexities of the relations among linguistic variation, social groupings, and the membership of the inhabitants in overlapping and criss-crossing 'communities' defined by shared features of language structure, language use, and language attitudes. The complex relationship between caste stratification and linguistic variation has repeatedly been explored in South Asia (cf. Bean 1974, Pandit 1972), and it provides an instructive example of both the value of the sociolinguistic working assumption A and the dangers of assuming a simple, direct relationship between any social grouping and language differentiation.

Like all other kinds of language variation, dialect variation changes through time. Both the social groupings and the language markings change, and the relations between the two change. The problem of dialect variation in language development is not often studied, although children often are exposed to dialect variation between different speakers of the ambient language, and it may be assumed that they may select one input as opposed to another or may innovate intermediate or divergent forms (cf. Local 1978, Payne 1976).

3. Register

The basic working assumption implicit in sociolinguistic study of register variation is B.

> **B.** *A communication situation that recurs regularly in a society* (in terms of participants, setting, communicative functions, and so forth) *will tend over time to develop identifying markers of language structure and language use, different from the language of other communication situations.*

People participating in recurrent communication situations tend to develop similar vocabularies, similar features of intonation, and characteristic bits of syntax and phonology that they use in those situations. Some of these registral features, such as special terms for recurrent objects and events, and formulaic sequences or 'routines', seem to facilitate speedy communication; other features apparently serve to mark the register, establish feelings of rapport, and serve other purposes similar to the accommodation that influences dialect formation. There is no mistaking the strong tendency for individuals and co-communicators to develop register variation along many dimensions. This basic characteristic of human language appears very early in the development of the individual child and is fundamental in understanding the process of conventionalization in speech communities.[4]

In an interim report on a project investigating eleven *sublanguages* of written English and French, Kittredge (1982) discusses four sample registers: the language of aviation hydraulics, cookbook recipes, regional weather forecasts, and stock market reports. Each shows unique features of lexicon, lexical collocations, sentence structures, and intersentential linking devices. Unfortunately, register studies do not usually explore the origin and development of the register variation they investigate, an approach that might offer a great deal in learning more about how the conventionalization develops.

In a rare exception of a register study with a diachronic component (Culy 1987), we learn a diachronic fact about the cookbook recipe register. Several observers have noted that a striking feature of recipe language is the omission of definite object noun phrases, or—as Culy puts it—"zero anaphors as direct objects, for example in 'Beat [∅] until stiff.'" Culy examined English-language cookbooks from the fifteenth century to the present and found that "the use of zeros . . . increased dramatically over time," especially in the period between 1830 and 1880. A speculative interpretation might be that the language of cookbook recipes was at first not very different from other written varieties of English, that it began to develop as the circulation of books increased, and that it took definitive form in the midnineteenth century with mass literacy and the popularity of cookbooks; such an interpretation would require of course a great deal of evidence to validate. Kittredge too notes the omission of definite articles in recipe language, a feature that characterizes many so-called simplified registers of English (Ferguson 1983). French recipe language shares both of these English register features to some extent, but the incidence of the omissions is much lower, and the history of the register, to my knowledge, has not been studied.

4. Genre

The basic working assumption implicit in sociolinguistic study of genre variation is C.

C. *A message type that recurs regularly in a community* (in terms of semantic content, participants, occasions of use, and so on) *will tend over time to develop an identifying internal structure, differentiated from other message types in the repertoire of the community.*

One of the fundamental characteristics of human language behavior is the formation of conventionalized message-forms, whether it is the form of the riddles exchanged by primary school pupils, the psalm-form of Hebrew religious poetry, or the legal form of a power-of-attorney document. For centuries the study of message-forms or genres was the province of the literary scholar and tended to have a universalist perspective, continuing the Aristotelian Greek-centered analysis of poetic creation. Only in the present century did it become clear that genre formation is rooted in everyday language and that a universal systematic of genre analysis must be based on broad cross-cultural and historical study. Every genre, whether literary or nonliterary, emerges in a specific sociohistorical context.

Sociolinguistic research on genre has been limited in scope, although the concept is widely accepted. A sociolinguistically oriented standard textbook on discourse analysis (Brown and Yule 1983) gives an indication of the accepted but unanalyzed status of genre in the field. The concept of message-form (the term *genre* is used interchangeably in the book) is defined only as 'what form is intended' (p. 38), and twenty-five examples are casually offered through the book in connection with various observations about other specific issues of discourse analysis. The twenty-five examples are collected and alphabetized here, as typical of the kind of examples of genres often cited in sociolinguistic work (including my own).

chat	love-letter
children's first reader	news broadcast
conversation	newspaper article
debate	nineteenth-century novel
description of the layout	obituary
of one's apartment	prayer
directions in a strange town	recipe
encyclopedic entry	repair manual

epic poem	salesperson's routine
examination questions in chemical	scientific textbook writing
engineering at degree level	scolding
fairy story	sermon
interview	sonnet

Unfortunately no space is given to the question of how to determine what constitutes a genre, and no example is given of the description of a genre, although several phenomena are mentioned as elements that distinguish particular genres from one another (e.g., paragraph structure, pattern of topic shift, distribution of WH-clefts, reference of pronouns to 'current' entities, distribution of pronouns versus definite noun phrases). And since Brown and Yule, like most sociolinguistic publications, is rigidly synchronic in orientation, there is no indication of how a genre comes into existence and changes through time, although there is a valuable discussion of how the listener or reader comes to learn to identify a genre.

As examples of genre description, I choose three, two from the Brown and Yule list plus the riddle, as a 'minor' folkloristic genre that has received considerable attention from folklorists, linguists, and literary scholars. The description of the layout of one's apartment was analyzed in Linde and Labov (1975), where it was not explicitly designated a genre but was referred to as "an unexpectedly well-formed speech act" and as "a well-practiced linguistic skill, a process of linguistic encoding in which speakers follow an intricate set of rules governing their syntactic choice," which is equivalent to recognizing it as a genre. I choose this example because it is clearly nonliterary, but it illustrates well the process of genre formation. The predominant form of the genre is the provision of an imaginary tour of the apartment beginning at the front door, making use of markers of directionality and room names. Since it is easy to imagine alternative ways of answering the question *Could you tell me the layout of your apartment?*, it is clear that this message-type has evolved into a shared (but unrecognized and unnamed) genre.

The sonnet is at the opposite extreme, a literary genre invented by a specific individual, the Sicilian Giacomo da Lentino, in the thirteenth century, which caught on in Italian literature; spread to Provençal then Portuguese and Spanish literature, and eventually to all the literatures of Europe and some Asian literatures; and is still composed and appreciated today. Fortunately we have a fine account of the history, variant forms, and present status of the sonnet by a linguist who has also composed sonnets (Friedrich 1988); this gives us a valuable feeling for the range of formal variants even in a genre that is regarded as highly specified and raises also the issue of the transfer of a genre from one speech community to another.

Finally, the riddle is somewhere between the layout of one's apartment and a sonnet in identifiability as a genre as well as in degree of literariness. As a widespread but by no means universal genre of folk literature it merits cross-cultural and functional analyses. Unfortunately, ethnographic studies have mostly been concerned with semantic content and the distribution of motifs, and linguistic and literary analyses have been mostly concerned with definitional questions. But the facts are that some societies perform riddles as a familiar message-form and some do not; in some societies that have riddles they are performed only by young children, but in others they may be the focus of adult riddle contests; in some societies riddle contests may be widely known and highly salient, while elsewhere they may be rare and marginal; particular formal features of syntax, meter, or rhyme may characterize a riddle genre in a particular speech community; particular features of content or game routine may equally characterize riddling in a given community. In short, a whole range of fascinating questions about the emergence, prevalence, and communicative functions of riddle genres arises, on which cross-cultural studies such as those of Roberts and Forman (1972) or Todorov (1978:223–45)[5] barely touch.

We are fortunate, however, to have a few studies of the acquisition of riddling competence in North America (notably Bauman 1977), which show us how children between the ages of five and eight gradually acquire the various pieces of the genre, until they become competent posers of and respondents to community repertoires of riddles. Discovery of this pathway of acquisition is of considerable importance because it decomposes the genre into features of structure, content, and function which are otherwise not obvious and suggests a line of inquiry that should be even more valuable for more complex genres.

Historical studies of genre are fairly common, but usually in connection with literary analysis rather than from a sociolinguistic perspective. An outstanding exception is Biber and Finegan (1989), which follows three English-language genres of written prose from the seventeenth century to the twentieth: fiction (chiefly novels), essays, and personal letters of literary figures. In their analysis Biber and Finegan use a quantified multidimensional approach that makes possible the discovery of a general, overall long-term *drift* in English style over the four centuries.

Before leaving the concept of genre, it is worth pointing out that genres may pass relatively easily from one speech community to another, to the extent that it raises the question of the actual locus of genres. It is traditional to regard the description of dialect variation and register variation as somewhere within the scope of a full-scale grammar of a language, but the issue of the extent to which a given genre may *belong* in a particular grammar arises since genres may be shared across languages (cf. Ferguson 1976).

5. Varieties

The basic working assumption implicit in the sociolinguistic identification of discrete language varieties is D.

> **D.** Sets of identifying markers of dialect, register, and genre variation vary greatly in the degree of cohesiveness they show as systems and the sharpness of the boundaries between them; *the more cohesive the systems, the sharper the boundaries, and the more they are perceived by the participants as separate entities, the more useful it is to analyze them as language varieties: dialects, registers, and genres, respectively.*

From the sociolinguistic perspective what are important are the existence of variation and the identification of the dimensions of variation: it is rarely possible to answer meaningfully such questions as how many dialects does language X have or how many registers or genres are there in the verbal repertoire of community Y. Assumption D is valuable partly for heuristic purposes, but it also has some validity in diachronic studies as these entities are seen to split and merge. This view of dialect, register, and genre is exactly parallel to the consensual view among linguists that the notion *a language* is largely arbitrary. The answer to the question of how many languages are spoken in country Z may be indeterminate, because of intermediate forms or because of disagreement in speakers' attitudes, yet the splitting and (less often) merger of languages over time is a recognized diachronic phenomenon. This issue has been particularly troublesome in genre analysis because of the salience of giving names to genres and the prescriptivism among authors, readers, and critics at various times and places. The issue is essentially the same, however, as that of correctness or appropriateness in language more generally.

As with the previous assumptions, it is important not to fall into the fallacy of exact parallelism or 'reflectionism' between the cohesiveness, sharpness of boundaries, and community perceptions of social groupings, occasions of use, and message types on the one hand and the cohesiveness, sharpness of boundaries, and community perceptions of the language counterparts of dialect, register, and genre on the other hand. Although there are tendencies for the cohesiveness of system, sharpness of boundaries, and perceptions of the community to be similar to the corresponding language measures, an otherwise cohesive, sharply bounded social group conscious of its identity may, for example, not show a correspondingly sharp dialect differentiation. An attempt has been made to construct a model of grammar writing that regards any language as the sum of a set of minimally different varieties (Klein and Dittmar 1979); one of the problems of such a model is the slippery, 'fuzzy' nature of boundaries between varieties.

6. Conversation

The basic working assumption implicit in sociolinguistic research on conversation analysis is E.

> E. While engaged in verbal interaction, *interlocutors tend to construct turn-taking, repairs, changes in deference expression, code-switching, and other sequential features of conversational activity in terms of their own communicative intentions of the moment.*

If we consider talk-in-interaction or conversation as the "primordial site of sociality and social life" (Schegloff 1988), any analysis of such activity is bound to include examples of dialect and register variation as well as the presence of particular genres with their own internal structure. For example, the genre (or family of similar genres) of the telephone conversation is characterized by certain conventionalized ways of initiating the conversation, identifying the speakers, exchanging messages, and managing to terminate the conversation. Such genres are, of course, conventionalized within particular speech communities, although like genres in general they may spread from one community to another and also may be constrained by universal tendencies. Like other genres, the telephone conversation came into existence at various times in different communities, has itself changed over time, continues to change, and is typically acquired by children systematically (Veach 1980).

What is intended by assumption E, however, is not this relatively static understanding of conversation activity, but the constructedness of each episode of conversation, the way each interlocutor makes use of the communicative resources of the community in order to achieve his or her communicative goals. Thus a speaker may at the beginning of a conversation use a form of address expressing a certain level of deference toward an addressee and then change the deference level in the course of the conversation even though the relative status of the interlocutors remains the same. The speaker may do this to achieve some communicative goal such as currying favor with or distancing himself or herself from the addressee, or changing the level of formality of the discourse because of the appearance on the scene of an unexpected auditor.

Perhaps the most extreme form of this local management of conversation is switching from one language to another in the course of the same conversation, a frequent enough occurrence, although with varying communicative intents, in communities that share two or more conventionalized language varieties (Gumperz 1982:59–99).

7. Multiple Determination

A basic working assumption that underlies sociolinguistic research of all these types of variation is F.

F. *Every utterance (in speaking or writing) simultaneously exemplifies dialect, register, genre, and conversational variation in the senses used here.*

Although four kinds of variation have been identified here as involved in the conventionalization process, it must not be assumed that they are completely independent. On the contrary, the working assumption is that they are all simultaneous, in the sense that any utterance is simultaneously determined by or exemplifies all four kinds of variation. All language users simultaneously signal membership in communities identifying their place in society as well as their recognition of more or less familiar communication situations and message-forms, and all exploit available resources to achieve communicative goals.

8. Attitudes

Another basic working assumption that underlies sociolinguistic research of all these types of variation is G.

G. *Users of variant forms of a language will tend to hold evaluative attitudes about such variants, rating them in terms of such attributes as relative beauty, purity, and effectiveness; most of these attitudes are unconscious and may differ from consciously held attitudes about the same variants.*

Many linguists (and sociolinguists) have been so concerned with demonstrating their own intended objectivity and nonjudgmental attitudes toward language that they neglect to investigate the attitudes, often very intense ones, that speakers have about the languages they speak (or, for that matter, the attitudes that the researchers have about their own use of language). A lesser but also significant reason for linguists' failure to investigate language attitudes is the difficulty in finding appropriate research methods, since direct questioning is so ineffective. Useful discussions about language attitudes in relation to aspects of conventionalization include Ferguson (1977:12–17), Finegan (1980), Labov (1972:308–17), Ryan and Giles (1982), and Woolard (1989:88–142).

9. Diachrony and Acquisition

A basic working assumption that underlies sociolinguistic research on conventionalization is H.

H. *Users of language tend, over time, to change patterns of language structure, language use, and attitudes toward language in patterned,* though not always well understood, *ways, largely unconsciously.*

Patterns of dialect variation change over time. Dialect areas may converge, diverge, change at different rates, or be radically restructured. Repertoires of register variation may contract, expand, or be radically transformed. Genres may come into existence, disappear, or be radically transformed. Evaluative attitudes toward particular variants may become more favorable, become less favorable, or shift in bases of rating. Preferred ways of exploiting the communicative resources of a community in episodes of verbal interaction may change.

Most diachronic studies focus on changes in linguistic structure narrowly defined (phonology, morphology, syntax) or changes in generic structure (genre identification, internal form/content structure, cross-genre modes). This is true even when the researcher acknowledges other kinds of variation. For example, Romaine in her detailed study of historical change in Middle Scots (Romaine 1982:24) recognizes the existence of register variation but focuses on syntactic variation, without examining possible shifts in register ("this type of stylistic [= register] variation is very similar to the stylistic continuum which operates today in the spoken language"). Changes in dialect variation and register variation, as well as associated changes in attitudes, are especially in need of investigation if we hope ever to understand the processes of conventionalization.

This problem is even more severe in studies of language development in child and second language acquisition. Research has focused on either linguistic structure or larger patterns of communicative interaction. Only recently has study begun of the early acquisition of dialect and register variation (see the review of research by Warren-Leubecker and Bohannon 1989), and the L2 acquisition of dialect and register variation is relatively little studied (but cf., e.g., Madsen and Bowen 1978).

10. Summary

One of the basic unanswered questions about language is just how conventionalization takes place, that is, how groups of language users come to share features of language structure and use, as well as evaluative attitudes toward language, and how such shared features change over time. Sociolinguists investigating phenomena of conventionalization typically look at patterns of synchronic variation to find clues, and in so doing they make certain working assumptions. They assume that social groupings of various kinds will tend to be marked linguistically (dialect variation), that particular occasions of use will tend to be marked linguistically (register variation), and that particular message-types will tend to emerge and be recognized (genre formation). The fact of variation is the important point here rather than the identification of units such as particular dialects, registers, or genres, although such identification may be justified if some areas of variation are relatively cohesive and sharply bounded.

Sociolinguists also assume that individual language users may, in verbal interaction, exploit the communicative resources (including dialect, register, and genre variation) of a community in order to achieve their own communicative goals. Such verbal interaction constitutes an important arena for change in patterns of variation.

Further, sociolinguistic researchers assume that language users hold evaluative attitudes about all utterances and texts, and in particular hold differential attitudes toward given variants as opposed to other variants. These attitudes are assumed to be somehow involved in users' choices in producing and interpreting variants, but since they are largely out of awareness and at times vacillating or ambivalent, they are especially difficult to identify and follow.

Finally, it is a firmly held assumption that the conventionalization of all linguistic patterns (whether of structure, use, or attitude) is typically in a state of flux and some changes may be long-lasting. Two perspectives are common: "an optimal time-lapse of say four or five centuries . . . is most favorable for the systematic study of change" (Bynon 1977:6) and "The only strong solutions to the problems of language change . . . are through the study of change in progress" (Labov 1972:274).

I hope that this attempt at making these sociolinguistic working assumptions explicit will serve to clarify both sociolinguistic and nonsociolinguistic research on language, and at the very least will bring responses from researchers or theoreticians who find reasons to disagree with the assumptions as stated.

Notes

1. The sense of *convention* used here is exactly Saussure's (de Saussure 1966:68); for a more recent treatment of conventions cf. Mailloux (1982:126–39). The term *community* is

used here to mean any group of human beings who share some characteristics of language structure, language use, or language attitudes; no attempt is made to specify a more extended meaning of community in the spirit of Gumperz (1968) or Labov (1972).

2. Biber (1988) may be the nearest, but it does not draw a sharp line between register variation and genre formation. The two anthologies in the *sublanguage* tradition (Kittredge and Lehrberger 1982; Grishman and Kittredge 1986) might also be candidates, but their papers mostly analyze scientific prose on specialized topics, considered as sublanguages of whole languages.

3. For a spirited argument against the parallelism and reflection fallacies, see Cameron (1990).

4. Note that in this discussion of register variation no mention is made of style. Partly because the term *style* is used with such a wide range of meanings, it has seemed better to avoid it here altogether. *Style* is sometimes used as roughly equivalent to register variation or as just that part of register variation that lies along the casual/formal dimension. Sometimes also it is used to mean individual variation as opposed to shared conventions or as variation within particular genres or registers. For a recent justification of several senses of *style* and an enthusiastic endorsement of the study of style compare Enkvist (1986).

5. Unfortunately, the insightful essay on the riddle ("La Devinette") in Todorov (1978) is one of the chapters omitted from the English translation (Todorov 1990).

References

Bakhtin, Mikhail M. 1986. *Speech Genres and Other Late Essays.* (trans. by V. W. McGee, ed. by C. Emerson and M. Holquist). Austin: University of Texas Press.

Bauman, Richard. 1977. "Linguistics, Anthropology, and Verbal Art: Toward a Unified Perspective, With a Special Discussion of Children's Folklore." In M. Saville-Troike, ed., *Linguistics and Anthropology* (GURT 1977). Washington, DC: Georgetown University Press. Pp. 13–36.

Bean, S. S. 1974. "Linguistic Variation and the Caste System in South Asia." *Indian Linguistics* 35:277–93.

Biber, Douglas. 1988. *Variation Across Speech and Writing.* Cambridge: Cambridge University Press.

———, and Edward Finegan. 1989. "Drift and the Evolution of English Style: A History of Three Genres." *Language* 65:487–517.

Brown, Gillian, and George Yule. 1983. *Discourse Analysis.* Cambridge: Cambridge University Press.

Bynon, Theodora. 1977. *Historical Linguistics.* Cambridge: Cambridge University Press.

Cameron, D. 1990. "Demythologizing Sociolinguistics: Why Language Does Not Reflect Society." In John E. Joseph and Talbot J. Taylor, eds., *Ideologies of Language.* London and New York: Routledge. Pp. 79–93.

Chambers, J. K., and Peter Trudgill. 1980. *Dialectology.* Cambridge: Cambridge University Press.

Culy, Christopher. 1987. "Cookbook Linguistics: Recipes and Linguistic Theory." Ms., Stanford University.

Ellis, Jeffrey, and Jean Ure. 1969. "Language Varieties: Register." *Encyclopedia of Linguistics, Information and Control.* London: Pergamon Press. Pp. 251–59.

Enkvist, Nils E. 1986. "What Has Discourse Linguistics Done to Stylistics?" In S. P. X. Battestini, ed., *Developments in Linguistics and Semiotics: Language Teaching and*

Learning, Communication Across Cultures (GURT 1986). Washington, DC: Georgetown University Press. Pp. 19–36.

Ferguson, Charles A. 1973. "'Short *a*' in Philadelphia English." In M. E. Smith, ed., *Studies in Linguistics: Essays in Honor of George L. Trager.* Westport, CT: Greenwood Publishing Corporation. Pp. 259–74.

———. 1976. "The Collect as a Form of Discourse." In W. J. Samarin, ed., *Language in Religious Practice.* Rowley, MA: Newbury House. Pp. 101–9.

———. 1977. "Sociolinguistic Settings of Language Planning." In Joan Rubin, Björn H. Jernudd, Jyotirindra Das Gupta, Joshua A. Fishman, and Charles A. Ferguson, eds., *Language Planning Processes.* The Hague: Mouton. Pp. 9–30.

———. 1082. "Simplified Registers and Linguistic Theory." In L. Obler and L. Menn, eds., *Exceptional Language and Linguistics.* New York: Academic Press. Pp. 49–66.

———. 1983. "Sports Announcer Talk: Syntactic Aspects of Register Variation." *Language in Society* 12:153–72.

———. 1990. "From Esses to Aitches: Identifying Pathways of Diachronic Change." In W. Croft, K. Denning, and S. Kemmer, eds., *Studies in Typology and Diachrony: Papers Presented to Joseph H. Greenberg on His 75th Birthday.* Amsterdam: Benjamins. Pp. 59–78.

———. 1991. "Individual and Social in Language Change: Diachronic Changes in Politeness Agreement in Forms of Address." In R. L. Cooper and B. Spolsky, eds., *The Influence of Language on Culture and Thought: Essays in Honor of Joshua A. Fishman on his 65th Birthday.* Berlin: Mouton de Gruyter. Pp. 183–97.

Finegan, Edward. 1980. *Attitudes Toward English Usage: The History of a War of Words.* New York: Teachers College Press.

Fowler, Alastair. 1982. *Kinds of Literature: An Introduction to the Theory of Genres and Modes.* Cambridge, MA: Harvard University Press.

Friedrich, Paul. 1988. "The Unheralded Revolution in the Sonnet: Toward a Generative Model." In D. Tannen, ed., *Linguistics in Context: Connecting Observation and Understanding (Advances in Discourse Processes XXIX).* Norwood, NJ: Ablex. Pp. 199–219.

Ghadessy, Mohsen, ed. 1988. *Registers of Written English: Situational Factors and Linguistic Features.* London: Pinter Publishers.

Goodwin, Charles. 1981. *Conversational Organization.* New York: Academic Press.

Grishman, Ralph, and Richard Kittredge, eds. 1986. *Analyzing Language in Restricted Domains: Sublanguage Description and Processing.* Hillsdale, NJ: Erlbaum Associates.

Gumperz, John J. 1958. "Dialect Differences and Social Stratification in a North Indian Village." *American Anthropologist* 60:668–82.

———. 1982. *Discourse Strategies (Studies in Interactional Sociolinguistics 1).* Cambridge: Cambridge University Press.

Hock, Hans H. 1986. *Principles of Historical Linguistics.* The Hague: Mouton.

Hymes, Dell. 1972. "Models of the Interaction of Language and Social Life." In J. J. Gumperz and D. Hymes, eds., *Directions in Sociolinguistics.* New York: Holt, Rinehart, and Winston. Pp. 35–71.

Kittredge, Richard. 1982. "Variation and Homogeneity of Sublanguages." In Richard Kittredge and John Lehrberger, eds., *Sublanguage: Studies of Language in Restricted Semantic Domains.* Berlin: de Gruyter. Pp. 107–37.

Kittredge, Richard, and John Lehrberger, eds. 1982. *Sublanguage: Studies of Language in Restricted Semantic Domains.* Berlin: de Gruyter.

Klein, Wolfgang, and Norbert Dittmar. 1979. *Developing Grammars.* Berlin: Springer.

Labov, William. 1972. *Sociolinguistic Patterns*. Philadelphia: University of Pennsylvania Press.

Levinson, Stephen C. 1983. *Pragmatics*. Cambridge: Cambridge University Press.

Linde, Charlotte, and William Labov. 1975. "Spatial Networks as a Site for the Study of Language and Thought." *Language* 51:924–39.

Local, J. K. 1978. *Studies Towards a Description of the Development and Functioning of Children's Awareness of Linguistic Variability*. Unpublished Ph.D. Dissertation, University of Newcastle-upon-Tyne.

Madsen, H. S., and J. D. Bowen. 1978. *Adaptation in Language Teaching*. Rowley, MA: Newbury House.

Mailloux, Steven. 1982. *Interpretive Conventions: The Reader in the Study of American Fiction*. Ithaca, NY: Cornell University Press.

Pandit, P. B. 1972. *Parameters of Speech Variation in an Indian Community: India as a Sociolinguistic Area*. Poona: University of Poona.

Payne, Arvilla C. 1976. *The Acquisition of the Phonological System of a Second Dialect*. Unpublished Ph.D. Dissertation, University of Pennsylvania.

Petyt, K. M. 1984. *The Study of Dialect: An Introduction to Dialectology*. Oxford: Basil Blackwell.

Roberts, John M., and Michael L. Forman. 1972. "Riddles: Expressive Models of Interrogation." In J. J. Gumperz and D. Hymes, eds., *Directions in Sociolinguistics: The Ethnography of Communication*. New York: Holt, Rinehart and Winston. Pp. 180–209.

Romaine, Suzanne. 1982. *Socio-Historical Linguistics: Its Status and Methodology*. Cambridge: Cambridge University Press.

Ryan, Ellen B., and Howard Giles, eds. 1982. *Attitudes Towards Language Variation: Social and Applied Contexts*. London: Edward Arnold.

de Saussure, Ferdinand. 1966. *Course in General Linguistics* (transl. by W. Baskin, ed. by C. Bally and A. Sechehaye). New York: McGraw-Hill.

Schegloff, Emanuel A. 1988. "Discourse as an Interactional Achievement II: An Exercise in Conversation Analysis." In D. Tannen, ed., *Linguistics in Context: Connecting Observation and Understanding (Advances in Discourse Processes XXIX)*. Norwood, NJ: Ablex. Pp. 135–58.

Schenkein, Jim M., ed. 1978. *Studies in the Organization of Conversational Interaction*. New York: Academic Press.

Todorov, Tzvetan. 1978. *Les Genres du Discours*. Paris: Editions du Seuil.

———. 1990. *Genres in Discourse*. Cambridge: Cambridge University Press.

Veach, S. R. 1980. *Children's Telephone Conversations*. Ph.D. Dissertation, Stanford University.

Warren-Leubecker, Amye, and John Neil Bohannon III. 1989. Pragmatics: Language in Social Contexts." In J. Berko Gleason, ed., *The Development of Language*, 2nd edition. Columbus, OH: Charles E. Merrill. Pp. 327–68.

Woolard, K. A. 1989. *Double Talk: Bilingualism and the Politics of Ethnicity in Catalonia*. Stanford, CA: Stanford University Press.

2

An Analytical Framework for Register Studies

Douglas Biber

1. Introduction

Despite the large number of register studies that have been completed to date, there is still need for a comprehensive analytical framework. Such a framework should clearly distinguish between linguistic and nonlinguistic characterizations, and it should allow a classification of registers using both types of information.

Hymes has argued that sociolinguistics should make "the systematic study of verbal repertoire" rather than "language" the "central scientific notion" (1984:44–45), and he has made repeated calls for taxonomic frameworks:

> We need taxonomies of speaking and descriptions adequate to support and test them. (1974:34)

> . . . it is essential to isolate the dimensions and features underlying taxonomic categories. These features and dimensions, more than particular constellations of them, will be found to be universal, and hence elementary to descriptive and comparative frames of reference. (1974:41)

Characterizing the state of research in 1974, Hymes notes that

> the fact that present taxonomic dimensions consist so largely of dichotomies—restricted vs. elaborated codes, . . . standard vs. non-standard speech, formal vs. informal scenes, literacy vs. illiteracy—shows how preliminary is the stage at which we work. (1974:41)

The present paper has gone through multiple drafts, with several colleagues making valuable comments on earlier versions: Dwight Atkinson, Ed Finegan, Randi Gilbert, and Bill Grabe. In addition, my thinking on the paper has been facilitated by interactions with members of the Corpus Workgroup of the Text Encoding Initiative: Jeremy Clear, Gunnel Engwall, Stig Johansson, and Lou Burnard.

This state of affairs was still largely true in 1982, when Tannen wrote:

> Linguistic research too often focuses on one or another kind of data, without specifying its relationship to other kinds. In order to determine which texts are appropriate for proposed research, and to determine the significance of past and projected research, a perspective is needed on the kinds of language and their interrelationships . . . discourse analysis needs a taxonomy of discourse types, and ways of distinguishing among them. (1982:1)

Although considerable progress has been made on both the situational classification of registers (e.g., Hymes 1974, Duranti 1985) and the linguistic classification of registers (e.g., Biber 1988, 1989), the concerns raised by Hymes and Tannen are still of central importance.

One important use of a taxonomic framework is to specify the level of generality for registers. Ideally, register comparisons should be on a single level, but often analysts compare registers from quite different levels of generality. At present, there is no system available to characterize the extent of similarity or difference represented by such comparisons. For example, monologues and sermons are registers that differ markedly in their level of generality. Monologues are spoken language having no interaction, unspecified for situational characteristics such as topic, purpose, and setting. Monologues thus represent a much higher 'evel of generality than sermons, which might be specified as planned, noninteractive spoken language in a religious domain on religious topics with primary purposes of informing and persuading. A comprehensive taxonomic framework should be able to identify differences in generality, specify the level of generality, and provide overall situational and linguistic characterizations for each register.

A separate issue is that there is considerable disagreement concerning the definition of *register* and its relation to the constructs of *genre, text type,* and *style.* I use the term *register* in this paper, as it is used in this book, as a general cover term for all language varieties associated with different situations and purposes. The framework developed here recognizes a continuum of varieties and describes the extent to which any particular register is specified. In contrast, other studies have attempted to restrict the usage of these terms to refer to textual constructs at discrete levels of generality. In the chapter Appendix, I give a brief survey of previous definitions of *register* in relation to constructs such as *genre, text type,* and *style.*

The remainder of the paper is organized as follows: I first describe general characteristics of register analyses (section 2) and the requirements of a comprehensive analytical framework (section 3), including both situational and linguistic characterizations of registers. Sections 4 and 5 then focus on situational descriptions. Section 4 surveys previous taxonomic frameworks, distinguishing between classificatory and descriptive frameworks, while in section 5, I attempt to develop an explicit situational framework, to provide a precise specification of both the level of generality and the particular situational characteristics of different registers. Finally, Section 6 discusses implications of this research for dialect studies and the possibility of developing a comprehensive theory of sociolinguistic variation, incorporating both register and dialect characterizations.

2. General Characteristics of Register Analyses

Typical register studies have three components: description of the situational characteristics of a register, description of the linguistic characteristics, and analysis of the functional or conventional associations between the situational and linguistic features. These are illustrated by the following:

FUNCTIONS

SITUATIONAL FEATURES   ⟷ and ⟷   LINGUISTIC FORMS

CONVENTIONS

Halliday (1978:31) describes this relationship in deterministic and unidirectional terms:

> Types of linguistic situation differ from one another, broadly speaking, in three respects: first, as regards to what is actually taking place; secondly, as regards what part the language is playing; and thirdly, as regards who is taking part. *These three variables, taken together, determine the range within which meanings are selected and the forms which are used for their expression. In other words, they determine the "register".* [emphasis added]

Other scholars see this relationship as correlational rather than deterministic, and they emphasize the bidirectional nature of the association, with situational characteristics influencing the choice of linguistic form, while the choice of linguistic features in turn helps to create the situation. Positing a functional association does not entail a one-to-one mapping between form and function. Rather, the mapping across form-function-situation often comprises complex many-to-many kinds of relations.

Associations between form and situation can be motivated by either functional communicative requirements (e.g., purpose, social relations, production constraints) or simple conventions. Differences in the relative distributions of common linguistic features typically have functional underpinnings, while the use of specialized register markers is often conventional. Finegan (1982) illustrates form/function associations in his analysis of last wills and accompanying letters; Zwicky and Zwicky (1980) illustrate conventional associations in their analysis of restaurant menus. Ferguson (1983) describes both types of associations in his analysis of baseball game broadcasts.[1]

3. Requirements of a Comprehensive Analytical Framework

A comprehensive framework for register analysis should provide tools for all three components identified in the last section: analysis of the linguistic characteristics of registers, analysis of the situational characteristics of registers, and analysis of the functional and conventional associations between linguistic and situational characteristics.

i. A comprehensive framework should allow analysis of all salient linguistic characteristics of registers, including specification of the relations among the linguistic features themselves. As Crystal and Davy (1969:13), who prefer the term *style* to *register*, put it, "A definitive book on English stylistics would provide a specification of the entire range of linguistic features entering into the definition of what we have been calling a variety of language, as well as a theoretical framework capable of accounting for them."

Two major types of linguistic characterization should be distinguished: First, there are register markers, which are distinctive linguistic features found only in particular registers. For example, the 'count' (balls and strikes) is a linguistic routine found only in broadcasts of baseball games (Ferguson 1983:165–67). Second, registers are distinguished by differing exploitations of core linguistic features (e.g., nouns, pronouns, subordinate clauses). The framework should include a specification of the full range of such features, as well as mechanisms for analyzing the relations among features in terms of their patterns of co-occurrence and alternation.

ii. A comprehensive framework should permit a complete situational characterization of individual registers, as well as a precise specification of the similarities and differences among registers. This requirement cannot be satisfied by descriptive frameworks that use open-ended parameters (e.g., purpose, field, tenor, and mode). That is, since these parameters have an undetermined set of possible values, they do not allow a precise characterization of individual registers.

In addition, open-ended parameters cannot be used to specify the extent of similarities and differences across registers. Since registers "can be identified at any delicacy of focus" (Halliday 1988:162), this is an important concern. Thus registers can range from extremely high-level varieties, such as formal versus informal, and spoken versus written; to varieties at several intermediate levels, such as conversations, narratives, essays, fiction, novels, science articles, and editorials; to extremely low-level varieties, such as methodology sections in psychology articles and newspaper headlines. These are clearly at very different levels of generality, but it is not obvious what those levels are or which registers are truly comparable.

For example, related registers such as fiction and novels, or academic prose and psychology articles, differ primarily in their level of generality. At present, though, we are not able to characterize those levels, and we thus cannot specify the extent or nature of the difference between related registers. Similarly, we have no basis for evaluating the appropriateness of cross-register comparisons; for example, can novels be appropriately compared to either academic prose or psychology articles?

iii. A comprehensive framework should provide formal apparatus to specify the relationship between situational characteristics and linguistic characteristics, as mediated by communicative functions and conventions. Such mechanisms should be able to cope with the continuous nature of register variation. In the multidimensional approach, this requirement is met through the analysis of linguistic co-occurrence patterns, as described in section 3.2.

3.1. *Linguistic Features Used for Register Analyses*

Although lexical items can be restricted topically (e.g., *home run* and *inning* are likely to occur in texts about baseball games), lexical choice itself does not typically mark a register. (Thus the term *home run* can occur in baseball game broadcasts, newspaper articles, and romance novels, among other registers.) Grammatical routines, on the other hand, can sometimes serve as distinctive register markers; for example, the phrase *the count is two and one* would provide a fairly distinctive marker of a baseball game broadcast (see Ferguson 1983).[2]

Core lexical and grammatical features are more pervasive indicators of register differences, as many registers are distinguished only by the relative distributions of core features. Any linguistic feature having a functional or conventional association can be distributed in a way that distinguishes among registers. Such features come from many linguistic classes, including phonological features (phones, pauses, intonation patterns), tense and aspect markers, pronouns and pro-verbs, questions, nominal forms (nouns, nominalizations, gerunds), passives (*by*-passives, agentless, postnominal passive clauses), dependent clauses (complement clauses, relative clauses, adverbial subordination), prepositional phrases, adjectives (attributive and predicative), adverbs, measures of lexical specificity, lexical classes (hedges, emphatics, discourse particles, stance markers), modals, specialized verb classes (speech act verbs, mental process verbs), reduced forms and discontinuous structures (contractions, *that*-deletions), coordination, negation, grammatical devices for structuring information (clefts, extraposition), cohesion markers (lexical chains), distribution of given and new information, and speech act types.

A comprehensive linguistic analysis of a register requires consideration of a representative selection of these linguistic features. Such analyses are necessarily quantitative, because register distinctions are based on differences in the relative distribution of linguistic features, which in turn reflect differences in their communicative purposes and situations.

3.2. Co-Occurrence in Register Analyses

On first consideration, it seems unlikely that the relative distribution of common linguistic features could reliably distinguish among registers. In fact, individual linguistic features do not provide the basis for such distinctions. However, when analyses are based on the co-occurrence and alternation patterns within a group of linguistic features, important differences across registers are revealed.

The importance of the notion of linguistic co-occurrence has been emphasized by linguists such as Firth, Halliday, Ervin-Tripp, and Hymes. Brown and Fraser (1979:38–39) observe that it can be "misleading to concentrate on specific, isolated [linguistic] markers without taking into account systematic variations which involve the cooccurrence of sets of markers." Ervin-Tripp (1972) and Hymes (1974) identify *speech styles* as varieties that are defined by a shared set of co-occurring linguistic features. Halliday (1988:162) defines a register as "a cluster of associated features having a greater-than-random . . . tendency to co-occur."

The notion of linguistic co-occurrence has been given formal status in the multidimensional approach to register variation (e.g., Biber 1988), where different co-occurrence patterns are analyzed as underlying *dimensions* of variation. There are three distinctive characteristics of the notion of dimension. First, no single dimension is adequate in itself to account for the range of linguistic variation in a language; rather, a multidimensional analysis is required. Second, dimensions are continuous scales of variation rather than dichotomous distinctions. Third, the co-occurrence patterns underlying dimensions are identified quantitatively rather than on an a priori functional basis.

Dimensions have both linguistic and functional content. The linguistic content of a dimension comprises a group of linguistic features (e.g., nominalizations, prepositional phrases, attributive adjectives) that co-occur with a markedly high frequency in texts. Based on the assumption that co-occurrence reflects shared function, these co-occurrence patterns are interpreted in terms of the situational, social, and cognitive functions most widely shared by the linguistic features. Studies by Biber (1986, 1988) and Biber and Finegan (1989a) illustrate this approach for analyses of register variation in English, while Besnier (1988) uses it to analyze register variation in Nukulaelae Tuvaluan; in the present book, the chapters by Kim and Biber and by Biber and Hared use this approach for register analyses of Korean and Somali.

3.3. *Register as a Continuous Construct*

One of the main distinguishing characteristics of the framework developed here is that it treats register variation as continuous rather than discrete. From a linguistic perspective, this means that the focus of analysis is on the relative distribution of common linguistic features, in terms of the patterns of co-occurrence and alternation. Registers are not equally well defined in their linguistic characteristics. Some registers (e.g., personal letters) have well-defined norms so that there is relatively little variation among the texts within the register; other registers (e.g., academic prose) are less specified linguistically, so that there are considerable differences among texts within the register (see Biber 1988:chapter 8, Biber and Finegan 1989a). In addition, registers are more or less specified with respect to different linguistic dimensions.

Similarly from a situational perspective, registers are distributed across a continuous range of variation, and they are not equally well defined. As mentioned above, registers exist at all levels of generality, and a primary function of an analytical framework is to specify the level for particular registers. In addition, it is possible in theory to analyze the co-occurrence patterns among situational features. Crystal and Davy (1969:89) note the existence of such co-occurrence patterns: "There are strong tendencies for certain categories from different [situational] dimensions to co-occur." Once such patterns have been identified, it will also be possible to analyze the correlational relations among linguistic and situational dimensions. The situational framework proposed in section 5 aims to be sufficiently explicit for such analyses.

In practice, most register studies have been atheoretical. In fact, Ferguson (1983) argues in support of an ad hoc approach, claiming that existing theoretical frameworks cannot adequately capture the differences among registers. Several useful frameworks have been developed, however, by researchers such as Halliday, Hymes, and Crystal and Davy. The following section surveys these previous frameworks.

4. Previous Frameworks for the Classification and Description of Registers

Previous frameworks for the situational characterization of registers have had one of two primary goals: classification or description. Classificatory frameworks are based on a closed set of discrete distinctions, so that the register category of any text can be specified. These frameworks typically include only a few general parameters and distinguish among only three or four major text categories. In contrast, descriptive frameworks attempt to provide complete situational characterizations of texts and registers; to accomplish this, they have utilized many open-ended parameters and thus have not been suitable for classificatory purposes.

4.1. Classificatory Frameworks

Several text typologies have been developed on a functional basis: first identifying one or two functional dichotomies and then describing the types defined by the poles of those distinctions. For example, much of the research on spoken/written differences can be considered as implicitly typological in this way, where the two modes represent two major text varieties. Functional text classifications date back at least to Malinowski (1923), who proposed the two-way distinction of pragmatic versus magical language varieties. Other functional typologies have been developed by rhetoricians such as Moffet (1968), Kinneavy (1971), and Britton et al. (1975). Within rhetorical theory, four basic *modes* of discourse are traditionally distinguished: narration, description, exposition, and argumentation. These text categories are based on a combination of differing purposes, topics, and text organizations. This four-way classification has been criticized, however, because its theoretical basis is not clear. In its place, Kinneavy (1971) argues for a four-way distinction based on static versus dynamic perceptions of reality: describing, classifying, narrating, and evaluating. Britton et al. (1975) propose a three-way functional distinction: transactional, expressive, and poetic.

Researchers using computer-based corpora have developed their own classificatory frameworks. The theoretical rationales underlying these frameworks are sometimes less clearly described, but the frameworks are well developed and have been widely used to classify texts. Some of the better known examples include the sixteen written categories distinguished in the Brown and Lancaster-Oslo/Bergen (LOB) corpora (including press reportage, learned prose, and general fiction); the eleven spoken categories distinguished in the London-Lund Corpus (e.g., face-to-face conversation, telephone conversation, prepared oration); the ten major topic-based categories distinguished in the Longman/Lancaster English Language Corpus (e.g., applied science, arts, fiction); and the six prototypical text categories (e.g., exposition, instruction, narration) and thirty-two text types distinguished in the Helsinki Diachronic Corpus of English. These and other corpus-based classification schemes are surveyed in Biber (1991).

The framework proposed by Chafe (1982) is based on two functional/linguistic parameters: 'involvement-detachment' and 'integration-fragmentation'. The first parameter refers to the ways that a speaker/writer participates in a communicative event (marked, e.g., by references to self and emphatic particles); the second refers to the way in which information is packaged into idea units and sentences (marked, e.g., by nominalizations, attributive adjectives, and prepositional phrase sequences). Chafe uses these two parameters to characterize the linguistic and functional differences among various spoken and written registers (cf. Chafe and Danielewicz 1987).

Only a few typologies start from a linguistic rather than a functional basis. Longacre (1976) proposes a four-way distinction of monologic texts that is similar to the traditional rhetorical modes, except that each type is defined in linguistic terms. Two linguistic parameters are proposed for the typology—projected time and temporal succession—and four basic text varieties are distinguished by these parameters: narrative, expository, procedural, and hortatory.

Using a multidimensional approach, Biber (1989) develops a typology of linguistically defined text types (cf. Biber and Finegan 1986). Eight text types in English are identified such that the texts in each type are maximally similar in their linguistic characteristics, while the different types are maximally distinct from one another. The types are identified on the basis of shared linguistic co-occurrence patterns, and therefore they represent important functional as well as linguistic differences among English texts (because linguistic co-occurrence reflects shared function). The order of analysis is reversed from that of most previous studies, however. The types are first identified on the basis of their linguistic characteristics and only subsequently interpreted functionally. The eight text types include two interactive types (labeled 'intimate interpersonal interaction' and 'informational interaction'), three expository types ('scientific exposition', 'learned exposition', and 'general narrative exposition'), and two narrative types ('general narrative exposition' and 'imaginative narrative').

4.2. Descriptive Frameworks

While descriptive frameworks are better developed than classificatory frameworks, they have not been sufficiently explicit to be used for a situational taxonomy of registers.

Malinowski (1982) was one of the first scholars to recognize the importance of the 'context of situation' for text analysis. Firth (1935, 1950) adopted this notion in his general theory of linguistics and developed it to include four components: participants (persons and personalities), action (verbal and nonverbal), effects (results of the verbal action), and other relevant features. Hymes (1974, especially chapter 2) developed a framework for studying the ethnography of communication, which distinguishes among sixteen components of the speech situation: message form, message content, setting, scene, speaker (or sender), addressor, hearer (or receiver, or audience), addressee, purposes-outcomes, purposes-goals, key (tone or manner), channels, forms of speech, norms of interaction, norms of interpretation, and genres. This framework has been very influential. Basso (1974) applies Hymes' framework to writing, focusing on a taxonomy of letters, while the other papers in Bauman and Sherzer (1974) apply the framework to descriptions of communicative events in different cultures. Studies such as Brown and Fraser (1979), Duranti (1985), and Biber (1988:chapter 2) develop this framework in greater detail. Grabe (1990), building on Basso's study, focuses on an ethnography of writing.

At about the same time, Halliday (1978—a collection of earlier papers; cf. Halliday and Hasan 1985) began developing his influential framework for analyzing the context of situation, built around the three features of *field* (what is happening), *tenor* (who is taking part), and *mode* (what part the language is playing). Gregory (1967) develops Halliday's framework in greater detail, while papers such as those in Ghadessy (1988) use this general framework to analyze particular registers.

A third major analytical framework was developed by Crystal and Davy (1969). (Crystal and Davy actually reject the term *register* and instead use *style* as a cover term for situational varieties.) Although it has not been as influential as either Hymes' or Halliday's, this framework is well developed and considers a wide range of theoretical issues. Crystal and Davy identify eight situational *dimensions* grouped into three broad categories: "relatively permanent" features of language use; "given, fundamental features of language in use"; and "relatively localised or temporary variations in language." The first category includes *individuality* (idiosyncratic characteristics of the speaker or writer), *dialect* (regional or social dialect), and *time* (historical stage of the language). The second category comprises discourse characteristics, including the *medium* (speech or writing) and *participation* (monologue or dialogue). The third category is considered to be of most interest for stylistic analysis (p. 71). The dimensions included in this category are *province, status, modality,* and *singularity. Province* refers to the professional or occupational activity being done; *status* refers to the relative social standing of the participants; *modality* refers to the specific purpose of an utterance; and *singularity* refers to the idiosyncratic preferences of each speaker or writer.

Although these frameworks are well developed, none of them can specify the extent to which two registers are truly comparable. Crystal and Davy (1969:71–72) discuss the problems posed by comparing varieties at different levels of generality. For example, varieties associated with the dimension of province can be specified at several levels of abstraction, as in the differences among advertising, television advertising, and television advertising of washing powders. Since it is not clear how these levels relate to one another, nor which levels are well defined linguistically, Crystal and Davy (1969:72) conclude that comparisons should be viewed "with the greatest suspicion, until further descriptive work has been done." Although we now have better mechanisms for analyzing linguistic differences among registers, there is still need for more precise situational analyses of registers.

5. Toward an Explicit Situational Framework

The situational framework presented in Table 2.1 is based on previous proposals by Hymes, Halliday, and Crystal and Davy, as well as my own earlier thinking along these lines (e.g., Biber 1988:chapter 2). In addition, it has been shaped by the thinking of corpus linguists (e.g., Oostdijk 1988, Clear 1992, Atkins, Clear, and Ostler 1992) and by my interaction with the members of the Corpus Workgroup

TABLE 2.1   Situational Parameters of Variation

I.   Communicative Characteristics of Participants

    A.   Addressor(s):
        Single/plural/institutional
    B.   Addressee(s):
        1.   Self/other
        2.   Single/plural/unenumerated
    C.   Audience: yes/no

II. Relations Between Addressor and Addressee

    A.   Social role relations—relative status and power of addressor and addressee:
        Addressor has more power/equal status/addressee has more power
    B.   Extent of shared knowledge
        1.   Specialist knowledge of topic: high/low
        2.   Specific personal knowledge: high/low
    C.   Interactiveness: extensive/slight/none
    D.   Personal relationship: like, respect, fear; kin, friends, enemies, colleagues, etc.

III. Setting

    A.   Characteristics of the place of communication:
        1.   Private/public
        2.   Domain:
            Business and workplace
            Education and academic
            Government and legal
            Religious
            Art and entertainment
            Domestic and personal
            Other
        3.   Audio/visual mass media (television, radio, cinema)
    B.   Extent to which place is shared by participants:
        immediate/familiar/removed
    C.   Extent to which time is shared by participants:
        immediate/familiar/removed
  *D.   Specific place and time of communication

IV. Channel

    A.   Mode (primary channel):
        written/spoken/signed/mixed/(other)
    B.   Permanence:
        recorded/transient
    C.   Medium of transmission:
        If recorded:
        1.   Taped/transcribed/typed/printed/handwritten/e-mail/other
        2.   Published/unpublished
        If transient:
        3.   Face-to-face/telephone/radio/TV/other
    D.   Embedded in a larger text from a different register: yes/no

V.   Relation of Participants to the Text

    A.   Addressor—production circumstances:
        revised or edited/scripted/planned/on-line
    B.   Addressee—comprehension circumstances:
        on-line/self-imposed time constraints

TABLE 2.1   (continued)

---

   *C.   Addressor's and addressee's personal evaluation of text:
          important. valuable. required. beautiful. popular. etc.
   *D.   Addressor's attitudinal stance toward the text:
          1.   Emotionally involved/removed
          2.   Reverence/everyday
          3.   Excitement
          etc.
   *E.   Addressor's epistemological stance toward the text:
          belief. conviction. doubt. etc.

VI.   Purposes. Intents. and Goals

    A.   Factuality:
          (Purported to be) based on fact/speculative imaginative mixed
    B.   Purposes:
          1.   Persuade or sell: high/medium/low
          2.   Transfer information: high/medium low
          3.   Entertain/edify: high medium low
          4.   Reveal self (including expression of personal feelings. attitudes. or efforts at enhancing interpersonal relations): high medium low

*VII.   Topic/Subject

    A.   Level of discussion:
          specialized/general/popular
   *B.   Specific subject: finance. science. religion. politics. sports. law. people. daily activities. etc.

---

*Parameters that are not specified as closed sets.

of the Text Encoding Initiative: Clear, Engwall, Johansson, and Burnard (see Biber 1991).[3]

The primary goal of the framework is to specify the situational characteristics of registers in such a way that the similarities and differences between any pair of registers will be explicit. There are two aspects of this characterization: the level of generality for each register and the particular values for the situational parameters that are specified. That is, the framework consists of several situational parameters, each having a closed set of values. Parameters can be left unspecified to mark the level of generality; the more unspecified values a register has, the higher the degree of generality.

Despite the need for closed parameters, I have also included a few open-ended parameters; these need further work before they can be specified as closed categories. In particular, the parameter of *topic* needs further analysis and is perhaps not specifiable as a closed set. The categories which are not yet fully developed are marked by an asterisk (*). In addition, many of the parameters that are specified in terms of discrete values actually represent continuums or clines. For example, factuality, purpose, and level of discussion are all of this type. Further, many situational characteristics can change within a text. For example, the personal relationships among participants can easily change during the course of a conversation, and the primary purposes can shift within both written and spoken texts.

The framework developed here is not hierarchical. That is, there is no attempt to rank situational parameters in terms of importance or precedence. Rather, any parameter can be (un)specified, so that registers differ not only in their overall level of generality but also in the particular parameters that are relevant. For example, 'writing' is a register at an extremely high level of generality in that only one parameter is specified: primary channel. 'Planned discourse' is a register at the same level of generality, but it differs from 'writing' in that the primary channel parameter is unspecified, while the only specified parameter is for production circumstances. Registers can thus be compared with respect to their overall level of generality, the particular parameters specified, and the values assigned for each parameter.[4]

An eventual goal for a situational framework is to specify quantitative values for each parameter, as continuous scales where possible (with values marking more-or-less relations), or as dichotmous scales (e.g., yes/no, high/low). Such specification would permit the use of correlational statistical techniques, allowing analysis of the co-occurrence relations among situational parameters, and a direct comparison of situational and linguistic characterizations in continuous terms. This is a long-term goal, however, and is not attempted in the present chapter.

Finally, it should be noted that the present framework does not include demographic characteristics of participants. Although these are important aspects of the overall situation, they can be regarded as dialect rather than register considerations.

'Communicative characteristics of participants' refers to the nature of the addressor (speaker or writer), addressee (listener or reader), and audience (participants who hear but are not intended addressees); this parameter could be extended to include demographic characteristics of individual participants. The addressor can be an individual, multiple persons (as in a co-authored paper), or an unacknowledged, institutional author (as in many government and industry documents). Addressees can also be single (as in a letter or dyadic conversation) or multiple. If there is only one addressee, it can be self (as in the case of notes or a diary) or some other person. If there are plural addressees, they can be enumerated (as in a class lecture or departmental memo) or unenumerated (as in a newspaper or novel). In some cases, it might be necessary to recognize the presence of an audience (onlookers) in addition to addressees—for example, in the case of a debate (with addressors and addressees) broadcast on television (to some audience).

'Relation between addressor and addressee' refers to the relative status, extent of shared knowledge, and amount of interaction among participants. Status and power relate to relative social position, including factors such as age and occupational differences. Shared knowledge can refer to specialist knowledge of particular topics or to specific personal background knowledge. (It can also refer to cultural world knowledge, which would be relevant in cross-cultural communication.) The amount of interaction can be extensive, as in typical conversations; moderate, as in many classroom discussions and personal letters; or nonexistent, as in most published prose and many formal lectures and speeches. If participants share personal background knowledge, they can also be characterized in terms of their personal relationship (e.g., kin, friends, acquaintances), and perhaps also their personal feelings toward one another (e.g., like, respect, fear). These seem to be open-ended categories and they are thus not explored further here.

'Setting' refers to the place and time of communication. The place can be identified with a particular 'domain' or context of use. Six primary domains are distinguished here: business and workplace, education and academic, government and legal, religious, art and entertainment, and domestic/personal. There are public and private settings within each of these domains; for example, a meeting versus a personal conversation in the workplace; or a dinner speech versus conversation at a party in one's home. Any of these domains can also be presented or represented via audio/visual mass media, for example, on television shows, movies, or radio shows.

The extent to which place and time are shared is another important difference among registers. Participants can directly share place and time (as in face-to-face conversations), can share time and be familiar with the place of communication (but not actually share that place, as in a telephone conversation), can be familiar with, but not share, both place and time of communication (as in many letters), or be completely unaware of each other's place and time (as in most kinds of expository writing).

The 'mode' (under 'channel') refers to the primary channel of communication, usually speech or writing. 'Mixed mode' refers to situations that use both channels, such as a scripted lecture. Other possible primary channels include sign language, Morse code, and drum talk. It is also possible to distinguish among the secondary channels available: speech typically uses prosodic and paralinguistic channels in addition to the linguistic channel, while writing uses various orthographic conventions. The permanence and medium of a text are further characteristics of its channel. For speech, a text can be recorded (i.e., taped or transcribed) or transient (the typical case). For writing, texts are always recorded and therefore relatively permanent. Both recorded and transient texts can occur in a variety of mediums. Recorded texts can be published or unpublished, and they can be classified according to their specific medium: taped, transcribed, printed, hand-written, e-mail, other. The mediums of transient texts can be classified as face-to-face, telephone, radio, television, or other.

In addition, a text from one register can be embedded in a larger text from a different register. For example, a story can be embedded in a conversation; a methodology section can be embedded in an academic article, which is in turn embedded in an academic journal issue.

'Relation of participants to the text' refers to the differing production circumstances for addressors, and differing comprehension circumstances for addressees. Writers typically can plan, revise, and edit their texts as much as they wish, while speakers typically must produce text on-line with much less opportunity for planning and different opportunities for revision and editing. Participants also have different 'stances' toward a text, including assessments of the importance of the communicative event, personal attitudes, and epistemological attitudes. This area needs more research; see Biber and Finegan (1989b) for one investigation of these factors.

Differences in 'purpose' (the goals or intentions of discourse) are very important in distinguishing among registers. Factuality can be considered one aspect of purpose. At one extreme are registers that purport to describe or explain facts, and at the other pole are registers that are overtly imaginative or fictional. However, there is a range of registers in between these poles (e.g., historical fiction, editorials, theoretical position papers, philosophical arguments). It is also possible to include here deliberate violations of Grice's maxims, and whether or not the addressee is aware of violations. (Such deliberate violations include lying, propaganda, and 'spin control'; sarcastic humor is a type of violation that requires awareness of the addressee.)

Purpose itself can be characterized along four parameters: 'persuade' (or sell), 'transfer information', 'entertain' (or edify), and 'reveal self'. Some registers can be marked by high attention to only one purpose, but registers frequently have multiple purposes. For example, advertisements are marked primarily by their focus on persuasion, but they might also have secondary purposes of transferring information and entertaining. A conversational narrative would likely combine purposes of revealing self and entertaining (and possibly transferring information). Using a four-dimensional specification of purpose allows characterization of these multiple goals. (Further research is required to determine whether these four parameters of purpose are adequate for all registers.)

Finally, the parameter of 'topic' (or subject of discourse) is a relatively open-ended category. This parameter is important, however, for distinguishing among subregisters (e.g., physics versus psychology articles). Subject distinctions are also used for high-level registers (e.g., scientific prose). Detailed subject classification systems have been developed by librarians, although it is not clear how adequate these systems are for unpublished written texts (e.g., merchandise catalogs, advertisements and other 'junk mail', office memos) or for spoken texts (e.g., a conversation about Uncle George).

Under the heading of topic, I also distinguish between specialized and general level of discussion, although this distinction overlaps with the assumed level of share background knowledge (II.B).

5.1. The Explicit Situational Characterization of Registers: Some Illustrations

Table 2.2 charts the major situational characteristics of eleven registers, representing varieties at several different levels of generality. I have included only thirteen of the parameters here (because of space limitations), so the table does not present complete characterizations. The framework and the characterizations are preliminary, and further research will doubtless show the need for additional or different parameters, or for revised characterizations of particular registers.

The first three registers in Table 2.2 are letters: personal letters, professional letters, and letters of recommendation. As the chart shows, letters of recommendation are more fully specified than the other two. All three have a single writer, but letters of recommendation differ from the other two in having multiple addressees (all interested parties at some target institution). Personal letters function in a personal domain, while the other two are work-related. Writers often assume that the reader is familiar with the place and time of writing in personal letters, and this is also possible in professional letters (thus deictic references such as *here* or *out in*

TABLE 2.2 Major Situational Characteristics of Eleven Registers

Register	I.A. Addressor	I.B. Addressee	III.A. Domain	III.BC Share Timeplace	IV.A. Mode	V.A. Production	VI.A. Factual	VI.B. Purposes: Persuade	Inform	Entertain	Reveal self	VII.A. Level	VII.B. Subject
Personal letter	sg/pl	sg/pl	pers	familiar	wr	rev	—	—	med	—	high	pop	—
Professional letter	sg	sg	work	—	wr	rev	—	—	high	low	low	spec	—
Letter of recommendation	sg	pl	work	no	wr	rev	fact	high	med	low	low	spec	candidate's qualifications
Face-to-face conversation	sg/pl	sg/pl	—	yes	sp	online	—	—	—	—	high	—	—
Lecture	sg	pl	—	yes	sp	planned	fact	low	high	low?	low	—	—
Sermon	sg	pl	rel	yes	sp	planned	spec?	high	high	med?	med?	pop	—
Novels	sg	uncn	art	no	wr	rev	imag	low	low?	high	—	pop?	—
Narration	—	—	—	—	—	—	—	—	—	—	—	pop?	—
Psychology article	sg/pl	uncn	acad	no	wr	rev	fact	med	high	low	low	spec	psychology
Expository prose	—	—	—	no	wr	rev	—	—	high	low	low	—	—
Academic prose	sg/pl	uncn	acad	no	wr	rev	—	—	high	low	low	spec	—

45

the hall are possible in both). Letters of recommendations do not assume any such familiarity with the place and time of writing (although the date is marked in the letter heading and can be used as a point of reference: e.g.. *Last year I had Jones in my class . . .*). All three types of letter are written and can be revised. although personal letters are often less carefully produced than the other two types. All three purport to present factual information. although they can be speculative as well. Purpose is least specified in personal letters: they typically convey some information and almost always convey personal feelings and attitudes. but they can adopt a number of different purposes relating to persuasion and entertainment. On the other hand. purpose is most specified in letters of recommendation: they are by definition persuasive and somewhat informative. but they are rarely entertaining or self-revealing. Personal letters typically adopt a popular or general level of discussion. although they assume a high degree of shared personal knowledge; the other two letter types assume more specialist knowledge. Finally. letters of recommendation have as their specified topic the individual being recommended. The other two letter types can deal with a wide range of topics.

Face-to-face conversations represent a register at a higher level of generality. They are characterized by a single addressor and addressee (although multiparty conversations are also common). speaking on-line in a shared time and place. Most other parameters, however, are unspecified: conversations can occur in any domain: they can be factual or speculative but rarely imaginative: they can be persuasive. informative, or entertaining, although they typically reveal self; and they can be on any topic at popular or specialized levels.

Narration is the least specified register on Table 2.2. Narratives range from imaginative fiction and personal stories to biographies. historical analytic prose. and even some methodology sections in experimental articles. They are defined primarily by their linguistic characteristics and discourse organization (see Labov and Waletsky 1967; Ochs this volume). Table 2.2 shows, however, that narration is not a well-defined register distinction situationally. (Distinctions such as fictional narrative, conversational narrative, and biography are more fully specified.)

Although the framework presented here is preliminary. it is immediately useful for assessing the comparability of register pairs. For example, personal letters are specified at a higher level of generality than letters of recommendation. and thus the two are not strictly comparable. Personal letters written to family members describing the writer's recent social life would be closer to the same level of generality.

Conversation and expository prose are both specified at a high level of generality, although Table 2.2 shows that they are unspecified on different parameters. Academic prose is more fully specified than expository prose (which includes academic prose, newspaper articles, business reports, and student essays). In fact, academic prose is nearly as specified as psychology articles. The main differences are that academic prose can be factual or speculative, while psychology articles purport to be factual; academic prose can deal with almost any subject; and academic prose can assume a variety of different mediums or formats (books, articles, working papers). Thus academic prose is at a comparable level of generality with personal letters and lectures, but it is more specified than face-to-face conversations.

TABLE 2.3 Dichotomous Coding for Mode
and Interactiveness

Value	Mode	Interactiveness
0	Speech	Interactive
1	Writing	Not interactive

5.2. Quantitative Measurement of the Functional Association Between Situational and Linguistic Parameters

The situational framework described here can be further developed to include quantitative scales (ordinal or dichotomous) for each situational parameters. This refinement would allow an empirical investigation of the relations among linguistic and situational parameters, exploring issues such as the situational correlates of underlying linguistic dimensions.

To illustrate, I recoded the 481 texts used in Biber (1988) for four inter-related situational parameters: mode (speech or writing), interactiveness (interactive or not), production circumstances (edited/revised, planned, on-line), and informational purpose (high, medium, low). Mode and interactiveness were coded as dichotomous scales, as in Table 2.3. Production circumstances (reflecting the degree of careful production) and transferring information as a primary purpose were coded as ordinal scales, as in Table 2.4. Each text should be coded separately with respect to situational parameters such as these, and in fact the situational characteristics of some parameters (e.g., purpose) can shift within a text.

Although there is a high degree of overlap among these four parameters, there are also important differences, illustrated by the values for six texts from different registers, as shown in Table 2.5.

Given this type of coding for each text, it is possible to correlate situational characteristics and linguistic characteristics as continuous parameters, to measure the degree of functional association between the two directly. For example, Table 2.6 presents Pearson correlation coefficients measuring the relationships among five linguistic features and the four situational parameters coded here. The columns labeled r present correlation coefficients, while the columns labeled r^2 present values for "R-squared," which should be interpreted as a direct measure of the

TABLE 2.4 Ordinal Scales for Production
Circumstances and Transferring Information

Value	Production Circumstances	Transfer Information
1	On-line	Low
2	Planned but not scripted	Medium
3	Scripted, revised, edited	High

TABLE 2.5   Values with Respect to Four Situational Variables for Six Texts

Register	Mode	Interactiveness	Careful Production	Informative Purpose
Face-to-face conversation	1	1	1	1
Business telephone conversation	1	1	1	2
Public lecture	1	0	2	3
Personal letter	0	1	2	1
Professional letter	0	1	3	3
Newspaper article	0	0	3	3

strength of association between two variables, representing the percentage of variation in one variable that can be predicted on the basis of the other.

The first row of Table 2.6 presents the correlations for contractions and shows a strong association between the distribution of contractions and the situational parameters of physical mode and interactiveness: a correlation of .74 in both cases, which translates into an r^2 value of 55 percent. The parameter of careful production shows an even stronger relation to contractions, with 71 percent ($r = .84$) of the variability in the distribution of contractions predicted by production circumstances. This finding supports the interpretation that contractions are due primarily to the pressures of on-line production; physical mode and interactiveness also show relatively high correlations because interactive, spoken discourse is commonly produced on-line. In contrast, informative purpose shows only a moderate relationship to contractions (38 percent), reflecting the fact that discourse with a high informative purpose can be produced under a variety of circumstances.

That-deletions show a similar pattern to contractions, except that the correlations are uniformly lower. Type/token ratio also shows a similar pattern, except that it does not have a strong relationship to any of these situational parameters. Mode and production circumstances have moderate associations with type/token ratio (both 26 percent), while interactiveness has a weak relationship (14 percent), and informative purpose shows essentially no relation to this linguistic feature (only 3 percent).

In contrast, informative purpose has the strongest relationship to prepositional phrases and passives (45 percent and 38 percent, respectively). Thus the distri-

TABLE 2.6   Correlations Between Linguistic Features and Situational Parameters

Linguistic Feature	Mode		Interactiveness		Careful Production		Informative Purpose	
	r	r^2	r	r^2	r	r^2	r	r^2
Contractions	.74	55%	.74	55%	.84	71%	.62	38%
That-deletions	.55	30%	.67	45%	.71	50%	.56	31%
Type/token ratio	.51	26%	.38	14%	.51	26%	.18	3%
Prepositional phrases	.42	18%	.46	21%	.52	27%	.67	45%
Passives	.43	18%	.39	15%	.44	19%	.62	38%

bution of contractions, *that*-deletions, and a varied vocabulary (type/token ratio) depends primarily on the production circumstances and physical mode, regardless of the primary purpose, while the distribution of prepositional phrases and passives depends primarily on purpose, regardless of production circumstances and mode.

These kinds of correlations can also be used to interpret the linguistic dimensions of variation investigated in multidimensional studies (e.g., Biber 1988, Biber and Finegan 1989a; cf. section 3.2). In previous work, dimension interpretations have been based on qualitative assessments of the underlying communicative functions. In contrast, the approach here allows direct measurement of the association between communicative functions (or situational parameters) and linguistic dimensions.

For example, Dimension 1 in Biber (1988) comprises linguistic features such as first and second person pronouns, contractions, *that*-deletions, hedges, and emphatics versus nouns, prepositional phrases, and type/token ratio; this dimension is interpreted as representing "Involved versus Informational Production." Table 2.7 shows that production circumstances have the strongest relation to Dimension 1 (74 percent), supporting that aspect of the interpretation. Physical mode and interactiveness also have quite strong correlations (58 percent and 59 percent, respectively). Informative purpose has a smaller but moderately strong correlation (36 percent), indicating that it is associated with Dimension 1 but less important than the other three parameters.

Dimension 3 comprises features such as relative clauses versus time and place adverbials, interpreted as "Explicit versus Situation-Dependent Reference." Dimension 5 comprises passive constructions (including main clause, postnominal modifiers, and adverbial clauses) and is interpreted as "Abstract versus Nonabstract Style." Both of these dimensions are most highly correlated with informative purpose (34 percent), although neither shows the very strong correlations characteristic of Dimension 1. Thus purpose is more important than mode, interactiveness, or production circumstances for Dimensions 3 and 5, but there may well be other situational parameters that show even stronger correlations.

As noted above, the particulars of this framework and these characterizations

TABLE 2.7 Correlations Between Linguistic Dimensions and Situational Parameters

Linguistic Dimension	Mode		Interactiveness		Careful Production		Informative Purpose	
	r	r^2	r	r^2	r	r^2	r	r^2
Dimension 1*	.76	58%	.78	59%	.86	74%	.60	36%
Dimension 3**	.42	18%	.28	8%	.45	20%	.58	34%
Dimension 5***	.43	18%	.36	13%	.44	19%	.58	34%

From Biber (1988).

*Dimension 1: "involved vs. informational production"
**Dimension 3: "explicit vs. situation-dependent reference"
***Dimension 5: "abstract vs. nonabstract style"

need additional research. However, even in its present form, the framework is useful for isolating the important situational characteristics of a register, for assessing the comparability of register pairs, and for analyzing the functional associations between linguistic and situational parameters.

6. Conclusion: Toward a Comprehensive Theory of Sociolinguistics

The framework described here could be extended to the analysis of dialects and dialect variation. Dialects are similar to registers in being defined by both linguistic and nonlinguistic characteristics. However, at present there are no frameworks that allow comprehensive analyses of dialects with respect to either set of characteristics. Other researchers have noted that the social/demographic characteristics of dialect groups could be described in more systematic and comprehensive terms than has been common to date. This shortcoming is even more striking with respect to linguistic characterizations: currently there is no framework for the overall linguistic description of social dialects, and in fact there is no indication that such characterizations are perceived to be an interesting research goal. Rather, research has been restricted to investigation of individual (socio)linguistic *variables,* and these variables have typically been further restricted to include only phonological and morphological features with semantically equivalent alternants.[5] Thus at present, although we know a great deal about the social distribution of some linguistic variables, we know very little about the overall linguistic characteristics of social dialects or the linguistic relations among dialects. Such research questions are clearly important and deserve future investigation.

In addition, the integration of register and dialect research into a single comprehensive theory of sociolinguistics would enhance our understanding of both fields. Traditional social dialect studies, such as Labov's research on New York and Trudgill's research on Norwich, have made a start toward this goal by comparing the patterns of variation across both social dialects and 'styles' (defined by the amount of attention paid to speech). Unfortunately, these styles represent only a very small proportion of the total range of situational/register variation within a community. Future investigations of linguistic variation in speech communities should include analysis of the full range of registers and dialects in order to be comprehensive (cf. the chapters by Rickford and McNair-Knox and by Finegan and Biber in this volume).[6]

In summary, the same analytical techniques can usefully be applied to both register and dialect studies. That is, issues of linguistic co-occurrence and alternation are central to the description of both kinds of varieties, and comprehensive descriptions are equally feasible and important for both dialect and register studies. In both cases, such descriptions should include social/situational characterizations, linguistic characterizations, and analysis of the functional/conventional associations between linguistic form and situational/social characteristics. Given an empirical base of this kind, the goal of a comprehensive sociolinguistic theory might finally become feasible.

Appendix. Definitions of *Register* and Other Related Constructs

The term *register* has been used in many different ways, as have the related terms *genre, text type,* and *style.* Most researchers agree in using *register* to refer to situationally defined varieties, as opposed to *dialect,* which refers to varieties associated with different speaker groups. For example, Ure (1982:5) states that the "register range of a language comprises the range of social situations recognized and controlled by its speakers—situations for which appropriate patterns are available."

Beyond this general association of register with situational variation, however, there is less consensus. The term *register* is sometimes used as a cover term for all situational varieties, with little discussion of level of generality. Other writers restrict register to occupational varieties (Wardaugh 1992, Trudgill 1974), such as computer programmer talk and auto mechanic talk. Crystal and Davy (1969:61) are so critical of the term that they discard it altogether; they write that register has been "applied to varieties of language in an almost indiscriminate manner, as if it could be usefully applied to situationally distinctive pieces of language of any kind," including, for example, newspaper headlines, church services, sports broadcasts, and advertising. For them, it is "inconsistent, unrealistic, and confusing" to group together this range of varieties under a single cover term, because they differ so markedly in their situational characteristics. (Instead, they use the term *style* to cover everything from conversation to legal documents to press advertising.)

For other researchers, the flexibility of the term *register* is an advantage. Thus Ferguson (1983:154) points out that "register variation, in which language structure varies in accordance with the occasions of use, is all-pervasive in human language," and the term *register* conveniently covers this range of variation.

Rhetoricians have usually used the term *genre* instead of *register.* However, literary genres often refer to varieties at an intermediate level of generality, such as essays, novels, short stories, and letters, in contrast to the traditional rhetorical *modes* of discourse—narration, description, exposition, and argumentation—which are text distinctions at a high level of generality, corresponding to differences in topic and purpose. These distinctions have also been referred to as *text types* (e.g., Faigley and Meyer 1983).

Several researchers working within Halliday's systemic-functional framework attempt to make a theoretical distinction between register and genre, reflecting two different levels of abstraction. Ventola (1984) and Martin (1985) refer to register and genre as different "semiotic planes": genre is the "content-plane" of register, and register is the "expression-plane" of genre; register is in turn the "content-plane" of language. Martin (1985) and Couture (1986) both describe registers as comprising particular configurations of the contextual categories of field, tenor, and mode (proposed by Firth and Halliday; see section 4.2). Martin (1985:250) further states that "genres are how things get done," listing poems, narratives, expositions, lectures, recipes, manuals, appointment making, service encounters, and news broadcasts as examples of genres. Gregory and Carroll's (1978:64) and Couture's (1986:80) characterization of register—"language in action"—is similar to Martin's characterization of genre. In contrast, Couture characterizes genre as "conventional instances of organized text." Couture's examples of genres and registers seem to be more clearly distinguished than in other studies of this type. For example, registers include the language used by preachers in sermons, the language used by sports reporters in giving a play-by-play description of a football game, and the language used by scientists reporting experimental research results. Genres include both literary and nonliterary text varieties, for example, short stories, novels, sonnets, informational reports, proposals, and technical manuals.

Swales (1990) differs from proponents of the systemic-functional tradition in preferring the term *genre* to *register,* and in focusing on purpose alone as the central parameter distinguishing among genres. A genre is defined as "a class of communicative events, the members of which share some set of communicative purposes. These purposes are recognized by the expert members of the parent discourse community and thereby constitute the rationale for the genre" (p. 58).

The IPrA Survey of Research in Progress (Nuyts 1988) uses a number of different terms. The survey exemplifies terms in a hierarchical presentation rather than explicitly defining the terms. At a high level of generality, the survey distinguishes between *language varieties* and *discourse types.* Register is considered to be a language variety, along with dialect, argot, slang, and jargon; examples of registers in this framework include aviation language, journalese, legalese, literary language, religious language, scientific language, technical language, and mythical language. The survey identifies two major discourse types: conversation types and text types. Conversation types include adult-child, classroom, interview, dinner, meeting, narrative, and courtroom. Text types include advertisement, comic strip, essay, joke, legal text, letter, literature, message, monologue, narrative, obituary, report, and summary.

The terms *genre* and *text type* have also been used in earlier multidimensional studies (e.g., Biber 1988, 1989; Biber and Finegan 1989a); *genre* has been used as an imprecise cover term in these studies, while *text type* has been given a more precise definition. The term *genre* is loosely defined as "text categorizations made by the basis of external criteria relating to author/speaker purpose" (Biber 1988:68) and "the text categories readily distinguished by mature speakers of a language; for example . . . novels, newspaper articles, editorials, academic articles, public speeches, radio broadcasts, and everyday conversations. These categories are defined primarily on the basis of external format" (Biber 1989:5–6). In practical terms, these categories are adopted because of their widespread use in computerized language corpora, but they are problematic in the same way that register distinctions are, in that they represent text categories at different levels of generality.

In contrast, the term *text type* has been used in multidimensional analyses to refer to text categories defined in strictly linguistic terms. That is, regardless of purpose, topic, interactiveness, or any other nonlinguistic factors, text types are defined such that the texts within each type are maximally similar with respect to their linguistic characteristics (lexical, morphological, and syntactic), while the types are maximally distinct with respect to their linguistic characteristics (see Biber and Finegan 1986, Biber 1989). After the text types are identified on formal grounds, they can be interpreted functionally in terms of the purposes, production circumstances, and other situational characteristics shared by the texts in each type.

The term *sublanguage* (Kittredge and Lehrberger 1982, Grishman and Kittredge 1986) has been used within computational linguistics to refer to "a subsystem of language that . . . [is] limited in reference to a specific subject domain"; each sublanguage is claimed to have its own"distinctive grammar" (Grishman and Kittredge 1986:ix). Sublanguages are quite restricted; for example, analyses of sublanguages have focused on medical articles about lipoprotein kinetics (Sager 1986) and navy telegraphic messages (Fitzpatrick, Bachenko, and Hindle 1986).

Finally, the term *style* has perhaps been used for a wider range of conceptions than any of the other terms. Crystal and Davy (1969) use the term in a similar way to the use of *register* here; Joos (1961) similarly uses the term *style* to refer to registers at a high level of generality.[7] Labov (1972) uses *style* to refer to language production under circumstances that require differing amounts of attention to speech (e.g., reading word lists versus an interview). More commonly, *style* has been treated as a characteristic way of using language. This usage often has an evaluative sense, as when writing handbooks discuss "writing with style" (which carries the implication that people can write without style). With regard to literary language, style in this sense has been studied as a characteristic of particular genres, particular periods, particular authors, and even particular texts (see discussion in Leech and Short 1981). A similar notion of style has been used to study conversational interactions, where each culture can be described as having a distinctive "communicative style" (e.g., Tannen 1984).

Notes

1. Atkinson (1990) surveys the role of conventional forms in register analysis.

2. This routine could occur in fiction or drama as well, but it would likely be part of a fictional sports broadcast embedded in a larger text.

3. The 100-million-word British National Corpus is currently being tagged on the basis of the explicit situational framework developed as part of the Text Encoding Initiative.

4. In this respect, the framework developed here is comparable to distinctive feature frameworks used in phonology. Phonological classes such as nasals, consonants, and voiced segments have a high level of generality (and are considered "natural") because they are specified for only a few distinctive features.

5. However, there have been exceptions to this trend, as some studies have used a traditional variationist approach to discourse characteristics (e.g., Dines 1980 on generalizing tags, and Schiffrin 1985 on causal sequences). Hasan (1989) argues for the need to analyze semantic variation in sociolinguistic studies.

6. It is unlikely that all members of a speech community will have the same register repertoire. Thus a comprehensive study of variation in a speech community would need to identify the differing repertoire ranges of particular speaker groups, as well as to analyze the linguistic patterns of variation among all registers and dialects.

7. Biber and Finegan (1989b) also use the term *stance style* to refer to the linguistically defined groupings of texts identified from differing patterns of stance markers. These styles are similar to text types in being defined on strictly linguistic grounds (and subsequently being interpreted functionally); they differ from text types in that they represent use with

respect to a restricted linguistic system—stance markers—rather than use with respect to the range of linguistic features available in English (the goal for text types).

References

Atkins, Sue, Jeremy Clear, and Nicholas Ostler. 1992. "Corpus Design Criteria." *Literary and Linguistic Computing* 7:1–16.

Atkinson, Dwight. 1990. "Discourse Analysis and Written Discourse Conventions." *Annual Review of Applied Linguistics* 11:57–76.

Basso, Keith H. 1974. "The Ethnography of Writing." In Bauman and Sherzer, eds. Pp. 425–32.

Bauman, Richard, and Joel Sherzer, eds. 1974. *Explorations in the Ethnography of Speaking.* Cambridge: Cambridge University Press.

Besnier, Niko. 1988. "The Linguistic Relationships of Spoken and Written Nukulaelae Registers." *Language* 64:707–36.

Biber, Douglas. 1986. "Spoken and Written Textual Dimensions in English: Resolving the Contradictory Findings." *Language* 62:384–414.

———. 1988. *Variation Across Speech and Writing.* Cambridge: Cambridge University Press.

———. 1989. "A Typology of English Texts." *Linguistics* 27:3–43.

———. 1991. "Final Report of the Text Corpus Work Group." Text Encoding Initiative, Document TR6 W1. University of Illinois at Chicago.

Biber, Douglas, and Edward Finegan. 1986. "An Initial Typology of English Text Types." In Jan Aarts and Willem Meijs, eds., *Corpus Linguistics II.* Amsterdam: Rodopi. Pp. 19–46.

———. 1989a. "Drift and the Evolution of English Style: A History of Three Genres." *Language* 65:487–517.

———. 1989b. "Styles of Stance in English: Lexical and Grammatical Marking of Evidentiality and Affect." *Text* 9:93–124.

Britton, James, Tony Burgess, Nancy Martin, Alex McLeod, and Harold Rosen. 1975. *The Development of Writing Abilities (11–18).* London: Macmillan Education.

Brown, Penelope, and Colin Fraser. 1979. "Speech as a Marker of Situation." In Klaus R. Scherer and Howard Giles, eds., *Social Markers in Speech.* Cambridge: Cambridge University Press. Pp. 33–62.

Chafe, Wallace L. 1982. "Integration and Involvement in Speaking, Writing, and Oral Literature." In Tannen, ed. Pp. 35–54.

Chafe, Wallace L., and Jane Danielewicz. 1987. "Properties of Spoken and Written Language." In R. Horowitz and S. J. Samuels, eds., *Comprehending Oral and Written Language.* New York: Academic Press. Pp. 82–113.

Clear, Jeremy. 1992. "Corpus Sampling." In Gerhard Leitner, ed., *New Directions in Corpus Linguistics.* Berlin: Mouton de Gruyter.

Couture, Barbara. 1986. "Effective Ideation in Written Text: A Functional Approach to Clarity and Exigence." In Barbara Couture, ed., *Functional Approaches to Writing: Research Perspectives.* Norwood, NJ: Ablex. Pp. 69–91.

Crystal, David, and Derek Davy. 1969. *Investigating English Style.* New York: Longman.

Dines, Elizabeth. 1980. "Variation in Discourse: 'And Stuff Like That'." *Language in Society* 9:13–33.

Duranti, Alessandro. 1985. "Sociocultural Dimensions of Discourse." In Teun van Dijk, ed., *Handbook of Discourse Analysis,* vol. 1. New York: Academic Press. Pp. 193–230.

Ervin-Tripp, Susan. 1972. "On Sociolinguistic Rules: Alternation and Co-Occurrence." In John J. Gumperz and Dell Hymes, eds., *Directions in Sociolinguistics*. New York: Holt, Rinehart and Winston. Pp. 213–50.

Faigley, Lester, and Paul Meyer. 1983. "Rhetorical Theory and Readers' Classifications of Text Types." *Text* 3:305–25.

Ferguson, Charles A. 1983. "Sports Announcer Talk: Syntactic Aspects of Register Variation." *Language in Society* 12:153–72.

Finegan, Edward. 1982. "Form and Function in Testament Language." In Robert J. Di Pietro, ed., *Linguistics and the Professions*. Norwood, NJ: Ablex. Pp. 113–20.

Firth, J. R. 1935. "The Technique of Semantics." *Transactions of the Philogical Society* 36–72.

———. 1950. "Personality and Language in Society." *Sociological Review* 42:37–52.

Fitzpatrick, Eileen, Joan Bachenko, and Don Hindle. 1986. "The Status of Telegraphic Sublanguages." In Grishman and Kittredge, eds. Pp. 39–51.

Ghadessy, Mohsen, ed. 1988. *Registers of Written English: Situational Factors and Linguistic Features*. London: Pinter.

Grabe, William. 1990. "Current Developments in Written Discourse Analysis." *Lenguas Modernas* 17:35–56.

Gregory, Michael. 1967. "Aspects of Varieties Differentiation." *Journal of Linguistics* 3:177–98.

Gregory, Michael, and S. Carroll. 1978. *Language and Situation: Language Varieties and Their Social Contexts*. London: Routledge and Kegan Paul.

Grishman, Ralph, and Richard Kittredge, eds. 1986. *Analyzing Language in Restricted Domains: Sublanguage Description and Processing*. Hillsdale, NJ: Lawrence Erlbaum.

Halliday, Michael A. K. 1978. *Language as Social Semiotic: The Social Interpretation of Language and Meaning*. London: Edward Arnold.

———. 1988. "On the Language of Physical Science." In M. Ghadessy, ed., *Registers of Written English*. London: Pinter Publishers. Pp. 162–78.

———. 1989. *Spoken and Written Language*. Oxford: Oxford University Press.

Halliday, Michael A. K., and Ruqaiya Hasan. 1976. *Cohesion in English*. London: Longman.

———. 1985. *Language, Context, and Text: Aspects of Language in a Social-Semiotic Perspective*. Oxford: Oxford University Press.

Hasan, Ruqaiya. 1989. "Semantic Variation and Sociolinguistics." *Australian Journal of Linguistics* 9:221–75.

Hymes, Dell. 1974. *Foundations in Sociolinguistics: An Ethnographic Approach*. Philadelphia: University of Pennsylvania Press.

———. 1984. "Sociolinguistics: Stability and Consolidation." *International Journal of the Sociology of Language* 45:39–45.

Joos, Martin. 1961. *The Five Clocks*. New York: Harcourt, Brace & World.

Kinneavy, James L. 1971. *A Theory of Discourse*. Englewood Cliffs, NJ: Prentice-Hall.

Kittredge, Richard, and John Lehrberger, eds. 1982. *Sublanguage: Studies of Language in Restricted Semantic Domains*. Berlin: De Gruyter.

Labov, William. 1972. *Sociolinguistic Patterns*. Philadelphia: University of Pennsylvania Press.

Labov, William, and Joshua Waletsky. 1967. "Narrative Analysis." In June Helm, ed., *Essays on the Verbal and Visual Arts*. Seattle: University of Washington Press. Pp. 12–44.

Leech, Geoffrey N., and Michael H. Short. 1981. *Style in Fiction: A Linguistic Introduction to English Fictional Prose*. New York: Longman.

Longacre, Robert E. 1976. *An Anatomy of Speech Notions.* Lisse: Peter de Ridder Press.
Malinowski, Bronislaw. 1923. "The Problem of Meaning in Primitive Languages." Supplementary essay in C. K. Ogden and I. A. Richards, *The Meaning of Meaning.* New York: Harcourt, Brace. Pp. 296–336.
Martin, J. R. 1985. "Process and Text: Two Aspects of Human Semiosis." In James D. Benson and William S. Greaves, eds., *Systemic Perspectives on Discourse,* vol. 1. Norwood, NJ: Ablex. Pp. 248–274.
Moffett, James. 1968. *Teaching the Universe of Discourse.* Portsmouth, NH: Heinemann.
Nuyts, Jan. 1988. "IPrA Survey of Research in Progress." Wilrijk, Belgium: International Pragmatics Association.
Oostdijk, N. 1988. "A Corpus Linguistic Approach to Linguistic Variation." *Literary and Linguistic Computing* 3:12–25.
Sager, Naomi. 1986. "Sublanguage: Linguistic Phenomenon, Computational Tool." In Grishman and Kittredge, eds. Pp. 1–17.
Schiffrin, Deborah. 1985. "Multiple Constraints on Discourse Options: A Quantitative Analysis of Causal Sequences." *Discourse Processes* 8:281–303.
Swales, John M. 1990. *Genre Analysis: English in Academic and Research Settings.* Cambridge: Cambridge University Press.
Tannen, Deborah. 1982. "Oral and Literate Strategies in Spoken and Written Narratives." *Language* 58:1–21.
———. 1984. *Conversational Style: Analyzing Talk Among Friends.* Norwood, NJ: Ablex.
———, ed. 1982. *Spoken and Written Language: Exploring Orality and Literacy.* Norwood, NJ: Ablex.
Trudgill, Peter. 1974. *Sociolinguistics: An Introduction.* New York: Penguin.
Ure, Jean. 1982. "Introduction: Approaches to the Study of Register Range." *International Journal of the Sociology of Language* 35:5–23.
Ventola, Eija. 1984. "Orientation to Social Semiotics in Foreign Language Teaching." *Applied Linguistics* 5:275–86.
Wardaugh, Ronald. 1992. *An Introduction to Sociolinguistics,* 2nd ed. Oxford: Basil Blackwell.
Zwicky, Ann D., and Arnold M. Zwicky. 1980. "America's National Dish: The Style of Restaurant Menus." *American Speech* 55:83–92.

II

INDIVIDUAL REGISTERS

3

On the Creation and Expansion of Registers: Sports Reporting in Tok Pisin

Suzanne Romaine

1. Introduction

This chapter examines a case of register creation in Tok Pisin, an English-based pidgin/creole spoken in Papua New Guinea, which has come to serve as the most important lingua franca spoken by more than a million people in a highly multilingual society. The register in question is sports reporting, as found in the newspaper *Wantok*. Begun in 1970 and published weekly, it is the country's most important secular publication and the only newspaper appearing today in Tok Pisin. All of the early written materials in Tok Pisin, which date from the 1920s, and the majority of published works today are religious in nature. *Wantok* carries most of the features one would expect of a newspaper: world and local news, letters to the editor, and so on. More recently, however, new items have appeared such as sports reports. The emergence of new registers and genres is a manifestation of more general stylistic expansion that has accompanied the nativization of the language over the past few decades.

I will look at the language of sports reporting through samples from an early year of *Wantok*, 1982, and later years, 1987 and 1990 (see the Appendix for two short sample texts). My discussion will focus on the lexical and syntactic features which make this register distinctive. I will also consider the extent to which conventionalization of this register can be detected in the later reports. Finally, I address the question of the extent to which the similarities of sports reporting in English and Tok Pisin are due primarily to the diffusion of conventions for the register across language boundaries, or to more general constraints imposed by the context of situation, subject matter, and so forth.

2. Brief History of Tok Pisin

One of the interesting aspects of this study will be the opportunity to document the rise and expansion of a new register in a relatively short period. The time frame in which Tok Pisin developed from its jargon roots to an expanded pidgin, then creole, and now postcreole, has been compressed into a period of 100 to 150 years. It is thus a young creole, by comparison with most of the Atlantic creoles such as Jamaican or Haitian Creole. Nevertheless, decreolization is already well under way in urban areas.

Tok Pisin was first learned by New Guineans working as contract laborers on plantations in Queensland, Samoa, Fiji, and later Papua New Guinea itself. The typical pattern of acquisition was for Melanesian workers to learn a rudimentary jargon variety of English which was widespread in the Pacific in the nineteenth century and used for trade between Europeans and Pacific Islanders. A more stabilized and expanded form of this jargon was in use on plantations where Pacific Islanders from many different language groups worked. When New Guineans returned to their villages, the plantation pidgin English was passed on to younger men and boys. While it was originally a language used for instrumental purposes in vertical, hierarchical, communicative encounters between Europeans and indigenous people, an expanded Tok Pisin later came to serve an integrative function at the horizontal level of communication among villagers.

Amid a highly linguistically diverse scene with more than seven hundred languages, Tok Pisin today stands as a lingua franca which cuts across the linguistic and social spectrum. Roughly half of the population of some three and a half million claim to speak it. It is known by villagers and government ministers, and most government and church communication at the grassroots level is in Tok Pisin. Indeed, Tok Pisin was the language used to make the public aware of voting, elections, and independence in 1975.[1] In 1982, 90 percent of the candidates campaigned in Tok Pisin. When the New Guinea legislature was established in the mid-1960s, Tok Pisin was accepted for use in the House of Assembly. In the first four years of its use it was restricted to certain topics and specific purposes. Now any business arising in the House can be and usually is discussed in Tok Pisin. Tok Pisin has in the past few decades become the main language of the migrant proletarian and the first language of the younger generation of town-born children.

One of the most important aspects of the expansion of Tok Pisin as a spoken language has been the emergence of socially determined varieties and new registers. Mühlhäusler (1979:140–54), for instance, identifies three major sociolects of Tok Pisin: rural Tok Pisin spoken by the majority of people living outside towns, bush Tok Pisin spoken in areas where Tok Pisin has only recently penetrated, and urban Tok Pisin spoken in the major towns since the late 1960s, when indigenous people were allowed to reside more freely there.

After years of development under German administration of the colony of New Guinea, when Tok Pisin had no direct contact with its superstrate, the language suddenly became subject to the influence of English again, particularly in urban areas. This has led to increasing anglicization. The most heavily anglicized Tok Pisin is spoken by those with the highest education residing in towns.

The urban environment has now become perhaps the most important one in terms of understanding future trends in the language and the country. The melanesianization of the town has gone hand in hand with the nativization of Tok Pisin. Tok Pisin has become no man's language in no man's land. This process is of particular interest to sociolinguists, given that most studies of urban speech varieties in Western industrialized societies take as their starting point the notion that social stratification will be an important dimension in accounting for linguistic variation. A basic premise is that inequalities in society will be reflected in the distribution of sociolects. Such models are, however, not immediately applicable in many postcolonial societies, such as Papua New Guinea, where the town itself is a colonial institution and an innovation in the Papua New Guinean context. Traditional society is based on the village. Even though class formation is incipient in Papua New Guinea, its basis is somewhat different from that found in Western industrialized nations. The most important dimension for variation in Tok Pisin today is the dichotomy between rural and urban, which overrides other regional differences. This linguistic division has its roots in colonization patterns and European ideologies of development (see Romaine 1992a). Urban Tok Pisin is a more anglicized variety reflecting the greater accessibility of the town to English speakers and better educational facilities. Rural Tok Pisin is also now seen by many as the "real" Tok Pisin, while the urban variety is stigmatized as mixed and impure.

3. Tok Pisin as a Written Language and the Emergence of Media Tok Pisin

Until the last few decades Tok Pisin was only a spoken language. Its development as a written language for use by Melanesians began in the 1920s when Catholic missionaries realized its potential as a valuable lingua franca for proselytizing among a linguistically diverse population and began using it for teaching. The Lutherans, who had a policy of using vernacular languages and developed two regional languages (Kâte and Yabem) for use in their mission schools, were nevertheless forced to accept the usefulness and necessity of Tok Pisin. The Lutheran church eventually recognized it officially in a conference in 1930 (Osmers 1981:96), where it was accepted that use of "pidgin English" was justified because of its wide distribution and ease of acquisition and neutrality. It recommended a knowledge of the language for all missionaries. However, the delegates also noted some problems, including the lack of standardization and lack of literature for teaching. Thus they, along with the Methodist mission, began publishing materials during the 1930s.

The Lutherans' acceptance and use of Tok Pisin increased over the years, largely through their conflict with the government over the use of English, which they opposed. Despite the government's withdrawal of support for non-English-medium schools, the Lutheran mission was resolved to teach Tok Pisin in its secondary schools and to produce the necessary literature. The Catholics approached them about which variety of the language to use, and the Lutherans agreed to cooperate to unify language practice.

Now the orthography used in the *Nupela Testamen* (New Testament) has come to serve as a de facto standard for Tok Pisin since its publication in 1966. It is based on Hall's (1955) system, which was approved by the Director of Education and the Administrator of the Territory of Papua and New Guinea and by the Minister for the

Territories in Canberra. A government publication issued by the Department of Education in 1956 recognized the orthography officially, and it was used with a few minor changes in Mihalic's (1957) grammar and dictionary. In 1969 an orthography committee was set up. It recommended that the slightly modified spelling system employed in *Nupela Testamen* be recognized as the official orthography, and the variety of Tok Pisin spoken along the north coast of mainland New Guinea be the standard. Mihalic's (1957) grammar and dictionary of Melanesian Pidgin was adopted for use in 1963 and made compulsory for production of written material in Tok Pisin and for teaching in the Vernacular Education program.

The *Nupela Testamen* had an initial printing of 40,000 copies and was the largest issue of any book in Tok Pisin. It has been reprinted many times since and is the best-selling book in Papua New Guinea with over 450,000 copies. Even those unable to read have probably heard it read aloud in church. The orthography used in this translation is still followed by the Kristen Pres (Christian Press), the major Tok Pisin publishing house, and *Wantok* newspaper.

The main production of written material in Tok Pisin was started at the beginning of the 1960s to cover the growing demand of the vernacular education program of the Lutheran Church. Today the Kristen Pres still produces most of the written material, both religious and more generally educational (Osmers 1981 lists 111 religious and 120 secular publications). The Summer Institute of Linguistics, a religious organization, also publishes in Tok Pisin.

Written Tok Pisin was first used for mass communication outside religious domains during World War II, when millions of propaganda leaflets were dropped by the Allies and the Japanese. After the war Tok Pisin newspapers began, and these and other periodicals proliferated in the 1970s, including *Bougainville Nius* (Bougainville News), *Toktok bilong haus ov assembli* (Discussions from the House of Assembly), and *Nius bilong Yumi* (Our News), but most ceased after only a few issues and did not survive after independence. *Nu Gini Toktok* (New Guinea Discussion), the first of these papers in Tok Pisin, was published weekly in Rabaul (see Frazer 1969) and ran from 1962 to 1970. It was originally *The Pidgin English News* and was published as a weekly supplement to the *Late New Guinea Times Courier*. Another shortlived paper called *Kundu* (Drum) was published in both Tok Pisin and English by the Catholic Press at Vunapope near Rabaul from 1966 to 1970. *Nius bilong yumi* ran from 1959 to 1982 and was a translation from *Our News* put out by the Department of Information and Extension Services. There was also a monthly journal called *Katolik:Buk bilong Tok Pitsin* (Catholics: Tok Pisin Book) published in 1940–41, which continued after the war as the *Katolik Nius* (Catholic News), and *Pangu Pati Nius* (Pangu Party News), a political newspaper that is still published.

Perhaps the most important of these periodicals is the weekly newspaper *Wantok*, which was founded by the Catholics in 1967 and appears only in Tok Pisin. The name means literally 'one language' and is a term widely used throughout Papua New Guinea to express solidarity in reference to those whom one regards as one's fellow clan members. The newspaper has a circulation of over 10,000 with more than 50,000 readers in Papua New Guinea. It has been in existence since 1970 and its staff now consists entirely of Papua New Guinea nationals.

While written Tok Pisin was originally used by expatriates for teaching the indigenous population, the contribution of indigenous authors writing for a Papua New Guinean audience has been steadily increasing.[2] The past twenty or thirty years have seen the appearance of a number of manuals on health, hygiene, agriculture, carpentry, cooking, and so on. There are already indications that secular publications are setting a new standard for the written language. The language is also written informally by those with little schooling and minimal exposure to the standard form. Such writings usually contain idiosyncratic spellings.

Thus after years of existing only in spoken form, Tok Pisin is now the language used in an increasing amount of literature. Brasch (1971) and Smith (1988) have discussed some of the creative coinages of Tok Pisin used for colloquial purposes. Tok Pisin already has a number of special named registers for particular speech functions (see Wurm and Mühlhäusler 1982). Thus *tok piksa* 'talk picture' is a general term for the use of similes and examples. For instance, a common Tok Pisin term for 'beer' is *spesel Milo* 'special Milo', where *Milo* is a brandname for a chocolate drink. Tok Pisin *switbisket* 'sweet biscuit' and *draibisket* 'dry biscuit' have metaphorical meanings. The former can refer to a sexually attractive woman and the latter to a woman past her prime. *Tok pilai* 'talk play' refers to the jocular use of metaphors, often over an extended period. In recent years a column called *Tok Pilai* has been added to *Wantok*. It contains jokes, amusing observations, and comments on Tok Pisin. *Tok bokis* 'talk box' uses familiar words in new senses to disguise meanings. This is often employed for discussing secrets. *Tok bilas* 'talk decoration' is used for saying things that can be potentially offensive and threatening, but later denied.

Euphemism is now widely used in advertising in Tok Pisin, where Western practice and models have been taken over (see Romaine 1990), and it has also begun to appear in everyday conversation. While many bodily functions do not have the same taboo surrounding them in Papua New Guinea as they do in Western culture, euphemisms for these things are beginning to appear. I was amazed when a young schoolgirl whom I was interviewing used a new euphemistic term I hadn't heard before, *troimwe excretia* 'to throw away excretia' instead of the normal Tok Pisin *pekpek* 'to defecate', which before was used in all contexts. Similarly, *pispis* is the normal term for 'urinate', though now there is a new euphemism, *kapsaitim wara* 'to capsize water'.

Many of these new idiomatic expressions in use in Tok Pisin today derive from similar English ones, as in a case where a young girl explained to me that her friend's mother was a *single meri* 'single mother.' Here the English term *single* has been borrowed and used along with the Tok Pisin word *meri* 'woman' to form a hybrid collocation modeled on English. Other new expressions like *lap indai* [laugh die] 'to laugh heartily', *kisim tamiok* [get ax] 'get the axe/be eliminated', and *kisim win* [catch wind] 'to rest' are closely related to similar English colloquialisms such as 'die laughing', 'get the axe', and 'catch one's breath'. The expression *no waris* is simply taken over from Australian English *no worries,* and *tu glas spak* [two glass drunk], according to Brasch (1971:19), is the local equivalent of the Australian expression *a two glass roarer,* that is, one too easily affected by alcohol. Sometimes these expressions are shortened to initials, as in *KBS* (<*kanaka big pela samting* [bush man big something]) 'bigshot'. Such usages are indicative of stylistic expansion and an increase in register range. A change in register range may be thought of as one of the most immediate ways in which a language can respond to social change. Much of the difference between developed and undeveloped languages is essentially one of register range.

4. Sports Reporting as a Register

My designation of the language of sports reporting as a register and its appearance as part of the more general process of stylistic expansion perhaps requires some specific comment. Insofar as the concept of register is typically concerned with variation in language conditioned by uses rather than users, its study will entail among other things a consideration of the situation or context of use; the purpose, subject matter, and content of the message; and the relationship between participants. It is in this sense that I have termed the language of sports reporting a register. That is to say, it is a recognizable language variety whose syntax and vocabulary have emerged and been shaped in response to these sorts of external conditioning factors. I have taken as my point of departure Ferguson's (1983) pioneering study of sports announcer talk, which he defines as a register or discourse genre:

> the sportscast is a discourse genre as identifiable as the sonnet, the bread-and-butter letter, the knock-knock joke, the professional paper in linguistics, or any of the hundreds of such forms of discourse in the total repertoire of communities of users of English. (154)

Ghadessy (1988:18), who has looked at the language of soccer reporting, states simply that there is no doubt that this variety constitutes a register.

Ferguson's venture into this area of linguistic variation has unfortunately not been followed up in any detail. Also seldom discussed by those interested in contextual variation have been problems such as the discreteness of registers and the extent to which register variation is distinct from stylistic variation (but see Ferguson this volume). I return to some of these issues later.

Ferguson (1983:167) notes that the

> emergence and conventionalization of registers includes not only the specialized use of particular lexical items and syntactic constructions, but the use of prefabricated modules, inserted as needed at appropriate points in the use of the register. Such routines serve, then, not only as convenient, streamlined, unobtrusive counters in well-worn patterns of discourse but also as markers of the register itself.

Conventionalization has been little studied (see, however, Halliday 1988 and Ferguson this volume). Of special interest in the case of Tok Pisin is the apparent wholesale transfer of some of the English conventions that make this register distinct. Indeed, Ferguson (1983:167) points out that the structure of routines is of special interest in the study of register since they may be easier to transfer via lexical borrowing, and thus they may diffuse across language boundaries more directly, than other aspects of a register. Many languages have borrowed the vocabulary of sports such as cricket and baseball, which have their origin in English-speaking countries, and even English has taken over French terms in gambling. There is thus a sense in which each sport or game has an international core vocabulary.

It will be evident from the examples I have already given that lexical expansion in Tok Pisin has relied heavily on English borrowing rather than on internal coinages, despite the existence of a productive word formation component. In many cases borrowing is resorted to as a means of filling a lexical gap, particularly where foreign institutions and ideas are involved. These concepts could be expressed in Tok Pisin but usually only by means of a lengthy circumlocution. I will show too that the lexicalization of sports reporting is primarily dependent on borrowing, at least as far as nouns having to do with technical aspects of the game are concerned. Verbs, however, which are used to describe the plays and events of various sports, draw on the latest Tok Pisin colloquialisms, not all of which are borrowed directly from English.

4.1. A Brief History of Sports Reporting in Wantok Niuspepa

According to Ferguson (1983:169), sports announcer talk began in the 1920s. As far as I can tell from examining previous issues of *Wantok*, sports writing in Tok Pisin begins in 1978. In the issue published for the week of 29 August a page labeled *spot pes* 'sports page' appears. During most of this year's editions the page carries mainly photos of men and women engaged in various sports and not much in the way of report of the actions or events in particular matches. A caption reads, *yu inap painim wantok bilong yu?* 'Can you find your friends?' The first reports of specific sports begin in 1979. For instance, *ragbi lig* 'rugby league' is featured on the sports page for the week of 24 February 1979, *basketbal* 'basketball' in the week of 3 March, and *soka* 'soccer' in the week of 19 March. This is not to say, however, that there were no reports about sporting events before this time. Both the Commonwealth and South Pacific Games received coverage as news items of general interest in previous editions. In the issue for the week of 28 January, boxing at the Commonwealth Games was the front page story because a Papua New Guinean, John Abu, was the junior lightweight champion (*Wol Feda Wet Sempion* 'World Feather Weight Champion').

In these early years, however, there is no play-by-play report, and sports coverage is not extensive, taking at most one or two pages. Although the standard orthography for Tok Pisin is used in the newspaper, spellings for some of the new sports terms are somewhat variable. For instance, 'player' appears as *pleya, pilaya,* and *plaia*. Sometimes glosses or synonyms are given for unfamiliar terms. For instance, in the week of 27 January 1979 the term *pul volt* 'pole vault' is introduced by the circumlocution *bikpela kalap ol i kolim pul volt* 'the big jump they call the pole vault'. In the week of 24 February, 1979 the term *Prisisen Kompetisen* 'preseason competition' is glossed for readers as *resis bilong taim i stap insait long dispela spot ragbi* 'competitions during the time of this sport rugby'.

This follows a practice which continues elsewhere in *Wantok* when other new English terms are introduced, for example, *wanpela bikpela mas em ol yut/yangpela bilong Lae siti i bin holim long las wik Fraide, 8 Jun 1990* 'a big march which the youth/young [people] held last week on Friday 8 June 1990'.[3] The introduction of the new term *yut* is followed by an already existing Tok Pisin equivalent, *yangpela*. Subsequently in the article the English term is used without its Tok Pisin gloss. In this next example a complete gloss is given for the term *pait politik* 'political fight': *Dispela i min olsem i gat tupela grup i wok long pait nau long winim pawa.* 'This means that there are two groups who are fighting for power.'

This practice of glossing is consistent with the founding editor's belief that *Wantok* is supposed to be aimed at the rural, colloquial Tok Pisin–speaking population. This is made clear in an editorial published in the first issue (5 August 1970, p. 3):

> *Tok Pisin em i tok bilong yu . . . inap nau i gat kain kain tok i save kamap long tok pisin. Tasol husat inap ritim? Em i hapkas tok pisin tasol. Man i hatwok long ritim. Dispela niuspepa Wantok em bai i spik olsem wantok tru bilong yu, em i no tanim tok pisin. Nogat. Em i tok olsem yu yet yu tok.*
>
> Tok Pisin is your language. There are already a lot of words coming into Tok Pisin now. But who can read them? That's half-caste Tok Pisin. It takes a lot of effort to read. This newspaper, *Wantok*, will speak as a true friend of yours. It won't transform Tok Pisin. Never. It speaks as you yourself speak.

Since then, *Wantok* has had a great influence on the way Tok Pisin is written. The founding editor, Mihalic (1986:2), published a style book which sets out norms to be followed. He writes:

> It is imperative for us at *Wantok* to write and spell correct Tok Pisin because unofficially we are considered the norm for usage and spelling throughout the country. Whether we like it or not, we are setting the standards for Tok Pisin writing, simply because no one else writes and prints as much material as we do in Tok Pisin. And what we write is spread all over the country.

Because *Wantok* is often read out to great numbers of people, it also influences spoken Tok Pisin. Similarly, the Tok Pisin editor of *Kristen Pres* commented (cited in Osmers 1981:112):

> We avoid anglicisms and the newest expressions one may hear in the towns (until they are widely known), as well as any expressions which may be peculiar to only one of the various dialects of Pidgin. We aim for no "learned" or "literary" style based on some English model, but for the *colloquial* language of the average Pidgin speaker, hoping to achieve the expressiveness of the oral language used daily by hundreds of thousands of speakers.

Nevertheless, despite its aim of using colloquial rural Tok Pisin, many of the items found in *Wantok* (and more generally in the media) are commonly used in town speech but are not intelligible to the average rural adult speaker. Many rural speakers whom I interviewed complained they could not understand urban Tok Pisin and the language of *Wantok*. Thus one man:

> *Em bilong taun. Sampela mi save, sampela ol miksim wantaim inglis em mi no save. Ol go pas long pisin tasol, mi save. Ol miksim wantaim tok inglis, em mi no ken klia. Long pisin bai mi klia, inglis mi no klia. . . . Sampela taim mi go long taun, mi sa baim na mi sa ritim. Em sem olsem redio ol sa toktok, sampela ol miksim inglis i go insait long*

dispela niuspepa. . . Inglis kam long hap bilong yumi na yumi save miksim. Miksim na toktok na i no gutpela.

[The Tok Pisin] of the town. Some people I understand, but some people mix English with it and I don't understand. Those who stick to Tok Pisin I can understand. Those who mix with English I am not clear about. In Tok Pisin I am clear. Sometimes I go to town, I buy [*Wantok*] and read it. It's the same way they talk on the radio. Some people mix English in this newspaper. English has come into our midst and we are accustomed to mixing. Mixing talk is not a good thing.

Complaints about anglicized Tok Pisin sent to the editor of *Wantok* have become more frequent since the 1970s.

Although most English borrowings found in *Wantok* have been orthographically adapted, they are still semantically and morphologically conspicuous and won't be intelligible to the average speaker who does not know the games and the English terminology. In later sports reports there is no glossing of unfamiliar words. This is of course indicative of another characteristic of registers with specialist terminology; the presumed audience is expected not to need an explanation of the terminology. I take this to be an indication of the conventionalization of the register.

In 1984 sports reporting in *Wantok* is expanded to three to four pages and appears much as it is found today. The spelling of terms such as 'player' stabilizes and is written as *pilaia* as it is found today. In the issue published for the week of 3 May 1984 a special section appears called *Rugby League News*. It covers rugby entirely in English, while the *spot pes* 'sport page' continues to report in Tok Pisin on other sports. In this edition mention is made of previous issues of *Rugby League News* which appeared earlier in *Wantok,* but I am not able to pinpoint its first appearance.[4] In September 1984 it ceases, but it reappears in June 1985. It also appears occasionally from that time on. Also during October 1984 a special section of some eight pages begins to appear called *Wantok Spot Nius* 'Wantok sports news'. It carries articles in both Tok Pisin and English and is featured alongside the English section *Rugby League News*. Some Papua New Guinean authors such as Ben Wauns write in both languages for *Wantok Spot Nius*. In 1990 *Rugby League News* appears in Tok Pisin as *Ragbi Lig Nius* and although most of its feature stories are in Tok Pisin, there are advertisements in English, and the Points Ladder, where the team rankings are given, is in English.

4.2. Some Features of Sports Writing

In my discussion of some of the linguistic features of sports writing I have focused on two aspects: lexis and syntax.

4.2.1. LEXIS

As I have already shown, the dependence on English borrowing for lexicalization of the sports register is immediately obvious (see, e.g., Balint 1969, whose sports dictionary lists two thousand entries, most of which are nonce borrowings). Special lexis is used for both the names of the games as well as technical moves associated with the games, players, and moves. As examples of the first type we have the following: *hoki* 'hockey', *soka* 'soccer', *ragbi* 'rugby'. The only example I found which was not imported wholesale from English was *netbal* 'netball' (volleyball). The term *volibal* does in fact appear in 1984 issues. Interestingly, Tok Pisin has the traditional term *umben* for 'net', taken from one of the indigenous languages of Papua New Guinea, and it is sometimes used in sports reporting to refer to nets.

As examples of technical terms associated with the game, we have the following: *fofit* 'forfeit', *gol* 'goal', *takel* 'tackle', *reperi* 'referee', *dro* 'draw', *fowat* 'forward', *sempionsip* 'championship', *tropi* 'trophy', *semipainal* 'semi final', *golkipa* 'goalkeeper', *tim menesa* 'team manager', *kosa* 'coach', *midfil* 'midfield', *straika* 'striker', *hom bes* 'home base', *kona kik* 'corner kick', and *bantim* 'to bunt'. The borrowing of these terms does have syntactic consequences in that some words such as *inning* then take English plurals, as in *inings*. The use of *-s* plurals has been generally increasing in the pasts few decades. The names of the clubs and associations are also often taken from English, sometimes with grammatical consequences, as in *Presiden bilong Wimens Sofbal Asosiesen* 'president of the women's softball association'. Normally the term for a woman in Tok Pisin is *meri*, although *gel* [<girl] is increasingly used too, and possessive constructions are normally phrased in Tok Pisin by using *bilong*, for example, *bilong ol meri* 'the women's'. Another example can be seen in *lainsman* 'linesman', where the linking suffix *-s* turns up in the compound (cf. also *batsman*). This term *lainsman* may have been borrowed, however, as a result of blocking conditions operating on productive Tok Pisin word formation processes. Although Tok Pisin has a word formation rule which produces compounds ending in *-man* with no linking suffix, for example, *spakman* [drunk + man] 'drunk' and *saveman* [knowledge + man] 'expert', it also already has the word *lain* meaning 'one's kin line'. If the equivalent term had been calqued as *lainman*, its meaning might not have been understood in its technical sense.

The team names are a mix of place names, for example *Lae Siti* (Lae City), English terms, for example, *Brothers, Sea Eagles, United,* and Tok Pisin terms, often animal names, for example, *Muruk* 'cassowary', *Wallabi* 'wallaby', *Dolfin* 'dolphin'. These have counterparts in the team names common elsewhere in the English-speaking world, for example, (Chicago) *Black Hawks* (United States ice hockey), *Oxford City/Leeds United* (English football), and (Los Angeles) *Rams* (United States football). The plurals of these team names in Tok Pisin end in *-s* as they would in English, for example *Muruks* and *Brothers*.

There were only a few instances where technical terms were calqued into Tok Pisin, for example, *haptaim* 'half time' and *nàmba tu hap* [number two half] 'second half'. I have also seen the borrowing *fes hap* 'first half' used in a sports cartoon, which like many cartoons in Tok Pisin, draws on a highly anglicized urban variety of Tok Pisin. There were quite a few semicalques or hybrids, where one of the terms is familiar, as in *birua tim* 'opposing team', where *birua* is from an indigenous language (with the meaning 'a piece of human flesh for a cannibal feast') and used in Tok Pisin to refer to 'accident', 'enemy', or 'opponent'. Another is *penalti bokis* 'penalty box'.

Another aspect to the lexical distinctiveness of sports reporting in Tok Pisin is the establishment of new collocations to refer to some of the plays, rules, and procedures. Again, some of these combine Tok Pisin terms with foreign lexis, such as *abrusim konversen* 'to foil a conversion', where *abrusim* 'to be apart' is already a familiar Tok Pisin term from one of the indigenous languages meaning 'get out of the way', 'pass by'. Other examples of this kind, where the verb is Tok Pisin and the noun a new borrowing, are *givim penalti* 'to give a penalty', *putim trai/poin/gol* 'to put a try, goal, point', *brukim difens* (or *brukim banis* 'to break fence'), *winim wisil* 'to blow a whistle', *go pas long poin/skoa* 'to go ahead to a point/score', *stilim bes* 'to steal a base'. In all of these cases, the new collocations extend the meanings of the Tok Pisin terms. They will be more easily intelligible in part to average readers because they draw on well established verbs already in the language. Thus *putim* is also used in idiomatic expressions such as *putim kiau* [put egg] 'to lay an egg', *brukim* in *brukim marit* [break marriage] 'to get divorced', and *go pas,* for example, in *tok i go pas* [talk which goes first] 'introduction'. Other expressions, however, are borrowed wholesale from English, for example, *kikim konversen* 'to kick a conversion' and *swingim bal* 'to swing the ball'. While most of these verbs are adapted to Tok Pisin morphology and take the transitive suffix *-im* when required, as do other well established borrowed verbs with origins in English phrasal verbs (e.g., *hansupim* 'to hold someone up' from the expression *put up your hands,* *bagarapim* 'to destroy' from 'bugger up'), there are other verbs which do not, for example, *tekova* 'to take over'. Many new phrasal verbs are being borrowed such as *kikov* 'to kick off'.

Another unusual feature of lexis is the use of terms which are nowadays found mainly in religious writing and among older rural speakers, for example, *beten* 'pray' or *dinau* 'debt', as in *sampela sapota i beten long gutpela san* 'some supporters are praying for sunny weather'. These probably reflect the fact that the newspaper was originally connected with the Catholic church.

Perhaps among the most interesting features of sports reporting is the use of a whole new range of idiomatic expressions, for example, *salensim/traim/sakim bun bilong birua tim* 'to challenge/try/sack the bone of opposing team'. Here *bun* [<bone] refers to the stamina or the backbone of the team and players. It is frequently used in everyday colloquial expressions such as *taitim bun* [tighten bone] 'to brace oneself/gather strength'.

Other idiomatic expressions are created through the use of already existing verbs in new metaphorical senses, for example, *kaikai* 'to eat' (i.e., 'devour one's opponents'), *autim* [out] 'to oust', and *daunim* [down] 'to defeat'. These verbs are already in use in expressions such as *autim wari* [out worry] 'to voice concern' and *daunim sik* [down sick] 'get rid of illness'. These and other newly created verbs such as *nekim* [<*nek* 'neck', 'voice', 'speech'] and *saitim* [<sait 'side'], *saitim long het* 'to propel the ball with a head kick in soccer' are now among the many new expressions used to describe the nature of one team's assault on or victory over the other. These verbs which are generally descriptive of combat and force dynamics add to the vividness of the sports reporting register, for example:

Royals i autim Brothers long tu poin.
'The Royals beat the Brothers by two points'.

Royals i nekim ol [Brothers] 20–18.
'Royals beat them 20–18'.

In addition, Smith (1988) has noted the use of the following synonyms for 'to win' in a *Wantok* sports report, *hamaim* 'to hammer', *nilim* 'to nail', *memeim* [<*meme* 'goat'] 'to butt', *krungutim* 'to twist/crush', *matmatim* [<*matmat* 'cemetery'], *kilim* 'to kill', *daunim* 'to down', *kapsaitim* 'to overturn', *autim tiket* 'out ticket'. Items like *autim, agensim, afterim* are all cases where English prepositions have been used to create new Tok Pisin verbs.

Other verbs with similar connotations are new borrowings from English, such as the following:

West i bomim *Difens*
'West bombed Difens'.

Gasel i blakaut *long Elkom 16–3.*
'Gasel blacked out Elkom 16–3'.

Wanzesi . . . bai wipim *ol kranki tru.*
'Wanzesi will really whip them senseless'.

These expressions, whether borrowed or created internally, have direct counterparts in sports reporting in the major English-speaking countries. For instance, we can take the following examples from the English, British, and Australian press coverage of major sports events. The choices of verbs or verbal expressions are all evocative of combat. There is a mix of colloquial spoken idioms such as *kill off*, *thump*, and *blow away* and more literary sounding phrases such as *administer a lethal blow*. Thus compare the following examples.

From football, that is, soccer, as reported in the British newspaper *The Guardian*):

He thumped *a final penalty high.*
They battered *forward.*
Steele's attempted clearance was charged down.
He struck *a hat trick past Coventry.*
He administered *a lethal blow.*
It killed *Sunderland* off.

From baseball and football (*San Francisco Chronicle*):

The underdog Cincinnati Reds ambushed *the A's.*
The Reds' clean-up hitter blasted *it well over the center-field fence.*
Jose Rijo . . . looked set to blow *him* away.
The A's have a fight on their hands.
The Bulldogs demolished *Miramonte last week.*

From cricket (*The Australian*):

The West Indies have pulverised *not only England but every side in the world for the past fifteen years or so.*

The main purpose of these terms is to introduce stylistic variation. This can be seen in particular when a team's record is being reviewed for readers, as in the following:

Guria i soim gutpela rekot long wipim Yuni (2) 3–0, krungutim Wanzesi (1) 4–0, na abrusim Sobou (1) 2–1. Wespac i bin pilai tupela taim tasol na memeim Tarangau (2) 5– 0 na laki long autim Rapatona (2) 1–0.

Guria has shown a good record in whipping Yuni 3–0, mangling Wanzesi, 4–0 and getting by Sobou 2–1. Wespac played only twice and butted Tarangau 5–0 and were lucky to oust Rapatona 1–0.

Ghadessy (1988:33) notes that the language of sports commentary is characterized by verbal as opposed to nominal style. Others such as Varantola (1984) have found the verbal style to be typical of specialized, technical, and scientific writing. Tok Pisin sports writing is consistent with these observations.

Many similes, metaphors, and idiomatic expressions are obviously calqued from English, as in *Peter Mundy i no ken kaunim ol kiau kwiktaim* 'Peter Mundy can't count the eggs quickly' (cf. "don't count your chickens before they hatch"; "don't put all your eggs in one basket"). It may be that some of these are the result of imperfect acquisition since I have often heard educated Papua New Guineans mix metaphors and produce such oddities as 'to be green behind the ears' (cf. "wet behind the ears", "to be a greenhorn"), "losing the boat" (cf. "missing the boat,' "losing a chance"). Other calques include *givim hat taim* 'to give a hard time', *sanap long* 'stand at' (in reporting the score), *katim pawa* 'to cut off the power', *givim wankain marasin gen* 'to give (a dose of) the same medicine again', *tanim tebol antap long* 'to turn the tables on'. There are, however, similes and analogies which are not calqued or borrowed directly from English, but obviously make reference to items or technology from English-speaking culture, for example, *Ol dispela pilaia i gat nem long mekim stail bilong piston masin long filding na givim siksti olsem Nisan trak long ol i kisim bat.* 'These players have got a reputation for being like piston engines in their fielding and they accelerate like a Nissan truck when they come up to bat.' The expression *givim/go siksti* 'to give, go sixty (miles an hour)' is widely used in urban speech for rapid movement.

4.2.2. SYNTAX

The most typical feature of syntax found in the sports reporting register is the complex or heavy NP construction, as in these examples from *Wantok:*

Kepten bilong Konepoti Wari Kini
'the captain of Konepoti, Wari Kini'

Kepten bilong Royals na huka bilong PNG nesenel tim, Kumul, Michael Matmilo
'Captain of the Royals and hooker of the PNG national team, Kumul, Michael Matmilo'

yangpela senta bilong Kumul Philip Boge
'the young center of Kumul, Philip Boge'

Dispela Koka Kola Soka Sempionsip bilong ol U10
'The Coca Cola Soccer Championship of U10 [division]'

Madang A Gret netbal gran painal
'The Madang A grade netball grand final'

United Ragbi Lig klap bilong Goroka   'United Rugby League Club of Goroka'

hatpela semi final kik bilong PMSA Kap pre-sisen nokaut resis
'hard semifinal kick of the Port Moresby Soccer Association Cup pre-season knockout
competition'

As can be seen, these complex NPs are of various types and include heads with
determiners, premodifiers, postmodifiers, appositives, or complements. A great
many of these consist of proper nouns. This style is also found in sports reporting in
English newspapers as can be seen in the following examples:
    From rugby (*The Guardian*):

England's flanker Gary Rees
fullback and record points scorer John Liley

    From baseball (*San Francisco Chronicle*):

pitcher coach Dave Duncan
Milwaukee Brewers' designated hitter Dave Parker

    From horse racing and cycling (*The Australian*):

bonny New Zealand staying mare Shuzohra
the gallant 22 year old Tasmanian Rice

    This style is often seen in its extreme in examples such as the following, where
nearly every NP consists of a proper name plus modification.
    From football (*San Francisco Chronicle*):

"The Colts have reached an agreement with veteran quarterback Joe Ferguson as a backup
to current starter Jack Trudeau," said coach Ron Meyer. The quarterback move was
prompted by injuries to rookie Jeff George and veteran Mark Herrmann.

    A similar style in Tok Pisin is immediately identifiable as part of sports reporting
register. For example:

Na 'trail blazer kid', Akwil Burat husat kisim nogut long skru tupela wik bipo bai sambai
olsem risev raitfilda o kamap designetet hita (D/H) nau. (1987)
'And the trail blazer kid, Akwil Burat who injured his knee two weeks ago, will stand by
as a reserve rightfielder or come in as designated hitter.'

    Ferguson (1983:163, 169) too notes the use of heavy modifiers such as preposed
adjectives, nonrestrictive relative clauses, and appositional NPs, as characteristic of
sports announcer talk. They are used, in his view, to pack more background information into event reporting sentence. This feature is, however, not dependent on
channel or medium since it is found in both spoken and written reports. Crystal and
Davy (1969:186), for instance, comment on the presence of much more complex
pre- and postmodification structures in what they call journalese than in ordinary
speech and writing. In Tok Pisin these heavy NPs found in sports reports are
especially striking because in the spoken language, nouns with no modification are
the norm; the most common NPs consist of heads only.
    Since NP marking is not obligatory, an unmarked NP may represent an entity
which is new or familiar, specific or nonspecific, singular or plural, and so on. Thus

in the next example from a spoken narrative I recorded, most of the NPs consist only of heads. Other simple NPs consist of a determiner plus head, for example, *ol dok* 'the dogs', where *ol* is the third person pronoun used as a plural marker. Complex NPs such as *bikpela ston* 'a large stone' and *haus bilong em,* where the genitive phrase functions as a determiner, are less frequent.

> *Krokodail tok olsem, "Nau bai mi go long wara na bai mi painim ol dok na ol dok bai sindaun, bai mi kissim em go long aus bilong em. Em bai wokabaut bilong mi", em tok, krokodail olsem. Krokodail tok olsem, "Bai mi go long wara na painim dok." Na em go long wara na em lukim bikpla ston na dok sindaun i stap.*

> The crocodile said, "I'll go down to the river and look for dogs. Dogs will be sitting there and I'll get him/them and take them/him back to his house. Then he'll/they'll come to mine," the crocodile said. The crocodile said, "I'll go down to the river and look for the dog(s)." He went to the river and saw a big stone and the dog(s) was sitting there.

While the reference of most bare NPs is clear from context, ambiguity does sometimes arise. In this extract from a narrative, the crocodile has already been introduced into the discourse and so is familiar. Its first occurrence in this extract is bare, but nevertheless its reference is definite and specific. The next noun is *wara,* which is also bare. The next animates to be introduced are the dogs, who are referred to as *ol dog.* Here the meaning seems to be plural, but since the dogs have not been mentioned before there is no indication that the crocodile is looking for a specific group of dogs. The story line then becomes more complicated because it is not clear whether the crocodile is making reference to a specific dog or the whole group when he uses the third person singular pronoun *em,* hence the indeterminacy of my gloss.[5] When the noun *dok* turns up again in the last line, it is unmodified and the hearer is not certain how many dogs are meant. While the reference is certainly definite and specific, it is indeterminate with regard to plurality.

In nineteenth-century Melanesian Pidgin texts, nouns occur most frequently with no modification. In a sample of speech of Melanesian plantation laborers recorded in the Queensland archives, Sankoff found that 82 percent of the nouns were 'bare'. Since then, however, the frequency of bare noun phrases has declined dramatically, although there are no fully grammaticalized noun modifiers (see Sankoff and Mazzie 1987).

4.3. Conventionalization of the Register

One can observe some changes in the sports reporting register by comparing earlier with later issues of *Wantok.* These are indicative of further conventionalization of the register. Words such as *reperi* 'referee' and *painal* 'final', which were used in the early issues, were more recently spelled as *referi* and *fainal* in 1987 and 1990 (see Romaine 1992b on the incorporation of the distinction between /p/ and /f/ in urban Tok Pisin). In other words, they had undergone what Mougeon and Beniak (1990) call "phonological disintegration." The result is that loanwords today may show less integration than they did at an earlier period. This can be considered to be an aspect of conventionalization in that /f/ is more generally being incorporated into urban Tok Pisin, and speakers' increased familiarity with English means there is less need for adaptation. Other phonological adaptations include *sempionship* in 1990 compared to *sempionsip* in 1982, as in *Bikos Madang i gat nem long autim Lae long gren fainal bilong Mamose rijonal sempionship long Madang las yia* 'Because Madang had the reputation to oust Lae in the Grand Final of Mamose Regional Championship last year'. Other words, however, such as *tropi* 'trophy' and *opisal* 'official', remain unaltered. The introduction of more anglicized spellings is of course a departure from the stated editorial policy of *Wantok*.

5. Universals of Register?

I return now to the question of the extent to which the similarities between sports reporting in English and Tok Pisin are due primarily to the diffusion of conventions for the register across language boundaries (which we might term *stylistic borrowing*), or to more general constraints imposed by the context of situation, subject matter, and so on. Of course, the posing of this question presumes some general agreement on the notion of register and its place within sociolinguistic theory. In particular, the relationship between style and register must be clarified. As yet, there is no consensus on these issues.

Crystal and Davy (1969:61), for instance, criticize the notion of register as vague because the situational variables of many registers mentioned in the literature are so varied that it is "inconsistent, unrealistic, and confusing to obscure these differences by grouping everything under the same heading." They are referring specifically to the classification of Halliday et al. (1964), who recognize as registers the following (among others): newspaper headlines, church services, sports commentaries, pop songs, advertising, and football. Nevertheless, Crystal and Davy then go on to present a taxonomy of named language varieties, including "the language of conversation," "the language of newspaper reporting," and "the language of legal documents," which look very much like what would otherwise be called registers.

Zwicky and Zwicky (1982:215–16) see register as a continuum. While they recognize clear cases of register (e.g., newspaper headlines and recipes), in their view the use of the term is dubious in cases such as the language of football. They also say that registers may exhibit stylistic variation on the dimension of formality and informality. The dimension of formality was criterial in Labov's (1972) concept of style, where it was taken to be unidimensional and referred to the amount of attention paid to speech. While Labov's view of stylistic variation has been criticized for its narrowness, it is at the same time too broad since it subsumes register in some cases and overlaps with it in others. Traugott and Romaine (1984), for instance, do not consider style to have a one-to-one relationship to any particular component of the speech event. In their view it is a relationship between participants in a speech event who are exemplars of social roles and have relationships in larger social institutions beyond the frame of dyadic interaction.

It is probably too soon to resolve boundary disputes about the extent to which style differs from register in all respects. In any case, Biber's (1988) work has shown convincingly that relationships among varieties of written and spoken English are so complex that no single dimension adequately captures the similarities and differences. A multidimensional analysis is required and Biber defines six dimensions which characterize a different relationship among texts. They provide an appropriate starting point for cross-linguistic analysis. (See also Kim and Biber this volume on Korean, and, on Somali, Biber and Hared this volume.)

It is worth considering some of Biber's findings for the language of the media in relation to Tok Pisin. The language of the media is of course not a monolithic category and contains many subgenres, both written and spoken. Biber's (1988:180–92, 196–97) analysis shows a wide range of variation on several dimensions within both press reportage and broadcasting due to the range of subgenres found in each of these categories (e.g., sports versus political report, personal editorials). Sports reports are more situation dependent in their reference than nonsports reports because they require the listener to construct a mental map of the playing field. In the spoken report there is no time to elaborate and give explicit reference. All broadcasts, both sports and nonsports, are not highly interactive, affective or involved, although sports broadcasting ranks higher on this dimension than nonsports broadcasting. Among the features of involvement which are used to express personal opinions are direct quotations and choice of terms which are evaluative, for example, *to slice* or *hack* as opposed *to kick* or *pass*.

Biber (1988:134–35) suggests that broadcasts which report events in progress have neither a primary involved nor a primary informational focus. They have relatively few verbs because many of them are deleted as a result of time constraints. This feature of broadcasting reflects the exigencies of being on-line and reporting rapidly unfolding events to an unseen audience. Not surprisingly, written sports reports do not display this feature and deploy many verbs to achieve a varied stylistic effect. However, written reports are also subject to space constraints and must compress information but still preserve intelligibility.

A number of scholars have noted that the noun phrase functions as a sensitive indicator of style (see, e.g., Raumolin-Brunberg 1991, Varantola 1984, Jucker 1989). Quirk, Greenbaum, Leech, and Svartvik (1985) examined a sample of seventeen thousand NPs in their Survey of English Usage. They found that fewer than one third were complex; these tended to occur in scientific writing rather than in prose fiction or informal spoken English. Varantola (1984) similarly observed a high density of premodification structures in engineering English. She (1984:85) found a frequency of ninety-nine complex NPs per one thousand words in engineering English compared to eighty-eight per thousand in a corpus of general English texts. Of fourteen properties which Chafe (1985:108–10) lists for idea unit expansion in written language, ten are found in complex noun phrases, including attributive adjectives, relative clauses, prepositional phrases, and pre- and postposed modifiers. Quirk et al. (1985:1351–52) and De Haan (1987:158) have found intertextual differences between prose fiction and informal spoken English, and between fiction and nonfiction. Compared to other varieties, prose fiction and informal spoken English are characterized by a much higher proportion of simple to complex NPs, and by a much stronger association between the grammatical relation of subject and simple NPs, and between nonsubjects and complex NPs. Jucker (1989:108) found stylistic differences between up-market and down-market British newspapers; the down-market papers showed a stronger tendency for simple NPs to be subjects. This distributional tendency has been explained in terms of discourse principles which favor light elements in thematic position, and more complex ones for introducing new information. Jucker (1989:93–108) also found that the up-market newspapers had greater NP complexity. The fact that not all newspapers have the same house style presumably reflects at least partly the different audiences they have in mind.

In Tok Pisin the appearance of complex NPs owes much to newspaper reporting, where they might be more generally considered a characteristic feature of what Siegel (1983) has called "media Tok Pisin" rather than of sport reporting specifically. The lexical and syntactic elaboration found in sports reports is indicative of the evolution of linguistic complexity in Tok Pisin, as it expands to meet the new demands put on it as a written and spoken medium. Syntactically more complex modifiers are semantically more explicit. Similarly, lexical diversity aids semantic precision. Words coined or borrowed in the sports reporting register such as *meme-im* and *krungutim* are not yet used more generally and have their origin in the register itself. From there they may diffuse more generally into spoken usage. Raumolin-Brunberg's (1991) work suggests that in English too there has been an increase in NP modification during the modern English period, but the extent to which this may be associated with an increase in literacy and the rise of particular registers is not yet clear. Languages such as Tok Pisin allow us a unique possibility for studying the extent to which specific registers act as sources for syntactic and lexical expansion.

While there can be no doubt that Tok Pisin has borrowed some of this lexis directly from English, the structural similarities between sports reporting in Tok Pisin and English must also derive at least partly from the common purpose underlying this register. It is no accident that the written styles of English and French tend to be more similar for specialized technical texts than for general texts, and further, that technical styles can even be more similar cross-linguistically than disparate registers within a single language (see Kittredge 1982).

Appendix: Sample Texts from *Wantok Niuspepa* 1982 and 1990

The following abbreviations are used in the texts:

PR Predicate marker
PL Plural
NEG Negative
FOC Focus
HAB Habitual
PERF Perfective
COMP Completive
PROG Progressive

Text 1. Wantok *1982*

Mormads Kwin   Bilong Madang
Mormads Queen of   Madang

Madang gret netbal gran painal i   kamap   namel long tupela
Madang great netball grand final   PR come up middle of   two
strongpela tim; Mormads   na Fly. Mormad i   wok   long go
strong   team Mormad PL and Fly Mormad PR PROG at   go
pas   long Madang Netbal long stat bilong sisen i   go inap
ahead of   Madang netball at   start of   season PR go until
long gren painal, taim ol   i   winim tim   bilong Fly. Fly
in   grand final   when they PR beat   team of   Fly Fly
tu i   save pilai strongpela gem   long olgeta taim na ol   i
too PR HAB play strong   game of   all   time and they PR
save stap long seken ples inap ol   i   kamap   namba tu
HAB stop in   second place until they PR come up number two
long gren painal. Long dispela gren   painal bilong tupela tim
in   grand final   in   this   grand final of   two   team
ya, Mormads i   win taim ol   i   givim 29 gol bilong Fly. Ful
FOC Mormads PR win when they PR give 29 goal of   Fly full
taim skoa bilong dispela gem   em, Mormads 29, na Fly 15. Em
time score of   this   game it   Mormads 29 and Fly 15 It
nau, ol meri   long Madang husat i   save skrap long pilai i
now PL woman of   Madang who PR HAB scrape at   play PR
mas lukluk long arapela kain pilai olsem, sofbal o soka.
must look to   other   kind play like   softball or soccer
Basketbal i   pinis nau wantaim netbal na ating   ol meri
basketball PR finish now with   netball and perhaps PL woman
i   mas pilai wantaim plet, kap na spun liklik pastaim na
PR must play with   plate cup and spoon little first   and
wetim neks yia.
wait next year

Translation:

Mormads are the Queens of Madang
In Madang the grand netball final between two strong teams has taken place: Mormads and Fly. The Mormads have gone ahead in Madang netball from the beginning of the season until the grand final when they beat the Fly team. The Fly team too has been playing a strong game and now they stand in second place since they were number two in the grand final. In this grand final between the two teams the Mormads won when they took 29 goals from the Fly team. The final score of the game was: Mormads, 29 and Fly, 15. So now the Madang women who long to play will have to look to other kinds of games like softball or soccer. Basketball has finished now along with netball and perhaps the women will play with plates, cups and spoons for a while first while they wait for next year.

Text 2. Wantok *1990*

Sea Eagles flai antap long Vanimo
Sea Eagles fly on top at   Vanimo
Sea Eagles i   kisim ples bilong Difens na paia stret   long
Sea Eagles PR get   place of   Difens and fire   straight at
Vanimo ragbi lig.   Ol i   bin   soim strong bilong ol   na
Vanimo Rugby League they PR PERF show strength of   them and

nekim Tigers 26-14 las wik   Sande.
neck Tigers 26-14 last week Sunday
Ol i   stap namba tu   long poin lata. Olsem na ol   i
they PR stay number two on   point ladder. Thus   and they PR
kamapim stret   strongpela gem taim ol   i   bungim Tigers.
come up straight strong   game when they PR meet   Tigers
Ol i   no   marimari liklik long ol boi bilong Tigers
they PR NEG pity   little for PL boy of
Dispela gem   las wiken   i   helpim tru Sea Eagle. Ol i
this   game last weekend PR help   true Sea Eagle they PR
mas winim dispela gem long go pas long poin lata. Gem
must win   this   game to   go first in   point ladder game
ya i   no isi. Ol Tigers i   putim strongpela banis na givim
FOC PR NEG easy PL Tigers PR put   strong   fence and give
hat taim stret   long ol Sea Eagles.
hard time straight to   PL Sea Eagles
Long hap taim, skoa bilong tupela tim   i   sanap long 0-0.
at   half time score of   two   team PR stand at   0-0
Tasol bihain long namba tu   hap, ol pilaia i   senisim ol
but   after in   number two half PL player PR change PL
posisen bilong ol. Ol Sea Eagles i   no   wet long putim
position of   them PL Sea Eagles PR NEG wait to   put
poin.
point
Magio Torima i   setim Kepas na em i   putim trai.
Magio Torima PR set   Kepas and he PR put   try.
Ol lain Sea Eagles i   no   malolo. Ol i   wok   long kapsaitim
PL line Sea Eagles PR NEG rest   they PR PROG at   overturn
trai olsem wara ya.
try like   water FOC
Wamut Wartovo na Chris Casmat i   go pas long fowat   bilong
Wamut Wartovo and Chris Casmat PR go first to   forward of
Sea Eagles. Ol Tigers i   no   was gut. Difens bilong ol   i
Sea Eagles PL Tigers PR NEG watch good. Defense of   them PR
slek na ol Sea Eagles i   putim trai long laik bilong ol.
slack and PL Sea Eagles PR put   try at   like of   them
Tigers tu i   soim strong bilong em   long namba wan hap.
Tigers too PR show strength of   them in   number one half
Olsem na tupela tim   i   dro. Tasol ol i   bin   traim long
thus   and two   team PR draw but   they PR PERF try   at
putim trai gen tasol ol   i   slek bikos   olgeta strong
put   try again but   they PR slack because all   strength
i   pinis long namba wan hap.
PR finish in   number one half
Yangpela fowat   bilong Tigers Ben Agore i   taitim bun
young   forward of   Tigers Ben Agore PR tighten bone
stret   bilong helpim tim   bilong em. Tasol em i   no
straight *to*   help   team of   him but   he PR HEG
bin kisim planti sapot tumas na tim i   lus.
PERF get   plenty support much and team PR lose

Translation:

Sea Eagles fly ahead at Vanimo
The Sea Eagles took Defense's place and headed straight for Vanimo Rugby League.
They showed their strength and got past the Tigers by 26-14 last Sunday.
They are now in second place. They put up a strong game when they met the Tigers.
They didn't show even a little mercy with the Tiger players.
Last weekend's game really helped the Sea Eagles. They had to win this game to advance
their ranking. The game was not easy. The Tigers put up a strong defense and gave the
Sea Eagles a hard time.
At half time the score stood at 0-0.
However, after the second half the players changed position. The Sea Eagles didn't wait
to score. Magio Torima set on Kepas and made a try.
The Sea Eagles did not rest. They tried to overturn the point like water.
Wamut Wartovo and Chris Casmat went past the Sea Eagles' forward. The Tigers weren't
watching. Their defense was slack and the Sea Eagles made the try they were after.
The Tigers too showed their strength in the first half. And so the two teams drew.
However, they tried to score again but they were careless and their strength had run out in
the first half. The Tigers' young forward, Ben Angore, went all out to help his team.
However, he didn't get too much support and the team lost.

Notes

1. Prior to independence in 1975, the southern half of New Guinea was an Australian
colony and the northern part was administered by Australia under a mandate from the United
Nations given after World War I, when the country ceased to be a German colony after only
thirty years of German rule.

2. As in other former anglophone colonies, a literary tradition in a locally distinctive
variety of English has begun to emerge.

3. This strategy of glossing borrowings was also widely used during the Middle English
period to explain new French borrowings to readers.

4. I was able to locate back issues of *Wantok* from its beginning in 1970 to 1979. For the
years 1980–81 I have no information. For the years 1982–83 I have only a few issues. From
1984 onward, I was able to examine continuously running issues.

5. In this respect Tok Pisin seems to contrast with other creoles in which the absence of
noun marking (i.e., zero determiner) has been claimed to carry the invariant meaning of
nonspecific (see Bickerton 1981).

References

Balint, A. 1969. *English Pidgin and French Dictionary of Sports and Phrase Book.* Port
        Moresby: South Pacific Post.
Biber, Douglas. 1988. *Variation Across Speech and Writing.* Cambridge: Cambridge University Press.
Bickerton, Derek. 1981. *Roots of Language.* Ann Arbor, MI: Karoma.
Brasch, E. 1971. "Tok Pilai, Tok Piksa na Tok Bokis (Imaginative Dimensions in Melanesian
        Pidgin)." *Kivung* 4:12–20.

Brown, Penelope, and Steven C. Levinson. 1978. "Universals in Language Use: Politeness Phenomena." In E. Goody, ed., *Questions and Politeness.* Cambridge: Cambridge University Press. Pp. 56–311.

Carrington, Lois. 1983. "Eye Witness Reporting." *Papers in Pidgin and Creole Linguistics. Pacific Linguistics* A–65:1–80. Canberra: Australian National University.

Chafe, Wallace. 1985. "Linguistic Difference Produced by Differences Between Speaking and Writing." In David R. Olson, Nancy Torrance and Angela Hildyard, eds., *Literacy, Language and Learning.* Cambridge: Cambridge University Press. Pp. 105–23.

Crystal, David, and Derek Davy. 1969. *Investigating English Style.* London: Longman.

De Haan, Pieter. 1987. "Exploring the Linguistic Database: Noun Phrase Complexity and Language Variation." In W. Meijs, ed., *Corpus Linguistics and Beyond: Proceedings of the Seventh International Conference on English Language Research on Computerized Corpora.* Amsterdam: Rodopi. Pp. 151–65.

Ferguson, Charles A. 1983. "Sports Announcer Talk: Syntactic Aspects of Register Variation." *Language in Society* 12:153–72.

———. 1984. "Repertoire Universals, Markedness, and Second Language Acquisition." In W. E. Rutherford, ed., *Language Universals and Second Language Acquisition.* Amsterdam: John Benjamins. Pp. 247–58.

Frazer, Thomas L. 1969. "A Study of the Development, Format and Content of the Nu Gini Toktok, Neo-melanesian Paper of New Guinea to April 13, 1966." M.A. Thesis, Louisiana State University.

Ghadessy, Mohsen. 1988. "The Language of Written Sports Commentary: Soccer—a Description." In Ghadessy, ed. Pp. 17–51.

———, ed. 1988. *Registers of Written English. Situational Factors and Linguistic Features.* London: Pinter Publishers.

Hall, Robert A. 1955. *A Standard Orthography and List of Suggested Spellings for Neomelanesian.* Port Moresby: Department of Education.

Halliday, Michael A. K. 1988. "On the Language of Physical Science." In Ghadessy, ed. Pp. 162–78.

Halliday, Michael A. K., Angus McIntosh, and Peter Strevens. 1964. *The Linguistic Sciences and Language Teaching.* London: Longman.

Jucker, Andreas H. 1989. "Stylistic Variation in the Syntax of British Newspaper Language." *Habilitationsschrift,* University of Zurich. [Published as Jucker 1992.]

———. 1992. *Social Stylistics: Syntactic Variation in British Newspapers.* Berlin: Mouton de Gruyter.

Kittredge, Richard. 1982. "Variation and Homogeneity of Sublanguages." In Richard Kittredge and John Lehrberger, eds., *Sublanguage: Studies of Language in Restricted Semantic Domains.* Berlin: de Gruyter. Pp. 107–37.

Labov, William. 1972. *Sociolinguistic Patterns.* Philadelphia: University of Pennsylvania Press.

Mihalic, Francis. 1957. *Grammar and Dictionary of Neo-Melanesian Pidgin.* Westmead, Australia: The Mission Press.

———. 1971. *The Jacaranda Dictionary and Grammar of Melanesian Pidgin.* Milton: The Jacaranda Press.

———. 1986. *Stail Buk bilong Wantok Niuspepa.* Boroko, PNG: Word Publishing.

Mougeon, Raymond, and Edouard Beniak. 1990. *Linguistic Consequences of Language Contact and Restriction: The Case of French in Ontario, Canada.* Oxford: Oxford University Press.

Mühlhäusler, Peter. 1979. *Growth and Structure of the Lexicon of New Guinea Pidgin.* Pacific Linguistics C-52. Canberra: Australian National University.

Nupela Testamen bilong Bikpela Jisas Krais na Buk bilong Ol Sam. 1966. Port Moresby: The Bible Society of Papua New Guinea.

Osmers, D. 1981. "Language and the Lutheran Church on the Papua New Guinea Mainland: An Overview and Evaluation." *Papers in New Guinea Linguistics. Pacific Linguistics* A–61:71–164. Canberra: Australian National University.

Quirk, Randolph, Sidney Greenbaum, Geoffrey Leech, and Jan Svartvik. 1985. *A Comprehensive Grammar of the English Language.* London: Longman.

Raumolin-Brunberg, Helena. 1991. *The Noun Phrase in Early Sixteenth-Century English: A Study Based on Sir Thomas More's Writings.* Helsinki: Société Néophilologique.

Romaine, Suzanne. 1990. "Advertising in Pidgin English (Tok Pisin) in Papua New Guinea." In L. Michaels and C. Ricks, eds., *The State of the Language.* Berkeley: University of California Press. Pp. 195–203.

———. 1992a. *Language, Education and Development: Urban and Rural Tok Pisin in Papua New Guinea.* Oxford: Oxford University Press.

———. 1992b. "Variability in Tok Pisin Phonology; Did You Say 'Pig' or 'Fig'?" In M. Rissanen, O. Ihalainen, T. Nevalainen, and I. Taavitsainen, eds., *History of Englishes: New Methods and Interpretations in Historical Linguistics.* Berlin: Mouton de Gruyter. Pp. 647–68.

Sankoff, Gillian, and Claudia Mazzie. 1987. "Determining Noun Phrases in Tok Pisin." Paper presented at NWAV-16. Austin, University of Texas.

Siegel, Jeff. 1983. "Media Tok Pisin." *Papers in Pidgin and Creole Linguistics.* Pacific Linguistics A–65:81–92. Canberra: Australian National University.

Smith, G. P. 1988. "Idiomatic Tok Pisin and Referential Adequacy." Ms.

Traugott, Elizabeth, and Suzanne Romaine. 1984. "Some Questions for the Definition of 'Style' in Socio-Historical Linguistics." *Folia Linguistica Historica* 6:7–39.

Varantola, Krista. 1984. *On Noun Phrase Structures in Engineering English.* Turin Yliopiston Julkaisuja, Sarja B, 168. Turku, Finland.

Wurm, Stephen A., and Peter Mühlhäusler. 1982. "Registers in New Guinea Pidgin." *International Journal of the Sociology of Language* 35:69–86.

Zwicky, Arnold M., and Ann D. Zwicky. 1982. "Register as a Dimension of Linguistic Variation." In Richard Kittredge and John Lehrberger, eds., *Sublanguage: Studies of Language in Restricted Semantic Domains.* Berlin: de Gruyter. Pp. 213–18.

4

Shared Thinking and the Register of Coaching

Shirley Brice Heath and Juliet Langman

1. Introduction

In the late 1980s, reformers in education, medicine, and engineering adopted the metaphor of coaching in efforts to reshape traditional instructional situations. Behind these reforms lay the premise that learners and the institutions in which they studied and worked would benefit by a move away from the transmission model of socialization which assumed a designated expert passing on information and skills to a passive but presumedly willing novice. New ideas about thinking and learning shifted the focus from·classrooms of individual learners to small groups being coached to construct knowledge jointly through collaborative and complex problem-solving in a variety of active learning situations.[1]

Experienced journalists now became coaches for less-experienced writers on the news, feature, or sports desk.[2] Within businesses ranging from high-technology firms to manufacturing, managers began to speak of coaching workers into new forms of behavior and innovative ways of communicating in groups to solve work-related problems.[3] Prodded by new plans for school reform, some public education reformers recommended a coaching model for instruction with the central focus on habituating learners to use their powers to observe, to judge, and to reshape and create knowledge collaboratively. Theodore R. Sizer, initiator of the "effective schools" movement of the late 1980s, argued that both students and teachers should learn by coaching: "The only way to learn to think well and usefully is by practice. The way a teacher assists this learning is by coaching" (1984:216). Support for such arguments came from studies of the rapid and generative learning seen in students working with computers and reported widely in journals devoted to the study of computers in education. The techniques students with different levels of expertise used with each other around computers inspired observers to equate their methods

Financial support for this project, codirected by Heath and Milbrey W. McLaughlin with associates Juliet Langman and Merita Irby, was provided by the Spencer Foundation.

with those of coaching. Education reformers quickly began to recommend peer-coaching and project-based learning that brought students together to learn in groups working on activities such as writing compositions, preparing science projects, or creating units of study for younger learners. Peer-tutoring and similar efforts, such as "reciprocal teaching," inspired the redesign of instructional situations away from individual learners working in isolation and dependent on the teacher as primary knowledge source (Palincsar and Brown 1984).

By the end of the 1980s, however, close studies of such shifts in learning situations revealed the complexities involved in enabling teachers and others previously involved in traditional top-down instruction to change their perceptions of their roles and their language. In essence, such studies suggested that the organization and guiding principles of any situation strongly influenced language uses, which in turn carried implications for cognitive and social development. Some scholars suggested that the hierarchical organization of schools created a chain of authority in which teachers met their "survival needs" through requiring only knowledge displays in short answers devoid of connection to "real" activities (McNeil 1986). Situations created with the intention of distributing learning across a small group (such as that composed of teacher and several students in writing conferences) more often than not reflected micromanagement strategies that led participants to reenact major features of traditional classrooms such that a single individual often emerged as the only active participant while others sat by passively. For example, when a specific set of objectives or "game plan" rested in the head of an individual who assumed a position of power early in the interaction, certain language uses (such as attentional imperatives—"now think," "see how it would . . .") shut down alternative perspectives and forms of knowledge display (Ulichny and Watson-Gegeo 1989).

Register features reflect choices of speakers who "index the moment" (Haviland 1979:389) through characteristics of language that are shared and conventionalized. Resulting language conventions are highly interdependent with a sense of role, title, and responsibility and are thus not easily dropped. Numerous studies of the register of teaching have shown, for example, that teacher talk is heavily marked by the instructors' sense of responsibility to transmit information; thus teachers often dominate classroom talk, ask a preponderance of questions to which they know the answers, and expect learners to display their knowledge primarily through specific genres—both written and oral (Cazden 1988).

2. Coaching as a Context for Talk

Though coaching is instructional in some sense, it seems to call for both organizational structures and language uses that differ from those of teaching. Sociolinguistic examination of the language of coaching to compare with studies of teacher talk can provide a sense of variation in what may be a range of registers of instruction. Moreover, a study of the language of athletic coaches can help fill a gap in research on sports language by sociolinguists who have examined sports announcer and narrator talk (Ferguson 1983), children's acquisition of the register of sportscasting

(Hoyle 1991), and the register of written sports commentary (Ghadessy 1988). Such studies have illustrated how these registers vary in accordance with occasions of *use* situated in specifiable contexts regularly populated by an identifiable set of language users. All of these studies emphasize the functional context for the use of language and suggest the extent to which individual speakers link their sense of role and context to their language choices.

This chapter looks specifically at the register of coaching to ask what are those linguistic features at all levels of the grammar, including discourse, that distinguish its use. We ask particularly about the nature of the language of coaching and how its use might be linked with assumptions that lie behind coaching. What are the relations that exist between coaches and players and between skills and information and the words and actions of coaching? We draw here from data collected from five different athletic teams of youths, two Little League Baseball teams of boys, one girls' softball team, one boys' basketball team, and one girls' basketball team in inner-city neighborhoods of three urban areas.[4] Unless otherwise indicated, conclusions drawn within this chapter apply to the language used by the coaches of all teams, regardless of type of activity or gender of players.[5]

Around the 1920s, when coaches came to be a regular part of sports teams, research on the process of coaching centered on the personality and background of the coach[6] (Coleman 1932, Lawther 1951). By the end of the twentieth century, physicians, psychologists, and sociologists lamented the absence of training for coaches, as well as their isolation from any systematic reporting of scientific research on children's development, the physiology of sports, or preventive sports medicine (Fixx 1985). Yet coaches, from neighborhood sports groups to collegiate and professional teams, have usually had practical experience in the sport they coach and have supplemented their knowledge through informal study of the game. In addition, they frequently have had managerial experience of some type, and they often bring a strong interest in the sport to their position (Neal 1969). Despite the fact that coaching is centrally involved in group dynamics, those who succeed as coaches seem to do so without explication or training in communication, a central part of the process of melding a group of disparate strangers into a team motivated to high performance through hard work, consistent practice, and sustained monitoring by peers. Thus it is appropriate to look closely at the language they use and the ways in which their language relates to their stated goals of working with individuals so that they become team players.

3. Locating the Register

Though numerous studies of register variation focus primarily on providing a taxonomic grid of several major dimensions or parameters of a register (Leech 1966, Halliday 1968), others merely label particular features of a register without offering a general framework for comparative purposes (e.g., Henzl 1974, Ferguson 1977). For this study, our approach is to "locate" the coaching register by identifying the organizational or functional features that lie behind the recognizable forms of the language (cf. Ferguson 1983 on sports announcer talk). This process of location is especially important for the register of coaching, because by the late 1980s the movement of coaching techniques into situations previously dominated by teaching brought with it the demand for attention to the features that characterize the occasions in which coaching generally occurs. By first locating the register situationally, we can check characterizing features for evidence that they are linguistically determinative and then relate these features to those of other registers in a systematic manner.

Four underlying organizational aspects of coaching provide the frame for its particular language characteristics. The first of these is that participation and demonstration—and hence activity—provide the primary contexts in which language is used. The second follows from the first, in that, to a great extent, action scripts the talk. The third provides the wider context of the first two: the primary goal of those engaged in the activities is to function as a group in order to accomplish a single jointly determined goal. The fourth relates to the rule-constituted and regulated nature of the activity for which coaching takes place: members regulate themselves by rules that derive from the nature of the activity that brings them together—whether it be baseball, production of a daily newspaper, or performance of a dance recital.

Coaching is then primarily the oral accompaniment to activities of practice and demonstration that prepare members of a group who intend to work together through a series of culminating events (often some type of contest, game, or performance). Coaches expect members to have different levels of experience, skills, and preparation in the array of tasks necessary to the culminating events; thus they view members as an ensemble of different individuals whose particular talents and abilities will have to play off each other in ways that will emerge through the course of the joint activity. The expectation of work toward a production, performance, or recognizable goal of an audience carries with it the need to develop into a cohesive unit within a definable time frame. Regroupings of teams may occur, but such regroupings are marked and involve the need to socialize new members into the group and the activity. The time element and the drive toward a culminating event or goal allow for language that intensifies the power of demonstration and elevates motivation—language uses that would not normally be sustainable over an undefinable period or for an unspecified task. This organizational feature differentiates the coaching register from kinds of talk that take place within groups where the focus is on transmitting a body of knowledge to individuals who will carry out tasks or demonstrate skills in isolation, with no responsibility for building group knowledge at a pace coordinated with a specific time span. The coaching register must simultaneously reflect the building of group relations and the incremental accumulation of participatory knowledge by each member of the group.

A second locating feature of coaching is that action scripts talk. Much of coaching talk during practice is a monologic scripting of activities as they occur or eventcast projections of possible scenarios that could emerge from an action just witnessed by all.[7] Coaches set up practices into specialized subactivities (such as bunting, hitting grounders or flies, catching grounders or flies) that they often first demonstrate and then orchestrate. For example, talk about bunting surrounds the coach's demonstration of several bunts, but when team members assume their position at bat, the talk of the coach backgrounds each bunt and extends actual events into other probable occurrences (e.g., a bunt along a baseline). This feature differentiates coaching register from related varieties, such as radio or television sports announcing or teaching, which do not have accompanying demonstrations and simultaneous eventcasting, and it places coaching closer to other demonstration talk, such as that taking place during a medical procedure performed as part of a clinical medical training program (Tannen and Wallat 1982).

A third locating feature of coaching is the level of commitment to group bonding for the purposes of the culminating activities. The diverse types of experience and skills in the group contribute particular features of the register that deemphasize hierarchical judgments of who is best or worst within the group, and that stress how group performance taken as a whole measures up to agreed-upon models outside the group. The central play of team and coach enters the imaginative realm of projecting the group beyond where and what it now is into what it can be and what it knows to be "best," "optimal," or "special." Added to those ideals that come from outside models or norms are those peculiar to the group, such as the use of special names for individuals or actions and secret codes in gesture, dress, or written representations. It is the coach who models these personalizing, praising, and reinforcing features in the talk of coaching. This location differentiates the register of coaching from that of teaching or other types of group activities, since the coach assumes (and often insists) that members of the group will not differentiate themselves through competition in particular highly specifiable skills (e.g., hitting home runs) or bits of knowledge (calculating statistics). Instead, group members will focus their differentiations within the framework of team work or play; they will heavily personalize all roles, including their own within the ensemble; and they will assess outcomes according to the external ideal for the group.

A fourth contribution to the location of the coaching register is the role of rules—those brought into the group to regulate its interactions as well as those that constitute the game or central activity that organizes the group.[8] Rules of the first type come with the players' prior knowledge of ways to regulate human behavior under very general conditions (such as being a "good sport," "hanging in there," or "sticking up for your friends"). The extent of shared knowledge of these regulative rules becomes clear early in the team's formation, quickly spreads among the group, and operates as a code for which all members hold responsibility and must therefore monitor. Thus the talk of coaches about these rules is extensive in the early stages of group formation and on occasions of crisis to the group as a whole, but not during the regular activities of the group.

Constitutive rules are those that make up the game (e.g., of baseball, basketball, soccer), and these, in contrast to regulative rules, echo consistently throughout practice beyond the opening sessions of the group and serve as the basis of frequent reminders from coaches to players to cite, demonstrate, or explicate. Coaches ask repeatedly for recitation of the specific rules for determining what a *ball* or a *bunt* is, the functions of a *forward,* and the rules for *time-out.* Moreover, coaches expect that recitation of the constitutive rules of the game before the group by both coach and players will help ensure automatic retrieval of these rules during actual performances. This direct commitment to rules in the register of coaching differs from that of other rule-regulated, role-differentiated registers, such as that of physicians to patients, teachers to students, or police officers to citizens, since the coach assumes that group members want to know and use the second type of rule because of their elective commitment to the normative ideals of the group and their joint goal of doing the best job possible for the team and thus for themselves.

These four characteristics lay out the role of the coach in building and sustaining the essentials of group collaboration as well as individual knowledge and skill development. Coaches are not direct players in the culminating activity, but through modeling, demonstrating, narrating and asking for recitation or recapping of rules, they bring about the participation and socialization to team membership of those who must practice, perform, and ultimately stand for assessment by team members and outsiders of the culminating event. Thus to a great extent coaches are both outside the team and full representatives of the team. The relative status of coaches depends on the extent to which they help create within the team norms of (co)opera-tion that draw attention away from individual performers and toward the activities themselves and the best possible coordinated execution of these. The communica-tive intentions of coaches lie within the ethos of the team's reason for being, namely its central activity. Moreover, since much of the language is scripted by ongoing demonstration and action, its effectiveness lies in the ability of team members to internalize the demonstration and action together with the accompanying language and to understand the extent to which specific practices relate to community-acknowledged rules and team-building expectations.

4. Discourse-Level Features of Coaching Talk

The discourse features of language identifiable in coaches' talk follow the course of both the season and the nature of practice and games. Certain speech styles mark coaches' talk at particular points in the season. At initial gatherings of the group or team (and throughout group sessions at times of crisis to the membership), coaches take the floor for chunks of uninterrupted language in which they lay out the group's philosophy (often reiterating regulative rules, such as those for good sportsmanship and team membership), additional rules of the current specific organization, and some personal elaboration or confirmation of these.

During practices, coaches provide eventcasts as openers, running commentary on the practices, and summative peptalks and reviews of skills practiced. Games provide relatively little time for talk except brief telegraphic reinforcements or reminders; at game end, coaches often recap highlights of the game and tie these back into the season's major philosophical themes.

4.1. Philosophical Setups

In the first sessions of the season, illustrated by (1), long segments of talk by the coach outline the call to team membership and responsibility, lay down and solicit the particular rules of the group, and remind players of their need to develop their skills and play with full knowledge of the actual rules of the game. Consistent throughout these talks are reminders of what may be termed the doubleness of the team's situation: they are *playing*, they are *in a game*, and yet within this play mode, they must operate according to some fundamental rules of *real life* relating to human interactions, future goals, and standards of judgment. Along with the rules that constitute the game of basketball or baseball come the rules of belonging to the team and the opportunity to extend what happens in team life to life in the world of work.

(1) There's rules to be followed. You gotta follow 'em in life; you're gonna have to follow 'em in baseball. You don't do what you wanna do. And the next one that talks. I'm gonna pull out of the line. [pause] It's one thing you learn, you have to listen. In any phase of life, you have to listen and, and follow rules and follow orders. I do. There's people tell me what to do and I listen. That's part of life. Now next week. I see I see a lot of progress in a lot of you. A lot of you are doing very good. By the time we get out on that field, you'll be, very good ball players, because I'm seeing a lot of progress.

The relationship established with the coach is more than that of source of rules and skills, but instead model, mentor, motivator for being a good team player and thus contributing to team camaraderie, and pride in the team as a whole.

One coach's three rules presented at the first meeting of the second season by the assistant coach hark back to the team membership the players shared the previous year and build on their strengths and weaknesses. He opens his address to the team by saying: "Last year I was kinda easy on you guys. This year I'm gonna really be mean." He adds the rules for this year:

(2) First, anybody caught fighting with ANYBODY, you're suspended for one game. Fight again, you're off the team. Second, I'll let you know the schedule. You are expected to be at all practices and games unless you call beforehand. Otherwise, you'll find yourself sitting on the bench. Third, when you get your uniform, you are always to come to games with a complete uniform. Part of the game of baseball is pride in your uniform and appearance. I want you guys coming to the games looking sharp.

To these hard and fast rules he adds the reminder that they are the defending champions, and they have to play their hardest, "look sharp," and be determined, if they are to retain their title.

The manager of one of the teams also lays out his set of rules for the beginning of the season. He greets his team on the first day with a pep talk, saying "I'm here to tell you we're gonna have fun; learn some fundamentals of baseball, sportsmanship; and learn to have fun and learn not to suck our fingers." While the emphasis is on having fun, he adds, "We're gonna be the best darn team in the league, right? Hopefully." He then invokes the relationship between the coaches and the players by adding, "We'll [the coaching staff] be with you every step of the way." After this introduction, he lays out some basic rules for play:

1. Be at least fifteen minutes early to make practice as good as possible. Maybe take a lap.
2. No horsing around; always be prepared to listen, as we have lots of teams and limited time on the field.
3. On the team, no laughing; always encourage your teammates. Remember every guy is doing his best. We want you to lose like a winner. You can be sad, you can be upset, but you always go and shake all hands at the end of every game.

The general philosophical precepts of team membership dictate how coaches and subsequently players learn to deal with preferred roles on the team. All the coaches and players stress the "basics" of throwing, running, hitting, and catching (all players have to learn the basics and then they can be creative). Players in all positions must have these skills and learn the techniques of strategizing when and how to play out the nuances of combinations of posture, timing, spacing, and cooperation that lead to success in a given play or game. Beyond these skills, however, as the course of the season moves along, individual players demonstrate expertise in particular roles. Coaches begin the season with numerous mentions of "We need some good catchers this year" or "We really have to have some strong outfielders"—creating a cluster of elements of need and features of play around each position.

One coach tells the team, "Everybody will have a shot at all the different positions; we'll spread it around. First we'll determine your skills so you can best help the team." Such generalized announcements of the qualifications for the team contributions of each position socialize all team members into a body of knowledge about how the choice of the appropriate players for particular positions will enhance the quality of the team as a whole.

Aside from these large blocks of talk about building teamwork at the opening sessions of the season, other such large chunks occur only at points of crisis and focus primarily on extended explanations of rules of the game. On most occasions of such extended talk, coaches remind players that they have heard this information before and are likely to hear it again.

(3) Now I told you I'm-o almost every practice I'm gonna keep sayin' this. If you're not gonna take a block or the target xxx during the game, I know you won't take it at the end of the game. That could be the difference between winnin' or losin'. Even if it is a charge and the referee calls a foul, that man still has to go to the free throw line and throw free throws. I'll take my chances. Some of you let the person go around you and just score a layup and tap him on the arm and then they get three points. Now you go to to get your bodies in front of them and you go to to take a charge. Now, if you don't take a charge you cannot play for me in important situations. It just will not happen. I don't care what you say. This game is made o-, if you don't if you can't take contact next you cannot allow your man just to roam free and go wherever they want to all over the basketball court. Some of you all just foul the man all around. You can't do that. You must cut the court in half.

In the remainder of this segment, the coach adds numerous conditions that might deter the players from wanting to charge—other players who are taller, particular run patterns of opposing team members, and so on. His talk ends with the admonition, "If you just let him run right across, he just gonna post you up every time."

The context of this talk was the need for the boys to "take the end of the game seriously in practice." Team members were not projecting ahead to the score results from each of their individual plays or hesitations in play, and the coach wanted the boys to think "game ending situations" as they played out every minute of practice.

At points such as these, when the team goals seem to slip away from players, coaches offer brief reminders of the need to stop thinking and moving as individuals and to unite as a team.

(4a) You guys are a bunch of individuals out there; you're not a team yet. You've got to support one another. All you guys care about when do I get to bat, and not how is my team doing.

(4b) All right, everybody give him five man; tell him he's gonna be all right. All right? [about a boy who was hit in nose with ball] Come on, that's your teammate; make sure he's OK.

To help promote sustained concentration by the whole team to the task at hand during practice, coaches often invoke fantasy play with the team by calling for "game conditions." For example, during an intersquad practice with the starting line-up in the field, minus the pitcher and the rest of the team batting, a coach says:

(5) I wanna see game conditions. It'll be just like a game. G., I want you to be umpire. OK? So that means, a walk you'll take first, we're gonna play it just like a game.

"Game conditions" extend to the request that the catcher put on all the catching gear. Here the coach shows his respect for some of the older players (the "vets" who are twelve years old) by giving the catcher the option of putting on his gear. "That's up to you. I know it's hot. You're gonna have to start getting used to it, OK? And it is game conditions." The catcher joins in on the discussion of what game conditions means by saying, "If this is a game, I need my suit." The instructions on game conditions complete, the team gets five minutes: "OK, do you guys wanna take five minutes, get the water, and then we're gonna go, OK? Like I said it's gonna be a hot summer, so you better start getting used to it, all right?" Such talk is often peppered with restatements of the fantasy condition (game end or game conditions) along with bits and pieces of the organizing rules of the group and reminders of the team as an entity.

4.2. Eventcasts and Routines

While the beginning of the season involves intensive team development, throughout the season, before both practices and games, coaches routinely set up what is to come for players by running verbally through the practice's events (drill for batting, catching, running, free throw practice, and so on).

(6) We're gonna practice going to first base, outfielders throwing to second base, throwing to third base. C., you listening? OK? and then I'm gonna pull a couple of you guys aside to see what you can do throwing the ball, see who's gonna be pitchers for this year, OK?

Such talk is punctuated with gestures, occasional movement about the field or court, and insertions of reminders of what has been done in previous practices or games. These chunks of language at the openings of events provide the only occasions during which coaches outline what is to come and remind players to keep the whole coming scenario in their heads. Phases of these eventcasts usually include the opening, enactment of the plan, any possible breaks, enactment of what will follow the break, and the closing.

The opening of each session or segment of activity invariably includes overt calls to membership and teamwork ("Let's go, gang," "Everybody in"). Before practices, such eventcasts lay out events and urge high effort; before games, coaches stir an image of finality or peak performance demand, offering abbreviated quick repetitions of what the game is, what the players know, and what they want.

Just before a girls' softball game, the coach gathers the players between the dugout and third base coach's box:

(7) This is it. Everybody has to go out there and attack the ball. Look at me. Attack the ball, girl. Go up there; you gotta go up there and take aggressive. You have to go up there thinking you want to get that ball. You don't go up there thinking—if you think you're going to get struck out, you're going to get struck out. You know who's pitching. You've nailed her a hundred times. Get out there and get on top of her quick. I mean quick. Hey, I want everybody talking up here. This is it, xxx. This is the game. Any game you want to win. This is a game you have to win. This is a game you have to win. Do what you want. It's up to you. Not to E (assistant coach). It's how bad you all want it. This is where it starts. Right here. This is where it starts.

The assistant coach echoes these thoughts in a follow-up talk, projecting several possible scenarios of specific actions:

(8) Jo, here. Hey, you've got to go on out there and be aggressive. Every play. On the bases. Norma, you gonna be here. Hey, you gonna play—look, look at the xxx. If I do this. If I go like this [imitating a wind-up for the pitch] the next pitch, the first pitch. Let's move. You know what that means. xxxx steal. If I go like this, during the second pitch. Anybody who goes base coaching, if I do like this or like that, first pitch or second pitch. Hear me. And when that pick up. Take it upon yourselves and, if she got a good pitch, don't make a break. Be sure she go the xxx. Get the xxxx. Go on in. Don't wait for nobody to get the ball. xxx and Go with her hard. [imitating a wind-up] xxx the baseline. OK. Go. Hey, stay with it girls. Stay with it xxx. It's your game. It's up to you all now.

These occasions of talk during games contrast sharply with the highly abbreviated talk (98 percent of which is between two and five morphemes in length) generally found during the actual playing of the game.

In contrast to what is possible during games, coaches use practices to model the running commentary that they hope players will run in their own heads during games. During practices, coaches urge players into action and script their actions with almost unceasing commentary, heavily laced with players' names, positive reinforcements, and rhetorical questions. This commentary takes the form of both imperatives that are often routinized and conditionals that remind players that under certain circumstances, other outcomes would be possible. These commentaries provide players with specific on-line feedback and instructions on skills with which they may be having trouble.

(9) Don't move back. Here do you wanna go that far, stand about right. [pause] Get the .bat up, choke up, choke up [hit]. There you go. Good job.

(10) That's right, OK good. [pause] You did the right thing. You couldn't get nobody so you held onto the ball. There's no reason to throw the ball if a man's already on the base.

This scripted action is interspersed with statements of positive assessment, reinforcement of correct behavior, and corrections of behavior the coach expects the player to know. The form of this talk is telegraphic and repetitive; the pace is that of the activity; the linking of statement to player is dependent on the frequent use of vocatives (either a given name, a nickname, or a position/role such as first baseman or catcher).

(11) OK infield, let's get one again. B. Str——, strong throw, no throwing up in the air, I wanna see a good throw, all right? Good throw, get one. [hit] Yeah. That's it, that's it, that's the way you throw the ball. Good catch, good catch, good catch. OK, C., get one. [hit] Get it, get it.

Once a drill is completed, the coach usually calls the players together for a brief retake, in which players and coach talk about what was seen and what improvement is needed. This point also reinvokes the concept of the team as joint monitors, continuous assessors, and team members who are consistently aligned to the achievement of the group goal.

(12) OK guys, out here, second base. Everybody come in to second base for a minute. [pause] Second base. Come on J. Come on Mr. B. hustle baby, hustle hustle. OK, you guys look sharp, all right? The infielders are doing what you want, the out-fielders, the only thing, only think I want you outfielders to do is remember, OK?, now and I know it isn't always comfortable, but I think M. and G. probably do the best job of it. Keeping the ball in front of you. OK? You don't always have to catch the ball, OK? But if the ball, if you can keep the ball in front of you, I mean if it hits your knee or if it hits you in the chest or in the side, I mean that's not the way you're supposed to catch, right? But the, you, the object is to keep the ball in front of you. OK?

During such retakes, the coach offers some "quick rules" and demonstrates what is meant (e.g., "Keep your knees bent," "Keep your eye on the ball at all times," "Keep your glove down"). The frequent call to "remember" comes with a fast-paced demonstration and frequently repeated encapsulation of the key points of the exercise. Mental state verbs, such as *remember* and *think*, as well as modals (*could, might,* and so on) and catenatives (such as *gonna*) occur on the average of thirty times in every one hundred turns of the coaches' talk and make evident the combination of cognition and action the coach intends for team members. These occasions remind the players that the sport rests on a small number of general rules that must be remembered and that have high transfer potential across positions and game conditions.

After games, coaches may wait until the next practice for a retake, and such retakes focus on specific incidents of the game as well as general principles of play and team membership.

(13a) Now listen. Now you all did pretty good yesterday. We come back when we had to, and you showed that you wanted to win. I like that. For a little while we were down on ourselves, but, like I told you all, we got on top of em quick, we let up and they came back on us. They went ahead. Bu I s-, I see it in your all's eyes last night you all wanted to win it. You wanted it. And took it. That's all that matters. So long as everyone out xxx, you can't take nobody lightly. I don't care if you've got twenty run lead. The game was early. That was only the second inning. We played five. We had to struggle for those last three innings. You cannot afford to let up. I'm tellin' you all. We can't afford to let up. They will come back. Hey, they're a hitting team. And they'll hit the ball. You all seen that last night. They scored ten runs just like that. I mean, just like that. [pause of eight seconds] Offense we did good. Everyone was hittin' the ball when we need to. You all hit it when we needed to.

Example (13a) contains only the first one third of the retake talk on this occasion by this coach. He closes the full sequence with a reminder:

(13b) Hey, let's start practicing today hard, and let's work on those mistakes. I'm telling you all, hey, the farther it goes along, it's going to get tougher, becuz everybody's getting better. I told you all that at the beginning. We'll go over everything today. We need a lot of work. A lot of batting practice.

Coaching language moves the players to practice the skills, remember and apply the rules, and, most important, see themselves as knowledge sources and skill displayers within an integrated unit of strategizers.

To these ends, coaches see a general developmental process as youngsters stick with a particular sport within the course of one season and certainly over several seasons. Early in the process, the players are to have fun, learn a few basics, and find out what it is like to be a member of a team unit. The next stage brings knowledge of rules specific to the game as well as a continuation of emphasis on the general philosophic principles of interaction that permeate the early process. At this point, distinction between one's own team and others becomes an integral part of the way in which competition figures in the players' sense of purpose or goals. The final developmental phase is maintenance of the basic precepts of the game as well as continuous invitations and reminders to the players to become strategizers and thereby frequent winners and good losers.

5. Syntactic Features

Five types of syntactic phenomena illustrate key features of the coaching register. Each of these features works to help the coach in his or her goals of invoking team membership, building up a set of skills in players, and ensuring that players learn to think of themselves as strategists.

5.1. Telegraphic Utterances

During segments of practice, as well as during games, coaches' utterances have a telegraphic character: short bursts of speech usually of no more than five morphemes, with those of three morphemes by far the most frequent. These utterances declare actions as positive, cue specific routinized parts of skills, or give imperatives in one of six forms:

1. V + pro or N prep phrase (optional ADV)
   get one, try it again, keep your eye on the ball
2. ADJ + N
   good job, nice throw

3. EXP pro V
   there you go
4. pro art N
   that's the way, that a way
   or
   pro N ADJ
   that's OK, that's all right
5. pro V pro
   I like that
6. Vphrase ADV
   let's get it together

These forms are either imperatives or evaluative declaratives. Optionally preceding or following any of these forms is a vocative addressing either an individual or the group.

Approximately 60 percent of the utterances within telegraphic scripted action talk are repeated at least twice within the span of eight seconds. Coaches think of this barrage of talk as a mental prod to get players to internalize the quality or feature of their current action. Such talk also serves as *back channeling* for the players' actions in ways similar to the "uh huh" and "yeah" of conversations. Such talk is either highly affective ("good play") or directive in very general terms ("all the way," "come on"). Approximately 10 percent include vocatives of a highly general type: "Sweetie," "Baby," "girls," "guys." Players say that this "chatter" lets them know someone is watching and tells them how they're doing at any given moment. Another 10 percent refers to individual players by name and highlights specific actions or features of that player's behavior.

5.2. Conditionals

Perhaps the most outstanding feature of all coaching talk (except for its telegraphic nature) lies in its creation of hypothetical conditions. Approximately 80 percent of eventcasts before practice and games and the running commentaries (excluding telegraphic utterances) during practices establish irrealis conditions. As noted, many of these assert "real game conditions" during practice, but others set up specific possibilities for the consequences of particular kinds of plays.[9]

The use of conditionals provides the players with alternatives and examples of causal environments which have an effect on the playing of the game. Within the *play* mode, the overarching frame is that of "what if?" and the accompanying expectation "You always have to be ready; anything can happen." Thus much of the talk of both coaches and players reshapes current actions into one or more possible extensions or outcomes. These conditionals exist not only in the form of "if-then" utterances, but also in utterances that appear in the form of directives but function as conditionals. Moreover, the juxtaposition of two declaratives often works as a conditional without the direct statement of either *if* or *then*. Following such statements is the implied question of "what now?" In addition to these abbreviated invitations to imagine "what if?" are longer sociodramatic bids that play out extended eventualities built upon the current configuration or one that can be fantasized.

5.2.1. IF-THEN CONDITIONALS

In extended chunks of discourse that are eventcasts for practices or retakes of practices, approximately one third of all utterances are if-then constructions. *If* appears on average nine times per one hundred turns of coaches' talk in girls' athletic events and ten in boys' activities.

Conditionals of the simplest type—stating only one condition and one result— refer primarily to state of affairs outside the game or practice itself.

(14) I think if there's rain coming again, we may uh xxx

if you, if you wanna get something [to eat] before, go ahead

if the pitcher's good enough to throw strikes, then you, then

if I have to get you a pizza after every win, I'll tell you, I'll be broke by mid midway

The primary location for simple conditionals that refer to the practice itself is at the end of extended chunks of coaching talk.

(15) if you just let him run right across, he just gonna post you up every time

if you drive to the basket, they're probably gonna foul you

if everybody calls that interference, they're not reading the rulebook

In approximately 50 percent of the if-then utterances, either the conditions or consequences are multiple, with branched possibilities of conditions occurring three times more frequently than a layout of numerous consequences. The conditions often work as a series of unstated if-then linkages.

(16a) And if I'm sticking him and [if] the ball's over there, before you can get over there, if he wants to get right there, [then] I make it so he has to fight to get around and I ain't just dead.

(16b) If the ball, say the ball gets to the-, passes the outfielder and [if] the ball hits the fence, OK, [then] there's no way that she can-, she can reach the ball from home or to second from where she's at, so second basemen, or say [if] the rightfield, second basemen has to go out and cut her off, and she'll hit the relay.

(16c) if you stay, if you stay, hey, hey, and relax and breathe deep, [then] you can swing as hard as you want, but you gon' like this [demonstrates], the ball's comin' in and you, hey, when you do that, xxx the ball xxx.

(16d) if the ball's a little bit slippery, maybe even dry off the ball. What you have to do, if you're gonna, step outside that circle, if you need to dry anything off or if the ball is really bad, show the umpire

(16e) OK, if you walk D., [if] you're on base, and uh you know, then you can start some action out there

Conditions are usually highly interdependent, while results include an array of outcomes that may or may not be linked and that cannot necessarily be predicted. Thus these multiply branched conditionals call for the players to hold several conditions in their minds and to anticipate alternative outcomes.

5.2.2. CONDITIONALS STATED AS QUESTION-DIRECTIVES

A fast-paced question with a follow-up directive usually functions as a conditional when coaches want to personalize heavily an outcome in a particular situation at a single point in time.

(17a) [Vocative], [if] this is your ball? [then] put it in your pocket.

(17b) [if] you wanna get to first base before him? [then] run, run like you're scared.

(17c) So [=if] they have some good hitters, huh? [then] you might have to go out six innings.

Coaches throw out these questions-directive conditionals very rapidly and appear to use them to target the attention of individuals. Most are accompanied by a vocative or a strong gesture directed to an individual (pointing to a youth's pocket, placing an arm around the shoulder, or giving a pat on the back). Their tone is sometimes sarcastic, especially in those utterances such as (17c) in which *so* functions as *if* and implies a challenge.

5.2.3. SOCIODRAMATIC BIDS

As indicated, during practice, coaches frequently draw players into the fantasy that they are in "real" game conditions.

(18) OK, the other thing is is this sort of applies to what's gonna have to happen in games. When we're playing a game, and you guys are out on the, in the defense, when you're in the outfield. We'll have to be ready all the time. You don't know where that batter's gonna hit the ball. OK? So when you guys are standing out here playing, I want you to be watching that batter. Now there may be times, like later this afternoon where the outfielders can play some catch in between pitches. But the infielders should always be ready. OK? If we have a hitter that we have to work with a little bit and it's taking some time, the outfielders can have a ball out there and play catch.

Later within this segment, the coach asks not only that the players imagine a game, but that they also imagine the limits of the field.

In addition, the coach wants them to join in a fantasy play within a fantasy play. They should suspend within their imagined game the "rule" that pitchers should try to throw so batters *cannot* hit the ball: "This is *batting practice*" (and thus those rules of real games that would conflict with this announcement are called off).

Other sociodramatic bids highlight critical turns of action in the hypothesized scenarios and often follow quick directives for team members to look and listen.

(19) All right, now. Now, listen, again. Listen again. HEY. J. Now, the skins' team is losin' 84 to 78. Both teams in the bonus. There's a minute on the clock. Which

means, cause I don't think some of you all know what that means. Which means that the skins' team must put pressure on the shirts' team to steal the ball. Not to do intentional fouls but to go for the ball. Now if you're in a man to man situation, if your man is in the front court and he gets by you, you try to run and pick him up. There's really no excuse for you to foul unless you're trying' to foul right away. Now in the this situation, you want to go for the ball hard where you probably will foul him in the front court. Not silly stuff.

In this case, the appropriate use of fouls can make the difference between winning or losing the game in the final moments. Consistently, these "clutch" sociodramas place the hypothetical scene near the end of the game when a cluster of conditions coming together can easily go either way—to the benefit or the detriment of the team's score. Such sociodramas are punctuated in the coach's elaboration with frequent expressions of *now, all right, OK,* as well as spatial deictics, such as *here.* These extended chunks of talk consistently take place in a mixture of present and present progressive tense. Past tense is generally reserved for comments of a par-enthetical type about the outcome of an action scripted in the present tense (e.g., "You denied them the ball").

Once the team moves out of the role of audience for such sociodramas and into practice, coaches test players on their understanding of the scenario by asking *why* questions.

(20a) Why would you foul him and put him in the bonus when he's winnin' by six?

(20b) How come you couldn't jump into him and shoot the ball rather fo-, fade away and shoot?

These questions continue the frame of the hypothetical "clutch" situation into practice, so that the conditions given in the drama persist and justify time-outs from practice to talk about the results of certain moves or plays.

5.3. Balanced Negatives and Directives

In spite of a public perception that coaches, especially those of baseball, are often highly negative with youngsters and constantly shout commands to players, data from the teams studied here show several patterns of use of negatives and directives among coaches that conflict sharply with the stereotypical view of coaches.

The first of these features is that of "balanced negatives"—negations followed immediately by positive assertions (usually more than one).

(21) don't call in the play. I'll call it

you can't be doin' this stuff, xxx put the pass, come on back for it, xxx, do it again.

don't reach for it, get over there and block him

Coaches rarely direct negatives to individual players; instead, they ask rhetorical questions, often tinged with a mixture of sarcasm and humor. During practice the majority of these questions ask for confirmation or explanation of an event that has just taken place and that all have either seen or heard.

(22) [Vocative] what did I just say?
     [Vocative] what are you afraid of?
     did you all hear that?
     you goin' to let it ride like that?
     what kinda pass is that?

Most of these questions are calls to attention, since listening, observing, and re-membering strategies must complement all other activities of the practice and game. Hence, coaches use both direct reminders ("Listen," "Keep your eyes open," "Lis-ten up," "You all keep a eye on the back court") throughout practices as well as in opening eventcasts of what is to come in either practices or games. Calls to *look* occur on the average twice as often as calls to *listen*.

Augmenting these direct reminders are frequent requests for clarification that check with players on the status of information and sustain the view that all mem-bers of the team are accountable for information that should be in common purview.

(23) OK, who are we missing here?
     Now, where is D.?

     Do you have money for it?

     Oh, you played the first game?
     Get fanned?

     OK, L., you still have that baseball?

     Who are we missing here? Where's D.? OK S., Where's S., S., where, where was
     that ball you guys were playing with?

Beyond these balanced negatives and checks on the status of knowledge is yet another way of lending a positive tone to practices. When infractions of safety, sportsmanship, or team image occur within practice, coaches usually set the nega-tive or unacceptable action against an understandable reason for such an action. When a player threw down his batting helmet with particular force after he struck out, the coach yelled: "We're not gonna have any of that, all right?" followed by a comment to lessen the blow of failure: "Everybody strikes out once in a while, OK?"

5.4. Tag Questions

Lessening the blow of an infraction is one of a number of occasions in which the coach makes use of tag questions (especially *OK?, all right?*). These are also used within the stream of running commentary during practices to mark points at which the players should check for themselves on what is happening.

Tag questions represent another attempt in which coaches try to get players to "see" how their thinking processes should work and to be in a constant state of self-monitoring. Coaches also explain their use of tag questions by indicating that they want the moment-to-moment directives to the team to fall into a general sense of acceptance of this information by all team members. (Note that examples [5], [6], [9], [12], and [18] show use of *OK?*, and [4], [5], [11], and [18] include *all right?*.)

5.5. *Pronoun Usage*

A fifth component of coaching talk centers on the use of first person plural and second person pronouns that draws the players into the talk by invoking team membership and a lack of distinction between players.[10]

This usage shows the unique position of the coach as a member/nonmember of the team. While not participating in the bulk of the activities, the coach invokes his identity with the group through talk that regulates positive team cooperation as well as talk that includes the coach only as far as planning and preparation are concerned. Hence we see both inclusive and exclusive use of first person plural pronouns with exclusive far more frequent.[11]

Our examination of pronouns focused on *we* and *us* and *you*, with the goal of determining the extent to which coaches used pronouns to consolidate individual identities of the youths into a group identity. Because English does not morphologically mark distinctions between the singular and plural of the second person pronoun, observational and follow-up interview data provided essential information about coaches' intended referents of *you*.

In addition to a focus on *you* (plural), we contrasted two primary uses of *we* and *us*.

5.5.1. WE/US-PRESENT-CENTERED, EXCLUSIVE, SINGULAR OR PLURAL

In this use of *we* and *us*, the coach excludes the speaker and addresses only listeners.

(24a) All right, now we gonna practice. We're not gonna do as m-, we not gonna do a lot of drills. We are gonna run so that you all stay in some kind of shape. And, uh, then we're gonna start practicin' and we're gonna be out of here by six o'clock, so that gives us about fifty minutes. OK, so start, y'all start runnin'

(24b) we all tend to be a little more aggressive about school when school is startin'

(24c) let's go, let's get started, let's get it together, guys

(24d) we're offsides here

In these cases, *we/us* functions as *you* (singular or plural) and appears most frequently in talk that has either a strong directive or nurturing and "checking-in" quality. Though the action to which the utterance refers may take place in the past, present, or future, the force of the utterance is a current directive or attempt to manage the behavior of another individual.

Even when the talk focuses on the specific action of a particular player, the use of the first person plural clearly places the talk within the frame of the group and implies that all members can benefit from the comment and should pay attention to everything that is said during practice. This applies in particular to chastising that follows infractions. The most frequent use of exclusive *we/us* occurs in such instances. The second most frequent use of exclusive *we/us* embraces all those occasions when the coach wishes to get the practice started (or restarted) and wants to draw the group together for talk which often includes an eventcast.

5.5.2. WE/US-INCLUSIVE PAST AND PRESENT, SINGULAR OR PLURAL

The second major use of *we/us* includes the addressee and recalls a shared experience or projects a future experience of which both speaker and listeners have some knowledge. This talk generally falls outside the play of the game and involves coordinating times and places for play.

> (25a) we'll have to get another one [said with reference to a test application needed in a tutoring program associated with the team]

> (25b) we were like three or four hundred miles over the four hundred miles that we were supposed to have [referring to the mileage on the van used to transport the team for the institution]

Within coaching talk, *you* (both plural and singular) appears far more frequently than either *we* or *us*, suggesting that coaches do not include themselves as team members in the sense that they can be directly involved in the winning of games. On the average, across all the girls' athletic events, *we* appeared 13.17 times per 100 turns of the coaches' talk, while *you* appeared 85.43 times; across all the boys' athletic events, *we* appeared 25.23 times per 100 turns of coaches' talk, while *you* appeared 107.63 times. The message of the coaches seems to be, It is up to *you, the players* to carry out the activities; I have to be separate, in the final analysis, from the actual game itself.[12]

6. Conclusion

Though the concept of *register* is slippery, it remains useful to identify the bundles of linguistic features that coalesce around certain types of social situations or uses. It is perhaps the most useful to compare the features of two registers often regarded either as very closely aligned or indeed as a single variant in the repertoire of a particular type of register (such as instructional registers or sports registers). The analysis here of the language of male and female coaches with young players (male and female) of baseball, softball, and basketball indicates numerous features that have not been found in instructional registers and several that appear often in sports talk (for example, telegraphic speech and hypotheticals).

The language of coaches is activity scripted, centered on practice and demonstration, and geared heavily to forming a group identity for a product or goal. Praise, rephrasing of rules, calls for future scenarios, and repetition of verbal props for participatory actions shape the bulk of coaching talk.

Coaches do not work on the basis of a transmission model of socialization; rather they are engaged in modeling and interpreting activities, which are supplemented with advice on ways to move as a team toward a group goal. Their primary goal is not to pass on bodies of knowledge, but to help learners develop competency in basic skills hand-in-hand with a sense of strategy and collaborative achievement as group members. Coaches also want to display and invoke in players positive attitudes, motivational incentives, and relish for participatory action. Coaches say that both skills and attitudes depend on practice over time, as does the habit of creating a mental picture of what can happen in future situations. Thus they set up practices that offer frames in which players can envision a series of potential environments that they may encounter in any possible game. The "game" then becomes a part of real life that extends over time and from which coaches draw further allusions to "the game of real life."

Coaches embrace a transitional model of socialization—even during a single season—believing that players will develop through practice, team participation, and the hard knocks of winning and losing "real" games. Coaches therefore see themselves as starting youths to learn particular skills, attitudes, and roles; they do this through reminding them of the *play* in which they are all engaged. Yet within this play, the roles are real in that they count toward the outcome of the team's reputation, identity, and final scorecard. Coaches cannot possibly elaborate all of the skills and bits of knowledge that individuals must have to bring about a successful practice or game; they see the outcome as emerging from the players themselves as collaborators solving mutual problems, monitoring and correcting each other, and producing a sense that they share their thinking and get better by doing so.

In the contexts of learning that promote the register of coaching, players internalize external activities, grow in interdependence with each other and with shifting situations, and develop as their verbal support and demonstration from coaches shift over time. The language in coaching—telegraphic feedback, emphasis on action by the players, and calls to think, look, listen, and hypothesize—reflects its strong cognitive functions. Moreover, the language of the coach underscores the idea that within practices that lead to the goal of successful games, the players need to prepare themselves to think and act in a constantly changing series of local perspectives, created through the combination of specific tasks and ensemble of talents on the court or field. The coaching register emphasizes for individuals their need to engage constantly in minute acts of perception, self-monitoring in highly participatory and shifting actions, and mental imaging of how the current scene can bring new situations for action. Such a combination of directive, socially integrative, and cognitive functions in language has rarely received attention in the language of instruction. As current educational and work-related reform movements take up the coaching metaphor for students and workers, close examinations of the organizational structure and language of coaching, as well as their implications for both individual and group participation, constitute a necessary preparatory step for such reforms.

Notes

1. In the 1980s, anthropologists and psychologists joined to "think through cultures" (Shweder 1991, Stigler, Shweder, and Herdt 1990) and center attention on competence, communication, and cognition in the everyday world (Rogoff and Lave 1984, Sternberg and Wagner 1986). Especially important in this work was attention to the means of mediation within small groups and the analysis of work as situated practice in multiactivity settings (see, for example, Suchman 1987 and Engeström 1990). Soviet psychologists earlier in the century had studied the role of language in collectives and small problem-solving groups and had also

identified the decisive role in such interactions of "work connections" that built "responsible dependence" (for reports of this research, see Chernyshev (1984) and Lomov and Kol'tsova (1984).

2. Primarily through the work of the Poynter Institute for Media Studies, the practice of coaching writers has spread through editing offices of major newspapers in the United States since 1985. *Coaches Corner*, a newsletter, circulates among editors, and periodic sessions on coaching writing take place at the institute. The "primer" of coaching writing characterizes the coach as a combination of teacher, critic, priest, therapist, and catalyst (Clark and Fry forthcoming).

3. In the 1980s, Tom Peters (Peters and Waterman 1982, Peters 1988) and sociologist Peter Drucker (1985) popularized key ideas underlying participatory management and the possibilities for coaching within business. Since then numerous journal articles, consulting firms, and educational units of business have offered workshops on coaching in which they promote its capacity to empower workers, to enable managers to get feedback from workers, and to motivate a team approach to recognizing and solving problems (Sujansky 1988, Margulies and Black 1987).

4. The five teams included the following: (1) a Little League team of predominantly African American inner-city working-class youngsters aged nine to twelve coached jointly by a middle-aged African American male from the community and a local European-American college student; (2) a Little League team of nine to ten year-old youngsters of working-class and middle-class parents, about half European-American and half African American, sponsored by a Boys and Girls Club and coached by an African American male; (3) an African American boys' basketball team, ages twelve to eighteen, sponsored by a grassroots inner-city community organization, with two coaches, both African American males—one a schoolteacher; (4) a primarily Latina Little League softball team, with two coaches—one Latino and one Latina; (5) a European-American girls' basketball team of working-class origin, sponsored by a Boys and Girls Club and coached by a European-American male.

Date for these athletic teams were drawn from a corpus of approximately a million words collected in a variety of artistic and athletic youth organizations in inner-city locations. Transcription conventions are modified from Tannen (1989), with CAPS indicating emphatic stress, and xxx indicating unintelligible portions of the tape. Transcriptions of the practices and games, once entered into a computer, were quantified according to the appearance of particular items (e.g., negatives, modals, *if-then* constructions) per one hundred turns of both coaches and players. In addition, conversation analysis, field notes, and follow-up interviews with coaches supplemented this quantitative overview.

5. It is not unusual for the general public to view coaches of voluntary out-of-school athletic activities as highly individualistic, autocratic, and even ruthless in their interactions with youngsters. We acknowledge that such coaches would in all likelihood be omitted from our data collection, since the larger study for which these data were collected had the goal of identifying youth-based inner-city organizations that neighborhood youths themselves viewed as effective. Thus we studied only those groups that regarded youths as resources and not as problems, and had relatively steady attendance and support from community youths. These organizations were not always those labeled as "the most successful" by local political leaders, social workers, youth counselors, or educators. For further discussion of these organizations, and their conception of youth, see Heath and McLaughlin (1991). Our findings that the coaching talk of male and female coaches differed little (regardless of whether or not they were coaching male or female teams) are, no doubt, influenced by the types of organizations studied. The philosophy of the youth-based organizations that inner-city youths selected would have eliminated highly autocratic coaches who put winning above all else. For discussions of differences in coaching philosophies—and resulting views on uses of aphorisms and

calls to strict discipline—between male coaches of male and female basketball teams, see Pratt and Eitzen (1989).

6. The origin of the English word *coach* is the name of a small town in Hungary where the first coaches were built; the word appears to have referred generally to "carrying others from place to place" until it came to be used to refer to academic tutors in the mid-nineteenth century, and by 1885, to those who both managed and trained players in athletic contests. From the late nineteenth century until well into the twentieth, clubs or teams had captains and managers but not coaches.

7. Such talk as script for action marks instructional talk that accompanies demonstration, but nuances, such as a sense of authority, shape particular types of such talk. For example, Niemloy (1988), in a study of the teaching of engineering in a research university, identified four uses of the first person singular pronoun: as classroom authority, as speaker's aside, as an inanimate object of manipulation, and as the voice of experience. In addition, special uses of modals and deictics mediated the professor's use of overhead transparencies and chalkboard drawings, as he emphasized degrees of importance of the visual material to his current action and the future actions of students.

8. The philosopher John Searle (1969:33–34) first distinguished between regulative and constitutive rules. The former exist independently of current behavior, such as rules of etiquette that regulate personal interactions. *Constitutive rules* are those whereby new forms of behavior—such as games—are created or defined.

9. For examination of the uses of conditionals by children and their various forms, see Traugott, Meulen, Reilly, and Ferguson (1986). Heath (1991) considers conditionals, including bids for sociodramatic play, in the practice and games of mainstream, middle-class, and upper-class Little League players.

10. For a comprehensive discussion of *we* and *us,* and the need to consider these in terms of the functions of language, see chapter 7 of Mühlhäusler and Harré (1990).

11. When we consider pronouns in the social events in which they appear, it is often impossible to determine their semantic and functional correlates. Since the corpus from which our analysis draws includes not only audiotapes, but also extensive field notes that detail the social practices and interviews that elicit rationales from the coaches for their ways of talking with the players, we can usually, though by no means always, determine their referents.

12. This notion of coach as outsider to athletic teams is paralleled among writing coaches: "Coaches occupy the privileged position of strangers in a community of shared assumptions, both of the immediate group and of the entire profession. As strangers, they tend to see with the clarity of the outsider, with sense less dulled by habit and preconception and personal politics" (Fry 1988:2).

References

Cazden, Courtney. 1988. *Classroom Language: The Language of Teaching and Learning.* Portsmouth, NH: Heinemann.

Chernyshev, Alexandre S. 1984. "Experimental Research on Self-Discipline of Collectives of Pupils and School Children." In Lloyd H. Strickland, ed., *Directions in Soviet Social Psychology.* New York: Springer-Verlag. Pp. 113–29.

Clark, Roy Peter, and Don Fry. Forthcoming. *Coaching Writers: The Human Side of Editing.*

Coleman, Griffith. 1932. *Psychology of Coaching.* New York: Scribner's.

Drucker, Peter F. 1985. *Innovation and Entrepreneurship: Practice and Principles.* New York: Harper & Row.

Engeström, Yrjö. 1990. *Learning, Working and Imagining.* Helsinki: Orienta-Konsultit Oy.
Ferguson, Charles. 1977. "Baby Talk as a Simplified Register." In C. E. Snow and C. A. Ferguson, eds., *Talking to Children: Language Input and Acquisition.* Cambridge: Cambridge University Press. Pp. 209–35.
———. 1983. "Sports Announcer Talk: Syntactic Aspects of Register Variation." *Language in Society* 12:153–72.
Fixx, James F. 1985. *Maximum Sports Performance.* New York: Random House.
Fry, Don. 1988. "Writing Coaching: A Primer." Mimeographed manuscript, Poynter Institute for Media Studies.
Ghadessy, Moshen. 1988. "The Language of Written Sports Commentary." In Mohsen Ghadessy, ed., *Registers of Written English: Situational Factors and Linguistics Features.* London: Pinter.
Halliday, Michael A. K. 1968. "The Users and Uses of Language." In J. Fishman, ed., *Readings in the Sociology of Language.* The Hague: Mouton. Pp. 139–69.
Haviland, John. 1979. "Guugu Yimidhirr Brother-in-Law Language." *Language in Society* 8:365–93.
Heath, Shirley Brice. 1991. "'It's about winning!' The Language of Knowledge in Baseball." In L. Resnick, J. Levine, and S. D. Teasley, eds., *Perspectives on Socially Shared Cognition.* Washington, DC: American Psychological Association. Pp. 101–24.
Heath, Shirley Brice, and Milbrey McLaughlin. 1991. "Community Organizations as Family." *Phi Delta Kappan* 72:623–27.
Henzl, Vera. 1974. "Linguistic Register of Foreign Language Instruction." *Language Learning* 23:207–22.
Hoyle, Susan M. 1991. "Children's Competence in the Specialized Register of Sportscasting." *Journal of Child Language* 18:435–50.
Lawther, John D. 1951. *Psychology of Coaching.* New York: Prentice-Hall.
Leech, Geoffrey. 1966. *English in Advertising.* London: Longman.
Lomov, Boris F., and Vera A. Kol'tsova. 1984. "Mental Processes and Communication." In Lloyd H. Strickland, ed., *Directions in Soviet Social Psychology.* New York: Springer-Verlag. Pp. 47–64.
McNeil, L. 1986. *Contradictions of Control: School Structure and School Knowledge.* New York: Routledge and Kegan Paul.
Margulies, Newton, and Steward Black. 1987. "Perspectives on the Implementation of Participative Approaches." *Human Resource Management* 26:459–79.
Mühlhäusler, Peter, and Rom Harré. 1990. *Pronouns and People: The Linguistic Construction of Social and Personal Identity.* Oxford: Blackwell.
Neal, Patsy. 1969. *Coaching Methods for Women.* Reading, MA: Addison-Wesley.
Niemloy, Araya. 1988. *Teaching Students to Do: Teacher Talk in Technical Classrooms.* Ph.D. Dissertation, Stanford University.
Palincsar, Ann S., and Ann L. Brown. 1984. "Reciprocal Teaching of Comprehension-Fostering and Comprehension-Monitoring Activities." *Cognition and Instruction,* 1:117–75.
Peters, Tom. 1988. *Thriving on Chaos.* New York: Alfred A. Knopf.
Peters, Thomas, and Robert Waterman. 1982. *In Search of Excellence.* New York: Harper & Row.
Pratt, S. R., and D. S. Eitzen. 1989. "Differences in Coaching Philosophies Between Male Coaches of Male and Female Basketball Teams." *International Review for Sociology of Sport* 24:151–59.
Rogoff, Barbara. 1990. *Apprenticeship in Thinking.* New York: Oxford University Press.

Rogoff, Barbara, and Jean Lave, eds. 1984. *Everyday Cognition: Its Development in Social Context.* Cambridge, MA: Harvard University Press.

Searle, John R. 1969. *Speech Acts: An Essay in the Philosophy of Language.* Cambridge: Cambridge University Press.

Shweder, Richard A. 1991. *Thinking Through Cultures: Expeditions in Cultural Psychology.* Cambridge, MA: Harvard University Press.

Sizer, Theodore R. 1984. *Horace's Compromise: The Dilemma of the American High School.* Boston, MA: Houghton Mifflin.

Sternberg, Robert J., and Richard K. Wagner, eds. 1986. *Practical Intelligence: Nature and Origins of Competence in the Everyday World.* Cambridge: Cambridge University Press.

Stigler, James W., Richard A. Shweder, and Gilbert Herdt, eds. 1990. *Cultural Psychology: Essays on Comparative Human Development.* Cambridge: Cambridge University Press.

Suchman, Lucy A. 1987. *Plans and Situated Actions: The Problem of Human Machine Communication.* Cambridge: Cambridge University Press.

Sujansky, J. G. 1988. "Performance Appraisals: Helping Managers Make It Work." *Allegheny Business News.* September.

Tannen, Deborah. 1989. *Talking Voices: Repetition, Dialogue, and Imagery in Conversational Discourse.* Cambridge: Cambridge University Press.

Tannen, Deborah, and Cynthia Wallat. 1982. "A Sociolinguistic Analysis of Multiple Demands on the Pediatrician in Doctor/Mother/Child Interaction." In R. J. DiPietro, ed., *Linguistics and the Professions.* Norwood, NJ: Ablex. Pp. 39–50.

Traugott, Elizabeth, Alice ter Meulen, Judith S. Reilly, and Charles A. Ferguson, eds. 1986. *On Conditionals.* Cambridge: Cambridge University Press.

Ulichny, Polly, and Karen Ann Watson-Gegeo. 1989. "Interactions and Authority: The Dominant Interpretive Framework in Writing Conferences." *Discourse Processes* 12:309–28.

5

Stories That Step into the Future

Elinor Ochs

1. Recollection and Anticipation

This chapter considers the role of future time within a particular genre of narrative generally referred to as 'narratives of personal experience'. While systematically linked to present-time conversational topics and concerns (Bauman 1986, Goodwin 1984, Jefferson 1978, Young 1987), narratives of personal experience have been generally characterized (with the exception of Goodwin 1990) as interpretive construals of *past* personal experience, in contrast to various other genres of narrative such as genres of science fiction or future planning narratives, which depict experiences which might take place at a *future* time. Labov, for example, notes that in producing narratives of personal experience, "the speaker becomes deeply involved in rehearsing or even reliving events of his past" (Labov 1972), and he defines such narratives as "one method of recapitulating past experience by matching a verbal sequence of clauses to the sequence of events which (it is inferred) actually occurred." Polanyi (1989) similarly uses past time in her analysis of stories: "In recounting a story, a teller describes events which took place in one specific past time world in order to make some sort of *point* about the world which teller and story recipients share." The centrality of past time experience is also evident in developmental studies of children's storytelling skills. In assessing children's storytelling competence, for example, developmentalists have used "consistent past tense" as an acquisition variable (cf. Applebee 1978, Pitcher and Prelinger 1963, Umiker-Sebeok 1979).

This essay argues that, while narratives of personal experience center around a

This essay has benefitted from the insightful comments of P. Gonzales, Sally Jacoby, Carolyn Taylor, and Sandro Duranti. The consideration of future time in this essay develops earlier collaborative research on family co-narration (Ochs, Smith, and Taylor 1989, Ochs, Taylor et al. 1992, Ochs and Taylor 1992a, 1992b). Data collection and analysis on which this study is based have been supported by the NICHD 1986–1990 (grant no. 1 ROH HD 2099201A1; Principal investigators E. Ochs, T. Weisner; Research Assistants: M. Bernstein, D. Rudolph, R. Smith, C. Taylor) and the Spencer Foundation 1990–1993 (Principal Investigator: E. Ochs, Research Assistants: P. Gonzales, S. Jacoby, and C. Taylor.)

specific past experience, such narratives share with other narrative genres a tendency to project *future* time experiences as well. Stories of personal experience regularly step out of the temporal domain of the past into the temporal domain of the future to make *story-coherent* predications of possible events to take place after the present moment. In many cases, these story-coherent predications consist of possible implications of past experiences for the future. In an incisive analysis of black adolescent storytelling, M. Goodwin (1990) details how storytellers may carefully lay the groundwork for future-oriented talk about implications in the telling of the past experience. In Goodwin's observations, the interlocutor who brings up the past experience structures the telling in a way that "instigates" other interlocutors to take future action or to talk about the future actions they intend to take or would like to take. The present essay argues that a concern for future time is not limited to the "instigating stories" of black adolescents: it is an existential dimension of *all* storytelling activity in the sense that storyteller's recollections of past events have the potential to evoke for participating interlocutors ideas and talk about future events/circumstances. Each verbal *recollection* of past events may lead interlocutors to *anticipate* ramifications of those events in the future. Talk about the future may be introduced at the very beginning of a story by the teller who initiates the story (henceforth 'Initial Teller') or may be introduced by some other teller (henceforth 'Other Teller') or the Initial Teller as the story events unfold (Ochs, Taylor, Rudolph, and Smith 1992).

Because talk about past personal experiences has the potential to evoke a sense of the future, it is not uncommon to find story-coherent predications about the future laced seamlessly in the storytelling activity. References to past- and future-oriented events as well as speech acts which are future-implicative (e.g., forecasts, warnings, prescriptions, advice) are often interwoven in the course of storytelling, at times within the same turn and at times even within the same clause (see section 4.2). An important claim of this essay is that such story-coherent future time references are integral to the story in the sense that they give meaning to its events. A defining feature of all stories is that they have a point (Labov and Waletzky 1967, Polanyi 1989, Ricoeur 1988). In many cases the point may be the relevance of the story's past events for future events. One or another teller may see the point of the story to include what certain past events mean with respect to their own or others' future experiences. A sense of the future may be fundamental to the design of the past events from the very beginning of the narrative, as Goodwin displays for black adolescent stories, or may be expressed at a later point in the course of storytelling. When interlocutors refer to story-coherent future-time events in the course of storytelling, they are not necessarily *exiting* from the story of personal experience and initiating a new discursive activity. Rather, they are furthering the construction of the story itself, using future ramifications to help shape what they see to be the *point* of the story's past events.

That narratives are Janus-like, with one face toward the past and one toward the present and future is recognized by Heidegger (1962) and Ricoeur (1988). Heidegger's chef-d'oeuvre *Being and Time* emphasizes that human "cares" (i.e., human concerns) structure our sense of time and hence our sense of ourselves, that is, what it means to be-in-the-world. Caring organizes narrative *recollection* of past events, including history. Ricoeur (1988) refers to this relation between care (in Heidegger's sense) and narrative events as the "configurational structure" of narrative, or the narrative "plot." The narrative configuration/plot selectively arranges narrative events according to some point of view (i.e., some "care"). Narratives bridge present and past time in that present cares influence the production and understanding of narratives about the past and in that narratives are discursive means of bringing the past into the experienced present. From a Heideggerian perspective, narratives help us to achieve a sense of continuity as we move through our lifespan by virtue of their capacity to extend the past into the present. In this light, our sense of ourselves is an outcome of how we tell the stories of our personal experiences. In addition, narrative recollection helps us to anticipate the future, including ultimately our death. One reason that narratives, including history, hold interest for us is that they help us to understand what may lie in wait for us—our destinies, our potentialities, our fates. In some cases, narratives provide new models, open up novel possibilities, for the shape of our lives to come. In other cases, narratives expose problematic events which we feel call for some response in the future.

While present time has been analyzed for its importance to stories (Bauman 1986, Goodwin 1984, Sacks 1970, Young 1987, among others), there has been little text analysis beyond Goodwin's research of the expression of future time in stories of personal experience. This essay examines texts of conversational stories for evidence that future time can be a deictic and experiential reference point of stories. An orientation either to the present or to the future may be in the form of a moral or lesson to be implemented in the present or future or in the form of a present or future payback for a past misdeed, for instance. Future time may be explicitly referenced or implicitly at work as an organizing principle for the design of the story. For example, M. Goodwin (1990) details how black adolescent storytellers may subtly craft stories with the implicit goal of co-opting interlocutors to perform some future action. From this point of view, stories are not only reconstructions of past experiences but *preconstructions* of future experiences as well. Stories may imply or make explicit what will, might, could, or should (not) happen next. They draft lives-in-progress, allowing interlocutors continually to (re)create their past, present, and future selves at once.

One might counterargue that while stories have relevance for the future, this temporal domain is not properly part of the stories of personal experience, even when explicitly mentioned. This line of argument might hold that stories are properly about past events and that when interlocutors leap to the future, they have switched into another genre—a future plan, for example. This position maintains a past-future temporal definitional distinction for narratives of personal experience. It has several advantages. First, it accounts for story narratives in which there is no explicit predication of future events. Second, it allows the analyst to talk about structural relations between past- and future-oriented narratives. For example, we can refer to embedding relations between story narratives (which predicate past time events) and future planning narratives (which predicate future time events), wherein stories may be part of a larger future plan. Thus, for example, black adolescent "instigating stories" can be analyzed as components of a future plan to carry out some future action. Third, preserving a time-based genre distinction allows the analyst to articulate possible functions of stories vis-à-vis (present and) future time narratives. For example, in the case of "instigating stories," they sometimes serve the function of introducing a problematic event which in turn "instigates" the addressee to initiate a future-oriented narrative about the actions she plans on taking to redress the narrated problematic event (Goodwin 1990).

These arguments are reasonable; however, when one examines everyday conversational storytelling, certain problems arise. First, switching among past, present, and future time can be recurrent and frequent in the course of storytelling. That is, storytelling is not always characterized by a lengthy continuous stretch of past time discourse followed by a lengthy continuous stretch of present or future time discourse. We can find predications about the present and future intermittent throughout some narratives that depict the past (see sections 3 and 4). Do we in these cases take out our analytic pencil and remove these present and future time threads from the story structure we are analyzing? Second, in cases where narratives of past events are analyzed as embedded in narratives of present or future events, the narrative of past events is nonetheless by implication a part of a future narrative. That is, such narratives can not be considered as just about past events. Third, from a Heideggerian perspective, present and future time are also part of the past time narrative in that one's sensation of the present and anticipation of the future organize one's sense of the story's past. Existentially (i.e., experientially) a story is past, present, and future at once.

This essay explores these arguments through an analysis of family dinner narratives. Many of these narratives journey back and forth between past and future time predications. The narratives often bring up past events that one or another interlocutor orient to as needing present or future attention. In all of these narratives, the narrative enactment of past and future events appears to be a single, coherent, discursive activity which interlocutors sustain with ease.

2. Data Base

The narratives analyzed in this essay are drawn from a larger study of family dinner discourse among twenty white, English-speaking, American families varying in socioeconomic status. All the families have at least two children, including a five-year-old and an older sibling. Our corpus consists of transcripts and videorecordings of dinnertime preparation, eating, and cleanup over two evenings for each of these families (a total of forty dinnertimes). During dinnertime recording, the researchers were present during dinner preparation. During the meal itself and the following cleanup, the researchers set up a videocamera on a tripod and then absented themselves from the dining area.

3. Narrative Past and Present Time

Before considering the expression of future time in storytelling, let us examine some dimensions of present time in stories of personal experience. The focus here is not on the use of present time markers (e.g., the historical present) in depicting past events but on predications of events taking place in the present moment of the storytelling. Present and future time have in common that they both occur at a temporal point after past time. When interlocutors are talking about either present or future events, they may retreat in time to a narrative past (what Young 1987 calls "the taleworld"). And complementarily, when storytellers are depicting past personal events, they may move forward to a time beyond that in which these events occurred to predicate present and future time propositions relevant to those past events (what Young 1987 calls "the story realm"). We turn now to a consideration of these temporal relations in stories of personal experience.

3.1. Present Retreats into the Past

Researchers have noted that stories of past personal experience may also incorporate the present into their telling. For example, storytellers often couch their evaluations of the events in the present tense (Labov and Waletzky 1967). Further, they design their narratives for *copresent* interlocutors and other circumstances (Bauman 1986, Goodwin and Goodwin 1989). And recollections are stimulated or "locally occasioned" (Jefferson 1978) often by some *present* time focus of attention (e.g., by a discourse topic currently under discussion or by something currently experienced in the physical environment). Example (1) illustrates two occasions in which talk about the past is occasioned by a current focus of family interaction. It is a continuous stretch of talk represented in four segments (1a–1d) for purposes of analysis. The example displays a family dinner conversation that includes Father, Mother, Oren (seven years, five months), and Jodie (five years). The family is eating guacamole dip. In this segment, the present activity appears to motivate Father to ask Mother whether she put chili peppers in the dip. After some hesitation, Mother reveals that she has included not only chili peppers but hot salsa:

(1a) Excerpt 1 from "Chili Peppers" (Conversation before "Chili Peppers" Story)[1]

Father:	whadid you put in (here/it) – chili peppers?
?:	heh
Mother:	no: ((*shaking head no*))
Father:	what
Mother:	uh yeah chili peppers – is it very spicy?
Father:	no? – it's not that spicy=
Jodie:	=Momma? ((*as she hands Mom back asparagus spear*))
	[
Father:	(It's spicy)
	((*Jodie chokes; Mom eats the asparagus*))
Mother:	(not a) lot though
Father:	(huh)
Mother:	(not a lot of it/it had a lot of em)
	(2.0) ((*Jodie choking*))
Mother:	you wanta know what I put in it?

Father: ((*slight raise of head—nod yes?*))
Mother: guacamo– I mean avocado. tomatoes. lemon juice, garlic powder? some
           <u>hot</u> salsa? and chili peppers

In this segment we find a small instance of how a current activity (eating
guacamole dip) leads to a return to a past event (what Mother put into the guacamole
dip). Mother's recollection is more a listing of ingredients than a full-fledged narrative consisting of two or more sequentially related clauses (unless we wish to
consider each ingredient as a separate event in the making of guacamole). In
addition, in (1a) Father's remarks (e.g., "whadid you put in (here/it) – chili peppers?", "<u>no</u>? – it's not <u>that</u> spicy") may be interpreted as complaints about the
guacamole being overly spicy) as well as a veiled challenge ("what") to Mother's
initial claim that she had not put chili peppers in the dip. In (1b), Mother's reluctant
revelation triggers a dramatization of a mock death by Oren:

(1b) Excerpt 2 from "Chili Peppers"

Oren: ((*as if gasping for breath, facing Mom*)) I ate hot salsa and chili?
           ((*Oren pretends to die in his chair*))
Mother: ((*leaning over to Oren, smiling, as if taking his protest as a joke*)) <u>ye:s</u>
           (1.0) ((*Oren flops back on chair, gasping as if expiring*))
Mother: <u>uh</u> – we lost Oren
           (0.4)
Mother: well: he was a <u>great</u> kid.

In (1b) Oren registers his surprise and dismay over the news, thereby reproduc-
ing and intensifying his father's negative stance toward Mother's making the guacamole peppery. At this point in the interaction, Oren initiates a narrative of personal experience of when, some years ago, his Mother inadvertently let him bite into a
hot pepper.

(1c) Excerpt 3 from "Chili Peppers" (Chili Peppers Story Begins)

Mother: well: he was a <u>great</u> kid.
           [   ]
Oren: (Mommy) – <u>wasn't it funny</u>? (when – wh–)
Oren: Wasn't it funny when you – thought that thing was a
           pickle? and I ate it?
Mother: no that <u>wasn't</u> funny. – I thought it was uh um:: ((*looks at
           Dad*)) – a green bean.
Father: ((*nods yes*))
           [
Oren: and – it was really a <u>chili</u>? – it was really a <u>chili</u>? – when I
           was about ((*turns to Mom*)) how old?
Mother: ((*looking to Dad*)) how old was he Don? when that happened?
                                                           [
Father: two

Mother:	was he even two?
	(1.0) ((*no noticeable affirmation from Dad*))
Oren:	yeah I was two:? – and then – and then you know what
	happened? – ((*to Jodie*)) I ate that chili pepper? .h ((*imitating*
	action of eating it)) and Mom thought it was a bean? – and I ate
	it? and I burned to death ((*turns to Mom*)) – what happened. –
	what=
Mother:	=you burnt your mouth
	(1.2) ((*Oren and Mom looking at each other*))
	((*Mom is eating asparagus spears from bowl, licking fingers,*
	eating another as she answers Oren's questions))
Oren:	(was/did) it all over?
Mother:	((*nodding yes*)) (it was/I thought)
	⌊
Oren:	Did I hafta go to the hospital?
Mother:	((*low*)) ((*Mom shakes head no once*)) (nah)
Oren:	what – (did they) hafta do?
Mother:	we gave you ice
Oren:	where
Mother:	in your mouth
Oren:	oh: my god – how long did I – keep it in
Mother:	(a few minutes) ((*very quiet, looking down at lap*))

In this passage the parallels that bind the present to the past are fairly evident. When Father asks Mother (in (1a)) whether she put chili peppers in the guacamole, she at first denies and then admits that she did. She goes on to list all the ingredients in the guacamole, putting off "hot salsa" and "chili peppers" till the end. In (1b) Oren reacts as if in shock, just now realizing that he ate hot salsa and chili. He collapses back into his chair, acting somewhat like a stereotypic Shakespearian actor who discovers he's been betrayed and poisoned. His mother enters into this dramatic footing, announcing to the world Oren's demise ("uh – we lost Oren"), even eulogizing him ("well: he was a great kid"). This dramatic enactment of a fictitious death calls to mind and presages the subsequent telling of narrative events of a similar nature that took place in another time and place.

When Oren turns to his mother and asks, "Wasn't it funny when you – thought that thing was a pickle? and I ate it?" this *present* time drama moves to a parallel *past, recollected* drama in which Oren unknowingly ate a hot pepper, trusting his mother's assumption that it was a benign food item. Although Oren initially frames this event as "funny," he subsequently alludes to more tragic elements in the narrative. Turning to his sister, Oren frames this event as one in which he was at death's door ("I ate that chili pepper? .h ((*imitating action of eating it*)) and Mom thought it was a bean? – and I ate it? and I burned to death"). With this statement, Mother is implicated as the perpetrator of his suffering, much in the way she is currently implicated for letting Oren eat hot salsa and chili peppers without forewarning him ("((*as if gasping for breath*)) I ate hot salsa and chili?").

3.2. Past Extends Forward into the Present

In addition to present time experiences occasioning stories of past experiences, stories of *past experiences can be extended forward to include present time* (Heidegger 1962:424–49). In these cases, it is not so much that present time falls back into a narrative past as much as that a narrative past progresses forward beyond a narrative 'then' to infiltrate a narrative 'now'. Indeed all stories of past experiences extend into present time in the important sense that their telling (i.e., storytelling) takes place in the present (see Young 1987 for discussion of this point). In this capacity, narratives allow persons and groups of persons to bring their pasts forward with them as they move through lifespans (Heidegger 1962, Ricoeur 1988). Narrative recollections discursively create for persons and communities a sense of continuity from past to present time.

In some cases, the narrative storyline does not stop with a recollection of past experience but rather *creatively evolves* (Bergson 1911) toward the present as a continuous discursive and/or physical activity (e.g., gestures, physical actions; that is, past and present predications are not separated by disjunctive markers, *oh, incidentally,* and the like—see Jefferson 1978 for a discussion of these constructions). The present time events dramatized in talk and action are incorporated *into* the story of personal experience rather than constituting a disjunctive genre or type of discourse. In such instances, predications about events that happened in the past progress into predications about events happening in the present or progress into some form of embodied actions (e.g., emotional events, action events). In (1b) we can see a brief illustration of this progression or creative evolution from the past into the present. In this passage, Oren moves from a narrated past experience ("((*as if gasping for breath*)) I ate hot salsa and chili?") seamlessly into a present-time dramatic enactment of the consequences of that past experience (Oren flops back on chair gasping as if expiring). In so doing, Oren produces a narrative that not only incorporates both talk and embodied action but also blends two temporal domains. The evolving character of narrative activity is even more vividly illustrated if we turn to the remaining moments of the "Chili Peppers" narrative presented in (1d):

(1d) Excerpt 4 of "Chili Peppers"

.
.
.

Oren:	did I love it [the ice] in?
Mother:	you were <u>crying</u>
	(0.8)
Oren:	I didn't like it (in there?)
Mother:	((*shakes head no*)) – you were <u>hurting</u> – your mouth hurt – it was burned=

Father: ((*leaning to Jodie*)) =Oren – I mean Jodie – (did) you=
                                                                        [
Oren: (I know)
Father: =(kids like the mango)?
           [
Mother: (it was like – I–)
Mother: we were (in a restaurant?)
           [
Jodie: ((*shakes her head no to Dad*))
Father: ((*to Jodie, pointing to piece of roll on Jodie's plate*)) Can I have
           this?
           [
Oren: YOUR FAULT – YOUR FAULT= ((*pointing at Mom and
           reaching over until he's touching her cheek with index finger*))
Jodie: ((*shakes head no to Dad, then picks up piece of roll in question,
           looks at it, and hands it to Dad*))
Mother: =It was my fault
Jodie: hhh ((*soft laugh at Oren's reaction to Mom?*))
Mother: I thought it was ((*Oren now pinching both of Mom's cheeks*)) a
           um – green pepper –.HHHHH– ((*pulling Oren's hands away*))
           ow that really hurts honey?
Oren: your fault – (I get to do whatever I want to do once)
           [
Jodie: ((*to Dad*)) No Don't eat it – put some of – put some of the=
           ((*Dad responds by buttering her piece of roll*))
Oren: =(that was my fee?)=
Jodie: =for me::=
Oren: =.he he .hh
           ((*Mom shakes her head no slightly*))
Oren: .hh ((*laugh*))
           ((*Dad teases Jodie by acting as if he's going to take a
           bite of roll he's buttered*))
Oren: ((*lolling back in chair, to Mom, laughingly*))
           just like (it) happened to me=
           [
Jodie: ah ((*shrill*))
           ((*Dad starts to put roll back on her plate, then starts to put it back
           in his mouth; Jodie doesn't see him, so he repeats motion*))
Oren: =it happens to you

In this passage, the narrative almost literally leaps from the *past* into the *present*
as Oren follows up his accusation "YOUR FAULT – YOUR FAULT" with a bolt toward
his mother and a rigorous pinching of her cheeks, the latter being carried out in the
midst of his mother's affirmation and renarrating of her past error.[2] In this movement, Oren switches from an orientation to the *past*—the accusation is rooted in the

past—to an orientation to the *here and now*—the action of pinching. It as if the events in the distant past have come alive to the point where Oren is emotionally aroused and reexperiences the past experiences in the time of their discursive portrayal, perhaps manifesting a form of transference (i.e., mapping feelings associated with a different set of circumstances on to the present circumstances). Mother's and Oren's subsequent turns sustain the orientation to the *present* (".ḤHHHH – ((*pulling Oren's hands away*)) ow that really hurts honey?", "your fault – (I get to do whatever I want to do once"). Then, in a final elegant narrative move, Oren returns to the narrative past to make explicit the narrative progression from *past* experience ("just like (it) happened to me") to *present* ("it happens to you").

The "Chili Peppers" sequence is a provocative segment of interaction in that the interlocutors have interactionally produced *one* story with at least *two* episodes. (For a structural analysis of this sequence, see Ochs, Taylor et al. 1992.) The first episode took place in a restaurant when Oren was around two years old; the second episode takes place in the present time in their own home sitting around the dinner table. In this second time and place, Oren is old enough to participate in the telling of the first episode and to take revenge for what Mother and Oren ultimately construct as Mother's wrongdoing in the first episode. The interlocutors do not close down the story at the end of the first episode, as evidenced by Oren's shouting of "YOUR FAULT – YOUR FAULT". Nor do the interlocutors isolate the second episode from the first as evidenced by Oren and Mother's discursive mingling of past and present time references.[3] The fluidity of the passage from past to present and present to past support the notion that temporal shifts do not necessarily signal exits from an otherwise temporally coherent past time story. Rather, interlocutors sometimes construct multiepisodic, multitime dimensional stories that have a single, complex story plot structure. In this case, episode two presents a "just desserts" ending to this story of personal experience.

4. Narrative Past and Future Time

4.1. Future Retreats into the Past

It is not only present time that both structures and is structured by narratives of past experience but *future time* as well. Just as a present concern for present circumstances and events both occasions and infiltrates the telling of past experience, so does a present concern for *future circumstances and events*. An interlocutor may drop back into a narrative past in the midst of considering the course of future events, for example. The return to a recollected past may provide evidence for or otherwise explain why a particular plan should be carried out in the future. Example (2) displays how a present concern for a future event may motivate and organize a narrative of past experience. In this example, Mother, Father, and three children— Dick (eight years seven months), Janie (five years eleven months), and Evan (three years seven months)—have just finished the main course of their dinner, and Father has just denied one of the children's (Dick's) request to eat some chocolate candy. In

the midst of this present discussion about a future event, namely the eating of
chocolates for dessert, Evan initiates a narrative recollection (i.e., drops back in
time) that before dinner Father had promised him ice cream for dessert:

(2) Excerpt from "Ice Cream"

```
Dick:      =Daddy? could we have those little chocolates – um af–
                      [                                    ]
Father:    ((to Evan?))        (wa– –     Dick's doin it)
Dick:      (uh) You said after dinner you'd save em for us?
Mother:    What little chocolates
                  [
Father:           What little chocolates
Dick:      That Daniel um – Daniel brought us?
Mother:    Oh: oh – yeah later
                     [
                     ((Mom raps spoon on pan — cleaning up))
Father:    Oh yeah. That's fer – later or tomorrow
                     [              [
Mother:           (not)        (That's for later)
           ((Evan is standing by Father, looking up at him))
"Ice Cream"
story begins→
Evan:      No – AN AND YOU 'MEMBER I COULD HAVE A –
                                           [
Father:                         (yeah/it's) – I think it's
           gonna be too late at night to have chocolates tonight
                                      [
Evan:                             DADDY?
Evan:      YOU (KNOW::/'MEMBER) IF I EAT A GOOD DINNER I–=
               [                        [
Father:      (have those tomorrow)
Dick:                            o:kay
Father:    =(You/Hey) (but see) in the morning? you get the energy?
                                  [
Mother:                        Janie don't touch that
           ((Janie is over by audio equipment?))
Father:    You go outside – you burn up that energy? s–
               [                              ]
Mother:      (that's                          )
                  [
Evan:              MO:MMY
Father:    Yeah don't le– – play with that ((to Janie))
           ((Evan is tapping Father's arm for attention))
Evan:      Mommy – you – you 'member – (um) if I eat a good=
                              [
```

Mother: (That's   )
                                     [
Janie?:   (Could I get my
purse?)
  [
Mother: No! (   )
         [
Evan: =dinner I could have a ice cream
Father: An ice cream? – Who? said that
                     [
Mother?:   Who said that?
Evan: You=
Dick?:   =You
       (0.4)
Mother: Oooooooo ((*barklike laugh*)) hehe
                              [
Father: I didn't? say that
      ((*Janie returns — Dick closes in toward Father too*))
Dick: Remember? – he – h–you said "Daddy – could I have a i:ce
crea:m?"
          [
Mother: Okay this is where you guys chant=
                       [
Dick: and
Father: =Where? was I
         [
Mother: "Haagen Dazs Haagen Dazs"
Dick: and then
       [
Mother: Haagen Dazs Haagens Haagen Dazs
       [
Janie: Haagen Dazs HAAGEN DAZS HAAGEN DAZS
           [
Evan: Haagen Dazs HAAGEN DAZS HAAGEN
DAZS HAAGEN DAZS

     .

     .

     .

Father: I don't even remember telling you that–What was I doing when
                                       [   ]
Dick: ((*moves to Father, drops ball*))   Daddy I'll tell you the
exact words you said
Father: Tell m– What was I doing – where was I first of all
                                      [
Dick: You were sitting right

```
                 in that chair where you are now
                                [
                                ((sound of Dick bouncing ball?))
                 (0.4)
Mother:          ((laughing)) hehehaha – It's o:n film – they have you.
                                          [        ]
Father:                                   (in/at dinnertime?)
Mother:          .hh hahaha
                 [
Janie?:          (he has a . . .)
                    [
Dick:               (You) watch ((moves to Father)) I'll ask em to play back
                 the film= ((everyone is looking at Father))
Father:          =No – ton't – don't do that – just tell me when – when I first sat
                 down for dinner?
Dick:            No – um you– we– it was before dinner .h when we were all
                 hungry Evan came up to you and said .h "Daddy? could I have a
                 ice cream" and you said "Yeah if you eat a good dinner you
                 can have a ice cream".
                                [
                                ((ball bouncing))
                 (0.4)
Father:          I – I did?
                 [
Mother:          Ooooooooooooooooo
                                 [
Janie?:                          Yes
Father:          I remember the conversation that I said that I'd–
                                 [
Mother:                          oooooooooo((like ghost))ooooooooooooooo
Evan:            Did I EAT a good dinner?=
Mother:          =You did so: we:ll: – chant "Haagen Dazs" ((uses hand to root
                 them on)) no huh huh huh ((laughing))
Dick:            Haagen Dazs Haagen DAZS HAAGEN DAZS HAAGENDAZS=
                                [
Janie:                          HAAGEN DAZS HAAGEN DAZS HAAGENDAZ=
                                   [
Evan:                              HAAGEN DAZS HAAGEN DAZS
                 HAAGENDAZS HAAGENDAZS
                                    [
Dick:                               =HAAGENDAZS
                                    [
Janie:                              =HAAGENDAZS
                                    [              ]
Father:                             Okay – I'm not gonna go to Haagen Dazs
                 ((raises hand again to signal stop))
                 (0.4) ((sudden silence))
```

Father:

      .

      .

      .

In this passage the children display a *present* concern for *future* events, first to eat chocolates and then to eat ice cream for dessert. Dick reminds Father of his promise to let them have chocolates, but Father finds a rationale to postpone that commitment. At this point Evan starts the ball rolling for eating ice cream by initiating a collective remembering of a *past* event that entails *future* events, namely that before dinner Father had promised Evan that if he ate a good dinner (future event 1), he could have ice cream for dessert (future event 2). Seemingly in an effort to minimize his commitment and avoid carrying out its implications, the narrative events are disputed by Father, who turns the narrative into a courtroomlike cross-examination of the purported facts concerning this set of events (e.g., "An ice cream? – Who? said that?", "I didn't say that", "I don't even remember telling you that – What was I doing when", "Tell m– What was I doing – where was I first of all"), whereupon Evan and Dick, egged on by Mother, rally together to support one narrative defense (e.g., "Remember? – he – h–you said 'Daddy – could I have a i:ce crea:m?'", "Daddy I'll tell you the exact words you said", "No – um you– we– it was before dinner .h when we were all hungry Evan came up to you and said .h 'Daddy? could I have a ice cream' and you said 'Yeah if you eat a good dinner you can have a ice cream'"). Mother and Dick even draw on the research team to shore up Evan's and Dick's narrative credibility (e.g., "I'll ask em to play back the film").

Example (2) supports the notion that future time can play a major role not only in warranting but in *structuring* stories of past experience. A present concern for some future event is not simply a spark that ignites a narrative that is otherwise about the past. Rather, similar to what Goodwin found in black adolescent stories, *anticipation of future events is a design element in the story itself:* First of all, *predications about future events* are made within the storyline itself (e.g., "Mommy. – you – you 'member – (um) if I eat a good dinner I could have a ice cream", "you said 'Yeah if you eat a good dinner you can have a ice cream'"). Second, the future events of eating a good dinner and eating ice cream are the *point* of the narrative from Evan's and his siblings' perspective: it organizes which events are *selected* for mention (e.g., father's past commitment to allow Evan to have ice cream), how the events are *implicationally related* to one another (e.g., how eating a good dinner is related to eating ice cream and therefore why it is important to establish that Evan did eat a good dinner), and how different interlocutors *affectively frame* the past events (e.g., the children's insistent support for one version of the narrative events in contrast to Father's doubting stance, Mother's delight at Father's predicament).

4.2. Past Extends Forward into the Future

In section 3.2., we considered how narratives of personal experience can evolve into present time narratives, wherein a sequence of recollected past events is continued into the storytelling moment. Storytelling evolves out of present concern/topic, turns to past events, and then back to the present time in which implications/consequences of past events are incorporated into the storyline. The perspective here is that a turn to the present in these instances is not outside the story but *part* of it. It is as if interlocutors continue a narrative of personal experiences to the point that they narrate present events or physically act out present events that are logically, causally, temporally, emotionally, or otherwise relevant to the past events just narrated.

In similar fashion, *narratives of personal experience can extend forward to include talk and actions that evidence a present, story-coherent concern with the future.* For example, in (2), the narrative of Father's *past* commitment to ice cream for dessert evolves into both Mother's present proposal to lobby again for ice cream in the relatively immediate *future* ("Okay this is where you guys chant 'Haagen Dazs Haagen Dazs'") and execution of that proposal as the kids and Mother repeat the chant to obtain the desired future experience—a future-oriented strategy that eventually moves Father to make good on his commitment to ice cream that evening. (Despite his stated refusal to take the kids to Haagen Dazs, Father in the end took the whole family along with the researchers and their recording equipment not to Pronto Market but to the Haagen Dazs store a number of miles away!)

Examples (3a)–(3c) illustrate storytelling activity that moves forward in time to include both present and future time predications and references. These future time constructions are enmeshed in the narrative of personal experience topically and structurally in the sense that they are referential expressions embedded in clauses that refer to the past, or they are predicates that relate causally or otherwise to a prior past time predicate. The narrative in (3a)–(3c) involves Mother (Patricia) and Father (Dan) as interlocutors as they are sitting around the dinner table at the end of the meal; their two children—Oren (seven years five months) and Jodie (five years)—are playing nearby. The passage in (3) occurs in the course of a narrative elicited by Dan about Patricia's day and concerns buying a dress for an upcoming wedding.

(3a) Excerpt 1 from "Patricia's Dress"

Mother: =and then we went to this other um – this dress store? – a:nd (my Mom) bought me a dress for the wedding – (for . . .'s wedding). (3.8) ((*kids outside talking; Dan looks at Patricia, then starts to eat, then looks back at Patricia*)

Father: (you're kidding)

Mother: hun uh ((*shaking head no*))

Father: (I thought you had a dress).

Mother: (my) mother didn't like it.

                       [

                     ((*phone rings; Patricia gets up*))

Father: ( )

Mother: (it's your mother).

        ((*phone rings second time; Patricia's voice on answering machine begins; Patricia picks up; it is his mother*))

.

.

.

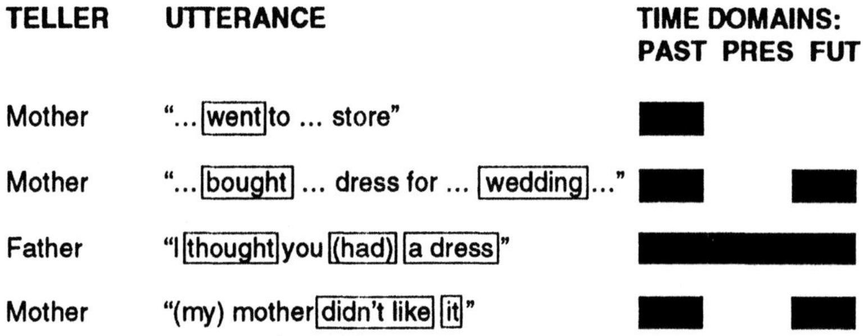

TELLER	UTTERANCE	TIME DOMAINS: PAST PRES FUT

Mother   "... went to ... store"

Mother   "... bought ... dress for ... wedding ..."

Father   "I thought you (had) a dress"

Mother   "(my) mother didn't like it"

FIGURE 5.1.

In this narrative excerpt, Patricia begins by predicating two *recent past* events ("and then we went to this other um – this dress store", "a:nd (my Mom) bought me a dress for the wedding – (for . . .'s wedding)"). In the second predicate, Patricia alludes to the *future* by referring within a prepositional phrase to a wedding that presumably is yet to take place ("for the wedding", "(for . . .'s wedding)"). At this point in the narrative, Patricia's primary linguistic focus of attention is on the *past* as evidenced by the use of the main-clause verbs *went* and *bought*. In the following turn, however, Dan brings the focus of attention in the narrative into the *present*. Although Dan uses verbs in the simple past (*thought, had*), Dan's predication ("I thought you had a dress") occupies a temporal domain that extends from a *more distant past up through the present* (I thought, i.e., think, you had, i.e., have, a dress for the wedding.). The predication implies that Dan not only thought that Patricia already had a dress for the wedding, but also that he still thinks that she has now in her possession a dress for the wedding. As this interpretation suggests, a sense of the *future* is implied in Dan's remarks. "I thought you had a dress" assumes the recipient's background knowledge that "a dress" refers not to any dress but to a dress for the wedding, which in turn both interlocutors know to be in the future. The *present* circumstance of having two dresses for the same event which was pointed out by Dan is addressed by Patricia in the subsequent turn. Her own predication, however, focuses on only that portion of the previous predicate that includes the more *distant past*. In this turn, Patricia predicates a stative event ("(my) mother didn't like it") that had motivated her mother to buy a second dress for her that day. It should be mentioned that Patricia alludes to the *future* event of the wedding in this proposition through the referential expression *it*. This term refers to the dress bought by her mother-in-law for the future wedding. Figure 5.1 displays the temporal domains alluded to in particular utterances by Patricia (Initial Teller) and Dan (Other Teller) in example (3a).

After being interrupted by a telephone call and intervening conversation, the narrative resumes:

(3b) Excerpt 2 from "Patricia's Dress"

Round 2   ((begins shortly after Patricia hangs up and sits at table again, sniffling from allergies and wiping nose; kids are outside playing ball))
     (2.2) ((Dan eats, looks around to camera))

Father: ((*looking away from Patricia, to l.r./camera*)) So as you were
           saying?
Mother: (what was I/as I was) saying ((*turning abruptly to face
           Dan*)) What was I telling you
                            [
Oren: ((*outside*)) (You can't get me:)
Father: I don't? know.
Mother: oh about the dress
Father: (the) <u>dress.</u>
           (1.2) ((*Patricia is drinking water; Dan looks to her, back to his
           plate, back to her*))
Father: you (had) a dress right?
Mother: ((*slightly nodding yes once*))your <u>mother</u> (bought me it/wanted=
                                                              [
Janie?:   ((*outside*)) (I'm not
           standing right here)
Mother: =me to) – (my mother didn't like it).
           (0.4). ((*Patricia tilts head slightly, facing Dan as if to say, "What
           could I do?"*))
Father: ((*shaking head no once*)) you're kidding
Mother: no.

This passage follows a similar temporal sequential pattern to that characterizing the
excerpt in (3a): attention to the *recent past (i.e., the recent purchase of the dress)
and future (i.e., the wedding) events* as implied by the phrases "oh about the dress"
and "(the) <u>dress</u>," followed by explicit attention to a period extending from a more
distant past up to the present ("you (had) a dress right"). As in (3a), *future* events are
implied through reference to the dress. Similarly, reference to recent past and future
is followed by attention to the *distant past* ("your mother (bought me it/wanted me
to) – (my mother didn't like it)"), with the continuation of an implied future carried
by the pronoun *it*. This pattern in temporal shifting is represented in Figure 5.2.
   Although both Initial (Patricia) and Other Teller (Dan) have alluded to the future

TELLER	UTTERANCE	TIME DOMAINS: PAST PRES FUT		
Father	"about the dress "	■		■
Mother	"(the) dress "	■		■
Father	"you had a dress "	■	■	■
Mother	"your mother bought me it ... my mother didn't like it "	■		■

FIGURE 5.2.

in (3a) and (3b), their subsequent turns in (3c) show them explicitly predicating future events:

(3c) Excerpt 3 from "Patricia's Dress"

Father:	you gonna return it?
Mother:	no you can't return it – it wasn't too expensive – it was from Loehmann's.
Oren:	((*outside*)) ( )
	(0.8)
Mother:	so what I'll probably do? – is wear it to the dinner the night before – when we go to the (Marriott)?

(1.8) ((*Dan turns head away from Patricia with grimace as if he is debating whether he is being conned, then turns back and looks off*))

.

.

.

(*narrative continues*)

In this passage, it is Dan—the Other Teller—who moves the narrative squarely into the *future* with his predication "you gonna return it?" This utterance relates to the past events narrated in that it describes a possible future effect/resolution of Patricia's past misdeeds. The *distant past* is not absent, however, in that once again the *it* in this predication refers to the dress his mother had bought for Patricia prior to that day. Nor is the *future* event of the wedding absent, in that once again the *it* concerns a dress for the wedding. In the following turn, Patricia continues to focus on this *future* time predication (along with the *distant past* and *future* events implied within this predication) when she responds "no" (i.e., No I am not gonna return it) to the previous question. The narrative has now evolved from a narrative about past events that are relevant to future events (e.g., the buying of a dress for the wedding by her mother, the buying of a dress for the wedding by his mother, her mother's not liking the dress bought by his mother) to a narrative that predicates future events. After this negative response, Patricia predicates a *timeless present* (Quirk and Greenbaum 1973) event ("you can't return it") with the *distant past* and *future* once again implied through the pronoun *it*. She then focuses on the more *distant past* ("it wasn't too expensive")[4] with the same *future event* implications carried through the continued use of *it*. Pausing for a moment, Patricia returns to an explicit focus on *future* events with the future predication "so what I'll probably do? – is wear it to the dinner the night before – when we go to the (Marriott)," reinforced by the *implied* future in the continued reference to the dress ("it"). In this turn, Patricia presents her own future resolution to the problem of having two dresses for the same future event. The temporal domains relevant to example (3c) are displayed in Figure 5.3.

Examples (1)–(3) support the notion that the activity of storytelling lends itself to temporal flows forward in time not only into the here and now but also into the future. While a story of personal experience may focus on past events, the past is

TELLER	UTTERANCE	TIME DOMAINS: PAST PRES FUT
Father	"you gonna return it ?"	██ ██
Mother	"no"	██ ██
Mother	"you can't return it"	████████
Mother	"it wasn't too expensive"	██ ██
	" ... what I 'll ... do ... is wear it ... the night before ... when we go to the (Marriot)"	██ ██

FIGURE 5.3.

not necessarily the exclusive center of attention throughout the storytelling. In example (1), we saw a narrative progress from predications about the immediate past (what Mother put in the guacamole dip) to the present (Oren acts out a fictional death) to the more distant past (Oren at two years old) back to the present (verbal and nonverbal acts of respite). In examples (3a)–(3c), we saw that a narrative may progress from predications about the past to predications about the future and present. And in example (2), predications about the past, present, and future share the spotlight from the very first turn of the narrative. The past may be a more or less ephemeral focus and may share the limelight with predications about the present and the future. Further, even when, within a narrative, a predicate specifies a past event, complements of that predicate often imply present and future temporal domains.

5. Stories as Unfinished Business

When Ricoeur (1988) considers Heidegger's (1962) notion of future time in the context of narrative, he emphasizes Heidegger's point that *anticipation of the future* drives human thoughts and action. Ricoeur argues this point from two perspectives. The first perspective is that of the protagonist. Within the past time storyline, the protagonist thinks and acts in ways that anticipate the future. The protagonist, that is, acts in goal-directed, purposeful ways, albeit sometimes unwittingly, or sometimes under the control of forces other than himself/herself. This premise is a critical component of the narrative plot. The second perspective is that of the narrators of and audiences to narratives. At the risk of seeming somewhat circular, Ricoeur notes that narrators and audiences organize their understandings and memory of narrative events in terms of their knowledge that there is a future which human beings need to anticipate. Narrators and audiences understand why a protagonist thinks and acts in a certain manner (including cause-effect relations between thoughts and actions), because they themselves think and act to anticipate the future (see Stein and Glenn 1979 for an analysis of children's narrative understandings and recollections).

The future that Ricoeur considers is anchored in the past (the protagonist) and in the present (the narrators/audience), with the task of those present being largely one of interpreting a future that has yet to come for the protagonist but that has already passed for those interlocutors presently involved in the storytelling. We can refer to this kind of future as a *future before the present*. Heidegger notes, in addition, that narratives help human beings to sort out their own futures, that is, their *future after the present*. Heidegger's views on the future import of narrative may be used to account in part for the *interest* an interlocutor takes in a narrative. Part of the interest value of a narrative may be its potential relevance to an interlocutor's own future. If a narrative appears to an interlocutor to be completely irrelevant to his or her future or is not providing new information regarding his or her future, then the narrative may be of diminished interest to the interlocutor. If the narrative does have relevance to one interlocutor's future, for example, that of the Initial Teller, but not to other interlocutors, the interest of the narrative for other interlocutors may depend on the existing relationship of other interlocutors to that interlocutor and/or on that interlocutor's ability to pique the interest of other interlocutors, at least for the narrating moment, to entertain the import of the narrative events for the future life of that interlocutor. The same situation may hold if the narrative has import only for the future of some third party. The interest of any interlocutor may depend on his or her relationship with that third party or on an interlocutor's ability to involve others copresent in that third party's future life.

An interlocutor's interest in the future relevance of a recollection of past events has relevance for the direction of the narrative in that those participating in the storytelling activity may make their interest in the future ramifications of past events explicit in the course of the storytelling. The present chapter demonstrates that a human preoccupation with the future after the present is not only a mental state integral to interpreting narrative, as Heidegger suggests: it is also manifest as *discursive structures* integral to the production of the narratives of personal experiences themselves. These discursive structures make mental inclinations toward the future visible to interlocutors and analysts alike. Let us now consider more closely how interest in the future may be provoked by the recollection of past time events in narratives of personal experience. In particular, let us consider how narrated past events may be framed as problematic and implicative for the future.

Stories have been widely analyzed as narrative structures that contain some past problematic event that in turn incited some response in the past (Bruner 1986, 1990, Labov and Waletzky 1967, Mandler 1979, Polkinghorne 1988, Schank and Abelson 1977, Stein and Glenn 1979). It is the play between the inciting event and the responses it has engendered that creates the dramatic tension and plot structure of a story. In these analyses, events are viewed as experienced by protagonists and problematic, and responded to by protagonists at a time before the present moment of storytelling. In this sense, stories present completed events. That the events are temporally completed, however, does not necessarily mean that the interlocutors presently engaged in telling a story necessarily treat the past problematic event and past responses as dead issues, as business that has already been taken care of. To the contrary, quite often in conversational storytelling among friends or family either an Initial or an Other Teller will take issue with some aspect of the past experience narrated (cf. Ochs et al. 1989, Ochs et al. 1992). In so doing, interlocutors define a *past* event as a *present* problem. And like protagonists in a narrative who provided *past* responses to a *past* event felt to be a problem in the *past,* the interlocutors presently involved in cotelling the narrative state *present* and *future* possible responses to a *past* event felt to be a problem in the *present.*

In cognitive science and cognitive psychology, stories have been analyzed as *plans* formulated and executed in the past (Schank and Abelson 1977), where a plan is a representation of a problematic situation along with consideration, evaluation, and execution of strategies for resolving the problem (Schank and Abelson 1977, Stein and Glenn 1979, Friedman, Scholnick, and Cocking 1987). The narratives of personal experience in the current study include not only *past plans* but *future plans* as well. The telling of the future plan may be a momentary discursive flash in the middle of the telling of the past plan, may be recurrent throughout the past plan, or may emerge after the past plan for a sustained conversational period.

Discursive turns to the future-after-the-present in the story narratives in our corpus characteristically frame some past event as *unfinished business.* In some cases, as in (2), the interlocutors (the children and Mother) problematize a protagonist's (Father's) past action as an unfulfilled past commitment (e.g., to have ice cream for dessert). In other cases, as in (3), the interlocutor (Dan) problematizes a protagonist's (Patricia's) past actions as leading to a present scandal (e.g., having two dresses to wear for the same event) which has yet to be resolved (Ochs and Taylor 1992a,b). In (3), the moral problems inherent in the protagonist's past actions are alluded to earlier in Dan's responses (e.g., "You're kidding") and they are further spelled out in the narrative activity that follows the discursive turn to the future, as illustrated in the following excerpt:

(3d) Excerpt 4 from "Patricia's Dress"

Father:	(doesn't that) (seem/sound) (like a helluva – waste)?
Mother:	no?:
Father:	no.
Mother:	((*with hands out, shaking head no*)) It wasn't even that expensive.
	(1.2)
Mother:	((*shaking head no, facing Dan*)) even if it were (a comp<u>lete</u> waste)
	(0.4) ((*Dan looks down at plate, bobs head to right and to left as if weighing logic, not convinced*))
Mother:	but it's not ((*looking away from Dan*))
	(0.6) ((*Patricia looks outside, then back to Dan*))
Mother:	(but the one) my Mom got me is grea:t=
	[
Father:	((*Dan picks food off Oren's plate next to him and eats it*))
Janie?:	((*outside*)) =(you're not letting me:))
Mother:	=it's (attractive-looking/a practical dress)
Father:	((*gesturing with palm up, quizzical*)) (Well why did) you have – Why did you let my Mom get you something (that you–)
Mother:	Your <u>mo:</u>ther bought it – I hh –

Father:	oh she just got it for you?
Mother:	((*nodding yes*)) (yeah)
Father:	you weren't there?
Mother:	I was there (and your mother said, "No no it's great. Let me buy it for you") – I didn't <u>ask</u> her to buy it for me?
	(5.0) ((*kids outside talking; Dad is eating*))
Father:	so they're fighting over who gets you things?
Mother:	((*nods yes slightly*)) – ((*smiling to Dan*)) tch – (cuz I'm/sounds) so wonderful.
	(9.0) ((*Patricia turns to look outside; blows her nose—allergies; kids talk outside, bouncing ball*))

In addition to framing past events as unfinished business, these discursive journeys to the future generally specify a means of *resolving the purported problem* (cf. Ochs et al. 1992 for a discussion of stories as problem-solving discourse). In (3c), Dan suggests one future way of handling the problem, namely returning the dress that his mother had purchased for the wedding, but Patricia points to the impossibility of this solution and goes on with her own solution, namely that she will wear the dress his mother had purchased to a dinner at the Marriott the night before the wedding. In (2), two different strategies are presented for resolving the problem of Father's unwillingness to let them eat ice cream for dessert that evening. The children's strategy is simply to get Father to admit his past commitment to the future event, but Mother's strategy is to get the children to lobby for ice cream by chanting "Haagen Dazs." The speech act of lobbying pragmatically implies an event that the speaker wants to take place in the future.

Examples (1), (2), and (3a)–(3d) suggest that the construal of a story event as unfinished business, that is, as something to be resolved, can be carried out by either the Initial Teller or Other Teller. In (1) and (2), it is the Initial Teller (Oren in (1), Evan in (2)) who frames the narrative past as unfinished business, but in (3) it is the Other Teller (Dan) who does so. (For discussion of example (1) as unfinished business see Ochs et al. 1992.) Examples (4a)–(4c) below present two contrastive framings of a set of story events by different interlocutors in different rounds of the story—*round* is defined here as one of a sequence of story segments interrupted by two or more turns dealing with other matters (e.g., passing food, table manners). In the first round (4a), the Initial Teller, Laurie (five years seven months), presents a somewhat mixed but generally positive framing of the narrative events, by integrating the narrative events into dinner grace. Copresent with Laurie are her mother and Laurie's siblings—Jimmy (four years four months), Annie (seven years ten months), and Roger (ten years eight months).

(4a) Excerpt 1 from "Grace Story"

Round 1

Laurie:	I wanna pray ((*clasps her hands*)) – Jesus?
Mother:	((*to Roger*)) ( ) ((*adjusting Laurie's chair*))
Roger:	((*mumbled, to Mom*)) ( )=

Laurie: =Jesus?
Mother: <u>Wait</u> a minute Laurie ((*irritated, throwing arms up in semidespair*)) <u>I'm</u> not
            sitting down= ((*Mother sits*))
Laurie: =kay – Jesus? – plea:se – um – help us to love and .hh um – thank
            you for letting it be a n:ice day and for taking a (fine/fun) nap? –
            a:nd – for (letting) Mommy go bye and I'm glad that I cwied
            today? cuz I like cwying .hh and I'm glad=
                                              [
Annie?:   ((*snicker*))
                                              [
Roger?:   ((*snicker*))
Laurie: =(that anything/everything) happened today in Jesus name
            ((*claps hands*)) A:–MEN!
Mother?:   amen ((*clapping lightly*))
                 [
Jimmy: A:MEN
            (1.0) ((*Laurie starts licking fork*))
Jimmy: amen bay<u>be</u> ((*baby*))
Mother: hohoho
            ((*general laughter—Mom, then Roger and Annie; Mom gets
            up*))
Jimmy: amen
                 [
Annie: <u>amen (honey bunch</u>?) ((*with southern accent*))
            (1.0)
Annie: <u>amen dahling</u>? ((*with glamour accent*))
                 [
Jimmy: <u>amen</u>
Jimmy: AMEN bay<u>be</u>.

In this round Laurie introduces a past event ("Mommy go bye") simultaneously
as one that was problematic in the past in that it provoked the event of crying ("I
cried today") and unproblematic at present (perhaps indicating that she has over-
come her earlier unhappiness) in that crying is something she claims to like doing
("I'm glad that I cwied today? cuz I like cwying and I'm glad (that any-
thing/everything) happened today in Jesus name A:–MEN"). This double framing of
unhappiness and happiness is somewhat a consequence of the story's also being a
grace and the requirements that a grace express gratefulness for events.

The narrative events are dropped for a while until Mother reintroduces them in
round 2 of the story.[5] In this second round, Mother, Laurie, and Laurie's siblings
restate the narrative events, and Mother and Laurie's siblings redefine them explicitly as problematic.

(4b) Excerpt 2 from "Grace Story"

Round 2

Mother: ((*addressing Laurie*)) Miss (Graw) said you cried and cried=

                                                    [
                                    ((*Laurie looks up
            from her spaghetti, momentarily pausing in her eating*))
Mother: =at nap time?
Laurie: ((*Laurie nods her head yes several times*))
                                    [
Annie: she did – she wanted (her) Mama
Mother: She said that was because – this was your first day to be at
            school? without me:?
            (0.6). ((*Laurie is visibly engaged in eating and spilling food*))
Mother: but honey? – I only work – this – it was only this week that I
            worked there all week? because it was the first week? of school
            but –
            [
Annie: she cried at three o'clock too
            (0.2)
Mother: but after this? – it – I only work one day a week? there and
            that's Tuesday
            (0.6)

In this excerpt, two different events are treated as problematic. First, the event
of Mother's absence from school is treated as allegedly problematic from Laurie's
point of view, as evidenced in reports by the teacher, by Laurie, and by Annie.
Second, Laurie's past response to that event is treated as problematic and as unfinished business by Mother. Here Mother begins to find ways of altering Laurie's
response to Mother's absence in the future. She tells Laurie what to expect in the
future, perhaps as a way of bracing Laurie for the coming school days. After a brief
interruption, the family returns once more to the story of Laurie's experience at
school, pointing out other problems and offering solutions to them. In this passage
(4c), Mother (and later Roger) indirectly makes Laurie responsible for her reaction
to Mother's absence by pointing out that Laurie had not taken her blanket to school
that day, indicating (especially through the use of the term *either* in turn 1) that she
had not taken the proper precautions to buffer herself for the day alone at school:

(4c) Excerpt 3 from "Grace Story"

Round 3

            (2.2)
Mother: Laurie? – you didn't take yer ((*shaking head no*)) – blanket to
            school either did you.
Laurie: No I (for)got it ((*petulant*))
            (0.4)
Jimmy: (you forgot it at a school)
Laurie: ((*nods yes once*))
Jimmy: (you left it at school?)
Laurie: ((*nods yes once again*))
Mother: No ((*shaking head no*)) – she left it at home

(1.0) ((*scraping plates sounds; Jimmy looking at Mom as if in a daze*))

Roger: She left it – here today

Mother: we'll hafta get it out of the closet – and put it over there with the lunch stuff

(2.0) ((*eating; Mom arranging hair*))

Jimmy: yes – so you could – bring it (with/to) school

                                                [

Mother: (as a warning/in the morning) – mhm?

Jimmy: yeah and you'd BETTER – ((*looks to Mom*)) take care of your – your – your – blankie because I am ((*looks to Mom again*))

Mother: mh:m:? ((*chuckles*))

          [

Roger: mhm ((*snickers*))

(1.0) ((*Roger finishes drink, wipes mouth*))

In this round, Mother turns to future ways of resolving Laurie's problem, namely making the family responsible to put the blanket with Laurie's lunch to take to school ("we'll hafta get it out of the closet – and put it over there with the lunch stuff"). Jimmy seconds this resolution, even intensifying it with his warning to Laurie about the future: "you'd BETTER – ((*looks to Mom*)) take care of your – your – your – blankie because I am ((*looks to Mom again*))."

The examples presented here suggest that at varying points throughout a story narrative an interlocutor may treat some past event as implicative for the future-after-the-present, that is, as unfinished business, and may alter the direction of the story to attend to those future implications. Sometimes the discursive expression of future implications appears right at the start of the story narrative, as in Evan's recall of Father's promise of ice cream in (2). But often the discursive turn to a future event implied by a past event is brought up in the course of a story's telling. Typically there is a two-step process in which a past event is first mentioned then framed as troublesome with respect to some future event. This process is illustrated in (3a)–(3d), where Mother's mentioning of the dress purchase is followed by Father's negative remarks and suggestions as to what Mother should do in the future, and in (4), where Mother first remarks on Laurie's crying at school and second makes a problem of her behavior in terms of future events.

6. Time and Narrative Genre

This chapter has been centrally concerned with narratives of past experience that creatively evolve (Bergson 1911) into narratives of future experiences in a discursively fluid manner. I have argued, following Heidegger (1962), that both past and future experiences comprise narratives of personal experience. Future time in narratives may be alluded to not only literally through noun phrases and predicates but also pragmatically through a variety of *speech acts* such as

Reminders ("Mommy. – you – you 'member – (um) if I eat a good dinner I
could have a ice cream")

Petitions ("Haagen Dazs HAAGEN DAZS HAAGEN DAZS")

Forecasts ("so what I'll probably do? – is wear it to the dinner the night before –
when we go to the (Marriott)")

Prescriptions ("we'll hafta get it out of the closet – and put it over there with the
lunch stuff")

Suggestions, admonitions, warnings ("you gonna return it?", "you'd BETTER –
((*looks to Mom*)) take care of your – your – your – blankie because I am
((*looks to Mom again*))")

Talk relevant to future and past time does not necessarily map on to discrete
segments of text. Rather, future and past time are often interwoven into the fabric of
a single narrative. As such, the same narrative text can be examined for its relevance
to both future and past events. In some cases, this might mean that the very same
text might be examined for its properties as a future plan (wherein future attempts to
respond to problematic events are expressed) and as a past plan (wherein past
attempts to respond to problematic events are expressed), or for its properties as an
agenda (a sequence of future events) and as a report (a sequence of past events). A
more overarching implication of this discussion is that *genre* (e.g., past plans,
future plans, reports, agendas, disputes) might best be considered as a *perspective*
on a text rather than as a discrete text itself. Genre might be seen as a linguistically
realized goal-structure (e.g., goals associated with planning for the future or reporting), and any single text might realize a multiplicity of such goal-structures (recollecting past events, projecting future events, engaging in a dispute, and more).

If interlocutors rarely made discursive journeys to the future in the course of
telling personal experiences, we might analyze such phenomena as exceptions to the
storytelling norm. However, interlocutors engaged in telling past personal experiences *discursively turn to future events regularly,* both in the sense that many stories
of personal experience contain references to and predications about the future and in
the sense that in a single story there may be several references to and predications
about the future. For example, the "Ice Cream" story paraphrases a similar future
event over and over throughout the narrative. The "Grace Story" contains a number
of different predications about the future, and "Patricia's Dress" abounds in references to upcoming events (e.g., repeated references to the upcoming wedding,
reference to the dinner before the wedding) and future time predications (e.g., about
returning one dress, about not returning one dress, about wearing one dress to the
wedding dinner).

If the discursive turns to the future were off-topic to the past story experiences
or were prefaced by topic-shifting disjunct markers (e.g., "oh," "incidentally"; see
Jefferson 1978) then we might analyze them as attempts to exit the story and begin
another discourse activity. However, the future-time predications that appear in the
course of a story's telling are *story-coherent* in the sense that they detail implications
of or are otherwise relevant to past experiences predicated thus far within the story,
and they appear without disjunct discourse markers. The future predications more
generally are prefaced by a logical connector such as "so" (e.g., "so what I'll

probably do? . . .") or, even more commonly, appear baldly, with no prefacing discourse marker at all. For the interlocutors engaged in storytelling, these discursive moves are treated as topically continuous and structurally expectable within the activity of storytelling.

If stories progressed in one evolutionary direction from past to future, then we might distinguish the future-oriented portion as a discursive product of the story, to be cut off and analyzed in its own right, perhaps as a discrete epilogue. However, there are at least two problems surrounding such a proposal:

> **1.** Stories may move not only forward to a future after the present but also *back to the past from a future time after the present.*

Consider, for example, "Patricia's Dress," in which Father's and Mother's references to and predications about the future in (3c) were immediately followed by more details about the past in (3d). And in "Grace Story," Mother's informing Laurie about the times she will be working in her school in the future is followed, after some interruption, by a return to another detail of the past experience, namely that Laurie forgot to take her blanket to school. Indeed, time-switchings between future-after-the-present and past predications can recur numerous times. In "Grace Story," for example, the interlocutors follow up Laurie's past forgetting of her blanket with another shift to future warnings and prescriptions. The "Ice Cream" story has interlocutors fluctuating between recollecting (e.g. "MEMBER", "What was I doing") and anticipating ("if I eat a goood dinner I could have a ice cream", "Haagen Dazs HAAGEN DAZS. . .") as parallel, shifting lietmotifs throughout the entire storytelling activity.

> **2.** Propositions about story events very often involve *past and future time at once.*

It is not easy to separate expressed propositions in a story into those that are "about the future" and those that are "about the past." First of all, as mentioned in the beginning of this essay, the future may underpin the telling of a past event even when no grammatical or lexical structures used index future after the present. Second, in Figures 5.1–5.3 we saw that references and predicates of past and future commingle within a single clause. In "Patricia's Dress," lexical items referring to different dresses implied a future event (an upcoming wedding), whereas the verbs in the same clauses specified past time events or circumstances. Third, even when the temporal constructions are consistently past or consistently future within a clause, the clause itself may be embedded within a larger multiclausal construction which traverses past and future. Thus, in "Ice Cream," Evan's construction "you "'member – (um) if I eat a good dinner I could have a ice cream" contains multiple temporal domains as a whole, even though each clause may be temporally consistent.

These considerations suggest that narratives of personal experience have one face toward the future. We may not see evidence of that face if we examine stories in experimental settings where the interlocutors typically have scant interest in the storyline or in the futures of the protagonists and copresent interlocutors (experimenters). And we may not see that face even in conversational narratives if we think of stories as mainly being told by entitled storytellers to story recipients, entitlement being by virtue of privileged access to some past events. In the larger corpus of family dinner stories used for this study, however, family interlocutors jumped into the telling of stories regardless of whether or not they had privileged prior knowledge or even any prior knowledge of the story's past events (Ochs et al. 1992). They contributed critical story parts such as psychological responses, outcomes, attempts, and consequences to the extent that they conarrated the story. In this framework, any copresent interlocutor helps to shape the point of the story. For any conarrator, the point of the story may be the import of the past events for future events. In some cases, coauthors rally around the same future import of past events, as do Mother and kids in the "Ice Cream" story and in later rounds of the "Grace Story". In other cases, coauthors are divided in their view of the relevance of the past to the future, as are Mother and Father in "Patricia's Dress" and Father and the rest of the family in "Ice Cream."

Finally, the future face of a story may be eclipsed if a story is not tracked and analyzed over sometimes lengthy interruptions and several rounds of narrative interaction. The "Grace Story" looks finished and is treated as finished by the Initial Teller at round 1 but reappears after lengthy intervening conversation. It is only in rounds 2 and 3 that the story is opened up to other family coauthors, who, as they narrate bits and pieces of the past events, begin to visualize possible future events. This process is at the very heart of the present argument. It is the perspective of this essay that story events are points along a temporal continuum of life, and that the activity of storytelling allows interlocutors continuously and creatively to move their lives forward in time (i.e., evolve) through a process of mentally and verbally stretching past life events into the future.

Notes

1. The transcription conventions used in the present chapter are:

[	open brackets indicate the start of an overlap between the utterances of two speakers
]	close brackets indicate the end of an overlap between two speakers
=	equal signs appear at the end of a line to indicate continuous speaking and at the beginning of a subsequent line to indicate that no pause or silence has intervened; this device allows the insertion of other turns or comments where the width of the page does not permit a line to be continued
–	a single dash attached to a word– indicates a cut-off utterance
–	a single dash with a space on both sides indicates an extremely brief pause: word – word
( )	single parentheses are used for two purposes. When they enclose a number they represent a silent pause in tenths of a second; (0.6) represents a silence lasting six tenths of a second. Otherwise parentheses enclose uncertain transcriptions.
(( ))	double parentheses are used to enclose ((stage directions and other comments by the transcriber)); the comments are *italicized* to indicate that they are not spoken by the participants
:	a single colon indicates a lengthening of one conversational beat

::   a double colon indicates a lengthening of two conversational beats
.h   a period preceding a breath marker indicates an in-breath
/   a slash is used within parentheses to separate alternative uncertain transcriptions
CAPS   CAPITAL LETTERS are used to mark loudness
____   underlining is used to mark emphasis

2. This move could be seen as paralleling Father's earlier dissatisfaction with and criticism of Mother for putting chili pepper in the guacamole dip.

3. It could also be argued that the drama (described in (1b)) surrounding Oren's realization that he has eaten hot salsa and chili peppers links the distant past narrative episode (described in (1c)) to the present time episode "just desserts" consequences (described in (1d)).

4. Patricia's comment here appears to be a response to her husband's utterance "You gonna return it?" which she takes to be a complaint. Her comment is an attempt to mitigate the gravity of the problem of having purchased two dresses for the same event.

5. This is a somewhat odd second round in that Mother initiates the round as if the events had not been narrated earlier, that is, as if she is the Initial Teller, not Laurie. This narrative is considered to be a second round in the sense that it is a second narrating of the same events, albeit from a different perspective.

References

Applebee, Arthur N. 1978. *The Child's Concept of a Story: Ages Two to Seventeen.* Chicago: University of Chicago Press.

Bauman, Richard. 1986. *Story, Performance, and Event: Contextual Studies of Oral Narrative.* Cambridge: Cambridge University Press.

Bergson, H. 1911. *Creative Evolution.* Boston: University Press of America.

Bruner, Jerome. 1986. *Actual Minds, Possible Worlds.* Cambridge, MA: Harvard University Press.

———. 1990. *Acts of Meaning.* Cambridge, MA: Harvard University Press.

Friedman, S., E. Scholnick, and R. Cocking. 1987. *Blueprints for Thinking.* Cambridge: Cambridge University Press.

Goodwin, Charles. 1984. "Notes on Story Structure and the Organization of Participation." In J. M. Atkinson and J. Heritage, eds., *Structures of Social Action.* Cambridge: Cambridge University Press. Pp. 225–46.

Goodwin, Marjorie H. 1990. *He-Said-She-Said: Talk as Social Organization Among Black Children.* Bloomington: Indiana University Press.

Goodwin, Marjorie H., and Charles Goodwin. 1989. "Story Structure and Social Organization." In J. Bergman, ed., *Kommunikative Formen und Kulturelles Milien* (Proceedings of the session on 'sprachsoziologie'). Zurich: German/Austrian/Swiss Sociological Association.

Heidegger, Martin. 1962. *Being and Time.* New York: Harper and Row.

Jefferson, Gail. 1978. "Sequential Aspects of Storytelling in Conversation." In Jim Schenkein, ed., *Studies in the Organization of Conversational Interaction.* New York: Academic Press. Pp. 219–48.

Labov, William. 1972. *Language in the Inner City: Studies in the Black English Vernacular.* Philadelphia: University of Pennsylvania Press.

Labov, William, and Joshua Waletzky. 1967. "Narrative Analysis." In June Helm, ed., *Essays on the Verbal and Visual Arts.* Seattle: University of Washington Press. Pp. 12–44.

Mandler, Jean H. 1979. "Categorical and Schematic Organization in Memory." In C. R. Puff, ed., *Memory Organization and Structure.* New York: Academic Press.

Ochs, Elinor, Ruth Smith, and Carolyn Taylor. 1989. "Dinner Narratives as Detective Stories." *Cultural Dynamics* 2:238–57.

Ochs, Elinor, and Carolyn Taylor. 1992a. "Family Narrative as Political Activity." *Discourse and Society* 3:301–40.

———. 1992b. "Science at Dinner." In C. Kramsch, ed., *Text and Context: Cross-Disciplinary Perspectives on Language Study.* Lexington, MA: D. C. Heath. Pp. 29–45.

Ochs, Elinor, Carolyn Taylor, Dina Rudolph, and Ruth Smith. 1992. "Storytelling as a Theory-Building Activity." *Discourse Processes* 15:37–72.

Pitcher, E. G., and E. Prelinger. 1963. *Children Tell Stories: An Analysis of Fantasy.* New York: International Universities Press.

Polanyi, Livia. 1989. *Telling the American Story: A Structural and Cultural Analysis of Conversational Storytelling.* Cambridge, MA: The MIT Press.

Polkinghorne, D. E. 1988. *Narrative Knowing and the Human Sciences.* Albany: State University of New York Press.

Quirk, Randolph, and Sidney Greenbaum. 1973. *A University Grammar of English.* London: Longman.

Ricoeur, Paul. 1988. *Time and Narrative.* Chicago: University of Chicago Press.

Sacks, Harvey. 1970. Class lectures. University of California, Irvine, CA.

Schank, Roger C., and Robert P. Abelson. 1977. *Scripts, Plans, Goals, and Understanding.* Hillsdale, NJ: Erlbaum.

Stein, Nancy, and C. G. Glenn. 1979. "An Analysis of Story Comprehension in Elementary School Children." In Roy O. Freedle, ed., *New Directions in Discourse Processing.* Norwood, NJ: Ablex. Pp. 53–120.

Umiker-Sebeok, D. J. 1979. "Preschool Children's Intraconversational Narratives." *Journal of Child Language* 6:91–109.

Young, K. G. 1987. *Taleworlds and Storyrealms: The Phenomenology of Narrative.* Dordrecht: Martinus Nijhoff Publishers.

6

Me Tarzan, You Jane: Linguistic Simplification in "Personal Ads" Register

PAUL BRUTHIAUX

1. Simplified Registers and Linguistic Theory

The study of register views language as dependent on its context of use.[1] Register is thus central to the study of language variation, and register variation may be seen, "not as a refinement in the use of language, but as a principal source of language structure itself" (Ferguson 1982:58). Yet, as Cheshire (1987:278) points out, even "after 25 years or so of analyzing language in its social context, we have achieved . . . little in the analysis of specific varieties." While no one doubts the reality of the phenomenon of register variation or questions its universality in human language, the problem is how to incorporate this variation into theories of language (Ferguson 1982). For the generative linguist, the difficulty lies in starting from an assumption that the language of an ideal speaker-hearer (Chomsky 1965) has a homogeneous and unified structure. Registers do not conveniently fit into tidy notions of linguistic competence. Seen as subsystems, they obey grammars which cannot easily be reconciled with the rules induced by generative linguists from the quasi-literary sentences which serve as their data. Yet they are undeniably central to every speaker's competence.[2]

To be truly illuminative linguistic theory must address the issue of those registers which appear to be "somewhere between the two extremes of order and chaos" (Ferguson 1982:51). A linguistic system may be deliberately (though not necessarily consciously) kept simple, among other purposes, "to reduce cognitive load, to save time and effort in communication, to give an appearance of ignorance, or to accommodate an interlocutor" (Ferguson 1982:59). Thus linguistic simplification might be defined as any strategy of language use which achieves optimal functional effectiveness while restricting form to what an encoder and/or decoder can handle.

If the criteria of simplicity are to be made explicit and the process of simplification explained, empirical studies of specific registers are needed, in order to reveal differences in the patterns of simplification and in the relationship between occurrence and function (Ferguson 1982). In addition, the study of simplified registers might illuminate general theories of language and help to reveal what is most unmarked, most deeply underlying in human language (Ferguson 1975). As Ferguson (1982:63) writes, the study of simplified registers

> has much to teach us about the human processing of marginal systems in language, the fundamental role of situational variation in the characterization of language structure, and the elusive family of notions called simplicity which enter into many crucial areas of language change, acquisition, and loss.

2. Language Handicap and Language Economy

In their most frequently studied forms, simplified registers can be described as varieties of speech typically aimed at listeners believed not to be fully competent in the language—young children, foreigners, or the hard-of-hearing. They assist communication by keeping the input simple and orderly, thus facilitating perception and comprehension. Janda (1985) reviews earlier work, essentially Ferguson's (1971, 1977), on the two most prominent varieties, namely Baby Talk (BT) and Foreigner Talk (FT). To these should probably be added pidgins, since they too assist comprehension between less than competent interlocutors. It is these varieties which I propose to label *handicap varieties.*

There is, Ferguson (1982) argues, a large measure of consensus over what linguistic simplification entails. Among representative sources are Meisel (1977) and Ferguson and DeBose (1977) for BT and FT, and Todd (1974) and Mühläusler (1986) for pidgins. All share a view of simplified registers as the products of reductive processes. These can involve a reduction in surface material or in grammatical complexity, or a minimization of both lexical repertory and semantic complexity due to, but possibly also causing, severe limitation in the scope of the variety's communicative use. Ferguson (1982) offers a typology of what he sees as the major features of these registers: smaller, generic rather than specific vocabulary; monomorphemic words and paraphrases of complex words; little or no subordination, but parataxis; invariant word order; invariant stems with little or no inflection; absence of copula, pronouns, and function words.

Simplified registers can also involve interlocutors with adequate linguistic competence. These registers are sometimes referred to as "little" or "condensed" (Halliday 1985) or "compressed" (Sinclair 1988). Among those previously studied are recognized registers, such as headlinese and telegraphese (Ferguson 1982), sports announcer talk (Ferguson 1983), and academic note-taking (Janda 1985). Since they all put a premium on economy for the fulfillment of a communicative purpose, I propose to gather them under the heading of *economy registers.* They share with simplified registers of the handicap variety some of the features listed in Ferguson's typology. Unlike them, however, they do not typically entail loss of referential potential or expressive power, although some specialization in subject matter is normally involved. In particular, Janda's (1985) study of note-taking (NT) identifies not only what he sees as reductive processes, but also a frequent use of more complex processes, including substitution, passivization, and nominalization.

3. Simplification and Personal Ads Register

In answer to Ferguson's call for further research, a step might be taken by examining processes of simplification in personal ads register (PAR). Although probably still a big-city phenomenon, the personal ads section has become a regular item in a wide variety of newspapers and magazines. In the Los Angeles area alone, personal ads appear on a daily basis in the *Los Angeles Times* (in English) and *La Opinión* (in Spanish). Another four major newspapers at least and countless ethnic publications also feature ads of this type on a regular basis. The international spread of personal ads can be gauged through the columns of the *Recycler,* a Los Angeles newspaper which, in a typical week, may print as many as two thousand personal ads. Electronically linked to over seventy-five similar publications in twenty-five countries, the newspaper reflects the growing worldwide appeal of the genre, with Brazil and Britain, and increasingly Hungary and Czechoslovakia, particularly well represented. Not surprisingly, wordings often suggest that motivations may be more migratory than matrimonial. Certainly, the large number of ads printed in the *Recycler* in languages other than English confirms that the phenomenon is much more than a local curiosity.

A typical, highly descriptive personal ad might look like the following[3]:

> Sultry, vivacious Latina, 35, seeking kind, sophisticated equal. Christian believing, provocative intellect, volcanic sensuality. Share arts, Andes, high-voltage romance. (137)

A characteristic of many English-language personal ads is the widespread reliance on descriptive acronyms. Thus readers need to know (or quickly learn) that *SBF* might stand for *single black female, BiWM* for *bisexual white male,* or *DJF* for *divorced Jewish female.* Some writers make highly imaginative use of literary techniques such as alliteration and assonance:

> Well, well, well! WSM, 6'1", 190, 40 years, well-educated, well-traveled, well-humored, well-situated Woodland Hills whereabouts, wonderful whysique, wants wanton wench for wholesome wedding. Well? (14)

> Very pretty, pretty witty SWF, 30, seeks intelligent, honest, attractive, marriage-minded SWM, 30–40. I know you're out there! (175)

Many more writers conventionalize the choice of opening words beginning with the letter *a* when this guarantees publication toward the top of the section:

> Accomplished, attractive, affectionate, athletic, professional, entrepreneur SWM 40s, 6', 190, educated, creative, intuitive, witty, sincere, loyal. Seeks younger, mature companion. (25)

Undoubtedly, the personal ads columns are a frequent source of amusement for many casual readers and could easily be dismissed for having only peripheral information to offer on language use. Yet PAR is the expression of genuine personal circumstances which motivate many language users in broadly similar fashion. The determining factor in selecting PAR for study is the fact that it is produced in naturalistic conditions under exceptionally tight constraints which should factor out many social and individual variables. One of the major characteristics of PAR is that it is not constrained by linguistic handicap of either encoder or decoder. It is in effect a monologue directed at an unknown reader who chooses to read but cannot coconstruct text through immediate feedback. It is also different from an economy register such as headlinese, in which the writer can risk a degree of opacity which will normally be disambiguated in the article which follows. In PAR, the user is allowed no such luxury. The register must convey a maximal amount of maximally appealing information about the writer. Stringent parameters constrain the producer spatially, just as the writer of NT is constrained temporally. In addition, since there is no pressure for on-line production, the writer enjoys considerable scope for editing. Editorial practice adds further constraints on what may be written. Although content and form undoubtedly vary across publications, both are likely to be highly consistent within each newspaper.

Studies of the language of advertising in general remain scarce. Leech (1966) and Toolan (1988) discuss the issue but tend to concentrate on the stylistics of conventionalized or formulaic aspects of the genre. In addition, their studies address mostly the language of professional writers, and they have little to say about patterns of linguistic simplification. With specific reference to classified advertising, Vestergaard and Schrøder (1985) point out that truly persuasive elements are absent and that very little can be done to persuade prospective readers to read an ad. Because of the assumed shared interest, classified ads are also quite close to being "communication between equals" (Vestergaard and Schrøder 1985:3), an observation which confirms the validity of making a distinction between the handicap and economy varieties of simplified registers.

4. Source and Nature of the Corpus

The corpus on which this study is based consists of two hundred ads drawn from the personal columns of the *LA Weekly,* which specializes in entertainment-oriented items but also reports social and political issues of local interest. Appealing to an affluent and trend-conscious readership, this newspaper features an extensive section devoted to classified advertising. The ads in the corpus were published 14–21 September 1990. Of the two hundred ads selected, half were placed by males seeking female partners and half by females seeking male partners. A key feature of these ads is that writers are constrained by a pricing system which offers a maximum of twenty words for a set fee, with the cost rising sharply with every extra word beyond the standard twenty. As a result, the ads in the sample adhere fairly closely to a mean length of 20.3 words, with a range of 15 to 25 words. In a typical issue of the *LA Weekly,* a number of advertisers try to achieve a degree of immediate saliency by ignoring spatial constraints and writing very short or very long ads. Thus in order to determine how this simplified register might be produced under near-identical spatial constraints, any ads which deviated markedly from the norm in length were not included in the corpus. Since deviant ads represented only 12 percent of the total available, the selected sample seems a fair representation of PAR at work. Although educated guesses can be made about the social identity of the language users in the sample, we should not assume an automatic link between register and social dialect or be sidetracked by issues of socioeconomic status, age, or even native-speaker competence. It seems reasonable to suppose that social variables will be largely factored out in the writing process by the exigencies of an identical language purpose, stringent spatial constraints, and powerful stylistic conventions. As expected, no such variables show up in recognizable patterns in the sample. This is not to say that systematic variation might not be present across publications aimed at different readerships. An examination of four other local newspapers with substantial sections devoted to personal ads (*Los Angeles Times, Orange County Register, Los Angeles Reader,* and *Recycler*) suggests that such variation may be editorially imposed (as in greater or lesser use of abbreviations) or imitatively transmitted (as in greater or lesser lexical creativity). Most probably, the *LA Weekly* is broadly representative of the medium in the sense that its set of conventions is not likely to be so powerful as to mask the operation of underlying simplification processes.

5. Analysis of Features

A total of 11 features were selected largely on the basis of their prominence in Ferguson's (1982) typology of features characteristic of simplified registers. Original typographical features (including punctuation) have been respected in all citations. The short conventionalized endings consisting mostly of a reference number have been removed, and original line breaks have not been retained.[4] Numbers in square brackets refer to the location in the corpus of each ad cited. Numbers [1–100] were placed by males seeking females, numbers [101–200] by females seeking males.

5.1. Definite and Indefinite Articles

One of the most prominent features of this and other economy registers is the very small number of articles, definite or indefinite, that appear in texts. In a corpus of 4061 words, there are just 49 occurrences of *a/an* and 19 of *the*. Typically, writers leave the field open to more than one possible referent:

1. . . . Young, blonde, cute, long hair, not conservative, lonely and looking for *a sweet partner?* [105]
2. Kind, exciting inside and out JSF, redhead, 35 would like to fall in love and live happily ever after with *a stable, secure mensch* 28–45. [164]
3. *An Oriental lady* wanted for friendship, fun and romance. . . . [2]

More interesting from the point of view of how language is made more manageable is the fact that conventionalized, formulaic sequences, not normally amenable to productive or reductive manipulation, show no sign of simplification. On the contrary, they often contain relatively rare examples of the definite article:

4. *What's the deal?* Looking for fun, action, adventure? SWM, 26, 5'11", 150 lbs. . . . [49]
5. . . . If you like to have fun, *you're the one!* [75]

6. . . . seeking pretty, 32–40, easygoing, classy, funky lady who wants to *live the good life.* [10]
7. . . . Need a fit and fun man, 33–40, ready for *the challenge of the road.* [179]

Some unsimplified formulaic sequences also contain the indefinite article:

8. I come from *a long line of love.* Audacious, charismatic, established artist wishes enduring relationship with 25–40, N/S, earthy, tactile, enchanting femme. [95]
9. Can you recognize *a great thing?* Redhead, 32, SWF, energetic, outdoorsy, creative, honest, adventuresome, nature oriented, jeep, stunt kites. [117]

More typically, however, the indefinite article occurs as part of a formulaic turn incorporated in a clause that is in some way incomplete:

10. Authentic, nice, Jewish girl seeking Jewish man, 30+ for fun and games? Relationship? *Honesty a must.* [187]
11. SWM sorcerer, 44, seeking sorceress for research on explosive chemistry. *Knowledge of ancient rites a must.* [72]

Even more common are cases in which a highly dispensable indefinite article appears to be missing, as in the following examples:

12. *Very attractive,* successful, athletic, educated, sophisticated, fun, adventurous *SWM seeks dark-eyed beauty.* . . . [11]
13. *Terrorist of love* will annex you. *SWM seeks siren of the Sahara.* 1001 Arabian nights await. . . . [1]
14. *Cute school teacher,* brown skin/hair/eyes, 5'5", 125, 30-something. Fun, bright, witty. *Wants man* who can appreciate it. [121]
15. *Attractive, slim, self-employed lady,* 40s. Seeking *long-term relationship* with *similar unencumbered male.* . . . [156]

5.2. Personal Pronouns

The absence of third parties from the interaction explains the extreme rarity in the corpus of personal pronouns other than for first (*I, me, my, our, us/'s*) or second (*you, your*) person deixis. Yet twenty-nine occurrences of first person and eleven of second person pronouns in a corpus of this size constitute strikingly low frequency. Of the ten first-person singular pronouns occurring in subject position, more than half co-occur with the otherwise rare *be* copula in clauses that, unusually for this register, tend to be fully formed:

16. *I'm ready and waiting!* Tall, attractive, N/S SJF, 31, seeks soul mate. . . . [163]
17. *I'm not perfect,* but parts of me are excellent. . . . [42]

Similarly with second person pronouns in subject position:

18. Truly nice gentleman with looks and confidence *that you'll appreciate.* SWJM, 40. *You're slim, long-haired and gorgeous.* [5]
19. *Are you bright?* SWM, 40, N/S, dramatist, desires personable SF without agents or therapists. . . . [27]

First person or second person pronouns in subject position also tend to co-occur in fully formed clauses with articles, suggesting that simplification processes may affect (or not, as the case may be) clusters of expendable features. This is consistent with the findings of Ervin-Tripp (1972), Chafe (1982), and Biber (1988), who stress the importance of empirically identifying salient patterns of co-occurrence in a variety of registers:

20. *Are you looking for a boy-friend?* Six foot tall, blue eyes, long hair, creative guy seeks romance. . . . [54]
21. Asian/Filipina wanted for friendship. Sincere, open-minded, affectionate. *I am in my 20s,* white, cute and a student. [32]
22. Young pretty female, athletically trim, desired by film exec, 51. *I'm extremely fit and an aerobics nut.* Let's get together for a mutually rewarding experience. . . . [20]

More typical of this corpus are cases of missing personal pronouns. The phenomenon can affect first person pronouns:

23. *Love younger men!* Pretty blonde wants 1970's born boy to recreate the 60's with. . . . [134]
24. Ebony beauty, 31, associate producer, ultra feminine. *Enjoy reading, theatre, weekends away.* Seeking SBM, . . . [123]
25. Happy blonde, blue, SJF, 30s, 5'8", good-looking, fit, outdoorsy, travelled, intelligent, unpretentious. *Seek counterpart* for fun, family, future. [129]

Here, overt deictic reference to the writer is probably seen as unnecessary since it can be unambiguously assigned exophorically.

Even more often, the third person inflection of the verb suggests that it is a third person pronoun in subject position that may be missing. This time, deictic reference can be unambiguously assigned anaphorically:

26. Attractive, slim, self-employed lady, 40s. Seeking long-term relationship with similar unencumbered male. *Enjoys social interaction and quiet times.* [156]
27. Cute, professional, vegetarian, SWM, 5'11", 165, 33, N/S, brown hair. *Seeks similar Japanese lady,* 21–33, for ever. [81]
28. Attractive SWM 35, 5'9", good income professional. *Loves attractive, dark skinned ladies* 25–35 for dating relationship. [37]

Already the analyst is faced with the difficulty of choosing between possible reconstructions of a text unaffected by a hypothesized process of deletion. Perhaps it is an underlying third person pronoun that was the target of deletion. If so, ad (26) can be reconstructed as follows (after adjustments to punctuation and capitalization):

[An] attractive, slim, self-employed lady, 40s, [is] seeking [a] long-term relationship with [a] similar, unencumbered male. [She] enjoys social interaction and quiet times.

Ads (27) and (28) lend themselves more readily to reconstructions that assume deletion of (among other things) a relative pronoun:

[I am a] cute, professional, vegetarian, SWM, 5'11", 165, 33, N/S, [with] brown hair, [who] seeks [a] similar Japanese lady, 21–33, for ever.

[I am an] attractive SWM, 35, 5'9", [and a] professional [with a] good income, [who] loves attractive, dark skinned ladies, 25–35, for [a] dating relationship.

But perhaps the most likely reading is that the period preceding the verb with third person singular inflection should be read as a comma, that the verb agrees with a more or less fully written-out subject noun phrase, and that no personal or relative pronoun deletion has taken place:

> [An] attractive, slim, self-employed lady, 40s, [is] seeking [a] long-term relationship with [a] similar, unencumbered male, [and] enjoys social interaction and quiet times. (26)

> [A] cute, professional, vegetarian, SWM, 5'11", 165, 33, N/S, [with] brown hair, seeks [a] similar Japanese lady, 21–33, for ever. (27)

> [An] attractive SWM, 35, 5'9", [and a] professional [with a] good income, loves attractive, dark skinned ladies 25–35 for [a] dating relationship. (28)

Thus in practice, reconstructing on the basis of a native speaker's intuitions what may have been the original form is largely a matter of guesswork.

5.3. Auxiliaries

Like the simplified registers analyzed by Ferguson (1982) and Janda (1985), PAR appears to be characterized by a relative rarity of function words, most apparent in questions formed without auxiliaries or modals. Of the 31 clauses ending with a question mark, not one makes use of the *do* auxiliary. In some, it is the *do* auxiliary that can be identified as most probably the missing segment:

> 29. . . . Seeks tall, intelligent, caring, monogamous man. *Still believe in romance?* [190]

More often, simplification is so extensive that it is not possible to decide with any degree of certainty what auxiliary or modal would have been contained in a fully formed sentence before the presumed application of deletion rules:

> 30. SWM, 40s seeks to meet young gals under 30. *Travel? Be my little girl?* Financially well off. [71]
> 31. . . . When I love, life becomes short, and then it's life. *Join me?* [67]
> 32. *More at home in the Sierras than on the 405?* Active, funny, handsome, professional SWM 27 seeks adventurous woman. . . . [66]
> 33. Voluptuous WF with long auburn hair. Like quiet evenings, goofy weekends. *Vice versa?* Ruggedly handsome, fit WM—surprise me! [101]

Although reconstruction is often impossible, referential assignment is never ambiguous. If the personal pronoun can be safely omitted there would be little sense in holding on to an auxiliary or one of a number of possible modals whose role is largely that of a function word. Thus dispensability appears to be rule-governed. That is, it is not the case that function words are randomly available for omission depending on the tightness of the spatial constraints. While an auxiliary or modal can be omitted even if the second person subject pronoun is present, the fact that the reverse is not possible suggests that implicational hierarchies may affect the production of simplified registers.

5.4. Negatives

In this corpus, the cluster of subject pronoun and copula is just as likely to be missing from negative clauses as it is from positive clauses:

> 34. . . . Myself: bright, sweet, attractive, young 45, unencumbered, successful. Yourself: attractive, *not loud, not overweight*, sweet person. [3]

In others, there is a strong sense that a fully elaborated version of the text would include a relative clause:

> 35. Writer, leftist, 57 *not short, fat, bald;* . . . [17]
> 36. . . . Brunette, long nails, sharp mind, artist with style seeks mature, creative man with substance, emotionally and financially *not afraid to spend.* [102]

But either way, simplification does not affect the expression of negation in the predicate.

In other negative predicates, attempts at reconstruction are frustrated by the wide range of structures which may be considered as the starting point of a presumed reduction process:

> 37. TV exec, SWM, 42, 5′8″, slim, *no dependents*, seeking serious relationship. . . . [6]
> 38. . . . seeks woman similar politics, feminist, intellectual, not too sweet, *no California metaphysical fruit cakes*. [17]
> 39. . . . Need: companion for concerts and parties. Nice guys must apply! *No drugs*. [109]

Superficially, there is here a suggestion of the fronting of the negative, said by Ferguson (1982) to be typical of the production of young children learning their first language as well as speakers of BT, FT, and pidgins. In such cases fronting produces forms (such as **No want!*) which are ungrammatical in any conceivable native speaker registers or dialects. In this corpus, on the other hand, reduced expressions remain grammatical with any number of possible readings (such as *[with] no dependents, no California metaphysical fruit cakes [need apply]*, or *[I want] no drugs*).

5.5. Copulas

Related to the phenomenon of missing auxiliaries is the relative rarity of copula verbs. In this corpus, the copula tends to appear in a small stock of fully formed clauses:

> 40. Handsome DWM single-parent, recently new to area would love to meet attractive Latina 25–35ish. *My interests are varied.* Kids OK. [92]
> 41. *A tender touch, knowing smile or indescribable feeling of unbridled joy can't be matched in words.* Or can they? [24]
> 42. . . . Let's talk and get acquainted. *Don't be shy.* [74]

Far more striking is the large number of cases in which a copula appears to be missing. In active clauses, describing the writer's primary motive, omission of the copula often clusters with omission of the subject pronoun:

43. *Looking for love.* SBM needs a special lady to share good times with and beyond. [43]
44. Bright, athletic, sweet, sexy UCLA student, 29, 5'7", 120. *Looking for jet pilot,* not rocket scientist. [113]
45. A free Mercedez!! (*Just kidding*). Attractive wealthy *boyfriend seeking girlfriend* for romance, travel, secret clubs. . . . [23]

In passive clauses, this often takes a conventionalized form:

46. Beautiful, educated, *black woman 21–29 wanted* by good-looking Preppie WASP. 36. [40]
47. Uncommon, *creative SF sought* by SM, 36. Likes art, music (real old, real new), lit, theater, and other heavy stuff. [7]
48. Attentive, energetic, romantic, *leading man required* to star in best-selling romance. . . . [155]

This phenomenon also occurs in clauses in which the writer typically requests, but also offers, descriptive information:

49. *2 gorgeous SWFs ready* for 2 gorgeous SWM, 40–50 years old. *Meaning of gorgeous: loving,* beautiful and affluent. [181]
50. *Up for grabs: sensual, sensitive, creative, eclectic female song-bird.* To be captured by tall, slender, blond for the marriage gig. [147]

In common with users of other simplified registers, PAR writers take advantage of the highly expendable nature of the copula whenever processing constraints require that attention be given to truly contentful components of the message.

5.6. Prepositions

Given the common aim of PAR users, it can be predicted that texts will tend to depend on the semantic field of intentionality. Looking at the frequency and distribution of prepositions such as *for* should therefore reveal the extent to which PAR writers expect meaning to be recoverable from more semantically contentful items and feel free to omit prepositions accordingly. On average every other entry in the corpus makes use of the preposition *for,* and examples abound in which purpose is expressed in fully formed prepositional phrases in spite of the fact that simplification of the form is apparent elsewhere in the clause:

51. . . . Athletic lover, wants to bond with fit, tender, wealthy woman *for blissful oneness.* [18]
52. Attractive, Latin professional, 30, gentle heart, affectionate seeks pretty lady, 25–45, *for discreet romance* based on friendship and trust. [56]
53. . . . Creative and unconventional SJM, twentysomething, seeks SJF *for deep conversation and light romance,* or vice versa. [61]
54. BiWM, 29, healthy, with a warm heart and an active mind, seeks an intelligent, non-feminine woman *for an emotionally and physically intimate friendship.* [58]

There are of course a number of alternatives to the use of *for* to express intention or purpose, such as passivization or listing:

55. *Artistic convergence desired.* SWM, 31, honest, communicative, athletic, conceptual designer seeks petite, zen-like, N/S N/D, fine visual artist 25–31. [29]

56. Real man who reads sought by pretty, loving writer 34. *Outback expeditions, sailing, urban fun.* If you're 28–35, 6', brilliant, Westside, do call! [169]

But there are few examples of these alternatives, which represent at best a marginal space saving over the preferred choice.

Similar patterns appear to be operating in the distribution of the preposition *with*, which occurs mostly in fully formed prepositional phrases, although simplification can take place on either side:

57. . . . Prefer affectionate, unpretentious, intelligent man *with a dry wit* and a penchant for hugs. [122]
58. . . . SJM warm and loving wants to share my life *with a nice lady,* 21–30. [96]

There are a few cases in the corpus of reliance on the most readily available alternative, namely, omission:

59. Pretty woman, 31, SWF seeks 30–35 SWM, attractive, considerate, responsible, *sense of humor,* marriage-minded. . . . [186]
60. Fairly nice man, 6'1", 33 *green eyes, hairy chest,* seeks fairly nice woman for friendship. . . . [84]

Yet these do not appear to offer significant savings over the preposition, which carries the bulk of the semantic weight. The reluctance in economy registers to dispense with prepositions does seem to indicate that their users view prepositions less as function words than as vehicles for both the assignment of thematic role and the transmission of meaning. This view is consistent with that of Janda (1985), who notes that NT writers also show a tendency to retain prepositions. It suggests that prepositions may be much more semantically crucial and less recoverable than (admittedly smaller) classes of function words such as articles, pronouns, and auxiliaries. It also fits in with the findings of Biber (1988), who notes the high co-occurrence of prepositions with other items (such as nominalizations and passives) which serve to integrate large amounts of information into a text.

5.7. Relativization

If relativization is the outcome of somewhat complex transformations, we would expect that under conditions of simplification it would not be a preferred option for PAR users. Surprisingly, the PAR corpus contains quite a number of fully elaborated relative clauses. All but one of the twenty-eight cases relativize a noun in subject position, with twenty-four opting for *who* and four preferring *that.* Even more interestingly, overt relativization appears to be in complementary distribution with missing copulas, articles, and uninflected verbs. In no case in this corpus does simplification take place within the relative clause itself, and the output is consistently fully elaborated:

61. . . . Looking for attractive, worldly, well-built gentleman *who is emotionally and financially secure.* [182]
62. Tall, dark, handsome, pensive, considerate, classy, kind SWM desires, SWF, thirty-something, adorable, sensual, spirited, feminine, *who appreciates fine gentlemanly qualities.* [70]

63. Good-looking PhD, 40, wants to talk to an intelligent woman *who has an interesting personality and a nice body.* [91]
64. . . . Seeks short, witty SWM *who looks beyond appearances* for inner beauty. [112]

This raises an intriguing question: why would writers who systematically ignore many of the grammatical requirements of more literary registers also choose to stay close to quasi-literary standards once they have opted for relativization? A possible answer is provided by Pawley and Syder (1983), who argue that the encoding of relativization follows distinct routes in vernacular and literary language use. In on-line vernacular production, speakers are cognitively constrained by a comparatively short attention span that forces them to tolerate greater fragmentation. In contrast, the more leisurely nature of the writing process offers encoders greater opportunities for the complex integration of ideas, a feature which is characteristic of the literary grammar of relativization. The relative clauses generated by that grammar, Pawley and Syder argue, are more suited to literary language use where encoder and decoder are in a better position to plan and scan language segments, and it may not even be part of any preliterate grammar. If so, writers who are under pressure to simplify may regard relative clauses as peripheral to their register. In PAR, recourse to relative clauses may be a brief digression into the literary grammar in which simplification is unnecessary and less acceptable. To the extent that they are used at all, relative clauses may resist internal simplification, as segments imported from the literary grammar are transferred wholesale, or not at all.

5.8. Attributive and Predicative Chaining

In practice, PAR writers often choose alternatives to relativization. Salient among these are the strings of adjectives or nouns that characterize the register. While the grammar of the fully elaborated language does not specify the number of consecutive items which can modify a noun phrase, the degree of chaining shown here would surely stretch the limits of acceptability in any other register. A few of the writers represented in the corpus try to keep the strings to a more manageable size by splitting the sequence into attributive and predicative segments, with relativization sometimes omitted in the latter:

65. *Accomplished, attractive, affectionate, athletic, professional,* entrepreneur SWM, 40s, 6', 190, *educated, creative, intuitive, witty, sincere, loyal.* [25]

Far more common, however, are cases of strings in attributive position only:

66. *Artistic, athletic, adorable* 18–32 y.o., race open sought by 26 y.o. SAM, graphic designer and financially secure, for sincere relationship. [30]
67. *Wealthy, happy, healthy, mature* DWM seeks uncommitted, discreet relationship with young, slim, beautiful female. . . . [47]
68. *Smart, silly, warm, witty, independent, imperfect, tempestuous* Thespian, 30, seeks sensual, humorous, communicative man who likes dogs. [196]
69. *Caring, feminine, fit, funny, gentle, gorgeous, happy, intelligent, loyal, sophisticated, together, unfettered* SWF seeks SWM counterpart/complement, play/soul mate. [160]

Since PAR specializes in describing writers and presumed readers, it is not surprising that it should make use of a higher than average number of adjectives. Yet unusually long nominal strings are also a feature of this register, though they are less frequent than adjectival strings:

> 70. Well-mannered, irreverent, fun-loving 30s guy seeks gal. *I love blues, jazz, classical, movies, food fests, travel.* [15]
> 71. Trim, attractive, liberal, heart/head combo, relaxed 40s, likes *zany humor, eclectic music, films, lit, outdoor sports, travel,* seeks similar. [145]

The striking frequency of these strings in the corpus suggests that they may be part of a strategy of wholesale omission of relative pronouns, articles, copulas, and verbal inflection, in return for maximal modification of the noun phrase. This preference for parataxis over conjunction is also noted by Ferguson (1982) in his typology of simplified features of BT and FT. In addition, the strategy becomes a conventionalized, perhaps self-perpetuating feature of this register, and one which cognitive constraints make highly unlikely in anything other than a written medium.

5.9 Vocabulary and Hyphenated Compounds

English is perhaps uncommonly generous in providing productive rules for the creation of semantically charged nouns and adjectives through a combination of morphemic transformations and hyphenation. Yet a much reduced vocabulary consisting of mostly monomorphemic, generic rather than specific terms is said by Ferguson (1982) to be characteristic of simplified registers. The question becomes whether PAR avails itself of the potential for combining economy with maximum communicative effect, or limits itself to the unelaborated, core vocabulary that appears to meet the needs of users of handicap registers.

Evidently, PAR writers take full advantage of the combinational possibilities of the language. Over half the entries in the corpus contain at least one hyphenated item. In addition, only five combinations appear more than once, all of them conventionalized items:

> 72. *fun-loving* [15, 45, 60, 65, 127, 183, 188, 190, 195, 197]
> 73. *good-looking* [10, 40, 44, 50, 68, 76, 88, 89, 91, 116, 129, 193]
> 74. *non-smoking* [26, 87][5]
> 75. *easy-going* [50, 182, 191]
> 76. *self-employed* [78, 82, 156]

By far the majority of hyphenated items occur only once. A few of the occurrences are clearly conventionalized:

> 77. *boy-friend* [54]

But PAR users are obviously skilled at using and, in many cases, creating a rich terminology which combines economy and content. Most of these creations can hardly be described as generic or typical of a register in which writers rely on a common stock of regularly used lexical items consisting of a single free morpheme:

78. *non-mothers* [35]
79. *zen-like* [29]
80. *non-heavies* [38]
81. *non-neurotic* [115]

Moreover, this degree of elaboration frequently co-occurs with signs of substantial simplification, mostly in the form of missing function words:

82. Elegant, exquisite, enticing, black beauty, 30, curvaceous, seeks healthy, affluent, white gentleman for *ultra-discreet* enduring relationship. . . . [124]
83. 29, artistic, into theatre, *self-development,* dancing, nature, music, seeks SF (24–34), for committed relationship. [21]
84. Serene, cerebral beauty, SWF, 34, journalist, wants to turn new page with sage, intrepid, winsome, *commitment-minded* professional. [125]
85. Never married, attractive Latina (34) seeks tall, *got-it-together* man w/sense of humor, who's not afraid of commitment. [165]

It is likely that PAR users respond to the constraints of the register by loosening the syntax as lexical and semantic complexity increases, to prevent more difficult processing if both were to be tightened simultaneously. It is this trade-off that may result in the co-occurrence of syntactic simplification and greater lexical density characterized by strings of adjectives and nouns and often novel hyphenated compounds.

5.10. Simplification and Ungrammaticality

One of the most salient features of PAR is that the often elaborate choice of semantically rich items tends to co-occur with widespread infringement of the norms of syntax as traditionally described. This shows up in the apparent mixing of constituents which would not be governed by the same verb phrase in the fully elaborated grammar. In many cases, these constituents are adjectives and nouns:

86. *I'm 31, brown hair, green-eyed romantic,* who enjoys sunsets, lots of laughter, good company, sweet music, and hopefully, you. [131]
87. 25, handsome, SJM, *likes biking, classical music, math, metaphysics, and literate,* seeks a cute, attractive and educated gal. [46]
88. 34, pretty, *Latina, red-head, 5'3", 110, hiking, sailing,* dancing, wants white, professional, attractive male, 40s, for romance. [153]
89. *Looks and soul, romantic dreamer* 33, seeks brainy guy into music, literature and film. . . . [151]
90. Mature, fun yogi seeks young vegetarian woman *to share life and love, pleasing God, trip to India, Ashram on beach.* [69]

It is of course possible to hypothesize a fully elaborated underlying form prior to systematic deletion of dispensable function words. If so, the simplified output would normally be expected to retain some skeletal outline of that underlying form. In practice, the high frequency of disjointed sequences suggests that syntactic consistency and the fully elaborated grammatical structures of more formal written language are low priorities for PAR users. The orallike fragmentation (Chafe 1982) resulting from this lack of preoccupation with the syntax of other registers is a feature which PAR, though written, shares with the largely unmonitored outcome of real-time speech.

5.11. Simplification and Shared Context

Given the constraints that shape this register, it is to be predicted that writers will make maximum use of what they take to be shared context between themselves and their eventual readers. From a Gricean perspective, the exigencies of both oral and written communication are such that encoders are able to cut corners by relying on decoders' willingness and ability to recover meaning even where none is overtly indicated (Cooper 1982). Just as the writer must not overtax the reader's ability to interpret the conventions of the register, the reader must be willing to find relevant meaning in opaque or even superficially incoherent messages. Thus, while a high degree of reliance on abbreviations might be predicted from the spatial constraints of PAR, the crucially interpersonal function of the register helps explain why nonstandard abbreviations are relatively rare, although *LA Weekly* editorial policy does not explicitly rule them out. Much more frequent in this corpus are cases of largely conventionalized abbreviations such as *N/S* (no/n-smoking, no/n-smoker) or *N/D* (no drugs), but even these depend for recovery on shared knowledge of local conditions and prevalent values.

In PAR, the most common type of conventionalized abbreviation consists of reducing some key feature of the identity of either party to a three-letter code. Thus frequent codes such as *SAM* can be assumed to stand for *single Asian male,* or *DBF* for *divorced black female.*[6] In this publication at least, only extreme confidence in the instinctive application of a cooperative mechanism can lead the writer to expect that *SJM,* for example, will be interpreted as *single Jewish male* and not as the theoretically possible *single Japanese male.* What the writer is doing is betting that social knowledge will enable the reader to recover the intended implicature, since nothing else in the ad suggests which interpretation is intended.

Similarly, only the application of a cooperative principle can account for the fact that referential assignment is often implicit. This, and knowledge of collocational conventions, is usually sufficient for the intended referent to be identified without difficulty:

> 91. *Nurse,* 39, 5'7", 135, blonde, desires love and marriage, baby optional. I have everything but *a husband. Healthy and pretty.* [139]

In more extreme cases, simplification strains the cooperative principle to such a degree that reference might equally be assigned to writer, reader, or possibly both:

> 92. *SWF,* attractive, young 40, seeks cool, off-beat *guy* 30–45 who likes film, literature, music, outdoors. *Secure and laid back.* [173]

In these examples, the economic constraints of the medium make it essential that space not be wasted on nonessential referential material. As a result, writers leave it entirely to readers to decide whether to apply key descriptive elements to themselves or to the writer.

6. Discussion and Implications

The analysis of PAR illustrates the fact that language use cannot escape from its temporal and spatial context. On the contrary, it strongly reflects the social norms and conventions of medium, location, and time. Thus conventionalization helps shape language use, as social groups develop norms appropriate to each occasion and as individual users acquire and modify these norms. As Ferguson (1983) points out, it is right that register analysis should emphasize not simply the functional basis but also the extent of conventionalization in language variation.[7] In PAR, this ritualization takes the form of standard abbreviations and clichés. It mirrors other forms of planned discourse and, like them, follows relatively predictable patterns that are likely to be socially and functionally conditioned (Ochs 1979).

PAR has also been shown to share some of the features found across the range of simplified registers. Although communicative function differs from one simplified register to another, it is impossible not to notice an "overall family resemblance" among them (Ferguson 1983:160). What seems to be happening is that pressure to simplify language for whatever purpose, to communicate with an infant or a foreigner, or to save time or space, may encourage language users to fall back on an unmarked linguistic core at least partly common to all simplified registers.[8]

One possible implication, raised tentatively by Ferguson (1982), is that competence in register variation, which subsumes linguistic simplification, may not be learned as part of normal language development but may be innate. Perhaps simplification processes are alike because human beings are innately equipped with the ability to dispense with fully elaborated forms whenever appropriate. This is not to say that speakers will universally tend toward simplification in identical situations. Indeed cultural norms may well constrain the situations in which simplification is appropriate. Ochs (1982), for example, has shown that while Samoan adults accommodate to foreigners through FT, they do not use a BT register when acting as caregivers. But when a society sanctions recourse to simplification strategies, speakers seem to have the competence to employ them effortlessly, using strategies that show signs of that family resemblance noted by Ferguson.

What remains to be addressed is the nature of the process by which simplified registers are produced. This study demonstrates that under pressure to condense, PAR users show a marked tendency to give low priority to the rules of the fully elaborated grammar. This links PAR with other simplified registers such as BT, FT, NT, and pidgins, all of which fall well short of orthodox grammaticality in some way. If it becomes apparent that simplified registers share a common reliance on an unmarked core, the notion may be incompatible with the prevalent view of linguistic simplification as a process of *top-down* reduction from the fully elaborated grammar in which deletion is assumed to play a major part. Undoubtedly, deletion can be shown to operate in linguistic simplification provided the result can be compared to an earlier, fully elaborated model. Janda (1985), for example, describes the changes that affect the form of lecture materials as they are converted to notes. Philips (1985) studies processes of clarification in spoken legal discourse. Lautamatti (1987) examines how a written text can be made more accessible through simplification of its rhetorical features. In all these cases, deletion can be seen to affect elements which are present in and recoverable from an earlier, more elaborated version of the text. This type of simplification can be accounted for within notions of top-down transformations from complete underlying structures.

But as Gunter (1963) makes clear, ellipsis is just as likely in cases where reconstruction of simplified material back to a fully elaborated model cannot be attempted. Weakening the assumption of top-down reductive mechanisms thus raises the intriguing question of the actual route followed by native speakers in the production of simplified language. Do language simplifiers cut back from elaborated underlying forms toward the unmarked common core proposed by Ferguson (1982), or is the core itself the default that language users begin with, adding structure in order to operate successfully in a more elaborated register? What the study of PAR suggests is that simplification mechanisms are not mere adjuncts to competence, and language that fails to meet the requirements of the fully elaborated, quasi-literary grammar is not simply an inferior by-product of deletion processes, convenient in performance, but unworthy of serious study. What a *bottom-up* view of linguistic simplification proposes instead is that, faced with constraints (of the handicap or economy type), language users may instinctively keep their output closer to the unmarked core that was characteristic of earlier stages in their linguistic development. Rather than being gradually replaced as learners progress, this core may be retained, to be relied upon as specific communicative conditions require (Ochs 1979). In brief, producing simplified language may be a matter, not of top-down reduction of underlying forms, but of bottom-up construction of text to the appropriate degree of elaboration over an ever-present linguistic core.

Ultimately a theory of language simplification must explain why language users operate so successfully in registers not subject to the requirements of the orthodox grammar, a problem to which the bottom-up approach offers a solution at least as plausible as assumptions of top-down processing. Whether the focus of further research is psycholinguistic or sociolinguistic, the suitability of the sentence as the basic unit of linguistic analysis cannot be taken as a given, as Pawley and Syder (1983), Hopper (1988), and others have suggested. With specific reference to PAR, further analysis of linguistic simplification as an instance of register variation should turn to broader samples of ads drawn from a wider range of publications and subject matters. Ideally, this should have a cross-linguistic dimension, already pioneered by van Dijk (1988) in his work on headlines in Arabic and Japanese. As Ferguson (1982) notes, an examination of a possible universal dimension to linguistic simplification has far-reaching implications for syntactic theory and psycholinguistics, as well as sociolinguistics, and must ultimately illuminate our understanding of the relationship between language as a property of mind and language in use.

Notes

1. The term *register* is used here to refer to "varieties according to use," in contrast with *dialects*, which are defined as "varieties according to user" (Halliday et al. 1964:48).

2. A comprehensive review of this issue can be found in Milroy (1987).

3. This and the following examples are drawn from the columns of the *LA Weekly*, 14 September 1990. Numbers in square brackets refer to the location of the ad in the corpus used in the subsequent analysis.

4. It is arguable that advance knowledge of where line breaks are to fall may affect the composition of the ad together with any simplification processes that may be operating. However, unlike that of other publications (the *Orange County Register*, for example), the *LA Weekly* mandatory application form does not allow the writer to preview the final appearance of the ad.

5. While the PAR corpus contains only two occurrences of the full compound *non-smoking*, it frequently appears in abbreviated form, either as *NS* or *N/S*.

6. The *LA Weekly* leaves the interpretation of these codes entirely to the reader. In contrast, the mandatory application form printed in the *Orange County Register* standardizes the practice further by listing and explaining the most common of these codes.

7. See Atkinson (1991) for a comprehensive discussion of theoretical and empirical aspects of conventionalized language, and for a model of written discourse conventions.

8. Markedness can be seen as both an abstract principle and a set of implications (Andersen 1989). As a result, identifying the possible content of an unmarked core common to all simplified registers is no easy undertaking, though Carter (1988) makes a start with his study of journalistic language.

References

Andersen, Henning. 1989. "Markedness Theory: The First 150 Years." In Olga M. Tomić, ed., *Markedness in Synchrony and Diachrony.* Berlin: Mouton de Gruyter. Pp. 11–46.

Atkinson, Dwight. 1991. "Discourse Analysis and Written Discourse Conventions." *Annual Review of Applied Linguistics* 11:57–76.

Biber, Douglas. 1988. *Variation Across Speech and Writing.* Cambridge: Cambridge University Press.

Carter, Ronald. 1988. "Front Pages: Lexis, Style and Newspaper Reports." In Mohsen Ghadessy, ed., *Registers of Written English: Situational Factors and Linguistic Features.* London: Pinter. Pp. 8–16.

Chafe, Wallace L. 1982. "Integration and Involvement in Speaking, Writing, and Oral Literature." In Deborah Tannen, ed., *Spoken and Written Language: Exploring Orality and Literacy.* Norwood, NJ: Ablex. Pp. 35–53.

Cheshire, Jenny. 1987. "Syntactic Variation, the Linguistic Variable, and Sociolinguistic Theory." *Linguistics* 25:257–82.

Chomsky, Noam. 1965. *Aspects of the Theory of Syntax.* Cambridge, MA: MIT Press.

Cooper, Marilyn M. 1982. "Context as Vehicle: Implicatures in Writing." In Martin Nystrand, ed., *What Writers Know: The Language, Process, and Structure of Written Discourse.* New York: Academic Press. Pp. 105–28.

Ervin-Tripp, Susan M. 1972. "On Sociolinguistic Rules: Alternation and Co-occurrence." In John J. Gumperz and Dell Hymes, eds., *Directions in Sociolinguistics.* New York: Holt. Pp. 213–50.

Ferguson, Charles A. 1971. "Absence of Copula and the Notion of Simplicity: A Study of Normal Speech, Baby Talk, Foreigner Talk and Pidgins." In Dell Hymes, ed., *Pidginization and Creolization of Language.* Cambridge: Cambridge University Press. Pp. 141–50.

————. "Toward a Characterization of English Foreigner Talk." *Anthropological Linguistics* 17(1):1–14.

————. 1977. "Baby Talk as a Simplified Register." In Catherine E. Snow and Charles A. Ferguson, eds., *Talking to Children*. Cambridge: Cambridge University Press. Pp. 209–33.

————. 1982. "Simplified Registers and Linguistic Theory." In Lorraine K. Obler and Lise Menn, eds., *Exceptional Language and Linguistics*. New York: Academic Press. Pp. 49–66.

————. 1983. "Sports Announcer Talk: Syntactic Aspects of Register Variation." *Language in Society* 12:153–72.

Ferguson, Charles A., and Charles E. DeBose. 1977. "Simplified Registers, Broken Language, and Pidginization." In Albert Valdman, ed., *Pidgin and Creole Linguistics*. Bloomington: Indiana University Press. Pp. 99–125.

Gunter, Richard. 1963. "Elliptical Sentences in American English." *Lingua* 12:137–50.

Halliday, Michael A. K. 1985. *An Introduction to Functional Grammar*. London: Edward Arnold.

Halliday, Michael A. K., Angus McIntosh, and Peter Strevens. 1964. *The Linguistic Sciences and Language Teaching*. London: Longman.

Hopper, Paul J. 1988. "Emergent Grammar and the A Priori Grammar Postulate." In Deborah Tannen, ed., *Linguistics in Context: Connecting Observation and Understanding*. Norwood, NJ: Ablex. Pp. 117–34.

Janda, Richard D. 1985. "Note-Taking as a Simplified Register." *Discourse Processes* 8:437–54.

Lautamatti, Liisa. 1987. "Observations on the Development of the Topic of Simplified Discourse." In Ulla Connor and Robert B. Kaplan, eds., *Writing Across Languages: Analysis of L2 Text*. Reading, MA: Addison-Wesley. Pp. 87–114.

Leech, Geoffrey N. 1966. *English in Advertising*. London: Longman.

Meisel, Jürgen M. 1977. "Linguistic Simplification: A Study of Immigrant Workers' Speech and Foreigner Talk." In S. Pit Corder and E. Roulet, eds., *The Notion of Simplification: Interlanguages and Pidgins and Their Relation to Second Language Pedagogy*. Neuchâtel: Faculté des Lettres. Pp. 88–113.

Milroy, Lesley. 1987. *Observing and Analysing Natural Language*. Oxford: Basil Blackwell.

Mühlhaüsler, Peter. 1986. *Pidgin and Creole Linguistics*. Oxford: Basil Blackwell.

Ochs, Elinor. 1979. "Planned and Unplanned Discourse." In Talmy Givón, ed., *Syntax and Semantics 12. Discourse and Syntax*. New York: Academic Press. Pp. 51–80.

————. 1982. "Talking to Children in Western Samoa." *Language in Society* 11:77–104.

Pawley, Andrew, and Frances H. Syder. 1983. "Natural Selection in Syntax: Notes on Adaptive Variation and Change in Vernacular and Literary Grammar." *Journal of Pragmatics* 7:551–79.

Philips, Susan U. 1985. "Strategies of Clarification in Judges' Use of Language: From the Written to the Spoken." *Discourse Processes* 8:421–36.

Sinclair, John. 1988. "Compressed English." In Mohsen Ghadessy, ed., *Registers of Written English: Situational Factors and Linguistic Features*. London: Pinter. Pp. 130–36.

Todd, Loreto. 1974. *Pidgins and Creoles*. London: Routledge.

Toolan, Michael. 1988. "The Language of Press Advertising." In Mohsen Ghadessy, ed., *Registers of Written English: Situational Factors and Linguistic Features*. London: Pinter. Pp. 52–64.

van Dijk, Teun A. 1988. *News as Discourse*. Hillsdale, NJ: Lawrence Erlbaum.

Vestergaard, Torben, and Kim Schrøder. 1985. *The Language of Advertising*. Oxford: Basil Blackwell.

III

REGISTER VARIATION

7

A Corpus-Based Analysis of Register Variation in Korean

YONG-JIN KIM AND DOUGLAS BIBER

1. Introduction

There have been numerous linguistic comparisons of speech and writing. Earlier studies often assumed a dichotomy between the two modes, while more recent studies have shown that there is considerable variation *within* each mode and considerable overlap in the linguistic characteristics of many spoken and written registers. However, few studies have analyzed the patterns of register variation in non-Western languages.

The present study helps to fill this gap by investigating the linguistic variation among spoken and written registers in contemporary Korean. We adopt the multidimensional approach to identify underlying dimensions of variation in Korean, and we analyze the relations among registers along these dimensions, with special reference to the spoken and written modes.

This study is the first attempt at a macroscopic discourse analysis of Korean; previous analyses of Korean have been microscopic. While a macroscopic approach seeks to define the overall parameters of variation among registers, a microscopic approach focuses on the discourse functions of individual linguistic features in particular registers. For example, Hwang (1981) discusses aspects of discourse structure in written narratives such as folktales and fiction; Lukoff (1986) studies tense variation in written narratives; Lee and Thompson (1987) study the variable deletion of accusative markers in spoken dialogues and narratives; Choi (1988) investigates textual coherence features in English and Korean argumentative essays; and Lee (1989) analyzes referential choices in conversations and personal letters.

Microscopic and macroscopic analyses have complementary strengths. A microscopic analysis can pinpoint the exact communicative functions of individual lin-

This chapter is based on a doctoral dissertation by Yong-Jin Kim (1990), completed at the University of Southern California. We would like to thank Edward Finegan, Nam-Kil Kim, and Donald Freeman for their extensive comments on this research project.

guistic features in particular registers, but it does not provide the basis for overall generalizations concerning differences among registers. In contrast, the macroscopic analysis presented here focuses on the overall patterns of variation among Korean registers, building on previous microanalyses to interpret those patterns in functional terms.

In addition, the present study is important from a cross-linguistic perspective. Although there have been several multidimensional analyses of English (e.g., Biber 1986, 1988, Biber and Finegan 1989), the only previous multidimensional analysis of a non-Western language is Besnier's (1988) study of register variation in Nukulaelae Tuvaluan. Until this type of analysis is applied to other languages, researchers cannot be sure of the extent to which their findings represent valid cross-linguistic generalizations. (More recently, this approach has been applied to register variation in Somali; see Biber and Hared this volume.)

English and Nukulaelae Tuvaluan represent two extremes: English is a highly developed language used in a complex, literate society; Nukulaelae Tuvaluan has a restricted range of registers and is used in a small, relatively simple society. In fact, Besnier describes the Nukulaelae speech community as representing a "restricted-literacy setting" with only two written registers: personal letters and church sermons. Korean is more similar to English than Nukulaelae Tuvaluan in that it has a wide array of spoken and written registers, and literacy has been an integral part of the culture for centuries. However, it was only recently (the end of the nineteenth century) that a native Korean literacy (as opposed to Chinese-based literacy) was fully implemented.

In other respects Korean is quite different from both English and Nukulaelae Tuvaluan. In particular, Korean has quite different cultural priorities. Hierarchical order and harmony in human relationships are regarded as central virtues in Korea, because of the influence of Confucian thinking. These values are realized linguistically and interactively. Special terms of address (pronouns and personal names) are used to mark the relation between speaker and hearer, and honorific infixes are used to mark the relation between the speaker and referents in a sentence. The so-called speech levels (sentence-final verbal suffixes) mark four levels of deference and condescension toward the hearer. As Kim (1990:28ff.) notes, most previous research on these devices has focused exclusively on spoken usage, and thus we know little about the use of these forms in written registers. They are required, however, in both speech and writing.

Thus the present study of Korean register variation is important in that it represents a quite different language situation from English and Tuvaluan; a comparative analysis of these three languages identifies potential cross-linguistic generalizations relating to the multidimensional patterns of register variation.

2. The Korean Corpus of Spoken and Written Texts

The composition of the corpus used in this chapter, which includes texts from ten spoken registers and twelve written registers, is summarized in Table 7.1. The

TABLE 7.1   Composition of the Korean Corpus of Spoken and Written Texts

Register	Number of Texts	Approximate Number of Words
Spoken Texts		
1. Private conversation	10	8,500
2. Public conversation verbatim-transcribed	8	7,000
3. Public conversation, edited for magazines	5	4,000
4. TV drama	6	6,500
5. Broadcast news	5	4,000
6. TV documentary	5	4,000
7. TV sportscast	5	4,000
8. Public speeches, unscripted	9	8,000
9. Public speeches, scripted	7	7,000
10. Folktale	10	9,000
Total Spoken Corpus:	70	62,500
Written Texts		
1. Newspaper reportage	6	6,000
2. Newspaper editorial	6	4,000
3. Novels	10	10,500
4. Literary criticism	5	4,000
5. College textbooks	6	6,500
6. Legal and official documents	10	10,000
7. Popular writing	7	7,000
8. Personal essays	5	5,000
9. Suasive essays	7	7,000
10. Political statements	7	6,000
11. Editorial letters	5	3,000
12. Personal letters	6	4,500
Total Written Corpus:	80	73,300
Total Corpus:	150	135,800

typical situations and purposes associated with each register are described in Kim (1990:chapter 2), and details about the particular texts collected for each register are given in Kim (1990:chapter 3.2.1 and appendix A).

Among the spoken registers, there are four types of dialogue: face-to-face private conversations, public conversations, published conversations, and TV drama. Private conversations are natural interactions among friends or peers, ranging over several topics. Public conversations are from professional seminars, radio and television talk shows, and a parliamentary hearing. These differ from private conversations in that they are more topic-focused and are conducted in the presence of a third party audience. Published conversations are interviews printed in monthly magazines; these have been edited and thus do not represent verbatim speech. Television drama also represents an edited kind of conversation, in this case reflecting the writer's perception of speech. These last two registers were included to investigate their relation to verbatim private and public conversations.

News broadcasting includes both radio and television reportage. In earlier periods, this register was almost always scripted, but reporters have recently begun to present the news live. Television documentaries are also a relatively recent development in Korean. Sportscasts in Korean seem relatively similar to those in English. Typically there is both an announcer, who describes the play-by-play action, and a commentator, who presents analyses of the actions or overall situation.

Public speeches have a short history in Korea, where they are restricted primarily to cultural activities adapted from Western cultures, such as political speeches and Christian sermons. Traditionally, the Confucian virtue of modesty discouraged people from developing fluent public speaking skills; in fact, listeners sometimes question the credibility of a fluent public speaker. Finally, the telling of folktales has become quite rare in Korean society, but it has a long and well-established history. Most of the folktales in this study were collected and transcribed by the Academy of Korean Studies; they were narrated by experienced storytellers, with local villagers and the researcher as a live audience.

Among the written varieties, two newspaper registers are included: reportage and editorials. Newspaper reportage is primarily narrative, recounting past events and dealing with a wide range of subjects (both international and domestic affairs). Editorials tend to be more argumentative, dealing with a wide range of topics (e.g., international relations, domestic politics, sports policies).

Novels include fictional works of varying length. This register evolved in the early part of the twentieth century; previous fictional texts were primarily folktales or Chinese classical texts. Korean novels are similar to English novels in that they can combine discourse of many types, including narration, description, dialogue, and even exposition. Literary criticism became popular around the same time as the modern Korean novel, but it differs markedly from novels in being a type of academic, expository prose.

College textbooks are also academic, but they are written with a didactic purpose. They are typically expository, but historical texts include considerable narrative portions, and texts in fields such as statistics or engineering can include considerable segments of procedural discourse. The category of legal and official documents comprises laws, regulations, and other official documents.

Popular writing includes various periodical articles written for the general public. Personal essays are also written for general readers, but they focus on personal reflections rather than descriptive information. Suasive essays are more didactic, presenting educational information relating to religion, marriage, and other social concerns. Political statements are overtly persuasive, dealing with issues relating to the existing political system, social and economic justice, national education, agriculture, and religion.

Finally, two kinds of letters are included. Editorial letters are taken from question-and-answer columns in magazines; these texts typically deal with personal, legal, or health problems. Personal letters are addressed to friends or relatives; these are truly interactive and personal in nature.

There is a total of 150 texts in the corpus, split almost evenly between twelve written and ten spoken registers. Texts are about 900 words long on average, and the total corpus comprises nearly 136,000 words.

TABLE 7.2   Linguistic Features Used in the Analysis

Lexical Elaboration	Cohesion Markers
1. Attributive adjectives	33. Explanative conjuncts
2. Derived adjectives (*-uj, -cek(in)*)	34. Conditional conjuncts
3. Manner or degree adverb	35. Coordinative conjuncts
4. Place adverb or noun	36. Adversative conjuncts
5. Time adverb or noun	37. Discourse conjuncts
6. Plural marker	38. Explanative verbal connectors
7. Possessive marker	39. Conditional verbal connectors
8. Informal postposition (*hako*)	40. Coordinative verbal connectors
9. Formal conjunct	41. Adversative verbal connectors
10. Contractions	42. Discourse verbal connectors
11. Total nouns	Tense/Aspect Markers
Syntactic Complexity	43. Nonpast tense
12. Long negation	44. Past tense
13. Short negation	45. Progressive aspect
14. Relative clauses	Sentence Types
15. Noun complementation	46. Direct questions
16. Verb complementation	47. Imperatives
17. Embedded or indirect questions	48. Declarative sentences
18. Nonfinite complementation	49. Fragmentary sentence
19. Quotative complementation	Verb Types
20. Sentence length	50. Psychological verbs
Information Structure	51. Speech act verbs
21. Passives	52. Dynamic verbs
22. Topic markers	Stance Markers
23. Subject markers	53. Hedges
24. *-ita* as copula	54. Emphatics
Situation Markers	55. Attitudinal expressions
25. Demonstrative or exophoric coreference	Other features
26. Coreferential expressions	56. Adverbial subordination
27. First person personal pronouns	57. Type/Token ratio
28. Second person personal pronouns	58. Postposition/Case-receivable noun ratio
29. Third person personal pronouns	
Sociolinguistic Indicators	
30. Honorifics	
31. Humble expressions	
32. Speech level 1—formal sentence ending	

3. Linguistic Features Used in the Analysis

Table 7.2 lists the fifty-eight linguistic features used in the analysis. These are grouped into ten major categories indicating their primary discourse function: lexical elaboration, syntactic complexity, information structure, situation markers, sociolinguistic indicators, cohesion markers, tense/aspect markers, sentence types, verb types, and stance markers. Kim (1990:chapter 3) provides a formal description of each linguistic feature.

Some of these categories are distinctive to Korean. For example, 'speech levels' and formality are marked structurally by several linguistic features (informal postpositions, formal conjuncts, Level 1 formal sentence endings), as are related phenomena indicating the relationship of speaker and hearer (e.g., honorifics, humble expressions). Information structure and cohesion are also well developed in Korean. For example, topic markers identify a word as topical, while subject markers identify a word as the focus of information; the various conjuncts (explanative, conditional, etc.) are sentence initial connectors marking logical relations in texts, while the verbal connectors (explanative, conditional, etc.) are clitics that attach to verbs and combine two clauses in a single sentence.

4. Methodology

The multidimensional approach used for the present study was originally developed for the analysis of register variation in English (Biber 1986, 1988), and it has also been used for analyses of Nukulaelae Tuvaluan and Somali. (See Biber and Hared this volume). Interactive computer programs were used to tag all texts in the corpus, so that each word was marked for its grammatical category. Then other programs performed frequency counts of the fifty-eight different linguistic features in each text, normalizing the counts to their frequency per one thousand words of text. A factor analysis was carried out on these frequency counts to identify the underlying co-occurrence patterns (i.e., the groupings of linguistic features that co-occur frequently in texts),[1] and these patterns were interpreted functionally as underlying *dimensions* of variation based on the assumption that co-occurrence reflects shared function. Finally, dimension scores were computed for each text. These are composite scores for each dimension, computed by summing the frequencies of the features having salient loadings on that dimension. The mean dimension scores for each register can be compared to analyze the relations among registers.

Six dimensions were identified as important for Korean. The following sections describe each dimension in terms of its defining linguistic features, functional underpinnings, and relations among spoken and written registers.

5. Korean Dimensions of Variation

5.1. Korean Dimension 1: 'On-Line Interaction Versus Planned Exposition—Fragmented Versus Elaborated Structure'

The co-occurring linguistic features grouped on Korean Dimension 1 are presented in Table 7.3. There are two groups of features, labeled *positive* and *negative*. Each of these represents a cluster of linguistic characteristics that frequently co-occur in texts, while the two groups have a complementary relationship. That is, if a text has frequent occurrences of the positive group of features, it will have markedly few occurrences of the negative group, and vice versa.

Most of the positive features reflect a reduced or fragmented structure. Contracted forms represent a reduction in surface form and a coalescence of morphemes. Fragmentary sentences are structurally incomplete, either missing the required

TABLE 7.3   Co-Occurring Linguistic Features
on Korean Dimension 1: 'On-Line Interaction
Versus Planned Exposition—Fragmented Versus
Elaborated Structure'

'On-Line Interaction (Fragmented Structure)'

Positive Features
   Direct questions
   Contractions
   Fragmentary sentence
   Short negation
   Informal postpositions
   Demonstratives
   Discourse conjuncts
   Discourse verbal connectors
   Hedges

'Planned Exposition (Elaborated Structure)'

Negative Features
   Postposition/noun ratio
   Relative clauses
   Attributive adjectives
   Sentence length
   Nonfinite clause
   Third person pronouns
   Noun complementation
   Possessive marker

speech level marker on the sentence-final verb or not ending in a verb at all. Discourse conjuncts and discourse verbal connectors are generalized devices for connecting clauses without specifying a particular logical relation between them. Hedges are related to these features in that they mark words or propositions as being imprecise.

Direct questions indicate an associated interactive function on this dimension. (First person pronouns are often omitted in declarative sentences, and second person pronouns are often omitted in questions, so these pronominal forms are not highly associated with interactiveness in Korean.) Demonstratives are somewhat related in that they can mark direct, deictic reference to the situation of communication. Finally, two features have conventional associations with colloquial, informal language: short negation and informal postpositions. These forms are considered inappropriate when used in formal written prose or formal spoken situations.

In contrast, the negative features are associated with an explicit and elaborated presentation of information. Many of these features reflect clause complexity and various types of structural embedding: relative clauses, sentence length, nonfinite clauses, and noun complementation. Attributive adjectives, relative clauses, noun complementation, and possessive (genitive) noun phrases are all devices for specifying and elaborating the identity of nouns. Postposition/noun ratio indicates the number of nouns that are explicitly marked for their case roles, since postpositions are frequently omitted in Korean. Because third person pronouns and genitive case markers are recent developments in Korean, they are rarely used; when they do occur, they function to specify referents explicitly.

Thus Dimension 1 reflects an opposition between reduced, fragmented structures and elaborated, explicit structures. In addition, the positive features show an association between interactiveness and fragmented structure. Figure 7.1 shows that these features are most common in Korean conversation, especially private conversations, but also in television drama and public conversations. This figure plots the mean Dimension 1 score for each register. A large positive Dimension 1 score reflects frequent occurrences of the positive features—direct questions, contractions, fragmentary sentences, and so on—together with markedly infrequent occurrences of the negative features—postpositions, relative clauses, attributive adjectives, and so forth. The large positive scores for the conversational registers thus reflect their frequent use of interactive and fragmented features together with the relative absence of structural elaboration features. These registers are all overtly interactive, and they are produced on-line, accounting for the fragmented and reduced structure. Text Sample 1 from a private conversation illustrates some of these characteristics.

Text Sample 1: Private Conversation

   1– ppalli wase ancayo.
   2– kamanhi isse.
   3– wuli cejswussi selkeci kkuthnakellang kathi chicako.
   4– ton isseyo, [name]-ssi?
   5– ton epse. ton epse.
   6– kulem senpaj-hanthej kkweyaci.
   7– mwe mathkil ke epsna? sikyej matha, sikyej-na.
   8– sikyej-to an chako osin ke kathaj.
   9– mwe, amukes-to epseyo?
10– phalcci isse, phalcci.
11– palcci hoksi ala, palcci?
12– phalcci isse. kuke mathkimyen twajci.
13– an twajyo.
14– an twajmyen 'contact lens' mathkitunci.
15– hahaha.

   1– come here and sit.
   2– hold on.
   3– (let's) play (cards) after our 'sister-in-law' finishes dishwashing.
   4– do you have money, [name]?
   5– no cash. no cash.
   6– then, borrow from your (senior) alumnus.
   7– do you have collateral? take a watch, watch.
   8– it seems as if she doesn't even have a watch.
   9– you don't have anything?
10– oh, (she) has a bracelet on, bracelet.
11– do you know about an ankle bracelet, an ankle bracelet?

12– she has a bracelet. that will do.
13– I won't do that.
14– if not, (how about) depositing your contact lenses?
15– hahaha.

This short sample has four direct questions (4, 7, 9, 11); five fragmentary sentences

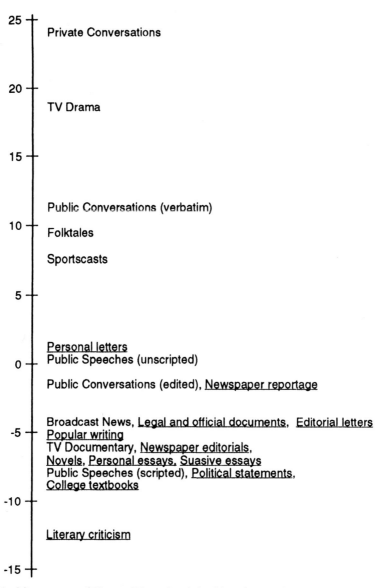

FIGURE 7.1. Mean scores of Korean Dimension 1 for 22 registers: 'On-Line Interaction versus Planned Exposition—(fragmented versus elaborated structure)' (speech/writing difference: $F = 78.39$, $p < .0001$, $r^2 = 34.6\%$).

(3, 7, 10, 11, and 14); short negation forms in lines 8, 13, and 14; and an informal postposition in line 6.

At the other extreme on Dimension 1 are written expository registers (e.g., literary criticism, college textbooks, essays, editorials) plus spoken informational monologues (e.g., prepared speeches, television documentaries). The large negative scores for these registers reflect frequent use of postpositions (explicit case marking), relative clauses, attributive adjectives, long sentences, and so on (the negative features), plus markedly infrequent questions, contractions, fragmentary sentences, and so forth (the positive features).

The functional basis of Dimension 1 is complex. On the one hand, Dimension 1 represents a distinction between interactive and noninteractive discourse. However, this function alone cannot account for the distribution of registers seen in Figure 7.1. For example, folktales and sportscasts are minimally interactive yet still have relatively large positive scores; edited public conversations are as interactive as nonedited public conversations, but the edited versions have a negative score. In addition, many of the linguistic features co-occurring on this dimension are not directly associated with interactiveness. Rather, several positive features indicate a reduced and fragmented structure (e.g., contractions, fragmentary sentences, hedges, and generalized discourse connectors); these features reflect the pressures of real-time production. In contrast, frequent use of the negative features, which are associated with structural elaboration and explicitness, reflects careful production circumstances having extensive time for planning and revision. The label 'On-line Interaction versus Planned Exposition—Fragmented versus Elaborated Structure' captures the complex functional bases of this dimension.[2]

This dimension is closely related to the mode difference between speech and writing. Only spoken registers, given without underscored letters in Figure 7.1, have positive scores reflecting 'on-line interaction'. In contrast, the written registers, which are underscored in Figure 7.1, all have negative scores, reflecting their 'planned elaborated exposition'. (Personal letters have a score near 0.) The overall mean score for speech is 6.6, while the mean score for writing is −5.8. The F-score at the bottom of Figure 7.1 shows that this is a significant and important difference, with 34.6 percent of the variation among dimension scores being predicted simply by knowing whether a text is spoken or written.

At the same time, there is considerable overlap among some spoken and written registers. In particular, scripted speech—public speeches, television documentaries, and broadcast news—shares many of the features of elaborated written exposition. This characterization reflects the fact that these registers originate in writing, even though they are eventually realized in speech.

5.2. Korean Dimension 2: 'Overt Versus Implicit Logical Cohesion'

The positive features on Dimension 2, listed in Table 7.4, relate primarily to textual cohesion, specifying the logical relations among propositions. Clause connectors and conjuncts clearly have this function, including explanative connectors (translated as 'because'), explanative conjuncts ('therefore'), general 'discourse' connectors ('and', 'but', 'by the way'), coordinate connectors ('and-then'), and conditional

TABLE 7.4   Co-Occurring Linguistic Features
on Korean Dimension 2: 'Overt Versus Implicit
Logical Cohesion'

'Overt Logical Cohesion'

Positive Features
   Explanative clause connectors
   Subject markers
   Explanative conjuncts
   Adverbial subordination
   Discourse verbal connectors
   Action verbs
   Coordinate clause connectors
   Coreferential expressions
   Manner adverbs
   Postposition/noun ratio
   Conditional clause connectors

'Implicit Logical Cohesion'

Negative Features
   Nouns
   Possessive markers
   Passive constructions
   Derived adjectives

---

connectors ('if'). Adverbial subordination similarly specifies a particular relation between the main clause and subordinate clause propositions (e.g., 'when . . .', 'as . . .', 'in order to . . .'). These devices result in an explicit marking of logical cohesion, overtly specifying the relations among clauses.

The co-occurrence of coreferential expressions with these positive features shows that there is a high degree of lexical cohesion—referring to the same referents repeatedly—associated with the explicit marking of logical cohesion. Action verbs, manner adverbs, and subject markers indicate that this is an active, clause-oriented style. (Subject marking, as opposed to topic marking, is the typical case in transitive clauses.) Postposition/noun ratio measures the proportion of nouns that have overt case markers, representing another way in which the logical relations among discourse entities are explicitly specified. Together, these positive features indicate highly cohesive text, with frequent active, transitive clauses; repeated references to the same participants; and an overt specification of the logical relations among clauses and phrases.

The negative features are fewer in number, but they show a nominal as opposed to a verbal style (frequent nouns, possessives, adjectives), and a frequent use of passive clauses as opposed to active, transitive clauses. Most importantly, no features mark logical relations among the negative features. This linguistic pattern indicates that highly nominal, passive texts tend to rely on an implicit system of cohesion in Korean, requiring readers and listeners to infer the logical relations among discourse entities for themselves.

The distribution of registers along Dimension 2, shown in Figure 7.2, is somewhat surprising. Spoken folktales have by far the largest positive score, reflecting

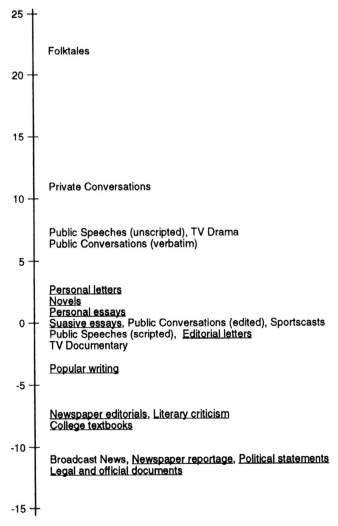

FIGURE 7.2. Mean scores of Korean Dimension 2 for 22 registers: 'Overt versus Implicit Logical Cohesion' (speech/writing difference: $F = 61.50$, $p < .0001$, $r^2 = 29.4\%$).

the most extensive overt marking of logical cohesion. Private conversations also have a relatively large positive score on this dimension, followed by public speeches, television drama, and public conversations. At the other extreme are several written expository registers, such as legal and official documents, newspaper reportage, and political statements, together with (scripted) broadcast news.

It is interesting that the explicit marking of logical and lexical cohesion (as measured by these features) does not correlate with the situational requirements for explicit, unambiguous meaning in Korean. For example, legal and official documents should be maximally clear and unambiguous, so that they can provide the basis for legal and official decisions. Despite this requirement, the distribution here shows that there is little overt marking of logical relations in this register, reflecting a reliance on other mechanisms for cohesion (such as punctuation and the implicit relations underlying adjacent clauses).

In sum, Dimension 2 represents the overt marking of logical cohesion versus other discourse organizations that rely on implicit relations among propositions; the label 'Overt versus Implicit Logical Cohesion' reflects this interpretation.[3] Extensive use of overt cohesion devices is common in texts that present a sequence of events, to specify the relations among the events (especially in folktales, conversations, television drama). Edited registers use less cohesive devices than corresponding unedited registers; thus compare edited and unedited public conversations, and scripted and unscripted public speeches. Similarly, spoken registers show a much greater tendency to use overt cohesive devices than written registers. Thus the mean score for speech is 5.6, while the mean score for writing is -4.8; this is a significant and important difference (F-score $= 61.5$; $r^2 = 29.4$ percent). Apparently the careful planning and editing possible in written registers allows a more integrated, implicit specification of relations among clauses, and readers have ample opportunity to infer logical relations in a written text; thus writing tends to omit overt surface markers of cohesion. In contrast, listeners require an overt specification of logical relations since they have less time for comprehension, and speakers also have less opportunity for an integrated, implicit specification of relations during production; thus many spoken registers show frequent use of these features.

5.3. Korean Dimension 3: 'Overt Expression of Personal Stance'

Dimension 3 comprises several features reflecting the personal attitudes and feelings of speakers and authors, as shown in Table 7.5. Hedges and emphatics measure the degree of commitment to a proposition: weak commitment in the case of hedges (e.g., *ama* 'perhaps', *keuj* 'almost') and strong commitment in the case of emphat-

TABLE 7.5   Co-Occurring Linguistic Features
on Korean Dimension 3: 'Overt Expression
of Personal Stance'

Positive Features
  Verb complementation
  Emphatics
  Attitudinal expressions
  Psychological verbs
  Hedges
  Short negation
  Embedded or indirect questions
  First person pronouns
  Noun complementation

Negative Features
  Nouns

ics (e.g., *punmyenghi* 'obviously', *chamulo* 'really'). These forms co-occur, even though they mark opposite attitudes; together, they contrast with the absence of any forms marking degree of commitment. Attitudinal expressions, or delimiters, are also grouped on this dimension (e.g., *-(i)ntul* 'even', *-(i)ya* 'as far as'). Private verbs and verb complements often occur together; private verbs are used to express a variety of personal feelings and attitudes (e.g., *ujsimhata* 'doubt', *musewehata* 'fear'). First person personal pronouns co-occur with these other features, indicating that these are the personal attitudes of the speaker/writer. (The only negative feature is nouns, apparently reflecting the highly nominal style of informational exposition, which has a minimal marking of personal stance.)

As Figure 7.3 shows, Dimension 3 features are most pronounced in those registers having personal expression as a primary purpose: private conversations, personal letters, and personal essays. Interestingly, these features are even more frequent in television drama than in private conversations. This distribution apparently reflects the dramatic nature of television dialogue, where personal feelings and attitudes are exaggerated to stimulate audience interest, resulting in a style that is even more *real* than real life!

The negative extreme of this dimension might be characterized as *faceless*, that is, a presentation of information with no acknowledgement of personal attitude. Figure 7.3 shows that legal documents and newspaper reportage have the largest negative scores. Legal documents have no acknowledged author, being a direct statement of laws or regulations (rather than opinion regarding those laws). Newspaper reportage is similar to (spoken) news broadcasts, television documentaries, and sportscasts in that it is a direct reportage of events and situations, purportedly factual rather than reflective of an individual's attitudes. It is interesting that political statements have a relatively large negative score on this dimension; even though these texts express individual opinions, they apparently adopt a direct, faceless stance.

In sum, Dimension 3 can be interpreted as marking the 'Overt Expression of Personal Stance'. Although Figure 7.3 shows that spoken registers are more likely to mark personal stance than written registers, it also shows that both speakers and writers can adopt a personal stance when it fits their purposes (as in conversation and letters); and that both speakers and writers can suppress all overt markers of stance when a faceless style is considered to be appropriate (as in broadcast news and press reportage).

5.4. Korean Dimension 4: 'Narrative Versus Non-Narrative Discourse'

Only a few features co-occur on Korean Dimension 4 (see Table 7.6), and their interpretation is straightforward. Three of the four positive features are verbal. These features mark a primary focus on the temporal succession of past events, or narrative discourse: past tense reflects the focus on past time, temporal adverbs indicate the temporal ordering among events, and action verbs are used to narrate active events (as opposed to static description or explanation). Type/token ratio co-

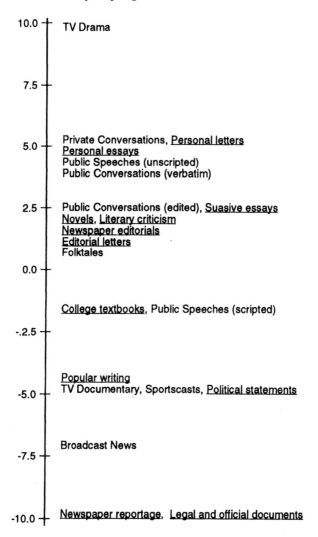

FIGURE 7.3. Mean scores of Korean Dimension 3 for 22 registers: 'Overt Expression of Personal Stance' (speech/writing difference: $F = 8.66$, $p < .005$, $r^2 = 5.5\%$).

occurs with these features, indicating that narrative discourse in Korean tends to have more varied vocabulary than non-narrative discourse.

Only two features have large negative weights on Dimension 4: present tense and formal conjuncts. These features are used to provide static descriptions and explanations, emphasizing the logical rather than temporal relations among clauses.

As Figure 7.4 shows, novels and folktales have two of the largest positive scores on Dimension 4. These registers are primarily narrative, marked by very frequent past tense verbs, time adverbs, and dynamic verbs. Text Sample 2 illustrates these features in a novel.

TABLE 7.6   Co-Occurring Linguistic Features
on Korean Dimension 4: 'Narrative Versus
Non-narrative Discourse'

'Narrative Discourse'
Positive Features
Past tense
Type/token ratio
Time adverbs
Dynamic verbs
'Non-narrative Discourse'
Negative Features
Nonpast tense
Formal conjuncts

Text Sample 2: Novel (*Yengwung sitaj,* a novel about the Korean War)

putulewun 'engine' soli-wa hamkkej catongcha-nun yathumakhan entek kil-lo cepetulessta. kajcen cikhwu Pukhan-ejse tajlyang-ulo nohojkhan chalyangtul-un cinan myech tal tonganej keuj somotojepelintejta twukkepkej ancun hukmenci-man takkanajmyen kumsaj tulenanun santtushan kwukpangsajk chachej-lo poa ujyongkwun-i kajiptojn twi-ej sajlo nohojkhan yenhapkwun-uj 'jeep' cha kathassta.

The car approached a road on a hill with a soft engine sound. Cars captured by the North Korean army during the first stage of the war were almost consumed, but this car had a bright brown color right underneath a thin layer of dirt: this jeep must have been captured from the allied forces very recently after the voluntary corps entered the war.

In addition to the exclusive use of past tense forms, this sample illustrates the extreme lexical diversity typical of Korean fiction. Actually none of the words in this sample is a repeated form; even 'car', which is repeated in the English translation, is referred to as *catongcha, chalyangtul,* and *'jeep' cha.*

In contrast, expository prose in Korean shows extensive lexical repetition (a low type/token ratio) in addition to a nearly exclusive use of present tense and static verb forms. Sample 3 illustrates these characteristics from a college textbook on statistics. The short sample shows several repetitions of *pyenin* 'variable', *yenkwuca* 'researcher', *yenkwu* 'research', and *toklip* 'independent'. These are all technical terms, which tend to be repeated to preserve the exact meaning (as opposed to the alternation among semantically related, but distinct, terms in narration).

Text Sample 3: College Textbook (a college textbook on statistics)

silhem yenkwu-ejse yenkwuca-ka imujlo cocakhanun pyenin-ul toklip pyenin-ila hako i toklip pyenin-ej yenghyang-ul patnuntako sajngkakhanun, yenkwuca-uj kwansim-uj pyenin-ul hunhi congsok pyenin-ilako pulunta. kulena kiswulcek yenkwu-ej isseseto pilok yenkwuca-ka yenkwuhakoca hanun pyenin-ul ujtocekulo cocak thongcejhal swu-nun epsciman . . .

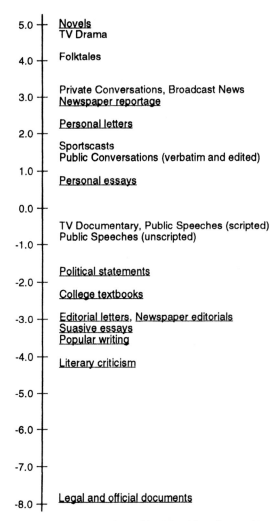

FIGURE 7.4. Mean scores of Korean Dimension 4 for 22 registers: 'Narrative versus Non-Narrative Discourse' (speech/writing difference: $F = 26.32$, $p < .0001$, $r^2 = 15.1\%$).

In an experimental study, the variable that researchers can manipulate at will is called independent variable, and the variable that is affected by the independent variable and that is the focus of the research is often called dependent variable. But even in a descriptive study, where researchers cannot manipulate variables at will . . .

Figure 7.4 shows that a number of registers besides novels and folktales are markedly narrative in orientation. Television drama has a positive score almost as high as that of novels, private conversations have a large positive score, and public conversations have a moderately large positive score. These characterizations indicate that narration is an integral part of Korean conversation. The relatively large positive score for personal letters shows that narration plays a key role in all personal, interactive discourse in Korean, whether spoken or written. In addition, informational reportage is marked for its reliance on narration, including both spoken (broadcast news and sportscasts) and written (newspaper reportage).

The complete exclusion of narration appears to be restricted to written registers in Korean. Figure 7.4 shows that spoken informational registers—television documentary and public speeches—are relatively unmarked on this dimension, having only a slight preference for non-narrative over narrative discourse forms. In contrast, several written registers are distinguished by the marked absence of narrative forms. These registers include several types of informational exposition, for example, textbooks, editorials, and literary criticism. The most extreme case is represented by legal and official documents, which show a nearly exclusive reliance on static, present tense verb forms, together with extensive repetition of technical vocabulary.

In sum, Dimension 4 reflects the reliance on narrative versus non-narrative discourse organizations. In Korean, this distinction has some relation to physical mode differences: the frequent use of narrative forms is common in both spoken and written registers, but the exclusive reliance on non-narrative forms is found primarily in written, expository registers.

5.5. Korean Dimension 5

The functional basis of Dimension 5 is not clear, so only a tentative interpretation will be given here. Table 7.7 presents the co-occurring linguistic features on the dimension, and Figure 7.5 plots the distribution of registers. Figure 7.5 shows that the primary distinction along this dimension is between sportscasts and the other registers. The large positive score for sportscasts reflects very frequent occurrences of declarative sentences, present tense verbs, copular verbs, formal sentence endings, adversative conjuncts (translated 'but' or 'however'), and short sentences. The other two sentence types included in the study (interrogative and imperative) are quite rare; imperatives were dropped from the factor analysis because they were too infrequent, and interrogatives are restricted primarily to the conversational registers. Thus the frequency of declarative sentences essentially represents the total frequency of sentences in a text, and sentence length occurs in a complementary distribution to declarative sentences (i.e., many, short sentences versus relatively few, long sentences). Figure 7.5 shows that these characteristics are apparently well

TABLE 7.7   Co-Occurring Linguistic Features
on Korean Dimension 5: Tentative Interpretation:
'On-Line Reportage of Events'

Positive Features
Declarative sentences
Nonpast tense
Copular verbs (-*ita*)
"Formal" sentence ending
Adversative conjuncts
Negative Features
Sentence length

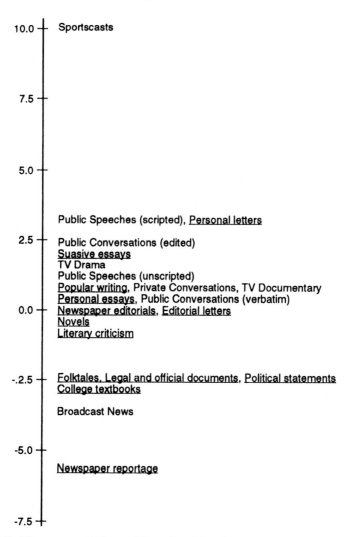

FIGURE 7.5. Mean scores of Korean Dimension 5 for 22 registers. Tentative interpretation: 'On-Line Reportage of Events' (speech/writing difference: $F = 9.68$, $p < .005$, $r^2 = 6.1\%$).

suited to the on-line reportage of events in progress, as in sportscasts, suggesting the tentative label 'On-Line Reportage of Events'.

At the negative extreme on Figure 7.5 is newspaper reportage, with registers such as broadcast news, college textbooks, and political statements having moder-ately large negative scores. Newspaper reportage and broadcast news were shown in the last section to rely on a past tense narration of events, and thus it is not surprising that they should be marked here by the absence of present tense forms. The charac-terization along Dimension 5 shows further that these registers have relatively few sentences that are often quite long, and that they rely on lexical rather than copular verbs for their reportage.

Most registers are relatively undistinguished along this dimension, however, and the scores for some registers seem at odds with the interpretation of on-line reportage. For example, it is not clear why suasive essays, personal letters, or scripted public speeches have moderately large positive scores, since they do not describe events in progress and are not produced on-line. A careful analysis of these features in particular texts from these registers is thus needed for a more satisfactory interpretation of Dimension 5.

5.6. Korean Dimension 6: 'Honorification'

Although relatively few features co-occur on Dimension 6, they are readily interpretable (see Table 7.8). Honorific expressions are used to express deference to the addressee or the person spoken about. Humble expressions are particular pronominal forms (first and second person) and particular verbs used with first person pronouns; these forms also show deference to the addressee relative to the speaker/writer. Speech levels (sentence-final particles) are yet another marker of deference; formal sentence endings (speech level 1) show the greatest deference to the addressee. First person pronouns are commonly omitted in Korean sentences; when they are included, they commonly co-occur with humble forms to mark explicit deference of the speaker/writer to the addressee.

From the distribution of registers seen in Figure 7.6, three main considerations seem to be involved in the extensive use of honorification devices: the existence of a particular addressee, the social distance between addressor and addressee, and a public setting. Thus apart from personal letters, all written registers have negative scores on Dimension 6, reflecting the relative absence of honorification devices. This characteristic is apparently due to the lack of a particular addressee in these registers, making the use of honorifics and self-humbling expressions less important. Personal letters are the only written register included in the Korean study that is addressed to an individual reader, and thus letters show extensive use of honorification.

The influence of a specific addressee can also be seen from a comparison of parallel spoken and written registers: verbatim and edited public conversations, unscripted and scripted public speeches, and broadcasts and newspaper reportage.

TABLE 7.8   Co-Occurring Linguistic Features
on Korean Dimension 6: 'Honorification'

Positive Features
Honorifics
Humble expressions
"Formal" sentence ending
Time adverbs
First person pronouns

[No negative features]

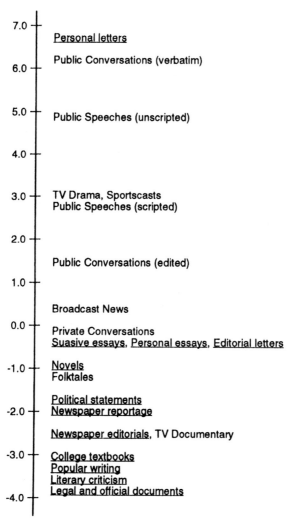

FIGURE 7.6. Mean scores of Korean Dimension 6 for 22 registers: 'Honorification' (speech/writing difference: $F = 35.42$, $p < .0001$, $r^2 = 19.3\%$).

In each of these cases, the spoken register is presented to a live audience: an individual addressee in public conversations (interviews), a physically present audience in the case of public speeches, and the television audience in the case of broadcasts. As the addressee becomes less identifiable across these three spoken registers, the use of honorification becomes less frequent. Thus public conversations have one of the largest positive scores here, while broadcast news is essentially unmarked. In addition, the written counterpart in each of these cases has considerably less honorification than the spoken counterpart; the honorific and humbling devices have apparently been removed by editors in the written registers, in recognition that the published version is being addressed to a wider, less specified audience.

Surprisingly, private conversations show much less use of honorific and humbling devices than (written) personal letters or public conversations. Private conversations are by definition not public, and the participants are commonly friends or peers. In contrast, public conversations (such as live interviews, radio talk shows, parliamentary hearings) occur in front of a live audience, and the individual participants are typically unacquainted. The public setting and relatively large social distance seem to be the main factors causing the greater use of honorification in public conversations. The personal letters in this study were addressed primarily to relatives across generational boundaries (e.g., son to mother, son-in-law to mother-in-law, daughter to mother, daughter-in-law to mother-in-law), so that the social distance is relatively large (in comparison to that in conversations among peers). In addition, a written letter is public in the sense that it is permanent, and this characteristic apparently also contributes to the careful use of honorific devices in this register.

It is interesting that even television drama shows a considerably greater use of honorification than private conversation. As with Dimension 3 ('Stance'), the characterization here identifies a difference between the perception of what conversational interactions *should* be like (i.e., television drama) and actual conversations. In addition, this difference reflects the fact that television drama occurs in a public forum; that is, these are private conversations viewed by a wide public audience. For this reason, they show considerably greater use of honorific devices than truly private conversations.

In sum, Dimension 6 shows the importance of social relations and setting in the characterization of Korean registers. The honorification system is one of the most studied aspects of Korean, and it is one of the most noticeable and problematic areas for foreign learners of the language. The analysis here confirms the importance of this system as a separate dimension of register variation in Korean.

6. Conclusion

In this chapter, six underlying dimensions of register variation in Korean are identified and discussed in terms of their discourse functions. The six dimensions are 'On-Line Interaction Versus Planned Exposition—Fragmented Versus Elaborated Structure', 'Overt Versus Implicit Logical Cohesion', 'Overt Expression of Personal Stance', 'Narrative versus Non-Narrative Discourse', 'On-Line Reportage of Events', and 'Honorification'.

Two of the dimensions (Dimensions 1 and 2) are related to informational aspects, and two others (Dimensions 3 and 6) are related to the presentation of self. Dimension 4 reflects the use of narrative discourse structures. The interpretation of Dimension 5 is problematic and requires further investigation.

This division of discourse concerns is different from that in English in interesting ways. Korean has two dimensions relating primarily to the presentation of self: in relation to the message (Dimension 3: 'Stance') and in relation to the addressee

(Dimension 6: 'Honorification'). In contrast, no dimensions in English have the presentation of self as their primary underlying function. However, stance is an integral part of several English dimensions, including Dimension 1: 'Involved Versus Informational Production', Dimension 4: 'Persuasion', and possibly Dimension 6: 'On-Line Informational Elaboration'; see Biber (1988). This difference reflects the different cultural priorities of Korean and English. Korean society has a well-established hierarchical structure, and that social organization is reflected in the linguistic characteristics of the underlying dimensions.

In contrast, Korean has only one dimension with the primary function of distinguishing informational, structurally elaborated exposition from other types of discourse (Dimension 1: 'On-Line Interaction Versus Planned Exposition'), while English has three such dimensions (Dimension 1: 'Involved Versus Informational Production', Dimension 3: 'Explicit Versus Situation-Dependent Reference', and Dimension 5: 'Abstract Style'). It is not the case, however, that Korean dimensions are insensitive to the mode difference between speech and writing. In fact, the spoken and written modes are more clearly distinguished in Korean than in English. Korean is similar to English, Tuvaluan, and Somali in that no dimension defines an absolute dichotomy between spoken and written registers; rather, there is some overlap on each dimension, as certain spoken registers have relatively literate characteristics, and certain written registers have relatively oral characteristics. However, most Korean dimensions show some relation to the spoken and written modes. Even Korean dimensions such as 'Narrative versus Non-Narrative Discourse', 'Personal Stance', and 'Honorification' distinguish between spoken interactive registers at one extreme and written informational registers at the other, although the functional underpinnings of these dimensions have no necessary relation to speech and writing. In contrast, the distribution of registers along comparable English dimensions relating to narration and persuasion shows no relation to spoken/written differences.

This difference between the two languages might be explained by reference to their histories. Diachronic register studies of English (Biber and Finegan 1989) and Somali (Biber and Hared 1991, this volume) suggest three stages in the evolution of written registers relative to spoken registers: (1) when written registers first enter a language, they are already quite distinct linguistically from spoken registers; (2) in the early history of written registers, they evolve to become even more sharply distinguished from spoken registers; (3) subsequently, written registers undergo a gradual transition toward more oral linguistic characteristics, while it is likely that many spoken registers gradually evolve toward more literate characterizations. Although Somali has a very short history of literacy, stage 2 trends are already well in evidence. English, on the other hand, passed through stage 2 in the eighteenth and early nineteenth centuries; since that time, English written registers have been evolving toward more oral linguistic characterizations. (It is not clear whether stage 3 is peculiar to English or common in other languages with a long literate tradition.) Korean appears to be in stage 2, although no diachronic register data are available at present. Positing this diachronic stage, however, can account for the relatively sharp distinctions that exist synchronically among spoken and written registers in Korean, in contrast to the considerable overlap among spoken and written registers in English.

Research tracing the diachronic development of written registers in Korean, from the introduction of popular literacy (c. 1900) to the present, would help to explain the current differences among spoken and written registers. In addition, multidimensional register analyses of other languages are needed to determine the extent to which the patterns observed in Korean, English, Tuvaluan, and Somali are shared cross-linguistically. The present study identifies and interprets six dimensions of register variation in Korean, laying the foundation for future research in these areas.

Notes

1. Six factors were extracted as the optimal solution in this case. Together, these factors account for approximately 58 percent of the total shared variance. The factorial solution was subsequently rotated using a Promax rotation.

2. Kim (1990) originally proposes the label 'Informal Interaction Versus Explicit Elaboration' for this dimension, emphasizing interactiveness over production circumstances.

3. Kim (1990) proposes the label 'Discourse Chaining versus Discourse Fragmentation' for Dimension 2.

References

Besnier, Niko. 1988. "The Linguistic Relationships of Spoken and Written Nukulaelae Registers." *Language* 64:707–36.

Biber, Douglas. 1986. "Spoken and Written Textual Dimensions in English: Resolving the Contradictory Findings." *Language* 62:384–414.

———. 1988. *Variation Across Speech and Writing*. Cambridge: Cambridge University Press.

Biber, Douglas, and Edward Finegan. 1989. "Drift and the Evolution of English Style: A History of Three Genres." *Language* 65:487–517.

Biber, Douglas, and Mohamed Hared. 1991. "Literacy in Somali: Linguistic Consequences." *Annual Review of Applied Linguistics* 12:260–82.

Choi, Yeon Hee. 1988. *Textual Coherence in English and Korean: An Analysis of Argumentative Writing by American and Korean Students*. Ph.D. Dissertation, University of Illinois at Urbana-Champaign.

Hwang, Shin Ja Joo. 1981. *Aspects of Korean Narration*. Ph.D. Dissertation, University of Texas at Arlington.

Kim, Yong-Jin. 1990. *Register Variation in Korean: A Corpus-Based Study*. Ph.D. Dissertation, University of Southern California.

Lee, Hyo Sang, and Sandra A. Thompson. 1987. "A Discourse Account of the Korean Accusative Marker." In Hyo Sang Lee and Sandra A. Thompson, ed., *Santa Barbara Papers in Linguistics*. Vol. I. *Korean: Papers and Discourse Data*. Santa Barbara: University of California at Santa Barbara. Pp. 23–49.

Lee, Won-Pyo. 1989. *Referential Choice in Korean Discourse: Cognitive and Social Perspec-*

tives, Ph.D. Dissertation, University of Southern California.
Lukoff, Fred. 1986. "The Use of Tenses in Korean Written Narrative." In Nam-Kil Kim, ed., *Studies in Korean Language and Linguistics.* Los Angeles: East Asian Study Center, University of Southern California. Pp. 1–36.

8

Linguistic Correlates of the Transition to Literacy in Somali: Language Adaptation in Six Press Registers

Douglas Biber and Mohamed Hared

1. Introduction

Stemming from a thought-provoking essay written by Goody and Watt (1963), many studies over the last three decades have investigated the social and intellectual consequences resulting from the introduction of literacy in a society (e.g., Goody 1977, Ong 1982, Scribner and Cole 1981). Few studies, though, have actually investigated the linguistic consequences of literacy—that is, the linguistic changes that result from the introduction of written registers in a language. One such study is Reder's (1981) analysis of spoken and written Vai (carried out as part of Scribner and Cole's study). Since Vai has an indigenous literacy that is transmitted apart from formal schooling, Reder could address the question of whether writing itself has any effect on the speech of literate adults. He found that there are systematic differences between speech and writing in Vai (e.g., certain medial consonants are deleted more frequently in speech, and indefinite noun phrases occur more frequently in writing), and that in their speech, literate adults use the forms associated with writing more frequently than nonliterate adults. A second study that directly addresses linguistic consequences of literacy is Kalmár's (1985) description of Inuktitut (in Canada). He found evidence there that new linguistic forms are developing under the influence of written language; in particular, true subordinate forms (complement clauses and relative clauses) seem to be developing in the written language at present.

Studies of language modernization, adaptation, and standardization also deal indirectly with the linguistic consequences of literacy. Ferguson (1968) proposes three stages of "language development" that a newly literate language can pass

Support for this research project has been provided by the National Science Foundation, grant BNS-8811720. We would like to thank Ann Beck and Ed Finegan for their helpful comments on earlier drafts of this paper.

through: graphization, standardization, and modernization. Graphization is the process of adopting a writing system, including spelling and orthographic conventions. Standardization is the process by which one variety of a language gains widespread acceptance as the "best" form of the language. (This stage apparently includes selection of a norm and codification of standard forms in grammars and dictionaries.) Finally, modernization refers to extensions that are required to meet the communicative needs of a modern society. Modernization has two aspects: expansion of the lexicon and "the development of new styles and forms of discourse."

Coulmas (1989a) discusses related phenomena under the rubric of *language adaptation,* which refers to language change in response to the changing communicative needs of a speech community. These changes can be completely natural or influenced by deliberate intervention (due to language planning). Coulmas notes that especially in situations where social development proceeds more quickly than language change (as, for example, with war or colonization), the communicative demands of a speech community can exceed the functionality of their language; the language then must either "adapt" or "decay."

Although Ferguson identified two separate domains of linguistic change—lexical and stylistic—nearly all empirical studies of language adaptation or modernization have focused exclusively on lexical processes (see, e.g., the papers in Coulmas 1989b). There have, however, been related studies in historical linguistics that focus on grammatical considerations. For example, Romaine (1980) analyzes the development of WH-relative clause markers in Scots English, showing how they entered the language in the most complex literate varieties. Rissanen (1986) describes the differing development of periphrastic *do* in formal written registers (e.g., chronicles) versus speech-based registers (e.g., sermons and records of meetings). Biber and Finegan (1989) trace the linguistic evolution of essays, fiction, and letters in English from 1650 to the present, describing linguistic developments associated with the trends toward wider literate audiences and more popular purposes. All of these studies describe ways that languages evolve in response to the introduction or development of literate varieties.[1]

The notion that a language can evolve or adapt runs counter to the commonly accepted tenet that all languages are "equal." This tenet can be traced to Sapir (1921:219), who claimed, "When it comes to linguistic form, Plato walks with the Macedonian swineherd, Confucius with the head-hunting savage of Assam." Sapir further discusses the relation between cultural change and linguistic change, claiming that languages do *not* develop as a consequence of cultural or social changes (pp. 218–19). He defines "the drift of culture" as "history, . . . a complex series of changes in society's selected inventory," and "the drift of language" as "changes in formal expression," excluding content and lexical changes. Sapir then goes on to assert that "the drifts of language and of culture [are] noncomparable and unrelated processes." Since the time of Sapir, linguists generally hold to this view that all languages are equivalent in structural complexity and that languages therefore do not evolve as a result of external stimuli (such as the introduction of literacy).

Only a few studies have described situations in which a functional expansion of a language has resulted in the addition of new linguistic structures (e.g., Kalmár 1985, Coulmas 1989a:18). Hymes (1974:73), however, raises another possibility that is probably more typical: that a language can change "even though the differences may not appear in the structure of the language within the limits of the usual description. The same formal linguistic system, as usually described, may be part of different, let us say, *socio*linguistic systems, whose natures cannot be assumed, but must be investigated." In a later programmatic article, Hymes (1984:44–45) argues that analysis of this kind of change is one of the two main tasks requiring attention within sociolinguistics. The first task is the systematic (synchronic) description of verbal repertoires, including "the organization of linguistic features in styles"; the second is "the description and analysis of the organization and change of verbal repertoires in relation to the main processes of societal evolution of our time . . . [analysis of] kinds of language in terms of function—the concomitants of use as a standard language, as a written language, as a literary language, as a language of religion, and the like." Ure (1982:7) stresses the importance of similar kinds of change:

> The register range of a language is one of the most immediate ways in which it responds to social change. The difference between developed and undeveloped languages (Ferguson, 1968) is fundamentally one of register range, and language contact, which contributes to language development . . . is mediated by particular registers. . . . This issue is concerned with both the pressures that make for change and the way in which these changes are realized linguistically.

The present chapter focuses on linguistic change of this type, represented here by shifts in the relative frequencies of co-occurring linguistic features across registers. We claim that the communicative-functional expansion associated with the introduction of written registers in a language will typically result in an expanded range of linguistic variability, reflecting new form/function associations.

We investigate these issues through an analysis of linguistic change in Somali written press registers over the first twenty years of their history. We include analysis of a broad range of lexical, morphological, and syntactic features, focusing on the variability in the relative use of forms rather than discrete formal alternants; and we contextualize our analysis relative to the range of spoken register variation in Somali, to focus on the impact of literacy following the addition of new written registers.

Specifically, we analyze the initial linguistic characteristics of written registers relative to spoken registers, the historical evolution of written registers, and the range of variability within and among written registers. Our findings show that (1) in their genesis, written registers are quite different from pre-existing spoken registers, and thus the mere addition of written registers greatly expanded the range of variability in Somali; (2) written registers have evolved over the last twenty years to become even more distinct from spoken registers, although there has not always been a steady progression away from oral linguistic characteristics; and (3) the variability among written registers has been reduced in some respects but expanded in others.

A Short Social History of Somali Literacy

The recent history of Somali (a Cushitic language spoken in Somalia, Kenya, Ethiopia, and Djibouti by five to six million people) makes it an ideal arena for the investigation of these issues: although it is currently the national language of Somalia, used for a large number of professional purposes, it has existed as a written language for less than twenty years. Somali had essentially no written tradition before 1972,[2] when the government of Somalia named it as the official language of the country. Before that time, Arabic, Italian, and English were used for official purposes. In a short time after 1972, however, there were many official and professional varieties of writing in Somali, including dictionaries, grammars, textbooks, newspapers, histories, biographies, storybooks, letters, and government documents. Because of the large number of written varieties that have been developed, coupled with the short time frame involved, Somali provides a unique opportunity for the study of the evolution of written language varieties relative to spoken varieties.

On 21 October 1972, Siyaad Barre, the president of Somalia, announced the development of a new standardized orthography for Somali and declared that Somali would be the sole official language of state, bureaucracy, and education from that time. This order was implemented rapidly. For example, mass literacy campaigns were conducted from October 1972 to January 1973 and from July 1974 to February 1975. During these periods, all students in the last two years of primary school and the first year of secondary school were recruited as literacy instructors. In all, approximately fifteen thousand instructors (including many civil servants and military officers) were active, some of them even traveling with nomadic villages.

By early 1973, there was a national newspaper (*Xiddigta Oktobaar*) and two periodical news magazines (*Waaga Cusub* and *Codka Macalinka*) in Somali. Folk stories, a number of nonfiction pamphlets, and government memos also appeared quickly in Somali, while textbooks and longer fictional or historical works began to appear after two or three years. Several studies describe the social processes involved in the introduction of mass literacy to Somali society (Andrzejewski 1974, Geshekter 1978, Laitin 1977, Mezei 1989). Ali and Gees (1979), Andrzejewski (1978, 1979), and Galeb (1979) further describe the overt language planning efforts needed to extend the lexical stock of Somali, to make it suitable for use in mathematics, science, politics, and so on. Taken together, these studies clearly document the remarkable implementation of literacy in Somalia. This rapid spread of native-language literacy makes Somali an ideal setting to study the linguistic evolution of written varieties and the extent to which a language can adapt in response to extended communicative demands.[3]

3. Three Dimensions of Variation Among Somali Registers

3.1. Linguistic Co-Occurrence and the Multidimensional Approach

The analysis here uses the multidimensional (MD) approach to genre or register variation (earlier referred to as the multifeature/multidimension approach), which is outlined in Biber (1986) and developed more fully in Biber (1988). The approach is based on the centrality of linguistic co-occurrence in analyses of text variation. Theoretical antecedents to this approach are provided by Ervin-Tripp (1972), Hymes (1974), and Brown and Fraser (1979). For example, Brown and Fraser (pp.

38–39) observe that it can be "misleading to concentrate on specific, isolated [linguistic] markers without taking into account systematic variations which involve the co-occurrence of sets of markers."

In the MD approach, linguistic co-occurrence is analyzed in terms of underlying *dimensions* of variation, with the explicit assumption that multiple dimensions will typically be required to adequately account for the range of linguistic variation among registers in a language. Dimensions are continuous scales of variation (rather than dichotomous distinctions), identified quantitatively by a factor analysis (rather than on an a priori functional basis).

Each dimension (or *factor*) comprises a group of linguistic features (e.g., nominalizations, adjectives, relative clauses) that co-occur with a markedly high frequency in texts. Factor analysis is used to identify the groups of linguistic features associated with each dimension. The interpretation of the factors as functional dimensions is based on the assumption that co-occurrence reflects shared function: that is, features co-occur frequently in texts because they serve shared, underlying communicative functions associated with the situational contexts of the texts. The functional interpretations are based on prior analyses of individual linguistic features and on the distribution of the co-occurring features across registers.

3.2. Somali Dimensions of Variation

In Biber and Hared (1992), we analyze the distribution of sixty-five linguistic features across 279 contemporary texts representing twenty-six spoken and written registers. The linguistic features are taken from eleven grammatical and functional categories: dependent clauses, main clause and verbal features, nominal features, pronouns, adjectival features, special lexical classes, features reflecting lexical choice, preverbal particles, reduced and interactive features, coordination, and focus constructions. The texts were taken from nine spoken registers (e.g., conversations, family and formal meetings, sermons, lectures) and seventeen written registers (e.g., press reportage, editorials, textbooks, fiction, folk stories, personal letters, memos).

Text samples of at least one thousand words were input into computers and then grammatically "tagged" by means of an interactive program written in Pascal.[4] After the tagging was completed, a second program compiled frequency counts of all linguistic features in each text; the counts were normed to a text length of one thousand words.

On the basis of a factor analysis of the distribution of linguistic features across the 279 texts, we identified and interpreted six basic dimensions of variation in Somali. In the present analysis we trace the evolution of written press registers with respect to the first three of these dimensions, summarized in Table 8.1. In the following paragraphs we provide brief descriptions of each of these dimensions, but readers are referred to Biber and Hared (1992) for a fuller account of the methodology, dimension interpretations, and analysis of the synchronic relations among Somali spoken and written registers.

Table 8.1 presents the major co-occurring features associated with the three dimensions analyzed here.[5] Features in parentheses are less strongly associated with the dimension in question (and not used in the computation of dimension scores; see later discussion), while features not listed for a dimension on Table 8.1 have negligible associations with that dimension.

Dimensions 1 and 3 on Table 8.1 consist of two groupings of features, labeled *positive* and *negative* features. Positive or negative grouping does not indicate the strength of the relationship; rather, these two groups represent sets of features that occur in a complementary pattern. That is, when the features in one group occur together frequently in a text, the features in the other group are markedly infrequent

TABLE 8.1   Summary of the First Three Dimensions Derived from Factor Analysis of 279 Contemporary Texts Representing 26 Spoken and Written Registers

Dimension 1	*Dimension 2*
Positive Features	Positive Features
Simple responses	Hapax legomena
Yes/no questions	Type-token ratio
Contrast-clause coordination (*eh*)	Nominalizations
Stance adjectives	Compound verbs
Contractions	Single case particle
Independent verbs	(Demonstrative relatives)
'What if' questions (*soo*)	(Clitic topic-coordination)
Time deictics	(Gerunds)
waa Focus markers	(Purpose clauses)
Main clauses	(Word length)
baa Focus markers	No Negative Features
Downtoners	
Imperatives	
WH questions	
(Conditional clauses)	
(Second person pronouns)	
(Verbless clauses)	
Negative Features	*Dimension 3*
Dependent clauses	Positive Features
Full relative clauses	Present tense
WH clefts (*waxaa*)	Predicative adjectives
ah Relative clauses	Possibility modals
Clause coordination (*oo*)	Concession conjuncts
Word length	(Verbless clauses)
Common nouns	(Attributive adjectives)
Derived adjectives	(Derived adjectives)
Phrase coordination (*iyo*)	(Impersonal particles)
-eed Genitives	(Conditional clauses)
Verb complements	(Dependent clauses)
(Case particle sequences)	Negative Features
(Single case particle)	Past tense
(T-unit length)	Proper nouns
(Agentive nouns)	Agentive nouns
(Compound nouns)	(Framing clauses)
(Attributive adjectives)	(Future modals)
(Purpose clauses)	(Speech act verbs)
(*ahaan* Adverbials)	

in that text, and vice versa. To interpret the dimensions, it is important to consider likely reasons for the complementary distribution of these two groups of features as well as the reasons for the co-occurrence pattern within each group.

3.2.1. DIMENSION 1: 'STRUCTURAL ELABORATION: INVOLVEMENT VERSUS EXPOSITION'

Consider the features grouped on Dimension 1 in Table 8.1. The positive features include nondeclarative, interactive, sentence types; interactive or involved lexical classes; main clause features; and other 'involved' features (e.g., contractions, conditional clauses, first and second person pronouns). The negative features include dependent clause features, nominal elaboration features, and elaborating phrases as marked by case particle sequences and single case particles.

The positive features tend to co-occur in texts. For example, when there are frequent questions and contrast-clause coordinators in a text, there also tend to be frequent stance adjectives, contractions, and so forth. Similarly, the negative features represent a set of co-occurring features; for example, when there are frequent total dependent clauses, relative clauses, and WH clefts in a text, there also tend to be high frequencies of common nouns, derived adjectives, and so on. The positive and negative groupings of features belong to a single dimension because they have a strong complementary relation to one another—when the positive features are markedly frequent in a text, the negative features are relatively absent from that text, and vice versa. Thus the interactive, involved, main-clause features (the positive features) have a complementary distribution to the dependent-clause and structural elaboration features (the negative features).

The interpretation of this dimension is facilitated by computing a Dimension 1 score for each text and then comparing the characterizations of spoken and written registers along this dimension. Dimension scores are computed by summing the frequencies of all major features associated with a dimension (in this case, all features not in parentheses).[6] Thus the Dimension 1 score for each text is computed by adding the frequencies of simple responses, yes/no questions, *eh*-coordination, stance adjectives, and so forth—the positive features—and then subtracting the frequencies of total dependent clauses, relative clauses, *waxaa* clefts, et cetera—the negative features (see Table 8.1). The resulting score provides an overall characterization of each text with respect to Dimension 1.

Table 8.2 presents the means and standard deviations of the Dimension 1 scores for twenty spoken and written registers. (This table also presents the scores for Dimensions 2 and 3, discussed later.) Conversations and family meetings have the largest positive Dimension 1 scores, reflecting very high frequencies of yes/no questions, stance adjectives, contractions, main clauses, and so on (the positive features on Dimension 1), together with markedly low frequencies of total dependent clauses, relative clauses, nouns, derived adjectives, and so forth (the negative features on Dimension 1). Informational written registers, such as editorials and news reportage, have the largest negative scores, reflecting the opposite linguistic characteristics: very high frequencies of dependent clauses, nouns, et cetera, plus low frequencies of yes/no questions, contractions, and so on. The two extremes of

TABLE 8.2   Synchronic (1987–89) Dimension Scores for 20 Spoken and Written Registers

Register	Dimension 1		Dimension 2		Dimension 3	
	Mean	Standard Deviation	Mean	Standard Deviation	Mean	Standard Deviation
Spoken						
Conversations	10.0	2.1	4.1	3.8	1.4	3.4
Family Meetings	9.1	1.0	4.0	2.5	5.2	2.2
Formal Meetings	−0.8	2.0	2.0	3.8	4.5	2.5
Quranic Sermons	2.4	2.1	3.0	3.8	1.4	3.2
University Lectures	−0.2	1.5	4.3	6.2	1.4	5.8
Sports Broadcasts	−0.7	0.7	7.9	2.9	−3.4	1.6
Written						
Editorials	−5.7	1.0	−9.9	3.5	−0.7	4.8
News Reportage	−4.8	0.7	0.7	6.1	−10.0	3.5
Analytical Press	−4.5	0.9	−6.9	3.8	3.2	3.5
Press Announcements	−4.1	0.8	−0.7	3.8	−0.5	2.4
Sports Reviews	−3.8	0.8	−4.4	3.9	−3.8	2.7
Published Speeches	−4.0	1.0	−10.0	4.2	1.6	3.4
Academic Essays	−4.0	1.0	0.7	4.3	2.7	3.8
Academic Theses	−4.2	1.2	0.3	3.7	0.8	3.8
Serial Stories	−0.1	2.8	−5.0	3.0	−2.6	1.8
Novels	−0.1	2.4	−5.9	2.8	−2.4	2.1
Folklore Stories	3.4	0.9	−1.7	2.3	−5.6	0.8
Government Memos	−3.5	0.5	−1.5	3.4	−2.0	1.5
Personal Letters	2.5	1.3	−1.4	2.2	0.0	1.5
Personal Petitions	−3.8	0.6	1.3	3.0	−2.5	0.9

Dimension 1 thus characterize personal involvement versus informational exposition. In between these two extremes, there are a number of spoken and written registers. The intermediate spoken registers include formal meetings, sermons, lectures, and sports broadcasting, which are all relatively informational. The intermediate written registers—serial stories, novels, folk stories, and personal letters—are involved and noninformational relative to the other written registers.

The mean Dimension 1 scores given in Table 8.2 show that this dimension does not reflect a spoken/written dichotomy (e.g., personal letters and folk stories have larger positive scores than lectures and formal meetings), and that it does not represent a dichotomy between interactive and noninteractive registers. Rather, we interpret the dimension as primarily reflecting author/speaker purpose: personal involved expression versus informational exposition. Linguistically, many of the features on Dimension 1 relate to structural elaboration, and we thus propose the interpretive label 'Structural Elaboration: Involvement Versus Exposition'.

3.2.2. DIMENSION 2: 'LEXICAL ELABORATION: ON-LINE VERSUS PLANNED/INTEGRATED PRODUCTION'

Dimension 2 has only positive features with large weights. The stronger features on this dimension are lexical characteristics: hapax legomena (once-occurring words), type-token ratio (the number of different words),[7] nominalizations, and compound verbs. Gerunds and word length are also grouped on this dimension. Thus this dimension distinguishes primarily between registers having careful and elaborated lexical choice (lexical diversity, rare words, and derivationally complex words) versus those using frequent repeated lexical forms which are short and derivationally simple.

A consideration of the Dimension 2 scores of spoken and written registers, presented in Table 8.2, shows that sports broadcasts have the least lexical diversity and elaboration of any register, although all spoken registers, whether informational or involved, are quite marked as lacking lexical elaboration. In contrast, written registers show a wide range of variation on Dimension 2. Some written registers, such as editorials and published political speeches, are markedly elaborated in their lexical choice, showing extreme lexical diversity and very frequent use of derived words and longer words. Other written registers, such as folk stories, memos, and personal letters, are less informational in purpose and thus have more moderate Dimension 2 scores, although they still show greater lexical diversity and elaboration than all spoken registers. Some informational registers (such as press reportage and academic essays) also have intermediate scores on this dimension, reflecting the frequent repetition of technical terms, which are often borrowed (from English or Italian) rather than derived from native Somali words.

Considering both the grouping of linguistic features on Dimension 2 together with this distribution of registers, we propose the label 'Lexical Elaboration: On-Line Versus Planned/Integrated Production'. This dimension seems to represent a basic difference between the production possibilities of speech and writing. All spoken registers, regardless of purpose or interactiveness, are produced on-line and thus show little lexical diversity or elaboration. In contrast, writers have extensive opportunity for careful word choice, and thus written registers *can* show extreme lexical diversity and elaboration. At the same time, writers can choose not to exploit the production possibilities of the written mode (as in personal letters and folk stories) resulting in relatively little lexical elaboration; or writers having a technical purpose (as in academic essays) can choose a deliberately restricted range of lexical diversity, as a result of the need for precise, technical vocabulary.

3.2.3. DIMENSION 3: 'ARGUMENTATIVE VERSUS REPORTED PRESENTATION OF INFORMATION'

Dimension 3 shows a basic opposition between present tense and past tense (see Table 8.1). However, as indicated by the co-occurrence of past tense verbs and future tense modals (both among the negative features), this dimension does not represent a simple difference between present and past events. In addition to present tense, the major positive features on Dimension 3 are adjectival forms and qualified statements (possibility modals, concession conjuncts, and conditional clauses). The major negative features on Dimension 3, in addition to past tense, are proper nouns and agentive derived nouns. The negative features represent projected time (past or future) with a focus on specific human referents; the positive features represent present time, with frequent elaborating details and qualifying conditions and concessions.

Table 8.2 shows that family and formal meetings have the largest positive scores on Dimension 3, together with written registers such as analytical press articles and academic essays. These registers are characterized by a heavy reliance on present tense forms plus frequent adjectives (predicative and attributive), possibility modals, and concessive conjuncts (the positive features), combined with a marked absence of past tense forms, proper nouns, and agentive nouns (the negative features). In contrast, press reportage has by far the largest negative score on this dimension, reflecting very frequent past tense forms, proper nouns, and agentive nouns (the negative features) combined with markedly infrequent present tense forms, adjectives, possibility modals, and concessive conjuncts (the positive features). Folk stories, sports reviews, sports broadcasts, serial stories, and novels also have relatively large negative scores on this dimension.

Considering the distribution of registers together with the linguistic features grouped on this dimension, we propose the label 'Argumentative Versus Reported Presentation of Information'. We intend the term *argumentative* to refer to a qualified presentation of information, comparing and contrasting various alternatives, while *reported* styles simply present the "facts," with little consideration of alternative possibilities.

3.2.4. ORAL AND *LITERATE* CHARACTERIZATIONS RELATIVE TO THE DIMENSIONS

Although none of these three dimensions defines an absolute distinction between speech and writing, Dimensions 1 and 2 are closely associated with the mode differences. Linguistically, these two dimensions are defined by features associated with interactiveness and personal involvement versus structural or lexical complexity and elaboration; and along both dimensions, conversations (stereotypical speech) are near one pole, expository prose registers (stereotypical writing) are near the other pole, and the range of spoken registers tends toward the conversational pole while the range of written registers tends toward the expository pole. Thus these two dimensions can be considered *oral* versus *literate,* in the sense of Biber (1988) and Biber and Finegan (1989).

The structural elaboration dimension (Dim. 1) shows that there is a limit on the extent to which spoken registers can be structurally elaborated, even when they have markedly informational purposes (as in lectures and formal meetings). Conversely, written registers are somewhat elaborated structurally, even when they have involved purposes (as in personal letters and folk stories). There is considerable overlap among spoken and written registers on this dimension, however, as the involved written registers have more *oral* characterizations than the informational spoken registers.

The lexical elaboration dimension (Dim. 2) nearly defines an absolute dichotomy between speech and writing; it shows that production differences in speech versus writing have an extremely strong influence in Somali in relation to linguistic features reflecting lexical diversity and elaboration. All spoken registers, regardless of purpose or interactiveness, are markedly nonelaborated in their lexical characteristics, because of their on-line production circumstances. Written registers, on the other hand, range from extreme lexical diversity and elaboration (as in editorials and published political speeches) to the relatively restricted range of vocabulary found in academic essays and press reportage.

In contrast, Dimension 3—'Argumentative Versus Reported Presentation of Information'—relates primarily to discourse purpose and is thus largely independent of mode considerations. In fact, written press registers are near both poles of this dimension: general interest press and analytical press near the 'argumentative' pole, and press reportage at the 'reported' pole.

The historical changes along Dimension 1 and 2, discussed in the following sections, can thus be related to differing degrees of personal involvement (or focus on information) and differing production demands of typical speech versus typical writing. These two dimensions relate directly to the historical expansion of variability resulting from the addition of written registers. There are also interesting historical changes along Dimension 3, but these reflect changed purposes rather than developments caused by the addition of writing per se.

4. Somali Registers Used for the Present Analysis

To investigate the initial impact of literacy on Somali, we restrict the scope of our historical analysis to seven written press registers, which are compared to seven spoken registers. The written registers are all from Somali newspapers, which were first written in 1973, while the spoken registers represent a wide range of the types of speech that existed in 1972–73.

Press registers are the best developed written varieties in Somali. Somali newspapers have been in continuous existence since January 1973, and in many years there were several newspapers. In 1989 there was both a daily paper (*Xiddigta Oktoobar*) and a weekly (*Ogaal*). (All Somali newspapers have been published, and primarily distributed, in the capital city of Mogadishu.) In addition, Somali press registers represent several different kinds of writing, ranging from news reportage and editorials to public announcements and serial stories; they thus allow analysis of the shared linguistic patterns across written registers as well as the particular developments of different types of writing.

The seven written registers used in our study are listed in Table 8.3. News reportage (*war*) was taken from the front page of newspapers; these were articles reporting on current events. Institutional editorials (*faallo*) were taken from a titled editorial page. These were commentaries with no acknowledged author, discussing a current event or situation and typically arguing in support of the official government position. Some example topics are the retreat of the Soviets from Afghanistan, the Somali business situation and problems with the black market, and an agreement between Ethiopia and Somalia to stop fighting at the border.

The situational characteristics of *ra'yiga dadweynaha* 'the opinion of the people' changed considerably from 1973 to the current period. In all periods, these were found on a separate, titled page of the newspaper. In earlier periods, these were true letters to the editor, written by interested readers and concerning local and national issues (such as family responsibility, the administration of local town governments, the importance of economic progress, and the repair of the city sports

TABLE 8.3   Composition of the Somali Subcorpus of Press Texts,
by Register and Historical Period

Register	Number of Texts in each Period			Total Texts
	1973–74	*1977–79*	*1987–89*	
War—News Reportage	11	10	14	35
Faallo—Institutional Editorials	11	10	10	31
Ra'yiga Dadweynaha—Letters to the Editor	10	10	5	25
Maqaal Gaar—Analytical Articles	10	10	11	48
Iidheh iyo Ogeysiis—Announcements	10	10	11	31
Faaqidaada Ciyaaraha—Sports Reviews	7	7	8	22
Taxane Sheeko—Serial Stories	7	7	7	21
Total Written Texts				213

stadium). In the current period, though, this page was renamed *ra'yiga iyo aqoonta* 'opinion and knowledge'. These are invited editorials and articles, written by experts on specialized topics such as the economy, international relations, and Somali culture and history.

Iidheh iyo ogeysiis are announcements and notices, which are presented in a special section of the newspaper. These include announcements about meetings and public events (e.g., new plays, new books, the opening of a new shop or hotel), as well as notices to individuals (e.g., a summons to appear in court or to pay an electricity bill). *Faaqidaada ciyaaraha* are sports reviews that appear regularly; these present relatively in-depth discussions of current sports news, including biographies, discussion of recent tournaments, and analysis of particular games. *Maqaal gaar* are informational articles that appear on the inside pages of newspapers but do not have their own titled sections. They are relatively long and analytical, dealing with specialized issues relating to international relations, politics, economics, social problems, scientific discoveries, the environment, and so forth.

Finally, *taxane sheeko* are serial stories that present an episode in each issue of the newspaper. These are sometimes later published as a single novel. Impressionistically, this register seems to have changed in purpose since 1973. Earlier works of fiction addressed serious issues relating to Somali national identity or social development, while most recent fiction presents variations on a love theme (a country girl comes to the city, falls in love, and has various adventures).

We collected press texts from three historical periods: 1973–74, representing the initial development of written registers; 1977–79, representing an early period of stability; and 1987–89, representing contemporary writing.[8] The first period was a formative period, when Somalis were developing new written registers. By the second period, nearly all writing in Somalia was done in Somali, and there was considerable enthusiasm and pride in Somali prose. Somali writing was well established in the domains of government, education, and popular information and entertainment, in addition to the press. By this period, all government memos and petitions were in Somali, school textbooks through secondary school had been written in Somali, and there were many novels and biographies, a dictionary, several grammars, and numerous popular informational pamphlets. Newspapers in

TABLE 8.4   Composition of the Somali Corpus of Spoken Texts
Typical of the 1973 Range of Variation

Register	Number of Texts
A. Sheekayn—Conversation and Storytelling	
Sheeko—Spontaneous/Conversational Narratives	20
Hadal Caadi—Non-narrative Conversation	21
B. Hadal Jeedin—Public Monologues	
Cashar Bixin Jamcadda—University Lectures	10
Wacdi and Tafsiir—Sermons	20
C. Hadal Raadiyo—Spontaneous Radio Broadcasts	
Ciyaaro Tebin—Live Sports Broadcasts	10
D. Hadal Shir—Formal Conversation and Meetings	
Shir Guddi—Formal Committee Meetings	11
Shir Qoys—Family Meetings	9
Total Spoken Texts	101

this period were quite long, with many articles in each issue and a professional format. The third period represents a decline in the production of written texts, due primarily to economic pressures (attributed by Somalis to war, rapid inflation, and government corruption). Comparatively few novels and information pamphlets were written during this period, and those that were written were shorter and less professional in appearance. All official or governmental writing continued to be in Somali, but no new reference works appeared in this period. With regard to press registers, newspapers became considerably shorter and less professional in appearance. (For example, fonts were commonly mixed in the text of articles, and characters were often set askew.)[9]

We compare these written registers with texts from seven spoken registers that existed in 1973, summarized in Table 8.4.[10] These texts were actually collected in 1988–89, and thus they do not truly represent speech as it existed in 1973. Our comparison here is thus based on the assumption that spoken registers have changed relatively little since 1973. However, our analysis does not require a strict assumption of spoken stability, since the expanded range of variation due to the addition of written registers is quite extensive (see later discussion).[11]

5. The Initial Expansion of Linguistic Variation Due to the Introduction of Written Registers

5.1. Expansion of Variation Along Dimension 1: 'Structural Elaboration: Involvement Versus Exposition'

Figure 8.1 shows the expansion of linguistic variation along the structural elaboration dimension (Dim. 1) that resulted from the addition of written press registers in Somali. Prior to the introduction of written registers, there was already a wide range of variation among spoken registers along this dimension. Involved, interactive

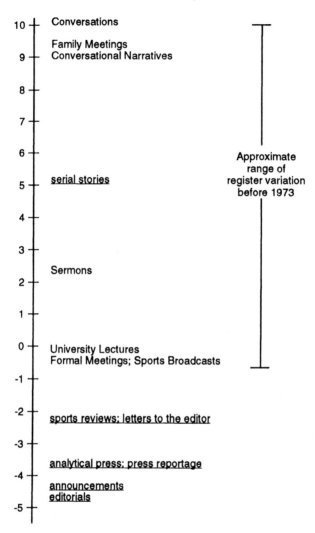

FIGURE 8.1. Distribution of registers along Dimension 1: 'Structural Elaboration: Involvement versus Exposition' (spoken registers are given in initial Caps; written registers are underlined).

registers, such as conversations, family meetings, and conversational narratives, have large positive scores on this dimension, reflecting frequent use of yes/no questions, stance adjectives, contractions, main clauses, and so forth (the positive features on Dim. 1), together with markedly low frequencies of total dependent clauses, relative clauses, nouns, derived adjectives, et cetera (the negative features on Dim. 1). Informational spoken registers such as university lectures, formal meetings, and sports broadcasts have values around 0.0, reflecting a lesser but relatively balanced use of both the involved features and structural elaboration features.

Text Sample 1 illustrates the extremely involved characterization of face-to-face conversations, while Text Sample 2 illustrates the mixed informational/involved characterization of university lectures.

Text Sample 1: Conversation[12]

Some young women discussing whether they had meddled in a relationship between a married couple; Speaker A feels unjustly accused

B: wallaahi   dee way   iska fiicnayd [pause]
   swear to God uh FM–she just was fine [pause]

   'I swear, she [i.e., the wife] was just fine'.

   suurahay   taqaan haye
   coyness–FM–she knew, isn't it?

   'She knew how to be coy, didn't she'?

D: walaal   meherkeedii   [unintelligible words]
   oh sister, legal wedding–her . . .

   'Sister, her legal–wedding . . .'

A: waxaa iigu   dambeyṡayba waa kaas
   What me–for last–time–was FM that [time].

   'The last time that I saw her was that time'.

   waxay   iigu   darnayd   ayaantay
   what–she me–for was the worst [was] day–the–she

   Aamina ku tidhi   ninkayga / ninkayga
   Amina to she–said "man–my [pause] man–my

   'What was the worst thing for me was the day that she said to
   Amina "my man, my man —"'

B: ninkaygay   igu   dirayaan
   "man–my–FM–they me–against they–set"

   '"— They are setting my man against me"'.

A: adduunka   kelmaddaasi weli waa   xasuustaa ka   warran!
   world–the, word–that   still FM–I remember, about report!

   'Can you imagine! I still remember that word, what do you think of that'?

B: dee horta   waa runoo   waan   ku dirnee
   uh first–the FM truth–and FM–we to we send–and

   'uh, first of all it is true and we set her against him'.

   ma og   tahay? Taasi ma been baa?
   QM know being? That QM lie   FM?

   'Don't you know? Is that a lie'?

A: kuma dirin
  to–NEG send

 'We didn't set her against him'.

B: Illaahay baan kugu dhaarshee ma been baa ?
 God-my FM–I from-with swore-and QM lie FM ?

 'I swear to you upon God, is it a lie'?

 laakiin adaa adaa gardarnaa Sacaado.
 But you–FM you–FM justice–without Sa'ado.

 'But you, you were at fault, Sa'ado'.

 markaan ku idhi ha u sheegin, ha u sheegin,
 Time–the–I to said OPT to tell–not OPT to tell–not,

 ma tidhi saaxiibaan nahay
 QM said friends–we being?

 'When I said to you "don't tell (her), don't tell (her),"
 didn't you say "we are friends?"'

 ma naag baa iyo ninkeedaa la dhexgalaa ?
 QM women FM and man–her–FM IMP middle–enter ?

 'Are a woman and her husband meddled with?'
 [i.e., isn't it wrong to meddle with a woman and her husband?]

Translation

[Talking about a woman who felt that Speaker A had meddled with her marriage]

 B: I swear, she [i.e., the wife] was just fine. She knew how to be coy, didn't she?
 D: Sister, her legal-wedding . . .
 A: The last time that I saw her was that time. What was the worst thing for me was
  the day that she said to Amina "my man, my man —
 B: — They are setting my man against me."
 A: Can you imagine! I still remember that word, what do you think of that?
 B: uhm, first of all it is true and we set her against him, don't you know? Is that a
  lie?
 A: We didn't set her against him.
 B: I swear to you upon God, is it a lie? But you, you were at fault, Sa'ado. When I
  said to you "don't tell (her), don't tell (her)," didn't you say "we are friends?" Are
  a woman and her husband meddled with? [i.e., isn't it wrong to meddle with a
  woman and her husband?]

Text Sample 2. University Lecture (economics)

Heerka 3aad wuxuu noqonaayaa [pause]
level–the 3rd what–it is becoming (is)

'The third stage is going to become —'

isla   maalgelin   ayuu   noqonaayaa [pause]
RFLX–with wealth–enter FM–it is becoming

'it is also going to be investment'.

laakiin waxa loo   fiirinaa maalgelinta   siday
But   what IMP-for looking wealth-enter-the (is) way-the-it

u saameyn kartaa ama u   faragelinaysaa dhismaha   guud   [pause]
affect   can   or for finger-entering building-the general,

'However, investment is considered for the way that it can affect or interfere with the
general structure —'

dhismaha   guud   oo dhaqaaalaha
building-the general of economy-the,

'the general structure of the economy —'

iyo siday   u   faragelin   kartaa ama u saameyn kartaa
and way–the for finger–enter can   or   affect   can

qofka   wax soo   saaraaya   [pause]
person–the thing from producing.

'and how it can interfere with or it can affect the person producing goods'.

Masalan waxaad   ka   soo qaadaysaa   siday
Example what-you from back are taking (is) way–which–FM–it

sawir uga   bixinaysaa   maalgelintani
picture for–from you are giving wealth–enter–this

guud   ahaan dalka   [pause]
general being country–the

'For example, what you are going to consider is [i.e., if you were an investment planner,
you would consider] the way in which you are going to give a picture about the country in
general from [analysis of] this investment'.

Translation

The third stage is going to become [pause] it is also going to be investment. However,
investment is considered for the way that it can affect or interfere with the general
structure, the general structure of the economy, and how it can interfere with or it can
affect the person producing goods. For example, you are going to consider [i.e., if you
were an investment planner, you would consider] how will this investment give a picture
about the country in general?

Sample 1 illustrates the high involvement style (Dim. 1) common in Somali conversation and conversational narratives, marked by frequent questions, first and second
person pronouns, and contractions (e.g., *suurahay* = *suuraha* + *ayaa* + *ay*
'coyness-the' + FM + 'she'; *runoo* = *run* + *oo* 'truth' + 'and'). This sample is
also quite unelaborated structurally, shown by the preponderance of main clause
constructions and focus markers, together with the marked absence of relative
clauses, WH clefts, and other dependent clauses. Sample 2, on the other hand,
illustrates the mixture of involvement and structural elaboration common in univer-

sity lectures. For example, there are frequent contracted forms (e.g., *siday* = *sidee* + *ayaa* + *ay* 'way-which' + FM + 'it'; *wuxuu* = *waxa* + *uu* 'thing-the' + 'it'), plus some WH questions and references to *aad* 'you'. Structurally, though, lectures are quite elaborated, relying on clefts and dependent clause constructions more than simple main clause constructions. Thus Sample 2 illustrates only one simple main clause with a focus marker, but it has three WH clefts, plus frequent relative clause and other dependent clause constructions (e.g., *qofka wax soo saaraaya* 'the person who is producing goods'; *siday sawir uga bixinaysaa* 'the way that you are going to give a picture'). These two samples illustrate the relatively wide range of variation that existed among spoken registers along Dimension 1 before the introduction of written varieties.

When written registers were added to Somali, the Dimension 1 range of variation was extended to include styles that use structural elaboration features more frequently than in lectures, with essentially no involvement features. Thus Figure 8.1 shows that all nonfictional press registers (in 1973) have larger negative scores than any spoken register. The linguistic characteristics of this extended range of variation are illustrated by the following text sample from an editorial.

Text Sample 3. News Editorial
11 May 1974
Xiddigta Oktoobar
Title: Gobanimadoonka Afrika iyo afgembiga ka dhacay dalka Bortuqiiska 'Independence movements of Africa and the coup d'état that occurred in Portugal'

> Haddii aan arrintaa   ka   eegno dhinaca dhaqdhaqaaqa
> If   we matter-that from look   side-the movement-the
>
> gobanimadoonka   Afrika waxaan oran karnaa
> independence-search-the Africa what-we say can   (is)
>
> in   isbeddelkaasi   ka   dhacay   Boortuqiiska
> that RFLX-change-that from happened Portugal-the
>
> uu yahay mid hore   u wadi doono siyaasadda
> it being one forward to take will policy-the
>
> isticmaariga   ah, hase yeeshee waxa dhici   karta   inuu
> colonialism-the is. Let be-but what happen can   (is) that-it
>
> la   yimaado tabo   cusub uu ula   jeedo inuu
> with come   tactics new   it to-with mean that-it
>
> waqti ku   kasbo markaa kaddibna   bannaanka uu
> time with benefit time-that from-after-and outside-the it
>
> ula   soo   baxo siyaasaddiisii is-addoonsiga ahayd.
> to-with towards go   policy-its-the RFLX-slavery was

Translation:

> If we look at that issue with respect to the liberation movements of Africa, what we could say is that the self-transformation [i.e., the coup] that happened in Portugal is one which

will continue the policy which is colonialism. However, what can happen is that it [i.e., the political change] would come with new tactics whose purpose is to gain time and then come out in public with its [old] policy which was enslavement.

This text sample has only two main clauses, both structured as WH clefts followed by complement clauses, rather than simple independent clauses (i.e., *waxaan oran karnaa in* . . . 'what we can say is that . . .' and *waxa dhici karta inuu* . . . 'what can happen is that it . . .'). The sample also illustrates the extremely dense use of relative clause constructions common in Somali written prose (e.g., *isbeddelkaasi ka dhacay Boortuqiiska* 'the change that happened in Portugal'; *mid hore u wadi doono siyaasadda isticmaariga ah* 'one which will continue the policy which is colonialism'). The only involvement features in this sample are the conditional clause and the use of rhetorical 'we' in the beginning, and a few contractions (i.e., *waxaan = waxa + aan, inuu = in + uu*). Overall, this sample is thus characterized by the markedly frequent use of structural elaboration features and the near absence of involvement features, illustrating the Dimension 1 characteristics of the expository styles that came into existence with the introduction of literacy.

5.2. Expansion of Variation Along Dimension 2: 'Lexical Elaboration: On-Line Versus Planned/Integrated Production'

The extension of variation due to the addition of written registers is even more striking on the lexical elaboration dimension (Dim. 2), plotted in Figure 8.2. Along the structural elaboration dimension (Dim. 1; discussed in the preceding section), spoken registers already occupied a wide range of variation, associated with the differences between interpersonal and informational purposes; although the addition of written registers extended that range, allowing a very dense use of structural elaboration features, the total differences among registers increased by less than half. In contrast, Figure 8.2 shows that spoken registers occupy a relatively restricted range of variation along the lexical elaboration dimension, and that the addition of written registers increased that range by almost a factor of three. (The poles of this dimension have been reversed, to facilitate comparisons across dimensions—see note 6.)

In Biber and Hared (1992), we interpret Dimension 2 as being associated with the differing production possibilities of speech and writing; thus all spoken registers, whether they are informational, involved, planned, or interactive, show very little lexical elaboration or diversity on this dimension. Sports broadcasts have the largest positive score here, reflecting the most lexical repetition and least lexical elaboration (because of very restrictive on-line production constraints), but the remaining conversational and informational spoken registers are all similar on this dimension in having little lexical elaboration.

Thus consider text Samples 1 and 2 again. Although they differ markedly in their structural elaboration features, they both have relatively restricted vocabularies and extensive repetitions. Sample 1, from a conversation, has almost no lexically complex forms (e.g., nominalizations or compound forms), and it relies heavily on common vocabulary (including frequent pronominal forms and elided references) plus frequent repeated forms (e.g., *dir* 'send'). Often, entire phrases are repeated in

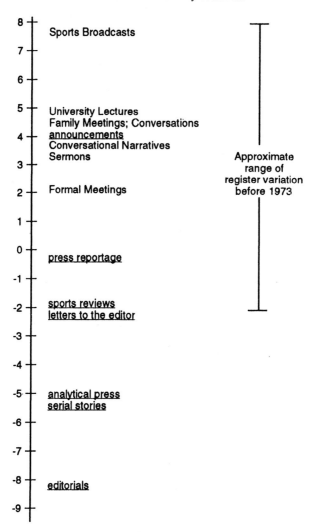

FIGURE 8.2. Distribution of registers along Dimension 2: 'Lexical Elaboration: On-Line versus Planned/Integrated Production' (polarity reversed) (spoken registers are given in initial Caps; written registers are underlined).

conversations (e.g., *ma been baa* 'is it a lie', *ha u sheegin* 'don't tell [her]' in Sample 1). Sample 2, although much more informational in purpose, also shows a frequent use of repeated forms (e.g., *noqonaayaa* 'is becoming', *faragelin* 'interfere', *dhismaha guud* 'the general structure'); these are sometimes relatively technical terms (e.g., *maalgelin* 'investment').

The addition of written registers greatly extended this range of variation. Some registers, such as press reportage, are relatively unelaborated in their lexical characteristics, although they are still considerably more elaborated than the most elaborated spoken register (formal meetings). Other registers, such as editorials, are extremely elaborated in their lexical characteristics, representing a style of text unlike any of the pre-existing spoken registers. (Interestingly, serial stories are quite elaborated lexically, although Figure 8.1 shows that they are unelaborated in their structural characteristics.) Thus Sample 3, from an editorial, shows extreme differences from both Samples 1 and 2 with respect to its lexical characteristics; there are few lexical repetitions, but a frequent use of long, relatively rare lexical forms, which are frequently compounded or derived (e.g., *dhaqdhaqaaqa* 'the movement', *gobanimadoonka* 'the liberation movements', *isbeddelkaasi* 'that self-transformation', *isticmaariga* 'the colonialism', *siyaasaddiisii* 'its policy', *is-addoonsiga* 'enslavement').

Sample 3 can also be contrasted with Text Sample 4, from a front-page press report.

Text Sample 4. News Reportage
25 May 1974
Xiddigta Oktoobar

Title: Jaalle Carte: Wadammada Afrika waxay muujiyeen kalsoonida iyo tixgelinta ay u hayaan dadka Soomaaliyeed
'Comrade Arte: The African countries, what they expressed [is] the confidence and the respect [that] they have for the people of Somalia'

Muqdisho, May, 24 (SONNA)
Mogadishu, May, 24 (SONNA)

Xoghayaha   Arrimaha   Dibadda   ee dalkan   Soomaaliya
Secretary-the Affairs-the Outside-the of country-this Somalia

Jaalle   Cumar Carte Qaalib shalay   ayuu   ku   soo   laabtay
Comrade Omar Arte   Qalib yesterday FM-he with toward came-back

magaaladan Muqdisho kaddib markii   uu socdaal ku
city-this   Mogadishu after   the time (that) he trip   with

kala   bixiyey   waddamo   ku yaal
from each he caused to go out countries (that) in are there

Qaaradda   Afrika iyo Aasiya.
continent-the Africa and Asia.

Xoghayuhu intii   uu booqashada
Secretary-the while he visit-the

ku marayey dalalka   ka   mid ah   Qaaradda Afrika
to going-on countries from one being (is) continent Africa

wuxuu   Madaxdooda u gudbiyey dhammbaalo uu uga   siday
what-he heads-theirs to conveyed messages   he from-to brought

Madaxweynaha GSK*, Jaalle   Maxamed Siyaad Barre.
President-the   SRC*, Comrade Mohamed Siad   Barre.

*GSK stands for Golaha Sare ee Kacaanka
'Council-the Supreme of Revolution-the'
SRC stands for Supreme Revolutionary Council

Translation:

> Mogadishu, May, 24 (SONNA). The Foreign Secretary of this country of Somalia, Comrade Omar Arte Qalib, came back yesterday to this city of Mogadishu after having paid visits to countries which are on the continents of Africa and Asia. While the secretary was visiting these countries which are part of the African continent, he conveyed to their heads [i.e., presidents] messages that he carried from the President of the SRC, Mohamed Siad Barre.

This sample differs from the editorial sample (3) in that the typical words are shorter, less complex, and more common. There are also more repeated lexical forms in the press reportage sample. However, the kinds and extent of lexical repetition are different from that found in conversations and lectures. In these spoken registers, it is rare to find distinct lexical items used for the same referent, and there is frequent repetition of phrases due to the constraints of on-line production (as well as the emphatic force achieved by repetitions). In the case of press reportage, repetitions are used to give the text a high degree of cohesion; for example, the following lexical roots are repeated in the two sentences contained in Sample 4: *xoghaya* 'the secretary', *dal* 'country', *Qaaradda* 'the continent', *Madax* 'head' or 'president'. A longer sample would illustrate additional repetitions of this type, as well as relatively frequent repetitions of proper nouns. However, this short sample also illustrates several cases where distinct lexical forms are used to refer to the same or overlapping referent; for example: *waddamo* and *dalalka* for 'countries', *socdaal* and *booqashada* for 'trip/visit', *bixiyey* and *marayey* for 'travel through (a place)'. Text Sample 4 thus illustrates the intermediate characterization of press reportage with respect to the lexical elaboration dimension—it has considerably more lexical diversity and complexity than the most informational spoken registers but considerably less lexical elaboration than registers such as editorials.

5.3. *Expansion of Variation Along Dimension 3: 'Argumentative Versus Reported Presentation of Information'*

Dimension 3, 'Argumentative Versus Reported Presentation of Information', differs from the other two dimensions in that nearly all written registers fall within the pre-existing range of spoken variation, as shown on Figure 8.3. Before 1973, meetings (family or formal) had the largest positive score on this dimension, reflecting very frequent present tense verbs, adjectives, possibility modals, and concession conjuncts. In contrast, sports broadcasts had large negative Dimension 3 scores, reflecting frequent past tense verbs, proper nouns, and agentive nouns (together with markedly infrequent present tense verbs, possibility modals, and so on).

Apart from press reportage, all written press registers fall well within this pre-existing range of variation. Figure 8.3 shows that most 1973 press registers have a moderately 'argumentative' presentation—less marked than in meetings, but considerably more argumentative than in sports broadcasts or conversational narratives. Announcements and press reportage differ from these other press registers. Announcements are relatively 'reported', although they are less marked than sports broadcasts. Press reportage, on the other hand, represents a dependence on 'reported'

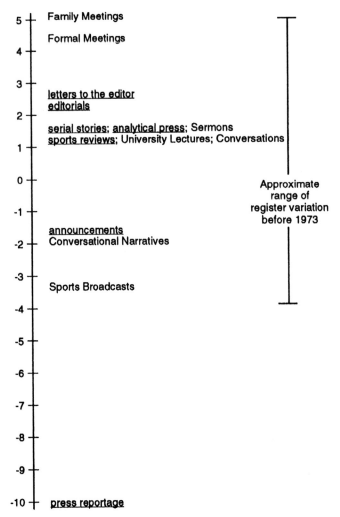

FIGURE 8.3. Distribution of registers along Dimension 3: 'Argumentative versus Reported Presentation of Information' (spoken registers are given in initial Caps; written registers are underlined).

presentation that is more extreme than in any pre-existing register. Text Sample 4 (above) illustrates these Dimension 3 characteristics, showing a very heavy reliance on simple past tense verbs as well as a very frequent use of proper nouns, both in accordance with the primary purposes of press reportage (typically a direct report of the past or future activities of national and community figures).

In contrast, both the lecture text sample (2) and the editorial sample (3) illustrate a more 'argumentative' presentation of information. Both illustrate a primary reliance on present tense forms, as well as the use of concessive conjuncts (*hase yeeshee* 'however' in the editorial; *laakiin* 'but, however' in the lecture) and possibility modals (in the editorial: *oran karnaa* 'we could say', *dhici karta* '(what) can happen'; in the lecture: *siday u saameyn kartaa* 'how it can affect', *siday u faragelin kartaa ama u saameyn kartaa* 'how it can interfere with or it can affect'). In both registers, these forms function to present various possible worldviews and to argue for or against a position, rather than simply to report known facts and past events as in press reportage.

Thus the addition of written registers extended the range of variation along Dimension 3 as along the other two dimensions; in this case, though, the extended range is due to the particular characteristics of one register, press reportage, rather than to any general characteristics of writing.

6. The Evolution of Somali Press Registers from 1973 to 1989

Processes of language standardization, defined as the reduction or suppression of optional variability (Milroy and Milroy 1985:8), often occur in a language at the same time as processes of modernization or adaptation. The more standardized a language becomes, the less variability it has.[13] This process has typically been described with respect to the regularization of low-level features such as spelling and morphological variants. That is, standardization describes situations in which there are competing variants of a single form, reflecting different pronunciations or different dialect patterns, and one of these variants is promoted in status to become the 'standard' form (see Milroy and Milroy 1985, Devitt 1989).

Registers can also undergo a type of standardization, a process that might be referred to as *register normalization*. For example, Biber and Finegan (1989) identify reductions, over time, in the range of variation *within* written registers of English. In historical periods when there is disagreement concerning the purposes of a register, there is also considerable linguistic variation among texts from that register. As agreement on the purposes of the register develops, however, the range of variation among texts of that register decreases, and, in this sense, the register itself can be described as undergoing a type of standardization or normalization.

At the level of speech and writing, there is a sense in which register normalization and register adaptation can be considered as competing processes that pull a language in opposite directions. Adaptation causes registers to diversify in accordance with the particular communicative demands of each. Thus it is possible for written registers to enter a language relatively similar to one another in their linguistic characteristics but subsequently to evolve so that they become more clearly distinguished as each one adapts to its particular communicative requirements. Register normalization, on the other hand, is a force pushing registers toward relative conformity, in response to the desirability of an overall written standard. Thus it might be the case that written registers enter a language relatively distinct from one another in their linguistic characteristics, lacking any prior written standard, and that subsequently they evolve to become more similar to one another as an overall written standard becomes established and accepted.

Within registers the same two processes can apply. Register adaptation at this level would eventually lead to either a marked shift in communicative characteristics or a split. That is, if multiple communicative demands are being served within a register, we would predict that over time the process of adaptation would result in either a shift of the register to some new set of characteristics (as happened with some English registers; see Biber and Finegan 1989) or a split into multiple registers, each serving different communicative needs.

For the purposes of our analysis here, we consider the processes of register normalization and adaptation from several perspectives. First, we analyze the development of written press registers relative to spoken registers. To the extent that written registers continue to adapt to the differing purposes and production possibilities of writing (versus speech), we would predict that they will evolve to become more different linguistically from spoken registers. Second, we consider the development of written press registers relative to one another. To the extent that they evolve in adaptation to the particular communicative demands of each register, we would predict that they will develop so that each register becomes more clearly distinguished. On the other hand, to the extent that they evolve in response to forces of normalization and an overall written standard, we would predict that written registers will become more alike. We show later that the movement toward diversity, motivated by adaptation, is seen with respect to Dimensions 2 and 3, while the movement toward suppression of variation, motivated by normalization, is seen with respect to Dimension 1. Finally, we briefly analyze changes in the range of variation among the texts within each press register. We show in this regard that there are no clear patterns of change either to extend or to reduce the range of internal variation, suggesting that register-internal norms are still developing—that these registers are still in a state of flux regarding their appropriate purposes and characteristic linguistic forms.

In the last section, we showed how the introduction of Somali written press registers—a type of language adaptation—greatly expanded the range of variation along three functional/linguistic dimensions. In the present section, we trace the linguistic evolution of those same written registers, to determine in what respects they become normalized and in what respects they further adapt.

6.1. Evolution of Press Registers Along Dimension 1: 'Structural Elaboration: Involvement Versus Exposition'

Figure 8.4 plots changes in the mean Dimension 1 scores for six press registers across the three historical periods. This figure can be compared to Figure 8.1, which presents scores for spoken and 1973 written registers. Most spoken registers, together with serial stories in 1973, have positive scores on this dimension, representing frequent questions, main clause constructions, stance adjectives, and so forth (the positive features on Dim. 1; see Table 8.1), together with infrequent dependent clauses, clefts, et cetera (the negative features on Dim. 1). The 1973 press registers, apart from serial stories, all have negative scores on Dimension 1, representing the opposite linguistic characteristics (i.e., considerable structural elaboration; few involved features).

With this background, Figure 8.4 shows that the press registers have undergone a steady progression toward more 'literate' characterizations, progressively becoming more sharply distinguished from spoken registers with respect to Dimension 1

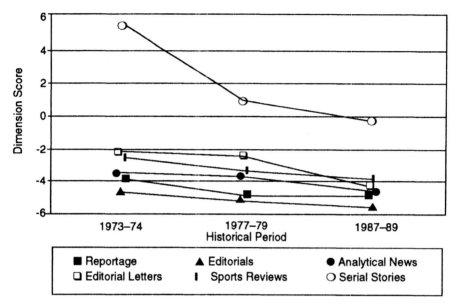

FIGURE 8.4. Historical change along the 'Structural Elaboration' dimension (1).

features. This shift is most pronounced in serial stories, but all press registers have undergone a shift in the same direction, representing more frequent use of structural elaboration features. This trend indicates that Somali continued to adapt across this timespan, extending the range of structural variation even further as writers developed proficiency and confidence in Somali discourse styles.[14]

Figure 8.4 can also be interpreted as showing a slight tendency toward register normalization, in that the range of variation distinguishing among the press registers has become more restricted. That is, the press registers have become more similar to one another in their Dimension 1 characteristics, representing a reduction in the distinctiveness of each register as they all move toward a 'standard' written style. This trend is most noteworthy in the case of serial stories, which undergo a quite marked change to become more similar to the other written registers; however, the trend is also evident among the expository press registers, which have become more similar to one another in the contemporary period than they were in 1973–74. Thus in this respect, normalization—the development of a unified written style—has taken precedence over register adaptation—the independent evolution of each register in response to its distinctive purposes and communicative requirements. The following sections show that this pattern does not hold for Dimensions 2 and 3.

6.2. Evolution of Press Registers Along Dimension 2: 'Lexical Elaboration: On-Line Versus Planned/Integrated Production'

The historical developments shown on Figure 8.5 are more complex. This figure shows changes along Dimension 2, representing lexical elaboration. The larger negative scores represent more frequent use of rare words, long words, and deriva-

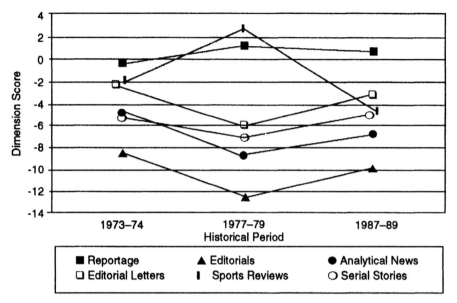

FIGURE 8.5. Historical change along the 'Lexical Elaboration' dimension (2).

tionally complex words (such as nominalizations and compound verbs). This dimension shows a parallel development in four of the press registers: editorial letters, serial stories, analytical news, and editorials. That development does not show a steady progression away from speech, however. Rather, there is a marked shift away from speech (toward extreme lexical elaboration) in the middle period, followed by a shift back toward slightly less lexical elaboration in the last period. News reportage follows a different pattern: in 1973, news reportage texts have relatively little lexical elaboration, and they change little over the timespan of the study, actually becoming slightly less elaborated lexically. Overall, though, there has been a general trend toward greater lexical elaboration with respect to Dimension 2, with editorial letters, analytical news, and editorials all more elaborated in the last period than in the first.

Consideration of the development of these written registers relative to conversations (compare Figures 8.2 and 8.5) shows the extent of the register adaptation along this dimension. Figure 8.2 shows that the initial addition of written registers greatly extended the pre-existing range of variation with respect to lexical elaboration; Figure 8.5 shows that these press registers have evolved to become even more different from speech, continuing to extend the range of lexical variation as writers learn to exploit the production possibilities of the written mode.

We have interpreted this dimension (in Biber and Hared 1992) as being directly influenced by the different production possibilities of speech and writing, and that interpretation is further supported by the development of editorial letters, serial stories, analytical news, and editorials seen in Figure 8.5. As noted in section 4, Somali newspapers in the middle period (1977–79) were more carefully produced than in either of the other two periods: the layout and formatting were professional, daily editions and individual articles were relatively long, and the coverage had more depth. Given these surface differences, it is likely that the prose itself was more carefully produced during this period, and it is thus reasonable to interpret the extremely elaborated lexical characteristics of these registers in the middle period as a reflection of this careful production. In the last period, then, newspapers were less carefully edited, the format became less professional, and articles became shorter. Newspaper staff frequently had to hold second jobs to earn enough money for basic needs, hampering their opportunity and motivation for producing carefully written articles. The shift back to less elaborated lexical characterizations in the contemporary period is apparently a reflection of this less careful production. In addition, Somali newspapers were acquiring a less specialized readership, educated entirely in Somali, over this same time span; thus the shift toward less literate styles might also be traced to the need to make press registers more accessible to this wider audience.

Despite the shift toward more oral styles in the last period, at that time the press registers are still more elaborated lexically than they were in the first period. We would not attribute this overall shift to increased care in production. In fact, there were fewer economic difficulties in 1973–74 than in 1988–89, and there was great nationalistic pride in Somali language literature, so we would predict that press articles were very carefully written in the first period. Rather, we interpret the more elaborated characterizations of the 1987–89 registers as reflecting adaptation in the language: that the lexical resources of the language expanded, and that writers learned to exploit the written mode in ways that were not possible before.

Considering all six press registers, Figure 8.5 shows greater diversity among the registers in the last period than in the first. This is in contrast to the development with respect to the structural elaboration dimension (Dim. 1; Figure 8.4), where these registers have become more similar over time. The diversification along the lexical elaboration dimension (Dim. 2) can be described as another form of adaptation, where press registers have evolved to become more distinct from one another. (In contrast, we noted in the last section that the pattern along the structural elaboration dimension can be described as a type of normalization, where the registers have evolved toward a single written standard.)

6.3. Evolution of Press Registers Along Dimension 3: 'Argumentative Versus Reported Presentation of Information'

It was shown in section 5.3 that there is a wide range of variation among spoken registers along the 'argumentative versus reported' dimension (Dim. 3), and that the only extension to that range due to the introduction of written press registers was caused by the peculiar characteristics of news reportage. Figure 8.6 shows that this register has remained remarkably stable over the three periods, retaining its markedly 'reported' style. The other five registers, however, have undergone considerable shifts in their Dimension 3 characterizations. These registers follow a parallel development: shifting to more 'reported' styles in the middle period, and then shifting back to more 'argumentative' styles in the last period. However, the extent of these shifts differs across the registers, so that by the last period there is consid-

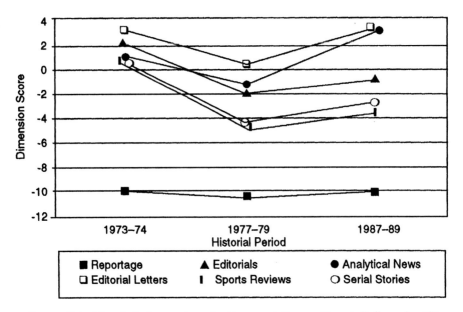

FIGURE 8.6. Historical change along the 'Argumentative vs. Reported' dimension (3).

erably more diversity among the press registers than there was in the first period. These registers thus show a strong pattern of adaptation, in that they become quite diversified rather than maintaining the written norm that existed in 1973–74 (when there were only minor differences among the registers, excluding press reportage).

The shifts along this dimension correspond to the changing political climate in Somalia over the period of our study. In the first period, writers were relatively free to present various opinions and to argue the relative merits of competing views. During the middle period, though, circumstances changed in two important respects. First of all, there was a very strong, and widely shared, feeling of cultural pride, due in part to an unambiguous external enemy: Ethiopia, supported by the Soviet Union and Cuba. There was actually an ongoing war with Ethiopia at the time, which had wide support among Somalis, engendering strong nationalistic feelings. During the same period, though, government control had become extremely tight, so that outspoken critics of the government were in danger of imprisonment. (Somalis during this time were cautious even in their conversations with acquaintances, because of fear of informers.) The press during this period thus resorted to a more 'reported' style of presentation, even in editorial and analytical writing. Some articles, motivated by nationalistic pride, presented slanderous accusations in a factual manner, often 'reporting' unfounded characterizations of Ethiopia and the Soviet Union. At the same time, writers were not free to present anything other than the "party line," so there was essentially no genuine dissent or argumentation. We interpret the marked shift to more reported styles in the middle period as a reflection of these circumstances.

As economic conditions worsened in the last period (1987–89), government control also became weaker, and dissent therefore increased, since there was little fear of retaliation. This greater freedom of speech was most obvious in everyday conversations, where Somalis openly criticized the government, but it was also found in some press writing (especially in the newspaper *Ogaal*). We interpret the marked shift toward more 'argumentative' styles in the last period as a reflection of this greater opportunity for dissent and argumentation.

The patterns in Figure 8.6 can thus be associated with two influences. The shifts toward more 'reported' styles in the middle period, and back toward more 'argumentative' styles in the last period, are tied to changing political and national circumstances, when dissent and argumentation became more or less feasible. At the same time, there was an overall movement toward greater diversification, so that the registers became more clearly distinguished in their Dimension 3 characteristics. For example, although sports reviews and serial stories follow the same general trend as the other registers, they end up with much more 'reported' styles in the last period than in the first. In contrast, editorial letters and analytical news are more 'argumentative' in the last period than in the first. The development along this dimension thus shows considerable adaptation in addition to the influence of purpose and external political constraints.

6.4. Register-Internal Variation

As noted above, an earlier historical analysis of register change in English (Biber and Finegan 1989) found that the amount of internal variation within registers changed systematically over time (in addition to systematic shifts in the typical characteristics of registers). In particular, the eighteenth century was shown to be a period when there was extreme internal variation among the texts within the English register categories of essays and fiction, indicating considerable disagreement concerning the appropriate purposes and styles of these registers. In contrast, the seventeenth century and modern period showed relatively little internal variation, indicating that there was a fairly strong norm for these registers at that time.

Patterns such as these led us to anticipate systematic shifts in the extent of internal variation in the development of Somali written registers. That is, we expected that the texts *within* each register would become more similar to one another over the span of our study, indicating a normalization of the registers. Table 8.5 shows, however, that there are no systematic patterns of this type, although there are some marked shifts. The table presents standard deviations for each register in each period; 68 percent of the texts in a register have scores in the range of plus or minus one standard deviation from the mean score. Thus larger standard deviations represent greater internal variation.

Dimension 1 ('Structural Elaboration') on Table 8.5 shows relatively small standard deviations across registers and periods. Dimension 2 ('Lexical Elaboration') shows larger standard deviations and some large shifts in internal variation across periods, but no systematic patterns across registers. For example, news reportage shows a steady progression toward greater internal variation, indicating the development of considerable disagreement concerning the appropriate lexical style for this register, and perhaps indicating a shift to a new norm. Sports reviews might have passed through a transition of this type in the middle period. Similarly,

TABLE 8.5   Change in the Range of Variation Among Texts Within Press Registers, 1973–88 (Represented by Standard Deviations)

Register	Dimension 1 (Structural Elaboration)			Dimension 2 (Lexical Elaboration)			Dimension 3 (Argumentative vs. Reported)		
	1973	1978	1988	1973	1978	1988	1973	1978	1988
Reportage	0.82	0.70	0.67	2.16	4.13	6.06	1.67	2.30	3.52
Editorials	0.96	1.40	1.03	3.25	4.09	3.54	2.48	2.04	4.84
Analysis	1.59	0.73	0.92	4.12	4.18	3.82	2.54	2.69	3.46
Editorial Letters	1.45	1.03	0.62	3.41	3.50	4.28	3.05	3.12	4.79
Sports	0.21	0.87	0.84	2.44	6.63	3.93	4.92	4.86	2.70
Fiction	2.29	1.20	2.83	5.03	3.47	3.05	3.96	1.70	1.81
Notices	0.59	0.44	0.85	3.21	2.67	3.81	1.26	1.32	2.40

there are some notable differences across periods with respect to Dimension 3 (argumentative versus reported), but again there are no systematic patterns across registers. Overall, there are thus no clear patterns in the evolution of internal variation across the time of this study. At this point, we attribute the difference between the Somali and English results to the differing time spans considered: one hundred-year periods in the case of English (and a total of over three hundred years), versus five- to ten-year periods for Somali (and a total of less than twenty years).

7. Summary and Conclusion

We have shown in this chapter that the evolution and extension of language use patterns in Somali are strongly influenced by the introduction of written varieties and the nativization of public institutions, and we have described the historical development of Somali press registers relative to the complementary forces of register adaptation and register normalization. Register adaptation has been particularly notable in the recent history of Somali, as reflected by (1) the extended range of variation along all three dimensions due to the addition of written registers in 1973; (2) the continuing evolution of written registers along Dimensions 1 and 2 ('Structural Elaboration' and 'Lexical Elaboration') to become even more different from spoken registers; and (3) the diversification of written registers along Dimensions 2 and 3 ('Lexical Elaboration', and 'Argumentative Versus Reported Style'), where the press registers have evolved to become more distinct. Register normalization has been a much weaker force in the evolution of these registers to date, being reflected primarily in the shift toward more similar characterizations among the press registers with respect to the structural elaboration dimension (Dim. 1).

In our ongoing work, we are examining these processes in a wider range of written registers, including novels, folk stories, academic theses, and government memos. We are also analyzing historical developments along additional dimensions of variation (e.g., 'Narrative Versus Non-Narrative Discourse Organization', 'Distanced, Directive Interaction', and 'Personal Persuasion'). Hared (1992) presents more detailed analyses of lexical, morphological, and grammatical changes in the press registers, in response to the complementary forces of standardization and modernization. And, finally, we are undertaking a fuller cross-linguistic analysis of these changes in Somali and English. Such analyses will provide a framework for additional cross-linguistic investigations, eventually allowing identification of universal tendencies in the adaptation and standardization of languages in response to changes in their social histories.

Notes

1. The related process of standardization, which refers to "the suppression of optional variability in language" (Milroy and Milroy 1985:8), also entails a type of linguistic change associated with the development of written varieties. For example, Devitt (1989) uses the "socio-historical" approach developed by Romaine (1982) to investigate the standardization of written English in Scotland. This approach includes analysis of the relative frequency of forms across registers from different historical periods; Devitt specifically analyzes the distribution of five major linguistic variables (e.g., relative clause markers: *quh-* in Scots-English versus *wh-* in Anglo-English) in five registers (e.g., religious treatises, personal letters, and official letters) across seven twenty-year periods extending from 1520 to 1659.

2. There actually were a few early indigenous scripts used for personal communication within Somali clans. The best known of these is Cismaaniya, created by Cismaan Yuusuf around 1920. This script was used primarily for personal letters within the Majeerteen clan of the Daarood clan family. Another indigenous script was developed in 1933 by Sheekh Cabduraxmaan Sheekh Nuur of the Gudabiirsi clan; and a third was developed in 1952 by Xuseen Sheekh Axmed Kaddare, from the Abgaal clan of the Hawiya clan family. The best published information on these scripts is in Laitin (1977), who indicates that all were used primarily for personal communication within their immediate clan. A thorough investigation of the range of language uses associated with these scripts is needed, as well as linguistic analyses of the written texts themselves (which are scattered across private collections).

3. Despite the successful transition from European to Somali literacy and the major literacy campaigns, literacy continues to play a relatively minor role in the daily lives of typical Somalis. Quranic literacy, which usually involves reading Arabic without comprehension, is still probably the most widespread literacy activity. There are few written materials available in rural areas, although there are some older adults who can read Somali folk stories or the newspaper, and the number of young adults who have been educated in Somali is steadily increasing.

In the 1970s, most writers of Somali were administrators, teachers, and journalists who had previously been educated in Italian or English. By the early 1980s, writers who had been educated in Somali began to enter the work force. There are still few actual producers of written texts, however. All published Somali texts are written in the capital city of Mogadishu by educated journalists, teachers, fiction writers, and government employees. Government employees in other cities write some memos and official letters, while the production of written texts by nonprofessionals is restricted to personal letters, petitions, and notes.

A fuller analysis of literacy practices in Somali is required, providing details of who actually produces and consumes written texts, and for what purposes. The focus of our study, however, is on the linguistic evolution of Somali written registers, rather than on the social correlates of Somali literacy. For this purpose, we collected and analyzed texts from all available spoken and written registers, even though relatively few Somalis actually produce some of those registers.

4. Since there were no pre-existing materials available for Somali, texts were tagged by an interactive program and an on-line dictionary. As new words were encountered in texts, they were analyzed interactively and then automatically entered into the dictionary for future reference.

5. We used a common factor analysis with a Promax rotation, extracting six factors for analysis. The first factor in the analysis accounts for 27.8 percent of the shared variance, while the six factors analyzed in Biber and Hared (1992) account for 53.3 percent of the shared variance. The major features on each factor have loadings over .45, while features in parentheses have loadings between .30 and .45.

6. We transformed the dimension scores to aid in comparability across dimensions. Following the practice in Biber (1988), all frequencies are standardized to a mean of 0.0 and a standard deviation of 1.0 before the dimension scores are computed. In addition, each dimension score was multiplied by a scaling coefficient so that all dimensions used a scale running from plus to minus 10. The scaling coefficients are

Dimension	Scaling Coefficient
1	.314
2	−1.693
3	1.067

Dimension 2 is inverted (reversing the positive and negative poles) to facilitate comparisons with Dimensions 1 and 3; after inversion, conversational registers are at or near the positive pole of all three dimensions, while expository registers are at or near the negative pole.

Dimension scores should not be interpreted in absolute terms; they are rather useful for relative comparisons among texts and registers. The transformations do not alter these relative relations or the strength of each dimension; their purpose is simply to facilitate comparisons across dimensions.

7. Hapax legomena and type-token ratio are both based on the first five hundred words in a text.

8. Biber and Hared (1991) analyzes a wider range of written registers (including government memos, folk stories, and general fiction) with respect to five dimensions of variation, but it considers texts from only the first period (1973–74).

9. With the revolution in Somalia in the winter of 1990–91 and the current state of turmoil, we expect that literacy production has declined to even lower levels.

10. We exclude conference lectures and conference discussions from the present analysis since these did not exist as Somali registers in 1972. University lectures and sports broadcasts also had marginal status as Somali registers in 1972. If we excluded these two registers as well, our results would be even more striking; we have chosen the more conservative approach of including the full potential range of spoken registers.

11. Comparison to actual speech from 1972 would of course be preferable, but it was not possible. There actually were a few tapes of early radio broadcasts archived at the Ministry of Information in Mogadishu, but we were unable to obtain copies despite repeated attempts.

12. The following abbreviations are used in our translations:
FM: focus marker
QM: question marker
OPT: optative marker
IMP: impersonal
NEG: negative
RFLX: reflexive

13. This generalization holds for the extent of variability within and among formal written registers; further research is required, however, to document the influence of standardization on spoken registers.

14. It is interesting to compare these historical changes in the patterns of use along Dimension 1 to the structural diachronic developments described by Givón (1979), associated with the movement from "discourse to syntax." For example, Givón discusses the historical development via "syntacticization" of the "looser, conjoined, paratactic constructions" in a language into "syntactic, tightly-bound, 'subordinated' constructions" (p. 97). The former set of features (paratactic constructions) are associated with the "pragmatic mode," while the latter set (subordinated constructions) are associated with the "syntactic mode." The pragmatic mode is in turn associated with informal registers, while the syntactic mode is associated with formal (written) registers. Givón further concludes that "the pragmatic mode was the *earlier* type of human communication, whereas the syntactic mode is a later outgrowth from it" (p. 106).

Although Givón focuses on structural change, similar patterns are seen in the historical extension of variability along Dimension 1 following the addition of written registers: much more frequent use of relative clauses, clefts, complement clauses, and other types of dependent clauses in the initial stage (Figure 8.1), and as Figure 8.4 shows, an even more frequent use of these "syntacticized" features in the written registers over time.

References

Ali, Issa H., and Mohamed S. Gees. 1979. "The Somali Language in Science Context." In Hussein M. Adam, ed., *Somalia and the World.* Mogadishu, Somalia: Halgan. Pp. 84–94.

Andrzejewski, B. W. 1974. "The Introduction of a National Orthography for Somali." *African Language Studies* 15:199–203.

———. 1978. "The Development of a National Orthography in Somalia and the Modernization of the Somali Language." *Horn of Africa* 1:39–46.

———. 1979. "The Use of Somali in Mathematics and Science." In Hussein M. Adam, ed., *Somalia and the World.* Mogadishu, Somalia: Halgan. Pp. 57–83.

Biber, Douglas. 1986. "Spoken and Written Textual Dimensions in English: Resolving the Contradictory Findings." *Language* 62:384–414.

———. 1988. *Variation Across Speech and Writing.* Cambridge: Cambridge University Press.

Biber, Douglas, and Edward Finegan. 1989. "Drift and the Evolution of English Style: A History of Three Genres." *Language* 65:487–517.

Biber, Douglas, and Mohamed Hared. 1991. "Literacy in Somali: Linguistic Consequences." *Annual Review of Applied Linguistics* 12:260–82.

———. 1992. "Dimensions of Register Variation in Somali." *Language Variation and Change* 4:41–75.

Bloomfield, Leonard. 1927. "Literate and Illiterate Speech." *American Speech* 2:432–39.

Brown, Penelope, and Colin Fraser. 1979. "Speech as a Marker of Situation." In Klaus R. Scherer and Howard Giles, eds., *Social Markers in Speech.* Cambridge: Cambridge University Press. Pp. 33–62.

Coulmas, Florian. 1989a. "Language Adaptation." In Coulmas, ed. Pp. 1–25.

———, ed. 1989b. *Language Adaptation.* Cambridge: Cambridge University Press.

Devitt, Amy J. 1989. *Standardizing Written English: Diffusion in the Case of Scotland 1520–1659.* Cambridge: Cambridge University Press.

Ervin-Tripp, Susan. 1972. "On Sociolinguistic Rules: Alternation and Co-Occurrence." In John J. Gumperz and Dell Hymes, eds., *Directions in Sociolinguistics.* New York: Holt. Pp. 213–50.

Ferguson, Charles. 1968. "Language Development." In J. A. Fishman, C. A. Ferguson, and J. D. Gupta, eds., *Language Problems of Developing Nations.* New York: John Wiley and Sons. Pp. 27–35.

Galeb, Mohamed H. 1979. "Brief Reflections on the Modernization of the Somali Language." In Hussein M. Adam, ed., *Somalia and the World.* Mogadishu, Somalia: Halgan. Pp. 53–56.

Geshekter, C. L. 1978. "Language Politics and University Teaching in Somalia." *Horn of Africa* 1:11–17.

Givón, Talmy. 1979. "From Discourse to Syntax: Grammar as a Processing Strategy." In Talmy Givón, ed., *Syntax and Semantics 12: Discourse and Syntax.* New York: Academic Press. Pp. 81–112.

Goody, Jack. 1977. *The Domestication of the Savage Mind.* Cambridge: Cambridge University Press.

Goody, Jack, and I. P. Watt. 1963. "The Consequences of Literacy." *Comparative Studies in History and Society* 5:304–45.

Hared, Mohamed. 1992. *Modernization and Standardization in Somali Press Writing.* Ph.D. Dissertation, University of Southern California.

Hymes, Dell. 1974. *Foundations in Sociolinguistics: An Ethnographic Approach.* Philadelphia: University of Pennsylvania Press.

———. 1984. "Sociolinguistics: Stability and Consolidation." *International Journal of the Sociology of Language* 45:39–45.

Kalmár, Ivan. 1985. "Are There Really No Primitive Languages?" In D. R. Olson, N. Torrance, and A. Hildyard, eds., *Literacy, Language, and Learning: The Nature and Consequences of Reading and Writing.* Cambridge: Cambridge University Press. Pp. 148–66.

Laitin, David D. 1977. *Politics, Language, and Thought: The Somali Experience.* Chicago: University of Chicago Press.

Mezei, Regina. 1989. "Somali Language and Literacy." *Language Problems and Language Planning* 13:211–21.

Milroy, James, and Lesley Milroy. 1985. *Authority in Language: Investigating Language Prescription and Standardisation.* London: Routledge & Kegan Paul.

Ong, Walter, J. 1982. *Orality and Literacy: The Technologizing of the Word.* New York: Methuen.

Reder, Stephen. 1981. "The Written and the Spoken Word: Influence of Vai Literacy on Vai Speech." In S. Scribner and M. Cole, *The Psychology of Literacy.* Cambridge, MA: Harvard University Press. Pp. 187–99.

Rissanen, Matti. 1986. "Variation and the Study of English Historical Syntax." In David Sankoff, ed., *Diversity and Diachrony.* Amsterdam: Benjamins. Pp. 97–109.

Romaine, Suzanne. 1980. "The Relative Clause Marker in Scots English: Diffusion, Complexity, and Style as Dimensions of Syntactic Change." *Language in Society* 9:221–47.

———. 1982. *Socio-Historical Linguistics: Its Status and Methodology.* Cambridge: Cambridge University Press.

Sapir, Edward. 1921. *Language.* New York: Harcourt, Brace and World.

Scribner, Sylvia, and Michael Cole. 1981. *The Psychology of Literacy.* Cambridge, MA: Harvard University Press.

Ure, Jean. 1982. "Introduction: Approaches to the Study of Register Range." *International Journal of the Sociology of Language* 35:5–23.

9

Stylistic Variation in a Language Restricted to Private-Sphere Use

Nancy C. Dorian

One of the fundamental principles of sociolinguistic investigation, according to William Labov, is that there "are no single-style speakers" (1970:19). Dell Hymes makes essentially the same point, asserting that "no normal human being talks the same way all the time" (1984:44). But dying languages have been included under the rubric "*exceptional* language" (Obler and Menn 1982), and some researchers have asserted that they are essentially "monostylistic" (Dressler and Wodak-Leodolter 1977:36–37, Dressler 1982:326, 1988:188–89). In invoking the notion of monostylism in language decay, Dressler specifies "restriction to a very casual style used with very familiar dialogue partners about restricted topics in routine speech situations" (1982:326). This paper represents an attempt to determine whether, in a language undergoing just that sort of restriction, the fundamental principle articulated by Labov and Hymes still applies, or whether in those unfavorable circumstances a lack of stylistic variation occurs which would warrant the term *monostylism*.

When a language moves close to a foreseeable point of extinction, it is inevitably spoken less and less frequently. Even those speakers who continue to use it regularly have ever fewer fellow-speakers to converse with, because the fluent-speaker population is aging and thinning out. Their own kin networks begin to be heavily populated by younger bilinguals who speak the expanding language of the region better than the original ancestral language, and eventually those same kin networks have expanding language monolinguals among their youngest members. Languages which die out gradually in this fashion, via the progressive failure of intergenerational transmission, usually retreat in the final generations to a few

I am grateful to Edward Finegan for encouraging me, both in general and with specific prompts and questions, to persist in working through my imperfect corpus to locate evidence of stylistic variation, and to Edward Finegan and Douglas Biber for helpful comments on the original draft of this paper and for suggestions on the relevant literature.

spheres of use: they persist in domestic settings among the older generation, and they are used for casual social intercourse among contemporaries who were school-mates or workmates in their young years. Occasionally some specialized use of the ancestral languages will remain in more formal spheres: religion, typically, and sometimes a few other more-or-less ritualized types of behavior.

This is certainly the profile presented by the East Sutherland dialect of Scottish Gaelic, still spoken in the last half of the twentieth century by a dwindling number of Gaelic-English bilinguals in three villages on the east coast of that very northerly Highland county, all fisherfolk or the offspring of fisherfolk. For East Sutherland Gaelic (ESG hereafter), the competition comes not from any more vigorous variety of Gaelic, but from English. In the local context the two languages, English and Gaelic, are in competition with one another, and I will therefore speak of ESG as a *language* approaching extinction, even though it is actually a regional dialect of Gaelic which is fading from the scene; there are certainly other forms of Gaelic which will survive the approaching demise of ESG. As would be expected, the competition between ESG and English has been a very unequal one. English has long had the unwavering support of the national state, so that education has been solely in English since the state took it on, and local people's experience of military service has also meant the use of English, in modern times, as has any contact with the court system or local administrative services. The one social institution which has favored Gaelic in the 20th century has been the church, with some denomina-tions (all Protestant in this region) persisting longer in the use of Gaelic than others.

It was the long-continued use of Gaelic in religious life which prevented the language situation among the ESG-speaking fisherfolk from becoming one of bilin-gual diglossia during the first half of the 20th century, in fact. So long as Gaelic remained the language of church services, scripture readings, psalm singing, and praying, it could not be said that English had usurped all H[igh] language functions or that Gaelic had retreated to L[ow] language functions. By the early 1960s, when I first arrived in East Sutherland to begin studying the dialect and its setting, only one village still had Gaelic church services available. All of the Gaelic speakers who were of fisherfolk background (which means all the indigenous Gaelic speakers who remained, by that time) had had their formative religious experiences through the medium of Gaelic, however. Active control of religious language was largely re-stricted to men, since only males were trained to precent (line out) the psalms during services, and only men had been expected to lead prayer spoken out loud in house-hold settings, at wakes, and so forth. Only men could serve as elders and thus take a limited leadership role in congregational life. (Ministers, too, were exclusively male, but since there were never any ministers of local origin this offered no verbal role for speakers of ESG.) As the number of men who could precent the psalms in the one remaining church with Gaelic services declined, a relatively young woman was sometimes persuaded to precent when no male precentor was available (though she did so from her pew, declining to take the precentor's seat facing the congrega-tion at the front of the church). She had a strong voice and was self-taught, but her example at least indicates that women could sometimes take a prominent role in using the rather archaic (and very nonlocal) Gaelic of religious usage, at least in the fixed and familiar language of the metrical psalms.

With the retirement of the last Gaelic-speaking minister in the late 1960s or early 1970s, Gaelic ceased to play any regular formal and public role for Embo villagers; it had ceased to play any such role for members of the other two former fishing communities of East Sutherland long since. Because it seemed neither appropriate nor congenial to explore merely as an observer the use of Gaelic in people's private devotional lives, I never tried to investigate the active control of religious language among the more than forty fluent speakers with whom I worked. In their work with me a few men demonstrated some control of Biblical vocabulary not in everyday use, and I noted also some occasional use of the language of benediction in formal partings among fluent speakers not in regular contact with one another (including the closing of tape-recorded messages). It seems likely that some individuals used Gaelic in private prayer, and some men were known as good psalm singers. It is possible that some few men read the scriptures in Gaelic.

For most ESG speakers in the latter half of the 20th century, and in particular for most women speakers, Gaelic was the language of hearth and home. There simply were no public spheres in which their native form of Gaelic could appropriately be used. The sole remaining public spheres for any Gaelic at all in these villages, when I began to do research there in the 1960s, were the church (for Embo village only) and the ceilidh. Ceilidhs were evening functions at which admission was charged, with performances of vocal and instrumental music, Highland dance, and sometimes also amusing monologues; they were usually held to benefit some cause or organization. For each ceilidh there was a *fear-an-taighe* (master-of-ceremonies), and if possible a Gaelic speaker served in this role. It was customary for any Gaelic-speaking *fear-an-taighe* to use some Gaelic, at least ceremonially (e.g., in welcoming the audience at the outset and in thanking the performers at the close), during the course of the evening. I am not aware of any Gaelic speakers native to the three fishing communities who served as *fear-an-taighe,* any more than as minister, however; these were roles performed by outsiders to the local communities, and consequently the Gaelic used was not the local variety. All the same, the Gaelic spoken from the platform at ceilidhs exposed local speakers to a relatively formal use of the language in a public function, as church services also did for those who still had them available. These local uses of a more formal Gaelic had some personal reality for ESG speakers, unlike the limited use of Gaelic in broadcasting, but it must be stressed that any variety of Gaelic used by a minister, a *fear-an-taighe,* or a broadcaster would inevitably be too different from the local East Sutherland variety to serve as a model for local imitation. ESG is radically deviant, from the point of view of the standard language, and the fit between ESG and any variety used in public spheres is too poor to allow any use of the other variety by local speakers beyond the odd adoption of lexical items or turns of phrase. ESG speakers who attempted more than this (and some few occasionally did) quickly came to grief through their inability to sustain the performance over more than a few phrases or sentences.[1]

When a language has retreated to the private sphere exclusively, as ESG has, there may well be some question about its stylistic range. If it is never used to make a formal speech, to introduce the speaker at a meeting, to give the vote of thanks to a guest performer or speaker at a public function, to debate the agenda of a local organization, to make a motion during a public meeting, to make an announcement of coming events, and so forth, how much capacity will it maintain to express stylistic differences at all?

My impression, from participating repeatedly over a fifteen-year period in some of the daily-life activities of fluent ESG speakers who became my friends, was that there remained a useful range of styles available to speakers, though a limited range certainly by comparison with that available to speakers of languages which are used to more public and formal purposes than ESG. In this chapter I try to substantiate my impression of the stylistic flexibility of ESG from tape-recorded but freely spoken data drawn from the single ESG speaker who was most available to me, my landlady over the entire fifteen-year stretch of my recurrent East Sutherland field-work.

Though it is the best I have available, this body of data is very far from ideal for the purpose of demonstrating the fullest possible range of styles in ESG. For one thing, it all derives from a single kind of verbal event, a very lightly guided variety of interview.[2] For another, it derives from a single main participant in that verbal event, with one unchanging lesser participant. These are certainly not ideal circumstances for plumbing the far reaches of style change. There are some redeeming factors, nonetheless. My landlady, whom I will call MMK,[3] was profoundly illiterate.[4] She was also remarkably uninclined to attempts at shifting in the direction of more standard Gaelic forms, which was striking in view of the fact that she had lived for a few years early in her married life on the west coast of Wester Ross, where she had heard a good deal of the Gaelic dialect (more nearly standard and definitely more prestigious) native to that region. She can be said to represent genuinely local ESG speech norms. She was also a wonderfully uninhibited speaker. That is, she was not only unpretentious in sticking strictly to local Gaelic usage, she was also much more impervious than most local speakers to the scorn of speakers of other dialects and to the disdain of many English monolinguals for speakers of Gaelic generally and for speakers of the local Gaelic particularly. She spoke Gaelic with pleasure and relish, and she was willing to speak it with normal audibility on the street, something a good many local women avoided. She liked to talk, in either of her languages, and had a great appreciation for conversation, gossip, and the recounting of stories. She was, in short, a great talker, harder to persuade to silence than to prompt to exuberant volumes of speech. For a linguistic fieldworker she had another splendid attribute: she had no qualms at all about being tape-recorded. Because of this, and because she and I lived under the same roof so often, she is better represented in my field recordings than most other speakers. And though I have perhaps as much material for two others, no other speaker romped so enthusiastically through as many stories and reminiscences as she. Consequently it was to the material which she spoke on tape for me that I turned when I became interested in stylistic variation, and her freely spoken tape-recorded material forms the basis for this study.[5]

During three recording sessions, in different years, MMK had an opportunity to display her verbal skills in Gaelic to good advantage.[6] As her audience I certainly felt that she was able to change her style to suit her topic, but I had not looked closely at her texts in order to discover whether my impression was supported by the data. Wishing to do that now, I have concentrated on the first two taping sessions, one of thirteen minutes' duration dating from 1964,[7] and another of twenty-five minutes' duration dating from 1968. She began the earlier of the two sessions with a particular story she had wanted to tell me, and the story in question had a somber theme. It was a story about a sign of ill luck, followed by drowning deaths among the fishermen in her own kin network, and she wanted to persuade me of the validity of her own belief in premonitions of death. She delivered the story in an unusually serious voice, slowly and with didactic emphasis, so it stood to reason that such a narrative might lean toward the more formal end of her stylistic range. Since most of her stories were far from soberly serious, the presence of this narrative made this first session, in contrast with any other, a good candidate for investigation. And though MMK knew me quite well in 1964, after many months of shared residence, and seemed thoroughly comfortable in talking with me in either of her languages, after much social interaction in both languages and many working sessions on Gaelic as well, she knew me still better in 1968, after intervening visits in 1965 and 1967, so that she could be expected to be still more at ease with me and with tape recording by the time of the second session. The later session could therefore be expected to show a special informality of long acquaintance, by comparison with the earlier one.

From the thirty-eight minutes of recordings made with MMK, I selected all of the material which seemed to me to constitute narratives: stories with particular themes, particular actors, and some degree of resolution.[8] There were eight such narratives, two in the first session and six in the second. Under short titles based on their themes, I offer brief summaries here:

1. The prefigured TRAGEDY (448 words).[9] Shattering glass leads to a prediction of tragedy to come. Soon thereafter two local fishermen are drowned. The body of one is recovered immediately, but the body of the other is found and buried only after a considerable interval.
2. Little boy LOST (339 words). While the family is at a herring fishing station MMK's youngest brother wanders away, but in the direction of the area where his aunt lives; she spots him and retrieves him.
3. The BATHER saved from drowning (974 words). MMK sees an acquaintance in difficulty while bathing and pulls her part of the way out of the water; others help to bring her the rest of the way in. The bather's sister claims that it was a dog who performed the rescue.
4. Past SINS exposed (144 words). While the bather is being dragged urgently out of the sea, more of her becomes visible than is polite; impolite inferences are drawn about her past history.
5. The Gaelic CLASS (308 words). MMK attends a Gaelic class in preparation for choral singing in a competition, but when she speaks her local Golspie Gaelic the instructor, not a local speaker, rejects it peremptorily. She leaves and refuses to return.
6. The choir COMPETITION (256 words). A strategy for defeating a neighboring village's choir in the Gaelic choral competition is successful and Golspie wins the challenge cup.

7. The unwelcome Gaelic COACH (860 words). A Gaelic speaker from the Hebrides is rejected as Gaelic choir coach in Golspie but coaches one or two neighboring choirs; the other villages pay her, but not Golspie. Singers from all the villages give her presents when she marries locally, but when the marriage is dissolved within a short time, she has the gifts auctioned off.
8. The defective Gaelic RECORD (214 words). The instructional record which a new boarder is using to help him learn Gaelic seems to MMK's ears to be teaching him incorrect Gaelic.

In referring to these narratives subsequently I will use the number and a single-word rubric: 1, TRAGEDY; 2, LOST; 3, BATHER; 4, SINS; 5, CLASS; 6, COMPETITION; 7, COACH; 8, RECORD. Each but the second (Lost) has a clear narrator's mood to it, matching the thrust of the story: number 1, serious/didactic; numbers 3, 5, and 7, indignant; numbers 4 and 8, hilarious; number 6, delighted. The second narrative (Lost) has a certain sober tone which carries over from the first, though it is perfectly cheerful and has a happy ending (the boy is swiftly found and was still alive as an elderly man when the story was told). It will become evident in due course that some 'soberness' carryover does appear in the stylistic features of the second story, and this is apparent also in such extralinguistic markers as the absence of any laughter on MMK's part.

The one stylistic marker in ESG of which I was well aware before I investigated MMK's eight narratives for this study was the handling of obvious loanwords from English.[10] I knew from long experience that when ESG speakers were on their best linguistic behavior they tried to avoid both code-switches into English, especially intrasentential ones, and the use of a lot of obvious loanwords from English. With a long history of close contact with English, Scottish Gaelic quite generally shows the effects of the contact in the presence of many English borrowings. Both Gaelic speakers and English speakers notice the more obvious borrowings, and English speakers are often scornful of Gaelic heavily laced with obvious English vocabulary when they hear it spoken. In East Sutherland belittling remarks are sometimes made, for example, "I could speak that Gaelic myself!" as if to deny the legitimacy of Gaelic as an independent language, and Gaelic speakers are self-conscious about the use of borrowings.[11] When I first began to gather tape-recorded texts from each of the East Sutherland fisherfolk villages, it was quickly apparent that those speakers who had the lexical latitude to do so made an effort to minimize their reliance on loanwords from English. One literate male Golspie speaker replaced the nearly universal /p'ɔlisxən/ 'policemen' with /ɫuxk ən ɫə/ 'people of the law', for example, when taping a narrative for me, and a male Embo speaker who needed to use the word /t'ramp / 'tramp' for his narrative carefully prefaced it with /mər ə xanu aǰ/ 'as they would say'. In view of all this I expected to see some change in MMK's handling of loanwords as she moved from the sober, didactic telling of her opening story to more relaxed stories in the later session.

In analyzing the use of loanwords in MMK's eight narratives, I looked at the following features: (1) the sheer number of recognizably English loanwords relative to the total number of words in the story, (2) phrasal switches to English, (3) use of loanwords in markedly Gaelic or markedly English fashion. Within the third catego-

TABLE 9.1   The Handling of Obviously English Loanwords and Phrases
in MMK's Gaelic Narratives, First or Last Instances of Significant Features
Indicated by Dividing Lines

		Loanwords as Percentage of All Words	No Mutation in Mutational Environment	English Plurals	Phrasal English Switches	Reversed Phrasal Switches
1964	1	3.4	0 of 4	0 of 3	0	—
	2	4.7	0 of 2	—	1	1
1968	3	5.3	5 of 13	0 of 2	1	1
	4	2.8	—	—	0	—
	5	3.2	0 of 8	—	1	0
	6	7.4	0 of 6	1 of 3	2	0
	7	3.8	2 of 10	1 of 7	4	0
	8	6.5	0 of 8	—	0	—

ry I looked in particular at the application of the initial consonant mutations so characteristic of Gaelic[12] to loanwords, in environments where a native Gaelic word would necessarily show mutation, and at the use of inflectional morphology with obviously English loanwords. Where inflectional morphology was concerned, the issue turned out to be whether an obviously English loanword was made plural by means of a Gaelic plural allomorph or an English plural allomorph, since only the plural proved to be variable; all other inflections used with loanwords were uniformly Gaelic. Switches to a wholly English phrase within the Gaelic narratives were also tallied, since it seemed likely that self-consciousness about dependence on English lexicon would extend a fortiori to phrasal switches. Table 9.1 shows MMK's handling of obviously English material in her eight narratives.

There is no indication in MMK's narratives that she is trying to limit her use of obviously English loanwords as such, since all her narratives have them; nor that a low percentage of such loanwords correlates with the relatively low-key delivery of her first two narratives, since narratives 4 and 5 have a lower percentage than even the first, deeply serious, narrative. The handling of the English material is conservative in the first two narratives overall, however. There are no failures of mutation in environments where mutation is obligatory in ESG until the third narrative; English plural formations first appear later still, in the sixth and seventh narratives. One phrasal switch to English appears in the second narrative and at least one in all but two of the subsequent narratives, but the early narratives (including 3, in this case) are distinguished from the later narratives by the fact that MMK shows self-consciousness about the phrasal switches, in that she immediately attempts to reformulate the phrasal switch to English as a Gaelic equivalent. In 2 (Lost) she uses the expression *Golspie holiday,* pauses momentarily, and then says /hɔlide: kəi:špi/. She's unable to come up with a Gaelic rendering of *holiday,* but she shifts to the Gaelic version of the place name and she reorders head and modifier to conform to the Gaelic word order rather than the English. In 3 (Bather) she finishes a Gaelic sentence with the phrase *a few years,* then follows it immediately with a precise Gaelic equivalent /anari vliənəxən/.

There are two further signs of lexical self-consciousness in MMK's two narratives from the earlier recording session. In the first narrative, she prefaces the deliberate use of an English borrowing with the Gaelic phrase /nɛ pun tɔ xatən/ 'or I could say'. She has just described the breaking of glass into "a few pieces" in her narrative, but "a few pieces" was evidently not strong enough to suit her, to describe the fragmentation of the glass, and she adds "or I could say 'smithereens'," using the English noun.[13] At the opening of the second story she uses two English-based loanwords, /kʼru:/ 'crew' and /anti/ 'aunt', without self-consciousness, but stops immediately after uttering the third, /wikɛnd/, breaking off her narrative to say to me in English, "What would I say for *weekend?*" As I murmur that *weekend* seems fine to me, she carries straight on with her story, but it's just after this that she uses the phrase *Golspie holiday* and then immediately offers a Gaelicized version of the phrase. She interrupts herself only once again, in these narratives or the later ones, with doubts about her use of an English word or phrase. In narrative 5, Class, where the acceptability of her Golspie Gaelic is the specific focus of the story, she uses the loanword /kʼwɛsčan/ 'question' in starting to describe the teacher's classroom request for the Gaelic version of an English sentence: /agəs hurd a rəm:əs ə gwɛsčan —/ 'and he said to me the question, —'. She then stops and repeats the offending noun in self-mockery, immediately reformulating the clause with the Gaelic verb 'ask'. The borrowed noun was well integrated phonologically, with the initial mutation (nasalization) appropriate to a masculine noun of its phonological class after the definite article, but it is evidently not suitable for use in preparing to quote the arrogant Gaelic teacher, even though she uses English loanwords freely and unselfconsciously later in the same story. This instance of corrective self-consciousness in 5 (Class) is spontaneous, while the first narrative remains unique in its deliberate introduction of an English loanword, self-consciously framed with the Gaelic phrase 'or I could say'.

The handling of obviously English loanwords as an index of self-consciously careful style was the first differentiating feature which I looked for in the eight narratives, but it seemed to me that the narratives might also be expected to differ in terms of features which contributed to their relative liveliness as stories, if there was a stylistic continuum of any sort among them. As indicators of liveliness I tallied seven features: the number of simple direct quotes or direct-quote interchanges; the number of those which were in fact interchanges rather than simple direct quotes; the number of interchanges which consisted of more than the minimum two turns; the number of direct quotes which used /(h)ɔrs/, the more vivid of the two quotative past-tense verbs of ESG;[14] the number of instances of doubled-up quotatives (akin to English "I sez, '_____', sez I"); the number of strong interjections (i.e., interjections other than the routine 'oh', 'well', 'ach', or 'och'); and the number of uses of 'adventurous' language (i.e., profanities and indelicate terms for body parts).[15] Table 9.2 presents the results of this tally.

As Table 9.2 indicates, none of the liveliness features of MMK's narratives except simple direct quotation appears in the first two of her stories (and only one of those in each story), but four liveliness features occur for the first time as of the third story. That third story is certainly a very lively one, but even so it has only one strong interjection and no instances of indelicate or profane language. The fourth

TABLE 9.2 Incidence of 'Liveliness Features' in MMK's Gaelic Narratives, First Instance or First Major Increase Indicated by Dividing Lines

		Simple Quotes and Interchanges #	Interchanges #	Interchanges of Three or More Turns #	/(h)ɔrs/ Quotatives #	Doubled-up Quotatives #	Strong Interjections #	'Adventurous' Language Uses #
1964	1	1	0	—	0	0	0.	0
	2	1	0	—	0	0	0	0
1968	3	6	3	—	11	1	1	0
	4	1	0	—	4	0	0	3
	5	2	2	1	0	1	0	0
	6	1	0	—	7	0	2	1
	7	1	1	1	0	0	1	2
	8	2	0	—	0	0	3	1

story, a very brief afterthought-anecdote connected with narrative 3 (Bather), is wholly indelicate in subject matter, and once she has told that story other 'adventurous' usages appear more freely. Of the subsequent stories only 5 (Class) is without them.

The combined evidence of Tables 9.1 and 9.2 seems to indicate that MMK is indeed using a relatively restrained style when she begins the earlier taping session, which produces the first two of the eight narratives, and that she opens the later taping session with a more relaxed and casual style. Although MMK is still sufficiently self-conscious about English material, at the opening of the 1968 session, to pause and reformulate a phrasal switch to English back into Gaelic, the third narrative marks the first failures of consonant mutation with an obviously English loanword in environments where mutation would be obligatory in a native Gaelic word. Narrative 3 also provides the first interchanges, in the use of direct quotes, and the vivid quotative /(h)ɔrs/ not only appears, but appears in large numbers. The first instance of doubled-up quotative verbs likewise characterizes this narrative. She uses no 'adventurous' language, but she does for the first time use a strong interjection. Though all but two narratives after the third have phrasal switches to English, no narrative after that one shows the reversal of such a switch. Only 5 (Class) among the subsequent narratives has neither a strong interjection nor any 'adventurous' language, but 5 does have a number of lively features associated with direct quotation (interchanges, use of /(h)ɔrs/, and the other instance of doubled-up quotatives).

Seven of the eight narratives involve MMK personally; only 4 (Sins) does not. She is a particularly central actor in the early part of narrative 3 (Bather), where she is the person who realizes that the bather is in trouble and makes the initial effort at rescue; and in the first half of 5 (Class), where she is the local Gaelic speaker who draws the teacher's scorn by speaking the Golspie variety of Gaelic. But she is also an actor in five of the six others. (For example, she is present when the glass shatters in 1, and it is she who runs to buy eau de cologne as an antidote to the terrible odor from the second body when it eventually washes up on the shore; she is among the older children who are supposed to be looking after the little boy in 2 when he wanders off.) Narratives 3 and 5, in which MMK plays a very central role, are especially lively stories, but so is 7 (Coach), in which she plays a far less crucial role: she takes a dislike to the Gaelic coach and states her intention to urge the local Gaelic committee not to engage the coach for the Golspie choir's tuition, but she is not a major figure in most of the story. Personal involvement motivates all of the narratives except 4 (in subject matter an addendum to 3), but degree of involvement does not fully account for degree of liveliness in the narratives.

It seems reasonable to look at the third narrative as the first in MMK's more casual style, which she then maintains to the end of that second taping session (to which the eighth narrative, Record, provides the close). Strictly in terms of Tables 9.1 and 9.2, there is nothing to distinguish the first two narratives from one another except for the absence of any phrasal switches to English in the opening story. For the listener, all the same, there is one characteristic of the first narrative which is uniquely its own, a feature I would term an artistry of repetition which MMK shows nowhere else in this taping session (or for that matter in the second and third). It lends an almost Biblical flavor to her Gaelic here, especially since she keeps her lexicon and her syntax very simple. In setting the scene for the breaking of the glass, for example, she relates that she was sitting with elderly relatives of her mother's: "Listening to their songs. And their singing." She repeats the possessive here, making two phrases out of what could easily be one (i.e., "their songs and sing- ing"). She does the same sort of thing several times again in speaking of the rescue attempt and the victims, after the capsizing of the fishing boat: "And my father was on *one,* and my uncle was on the other *one*" (instead of "on the other," i.e., of the boats going out to try to rescue the men in the water); "And they *caught* the old man, but they didnt *catch* his son"; "And the police *came,* and they all *came*"; "but one *boot* was off him and the other *boot* was on him." In each case the italicized second instance of a word could have been avoided, and in more ordinary style probably would have been. The example involving the repetition of the verb 'catch' is especially notable, because that particular verb is regular, so that repeating it produces identical-sounding verb forms in rapid succession. The more common and less marked verb here would have been 'get/find'. But 'get/find' is suppletive and in the preterite is /h/-initial; because initial /h-/ is unstable in this context and would have disappeared in the second clause, using 'get/find' would have produced less similar-sounding verbs in the positive preterite (first clause) and the negative pre- terite (second clause).

One other phrasal oddity appears in this short story, one which resembles the other overly complete repetitions but is actually still more striking, when MMK says, "And the old man was drowned, *and his son.*" Gaelic is a verb-initial lan- guage, and the passive MMK uses to start the sentence would be inflected for third person *plural* possessive if she had meant "the old man and his son" to act as a compound subject of the passive.[16] She inflected it for third person *singular* mas- culine possessive, making it clear (as do the suprasegmentals) that "and his son" is intended to be a second but separate third person singular subject, agreeing with the third person singular masculine passive (or with an elliptical second such passive). The phraseology is unusual, and is the more effective for that reason. In none of the subsequent narratives does MMK use phrasal repetitions in this way. When she uses repetitions in these other stories, they are simply expansions and afterthoughts, as is the case in this example from narrative 7 (Coach), "MacLeod was in the army along with Bob. Along with my husband. He was in India along with my husband." There are opportunities to use the same sort of repetition effect seen in narrative 1 again, but MMK does not take them. In 3, Bather, for example, a narrative which opens with a near-tragedy resembling the tragic scene of the first narrative, she tells of pulling an almost drowned woman from the sea: "And her mouth was full of green foam. And white. And I caught her, and I was pulling her in, but she was too heavy, and I couldn't get her in." In this passage MMK does not repeat the noun 'foam', to produce ". . . of green foam. And white foam"; and instead of repeating the verb 'pull', as she perfectly well could here, she makes a switch from 'pull' to 'get' when speaking of retrieving the body from the sea. She is using language quite differently from the way she used it in the first narrative of the earlier session, although she is describing a similar scene.

The handling of English loanwords and phrasal switches to English and the use of liveliness features constitute two sorts of dimensions along which MMK is able to vary the degree of formality versus casualness in her narratives. By observing the variations along those dimensions the listener can distinguish between the two opening narratives in her first taping session, which are both relatively formal, and the six subsequent narratives, from the second taping session, which are more casual. By attending to the high degree of purposeful phrasal repetition in the first narrative, the listener can recognize in it a more crafted formality than in the second narrative, even though the second narrative, too, is less casual than those which follow.[17]

MMK is not the speaker whom I would have chosen if I had been setting out specifically to explore the fullest range of stylistic variation which an ESG speaker in Golspie village could muster. I would have opted instead for one of the three males with whom I worked in Golspie, since I would have expected them to control some of the lexicon and phraseology of religious usage in ESG, giving them an outer limit of formal style more extreme than MMK's. Neither would I have chosen to use two recording sessions with myself as interviewer/audience as my test case, in exploring MMK's stylistic range or anyone else's. I would have tried to set up situations in which the individual was speaking to a variety of persons with whom s/he was on more intimate footing or less, in settings of greater or lesser familiarity, and to a variety of purposes. There is one advantage to having less than ideal material to work with, however: if variation in style is identifiable under such conditions, then it becomes that much the more certain that stylistic variation can reliably be claimed for this very "domestic" language which is already close to extinction.

It is important to establish the presence of a moderately broad stylistic range in terminal ESG, because it indicates that natural languages, even when restricted by decline in functions and domains to the private sphere, and hence to speech situations which are on the whole informal ones by comparison with those characteristic of languages in vigorous use across an entire society, can still be spoken by the fully fluent in ways appropriate to their various stylistic needs. The evidence of MMK's narratives, all drawn from two same-setting speech events, does not bear out the "monostylistic" label which Dressler applies to dying languages, for example, in a recent reference work:

> Terminal language decay seems to show a tendency towards monostylism. . . . That is, recessive languages are more and more used in casual styles only, for example, those which are appropriate for intimate routine interactions at home. This stylistic change is yet another dysfunctional change in so far as the recessive language becomes inadequate for certain speech situations, domains, and functions. (Dressler 1988:188–89)

While it is true that a speaker like MMK uses her Gaelic almost entirely for "routine interactions at home," it is not true that her Gaelic is "monostylistic." She can vary it according to her intention in telling a story, so that a serious story which is told for purposes of impressing and convincing shows quite different stylistic features from a hilarious story which is told for its entertainment value above all. No doubt her

Gaelic is "inadequate for certain speech situations, domains, and functions." She probably could not, in Gaelic, pray aloud, welcome a guest speaker to the Women's Rural Institute, or repeat the multiplication tables. These limitations have a great deal to do with MMK's range of activities, however; I doubt that she could easily do any of these things in English, either, or would undertake to do so willingly. She would (and did, once I replaced the interviewer whose western dialect she couldn't understand) do an interview for broadcast on the radio, and I'm certain that she would have had no difficulty whatever in lodging a protest in Gaelic about traffic safety for children, or other such daily-life matters, with the village authorities, assuming only that she had a speaker of a Gaelic mutually intelligible with hers to lodge it with. That is, the limits of her Gaelic style range reflect to a considerable degree the limits of her range of activities and not any drastic poverty of her Gaelic, which is rich and fluent by local standards.

One of my male sources in Golspie was highly political and quite prepared to engage in serious political discussions in Gaelic. He was not in late adulthood a churchgoer, but though I never heard him pray in Gaelic I suspect he was capable of it because of the religious upbringing which young males of his day experienced. He was an intelligent and resourceful speaker in both Gaelic and English, intellectually inclined despite limited education, and absolutely fearless in verbal interactions regardless of any differences in social status between him and his interlocutor. Listening to Gaelic speakers like this man, and listening to any group of ESG speakers moving from topic to topic and mood to mood, was more than sufficient to convince me that their Gaelic should be termed *polystylistic* rather than monostylistic:

> One can locate styles within [both the East Sutherland English and the East Sutherland Gaelic of the Brora, Golspie, and Embo bilinguals] which are appropriate to formality or informality, to vulgarity, to humor, to anger, and the like. Speakers differ in their ability to perform vividly in these styles, but they can certainly shift in the appropriate directions. (Dorian 1981:85)

I believe that it is a mistake to suppose that even a restriction to "routine intimate interactions at home" produces such radical loss of stylistic range in a language as to warrant the label "monostylistic," at least among speakers who remain fluent. Without leaving the hearthside, fluent last speakers of a fading language are quite likely to speak about subjects as different as their grocery shopping and a recent bereavement, to mention two which I've heard women discussing among themselves. The speech style shifts markedly in the course of a casual conversation when a bereavement becomes the topic of discussion. If it does not go over altogether to the religious register of ESG, it certainly moves to the formal end of the range of styles in use among illiterate female speakers of the language.

MMK was not literate in Gaelic, was not trained (as the boys of her generation often were) in the use of Gaelic religious language, and did not use either of her languages in the public sphere proper, since she did not take on roles that would have required that of her. Nonetheless her narrative Gaelic speech can be shown to display stylistic differences which are in keeping with topic and purpose in her narrations and also with the increasing ease of the interview situation over two tape-recording sessions. She is a testimony to the versatility of speaker and language both, late in the life of each.

Notes

1. I should note that this is just as true of me as of other ESG speakers. Though I've often tried, in unavoidable interactions with speakers of more standard varieties, and especially with Gaelic intellectuals, to make some active use of my passive and partial knowledge of standard Gaelic, I've been unable to sustain it. Since I have a large advantage over most ESG speakers in passive literacy and in conscious knowledge of the structure of the standard language, my own failures in this respect make me deeply aware of the difficulties of adopting nonlocal models in active Gaelic use.

2. I term these speech events *interviews* in recognition of the fact that two people were present, one of whom operated a tape recorder and sometimes asked questions or made comments. In actual fact one speaker did the vast majority of the talking, chose the topic a good part of the time, and was relatively seldom interrupted. Linguists sometimes present themselves as power figures in any situation involving their use of a tape recorder (Briggs 1986:89, 120) and in theory I could of course have terminated the session by turning off the tape recorder; but the reality of these sessions is that the other participant was the dominant party in most respects: she controlled the language being spoken far better than I, she chose most of the topics for presentation, she held the floor uninterrupted the majority of the time. Where I affected the topic it was by asking that she repeat for the tape recording a story which she'd already told me. Where I affected the form of the story it was generally by interrupting to ask for more information about something she'd said.

3. She is G2, that is, the second-oldest of my Golspie village sources, in many of my other publications. That seems an excessively impersonal designation for the present paper, however, where the individual aspects of her speech are at issue.

4. The adverb reflects the fact that she could not so much as recognize written Gaelic when she saw it; she used to give me the weekly radio bulletin so that I could tell her which program titles were Gaelic as opposed to French, because both looked equally unfamiliar to her.

5. I was not interested in register variation as such at any point in my original study of ESG and made no effort to gather materials which would be useful for that purpose. By the time I *was* interested, I was prevented by health problems from returning to East Sutherland to collect material specifically to that end. I have not been able to visit East Sutherland since 1978, and most of the fluent speakers with whom I worked (all, in the villages of Brora and Golspie) have died since then.

6. She provided other tape-recorded material on other occasions, including songs, phonologically contrastive words and phrases, and two sections of a letter-tape, but these three sessions contain all of her narrative material.

7. This session takes less time on tape than it took in the event, because I stopped recording each time I myself spoke. The tape was made late in 1963–64, my first year in East Sutherland, and my Gaelic was not yet comfortable. I evidently preferred not to have my own efforts at Gaelic interviewing immortalized on the tape, since I stopped the recording whenever I spoke and restarted it as MMK began to speak.

8. A question from me interrupted narrative 5 before it had reached its natural conclusion.

9. The word counts are approximate. ESG is an unwritten dialect and though I have

sometimes contrived to write it in Gaelic orthography for publication purposes, I do not normally, or willingly, do so. All of my ESG tape transcriptions are in quasi-phonemic renderings, and in many cases I followed phonological boundaries rather than those of the traditional orthography. For example, the expression *bha aid* 'they were' has a single long vowel with no rearticulation in ESG: [vaːj̃]. I always wrote it as a unit in my field notes, and I reckoned it as a single word in making the word counts for MMK's narratives here. There are so many such cases, all involving short words, mostly of high frequency, that I did not trust myself to take these phrases apart with any consistency while counting. Consequently the word counts given here are all lower than they would be if someone more comfortably literate in Gaelic than I were to translate the texts into written ESG, following the word-division conventions of the standard written language.

10. Here and subsequently I consider only recognizability, to East Sutherland perceptions, of the English origins of the word. Whether or not the word was borrowed recently or some centuries ago is not relevant to the potential self-consciousness of the ESG speaker using the word.

11. See the discussion in Dorian (1981:100–2).

12. The initial consonants of nouns, verbs, and adjectives can be altered to show grammatical distinctions, as the sole sign of the category in some instances but in conjunction with suffixal morphology in others. In addition, mutations are sometimes an obligatory though grammatically nonsignificant feature of certain constructions. Some ESG examples: /maru a, xə̃nʹãəx/ 'Kill him, Kenneth!' versus /varu a kə̃nʹãəx/ 'He killed Kenneth'; /hũnig mi ə praːr/ 'I saw her brother' versus /hũnig mi ə vraːr/ 'I saw his brother.' The initial mutations are pervasive in all of the Celtic languages, and ESG is no exception. Some consonants are simply not susceptible to mutation, however, and of course some loanwords appear in environments which do not call for mutation, so that this criterion of loanword adaptation does not apply universally to the handling of every loanword which appears in the texts, despite the high frequency of initial mutations.

13. The sibilant plural of this noun was not counted as an English plural inflection for purposes of Table 9.1; since the noun has no singular, there is no independent base to be inflected. *Smithereens* is in origin an Irish loanword in English, but it has no Scottish Gaelic counterpart, nor does Scottish Gaelic use the same suffix (anglicized as *-een*) to form diminutives.

14. MMK is the major user of /(h)ɔrs/ in all freely spoken tape-recorded speech in my corpus. Only one other speaker ever uses it at all in tape-recordings; tellingly, he uses it only in performing jokes.

15. MMK is by no means the most profane or indelicate ESG speaker I've heard, but she is more likely to use profane or indelicate language *on tape* than most. This probably reflects both her ease with tape-recording and her particular ease with me as her long-standing boarder.

16. The passive in question is a partially nominal structure, requiring a possessive pronoun inflected for person and number, and in the third person singular also for gender.

17. Tannen (1987:576) recognizes the repetition of a word, phrase, or longer syntactic unit as part of the "poetics of talk."

References

Briggs, Charles L. 1986. *Learning How to Ask: A Sociolinguistic Appraisal of the Role of the Interview in Social Science Research.* Cambridge: Cambridge University Press.

Dorian, Nancy C. 1978. *East Sutherland Gaelic: The Dialect of the Brora, Golspie, and Embo Fishing Communities.* Dublin: Dublin Institute for Advanced Studies.

———. 1981. *Language Death: The Life Cycle of a Scottish Gaelic Dialect*. Philadelphia: University of Pennsylvania Press.

Dressler, Wolfgang U. 1982. "Acceleration, Retardation, and Reversal in Language Decay?" In Robert L. Cooper, ed., *Language Spread*. Bloomington: Indiana University Press. Pp. 321–36.

———. 1988. "Language Death." In Frederick J. Newmeyer, ed., *Linguistics: The Cambridge Survey*. Vol. IV. *Language: The Socio-Cultural Context*. Cambridge: Cambridge University Press. Pp. 184–92.

Dressler, Wolfgang U., and Ruth Wodak-Leodolter. 1977. "Language Preservation and Language Death in Brittany." *International Journal of the Sociology of Language* 12:33–44.

Hymes, Dell. 1984. "Sociolinguistics: Stability and Consolidation." *International Journal of the Sociology of Language* 45:39–45.

Labov, William. 1970. *The Study of Nonstandard English*. Champaign, IL: National Council of Teachers of English.

Obler, Loraine K., and Lise Menn, eds. 1982. *Exceptional Language and Linguistics*. New York: Academic Press.

Tannen, Deborah. 1987. "Repetition in Conversation: Toward a Poetics of Talk." *Language* 63:574–605.

IV

REGISTERS, SOCIAL DIALECTS, AND SOCIOLINGUISTIC THEORY

10

Addressee- and Topic-Influenced Style Shift: A Quantitative Sociolinguistic Study

JOHN R. RICKFORD AND FAYE MCNAIR-KNOX

1. Introduction

This chapter is a study of addressee- and topic-influenced style shift in language, within the framework of quantitative or "variationist" sociolinguistics.

The first section is written from a theoretical, history-of-science perspective; we begin by contrasting the taxonomic, polydimensional approach of sociolinguists like Hymes (1972) and Halliday (1978) with the empirical, unidimensional approach of Labov (1966:90–135, 1972a:70–109), for whom styles were ordered on a single dimension, involving *attention* paid to speech. We suggest that the neglect of style within the American variationist school from the 1970s onward was due in part to methodological and theoretical difficulties with this approach. As we note, an alternative unidimensional approach, considering style as *audience* accommodation (Giles and Powesland 1975, Bell 1984), is more promising, but although several quantitative studies within this framework have been made over the past decade and a half, most of them were done outside the United States, primarily in Britain.

In the second section, we introduce some new data on addressee and topic style

This paper was prepared while the senior author was a Fellow at the Center for Advanced Study in the Behavioral Sciences, at Stanford. The financial support provided by NSF grants BNS-8700864 and BNS-8913104 is gratefully acknowledged. It is a pleasure to acknowledge, too, the assistance and encouragement which we have received from Renee Blake, Daria Ilunga, Rashida Knox, Anakela Rickford and Angela Rickford, and our forbearing families. We would like to thank those who provided feedback on the first draft of this paper, regretting only that we were not always able to incorporate their suggestions or follow their advice: John Baugh, Allan Bell, Doug Biber, Ed Finegan, Nik Coupland, Greg Guy, Dennis Preston, Suzanne Romaine, Elizabeth Closs Traugott, and Malcah Yaeger-Dror. We would also like to thank others who sent relevant papers: Marianna Di Paolo, Barbara Horvath, and Keith Walters.

shift in language, drawn from our ongoing study of sociolinguistic variation in East Palo Alto (EPA), California, a multiethnic, low-income community of over eighteen thousand people, located just east of Stanford University. The data are from our two most recent interviews with Foxy Boston, an eighteen-year-old African American teenager whose vernacular language use we have been chronicling, through successive recordings, since she was thirteen.[1] The two interviews which form the empirical focus of this paper were recorded about eight months apart in 1990 and 1991 within the same setting (Foxy's home), but with different interviewers. The 1990 interview was done by Faye (coauthor of this paper), a forty-one-year-old African American lecturer at Stanford, who was familiar to Foxy as a community resident and from earlier interviews. Faye was accompanied by her sixteen-year-old daughter, Roberta (a pseudonym), a native of East Palo Alto, who served primarily as cointerviewee and peer for Foxy (see section 2.1). Since this was the third interview of Foxy, we'll refer to it as interview III. The 1991 interview (referred to as IV) was done by Beth (a pseudonym), a twenty-five-year-old European American who was a graduate student at Stanford and a stranger to Foxy. Although the latter interview was ostensibly being done for Faye, and Beth was able to trade on "inside knowledge" from Faye's earlier interviews, Foxy's language in the second interview was less vernacular and more standard than it was in the former.

We investigate Foxy's style shift across the two interview contexts by means of quantitative analyses of her usage of several variables, including zero copula, invariant *be*, plural *-s*, third singular present *-s*, and possessive *-s*. The fact that (most of) these variables *are* sensitive to style-shifting is itself of interest, since the earlier literature on African American Vernacular English (AAVE) is either ambiguous or negative on this point. The fact that the style-shifting is primarily a function of the race of the interviewer(s) is also of methodological interest, for, with only a few exceptions (Anshen 1969, Fasold 1972, Terrell et al. 1977, Edwards 1986), race-of-interviewer or -addressee effects have been neglected within sociolinguistics,[2] although they have been the focus of lively discussion in other social sciences, where the focus is on the content of interviewees' responses rather than their language (see, for instance, Schumann and Kalton 1985, Anderson et al. 1988). In fact, the effect of interviewer attributes on interviewee speech—although privately recognized as important by everyone—has received little systematic discussion in the sociolinguistics literature. The primary exceptions have been studies of the effects of addressee status or solidarity (Brown and Gilman 1960, Payne 1976, Baugh 1979, Hindle 1979, Coupland 1984), gender (Walters 1989a, b), and insider versus outsider status (Van den Broeck 1977, Bickerton 1980, Russell 1982, Rickford 1983).

We also argue that the variable rule computer program, which we use for the analysis of zero copula, allows us to disentangle the effect of audience-design from the effect of internal grammatical constraints with a precision that other approaches do not, and we recommend it as a general means of studying stylistic variation. Finally, we consider variation by topic within each interview, attempting to assess whether this can be related to audience-design, as Bell (1984:178–82) suggests, and its relative importance vis-à-vis addressee-influenced style shift.

In our conclusion, we summarize our main findings and stress the importance of encouraging quantitative sociolinguists to return to the study of stylistic variation and of encouraging students of style in spoken language to exploit the assets of the quantitative approach.

2. The Study of Style in Quantitative Sociolinguistics

Stylistic or intraspeaker variation has certainly received less attention within American sociolinguistics than has social or interspeaker variation.[3] This is less true of British sociolinguistics, where the concept of *register* (variety "according to *use*") has been as firmly established as the concept of *dialect* (variety "according to the *user*"), and where the concepts of *field* (subject-matter), *tenor* (addressee and other participant relations), and *mode* (communication channel) have encouraged attention to the subdimensions of register (Gregory and Carroll 1978:7–11, Halliday 1978:33).

Within American sociolinguistics, heuristic sociolinguistic taxonomies (for instance, Ervin-Tripp 1964, Hymes 1972, Preston 1986) have also provided for the analysis of stylistic or intraspeaker variation, via their inclusion of categories such as message content, setting, purposes, and key, alongside interspeaker categories such as speaker's age, sex, ethnicity, and region. Such taxonomies are typically wide-ranging; for instance, Hymes (1972) includes sixteen components, while Preston (1986) expands the number of potentially relevant categories to fifty.

By contrast, empirical studies within the framework of quantitative sociolinguistics, whether in Britain or the United States, have usually taken a more parsimonious approach, attempting to relate stylistic variation to one primary underlying dimension.[4] In the 1960s and early 1970s, *attention paid to speech* (Labov 1966) reflected in varying degrees of formality, was the underlying dimension on which styles ranging from casual to careful to reading and wordlists were delimited. In the late 1970s and 1980s, to the extent that stylistic variation in speech has figured in quantitative sociolinguistics, it has primarily involved the study of the effects of the *addressee*. However, as noted, most of this work was done outside the United States.

2.1 Attention Paid to Speech

It is instructive to trace the rise and fall of style as a central area of interest in American quantitative sociolinguistics, and of attention paid to speech as its principal theoretical conceptualization. Labov is clearly the major pioneer in this framework, but in his earliest (1963) study, of Martha's Vineyard, style-shifting was basically ignored, because the majority of his subjects did not show stylistic variation for the variables under investigation: "Sometimes the conversation will take a livelier tone, or a more formal aspect, but the percentage of centralized forms is not significantly affected" (Labov 1972:21).

In his subsequent (1966) study of the pronunciation of (*r*) and other variables in New York City, however, Labov found that it was critical to attend to stylistic variation, and particularly to net *casual speech,* "the everyday speech used in informal situations, where no attention is directed to language" (p. 100), for only casual speech adequately revealed the regularity of everyday synchronic and diachronic processes—the nature of social stratification, for instance, or the direction and status of ongoing linguistic change. Although casual speech (appropriately called style A) could be easily separated from *reading* style (style C), *word-lists* (style D), and *minimal pairs* (Style D), the task of distinguishing it from *careful speech* (style B), "the type of speech which normally occurs when the subject is answering questions which are formally recognized as 'part of the interview'" (p. 92), was more difficult, and it was to this problem that Labov devoted most of his attention.

Labov's solution, well known by now, was to define certain contexts—for instance, speech with a third person (A2), speech on the topic of childhood rhymes and customs (A4), and speech on the topic of the danger of death (A5)—as *potential* casual speech contexts, and to classify speech in these contexts as *actual* examples of style A when it was accompanied by "channel cues" such as a change in tempo, pitch, volume, breathing, or laughter.

One problem, however, was that researchers usually found this method of distinguishing casual speech difficult to apply in an objective and reliable way. As Wolfram (1969:58–59) noted in discussing the Detroit dialect survey:

> An exploratory attempt to distinguish careful from casual speech based on Labov's criteria was *rejected* for several reasons. [i] In the first place, any of the paralinguistic channel cues cited as indications of casual speech can also be indications that the informant feels an increased awareness of the artificiality or formality of the interview situation. Can nervous laughter reliably be distinguished from relaxed or casual laughter? [ii] Also, the subjective interpretation of the paralinguistic cues tends to bias the interpretation of casual speech even though the channel cues are theoretically supposed to be independent of the measurement of linguistic variables. To what extent must there be a change of pitch or rhythm and how close to the actual feature being tabulated must it occur? [iii] Further, for some informants, the incidence of casual speech, based on Labov's cues, is so infrequent that it is difficult to base statistics on so few examples. [emphasis and numbering added]

Other researchers, like Trudgill (1974), avoided the indeterminacy of channel cues altogether, depending instead on earlier versus later sections of interviews or topical contexts alone to separate careful and casual speech. But most overcame the methodological problem by ignoring the distinction between these styles altogether. This was true even in the Philadelphia neighborhood studies of the Linguistic Change and Variation (LCV) project—the principal research focus of Labov and his associates from 1980 onward. As Labov (1989:11) notes, in a paper originally presented in 1982, "The main data base is the set of tense/lax ratings of all short a words in the *spontaneous speech* recorded from the 100 subjects. *This includes both 'casual' and 'careful' speech as defined in Labov 1966*" [emphasis added]. What came to define the sociolinguistic/variationist approach to language was its use of recorded corpora of *spontaneous* (real, natural, conversational) speech in the new (Labov 1989) sense. There was an unspoken consensus that while it was valuable to try to get as much *casual* speech (in the old sense) as possible, the operational difficulties of separating casual from *careful* speech made further attachment to the theoretical distinction unrealistic. In any case, even where the recordings of quantitative sociolinguists were primarily careful speech, in the old sense (Labov 1989:50), they were still able to identify regular internal and external constraints on linguistic variation and change, and to distinguish themselves theoretically from those who depended instead on "introspection—and the elicitation of others' introspections" (Labov 1989:51).

Although most quantitative sociolinguists came to ignore the casual/careful distinction—and to attend less and less to stylistic variation in general—for practical, operational reasons like these,[5] there were also empirical and theoretical arguments against studying stylistic variation principally or only in terms of attention paid to speech.[6] Many of these arguments have been summarized by Milroy (1987:172–83), but the primary ones are worth repeating. Wolfson (1976) expressed the view that the "spontaneous" speech produced in response to requests for danger of death narratives often had a "performed" quality and challenged the assumption that natural/absolute speech existed as an absolute entity. Macaulay (1977), Romaine (1978, 1980), and Milroy (1980) presented evidence which suggested that reading did not lie on the same continuum as speech, at least not in the British varieties they investigated.[7] Baugh (1979:25) noted that styles delimited according to attention paid to speech were the products of linguistic inquiry rather than social circumstance and chose to study situational style-shifting because it was likely to be closer to realistic stylistic variation in everyday conversation. Cheshire (1982), Dressler and Wodak (1982), and Finegan and Biber (1989) questioned whether "attention paid to speech" really underlay the kinds of formality Labov distinguished. In a related vein, Traugott and Romaine (1985) criticized the attention-paid-to-speech approach for its unidimensionality (see also Irvine 1979, 1985:560) and for its implicit view of the speaker as passive respondent rather than active strategist. And Bell (1984), critiquing the experimental work on monitoring by George Mahl which Labov (1966:134, 1972:97–99) had cited, and summarizing empirical evidence from other researchers, concluded that "empirical foundation for the attention variable is notably lacking" and that "attention is at most a mechanism of response intervening between a situation and a style. This explains both why it seemed a plausible correlative of style shift, and why it could never be a satisfactory explanation of style" (1984:148). By and large these critiques came from outside the main tradition of American quantitative sociolinguistics, and they came *after* most quantitativists had already begun to shy away from distinguishing styles in terms of interview contexts and channel cues, but they perhaps contributed to the decline in the study of style in terms of attention paid to speech.

2.2 Addressee and Other Audience Design Effects

When Labov et al. (1968) turned to the study of AAVE in Harlem, they were still interested in eliciting casual or vernacular speech, for "the most systematic and regular form of language is that of basic vernacular" (p. 167). But as their primary means of achieving this goal, they adopted a new approach—recording group-sessions, in which adolescent and preadolescent AAVE speakers were "in spontaneous interaction with each other" (p. 57).[8] To the extent that Labov et al. discuss stylistic variation in this study, it is by comparing speakers' outputs in the individual interviews with their outputs in the group sessions ("single style" versus "group style"). Theirs is actually one of the earliest empirical sociolinguistic studies of stylistic variation to use addressee rather than topic or attention as the primary variable. Anshen (1969) and Fasold (1972) also reported quantitative variation in the output of AAVE speakers according to (race of) addressee, although it was not a major theme of their work. However, for Blom and Gumperz (1972), stylistic variation among Norwegian speakers in Hemnesberget according to whether they were speaking to locals or outsiders was of central significance, leading them to introduce (pp. 424–25) the theoretical distinction between *situational* switching, primarily influenced by addressee, and *metaphorical* switching, primarily influenced by shifts in topic and role relationship while addressee and other situational features remain constant.[9]

From the late 1970s on, there have been several quantitative studies of stylistic variation in the recorded speech of individuals according to addressee. The list includes, in chronological order, Bell (1977, 1982, 1991), Van den Broeck (1977), Douglas-Cowie (1978), Baugh (1979, 1983), Payne (1976), Hindle (1979), Rickford (1979, 1983), Bickerton (1980), Coupland (1980, 1981, 1984), Trudgill (1981), Russell (1982), Thelander (1982), Purcell (1984), Lucas and Borders (1987), Walters (1989a,b), and Youssef (1991). The typical approach was to record one or more individuals speaking to someone who was a local insider or someone relatively familiar and compare this with their recorded outputs when speaking to an outsider or a stranger. The parallels with the work of Labov et al. (1968) and Blom and Gumperz (1972) are striking, but while some of the new studies (for instance, those by Baugh and Rickford) acknowledged an intellectual link with these earlier works, others (for instance, Douglas-Cowie and Bickerton) did not, almost as if their authors had independently hit upon an operationally clear-cut way of distinguishing styles which they knew from informal observation and experience to exist. Moreover, with only a few exceptions, the new studies drew on data from Great Britain and other communities outside the continental United States, and some were also outside the American variationist/Labovian tradition.[10]

One theoretical source of this approach to stylistic variation which *was* acknowledged by some of the researchers (Coupland, Russell and Trudgill, for instance) was the speech accommodation model of British social psychologist Howard Giles and his associates (Giles and Powesland 1975, Giles and Smith 1979, Thakerar et al. 1982, Giles 1984). In this model, the theoretical significance of the addressee is paramount, since speakers are seen either as converging with or diverging from their addressees depending on their relationship to them and their desire to gain social approval or achieve "communication efficiency." The speech accommodation model, recently reconceptualized in broader terms as "communication accommodation theory" (Coupland and Giles 1988:176), makes explicit links with theoretical frameworks in psychology and other behavioral sciences and has undergone several revisions and refinements over the years. It has inspired many empirical studies—

see Giles, Coupland and Coupland (1991) for some of the most recent—although critiques have been made of the limited linguistic analysis in some studies and of the tendency to refer to accommodation theory post hoc.

Bell's extended (1984) discussion of style as audience design, which provided an integrative review of many of the addressee-based studies mentioned above, and has undergone some refinements of its own (see Bell 1986), has received relatively little attention at variationist conferences (like NWAVE) or in the quantitative sociolinguistics literature.[11] This neglect is unfortunate, however, for in its integration and explication of diverse strands of earlier sociolinguistic work, and in its bold hypotheses and predictions, Bell (1984) strikes us as one of the most theoretically interesting works to emerge in the study of style-shifting—and in sociolinguistics more generally—since the work of Labov in the early 1960s.

Space will not permit us to recapitulate all the ideas and data that Bell (1984) presented—and we would, in any case, encourage readers unfamiliar with the paper to read it themselves—but we summarize some of its key elements and explain how it relates to the empirical study to be presented in this paper.

A central feature of Bell's paper is its attempt to relate interspeaker (social) and intraspeaker (stylistic) variation by means of the *style axiom:* "Variation on the style dimension within the speech of a single speaker derives from and echoes the variation which exists between speakers on the "social" dimension" (p. 151). As Bell notes, this axiom explains a number of previously unexplained facts about sociolinguistic structure, including the fact that "some linguistic variables will have both social and style variation, some only social variation, but none style variation only" (p. 151); the fact that the degree of style variation never exceeds the degree of social variation (pp. 152ff.); the fact that audience effects are most strongly marked for addressees and are progressively weaker for auditors, overhearers, and eavesdroppers (pp. 162 ff.); and the fact that stylistic variation by topic and other nonaudience factors presupposes and is weaker than variation according to addressee (pp. 178 ff.). While these generalizations are shown to be tenable as "facts," on the basis of earlier studies, they also constitute working hypotheses against which all current and future work can be judged. They are therefore empirical and falsifiable claims, with theoretical import. Although it is easy to criticize an essentially monodimensional approach to style like this one for neglecting potentially relevant factors, we believe that sociolinguistics needs the integrative and predictive approach to theory testing and development which Bell's paper represents.

Before turning to the empirical East Palo Alto study which will occupy us for the rest of this paper, we should note some of the questions which Bell's paper specifically led us to pursue. Why do some variables show significant addressee-based shift between the two interviews while others do not? Can we account for this differential accommodation by appealing to the variables' role in social or *interspeaker* variation, as Bell (pp. 166–67) suggests? What is Foxy reacting to as she style shifts between one interview and the other—her interlocutors' personal characteristics (race and familiarity, for instance) or their specific linguistic usage (Bell, pp. 167–69)?[12] What of the role of *topic shifts* within each interview? Can these be viewed as proxies for audience-design, as Bell (pp. 178–82) asserts? And does

Foxy's vernacular use in our very earliest interviews (1986, 1988) square with the evidence and analyses we present from interviews III and IV? These are some of the questions we attempt to answer in the next section of this chapter.

3. Empirical Study of Style Shift in Foxy's Interviews

Following Bell (1984:146–46), we treat linguistic differences in the speech of a single speaker (*intraspeaker* variation) as stylistic, in contrast with differences between the speech of two or more speakers, which is *interspeaker* or social variation (as, for instance, in social class or ethnic dialects). Stylistic differences between Foxy Boston's speech in interviews III (EPA 55–56) and IV (EPA 114 B), taken as wholes, will be regarded as instances of addressee-influenced style shift, since the primary situational differences between the interviews are the race and familiarity of the interviewers.

Section 3.1 gives further information about the two interviews which provide the new data for this paper. Section 3.2 discusses *addressee*-influenced differences in Foxy's quantitative usage of five vernacular variables, comparing them with earlier studies of these variables in relation to race and style. Section 3.3 considers the interviewers' usage of the same variables to see whether Foxy is accommodating to the linguistic usage of her addressees, or their personal/social characteristics (Bell 1984:167). Section 3.4 explores *topic*-controlled variation in vernacular usage within Foxy's two interviews, assessing whether such nonpersonal style design can be related to and derived from interpersonal addressee design (Bell 1984:178–82). Finally, section 3.5 briefly discusses Foxy's usage in two earlier interviews with Faye and Roberta, one of which suggests that the setting, scene, and key (Hymes 1972), as well as the strategic use of style, have to be given more prominence than Bell's approach perhaps allows them.

3.1 Further Information About the Two Interviews

The two interviews described in general terms in the introduction were comparable insofar as both were conducted in Foxy's home and focused on conversing with Foxy as the primary interviewee. However, they differed with respect to logistics, tempo and key, participants, and topics. Interview III was recorded in June 1990 on a UHER 2600 stereo reel-to-reel tape-recorder; it lasted about ninety-six minutes and produced a one-and-a-half spaced transcript of eighty-eight pages. Interview IV was recorded in February 1991 on a Sony TCD-5M stereo cassette recorder; it lasted seventy-five minutes and produced a one-and-a-half spaced transcript of forty-two pages. The fact that the transcript of interview III is twice as long as that of interview IV while the recording itself was only slightly longer indicates that III was a livelier and more informal interaction, with a faster tempo and more give-and-take among the participants. This was in turn related to differences in who the participants were, their relation to Foxy, and the distribution of topics in each interview, which the next two subsections discuss.

3.1.1. INTERVIEW III

Besides Foxy (F), the primary participants in interview III were two African American females who were familiar to Foxy from the community and from previous
interviews. Faye, the adult, served as the interviewer (I), introducing most of the
initial topics, but she employed a bantering approach which encouraged informality
and often led to laughter, for instance, from an early section of the interview (p. 2,
transcript), dealing with college plans:

(1) I: What kinds of plans you have for college? Where—Where have you been
        thinking about going?
    F: Prob—. . . I don' wanna go far away.
    I: Really? You wanna hang around with mom?
    F: Mm–hmm[=yes] [Laughter]
    I: Are you scared to get out there on your own?
    F: No! [laughter] I's jus' that . . . we just too close, I guess.

Faye's intimate knowledge of places, people, and events in the community also
stimulated Foxy to talk excitedly about events and individuals which she might not
have mentioned to a stranger.[13] For instance, Faye's reference to a recent gang-
related killing on Xavier Street led Foxy to note (p. 15, transcript) that three of her
friends had been killed similarly, including, most recently, Jimmy [name changed]:

(2) F: Oh, and then Jimmy. . . . Jimmy got killed at Shakedown's.
    I: Is that that shooting they had over there? [high-pitched]
    F: Yeah, that— that was my good— good friend. I was like, "WAIT A
        MINUTE!" . . . I was like, "Y'all lying! No! I just talked to Jimmy, the
        other night."

Another factor which contributed to the animated conversational quality of
interview III was the presence of Roberta (R), Faye's daughter. Roberta was primarily a cointerviewee, talking about her own teenage experiences in Oakland (where
she had attended high school) and often stimulating Foxy to use teenage slang
spontaneously and to share aspects of their peer-group knowledge about boys and
other topics, as in this extract (p. 23, transcript):

(3) F: This one [Black Student Union (BSU) convention] was in Bakersfield. And
        we met so many GUYYYS, from uh —ooh, now lemme tell you what high
        school got—got it going on.
    R: Saint Mary's! Saint Joe's!
    F: YES, YES! St. Mary's! [laughter]
    I: Oh yeah!
    F: St. Mary's is HITTIN! IT'S HITTIN!
    R: [To I] St. Mary's is an all boy's school in Oakland—
    F: [Overlapping with R] St. Mary's is HITTIN! They be like, "Ooh, yes. Wha's
        your name?" Ooh! Blah, blah, blah, this. [laughter] I be like, "Ooh, yeah —
        you— you come here?" I be like — Tanya was like "Wha—wha's your
        name? Uh, WHERE YOU GOING TO SCHOOL AT NEXT YEAR?!
        [laughter] . . . I'm like, "Y'all is a fool."

In this informal atmosphere, Foxy produced long stretches of excited speech, often overlapping with or interrupting other participants' turns, and bringing narrated events to life through extensive use of direct quotations and sound effects, as in the preceding quotation and in this account of repeated phone calls from an admirer (pp. 49–50, transcript):

(4) F: an' she—ma —I be on the telephone and he be going, [breathlessly and fast] "Where you went today? I— I know you wasn't at home! I called you. You wasn't at home! I left a message! You wasn't at home. Where you was at today? Uhn-uhn, Uhn-uhn, you got to get a beeper or something so I can page you. You have to call me back. Where was you?!" [laughter] And everyday— everyday, "Did you go shopping today? What you go buy? You bought this? You bought that? You like it?" And I be going, "Yep, yep, yep."

   I: Mm–mm–mm–mm.

   F: Okay." Then he hang up.

   I: Mm–mm–mm–mm.

   F: Then [pause] — THIRTY minutes later—, BRRINNNG [telephone]! "Hello." "Oh, I'm just calling to see if you in the house." My ma be like, "DANG! That boy on your TIP!"

Most of interview III was occupied by personal and/or controversial topics (see section 3.4 for further details), such as male-female relationships and drug-dealing and related violence in the community, and these succeeded in engaging the interviewee's enthusiastic participation.

3.1.2. INTERVIEW IV

Beth's interview IV was actually modeled quite closely on interview III (to which Beth had listened beforehand), so that many of the topics and subtopics overlapped, including high school life, college and career plans, boyfriends, girlfriends, teenage pregnancies, recreation activities, race relations, boy-girl relationships, and slang terms. Both interviews naturally included distinctive topics of their own (community homicides in III, the Persian Gulf War in IV), but this was less significant than the relative time spent on related topics, Foxy's personal and emotive involvement in each, and her relation to her interlocutor as she talked. For instance, both interviews began with school life and college plans, a relatively formal and nonpersonal topic, exemplified by the following extract (p. 7, transcript interview IV):

(5) F: . . . my teacher, his name is Mr. Segal and he's like— really hard. And he's like, "You guys [??]" He teaches you— he teaches us like we're in college, and my um Biology— when I had Biology? This guy named Mr. Cross— I mean he teaches you like you're in college. He gives you — he gives you all your book and he assigns you ALL this work. It's like sooo much work . . . and it's— it's done in a week and you're like, "OH MY GOSH!"

However, this topic constituted only 7 percent of interview III but 19 percent of interview IV (see section 3.4). The next topic in IV, the Persian Gulf War and related events at school, produces the same information-giving register from Foxy and goes on for another 13 percent of the transcript, whereas the next topics in III are drugs, murders, and thefts in the community, producing much more excitement and involvement on Foxy's part. As we'll see in a moment and explore further in section 3.4, the topic of boy-girl relationships ("wives and slamming partners") produces equally involved dialogue and vernacular usage in both interviews, but Foxy simply gives more topics this personalized, animated treatment in interview III than she does in interview IV.

This is in turn related to the fact that Foxy's interlocutor in interview IV is European American and a stranger, and the fact that she is unaccompanied by a teenager like Roberta to whom Foxy can relate as a peer-group insider. Although Beth opens the interview by saying that Faye "asked me to talk to you" and draws artfully on terms and events which Foxy had mentioned in her previous interview, her status as an outsider is clear from the fact that she doesn't know specific individuals and institutions that Foxy mentions, as in this excerpt (p. 3, transcript):

(6) F: You might know Alice [name changed]. She used to work at Stanford with
    Faye?
   B: I haven't met her.
   F: Oh. Well, she goes to Howard.

Moreover, while she is skillful at keeping up her end of the conversation and usually reacts fluidly to what Foxy says in any one segment of the interview, Beth's transitions between topics are sometimes awkward, marked by long pauses and hesitation fillers as she tries to decide what to turn to next. And sometimes, perhaps because of dialect differences, Beth's questions are misunderstood, as in this excerpt (p. 16, transcript):

(7) B: I mean, do you think they maybe talk more to girls than they—
   F: Talk to girls?
   B: Do you think they're like, yeah, like more open with other—with girls than
    they are with other guys? You see what I'm saying? Like do you think they,
    um—
   F: Do I think, um, guys are open with—girls than guys?
   B: Yeah.

These misfirings in interlocutor communications, added to their ethnic distance, help to hold interviewer and interviewee at arm's length, so to speak, for at least the first third of interview IV. Even where Foxy goes *on* about something at some length, as in her account of acquaintances who are in the Persian Gulf or scheduled to go there, she doesn't get *into* it as fully as she might, as she often does in interview III. And she sometimes deals with topics sparingly in interview IV, as in this discussion of teen pregnancies, which occupies only a few lines (p. 15, transcript):

(8) B: Do you have many friends who are pregnant?
   F: Yeah, a lot of my friends do have kids—[pause] or are pregnant, yeah.
   B: How do you feel about that?
   F: I don't know. I was like, "They're CUTE," but then, I was like, "I'm not
    ready to have kids, oh my gosh."

B: Do you think they're ready—do you feel like they're ready to have kids?
F: No, but [laughter]—I 'on know. [laughter]

In interview III, by contrast, the same topic goes on for one and a half pages; Foxy's contributions to this topic are not only longer, but more personal (note her references to specific individuals), and animated with more dialogue and sound effects (p. 6, transcript):

(9) F: . . . when I be driving, it ['ll] seem like every corner I drive around— there go somebody you know pushing a baby.
I: Mm. Mm. Mm.
F: [Quoting] "Hi, F.! Beep-beep!" [Car horn; laughter]
I: Mm. Mm. Mm. Mm-hmm.
F: Me and T. and them be like, "Tha's a SHAME, huh?!" . . . Cause like, you know Elizabeth? [Name changed] I be like, "Dang, T., she in the same grade with me and SHE HAVE 3 KIDS!"
I: Oh my GOD!
R: She got three kids?!
F: She got three kids!!

Interview IV does have its animated highlights, however. The most notable one is Foxy's discussion of "wives and slamming partners," which, interestingly enough, occurs in response to Beth's question about whether these terms, which she said Faye had told her about, were still in use. Foxy's response to this display of insider knowledge is not only long (going on for five full pages) but also lively, packed with as much dialogue as in interview III, with as much copula absence, and with even more risqué lexicon (a point we return to in section 3.4), as this segment (from p. 21–22, transcript B) illustrates:

(10) F: Well, all guys have a main girl that they really like— that they really, you know, spend time with ['n] stuff, and that's the one they call—their *wife*. And it's like, the other girls, they just . . . It's just like— you know, it's just that, they don't really care about 'em, they just—they just *slam*—that's just they work. [Background laughter] *Work* just means 'sex' too. That's just they work and stuff like that. But, like—if you talking to a guy on a phone and all his friends come in, "Hey blood, blood! Who you talking to? Who's that on the phone? Who's that on the phone?" They be like, ". . . Maybe I can get my hit in." [background laughter] *Hit* means 'slam.' And then the boy be saying, "Blood, you better go on. This the wife. This the wife. I'm talking to my wife on the phone." Then they be like, "Oh for real? I'm sorry, I'm sorry, I'm sorry, blood, I'm sorry. I didn't know it was the wife."

3.2. Addressee-*Influenced Style Shift: Differences Between Foxy's Vernacular Usage in Interviews III and IV*

In this section we'll consider Foxy's addressee-influenced style shift between interviews III and IV, as reflected in quantitative differences in her use of the following variables.[14]

TABLE 10.1   Foxy Vernacular Usage Interviews III and IV

Variable	Foxy: Interview III (1990, African/ American Interviewer)	Foxy: Interview IV 1991, European/ American Interviewer)
Possessive -s absence	67% (6/9)	50% (5/10) N.S.
Plural -s absence	1% (4/282)	0% (0/230) N.S.
Third singular present -s absence	73% (83/114)	36% (45/124)*
Copule is/are absence	70% (197/283)	40% (70/176)*
Invariant habitual be	385 (= 241 per hr)	97 (= 78 per hr)*

Note: Number of tokens in parentheses; *significant by chi-square test, < .001; N.S. = Not Significant.

a. Possessive -s absence, as in: "the teacher'Ø clerk" [Int IV];[15]
b. Plural -s absence, as in: "They just our friendØ" [Int III];
c. Absence of third person singular present tense -s, as in: "At first it seemØ like it wasn't no drugs" [Int IV];
d. Absence of copula/auxiliary is and are, as in: "He Ø on the phone" [Int III]; "You go there when you Ø pregnant" [Int IV];[16]
e. Use of invariant habitual be, as in: "He always be coming down here" [Int III] and "I be tripping off of boys" [Int IV].

Table 10.1 shows the relative frequency with which Foxy used the vernacular variants of these variables in each of the two interviews, without regard to internal constraints.[17] We discuss each of the variables in turn, relating our findings concerning style-shifting to the findings of earlier researchers (including Bell 1984) and discussing the effects of internal constraints where known.

3.2.1. POSSESSIVE -S ABSENCE

Although Foxy's possessive -s absence is 17% higher in interview III than in interview IV, indicating a style shift in the hypothesized direction, the difference is not statistically significant, because of the small number of tokens on which the percentages are based.[18] This case illustrates the need to provide both the number of tokens on which relative frequencies are based and chi-square or other measures of statistical significance, information which is not always provided in variationist studies of AAVE and other dialects.

Labov et al. (1968:169–70) was the first study of AAVE to provide information about possessive -s absence in relation to style. Combining data from all their African American New York City peer groups (forty-four youths, excluding the "Lames"), the authors reported 72 percent (23/32) possessive -s absence for single style, and 57 percent (32/56) for group style. Again, the percentage gap seems relatively large, but it is statistically insignificant (chi-square = 1.89, $p > .05$).

How can we explain the absence of statistically significant style-shifting for this variable?[19] Bell (1984:167) has advanced the following strong hypothesis:

(11) A sociolinguistic variable which is differentiated by certain speaker characteristics (e.g. by class or gender or age) tends to be differentiated in speech to addressees with

those same characteristics. That is, if an old person uses a given linguistic variable differently than a young person, then individuals will use that variable differently when speaking to an old person than to a young person . . . and mutatis mutandis, for gender, race and so on.

Since urban European American vernaculars typically show little or no absence of possessive -*s*, in contrast with urban AAVE (Ash and Myhill 1986:38–39, Labov and Harris 1986:11–12), one might expect from Bell's hypothesis that AAVE speakers would show significantly lower rates of -*s* absence when speaking to European Americans than to African Americans. The fact that Foxy does not do so, at least not to a statistically significant degree, suggests the need for a rider to Bell's hypothesis: If the variable is relatively rare in speech, its value and exploitation as a symbolic counter in style-shifting may be reduced.[20]

Another tack we might take on this problem is to interpret the evidence of Labov et al. (1968) as suggesting that possessive -*s* absence in AAVE is an *indicator*, showing social but not stylistic differentiation, instead of a *marker*, showing differentiation by social class *and* style (Labov 1972:179). As Bell notes (1984:166), features established as indicators on the basis of limited style shifting among speech, reading, and word lists will tend to show little or no addressee style shift. This argument is somewhat tautologous, however, and it also potentially contradicts the hypothesis in (11), since features that are indicators insofar as they show little differentiation in terms of more monitored or less monitored speech might still show addressee style shift if they are differentially used by a speaker's interlocutors or the ethnic/class/gender groups to which the interlocutors belong. A final reason for not allowing the evidence of earlier data sets to *define* the status of variables in new data sets (as indicators or markers) is that the evidence of previous studies might be limited or mixed, and there is always the possibility that the older and newer data sets might differ regionally, or in terms of social class and recording situation, or insofar as they represent change in the intervening time period.

Baugh (1979:215–17) in fact provides quite a different kind of evidence from Labov et al. (1968), because possessive -*s* absence among his Pacoima (Los Angeles) AAVE speakers is influenced most strongly by a situational/stylistic factor— whether the addressee is familiar to the interviewer (favoring *s*-absence) or not (disfavoring -*s* absence). We don't have the Ns on which Baugh's probability coefficients are based, but he does note that "possessive -*s* occurs less frequently than plural -*s* or third person singular -*s*" (p. 215). Whether tokens of this variable occurred *more* frequently in Baugh's study than in our study or Labov's, allowing us to attribute its stylistic significance to this, is unclear.

3.2.2. PLURAL -*S* ABSENCE

In the case of plural -*s* absence, sample size is not a problem, but the one percentage point (1 percent) difference between Foxy's usage in interviews III and II is too slight to achieve statistical significance.[21] Here we can argue, however, that we would *not* expect significant addressee shift on the basis of Bell's hypothesis (11), since AAVE usage rates on this variable tend to be low. Labov and associates' (1968:161) New York City peer-group members displayed 7 percent (75/1059) plural -*s* absence overall in single style and 9 percent (57/648) for the same members in group style; Wolfram's (1968:150) upper- and lower-working-class Detroit teenagers had 3 percent and 7 percent plural absence, respectively; and, more germanely, AAVE speakers recorded in East Palo Alto in 1986–87 (Rickford 1992) showed frequencies of plural -*s* absence ranging from 1 percent to 13 percent.[22] This is not a major vernacular variable for AAVE speakers, and as such its insignificant role in style-shifting between European American and African American addressees in interviews III and IV is not surprising. Bell (1984:166) cites a similar case from the work of Douglas-Cowie (1978:41–42); five of her speakers rarely used the local variant of two variables, (ɔ:) and (aye), so, as Bell notes, "had little distance to shift when addressing the English outsider." However, Baugh (1979) points in a different direction; although he notes (p. 223) that "the plural marker, as has been observed in many BEV communities, is very rarely deleted," he nevertheless finds style-shifting significant for plural -*s* absence in the speech of his Pacoima (Los Angeles) AAVE speakers (p. 219).

3.2.3. THIRD SINGULAR -*S* ABSENCE

Unlike the preceding two variants, this variable and its vernacular variant occur frequently enough to allow us to consider its internal conditioning, a potentially significant factor which many quantitative studies of style (for instance, those by Douglas-Cowie, Bickerton, Coupland, Russell, and Thelander referred to earlier) unfortunately do not take into account. The omission is unfortunate because a shift in a speaker's usage from one situation to the next might have little relation to addressee or other differences, and more to the effect of internal constraints, differentially distributed in the two situations. Without systematic data on internal constraints, it is difficult to know for sure.[23] Without such data, it is also impossible to test the "status" extension of Bell's "style" hypothesis, in which Preston (1991:36) proposes, "Variation on the 'status' dimension derives from and echoes [and will be less than/contained within] the variation which exists within the 'linguistic' dimension."

Table 10.2 shows the percentage of third singular -*s* absence in Foxy's two interviews in relation to the primary internal factor which seems to affect this variable locally (cf. Rickford 1992): verb type. The percentage of -*s* absence is higher in interview III than interview IV in every case except *say*, and the relative

TABLE 10.2   Foxy's Third Person Singular Present
-*s* Absence by Verb Type

Verb Type	Interview III	Interview IV
Regular verbs (*walk*)	67% (57/85)	31% (27/87)
Have	75% (3/4)	11% (1/9)
Do	60% (3/5)	40% (2/5)
Don't	100% (15/15)	50% (8/16)
Say	100% (5/5)	100% (7/7)
TOTAL, all verbs	73% (83/114)	36% (46/124)

effect of verb type is similar in both interviews, with *don't* (versus *doesn't*) and *say* favoring *-s* absence more than regular verbs and *have* (versus *has*) do. Furthermore, the distributions of verb types within each interview are comparable—the verbs less favorable to *-s* absence (regular verbs and *have*) constitute 78 percent (89/114) and 77 percent (96/124) of the total set of third singular present stems in interviews III and IV, respectively, and the stems more favorable to *-s* absence (*don't* and *say*) account for 18 percent of the total in interview III (20/114) and 19 percent in interview IV (23/124). Clearly, the tendency for Foxy to omit third singular *-s* more often in interview III than interview IV remains true when the effect of verb type is taken into account; we can conclude that the overall percentages of *-s* absence in interviews III and IV are robust indicators of a fundamental style shift between the interviews.

Given what we know about the very limited third singular *-s* absence in European American Vernacular English (Ash and Myhill 1986:38–39), a marked style shift of this type is again consistent with Bell's "differential accommodation" hypothesis (see [11] above). But what do earlier studies indicate about AAVE style-shifting in relation to this variable?

The most directly comparable study is Fasold (1978:214), which reports race-of-interviewer effects on the speech of forty-seven working-class AAVE interviewees from Washington, D.C. Those who were interviewed by African Americans exhibited higher rates of third singular *-s* absence (68 percent) than those who were interviewed by European Americans (63.8 percent), but the difference was not statistically significant.[24] The fact that Fasold's African American interviewers were mostly "middle-class, standard English speaking young women (a few were conducted by a working class black man)" may have had something to do with this unexpected result, especially if they failed to establish the kind of insider's rapport which Faye and Roberta had with Foxy Boston.

Although Baugh (1979) does not provide data on the effects of African American versus European interviewers—an African American, he interviewed all his Pacoima speakers himself—his important study of style-shifting in AAVE also includes data on third person *-s*. Styles in Baugh's study were delimited along the intersections of two dimensions. The first was the relative *familiarity* (or solidarity) of interviewer and interviewee, ranging from his outsider status during the first year of his fieldwork to his insider status in the third or fourth year, when he was living in the community itself, had "gained access to a number of social domains," and had become "active in the day to day lives" (p. 30) of community members.[25] The second, related to the first, was whether the speech events that were being manifested in the presence of the interviewer were primarily vernacular or nonvernacular. Baugh found significant stylistic variation for suffix *-s,* especially third singular present *-s* (pp. 212–15). Baugh's variable rule probability coefficients for stylistic factors for third person *-s* absence (see Table 10.3) in fact outweigh and contain those for internal linguistic factors (the variation space or range for style is .184, compared with .092 for following phonological environment and .158 for preceding phonological environment), contrary to Preston's (1991:36–37) predictions that the scope of the latter would outstrip that of the former. After noting that stylistic factors are also significant for postvocalic *r*-deletion, but not for copula absence or

TABLE 10.3   Constraints on Third Singular *s*-Absence, Pacoima

Situation/Style	Foll. Phon. Env.	Prec. Phon. Env.
Familiar Vernacular: .601	—Consonant: .546	Nasal—: .490
Unfamiliar Vernacular: .443	—Vowel: .454	Voiced Consonant—: .567
Familiar Non-Vernacular: .538		Voiceless Consonant—: .427
Unfamiliar Non-Vernacular: .417		ts-cluster—: .430
		Vowel—: .585

From: Baugh (1979:215).

t, d deletion, Baugh suggests (p. 225) that *r*'s "lack of grammatical function" allows it to be used as a stylistic device, since "little if any confusion results from post vocalic /r/loss." The argument with respect to suffix *-s* is similar, though not made as directly (pp. 225–27): Discourse context can usually provide the grammatical information provided by suffix *-s*, so it is free to be variably absent in accord with situational or stylistic factors. This is reminiscent of Hymes' (1974:160) observation that strong versus weak aspiration of an initial stop in English has stylistic but not referential meaning—in fact, it is free to have the former because it lacks the latter. However, nothing in Bell's theory would predict the general argument, and since it isn't confirmed by our results (third singular *-s* absence, copula absence, and invariant *be* all show significant style-shifting although they are bearers of potentially significant grammatical information), we do not pursue this interesting hypothesis any further.

However, it is worth noting that, contrary to his expectations, Baugh found more significant style-shifting for *-s* absence according to whether he was familiar or nonfamiliar to his interlocutors than whether he used AAVE or not (p. 235).[26] As we will see later, Faye used some of the AAVE variants, but nowhere near as often as Foxy did, and Foxy's differential vernacular usage in interviews III and IV must be taken as a combined accommodation to the race and familiarity of her interviewers. Since Beth is both non–African American and a stranger, it's difficult to say which feature Foxy is primarily responding to, but Baugh's study reminds us that familiarity can be a significant addressee variable in and of itself.

Another study which reports style-shifting data for third singular *-s* absence in AAVE is Wolfram (1969), which reported (p. 147) a significant style shift effect among his working-class Detroit speakers, who had much higher third person *-s* absence rates in spoken interview style (61.3 percent) than in reading style (15.6 percent). Of course, since the text of his reading passage was fixed and did not deliberately exclude instances of third person *-s*, the scope for stylistic variability was limited, and this method does not in any case provide direct information on style as *audience design*. However, Wolfram's results are of interest because they led him to exactly the opposite conclusion from Baugh (1979). After noting (p. 177) that zero copula also shows significant style-shifting among his working-class speakers, Wolfram comments, "For other grammatical features, the working class showed significant stylistic shift between the interview and reading styles but in the phonological variables there is generally slight variation between interview and reading style." Since our study did not look at phonological variables, we're in no position to arbitrate on this issue, but it's an interesting one which deserves further research. As Wolfram (1969:204) notes, grammatical variables generally show sharp stratification while phonological variables show gradient stratification. If Bell's hypothesis ([11]) is right, the former would therefore be more likely to show marked style shift.

The final study of relevance is Labov et al. (1968), who, discussing third person present -*s* absence in the speech of their New York City adolescent peer groups, observe (p. 164), "There is no stylistic shift observable in moving from group style to single sessions." This statement is corroborated by combined data from the T-Birds, Aces, Cobras, Jets, and Oscar Bros, across both preconsonantal and pre-vocalic environments, which show a third singular -*s* absence rate of 66 percent (208/316) in group style, compared with 69% (384/560) in single interview style (p. 161). The absence of style-shifting for this variable runs counter to the findings of the present study as well as to the results of Baugh and Wolfram reported earlier, but it may be related to Labov et al.'s claim, based on a high overall percentage of third singular present -*s* absence and the irregular effects of following phonological segments, that "there is no underlying third singular -*s* in AAVE" (p. 164).

3.2.4. ABSENCE OF COPULA/AUXILIARY *is* AND *are*

In the case of copula absence, the set of internal factors which could affect the distribution of the variable is too large to keep track of with percentages and one-dimensional tables.[27] So we turned instead to the variable rule program (Gregory Guy's MACVARB, based on David Sankoff's VARBRUL 2S), which, on the basis of inputted information about observed frequencies of copula absence in different environments, estimates the independent contribution of each factor to rule application, expressed as a probability coefficient (see Sankoff 1988).[28]

Table 10.4 shows the outputs of three analyses of Foxy's copula absence data using the variable rule program.[29] The first two runs are for interviews III and IV considered separately; they show us first of all that Foxy's copula absence is similarly affected by internal constraints in both interviews; the same factor groups are selected as significant by the regression routine of the program, and the ordering of factors within each group is comparable, with second person and plural *are*, for instance, much more likely to be absent (.74, .67) than third singular *is* (.26, .33).[30] But what is even more significant are the input probabilities (corrected means), shown in the first row of this table: .49 for interview III and .20 for interview IV.[31] These represent "the probability that the rule will apply regardless of environment" (Guy 1975:60) and indicate that there remain big differences between interviews III and IV even when the cross-cutting effect of internal factors is taken into account. The final column of Table 10.4 provides a similar indication, in a different way—by pooling the data from both interviews and contrasting interviews III and IV as factors in a new INTERVIEW factor group. The effect of this external constraint is shown to be as pronounced as the effect of the PERSON/NUMBER factor group, with interview III much more favorable to copula absence (.72) than interview IV (.28).[32]

Given the much higher frequencies of copula absence in AAVE than in European American Vernacular English (Wolfram 1974, Ash and Myhill 1986:38–39,

TABLE 10.4   Probability Coefficients for Foxy's Copula Absence,
Interviews III and IV Separately and Combined

Factor Group Constraints		Interview III	Interview IV	Interview III + IV
Input probability		.49	.20	.33
Following grammatical	Gonna	[100%]	.79	.90
	Verb-*ing*	.59	.66	.59
	Locative	.87	.52	.61
	Adjective	.39	.29	.29
	Noun phrase	.24	.32	.21
	Miscellaneous	.34	.40	.31
Subject	Personal pronoun	.81	.81	.83
	Other pronouns	.27		.26
	Noun phrase	.39	.19	.37
Person/number	Second person plural	.74	.67	.71
	Third person singular	.26	.33	.29
Interview	III (African American interviewer)			.72
	IV (European American interviewer)			.28
Overall %'s (Ns)		70% (283)	40% (176)	58% (459)

McElhinny, in press), we would of course expect higher rates in speech to African Americans than European Americans, given Bell's hypothesis (11), and Foxy's behavior in interviews III and IV conforms perfectly to this prediction. However, earlier studies are quite mixed with regard to the significance of style-shifting for copula absence in AAVE more generally. As noted, Baugh (1979:183–91) found that situational factors were of minimal importance for this variable as used by his Pacoima interviewees, less influential than the internal linguistic constraints, and less influential than in the case of suffix -*s* absence. By contrast, Wolfram (1969: 177) found a sharp decline in copula absence among his working-class Detroit interviewees between their spoken interview style (41.8 percent) and reading style (7.9 percent).

Labov et al. (1968:191), who considered only absence of *is*, not *are*, suggested that "stylistic shifts are minor effects among the [NYC] pre-adolescent and adolescent peer-groups, and only begin to assume importance with the older adolescents and adults." This appears to be generally true of their data in Table 10.5, although

TABLE 10.5   % *IS* Absence, by Style, Central Harlem, New York

Peer-group	T-Birds (9–13 yrs)	Cobras (11–17 yrs)	Jets (12–16 yrs)	Oscar Bros (15–19 yrs)	Adults (20+ yrs)
Single style	36%	44%	27%	31%	11%
Group style	41%	42%	45%	44%	17%
Style effect	5%	2%*	18%	13%	6%

Adapted from Table 3.12, Labov et al. (1968:192).

*Instance in which group style shows less copula absence than single style, rather than more.

TABLE 10.6   % *Is* Absence, by Subject and Style, Central Harlem, New York

	T-Birds		Cobras		Jets		OscarBr		Adults	
Peer-group	NP	Pro	NP	Pro	NP	Pro	NP	Pro	NP	Pro
Single style	12%	51	18	67	18	61	04	15	08	16
Group style	42%	60	36	77	27	58	26	64	14	27
Style effect	30%	09	18	10	09	03*	22	49	06	11

Adapted from Table 3.12a, Labov et al. (1968:194).
*Instance in which group style shows less copula absence than single style, rather than more.

the adults show less style-shifting than they'd lead us to expect,[33] and it is certainly true from other evidence in their study that internal linguistic constraints have a greater effect on variability in copula absence than external factors do (as in Baugh's study).

Note, however, that when the effect of a noun phrase versus pronoun subject is controlled for, as in Table 10.6, the style effects generally *increase:*[34]

This supports our general point that it is critical to control for the effects of internal constraints when considering style-shifting. Since we don't have a variable rule analysis of the New York City data which includes style as a constraint (Labov 1972 and Cedergren and Sankoff 1974 consider internal factors only), we can't tell for sure whether it would remain significant when all the cross-cutting internal constraints are controlled for, but Table 10.6 at least suggests that it might have been more important than Labov et al. (1968) originally suggested, and more in line with what Bell's differential accommodation hypothesis would lead us to expect.

3.2.5. INVARIANT HABITUAL *be*

The first thing that must be said about Foxy's use of invariant habitual *be* in these interviews is that it exceeds anything reported in the literature to date. For instance, Labov et al. (1968:236) recorded a total of 95 *be* tokens from 18 members of the Thunderbirds gang in New York City; Wolfram (1969:198) recorded 94 from his sample of 48 speakers in Detroit (most were from younger, working-class speakers); and, more recently, Bailey and Maynor (1987:457) reported a total of 119 from their sample of 20 twelve- and thirteen-year-old children in the Brazos Valley, Texas. Foxy had singlehandedly surpassed these group totals since Faye's first interview with her in 1986, producing 146 tokens of invariant habitual *be* on that occasion. Her *be* frequency of 385 in her most recent reinterview with Faye (interview III) surpasses even this earlier high-water mark, and her 97 tokens with Beth (in interview IV), although representative of a style shift away from AAVE, is still higher than reported for African American individuals in other studies.

As first noted by Wolfram (1969:196), invariant *be* "presents special problems" if one attempts to quantify its occurrences in relative terms, that is, "on the basis of actual and potential realizations of particular variants of a variable." Bailey and Maynor (1987) quantify it as a percentage of all present tense forms of *be*, including *is, are,* and zero copula, but this ignores the fact that *be* is a variant of noncopula forms as well, in particular, the English present tense (Richardson 1988, Rickford 1989). Until the relationship of *be* to the full set of its potential alternants is better understood, it is best to report its occurrence in absolute terms.

Because we have absolute rather than relative data on this variable, we cannot analyze the effect of internal constraints on its occurrence as we did for third singular present -*s* of copula absence. But the statistical significance of Foxy's per hour rate of invariant *be* usage (230 in interview III versus 78 in interview IV) is, in any case, so massive as to make it unlikely that it would be due entirely to any internal factors.

Although they shed no light on style-shifting per se, two correlates of Foxy's *be* usage in these interviews are worth noting briefly for their potential interest to other researchers. One is that, as in earlier studies by Labov et al. (1968:234) and Bailey and Maynor (1987:453–54), Foxy's *be* in both interviews is most frequent with second person and plural subjects, next with first person singular subjects, and least with third person singular subjects. Second, in terms of following grammatical environments, Foxy uses *be* in both interviews much more often with a following verb + *ing* than with a following noun phrase, locative, or adjective. This much is consistent with earlier findings (see Bailey and Maynor 1987:457–59). However, what is new is that many of those verb + *ing* forms are *going* and *saying,* used as quotative introducers, as in

(12) My mother jus *be* going, "You—tha's a shame." (III, line 56–481.5b)
(13) They *be* saying, "If I can't be with you . . ." (IV, line 876)

And there is a huge set of invariant *be* tokens before *like* (44 percent interview III, 54 percent interview IV), used as a quotative introducer, as in[35]

(14) He be like, "What you talking bout?" (III:56–028d)
(15) I be like, "FOR REAL?!" (IV, line 852)

This latter feature was not characteristic of Foxy's *be* use when she was first interviewed.

With the exception of speakers over seventy-five years old from east Louisiana and Mississippi whose dialect atlas data are discussed in Bailey and Bassett (1986), European Americans generally do *not* use invariant habitual *be* (Labov et al. 1968:235, Wolfram 1974, Sommer 1986, Nichols 1991). On the basis of this fact, together with Bell's (1984) differential accommodation hypothesis ([11]), we would expect the decreased use of the form between interview III and IV which Foxy displays. But do earlier studies similarly indicate that this feature is sensitive to style shift?

Labov et al. (1968:235) report some style shift for invariant habitual *be* (called *be₂*) use in New York City, but it is the opposite of what we'd expect from a vernacular feature, with "very little use of *be₂* in the group sessions" and more in single style, as Table 10.7 shows. The authors conclude that, for the peer group members, "*be₂* is an emphatic form used in deliberate speech." Whether or not this analysis was valid for New York City peer groups at the time (it is certainly not valid for Foxy and her peers today), one possible explanation for the unexpected result may simply have been the fact that Labov and his colleagues may have had more

TABLE 10.7   Invariant Habitual *be*, Central Harlem, New York

Peer-group	T-Birds (9–13 yrs)	Cobras (11–17 yrs)	Jets (12–16 yrs)	Oscar Bros (15–19 yrs)	Adults (Over 20 yrs)
Single style	83	95	100	18	00
Group style	12	6	29	09	00

From: Labov et al. (1968:236).

data from individual interviews than group sessions, producing more opportunities for tokens of *be* to occur. With an absolute rather than relative frequency count, the relative length of the interviews can make a critical difference. Given the magnitude of the single versus group style distributions in Table 10.7, this clearly cannot be the only explanation, but it is worth considering.

A more significant factor is that invariant *be* use has simply increased by leaps and bounds since the 1960s (either that, or we have better data), and its increased frequency and salience (Butters 1989:15, Bailey and Maynor 1987) may make it available as a counter in strategic style shifting to an extent that was simply not possible in the 1960s. This hypothesis receives some support from the studies by Fasold (1972) and Baugh (1979) reported on below, which show increased use of *be* with African American and familiar addressees, although the extent of the style shift is less dramatic than in the case of Foxy Boston. To the extent that this hypothesis receives further support, it would of course complement and strengthen the related hypothesis which we suggested in relation to possessive *-s*—that a variable which is relatively rare in speech will tend to be exploited less frequently and regularly in strategic style-shifting.

Wolfram (1969), who depended on spoken versus reading contexts for his analysis of style, had nothing to report about invariant *be* in relation to style, because "no instances of invariant *be* occur in the reading passages" (pp. 199–200). Fasold (1972:214), whose Washington, D.C., data were most similar to ours insofar as they used both African American and European American interviewers, noted that

> a higher percentage of speakers who were interviewed by white interviewers used *be* than those who were interviewed by black interviewers—67.7 percent, as against 62.5 percent. However, *the speakers who used* be *at least once were somewhat freer in their use of the form when talking to a black interviewer. Those interviewed by black interviewers averaged 4.7 instances per speaker; those who talked with a white interviewer had an average of 3.4.* [emphasis added]

The italicized portion of this quotation certainly agrees with our data on Foxy Boston, although the extent of the difference in *be* use was much weaker in Fasold's data than in ours. Baugh's (1979:144) comment that invariant *be* "occurs with much greater frequency in colloquial contexts where all interactants are aware of the non-standard form" also matches Foxy's behavior in interviews III and IV. Overall, we can take Fasold's and Baugh's studies as evidence of a trend which reaches its high point in Foxy's 1990s data—for *be* to function more systematically as a vernacular style marker as its frequency of use increases.

3.3. Interviewers' Usage: What Is Foxy Accommodating to?

We have seen from section 3.2 that Foxy's vernacular usage is significantly lower in interview IV than it is in interview III, for three of the variables we considered: third person present -*s*, *is/are* (copula) absence, and invariant habitual *be*. We attribute this intraspeaker or stylistic variation, plausibly enough, to Foxy's accommodation to the different addressees whom she faces in each interview. But Bell's (1984:167) question then arises: "What is it in the addressee (or other audience members) that the speaker is responding to?" Bell (1984:167) suggests three "increasingly specific" possibilities:

(16) 1. Speakers assess the personal characteristics of their addressees and design their style to suit.
2. Speakers assess the general level of their addressees' speech and shift relative to it.
3. Speakers assess their addressees' levels for specific linguistic variables and shift relative to these levels.

As Bell notes (p. 168), it is difficult to distinguish between possibilities 2 and 3, "since the general speech impression of level (2) largely derives from the combined assessment of many individual variables." Operationally, we will consider level 3 to be satisfied to the extent that we can show that there is specific matching between interviewer and interviewee speech with respect to the variables under investigation, even while admitting that the influence could have been, in theory and to some extent, bidirectional.

Table 10.8, showing the vernacular usage of Foxy's addressees in interviews III and IV,[36] suggests that the third possibility is not tenable in our case. Although Beth essentially follows Standard English grammar for the variables in question, while Faye and Roberta use the AAVE variants to some extent, their levels are considerably lower than those of Foxy in the same interview. One might still maintain that Foxy was shifting *relative* to her addressees' levels (about 30 percent to 40 percent higher, for third person -*s* and copula absence, in each case), but the absolute differences are so great, especially for invariant *be*, that possibility 2 is more likely.[37]

Possibility 2 and possibility 1 seem to represent the more valid general statement in the light of Fasold's (1972:214) finding that African American interviewees from Washington, D.C., used vernacular variants more frequently with African Ameri-

TABLE 10.8   Interviewers' Vernacular Usage, Interviews III and IV

	Third Person Present -s	is + are *Absence*	*Invariant* be
Foxy: Interview III	73% (83/114)	70% (197/283)	385
Faye: Interview III	30% (13/43)	22% (29/130)	5
Roberta: Interview III	12% (2/17)	30% (14/46)	12
Foxy: Interview IV	36% (45/124)	40% (70/176)	97
Beth: Interview IV	0% (0/17)	1% (1/81)	0

can interviewers than with European American interviewers (significantly so in the case of past tense [*d*]-deletion). This was so, Fasold noted, "despite the fact that most of the black interviewers were middle-class, standard English speaking young men (a few were conducted by a working-class black man)."

But although it may be the personal characteristics of her addressees that Foxy is responding to, it is impossible to say without further interviews and experiments how much of Foxy's vernacular use should be attributed to the various distinctive aspects of her addressees. Their race and relative familiarity seem significant enough, from this study and from the earlier work of Anshen (1969), Fasold (1972), and Baugh (1979), but how *much* to attribute to race and how much to familiarity is difficult to say, and the contributory effects of residential community membership, personality, and age are even harder to assess (see Bell 1984:168–69 on this point).

3.4. Topic-Influenced Style Shift in Foxy's Vernacular Usage, Interviews III and IV

Although Bell (1984) suggests that the nature of the addressee and other audience members is the primary factor in a speaker's style shift, he does acknowledge that "nonpersonal" factors such as topic and setting also have some influence. However, he argues that "the direction and strength of style shift caused by these factors originate in their derivation from audience-designed shift" (p. 178). This general argument leads him to these three specific hypotheses which can be tested against Foxy's data:

(17) 1. Variation according to topic . . . presupposes variation according to addressee. (p. 179)
  2. The degree of topic-designed shift will not exceed that of audience-designed shift. (p. 180)
  3. Speakers associate classes of topics or settings with classes of persons. They therefore shift style when talking on those topics or in those settings as if they were talking to addressees whom they associate with the topic or setting.

Hypothesis 17.1 is trivially correct. Since we know from section 3.2 that Foxy does show addressee style shift, the presupposition which the hypothesis embodies is satisfied, and any variation by topic which we find in her data would be consistent with it.

As Tables 10.9 and 10.10 show, Foxy does display variation by topic in both interviews III and IV, and the data they contain allow us to address hypothesis 17.2. This hypothesis does not fare as well as the first, however, since the amounts of zero copula shift caused by addressee differences (calculated by subtracting the percentages in the Total row of Table 10.10 from their counterparts in Table 10.9) range from 22 percent (zero *is*) to 30 percent (zero *is* + *are*), while the amounts caused by topic changes within each interview are much higher: for instance, 75 percent for zero *is* in Table 10.9 (from 0 percent for topic I to 75 percent for topic G) and 73 percent for zero *is* + *are* in Table 10.10 (from 9 percent for topic G to 82 percent, topic F).[38]

One of the speakers in Douglas-Cowie's (1978:41, 42, 45) study similarly

TABLE 10.9   Foxy's Zero Copula and Invariant *be* Use by Topic,
Interview III, with Faye and Roberta

Topic	Zero is	Zero are	Zero is + are	be₂
A: School, including teen pregnancies (6 & ½ pages, 7% transcript)	60% (5)	50% (4)	56% (9)	7
B: Drugs, thefts, murders, EPA (11 pages, 12% transcript)	10% (10)	96% (26)	72% (36)	12
C: Skating, meeting boys, slang (7 & ½ pages, 9% transcript)	25% (4)	100% (4)	63% (8)	19
D: School, including teachers and drugs (3 & ½ pages, 4% transcript)	40% (10)	100% (5)	60% (15)	1
E: Graduation, college/career (5 pages, 6% transcript)	33% (6)	100% (1)	43% (7)	0
F: Wives, slamming partners (10 & ½ pages, 12% transcript)	54% (13)	90% (20)	76% (33)	53
G: Boy-girl conflicts and relations (7 & ½ pages, 9% transcript)	75% (16)	95% (21)	86% (37)	78
H: Foxy's friends: girls, guys (9 pages, 10% transcript)	31% (26)	96% (28)	65% (54)	61
I: Vietnamese/foreign friends (4 pages, 5% transcript)	0% (3)	100% (7)	70% (10)	10
J: Boys, and how to treat them (9 pages, 10% transcript)	30% (10)	69% (16)	54% (26)	61
K: Race relations at school (9 pages, 10% transcript)	44% (9)	88% (24)	76% (33)	48
L: Fun at school (5 pages, 6% transcript)	3% (6)	100% (9)	73% (15)	37
Total, all topics (87 & ½ pages, 100% transcript)	39% (118)	91% (165)	70% (283)	387

showed more topic shift than addressee shift, and Bell (1984:180), commenting on this exception, suggested that the expected ratios were more likely to hold for grouped data, as in Coupland (1981). To the extent that this means that cells with low token counts can be expected to show random variability, Bell is right, and we might note that the categorical cells in Tables 10.9 and 10.10—the ones with values of 0 percent and 100 percent which could be interpreted as indicators of extreme topic shift—all contain ten or fewer tokens (one cell has twelve). But individuals with sufficient data should be expected to exemplify the expected ratios as well as groups. If we followed Guy (1980:26) and accepted thirty tokens per factor as the cut-off point for reliability, hypothesis 17.2 would be sustained; Table 10.10 has only one such cell for zero *is/are* (topic F), and the five qualifying *is/are* cells in Table 10.9 (topics B, F, G, H, K) between them show a maximum topic-influenced shift of only 21 percent (from 65 percent for topic H to 86 percent for topic G)—less than the 30 percent addressee-influenced shift in *is/are* absence which separates

TABLE 10.10   Foxy's Zero Copula and Invariant *be* Use by Topic,
Interview IV, with Beth

Topic	Zero is	Zero are	Zero is + are	be₂
A: School, college/career plans (8 pages, 19% transcript)	9% (11)	23% (13)	17% (24)	0
B: The Persian Gulf War (5 & ½ pages, 13% transcript)	11% (9)	10% (10)	11% (19)	0
C: Foxy's boyfriend, girlfriends (2 pages, 5% transcript)	0% (3)	33% (6)	22% (9)	1
D: Boy-girl differences (3 pages, 7% transcript)	0% (0)	14% (7)	14% (7)	2
E: Slang terms (2 & ½ pages, 6% transcript)	0% (3)	100% (12)	80% (15)	13
F: Wives, slamming partners (5 pages, 12% transcript)	60% (15)	96% (24)	82% (39)	46
G: Recreation, F as role model (2 pages, 5% transcript)	10% (8)	33% (3)	9% (11)	16
H: AIDS, other teen problems (3 & ½ pages, 8% transcript)	17% (12)	29% (7)	21% (19)	0
I: Races, other groups at school (7 pages, 17% transcript)	10% (6)	58% (12)	39% (18)	16
J: Popular music and dances (3 & ½ pages, 8% transcript)	0% (8)	71% (7)	31% (15)	3
Total, all topics (42 pages, 100% transcript)	17% (75)	56% (101)	40% (176)	97

interviews III and IV. However, if we also accepted the evidence of cells just slightly below Guy's cut-off point—specifically, the cells with twenty-six and twenty-four tokens in the zero *is/are* columns of Tables 10.9 and 10.10—hypothesis 17.2 would *not* be sustained, since the maximum topic shift in Table 10.9 would be 32 percent (from 54 percent for topic J to 86 percent for topic G), and the maximum topic shift in Table 10.10 would be 65 percent (from 17 percent for topic A to 82 percent for topic F), both higher (the former admittedly just slightly higher) than the addressee shift of 30 percent between interviews III and IV. We feel that the evidence of such cells should be accepted. In the case of the twenty-four-token cell in Table 10.10 (interview IV) at least, an additional six tokens would not alter the picture, whatever their realization, and zero copula fluctuations in this table accord with the very strong impression we get from listening to the tape (and attending to other variables) that Foxy makes some remarkable topic shifts within interview IV.

In the rest of this section, we concentrate on Foxy's shift between topics A and F in interview IV, using it to consider hypothesis 17.3, and comparing it with a smaller but related shift in interview III.

Elaborating on 17.3, which he offers as an *explanation* for the direction of topic style shifts rather than as a *hypothesis*, Bell (1984:181) suggests, "Topics such as occupation or education . . . cause shifts to a style suitable to address an employer or teacher. Similarly, intimate topics . . . elicit speech appropriate for intimate addressees—family or friends." Foxy's shift between topics A and F in interview IV corresponds perfectly to Bell's hypothetical example, since A deals with school, college, and career plans and is predictably more standard, while F deals with "wives and slamming partners" (see quotation [10]), the kind of topic one is most likely to discuss with friends, and one which predictably elicits the most vernacular speech. Foxy's shift in interview III between topics A and E, which deal with her academic progress and plans, and topic F, which deals with "wives and slamming partners," is comparable, although the shift is quantitatively smaller, since Foxy's baseline vernacular use with Faye and Roberta in this interview is higher.

But while the direction of shift which Foxy displays in both interviews fits Bell's predictions, it doesn't really show that Foxy style shifts when talking on various topics *as if talking to addressees associated with the topic.* If we had data on Foxy's actually talking to her teachers and closest friends, and those data matched her language use on academic versus "slamming partners" topics in our two interviews, that would provide some support for hypothesis 17.3, although Bell is careful to note (p. 182) that the association between addressee and topic shift is relatively abstract; speakers need not be "conscious of an associated addressee when style shifting for a particular topic."

One relevant difference between Foxy's language in the college/career and "wives/slammin partner" sections of both interviews is the absence of direct quotes in the former and their prevalence in the latter. The absence of quotes, the absence of invariant habitual *be,* and the low zero copula rates in the college and career sections are all manifestations of a relatively detached information-presenting style, the kind that one might use when talking to a teacher or a stranger:

(18) F: Miss R. *is* the one that—[laughter] Miss R Ø the one help me get into this program, and my—and this guy name Mr O at our school, he's Chinese. [interview III, with Faye and Roberta]
(19) F: M., she goes to DeAnza's nursing school. And R. and T., they're going to, um, CSM, and my friend A, she's going to be going with me when I go. . . . [interview IV, with Beth]

By contrast, in the "wives and slamming partner" sections (F) of both interviews, Foxy is extremely animated and involved, frequently quoting the remarks of real and hypothetical teenagers, as in extracts (4) and (10) above. Significantly enough, both sections contain high frequencies of invariant habitual *be* (fifty-three in interview III, forty-six in interview IV), and most of these (60 percent in interview III, 72 percent in interview IV) precede quotative introducers, as in

(20) F: I *be* like, "for real?" I *be* going, "Tramp, you're stuuupid. You Ø just DUMB! Uhhh! Get away from me! You Ø stupid!" [C]
(21) F: You be in your car with your friends and they *be* like, "Hey, F, ain't that that girl they—um—B slammed the other night?" You *be* like, "Yeah, that IS her." [D]

In the sections in which Foxy's vernacular language use reaches its peak, therefore, Foxy is not just behaving *as if* speaking to teenagers; she is, through extensive quotations, dramatically reenacting the speaking *of* teenagers.[39]

Many of the copula tokens in the "slamming partners" (topic F) sections of both interviews in fact occur within quotations. And, in interview III, copula tokens within quotations show a higher *is/are* absence rate (13/15 = 87 percent) than those not in quotations (12/18 = 67 percent), although this is not true for interview IV: 7/9 (78 percent) zero *is/are* within quotations, versus 25/30 (83 percent) zero *is/are* outside quotations. In any event, it seems reasonable to interpret the heavy use of quotations in these sections of the interviews as providing some support for Bell's hypothesis 17.3; to attribute Foxy's high zero copula and *be* use frequencies in these sections to her speaking as if speaking to (and on behalf of) her teenage friends and peers.

Whether it is theoretically *necessary* to do so is another matter. One could alternatively appeal to differences in one or more of Finegan and Biber's (1989) situational parameters (for instance, an informational communication purpose for the academic topic versus an interpersonal, affective purpose for the slamming partner topic) to characterize the topic-influenced variation which Foxy displays in these interviews. But it must be admitted that there are theoretical benefits to Bell's approach (the linking of previously unconnected social and stylistic variation), and that it squares with the empirical evidence.

One point which remains to be made before we leave this issue is that whatever vicarious identification with typical but absent addressees various topics might involve, the effect of the actual and present addressees remains stronger. (What we're doing here is essentially returning to 17.2 from a different perspective.) This is evident in the fact that although the race and familiarity of Faye and Roberta elicit more vernacular grammar, Faye's role as an adult and mother appears to lead Foxy to refer to sex allusively and indirectly in interview III (you just *do everything with 'em except that*), while using four-letter words (in quotation) with the younger Beth in interview IV:[40] Note that topic does not override addressee. For all that Foxy talks animatedly about sex and boy-girl relations in interview III, she never uses obscenities with Faye. Contrariwise, even when playing a profane rap song and discussing music and dances with Beth at the end of interview IV, Foxy's zero *is/are* and *be* rates remain low.[41]

3.5 Foxy's Earlier Interviews (1986, 1988)

We have now explored the salient aspects of Foxy's stylistic variation, as influenced by addressee and topic, in interviews III and IV. One could obviously attempt to squeeze other insights from these interviews—by considering phonological variables, for instance, or alternative influences on style shift—but it's more theoretically fruitful to look briefly at Foxy's style levels in her two earlier interviews with Faye and Roberta, as reflected in copula absence and invariant *be* use, the main variables explored in this paper.

The very first interview, which we'll refer to as interview I (= EPA 7, 8), was recorded in 1986, when Foxy was thirteen. Up to this point, she had been schooled entirely in East Palo Alto, in schools with exclusively or primarily African American populations, and her vernacular usage was at a peak. Interview I lasted about an hour and a half, and in it Foxy used 146 tokens of invariant *be* and exhibited whopping copula absence rates: 79 percent (N = 72) for zero *is,* 99 percent (N = 82) for zero *are,* and 90 percent for zero *is* and *are* combined (N = 154). Although these rates differ somewhat from those in interview III, it is possible to attribute the latter to change over time, especially since the intervening four years represents the teenage years—a period in which, as Eckert (1988) shows, major readjustments in an individual's social identity and linguistic usage can take place. Moreover, interview I, when contrasted with interview IV, still shows significantly higher rates of vernacular usage, and we could attribute the stylistic contrast between them to differences in the race and familiarity of the addressees, as we did in contrasting interviews III and IV above.

However, the second interview, which we'll refer to as interview II (= EPA 42, 43), is another story. This interview, recorded in 1988, when Foxy was fifteen, was shorter than the other interviews (fifty-five minutes), and in it Foxy used eighty-one tokens of invariant *be* (= eighty-eight per hour) and exhibited relatively low copula absence rates: 18 percent (N = 48) for zero *is,* 48 percent (N = 46) for zero *are,* and 34 percent (N = 94) for zero *is* and *are* combined. These rates are not significantly different from those in interview IV, when Foxy was addressing Beth, a European American stranger, and they therefore require some explanation.

There are several potential explanations for Foxy's reduced AAVE use in interview II. At this point she had completed her first year at a predominantly European American high school outside the EPA community. She had also taken part in a live-in summer Upward Bound program at Stanford and had been involved in several tutorial, college motivational, and preprofessional programs (Higher Horizons, MESA, TOPS, SASI) which exposed her to consistent Standard English models. We wouldn't want to overestimate the influence of these factors on her language development, but Foxy mentions in interview II that African American students at school are beginning to say that she sounds "like a white person." She does not believe that she does, but she concedes that the extensive contact she's been having with European Americans outside EPA may have had some effect.[42] For all her attempts to rebuff it, Foxy may also have been affected by the apparent prejudice she encountered at her school against her race and community; she talks of schoolmates who say they are forbidden to go to East Palo Alto because "the black people's gonna get us!" and of the school's spirit squad rejecting *all* the African American girls who try out for it. One response to such prejudice might have been a temporary diminution in her distinctively African American language and behavior.[43] By the time Foxy is interviewed again, in 1990, she seems much more secure about her background and identity; she is president of the BSU, has won respect from teachers and students on her own terms, and has seen her African American friend T. crowned as homecoming queen ("We was all happy. . . . All of us was cryin"— interview III). And her language has returned close to the vernacular levels of her early adolescent years.

There are also a number of factors within the interview situation which may have produced the reduced vernacular usage which Foxy exhibits in interview II. For one thing the setting was different. This was the only interview conducted in Faye's home, and neither Faye nor Foxy appears to relax as much as in the interviews conducted at Foxy's. Faye's status as mother and authority figure comes across much more clearly as she attends to household matters, and her role as interview director is much more sharply delineated, as she deploys more prefabricated questions than usual ("If you could pass a message on to a fifteen-year-old in Nigeria about life in America, what would you tell her to look out for?") and switches abruptly from one topic to another when they fail to elicit much interest ("I see I ain't gettin no information outta y'all 'bout the boys, so I'ma drop that subject"). Foxy does get more excited about some topics—sexuality, teen pregnancies, and teen slang predictably lead to elevated copula absence and invariant *be* rates—but in general she is more subdued and detached than she is in her other interviews with Faye and Roberta, and her reduced AAVE use is very much in keeping with that.

One way of accounting for Foxy's reduced vernacular usage within interview II is to consider it *initiative* style design, which, instead of occurring "in response to a change in the extralinguistic situation . . . itself initiates a change in the situation" (Bell 1984:182). As in the cases of metaphorical switching discussed by Blom and Gumperz (1972), Foxy's more standard usage might be seen "as a claim to intellectual authority" (Bell 1984) or as a reflection of the fact that, because of her exposure to Stanford and the motivational programs referred to previously, she is now responding to Faye more in terms of her association with this institution than in terms of her race or community membership. It might even be argued that her initiative style shift in this case is partly an instance of "outgroup referee design" (Bell 1984:188–89)—that she is now more conscious of absent Stanford people who might listen to the interview than she was in interviews I and III. To the extent that Foxy's stylistic level in interview II represents initiative style shift, the most we can do is attempt to interpret it after the fact (cf. Bell 1984:185).

Despite our extensive discussion of this issue, our purpose is *not* to explain away the unusualness of interview II or to view it as aberrant. Whatever the stage-of-life, intrainterview, or other factors which made it happen in interview II, Foxy has as much "right" to shift away from the vernacular with familiar African Americans like Faye and Roberta as she does with unfamiliar European Americans like Beth. We can't say that Foxy has one fixed register for African Americans and another for European Americans, or that she has one register for familiars and another for nonfamiliars, any more than we might expect anyone *always* to talk to a spouse or workmate in the same way. While these addressee variables do set up some valid expectations about the kind of language that Foxy (or anyone else) might use, we have to allow for the use of style as a resource and strategy, as an interactive and dynamic process (Coupland 1984, Traugott and Romaine 1985) which can vary between different situations, and for the intersecting effects of setting, scene, key, and the other multidimensional factors that Hymes (1972) and others have identified. This recognition may help us account for the fluctuating views of their intersection with style which earlier studies of AAVE variables have yielded (see sec. 3.2). It's not enough to say that groups A and B differ significantly with respect to a specific feature and *therefore* we should always expect the feature to display significant style-shifting when addressees from groups A versus B are involved. The features of a dialect are a resource which individuals and groups have some freedom to use as their mood and inclination dictate, although Bell's addressee-based principles do help us to predict in general ways what they are likely to do.

4. Summary and Conclusion

We have documented and attempted to explain the decline of intraspeaker or stylistic variation as a focus of research in quantitative sociolinguistics. We suggested that a primary reason for this decline was the fact that investigators found it difficult to separate "careful" from "casual" speech in reliable and objective ways, and that they also found it possible to continue doing quantitative "sociolinguistics" (identifying internal and external constraints on linguistic variation, for instance, or studying ongoing linguistic change) *without* attending to this operationally difficult distinction.

Whether other quantitative sociolinguists will agree with the explanation or not, it is clear that style is too central to the methodological and theoretical concerns of our subfield for us to neglect it any longer. For one thing, Labov's original assertions that the most informal or peer group–influenced speech offers the clearest view of social differentiation and linguistic change have never been refuted, and in a subfield where recorded corpora are the primary means of studying such phenomena, the styles represented in such corpora can hardly be ignored. If, for instance, we had used Foxy's copula and third singular -*s* absence rates in interview IV (40 percent and 36 percent, respectively) to assess the nature of current adolescent usage of African American Vernacular English in East Palo Alto, we would have had a very different picture than if we had used her corresponding rates in interview II (70 percent and 73 percent, respectively), leading us to radically different inferences about the nature of regional differences in the dialect and its convergence with or divergence from other ethnic vernaculars.[44] Douglas-Cowie's (1978:39) motivation for studying addressee-influenced style shifts among villagers in the Northern Irish village of Articlave was also rooted in a methodological concern—"to reveal the possible linguistic limitations of being a well-educated English investigator in a Northern Ireland rural community." Quantitative sociolinguists simply do not discuss these issues these days. We have become almost as bad as generative syntacticians in avoiding critical discussions about our data, making us perhaps as vulnerable to the charge of developing strong theories with weak foundations (cf. Labov 1975).

With respect to theory development, stylistic variation seems to offer more potential for the integration of past findings and the establishment of productive research agendas than virtually any other area in sociolinguistics. This is because of its ubiquity (maybe even universality) and its relation to other central topics within our field, including social or status variation and internal linguistic conditioning, as explored in recent articles by Bell (1984), Finegan and Biber (1989), and Preston (1991). By the same token, quantitative sociolinguistics offers a precision to the study of style shift and accommodation that is unmatched by other approaches (cf. Coupland 1984:53), and a means of disentangling the effects of internal and external constraints, via the variable rule program, that other approaches could fruitfully adopt. We hope that these benefits have been exemplified in our discussion of Foxy's style-shifting, particularly with respect to copula and third singular -*s* absence.

If quantitative sociolinguistics is to return to the study of style, as we urge, an approach based on the re-recording of speakers with different addressees (Rickford 1987) seems most promising, especially if coupled with the theoretical conceptualization of style as audience design which Bell (1984) offers. Several of Bell's hypotheses and predictions about addressee design were confirmed by the data on Foxy's style-shifting examined in this chapter. His predictions about differential accommodation (which variables might be expected to show significant style shift with different classes of addressees and which might not) were generally confirmed, once riders about absolute and relative frequencies of occurrence were added: that low rates (as with possessive and plural -*s* absence) reduce the probability that a variable will figure significantly in style shift, and high rates (as with *be* use in the 1990s) increase that probability. Preston's "status" axiom was also confirmed, along with Bell's "style" axiom.

Bell's hypotheses about the primacy of addressee over topic shift were also confirmed, more or less; more if thirty tokens per cell (Guy 1980) was accepted as a minimum cut-off point, less if cells with slightly fewer tokens were also considered. We were impressed by the dramatic topic shift (17 percent to 72 percent copula absence) which Foxy displayed when talking about "school and career" versus "wives and slamming partners" with Beth in interview IV (recorded in 1991), but we were convinced about the primacy of addressee by the fact that she generally used higher frequencies on each topic when talking to Faye and Roberta in interview III (recorded in 1990).

Bell's hypothesis that speakers shift style when talking on particular topics *as if* talking to addressees whom they associate with that topic was more difficult to investigate empirically, but it seemed to receive some support from the fact that Foxy's most vigorous vernacular usage in both interviews occurred where she was quoting extensively from teenage friends and peer group members, dramatically re-enacting their actual and hypothetical conversations. Whether it was theoretically necessary to appeal to Bell's hypothesis to explain the increased vernacular usage in such sections was, however, less clear.

The single greatest challenge to Bell's audience design approach came from consideration of interviews I and II, which Faye and Roberta recorded with Foxy in 1986 and 1988. The former was no problem, since Foxy's style remained closer to the AAVE vernacular than it did in interview IV, as Bell's hypotheses would predict for an African American versus European American addressee. However, Foxy's stylistic level in interview II was *not* significantly closer to the vernacular than in interview IV, and this ran counter to Bell's predictions about responsive addressee style shift. We proposed several possible explanations for this unexpected result, including appeals to Bell's notion of "initiative" style shift (cf. Blom and Gumperz's "metaphorical switching") and consideration of components such as setting, scene, and key (Hymes 1972), which we had previously ignored. However persuasive our arguments, we were clearly engaging in post hoc interpretation by this stage and moving away from the powerful predictions which lie at the heart of Bell's (1984) approach. This may be acceptable, even necessary, for some kinds of stylistic variation, as Bell himself (1984:185) suggests. But we would urge in closing that sociolinguists who return to or enter into the study of style attempt to push the predictive parts of Bell's model as far as possible, testing them against other data sets, and revising and refining them where necessary. Sociolinguistics needs fewer laissez-faire generalizations and more falsifiable predictions if it is to answer to recent calls for more explicit theory building (Cheshire 1987:257, Finegan and Biber 1989:3), and style is one area in which we have already begun to make good progress toward this goal.

Notes

1. Foxy's father, who does not live with the family, is a construction worker. Her mother, a single parent household head, is a construction planner at a Bay Area aeronautical corporation. "Foxy Boston" is a pseudonym.

2. Dubois and Horvath (1991) approach the issue from another direction, varying not the race of the interviewer, but the race of the interviewee. The questioning strategies of their Anglo interviewers in Sydney, Australia, turned out to be significantly different with Greek, Italian, and Anglo/Celtic interviewees. Their conclusion that "the negotiation of tension is most easily achieved when both members of the interview come from the same culture" (ms., p. 11) parallels the finding of Terrell et al. (1977:381) that "speaking to one's own ethnic group has a facilitating effect on both the total number of words used and the complexity of the sentences used." These experimental results do not of course imply that same-race interviewers will always have a facilitating effect nor that different-race interviewers will never have a facilitating effect.

3. Of course several individual sociolinguists—Labov (1972), Baugh (1979), Irvine (1979, 1985), Biber (1988), to name only a few—have provided important theoretical or empirical studies of stylistic or intraspeaker variation, but the major focus of attention in the United States has been on intergroup variation—by socioeconomic class, ethnicity, sex/gender, and age. In this respect, one might say that the (partial) roots of American sociolinguistics in dialect geography have remained evident, with social groups replacing geographical regions as the primary external variable.

4. See, however, Biber (1988), who emphasizes that a multidimensional perspective is essential to adequate analyses of register (or style) variation.

5. The diminution in American quantitativist studies of stylistic variation had started since the mid-1970s, but as shown by the published proceedings of recent NWAVE conferences (for instance, Denning et al. 1987, Ferrara et al. 1988), or the new variationist journal, *Language Variation and Change,* it is really marked over the past half decade, since variationist papers in these publications contain little or no reference to style.

6. However, some researchers—for instance, Tarone (1985), Di Paolo (1992), and Yaeger-Dror (1991)—have continued to make productive use of a Labovian-like distinction between relatively monitored and unmonitored or prescriptive and vernacular styles, involving attention paid to speech. Yaeger-Dror (1991) distinguishes terminologically between "attention-related 'style' and target-related 'register'."

7. Nikolas Coupland (personal communication) notes additional evidence in this regard, from recent research in Wales conducted by one of his students, Penny Rowlands, on stylistic variation in young children's speech, especially in relation to addressee effects over different

ages: "One point to emerge very clearly in her work is that 'reading aloud' does have truly generic characteristics in that kids quickly learn prosodic and, it seems, segmental phonological conventions for doing it."

8. Labov has noted (personal communication) that his decision to use group recordings in Harlem was directly influenced by the successful use which Gumperz had made of this technique in Hemnesberget, Norway, as reported in Gumperz (1964) and elsewhere.

9. The distinction between situational and metaphorical switching—although in practice often involving change of addressee and topic, respectively—is theoretically more complex. The former "involves clear changes in the participants' definition of each other's rights and obligation," while the latter does not involve "any significant change in definition of participants' mutual rights and obligations," but usually occurs in situations which "allow for the enactment of two or more different relationships among the same set of individuals" (Blom and Gumperz 1972:424–25). Dennis Preston (personal communication) restates it as follows: "Situational shifting occurs when a change exploits the range of options predicted by the linguistic, status, and style boundaries of an interaction. Metaphoric shift occurs when such shift occurs outside this predictability . . . it is an exploitation of the unexpected."

10. This was not true of the studies by Baugh, Hindle, Payne, and Rickford, whose dissertations were supervised by Labov.

11. Exceptions include Milroy (1987), Wilson (1987), Finegan and Biber (1989), and Preston (1991). Bell himself (personal communication) offers the following comment: "I guess if I am disappointed in anything about the lack of follow-up on audience design it is the lack of theoretical building on or critique of it rather than of empirical studies within the framework (although the two are probably linked)."

12. Bell notes (personal communication) that the question of whether speakers style shift in reaction to the general persona of their interlocutors or in relation to their specific linguistic performance was first raised by Coupland (1981, 1984) before he picked it up. For a subsequent and more detailed analysis of the motivations for code-switching, see Coupland (1985).

13. As Labov (Ms. 52) notes, in discussing the importance of the feedback principle, the more an interviewer knows when talking about a topic, the more interviewees are likely to tell you: "Once he [the investigator] has entered far enough into the subject to ask an 'insider's question,' he will obtain richer results." Gossip, of course, exemplifies the principle perfectly.

14. All variables were tabulated in accordance with Labov's (1969:738, 1972:72) accountability principle, which requires the observer to report the actual occurrences of a variant against the total of all the possible cases in which it might have occurred, excluding categorical or indeterminate contexts (see notes 15 and 16).

15. In the case of possessive, plural, and third person singular -s absence, tokens followed by a word beginning with s (as in "John's son") were not counted, since these make it difficult to tell whether the inflectional -s is present or not.

16. The list of "don't count" cases excluded from consideration in the analysis of copula absence is quite large (see Labov et al. 1968, Wolfram 1969, Blake 1992, Rickford et al. 1991), but they include the following cases in which the variable is either categorical or indeterminate: clause-finals; tokens under primary stress; instances of "what's," "that's," or "it's"; negatives; tokens of *is* preceded or followed by s; tokens of *are* followed by r.

17. In the case of invariant *be*, for which we have absolute rather than relative frequency data (see section 3.2.3), significance was calculated on the per hour rate of *be* use.

18. As noted by Rickford (1992), the relative rarity of nominal possessives in speech has been a problem for most studies of AAVE.

19. In response to this point, Suzanne Romaine (personal communication) has raised some interesting questions about the differences between production and perception and

between statistical and other kinds of significance. We do not as yet have definitive answers but think her remarks on this issue are worth quoting in full: "This point raises a question that hasn't been addressed in the literature on style shifting: How much of a difference is significant in terms of *perception* by the listener? One needs to know this to determine if the variable is being used symbolically in a successful way. Tests of statistical significance only indicate *production*-related differences."

20. Of course, we also know that even a single occurrence of a stereotyped, salient (Trudgill 1986), or strongly marked feature can be enough to register a style shift, or to mark its user as speaking in a special (preferred or dispreferred) style. See Gumperz's (1983) discussion of the student who said "Ahma git me a gig," and note the following quote from Reggie, an African American teenager (cited in Rickford 1992): "Over at my school, if they—first time they catch you talkin' white, they'll never let it go. Even if you just quit talking like that, they'll never let it go!" (EPA50:A530–532). Finally, Allan Bell (personal communication) notes that in his analyses of initiative style shift in media language, "rare variants are all the more valuable just because of their rarity. Just one token can act as a marker of identity." Together these "counterexamples" to the proposed frequency rider indicate that one task for a theory of style is to determine in a principled and predictable way the difference between rare but stylistically salient variables and rare and nonsalient ones.

21. However, it could be argued that the difference is, in this case, *qualitatively* interesting, insofar as Foxy *never* omits plural -*s* in interview IV.

22. Foxy's plural absence rate, when she was first interviewed in 1986, was 13 percent (14/107), so she has become more standard in the interim. This is also true of her copula absence rate; see section 3.5.

23. LePage and Tabouret-Keller's (1985) "Acts of Identity" model, which treats linguistic behavior "as a series of acts of identity in which people reveal both their personal identity and their search for social roles" (p. 14), is admirable in several respects, but it tends to slight or ignore internal constraints in favor of external or sociopsychological ones.

24. The difference *was* significant for percentage of [*d*]-deletion but not for cluster simplification, the other variables discussed with respect to race-of-interviewer effects (ibid.).

25. As Baugh notes (1979:106–8), the familiarization process does not proceed uniformly for all individuals; some, like David W., became familiar with the interviewer and used vernacular styles relatively rapidly; others, like James D., remained suspicious for a longer period and took correspondingly longer to begin using his vernacular.

26. Baugh (1979) states it more generally: "The adults under analysis therefore consistently altered their speech toward SE in the presence of people with whom they were newly acquainted, regardless of their race." But since Baugh was the principal interviewer in each case, and non–African Americans were only present in peripheral roles in some of his interviews, the statement should not be taken to imply that variation by race of *addressee* is unimportant.

27. In addition to the factor groups in Table 10.4, we also considered the effect of the preceding and following phonological environment, but these turned out to be nonsignificant.

28. The particular model we used is the logistic model (ibid.), in which "values above .500 favor the rule, values of less than .500 disfavor the rule and a value of .500 means a constraint has no effect" (Fasold 1978:93).

29. In Table 10.4, as in Table 10.1, copula absence is calculated as "straight deletion"— the proportion of zero copulas against the total of all zero, contracted, and full forms, excluding "don't count" cases (see note 16). See Rickford et al. (1991) for further discussion of "straight deletion" and for comparison with "Labov deletion," which calculates the proportion of zero copulas against the total of zero and contracted forms only, for reasons outlined in

Labov (1969). Although space prevents us from presenting all the results, we have in fact made "Labov deletion" runs for interviews III and IV; these modify the significance and ordering of some of the internal factors but do not affect the external factor (addressee-based style shift) under consideration. Interviews III and IV have input probabilities of .73 and .44 in separate "Labov deletion" runs; in the pooled (III + IV) interview run, they remain sharply differentiated as factors within a factor group, with associated factor weights of .74 and .26, respectively.

30. The only differences are in the following grammatical factor group, where minor differences from the usual ordering and from each other are shown.

31. The percentage and raw frequency data at the bottom of Table 10.4 are based on the copula absence data prior to the removal of knockout (categorical) factors. The coefficients are taken from the variable rule runs containing only the significant factor groups.

32. Note that the data in the "Interview III + IV" column of Table 10.4 confirm Preston's (1991:36) prediction, since the range and limits of two of the three internal factors (FOLLOWING GRAMMATICAL = .21–.90, SUBJECT = .26–.83) exceed the range and limits of the single external variable (INTERVIEW = .28–.72). Dennis Preston (personal communication) has made the following additional observation about these data: "Foxy's data here shows that her stylistic performance (.28–.72) . . . is contained within the variation space for age within her speech community (.22–.83, as presented in Rickford et al. 1991:117, table 6; and cited in Preston 1991:40, table 5). This suggests that Foxy's 'models' for speech behavior, although perhaps triggered by audience factors, need not have been derived from the audience of interview IV since her own speech community (namely older speakers) provide a score (.22) which could predict her performance in setting IV (.28)."

33. To make it consistent with the data of Table 10.4, Tables 10.5 and 10.6 consider the ratio of deleted forms to full, contracted, and deleted forms (=Rickford et al.'s 1992 "straight deletion"). Although Labov et al. claim (p. 191) that "the feature which is correlated with style shift from single to group sessions is the ratio of deleted to originally contracted forms—that is, D/D + C" ["Labov deletion" in our terms], these alternative computations do not significantly affect their argument. The "straight deletion" data in fact support their claims about older/younger style-shifting differences better than the "Labov deletion" data do.

34. It should be noted that the data in Tables 10.5 and 10.6 are not completely comparable because the number of forms and subjects represented in each group sometimes changes from one table to the other. For instance, the single style figure for the Cobras in Table 10.5 is based on 230 tokens from eleven subjects, while the single style figure for the Cobras in Table 10.6 is based on 141 tokens from nine subjects.

35. For analysis of constraints on variation between *say, go,* and *be like* as quotative introducers in American English, see Blyth et al. 1990.

36. For shorthand we say "interviewers' usage" in the Table 10.8 title but Roberta was of course a cointerviewee rather than an interviewer in interviews I, II, and III.

37. Of course, there's a certain amount of mutual accommodation—Roberta and Faye's accommodating to Foxy, and vice versa (cf. Coupland 1984:54)—but in the absence of independent data on Roberta and Faye's (or Beth's) speech in other contexts, we can't measure the extent of *their* accommodation, and our focus is, in any case, on *Foxy's* style shifts.

38. Since the invariant habitual *be* data are absolute rather than relative, they have no bearing on this issue; the overall "addressee" difference between interviews III and IV (290 tokens) will always exceed the maximum topic shift within either interview.

39. As Bell (personal communication) notes: "This is very much what I would regard as an initiative use of language: Deliberate declaring of an ingroup identity."

40. At the end of interview IV, Foxy also plays a rap song called "Bitches" for Beth, which, by Foxy's own admission, is extremely "profane."

41. One could also point to the fact that when Foxy's copula absence for equivalent topics in interviews III and IV is compared, it is higher in interview III than in interview IV (e.g., 76 percent versus 39 percent for race relations), but the status of these comparisons is questionable insofar as none of them passes the minimum thirty-token requirement in both interviews.

42. Foxy returns to this theme in 1991 in interview IV, observing that "When I get home, I use slang and everything; when I'm at school, I talk different," and that friends still accuse her of "talking like a white girl." It appears that the latter impression might derive primarily from her phonology, from her adoption of some of the distinctive characteristics of European American pronunciation in the area.

43. And an interview with Beth or any other European American, at the time, might have shown even lower rates of vernacular usage than Faye and Roberta elicited, posing no problem for Bell's hypothesis ([11]).

44. There is every reason to believe that the problem would remain whether we used individual or group data, as long as we did not measure and take into account the addressee/interviewer effect.

References

Anderson, Barbara A., Brian C. Silver, and Paul R. Abramson. 1988. "The Effects of the Race of the Interviewer on Race-related Attitudes of Black Respondents in SRC/CPS National Election Studies." *Public Opinion Quarterly* 52:289–324.

Anshen, Frank. 1969. "Speech Variation Among Negroes in a Small Southern Community." Ph.D. Dissertation, New York University.

Ash, Sharon, and John Myhill. 1986. "Linguistic Correlates of Inter-Ethnic Contact." In David Sankoff, ed., *Diversity and Diachrony.* Amsterdam: Benjamins. Pp. 33–42.

Bailey, Guy, and Marvin Bassett. 1986. "Invariant *Be* in the Lower South." In Michael Montgomery and Guy Bailey, eds., *Language Variety in the South.* University: University of Alabama Press. Pp. 158–79.

Bailey, Guy, and Natalie Maynor. 1987. "Decreolization?" *Language in Society* 16:449–73.

Baugh, John. 1979. "Linguistic Style-shifting in Black English." Ph.D. Dissertation, University of Pennsylvania.

———. 1983. *Black Street Speech: Its History, Structure and Survival.* Austin: University of Texas Press.

Bell, Allan. 1977. "The Language of Radio News in Auckland: A Sociolinguistic Study of Style, Audience and Subediting Variation." Ph.D. Dissertation, University of Auckland.

———. 1982. "Radio: The Style of Language." *Journal of Communication* 32:150–64.

———. 1984. "Language Style as Audience Design." *Language in Society* 13:145–204.

———. 1986. "Responding to Your Audience: Taking the Initiative." Paper presented at the Minnesota Conference on Linguistic Accommodation and Style-Shifting. (Published in *Language & Communication* 12 (1992):327–40).

———. 1991. "Audience Accommodation in the Mass Media." In H. Giles, J. Coupland, and N. Coupland, eds., *Contexts of Accommodation: Developments in Applied Sociolinguistics.* Cambridge: Cambridge University Press. Pp. 69–102.

Biber, Douglas. 1988. *Variation Across Speech and Writing.* Cambridge: Cambridge University Press.

Bickerton, Derek. 1980. "What Happens When We Switch?" *York Papers in Linguistics* 9:41–56.

Blake, Renee A. 1993. "Accounting for the Don't Count (DC) Cases in Variable Rule Analyses of the Afro-American English Copula." Ms., Department of Linguistics, Stanford University.

Blom, Jan-Petter, and John J. Gumperz. 1972. "The Social Meaning of Linguistic Structures: Code-Switching in Norway." In John J. Gumperz and Dell Hymes, eds., *Directions in Sociolinguistics,* New York: Holt, Rinehart and Winston. Pp. 407–34.

Blyth, Carl, Jr., Sigrid Recktenwald, and Jenny Wang. 1990. "I'm like, 'Say What?!': A New Quotative in American Oral Narrative." *American Speech* 65:215–27.

Brown, Roger, and Albert Gilman. 1960. "The Pronouns of Power and Solidarity." In T. A. Sebeok, ed., *Style in Language,* Cambridge, MA: MIT Press. Pp. 253–76.

Butters, Ronald. 1989. *The Death of Black English: Divergence and Convergence in Black and White Vernaculars. (Bamberger Beitrage zur Englischen Sprachwissenschaft,* 25.) Frankfurt: Peter Lang.

Cedergren, Henrietta, and David Sankoff. 1974. "Variable Rules: Performance as a Statistical Reflection of Competence." *Language* 50:333–55.

Cheshire, Jenny. 1982. *Variation in an English Dialect.* Cambridge: Cambridge University Press.

Coupland, Nikolas. 1989. "Style Shifting in a Cardiff Work-Setting." *Language in Society* 9:1–12.

———. 1981. The Social Differentiation of Functional Language Use: A Sociolinguistic Investigation of Travel Agency Talk." Ph.D. Dissertation, University of Wales Institute of Science and Technology.

———. 1984. "Accommodation at Work: Some Phonological Data and their Interpretations." *International Journal of the Sociology of Language* 46:49–70.

———. 1985. "'Hark, Hark, the Lark': Social Motivations for Phonological Style-Shifting." *Language & Communication* 5:153–71.

Coupland, Nikolas, and Howard Giles, eds. 1988. "Communicative Accommodation: Recent Developments." *Language & Communication* 8:175–327.

Denning, Keith M., Sharon Inkelas, Faye C. McNair-Knox and John R. Rickford. 1987. *Variation in Language: NWAV-XV at Stanford.* Stanford: Dept. of Linguistics, Stanford University.

Di Paolo, Marianna. 1992. "Hypercorrection in Response to the Apparent Merger of (ɔ) and (ɑ) in Utah English." *Language & Communication* 12:267–92.

Douglas-Cowie, Ellen. 1978. "Linguistic Code-Switching in a Northern Irish Village: Social Interaction and Social Ambition." In Peter Trudgill, ed., *Sociolinguistic Patterns in British English.* Baltimore: University Park Press. Pp. 37–51.

Dressler, Wolfgang U., and Ruth Wodak. 1982. "Sociophonological Methods in the Study of Sociolinguistic Variation in Viennese German." *Language in Society* 11:339–70.

Dubois, Sylvie, and Barbara M. Horvath. 1991. "Examining the Effect of Interaction on Text Variation." Paper presented at the Twentieth Annual Conference on New Ways of Analyzing Variation (NWAV-XX), Georgetown University, Washington, DC.

Eckert, Penelope. 1988. "Adolescent Social Structure and the Spread of Linguistic Change." *Language in Society* 17:183–207.

Edwards, Viv. 1986. *Language in a Black Community.* Clevedon, Avon: Multilingual Matters.

Ervin-Tripp, Susan M. 1964. "An Analysis of the Interaction of Language, Topic and Listener." In John Gumperz and Dell Hymes, eds., *The Ethnography of Communication. (=American Anthropologist* 66.6, pt. II). Pp. 86–102.

Fasold, Ralph. 1972. *Tense Marking in Black English: A Linguistic and Social Analysis.* Arlington, VA: Center for Applied Linguistics.

———. 1978. "Language Variation and Linguistic Competence." In David Sankoff, ed., *Linguistic Variation: Models and Methods.* New York: Academic Press. Pp. 85–95.

Ferrara, Kathleen, Becky Brown, Keith Walters, and John Baugh, eds. 1988. *Linguistic Change and Contact: Proceedings of the Sixteenth Annual Conference on New Ways of Analyzing Variation (NWAV-XVI).* Austin: Dept. of Linguistics: University of Texas at Austin. (=*Texas Linguistics Forum,* 30.)

Finegan, Edward, and Douglas Biber. 1989. "Toward an Integrated Theory of Social and Situational Variation." Ms., Dept. of Linguistics, University of Southern California. [revised version published as Finegan and Biber this volume]

Giles, Howard, ed. 1984. "The Dynamics of Speech Accommodation." *International Journal of the Sociology of Language* 46.

Giles, Howard, Justine Coupland, and Nikolas Coupland, eds. 1991. *Contexts of Accommodation: Developments in Applied Sociolinguistics.* Cambridge: Cambridge University Press.

Giles, Howard, and Philip M. Smith. 1979. "Accommodation Theory: Optimal Levels of Convergence." In Howard Giles and Robert N. St. Clair, eds., *Language and Social Psychology.* Oxford: Basil Blackwell. Pp. 45–65.

Giles, Howard and P. Powesland. 1975. *Speech Style and Social Evaluation.* New York: Academic Press.

Gregory, Michael, and Susanne Carroll. 1978. *Language and Situation.* London: Routledge and Kegan Paul.

Gumperz, John J. 1964. "Linguistic and Social Interaction in Two Communities." In John J. Gumperz and Dell Hymes, eds., *The Ethnography of Communication.* (=*American Anthropologist* 66.6, pt. II). Pp. 137–54.

———. 1983. *Language and Social Identity.* Cambridge: Cambridge University Press.

Guy, Gregory R. 1975. "Use and Applications of the Cedergren/Sankoff Variable Rule Program." In Ralph W. Fasold and Roger W. Shuy, eds., *Analyzing Variation in Language.* Washington, DC: Georgetown University Press. Pp. 59–69.

———. 1980. "Variation in the Group and the Individual: The Case of Final Stop Deletion." In William Labov, ed., *Locating Language in Time and Space.* New York: Academic Press. Pp. 1–36.

Halliday, M.A.K. 1978. *Language as a Social Semiotic: The Social Interpretation of Language and Meaning.* London: Edward Arnold.

Hindle, Donald M. 1979. "The Social and Situational Conditioning of Phonetic Variation." Ph.D. Dissertation, University of Pennsylvania.

Hymes, Dell. 1972. "Models of the Interaction of Language and Social Life." In John Gumperz and Dell Hymes, eds., *Directions in Sociolinguistics.* New York: Holt, Rinehart and Winston. Pp. 35–71.

———. 1974. *Foundations in Sociolinguistics: An Ethnographic Approach.* Philadelphia: University of Pennsylvania Press.

Irvine, Judith. 1979. "Formality and Informality in Communicative Events." *American Anthropology* 81:773–90.

———. 1985. "Status and Style in Language." *Annual Review of Anthropology* 14:557–81.

Labov, William. 1963. "The Social Motivation of a Sound Change." *Word* 19:273–309.

———. 1966. *The Social Stratification of English in New York City.* Arlington, VA: Center for Applied Linguistics.

———. 1969. "Contraction, Deletion, and Inherent Variability of the English Copula." *Language* 45:715–62.

————. 1972. *Sociolinguistic Patterns.* Philadelphia: University of Pennsylvania Press.

————. 1975. "Empirical Foundations of Linguistic Theory." In Robert Austerlitz, ed., *The Scope of American Linguistics.* Lisse: Peter De Ridder Press. Pp. 77–133.

————. 1989. "The Exact Description of a Speech Community: Short *a* in Philadelphia." In Ralph W. Fasold and Deborah Schiffrin, eds., *Language Change and Variation.* Amsterdam: Benjamins. Pp. 1–58.

————. Ms. "The Design of a Sociolinguistic Research Project." Paper presented at the Sociolinguistics Workshop, Central Institute of Indian Languages, Mysore, India. May-June 1972.

Labov, William, Paul Cohen, Clarence Robins, and John Lewis. 1968. *A Study of the Non-Standard English of Negro and Puerto Rican Speakers in New York City,* I. Final Report, Cooperative Research Project 3288. Philadelphia: US Regional Survey.

Labov, William, and Wendell Harris. 1986. "De Facto Segregation of Black and White Vernaculars." In David Sankoff, ed., *Diversity and Diachrony.* Amsterdam: Benjamins. Pp. 33–42.

LePage, Robert, and Andrée Tabouret-Keller. 1985. *Acts of Identity: Creole-Based Approaches to Language and Ethnicity.* Cambridge: Cambridge University Press.

Lucas C., and D. Borders. 1987. "Language Diversity and Classroom Discourse." *American Research Educational Journal* 4:119–41.

Macaulay, Ronald K. S. 1977. *Language, Social Class and Education: A Glasgow Study.* Edinburgh: University of Edinburgh Press.

McElhinny, Bonnie. In press. "Copula Auxiliary Contraction by White Speakers of English." *American Speech.*

Milroy, Lesley. 1980. *Language and Social Networks.* Oxford: Basil Blackwell.

————. 1987. *Observing and Analyzing Natural Language.* Oxford: Basil Blackwell.

Nichols, Patricia C. 1991. "Verbal Patterns of Black and White Speakers of Coastal South Carolina." In W. F. Edwards and Donald Winford, eds., *Verb Phrase Patterns in Black English and Creole.* Detroit: Wayne State University Press. Pp. 114–28.

Payne, Arvilla. 1976. "The Acquisition of the Phonological System of a Second Dialect." Ph.D. Dissertation, University of Pennsylvania.

Preston, Dennis S. 1986. "Fifty Some-odd Categories of Language Variation." *International Journal of the Sociology of Language* 57:9–47.

————. 1991. "Sorting Out the Variables in Sociolinguistic Theory." *American Speech* 66:33–56.

Purcell, A. 1984. "Code Shifting Hawaiian Style: Children's Accommodation Along a De-creolizing Continuum." *International Journal of the Sociology of Language* 46:71–86.

Richardson, Carmen. 1988. "Habitual Structures Among Black and White Speakers in East Palo Alto." M.A. thesis, Stanford University.

Rickford, John R. 1979. "Variation in a Creole Continuum: Quantitative and Implicational Approaches." Ph.D. Dissertation, University of Pennsylvania.

————. 1983. "What Happens in Decreolization." In Roger Andersen, ed., *Pidginization and Creolization as Language Acquisition.* Rowley, MA: Newbury House. Pp. 298–319.

————. 1987. "The Haves and Have Nots: Sociolinguistic Surveys and the Assessment of Speaker Competence." *Language in Society* 16:149–78.

————. 1989. "Continuity and Innovation in the Development of BEV be₂." Paper presented at NWAV-XVIII, Duke University, Durham, North Carolina.

————. 1992. "Grammatical Variation and Divergence in Vernacular Black English." In Marinel Gerritsen and Dieter Stein, eds., *Internal and External Factors in Syntactic Change.* The Hague: Mouton. Pp. 175–200.

Rickford, John., Arnetha Ball, Renee Blake, Raina Jackson, and Nomi Martin. 1991. "Rappin on the Copula Coffin: Theoretical and Methodological Issues in the Analysis of Copula Variation in African-American Vernacular English." *Language Variation and Change* 3:103–32.

Romaine, Suzanne. 1978. "Post-vocalic /r/in Scottish English: Sound Change in Progress." In Peter Trudgill, ed., *Sociolinguistic Patterns in British English*. London: Edward Arnold. Pp. 144–57.

———. 1980. "A Critical Overview of the Methodology of Urban British Sociolinguistics." *English World-Wide* 1:163–98.

Russell, Joan. 1982. "Networks and Sociolinguistic Variation in an African Urban Setting." In Suzanne Romaine, ed., *Sociolinguistic Variation in Speech Communities*. London: Edward Arnold. Pp. 125–40.

Sankoff, David. 1988. "Variable Rules." In Ulrich Ammon, Norbert Dittmar, and Klaus J. Mattheier, eds., *Sociolinguistics: An International Handbook of the Science of Language and Society*. Berlin: Walter de Gruyter. Pp. 984–97.

Schuman, Howard, and Graham Kalton. 1985. "Survey Methods." In Gardner Lindzey and Elliot Aronson, eds., *Handbook of Social Psychology. I. Theory and Method*, 3rd ed. New York: Random House. Pp. 635–97.

Sommer, Elisabeth. 1986. "Variation in Southern Urban English." In Michael B. Montgomery and Guy Bailey, eds., *Language Variety in the South*. University: University of Alabama Press. Pp. 180–201.

Tarone, Elaine. 1985. "Variability in Interlanguage Use: A Study of Style Shifting in Morphology and Syntax." *Language Learning* 35:373–403.

Terrell, Francis, Sandra L. Terrell, and Sanford Golin. 1977. "Language Productivity of Black and White Children in Black Versus White Situations." *Language and Speech* 20:377–83.

Thakerar, J. N., H. Giles, and J. Cheshire. 1982. "Psychological and Linguistic Parameters of Speech Accommodation Theory." In C. Fraser and K. R. Scherer, eds., *Advances in the Social Psychology of Language*. Cambridge: Cambridge University Press. Pp. 205–55.

Thelander, Mats. 1982. "A Qualitative Approach to the Quantitative Data of Speech Variation." In Suzanne Romaine, ed., *Sociolinguistic Variation in Speech Communities*. London: Edward Arnold. Pp. 205–55.

Traugott, Elizabeth Closs, and Suzanne Romaine. 1985. "Some Questions for the Definition of 'Style' in Socio-Historical Linguistics." *Folia Linguistica Historica* VI/1:7–39.

Trudgill, Peter. 1974. *The Social Differentiation of English in Norwich*. Cambridge: Cambridge University Press.

———. 1981. "Linguistic Accommodation: Sociolinguistic Observations on a Sociopsychological Theory." *Papers from the Parasession on Language and Behavior*. Chicago, IL: Chicago Linguistics Society. Pp. 219–317.

———. 1986. *Dialects in Contact*. Oxford: Basil Blackwell.

Van den Broeck, Jef. 1977. "Class Differences in Syntactic Complexity in the Flemish Town of Maaseik." *Language in Society* 6:149–81.

Walters, Keith. 1989a. "Social Change and Linguistic Variation in Korba, a Small Tunisian Town." Ph.D. Dissertation, Austin: University of Texas.

———. 1989b. "The Interviewer as Variable in Quantitative Sociolinguistic Studies." Paper presented at the annual meeting of the Linguistic Society of America, Washington, DC.

Wilson, John. 1987. "The Sociolinguistic Paradox: Data as a Methodological Product." *Language and Communication* 7.2:161–77.

Wolfram, Walter. 1969. *A Sociolinguistic Description of Detroit Negro Speech.* Washington, DC: Center for Applied Linguistics.

————. 1974. "The Relationship of White Southern Speech to Vernacular Black English." *Language* 50:498–527.

Wolfson, Nessa. 1976. "Speech Events and Natural Speech: Some Implications for Sociolinguistic Methodology." *Language in Society* 5:189–209.

Yaeger-Dror, Malcah. 1991. "Linguistic Evidence for Social Psychological Attitudes: Hyperaccommodation of (r) by Singers from a Mizrahi Background." *Language & Communication* 11:1–23.

Youssef, Valerie. 1991. "Variation as a Feature of Language Acquisition in the Trinidad Context." *Language Variation and Change* 3:75–101.

11

Situational Variation in Children's Language Revisited

COURTNEY B. CAZDEN

1. Introduction

When I reviewed research on situational variation in children's language more than twenty years ago (Cazden 1970), I was not just contributing to a gap in scholarly attention; I was also deliberately intervening in a continuing debate about valid descriptions of how children's communicative competence varies with differences in their cultural background and/or social class. In a still earlier article (Cazden 1966), I had argued against the adequacy of then prevailing "deficit" explanations of lower-class children's vocabulary and syntax, and for more serious attention to "differences" in language use that were beginning to be studied in the then very young fields of sociolinguistics and ethnography of communication. In 1970, this contrast was termed the "less language" explanation versus the "different language" explanation, and both were judged inadequate:

> The inadequacy of both the "less language" and the "different language" character-
> izations is two-fold. First, both refer only to patterns of structural form and ignore
> patterns of use in actual speech events. Second, they assume that the child learns
> only one way to speak which is reflected in the same fashion and to the same
> extent at all times. On both theoretical and practical grounds, we can no longer
> accept such limitations. We must attend not only to the abilities of individuals and
> how they develop, but to qualities of the situation, or temporary environment, in
> which those abilities are activated. (Cazden 1970:40–41)

In the intervening decades, we have accumulated more studies of situational variation in children's language, and even several research reviews. Romaine (1984) reviews the development of children's stylistic variation, primarily in phonological features. Warren-Leubecker and Bohannon (1989) divide register variation into two dimensions—adaptations to listener knowledge and to listener status—and review children's development of those adaptations in both production and judgments. Andersen (1990) adds an updated research review to the publication of her important 1978 doctoral dissertation. By means of role-playing activities, she brings to light children's knowledge of registers, such as how doctors talk on the job, that might never be evidenced in their spontaneous speech.

Over these two decades, this body of research has changed in quality as well as grown in quantity. In 1970, my review presented the studies within a correlational framework. Features of situations (the "independent variables") were categorized: topic, task, listener(s), and interaction (aspects of discourse such as who initiates and how long a topic is pursued). Then features of children's language (the "dependent variables") that covaried with these situational variables were also categorized: fluency/spontaneity, length/complexity, content or style, and approximation to Standard English. Now, such a reductionist framework seems too behavioristic: it doesn't allow for the cognition—both linguistic and social—that presumably underlies the cluster of language adaptations that children make. And it construes the children as only passive responders, rather than active adapters of their language to create, as well as accommodate to, changing contexts.

Today both questions and answers about children's register knowledge are articulated in different terms. But one problem for research and analysis remains the same:

> Our eventual goal is to understand how a person's previous experience (of which his [sic] social class is simply a rough and composite index) interacts with factors in the momentary situation to affect his behavior. At any one moment, a child decides to speak or be silent, to adopt communicative intent *a* or communicative intent *b*, to express idea *x* or idea *y*, in form *1* or form *2*. The options the child selects will be a function of characteristics of the situation as he perceives it on the basis of his past experience. (Cazden 1970:42)

Although this problem statement speaks of "interaction" (i.e., influence) between previous experience and current speaking situation, little of the early research illuminated that interaction. In this article, I will try again. I begin by presenting three recent studies, all conducted in the greater Boston area, that examine the interaction between the speech situation and some index of the background experience children bring to it. As in the research selected for review in 1970, these three studies analyze differences in the way the same child, or group of children, speak in different situations.

Considered together, the three studies span a wide age range: Wolf (1985) describes how a diverse group of twenty-four five-to-seven-year-old children retell a silent movie in two task formats; Gee (1989a, b) analyzes the personal narratives of two fifth grade girls, one working-class black and one middle-class white, told to adult or peers; Hemphill (1986) reappraises social class differences in the speech of working-class and middle-class adolescent girls as they discuss a controversial topic in two participant structures.

At the end, I return to a hypothesis from the 1970 review for integrating these separate studies: all children make qualitatively similar adjustments in their adaptations to changing task formats that do not require a shift in self-identity and participant role (including what Warren-Leubecker and Bohannon [1989] call "listener knowledge"), while children from different cultural and even individual backgrounds (influenced by social class, ethnicity, gender, and so on) make qualitatively different adjustments when such a shift in identity and role (which Warren-Leubecker and Bohannon [1989] call "listener status") is entailed.

Throughout, I have retained the older term *situational variation* because the changes in children's language seem to go beyond the usual referents of *register*.

2. Movie Enactments and Retellings

Wolf (1985) was interested in how children from different experiential backgrounds adapt their speech to shifting communicative demands. Initially, personal narratives were elicited from fifty children in kindergarten or first grade from "diverse neighborhoods." These narratives were then analyzed for what she considered more "oral" and more "literate" features, and the twelve children with the most extreme differences in style were selected for a film study. Children identified as having the more oral style were, by definition, those who did less spontaneous editing to improve the adequacy of the message; encoded more nonverbal information in gestures; and used fewer explicit connectives (other than *and*) and descriptive terms. Children identified as having a more literate style showed the maximum contrast on all three features.

Children in both groups were individually shown a two-minute silent film about three children teasing each other with a yellow hat and, in randomized order, asked to talk about it in two task formats: (1) "show what happened in the movie" with the help of a set of toy figures, and (2) without any props, make an audiotaped "story about the movie for other children who didn't get to see it." The children's enactments and retellings, which Wolf terms "situated" versus "autonomous," were then analyzed for the relative presence (frequency divided by number of independent clauses) of the features listed. Tables 11.1–11.3, which present Wolf's tables 1 to 3, give the results.

As Wolf summarizes them: "These findings bear a strong resemblance to phonological findings which demonstrate 'one speech community' (Labov 1972a)." All the children shift toward what Wolf calls the more literate style in the more autono-

TABLE 11.1   Spontaneous Editing in Narrative Tasks

	Play Narratives (%)	*Entirely Oral Narratives* (%)
Kindergarten		
Literate style children	3	8
Oral style children	4	14
First Grade		
Literate style children	3	16
Oral style children	4	14

From Wolf (1985:81).

TABLE 11.2   The Use of Contextual Information in Narrative Tasks

	Play Narratives (%)	Entirely Oral Narratives (%)
Kindergarten		
Literate style children	8	5
Oral style children	15	8
First Grade		
Literate style children	3	4
Oral style children	12	8

From Wolf (1985:82).

mous retelling task: they do more self-editing, use less contextual information, and provide more explicit descriptors than in the more situated enactment.

3. Personal Narratives

Four years after recording oral Sharing Time narratives of a first grade black girl whom we called Leona (Cazden 1988), Sarah Michaels and I renewed contact with Leona and recorded her telling a narrative of personal experience to a sympathetic but unfamiliar white adult (then doctoral student Charles Haynes) and later to a small self-chosen group of her peers. Unlike Sharing Time, these stories were told outside the classroom, though still in school, and the dual audience of teacher and peers present together in the classroom (Cazden 1988) was separated.

Following Labov (1972b), we asked Leona to tell about "the scariest thing that happened to you," and then asked her to retell one of the resulting stories, about an earache, in a story-swapping session with her friends (school peers she selected). The result was two versions of a single story (which she may or may not have told to others before). In the discussion that follows, the two versions, formatted into stanzas by Gee (1989a, b), are lined up so that the topically similar stanzas are placed opposite each other to facilitate comparison. (The Gee [1989a, b] references are to the same article, differing only in minor editorial details; my page numbers all refer to 1989b.[1])

TABLE 11.3   The Use of Explicit Language in Tasks

	Play Narratives (%)	Entirely Oral Narratives (%)
Kindergarten		
Literate style children	11	25
Oral style children	5	15
First Grade		
Literate style children	12	27
Oral style children	11	24

From Wolf (1985:83).

TABLE 11.4 Informational Expressive and Contextual Design

	Leona to Peers (%)	Leona to Adult (%)	Sandy (%)
Informative lines	56	56	86
Expressive lines	24	7	2
Other	20	37	12
Line Links			
Temporal	48	58	59
Logical	9	25	31
Expressive	30	9	1
Unlinked	13	9	9
Speech and Sound	33	11	16
Performed Narrative			
Features	11	6	6

From Gee (1989b:107).

Thematically, in both versions Leona contrasts the familiar world of home, mother, and food with the hostile institutional world of hospitals, nurses, and medicine as she and her mother travel between them, first via a "long dark street" and then via a cab that her mother had no money to pay for. There is humor in the telling, but also poignancy when the story is heard as a representative anecdote of societal racism.

Our interest here is in the differences between the two versions. In Table 11.4, Gee (1989b) summarizes his quantitative comparison in terms of percentages of lines in each version that have particular informational, expressive, and textual features. Although the peer version is one-fourth longer (eighty-eight lines versus seventy to the adult), they have the same informational density (56 percent of the lines). But there the similarity ends. As Gee's table shows, the most important addition in the peer story is in expressive and performative features: for example, more direct speech, plus speech sounds (as in stanzas 2 and 3) that are not included in the adult version at all.

Other changes are not included in Gee's analysis. One is in the way direct speech is introduced. In the adult version, there is one instance of "she goes 'X'" (11), and all the rest is introduced by some form of *say*. (Note that some words that might be direct speech are not enclosed in quotation marks in Gee's transcription; they are spoken without speech intonation as if reported rather than quoted.)

In the peer version, there is more variety: two occurrences of *goes*, six forms of *say*, one *yelling*, one quote with no introducer, and eight forms of what Ferrara and Bell (n.d.) call "innovative dialogue introducers": either "was all 'X'" (as in 2 and 10) or "was like 'X'" (as in 15 and 16). Ferrara and Bell's corpus is from the speech of middle-class Anglo adults in Texas, so Leona's use should not be considered a black dialect form. But, from its distribution in this small speech sample, we can conclude that it is marked in her repertoire as a part of her more informal style.

Another difference is in Leona's word choice. Because we have two narratives

Leona's Hospital Story as Told to White Male Adult

Leona's Hospital Story as Told to Peers

FRAME:
oh god, this is so hard for me to tell
it just happened a little while ago

BEGINNING
1. AT GRANDMOTHER'S
all right, I had spent the night at my grandmother's house
for like two days—two or three days—two days, yeah, two days
it was on a weekend
you know how you go up to your grandma's house for a weekend so something like
that, right

2. EARACHE
an I don know, after Edna an me getting ready to go home
gettin all our stuff ready
I had this terrible earache, right
and I was cryin and ?? everything
an I hadda put all this cotton in my ear and some peroxide

3. ICE CREAM
an then I was thinkin that it was feelin better
I was feelin better
so my mother bought me an ice cream
and I ate that
an then I started feelin real sick

4. BUS/TRAIN
then we got on the bus first
then we got on the train

FRAME:
I'll tell you about my earache, o.k.?
all right, this is what happened

BEGINNING
1. AT GRANDMOTHER'S
I was just up there
I was up my grandmother's house
especially for like like two weeks, or three
well not two weeks, two days or three, or more like that, a couple of days
ah shoot, I should say

2. EARACHE
all right, I got this thing
my ear's all buggin me an everything
my ear was all buggin me
and I was cryin
I was all: oooh oooh oooh, oooh oooh
I was doin all that
and my mother put alcohol on though

3. ICE CREAM
and then what happened was
and then what happened
I was just let alone
an I bought myself an ice cream
I thought that would make me feel better
I was all shuup, shuup, shuup, you know

4. EARACHE
and then, you know, just all of a sudden
I just got this terrible feelin

you know how children's hospital is right near when you get on the Park Street train

an I got on the train

5. TO THE FIRST HOSPITAL

my mother said "you better go to the hospital"
so we went to the hospital
walked down this dark long street
I thought I was dyin:

6. TALK TO RECEPTIONIST

all right, so we went in the hospital, right
I was cryin an everything
the lady goes what's the matter
so we sat down and started talkin right

7. ASK FOR HELP

an um my mother says "my daughter has a terrible earache
could you take care of it for us"
so she said something like that
and I didn't quite hear cause I was cryin an everythin

8. YOU HAVE TO PAY

and the lady gave us some tissue and everythin
an I stopped cryin for awhile
an next thing you know they said
they said you have to pay money

after I stopped eatin ice cream, and what not
like, oh shoot, oh go::d
my ear was killin me
an I was sayin: "ma:: ma::"

5. GOING TO FIRST HOSPITAL

an we got on the train to go home
an my mother said: "let's go to the hospital"
we had to walk down this LONG DARK street
about FIVE MILES, or somethin like that

— ???[aside—line cannot be heard]

we had to walk down this long street
an then the hospital was there

6. TALK TO RECEPTIONIST

and this is the funny part
"All right, you wait in there"
I'm sittin there, oooh oooh oooh
my mother's sittin there, talking to this lady and all
an, she's all, "excuse me, madame can I help you at all", oooh oooh oooh

7. INTO THE EMERGENCY

an then we went in the emergency
because we didn't make an appointment or notin
my mother's in there, for about ten minutes, or what not
I'm still cryin

8. WE CAN'T HELP YOU

she's talkin to this lady
and they said: "well we can't help you here
cuz this is a here regular hospital"
we're blaa blaa blaa
and they kept goin on and on

(continued)

Leona's Hospital Story as Told to White Male Adult	Leona's Hospital Story as Told to Peers
9. HARVARD HOSPITAL you know how you have Blue Cross or somethin like that Blue Shield somethin like that so you have to go to a Harvard hospital like it's produced in Harvard or somethin so we had to go to Harvard, right all the way to Harvard	**9. MOTHER GETS MAD** my mother got real mad start steamin at that lady she was all cussin her out yellin naa naa naa
10. WE CAN'T HELP YOU they said we can't treat you here so we went //	**10. MOTHER-NURSE ARGUE ABOUT TREATMENT** and then she goes: "what happened if my daughter was die'in", an all that stuff she was all: "well um excuse me miss if you want to pay the bill we can see you right away, my way"
11. NURSE AND MOTHER ARGUE ABOUT THE CAB my mother talks to this lady on the phone she was yellin at her an everythin my mother was sayin "I have no money for no cab," right she goes "could ya take a cab down there" my mother was sayin "I don't have no money for no cab"	**11. MOTHER-NURSE ARGUE ABOUT CAB** an then she called my hospital doctor up on the phone I was like ooooooh, still me cryin and my mother was cussin that lady out an then this lady goes: "why don't you take a cab?" my mother say: "I ain't got no *money now*"
12. GO TO ANOTHER HOSPITAL so then we went all the way to another hospital I was cryin and everythin I said "Ma I coulda been goin deaf you know" I coulda died	**12. MOTHER AND THE CAB** an then they sent a cab down for her cuz she have no money she didn't pay that cab driver she jus' walked out she jus' slammed that door she said: "come on Rona" [increasing rate over these lines]
13. HAD TO WAIT an so I hadda sit in this hospital and wait for like fifteen twenty minutes, right	**13. GETTING THE "BILL"** an then they gave me this consumation, or something like that, for the bill this lady wrote it up

next thing you know
my earache's killin me an killin me

14. DIDN'T PAY FOR CAB
an so we didn't pay for the cab
you know how you sorta give them a slip a paper
so they can go on their way
from a check or somethin
gave him one of those
an he left

15. HAD TO WAIT
so we hadda come all the way to another hospital
we hadda ?we waited fifteen or twenty minutes
just to get in a room
for me to get my earache

16. MEDICINE
an all I needed was some medicine
an I went through all that fuss
an I coulda got it at the store

(laugh) that was so funny though
I laugh at it now

an spit it in my mother's face
??? pssst [kissing sound] "thank you", like that
boy I was upset

14. HAD TO WAIT
and then we had to wait for a good fifteen minutes
just to get help
now isn't that, come on, what if I was goin deaf, or something
you know what I mean

15. REPRISE
that's when I had that bad earache
I was like:"oh god, am I gonna die?"
I says: "no what if I die?", oooooh
I was just cryin there like that

16. LEONA AND THE NURSE CLEANING HER EAR
this lady was all cleanin, an like that
she said: "you have an ear inFECTION
an everything is going well
but there's something in your ear, you know"
an I was like: "yeah, I know"

STANZA 17. GRUBBING OUT ON FOOD
an that's about all
we went home
I: grubbed out on SOME FOOD
wait you see

put that medicine in my ear
an I was grubbin out on that food
I was grubbin out, shuuk shuuk, mmm mmm
an I was grubbin out on the food, an everything, mmm

285

of the same experience, we can compare alternative expressions of the same propositional content (with stanza number given on the left):

Adult version	Peer version
1. spent the night at	1. was up
2. I had this terrible earache	2. I got this thing
2. put . . . some peroxide	2. put alcohol on
3. I ate that	3. I was all shuup, shuup, shuup
10. we can't treat you here	8. "we can't help you here."

In all these contrasts, the vocabulary spoken to the adult includes more precise and/or lower-frequency words. The adult version also mentions *Blue Cross* and *Blue Shield*, which is omitted in the version to peers.

There is also an interesting contrast in the function of a single phrase, *you know*. In the adult story, *you know how* is used four times to introduce propositional content (in 1, 4, 9, and 14); twice in the idiom, "next thing you know" (8 and 13); and only once as a phrase-final tag, and that within Leona's own quoted speech (12). In the peer version, there are four instances: three as a phrase-final tag (in 3, 4 and 16, fourth line) and once in its literal meaning (16, last line).

In the adult story, a function similar to the introducer *you know* is served by the seven instances of *right* as a tag (as at the end of 1). Both are confirmation checks, and evidently Leona feels neither is needed with peers. On the other hand, the peer use of the tag *you know,* labeled by Bernstein (1971) as a "sociocentric" or "sympathetic circularity" sequence, seems functionally related to phrases Gee includes in his category of performed narrative features. These are the "semantically empty expressions like '*and all that stuff,*' '*and like that,*' or '*and all*' that encourage hearers to add their own equivalent experience as to what '*stuff like that*' is like" (1989b:108).

I have gone into this much detail about these two stories because they exemplify so vividly the phenomenon of situational shift, here of an African American girl of elementary school age. Leona is clearly drawing on, and silencing, different parts of her total speech repertoire in narrating the same personal experience to her two audiences.

The third column in Gee's table gives his quantitative analysis of a story told by Sandy, a middle-class white girl whom we had also taped during first grade Sharing Time and now found again. (In an all-too-typical contrast in their school biographies, Leona was still in the same elementary school, reputedly the most barren in town, while Sandy had transferred to a computer magnet school in the same district.)

Leona and Sandy's stories contrast thematically in ways that typify the perceived sources of danger in their lives: Instead of the problems of getting help for an illness without Blue Cross or money, Sandy tells of the danger that lurks in a "dumb" boy she and her friend encounter in the neighborhood park and finally chase away—the danger thus residing in strangers encountered outside the protection of her middle-class home.

Sandy told her park story only once, to a sympathetic but unfamiliar adult (Dennie Wolf), so we cannot assess her register shift to peers. But we can ask, as Gee does, whether Leona's style to the adult is closer to Sandy's style than the style she adopts with her peers.

Gee's quantitative comparisons suggest that it is. But he goes on to argue against such a simple interpretation, even though it would fit Labov's (1972a) findings of a single speech community defined not by the absolute values of variables (in his research, phonological) but by the direction of their situational change:

> When Leona tells her story to the white male, she appears to switch to Sandy's style. . . . In fact, as Table [11.4] shows, Leona does not actually increase the number of her informative lines—instead, she greatly lowers the number of expressive ones and increases lines that are neither informative nor expressive ("other"). . . . They are nonexpressive sorts of repetition and extra-narrative comments, mainly "knowledge checks" she runs on the adult ("you know how . . ."). Thus, it is not so much that Leona switches to new devices as she speaks to the adult, but rather that she drops performance aspects of her style. . . . [T]he content of seven of the stanzas in the story to the peers is simply missing in the story to the adult. . . . And all these missing stanzas involve the expression of anger, antagonistic relations, or Leona's fear and dismay; in other words, emotive and expressive information. (1989b:108–9)

4. Group Discussions

Hemphill set out to replicate and extend Bernstein's earliest research (1971, originally published in 1962) on social class differences in speech. In Bernstein's study, working-class and middle-class adolescent boys were asked to discuss whether capital punishment should be abolished. The participant structure of the discussion situation was not described, and the resulting speech was analyzed primarily for the frequency of certain lexical and syntactic features.

In Hemphill's research, two separate small groups of working-class inner-city and middle-class suburban girls, all white, were asked to discuss, in two contrasting discussion situations, whether women should have to register for the draft (informal discussion), and whether the drinking or driving age should be raised (formal discussion); the participant structures of the two situations are fully described, and discourse patterns are analyzed as well as syntax. Hemphill's hypothesis is that social class influences on individual speech patterns are mediated by, or have as their intervening variable, different conversational styles.

The informal discussions began with a "theater game" that involved the participants in discovering mutual interests. Hemphill spoke as a teacher only by probing for generalizations; otherwise, she spoke as a participant in offering opinions and anecdotes and deliberately avoided nominating speakers or evaluating student comments. To lead each formal discussion, a graduate student was trained in *teacher-talk:* controlling topic, nominating speakers, filling pauses with questions, and evaluating and/or summarizing student turns.

In the change from informal to formal situation, the middle-class girls shifted some of their lexical and syntactic choices. Lexically, colloquialisms like *shitless* dropped out, and more school-like words like *repugnant, tangible, invincible,* and *statistics* appeared; syntactically, subjunctives were used in several turns. Other changes were more directly attributable to the changed participant structure, particularly the more active role of the teacher. In the formal discussion, the middle-class girls used more cross-speaker anaphora, which had been noticeably infrequent in their informal discussion; now they tied their utterances to the teacher's previously given topic. For the same reason, the middle-class girls uttered more back-channels, expressing agreement with the teacher, than they had uttered to their peers.

For the working-class girls, the shift to a more typical teacher-led discussion brought qualitatively different changes in their speech. In the informal discussion, their style had been much more collaborative than that of the middle-class girls, with significantly more cross-speaker anaphora and supportive back-channels that were not bids for the next turn to speak. With the more teacher-like role of the adult in the formal situation, both cross-speaker anaphora and back-channels decreased in frequency. Metacommunicative functions of commenting, summarizing, and questioning also decreased significantly in the working-class girls' speech (from 18 percent of their turns in the informal discussion to 3 percent in the formal), whereas these same functions remained in the middle-class girls' speech (from 22 percent to 24 percent, respectively). The working-class girls paused longer and more often in the formal discussion, giving the appearance of "reticence."

These shifts in participant structures and their conversational constraints also brought different changes in the syntax of the two groups of speakers. In the formal discussion, the middle-class group reduced their ratio of noun subjects to third person pronoun subjects; this was related (like their increased cross-speaker an-

TABLE 11.5   Cross-Speaker Anaphora Across Contexts

	Formal Context	*Informal Context*
Middle class		
Turns with cross-speaker anaphora / All turns	.31	.15
Teacher-dominated cross-speaker anaphora / All instances of cross-speaker anaphora	.74	0
Working class		
Turns with cross-speaker anaphora / All turns	.26	.32
Teacher-dominated cross-speaker anaphora / All instances of cross-speaker anaphora	.67	.32

From Hemphill (1986:104).

TABLE 11.6   Syntax Across Contexts

	Formal Context	Informal Context
Working class		
Noun subjects / Third person pronoun subjects	.49	.53
Subordinate clauses / Finite verbs	.16	.21
Middle class		
Noun subjects / Third person pronoun subjects	.50	.80
Subordinate clauses / Finite verbs	.36	.36

From Hemphill (1986:105).

aphora) to the more dominant role of the teacher. Whereas in the informal discussion these girls spoke independently, even competitively, introducing anecdotes or opinions without tying their turn to the previous peer's, in the formal context their speech was more closely tied to the topic introduced by the teacher. Their elaborated syntax (as measured by the ratio of subordinate clauses to finite verbs), which functioned to delay transition-relevant points when someone else—peer or teacher—could take the floor, stayed the same in both situations.

In the speech of the working-class girls, by contrast, there was a small drop in the ratio of noun to third person pronoun subjects in the informal context, as the girls now tied their turns even more to the teacher than they had to their peers. And there was a relatively larger drop in the subordination ratio that accompanied their drop in metacommunicative comments and in the peer back-channels that, in this group, had served in the informal discussion not to bid for the next turn but to support the further development of the current peer speaker's idea.

Tables 11.5 and 11.6 show Hemphill's findings for cross-speaker anaphora and syntax. In summary, Hemphill "argue[s] from the group discussion data that these features of the groups' conversational styles form different environments for use of full NPs or pronouns and for the use of subordinate constructions and complex syntax" (1986:109).

5. Discussion

In the research reviewed in 1970, there were indications of two contrasting relationships between previous experience and current speech situation:

> Differential responses according to aspects of the situation may be intensified for lower-class speakers (an ordinal interaction). So for example, all children may be constrained in a testing situation and lower-class children especially so. . . . Alternatively, there may be interactions between language and situation in which the relationships are reversed (disordinal interaction). . . . Middle-class children

may be more fluent in one set of situations [e.g., with adults], while lower-class children talk more fluently in another [e.g., with peers]. (Cazden 1970:55)

This still seems a useful summary. Without the statistical terminology of ordinal/disordinal interactions, it makes two assertions: (1) In response to some situational variations, people make similar adaptations in their ways of speaking; in response to other situational variations, people adapt in different ways, influenced by prior group and individual experience. (2) More specifically, situational features in the first category are exemplified by the shift from conversation to oral language test; situational features in the second category are exemplified by talking with adult versus peers.

Relabeled in more general terms, this hypothesis contrasts changes in task format with changes in participant status and structure. Where situational variation is only in task format, as when situated enactments versus autonomous movie retellings are both requested by the same teacherlike adult, changes in language will be qualitatively similar in kind (though not necessarily in frequency or amount) across children, regardless of previous experience. But where the situational change involves a significant change in participant status and structure, as in informal versus formal group discussions or a narrative of personal experience told to adults versus peers, changes in language will vary with previous experience in kind as well as frequency.

5.1. Speech Adaptations to Changes in Task Format

Consider again the first category, for which I will now adopt the label of *task format*. In the three studies cited, this type of adaptation is exemplified in the changes Wolf's young children made in shifting between movie enactment and retelling. The kind, or direction, of change is the same for all: at both grade levels, the children initially assessed as having a more literate style used more explicit language and fewer gestures than the children with the more oral style in both their enactments and their retellings (to be expected, given the original groupings), but all the children used more explicit language and fewer gestures in the retellings than in the enactments. The one exception to this pattern is the older literate style children's gestures, which did not decrease in frequency in the enactments, presumably because there were so few overall.

This particular change in task format fits Warren-Leubecker and Bohannon's (1989) dimension of changed "listener knowledge." Other influential aspects of task format can be related to Labov's (1972a) dimension of attention to speech (in his research, from emotional talk outside the interview to the monitored reading of word lists).

Informal evidence of situational variation due to a change in the degree of self-monitoring (in children the age of Wolf's) comes from the primary classroom I taught years ago in San Diego (Mehan 1979). One day, I spent a few minutes trying out a new oral language test that might be useful in California's early childhood education program. One of the subtests asked children to complete orally such statements as *Here is a child; here are two—* . . . Eight of these items asked for such irregular forms, and the seven first- and second-graders in the classroom who were native speakers of English (all African American) gave thirty-five overgeneralizations out of fifty-six possible responses: *childrens, feets, mines, morest, gooder,* and so on. In contrast, on items asking for regular plurals, possessives, and comparatives, the children got seventy-four out of ninety-eight right. Having spent months of my graduate student life coding transcriptions of child speech for just such overgeneralizations, I felt sure that I would have noticed them if they were that frequent in these children's spontaneous conversation.

I could think of no way to obtain tokens of *mine, most, better,* and *best* in a more casual and less contrived situation, but eliciting plurals seemed possible. From *Ebony* magazine, I cut out pictures of a group of children and a group of men; for pictures of feet, I drew around my own. A few days after completing the tests, I found moments to ask the same seven children individually and as casually as possible, "What's that a picture of?" Of twenty-one possible overgeneralizations, the children gave only six. This large decrease in overgeneralizations in the more casual speech situation suggests that the test elicited from these black children what Labov (1972a) termed "hypercorrections" (Cazden 1975).

5.2. *Speech Adaptations to Changes in Participant Status and Structure*

When Hemphill's adolescent girls experienced the situational change of informal to more formal, teacher-led discussion, this was a change in participant status and structure (what Warren-Leubecker and Bohannon [1989] call "listener status"). It led to qualitatively different speech adaptations in the two social-class groups. The middle-class girls, who competed with each other for turns to speak in the informal discussion (as indicated by back channels that predicted bids for the floor), increased their anaphora with, and back channels to, the teacher in the teacher-led discussion. The working-class girls, who were more collaborative in the informal discussion (using back channels to affirm each other's propositions rather than bid for a turn), decreased both anaphora and back channels when the teacher played a more dominant role.

Categorizing Leona's shifts in narrative style is more difficult—in part because we don't know how Sandy would have adapted her story to the adult and so do not have the full contrast picture, and in part because Leona's adaptations seem intrinsically a mix. Her use of more low-frequency words to the adult in contrast to more expressive speech sounds to her peers is an adaptation to listener that most children may learn to make. On the other hand, her confirmation checks to her peers, and her addition of more emotional content to her peers, seem more influenced by her social class, ethnicity, or low academic status. As Gee suggests at the end of his analysis:

> Presumably, Leona has dropped the enactive/performative aspects of her style because she lacks "social permission" in the face of the white male to fully utilize her own style—the style that reflects her cultural identity and sense of self. . . . [And the school] does not give her access to the instruction that would ensure she could so switch, let alone do so in a way that does not threaten her own sense of self. (1989b:109)

Having suggested, for the sake of discussion, a hypothesis of widely shared adaptations to differences in task formats versus more differential adaptations to differences in participant status, I want to blur that contrast. Even young speakers make some shifts in participant status—for example, in speaking more politely to family elders or more simply to toddlers; perhaps within any single speech community, self-identity is not at issue.

Conversely, for older speakers, tasks (in school and out) become associated with, and symbolic of, different contexts in the larger social world; they are felt to be different language games, played by members of different clubs, with seemingly strict language-using rules for admittance. As (African American) Patricia Williams begins the opening allegory in *The Alchemy of Race and Rights: Diary of a Law Professor:* "Once upon a time there was a society of priests who built a Celestial City with gates secured by word-combination locks" (1991).

Writing tasks constitute a special case in point. In a simplistic external picture of writers at work, there is no participant status or structure at all, only individual writers alone with their writing tools. But if we consider the context in the mind of writers as they try to adapt their writing to the expected conventions of different audiences, or resist (as Williams explains in her chapter "The Death of the Profane: A Commentary on the Genre of Legal Writing") the limitations that those conventions place on expressable meanings, the picture changes. We see how readers become active participants, even censors, in writers' minds as they set to work. Some writers approach writing tasks with feelings of competence and confidence, but others feel incompetence, ambivalence, conflict, and resistance. (See the chapter on "Vygotsky, Hymes, and Bakhtin—From Word to Utterance and Voice" in Cazden 1992 for comments to this effect from other writers, especially those writing "from the fringe.")

Even with this qualification of some blurring of the suggested contrast between adaptations to task format versus participant status, the contrast is useful for considering implications for education. Both kinds of adaptations can be assisted in school, but different kinds of assistance will be helpful. Very briefly, I think that techniques for adapting to new task formats can be taught more directly, whereas adaptations to shifts in perceived participant status may require discussion of larger social, racial, and political issues of language use and language change in society— what in Britain is called "critical language awareness."

We should not be surprised at this political aspect of situational variation. Register is, after all, the category of language use associated most closely with social roles, and no democracy is yet complete enough for all roles to be open to all people.

Notes

1. Leona's story as told to the adult male does not appear in Gee 1989a, and is cited from an earlier unpublished paper entitled "Commonalities and Differences in Narrative Construction: A Linguistic Examination of a Black and a White Girl's Stories" (1987).

References

Andersen, Elaine S. 1990. *Speaking with Style: The Sociolinguistic Skills of Children.* London: Routledge.

Bernstein, Basil. 1971. *Class, Codes, and Control,* Vol. 1. London: Routledge.

Cazden, Courtney B. 1966. "Subcultural Differences in Child Language." *Merrill-Palmer Quarterly* 12:185–219.

———. 1970. "The Situation: A Neglected Source of Social Class Differences in Language Use." *Journal of Social Issues* 26:35–60.

———. 1975. "Hypercorrection in Test Responses." *Theory into Practice* 14:343–46.

———. 1988. *Classroom Discourse: The Language of Teaching and Learning.* Portsmouth, NH: Heinemann.

———. 1992. *Whole Language Plus: Essays on Literacy in the United States and New Zealand.* New York: Teachers College Press.

Ferrara, Kathleen, and Barbara Bell (n.d.). "Variation and Innovation in Constructed Dialogue Introducers: The Evolution of *be + like.*" Texas A&M University, Department of English. Ms.

Gee, James P. 1989a. "Two Styles of Narrative Construction and Their Linguistic and Educational Implications." *Discourse Processes* 12:287–307.

———. 1989b. *Literacy, Discourse, and Linguistics: Essays by James Paul Gee. Journal of Education* 171:97–115.

Hemphill, Lowry. 1986. "Context and Conversational Style: A Reappraisal of Social Class Differences in Speech." Ed.D. Dissertation, Harvard University.

Labov, William. 1972a. *Language in the Inner City.* Philadelphia: University of Pennsylvania Press.

———. 1972b. *Sociolinguistic Patterns.* Philadelphia: University of Pennsylvania Press.

Romaine, Suzanne. 1984. *The Language of Children and Adolescents.* New York: Basil Blackwell.

Warren-Leubecker, Amye, and John Neil Bohannon III. 1989. "Pragmatics: Language in Social Contexts." In Jean Berko Gleason, ed., *The Development of Language, 2nd ed.* Columbus, OH: Merrill. Pp. 327–68.

Williams, Patricia. 1991. *The Alchemy of Race and Rights.* Cambridge, MA: Harvard University Press.

Wolf, Dennis P. 1985. "Ways of Telling: Text Repertoires in Elementary School Children." *Journal of Education* 167:71–87.

12

Diglossia as a Special Case of
Register Variation

ALAN HUDSON

1. Introduction

The three basic premises upon which the following discussion of diglossia is founded may be stated at the very outset. First, diglossia, in its original and most theoretically productive sense, is a dramatic instance of the apparently universal opposition between formal and informal language use. Second, the situational differentiation of registers of the same language is not of the same order as the asymmetric functional allocation of distinct languages within the same speech community, but rather differs from the latter in terms of its sociogenesis and evolutionary course of development. Third, and following from the first two premises, the phenomenon of diglossia is more fruitfully investigated from the perspective of a theory of formal language use and formal social behavior generally than from the perspective of a theory of language contact and societal bilingualism.

Two largely independent views of the notion of formality predominate among students of language use in social context, the first an anthropological, or sociocultural, view, and the second a discourse-functional, or psychopragmatic, view. From the anthropological standpoint, formality of discourse is typically viewed in terms of "a prevailing affective tone," such as seriousness, politeness, or respect (Irvine 1984:212). Within the more psycholinguistic framework of discourse pragmatics, however, formal-informal variation in linguistic form is understood in terms of the interaction between the physical and psychological exigencies of the communicative context, on the one hand, and the cognitive mechanisms engaged in the planning, production, and processing of discourse, on the other (Givón 1979:105–06).

2. The Ethnography of Noncasual Discourse

The anthropological, or sociocultural, view has perhaps been most succinctly articulated by Judith Irvine, who conceives of formality as being defined cross-culturally by four parameters of social occasions and of the behavior, both linguistic and nonlinguistic, associated with them. In the first instance, the various systems of social behavior, including the proxemic, kinesic, gestural, and linguistic systems, are claimed to be subject to "the addition of extra rules or conventions" in formal settings; linguistically, the rule elaboration characteristic of formal discourse may be manifested jointly or severally in the phonological, syntactic, lexical, and prosodic subsystems (Irvine 1984:214). Second, formal situations generally are held to be governed by stricter co-occurrence restrictions on the realizations of socially significant behavioral variables; linguistically, this means that selection of a particular socially meaningful phonological, syntactic, lexical, or prosodic variant in one instance is more likely to constrain the choice of a subsequent variant in a formal context than in an informal one (p. 215). Third, positional identities, that is to say, social identities whose existence, attributes, and incumbents are widely recognized throughout the community, are more frequently appealed to in formal than in informal situations (p. 216), and "the wider, or more public, the scope of the social identities invoked on a particular occasion, the more formal the occasion is" (p. 217). Finally, formal occasions are characterized by the emergence of a central situational focus, "a dominant mutual engagement that encompasses all persons present" and that distinguishes the main focus of attention from various peripheral interactions (p. 217).

Like Irvine, John Gumperz (1964:140) also has argued that in more formal types of interaction, "modes of speaking are narrowly prescribed," while in more informal types of interaction, there is a loosening of co-occurrence restrictions, and "forms which would not appear together in transactional encounters may now co-occur" (p. 149). Irvine's notions of the invocation of positional identities and the emergence of a central situational focus are in large measure foreshadowed in Gumperz' distinction between transactional and personal interaction. Transactional interaction "centers about limited socially defined goals," as in the case of religious services or job interviews, where participants "in a sense suspend their individuality in order to act out the rights and obligations of relevant statuses" (p. 149). In personal interaction, on the other hand, typified by casual conversation between friends and peers, participants "act as individuals, rather than for the sake of specific social tasks" (p. 149).

Among the earliest attempts to characterize the differences between formal and informal discourse was Carl Voegelin's (1960) essay on the distinction between casual and noncasual utterances. Concluding that no universal grammatical features which systematically distinguished the former from the latter could be identified, Voegelin was led to the position that such a distinction had to be drawn in general cultural, rather than in linguistic, terms (1960:60–64). Three cultural criteria in particular were adduced in order to distinguish noncasual from casual utterances: (1) Noncasual utterances are clearly restricted to very particular times and places, whereas casual utterances are appropriate across a wider range of social contexts; (2) there is more general agreement among persons-in-the-culture in evaluating the appropriateness of noncasual utterances with reference to participants, occasions, locales, and choice of language variety, while there is less agreement, across fewer criteria, regarding the identification, interpretation, and evaluation of casual utterances; and (3) some kind of formal training, or specialized interest, is prerequisite to the acquisition of proficiency in the different varieties of noncasual language, while proficiency in casual language is acquired by imitation and without any deliberate instruction.

The situations in which the high variety in diglossia is appropriate are clear instances of formal or noncasual contexts in the sense in which these terms are employed by Irvine, Gumperz, and Voegelin. The high variety is traditionally used in religious sermons, in parliamentary debates and political speeches, in university lectures, and in news broadcasts, as well as in other communicative settings (Ferguson 1959:329). These are all occasions characterized by dominant central foci where positional identities are invoked by individuals specifically licensed by the community: priests and mullahs, professors, politicians and government bureaucrats, broadcasters, and so forth. In Gumperz' terms also, the social interaction which takes place in these contexts is transactional in nature, involving as it does the suspension of individual personal identities and the accomplishment of limited, socially defined goals.

Voegelin's so-called cultural attributes of noncasual utterances also bear some considerable resemblance to Ferguson's account of the social contexts in which the high variety is appropriate in diglossia, as well as to the circumstances whereby proficiency in the high variety is attained. As Voegelin (1960:61) points out, compared with casual utterances, noncasual utterances are more restricted to particular times and places, and use of noncasual linguistic forms by inappropriate individuals, or on inappropriate occasions, is considered shocking or humorous by persons-in-the-culture. In a similar vein, use of the elevated variety in diglossia is essentially confined to situations characterizable as formal in the sense that the role relationships, social settings, and individual speech acts of which they may be constituted are more narrowly and more explicitly constrained by the culture than in informal situations. As with noncasual utterances, use of the high variety in informal communication is regarded as incongruous, if not ridiculous, by the members of the diglossic speech community (Ferguson 1959:329). Moreover, just as proficiency in noncasual varieties is typically attained through formal training and deliberate instruction (Voegelin 1960:62), mastery of the high variety in diglossia is attained by means of formal education, whether in religious schools, in government schools, or at the hands of private tutors, rather than as a result of natural exposure in the home environment (Ferguson 1959:331).

As to the structural properties of formal linguistic codes, Irvine (1984:214), as noted above, identifies increased code structuring, or "the addition of extra rules or conventions to the codes that organize behavior in a social setting," as one possible marker of formality. A second indicator of relative formality is the level of consistency obtaining between the choices of successive linguistic variants throughout the course of a given speech event: "In the kinds of discourse that ethnographers have labeled more formal, consistency of choices (in terms of their social significance) seems to be greater than in ordinary conversation, where speakers may be able to recombine variants to achieve special effects" (Irvine 1984:215). Essentially the same position is taken by Gumperz (1964:140), who notes that, while all discourse is subject to some degree of restriction on the co-occurrence of linguistic alternants, some speech events, such as public ceremonies and religious rituals, are subject to more restrictive co-occurrence requirements than others, such as conversations among personal friends.

On the matter of co-occurrence restrictions on grammatical and phonological variation in diglossia, however, Ferguson (1959:332) is essentially silent, except to note that the high variety (H), which is the only codified variety, tolerates less variation in phonology, grammar, vocabulary, and orthography than does the vernacular, or low variety (L). Furthermore, a well-known feature of diglossia is the existence of phonologically unrelated lexical doublets referring to fairly common concepts in H and in L (Ferguson 1959:334). Lexical choice is constrained in H, being limited only to the H-appropriate members of the doublets, as it is in L, where it is limited strictly to the L-appropriate members of the doublets, and so the sets of socially equivalent lexical alternants in diglossia function as sharply diagnostic indices of style. However, since the lexical co-occurrence restrictions appear to apply as rigorously in H as in L, they cannot be used to argue for the greater formality of H relative to L. Instead, the rigid co-occurrence restrictions found in diglossic code repertoires may distinguish the latter from other types of situationally differentiated monolingual speech repertoires where tolerance for stylistic interpenetration is considerably greater (Ervin-Tripp 1964:91, 1971:44–45, 1972:240–41). Thus lexical alternation in diglossia differs from somewhat similar kinds of alternation in English, such as *purchase/buy* and *children/kids*, where the alternants represent points on a continuum of formality-informality and where the range of formality to which one alternant is appropriate is not necessarily identical with the range to which another alternant is appropriate (Ferguson 1959:334).

To summarize the discussion to this point, Ferguson's account of the social functions of the elevated variety in diglossia is consistent with its being regarded as a formal or noncasual variety according to the situational and cultural criteria proposed by Irvine, Gumperz, and Voegelin. The situations in which the high variety is appropriately used are all situations in which there is indeed a dominant central focus and in which the principal actors, duly sanctioned by the speech community, invoke positional identities for the purposes of conducting limited social transactions. With regard to the structure of the linguistic codes, the tendency discussed by Ferguson (1959:334) for the elevated variety to exhibit greater grammatical complexity than the vernacular might be construed as a case of rule addition or rule elaboration, but this is far from clear. On the other hand, the lexical co-occurrence restrictions which are so prominent a feature of classical diglossia, while they cannot be said to mark the greater formality of the high variety relative to the low, may prove diagnostic in distinguishing diglossic code repertoires as a class from other types of stylistically differentiated repertoires. For reasons to be discussed later, however, it may as yet be premature to foreclose, as Voegelin does, on the prospects for discovering features of linguistic structure, of a suitably abstract character, which might reliably distinguish casual from noncasual utterances cross-linguistically, and therefore distinguish elevated varieties from vernacular ones in diglossic contexts.

3. The Discourse Pragmatics of Formal and Informal Registers

The discourse-pragmatic approach to the analysis of formality-informality is represented in the work of Kay (1977), Ochs (1979), Givón (1979), and Pawley and Syder (1983), among others, and, explicitly or otherwise, in the work of many students of the relationship between spoken and written language (e.g., Besnier 1988, Biber 1988, Chafe 1982, Tannen 1982). In a sense, Basil Bernstein's (1964) distinction between restricted and elaborated codes can also be considered an early statement, if not a forerunner, of this point of view, in that it relates cultural context, by way of social structure, socialization processes, and family role systems, to the social and psychological demands of local social interaction.

A distinction of some significance to the study of the elevated and vernacular varieties in diglossia is that drawn by Paul Kay (1977:21–22) between autonomous and nonautonomous speech. In characterizing this distinction as "that which exists between the speech of an educated speaker in a formal academic context . . . and [the] speech of the same person when playing baseball, making love, or quarreling," Kay implies a distinction not totally unlike that between noncasual and casual speech, or between H and L in diglossia. In point of fact, however, the functional relationship between autonomous and nonautonomous speech is far more akin to that between elaborated and restricted codes (Bernstein 1964), in that autonomous speech is a precise, logically explicit, style of communication which is minimally dependent upon simultaneous transmission over nonlinguistic channels or upon prior understandings resulting from the overlapping backgrounds of the interlocutors (Kay 1977:21–22). As described by Kay, autonomous speech "is suited to the communication of novel, exact, emotionally neutral information to an unfamiliar addressee" (p. 22). Structurally, autonomous speech is distinguished from nonautonomous speech by the use of longer and syntactically more complex sentences, by more explicit and more varied vocabulary, and by more paused and more edited delivery (p. 21).

In an analysis strikingly reminiscent of Kay's distinction between nonautonomous and autonomous speech, Talmy Givón proposes that "every language has a wide range of DISCOURSE REGISTERS, from the loose-informal-pragmatic to the tight-formal-syntactic" (1979:84), and further, that every adult commands an entire repertoire of communicative modes, ranging from the extreme pragmatic to the extreme syntactic, among which he or she is capable of shifting as the demands of the situation require (1979:102, 104, 107). Prototypical examples of pragmatic, or paratactic, discourse are characterized, in particular, by topic-comment sentence structure, by thematically determined word order, by loose conjunction between related clauses, by a roughly one-to-one ratio of nominal arguments to verbs, and by the absence of grammatical morphology (Givón 1979:98, 1991:338). By contrast, prototypical syntactic discourse is characterized by subject-predicate sentence structure, by semantically determined word order, by tight subordination of related clauses, by a higher ratio of nominal arguments to verbs, and by elaborate use of grammatical morphology (Givón 1979:98, 1991:338). The quintessential example of the pragmatic communicative mode is early childhood discourse (Givón

1979:107); the extreme example of the syntactic communicative mode is adult, formal, educated, written language (Givón 1979:102–7).

The emergence of the syntactic mode of communication may be explained by reference to the interactional constraints operating in a given communicative context. As in child language and in pidgin varieties of speech, use of the pragmatic, or paratactic, mode of communication is precipitated when planning of discourse is either impossible or unnecessary (Givón 1979:100, 102, 105); the syntactic mode employed in formal language use, on the other hand, is made possible by the availability of ample opportunity for the preplanning of discourse (Givón 1979:106; cf. Ochs 1979:57–58). Where, as in child language, pidgins, and informal speech, the interlocutors either are engaged in discourse concerning immediately obvious topics and tasks or share a considerable degree of pragmatic suppositional background, use of the pragmatic mode again becomes possible (Givón 1979:100–102, 105–6); in the most extreme cases of formal language use, by contrast, there may be relatively little shared presuppositional background to begin with and "virtually no immediately obvious context, topic, or task" (Givón 1979:106; cf. Ochs 1979:62). Finally, whereas informal speech typically occurs in situations where constant monitoring of the addressee is possible, the most formal speech occurs in situations where "there is a total absence of face-to-face monitoring" (Givón 1979:105–6).

The diachronic process whereby "loose, paratactic, PRAGMATIC discourse structures develop . . . into tight, GRAMMATICALIZED syntactic structures" (Givón 1979:83), evident also in the maturation of communicative competence in children and in the nativization of pidgins as creoles, is apparent synchronically in the grammatical distinctions between informal-unplanned discourse and formal-planned discourse (Givón 1979:98, 104). In particular, paratactic expression of sentence topic, as in left-dislocation accompanied by disruption of the overarching intonational contour, is more characteristic of informal than of formal speech; on the other hand, syntactic devices, such as the passive voice, clefting, and pseudoclefting, are more likely to be employed as explicit markers of informational relations in formal than in informal language. Second, formal language may be expected to exhibit a higher incidence of clause embedding than informal language, accompanied by a more complex argument structure. Finally, to the degree that there are significant differences in grammatical morphology between formal and informal language, the grammatical morphology of the formal varieties is predicted to be more extensive than that of the informal varieties.

From the point of view of diglossia research, the most striking difference between formal and informal language concerns the relative reduction of grammatical morphology in the latter. In Givón's (1979:104) account, informal discourse tends to "involve a considerable reduction and simplification of the grammatical morphology, that is, reduced tense-aspect systems and less complex case-morphology, thus dispensing with subordinating morphemes for both verb complements and relative clauses, and an increased use of zero anaphora over anaphoric pronouns." This claim may be compared with Ferguson's (1959:333) statement regarding grammatical morphology in the elevated and vernacular varieties in diglossia: "H has grammatical categories not present in L and has an inflectional system of nouns and verbs which is much reduced or totally absent in L." Thus according to Ferguson, Classical Arabic has three overtly marked nominal cases where colloquial Arabic has none, *katharevousa* has four cases compared with three in demotic Greek, and Standard German has four nominal cases and two nonperiphrastic tenses in the indicative of the verb, where Swiss German has three cases and one nonperiphrastic indicative tense. Moreover, in all of the instances of diglossia examined by Ferguson, "there seem to be several striking differences of word order as well as a thorough-going set of differences in the use of introductory and connective particles" (p. 333).

Commonly in diglossia, though not universally if the contrast between Classical Chinese and modern spoken Mandarin may be regarded as a valid counterexample (Li and Thompson 1982), it appears that the grammatical structure of the low variety is less complex than that of the high variety, in the operational sense that fewer grammatical categories are obligatorily marked in the low variety, government and agreement are more regular in the low variety, the paradigms of the low variety are more symmetrical than those of the high, there is less morphological alternation in the low variety, and the conditioning of such alternation as is found in the low variety is more regular than that found in the high (Ferguson 1959:333–34). The differences in grammatical morphology between the high and low varieties in diglossia, therefore, appear to be of a single nature with those distinguishing formal-planned language from informal-unplanned language generally. What seems to set diglossia apart from more typical instances of formal-informal stratification, such as that involving the opposition between formal written English and colloquial spoken English, is the extent rather than the basic nature of the grammatical differences between the formal and the informal varieties, and the relatively greater susceptibility of the formal variety, in the more typical nondiglossic situations, to influence from the informal variety over a given period.

Kay's distinction between autonomous and nonautonomous codes and Givón's distinction between syntactic and pragmatic modes of discourse are highly evocative of Basil Bernstein's well-known contrast between elaborated and restricted codes, the relevance of which to the study of diglossia has already been noted by Tannen (1982:15, n. 3) and Fasold (1990:270). Bernstein's distinction between elaborated and restricted codes, on the one hand, and between two distinct types of restricted codes, on the other, yields a tripartite functional categorization of linguistic varieties. The primary function of an elaborated code is the verbally explicit transmission of a speaker's unique experience and discrete intent (Bernstein 1964:57, 63–65). Elaborated codes are born of, and in turn reinforce, the expectation of psychological differences between the participants in a given social relation, taking into account the perspective of the addressee in addition to that of the addressor (1964:63, 65). Stated differently, elaborated codes arise in circumstances where the participants in a given context are to some extent interacting as individuals differentiated from their respective social groups and local cultures and where their discrete intent may not therefore be taken for granted. Structurally, elaborated codes are distinguished from restricted codes in that, in the case of the former, speakers select from a wide range of syntactic alternatives, with the consequence that the particular syntactic options likely to be exercised in a given range of speech are less predictable (Bernstein 1964:57, 63).

In the case of restricted codes, by contrast, the explicit verbal expression of discrete intent is either socially unnecessary or socially proscribed, and discrete intent, if it is to be expressed at all, is communicated implicitly through nonverbal channels (Bernstein 1964:59–63). One variety of restricted code is employed in situations where social roles are constrained by rigid and extensive prescription and where there is a minimum of discretion available to the participants for the expression of individual identity, as might be the case, for instance, within certain religious, legal, or military hierarchies (Bernstein 1964:58). In the most ritualistic form of this code, "the messages transmitted through all channels (verbal and extraverbal) approach maximal redundancy from the perspective of both transmitter and receiver," and any departure from maximal redundancy is regarded by members of the speech community as a breach of interactional etiquette, indeed even as profanity (Bernstein 1964:58). Under such conditions, to quote Bernstein's (1964:58) apposite synopsis, "the individual is transformed into a cultural agent."

A second variety of restricted code is employed in circumstances where the communicative exchange "is played out against a backdrop of assumptions common to the speakers, against a set of closely shared interests and identifications, against a system of shared expectations"; in sum, in circumstances where the interaction "presupposes a local cultural identity which reduces the need for the speakers to elaborate their intent verbally and to make it explicit" (Bernstein 1964:60). Such a code might be expected to arise in closed communities such as prisons, combat units of the armed service, criminal subcultures, and peer groups of children and adolescents (p. 61). The messages conveyed in this type of restricted code tend to be concrete, descriptive, and narrative, in contrast with the abstract and analytical nature of discourse in elaborated code (pp. 62–65). Formally, the code is characterized, like all variants of restricted code, by the use of a considerably reduced range of syntactic and lexical alternatives, and, more specifically, by more "dislocated" or "disjunctive" speech sequences, by the occurrence of fewer qualifiers, by the almost exclusive use of the active voice, and by more frequent appearance of tag questions, hedges, and certain pronouns which "emphasize the communality of the speakers" (Bernstein 1964:56–61). The structural properties of this type of restricted code reflect the general principle that the more the intent of the other participants in a verbal interaction may be taken for granted, "the more likely that the structure of the speech will be simplified and the vocabulary drawn from a narrow range" (pp. 60–61).

4. Synthesis: Casual, Autonomous, and Transactional Modes of Communication

The attempts to differentiate the varieties of discourse discussed have a great deal in common with each other as well as with the distinction between the H and the L varieties in diglossia. Above all else, each categorization, including the H and L of diglossia, represents a functional categorization of linguistic varieties, in the sense that the varieties in question are defined externally by reference to certain aspects of the social context in which they occur, rather than by reference to the social identities of the individuals who characteristically use them most. Following Britto (1986:37–39), they may be thought of in this respect as diatypic code ranges rather than as dialectal code ranges. Emphatically, the H and L opposition of classical diglossia also is fundamentally diatypic, rather than dialectal, in nature. Beyond this, it is abundantly clear that the underlying dimension of functional variation which is implicit in each of the previously discussed categorizations is anchored at one extreme by the variety of language universally employed in everyday, personal, face-to-face intercourse between intimates. This is as true of informal and casual speech as it is of restricted code (peer group variety), nonautonomous speech, pragmatic communicative mode, unplanned discourse, and, in particular, the vernacular variety in diglossia.

By contrast, the polar opposite of unguarded oral conversation is variously characterized. There is general agreement, however, that it is acquired later in life as a superposed variety (or range of varieties), usually through the agency of some formal institutional or apprenticeship structure (Bernstein 1964:64, Feldman 1991:47–48, Ferguson 1959:331, Givón 1979:101–03, Ochs 1979:54, Pawley and Syder 1983:552, 557, Voegelin 1960:62). Within the more psycholinguistic framework of discourse pragmatics, the grammatical structure of formal discourse is interpreted as a consequence of the interaction between the exigencies of the communicative situation and the psychological mechanisms involved in the planning, production, and processing of discourse. Thus the structural characteristics of what might be referred to generically as noncasual discourse are explained by the lack of opportunity for discourse planning (Ochs 1979), the absence of shared presuppositional background between the interlocutors (Bernstein 1964, Givón 1979, Kay 1977), the relative lack of opportunity for immediate audience feedback (Givón 1979, Kay 1977, Labov 1972), the degree of monitoring of one's own discourse production (Labov 1972), the physical character of the available communicative channels (Kay 1977), or combinations of several of these factors (Givón 1979). Within the framework of the ethnography of communication, however, noncasual discourse is more typically viewed in terms of "a prevailing affective tone," such as seriousness, politeness, or respect, to quote Irvine's (1984:212) summary. As noted previously, formal occasions, in this sense, "invoke positional and public, rather than personal, identities" and involve "a dominant mutual engagement that encompasses all persons present" (Irvine 1984:216–17).

The distinction drawn here between sociocultural and psychopragmatic determinants of linguistic form seems virtually identical to that drawn by Besnier (1988:731) between "the norms of communication at play in each context," or "the cultural 'value' of a communicative context," on the one hand, and "the physical and psychological characteristics surrounding the situation of use," on the other hand. The same idea is to be found in Bartsch's (1989:207) observation that communicative efficacy alone does not uniquely determine linguistic form: "What are considered to be the adequate linguistic forms for performing a certain function is partly determined by what is rational, i.e. goal directed and goal adequate, but for another part it is determined conventionally." Interestingly, the same distinction was recognized much earlier in Bernstein's opposition between restricted code (lexicon prediction), employed when "the organization and selection of all signals is bound by rigid and extensive prescriptions," which is to say when the individual is performing strictly as "a cultural agent" (1964:58), and elaborated code, employed when there are fewer shared expectations between the interlocutors, and when the discrete intent of one may not be taken for granted by the other (1964:63–64). Both restricted code (lexical prediction) and elaborated code are in turn opposed by Bernstein (1964:60) to restricted code (high structural prediction), employed in contexts presupposing a set of closely shared interests, identifications, and expectations among the interlocutors.

In summary, the psychopragmatic and sociocultural dimensions of linguistic variation constitute separate axes of alternation across styles, registers, or genres. In principle, these axes may be totally independent of each other; in practice, they are at least partially so, and their relative prominence in accounting for situational variation in linguistic form may vary from one discourse context to the next and from one speech community to another. The psychopragmatic axis is concerned first and foremost with communicative efficacy, in large measure a function of the degree of presuppositional background shared by the interlocutors, and of the situational constraints upon establishing sufficient common background to permit the discourse to continue. Underlying the sociocultural axis of variation, on the other hand, is the concern of the speech community with communicative decorum, as reflected in the extent to which a speaker or writer is at liberty to express discrete, personal intent, or is required to suspend personal identity in order to perform as a duly licensed agent of the culture. At the common origin of these two axes lies casual conversation, "the everyday talk used for getting on with, getting things done with, and gossiping with others" (Feldman 1991:48), where interlocutors are free to engage in personal rather than purely transactional interaction, and where there is considerable overlap of identity, expectation, and experiential and cultural background between them.

Following Voegelin's (1960) terminology, everyday conversation, with regard to the social contexts in which it occurs, its content, and its structural characteristics, will be referred to here as *casual,* and its opposite, whether formal, high, transactional, autonomous, syntactic, planned, or elaborated, as *noncasual.* The choice of terminology reflects, in part, agreement with Givón's (1991:339) claim that informal face-to-face communication about human affairs "is the more frequent, unmarked, human-universal cultural norm," while written or formal spoken discourse about abstract subject matter "is the less frequent, marked counter-norm." It also, of course, reflects the need for further differentiation of noncasual discourse along the psychopragmatic and sociocultural dimensions referred to previously.

Of the noncasual varieties of discourse, autonomous, syntactic, or elaborated modes of communication may be differentiated from casual discourse by a relative absence of shared presuppositional background among the participants, whether due to the absence of an immediately obvious context or task, of commonly held experiential or cultural expectations, or both. While Givón's term "syntactic" (unlike its opposite, "pragmatic") captures the structural quality of this type of noncasual discourse, and Bernstein's term "elaborated" is somewhat ambiguous in the distinction between structure and function (with certain evaluative overtones besides), Kay's functional term "autonomous" best seems to reflect the notion of a

TABLE 12.1   Conceptual Relationships
Among Three Modes of Discourse

Discourse Mode	Shared Background	Individual Discretion
Autonomous	−	+
Transactional/Formal	+	−
Casual	+	+

mode of discourse relatively free of the requirement of common presuppositional background.

By way of contrast, formal, high, transactional, or, in the extreme case, ritual discourse may be distinguished from casual discourse by the degree to which the participants in the interaction enact roles as agents of the culture rather than as individuals with the discretion to express personal perspective or intent (Bernstein 1964:58), or, in Gumperz' (1964:149) terms, "suspend their individuality in order to act out the rights and obligations of relevant statuses." While the label "formal," though variously ambiguous, is commonly used for this type of discourse in the ethnographic literature, and the term "high," reflecting the typically exalted status of such codes within their communities of users, is the term most commonly employed by students of diglossia, in many ways it is Gumperz' term "transactional" which best embodies the functional meaning of situational restriction on individual personal expression. The conceptual relationships among casual, autonomous, and transactional modes of discourse are summarized in Table 12.1.

As far as diglossia is concerned, the domain of casual discourse is clearly also the domain of L, or the "low" variety, since "no segment of the speech community in diglossia regularly uses H as a medium of ordinary conversation" (Ferguson 1959:336–37). Use of the H variety in diglossia, on the other hand, above all else is high in its connotations of cultural agency and transactional interaction, bearing less of a relationship, so it seems, to the psychopragmatic constraints operating in a given communicative context.

The discussion up to this point has focused largely upon the external, functional definition of linguistic varieties, which is to say their characterization in terms of the physical, psychological, and social properties of the communicative contexts in which they occur. A second topic, inseparable from the first, concerns whether and to what extent there might exist a causal nexus between the recurring structural features of noncasual codes and the interactional properties of the situations in which they are used. More generally still, there is the question of which aspects, if any, of the social structure and ideology of a speech community are reflected in the linguistic organization of noncasual speech events (cf. Irvine 1984:213, 220–24). Two themes, in particular, recur with unrelenting persistence throughout the scholarship discussed above: the general notion that noncasual codes are characterized either by additional or more elaborate structure than casual codes, and the more specific notion that grammatical morphology and syntactic embedding are reduced in casual codes relative to noncasual.

In diglossia too, as noted, the claim has been made that "H has grammatical categories not present in L and has an inflectional system of nouns and verbs which is much reduced or totally absent in L" (Ferguson 1959:333). Much more comparative research remains to be done before a verdict can be returned on the greater morphological complexity of H relative to L, not to mention on whether such complexity is reproduced in the phonology, syntax, or semantics of H; however, recent research on register differentiation in a variety of unrelated languages suggests that the forms and structures of noncasual registers, in the generic sense of the term, may well turn out to be more complex than those of more casual registers (Besnier 1988, Biber 1988, Kim and Biber this volume, Biber and Hared this volume). To the extent that such a generalization can be sustained cross-linguistically for the synchronic contrast between casual and noncasual varieties, including that between the vernacular and elevated varieties in diglossia, and to the extent that it may be revealed also in the diachronic processes of language change, language acquisition, and creolization, and, in reverse, in language obsolescence and attrition, the functional common denominator of all of these processes may provide the necessary clue to the nature of the causal relationship between linguistic structure and communicative function.

5. The Sociogenesis of Functional Differentiation

Paul Kay has proposed that nonautonomous speech is phylogenetically prior to autonomous speech, and that linguistic repertoires, as they evolve, tend to develop the lexical and syntactic resources necessary "for more precise and explicit (i.e., more autonomous) communication at whatever level of abstraction is desired by the addressor" (1977:24). Nonautonomous speech is not ultimately replaced by autonomous speech; instead, verbal repertoires, in the course of accommodating to the communicative demands placed upon them, develop the resources of autonomous speech in addition to the already available resources of nonautonomous speech. The fundamental mechanism driving this process of linguistic evolution is the adaptation of language "to an increasingly complex and diversified speech community whose members collectively control a body of knowledge beyond that which any one speaker can control" (Kay 1977:30). The growth in size of local speech communities, the shift from genealogical to territorial social group definition, and the emergence of occupational, regional, and other subcultures diminish the opportunity for constant face-to-face interaction among all the members of the community and increase the likelihood of communication between interlocutors who have little background in common. The division of labor within the community also results in the creation of expert bodies of knowledge as well as the specialized terminologies required to communicate about them. In short, the general process of social evolution "produces speech communities in which situations calling for autonomous speech occur with increasing frequency" (Kay 1977:29).

There are many remarkable points of similarity between Kay's account of linguistic evolution and Givón's functional-evolutionary explanation for the outgrowth of the syntactic communicative mode from the more primitive pragmatic mode. Givón, like Kay, sees the pragmatic mode of communication as being "phylogenetically earlier, and, in terms of cross-language attestation, more universal than the syntactic mode" (Givón 1979:107). Again like Kay, Givón attributes the coexistence of pragmatic and syntactic modes of communication in all known speech communities to the fact that the human species has evolved "to the point where nonimmediately obvious contexts, topics, and tasks can be dealt with and where one may communicate with strangers as well as . . . with familiars" (1979:106, n. 50). In Kay's view, "the direction of linguistic evolution is toward the precise and explicit speech of the analytic philosopher, the scientist, and the bureaucrat" (1977:30), while in Givón's view, "the written register, much like the formal public-address register, is . . . the utmost mode of communication in the MASS SOCIETY OF STRANGERS" (1979:106).

A similar principle involving the selective adaptation of linguistic form to the conditions of language use has been advanced by Pawley and Syder (1983) in order to account for certain systematic differences between the grammar of vernacular conversation and that of formal written style. The basic premise of this position is that the "forms of [syntactic] construction are molded to suit the constitutive conditions and purposes of face-to-face talk, on the one hand, and impersonal written communication on the other" (Pawley and Syder 1983:552; cf. 551, 577). The circumstances surrounding conversational language use, and therefore the form of grammar to which they give rise, are regarded as universal and as phylogenetically and ontogenetically prior to the conditions and the forms of literate style. Literary register, by contrast, is argued to have evolved more recently than vernacular register in response to the requirements of specialized modes of communication and, like the H variety in diglossia, to be acquired as a superposed variety rather than in the manner of a first language (Pawley and Syder 1983:551–52, 557, 570, 577).

What remains to be added to these proposals is that to the extent that occasions for interaction between strangers, and therefore for autonomous speech, are by and large formal situations, and frequently status-sensitive, it is likely that a cachet of formality will eventually attach also to certain of the structural features of autonomous speech. By the same token, to the extent that access to social occasions calling for autonomous speech is asymmetrically distributed across the speech community, with higher-status individuals typically commanding greater access to such occasions, the structural features of autonomous speech, and, derivatively, of formal speech, may come to represent the social group membership of those who use them, irrespective of the social or communicative context in which they do so (cf. Kay 1977:31, n. 1).

The intimate association between class differentiation and functional differentiation of linguistic varieties has also been noted by Renate Bartsch (1989:206), who claims that "high evaluation of a kind of linguistic usage is a function of the high evaluation of the business conducted in this linguistic usage and of the high evaluation of the officials involved," who "to some degree adopt the language used in these functions also for other areas of life." Similarly, the structural homology between linguistic varieties used by more highly ranked social groups, on the one hand, and those used in more literate or more formal contexts, on the other, has been attributed by Finegan and Biber (this volume) to the unequal distribution of communicative tasks and activities across social groups and to the tendency for each social group to develop "a linguistic norm, representing a kind of average of its register range, with higher-ranked social groups developing norms closer to literate registers than lower-ranked social groups." Thus what begins as a pragmatically determined distinction between written and spoken text may first become an indicator of situational formality and, in a second development, transpose itself vertically into a marker of social identity.

If cross-cultural comparison is any guide to phylogeny, then functionally differentiated speech repertoires must have emerged very early on in the process of formation of speech communities. Even in small bands of hunters and gatherers, characterized by face-to-face communication, minimal social stratification, and limited outgroup interaction, there are perceptible, if relatively small, differences between "casual every-day speech and non-casual styles used in singing, recitation, myth-telling and similar ritually defined situations" (Gumperz 1968:466). In the speech economies of these least complex of societies, noncasual styles are not the exclusive province of any particular group, though they may become so as a consequence of the tendencies toward increasing specialization of ritual activity found in tribal societies. Only in more advanced tribal groups, however, with the expansion of the economic base and the advent of economic stratification, does the development of major stylistic variance become possible (Gumperz 1968:466–67). It is this major stylistic variance that provides the raw material for the potential development of diglossia, under favorable conditions, in more complex, intermediate societies.

6. The Evolutionary Course of Diglossia

The opposition, central to diglossia, between a vernacular variety learned in the home and a superposed variety learned after childhood reaches prominence in intermediate societies constituted of peasant, herder, or even tribal populations integrated to varying degrees into the dominant society and exhibiting a high degree of social stratification and occupational specialization (Gumperz 1968:467–68). Such societies are likely to develop special sacred and administrative codes, in addition to other special parlances, which are "characterized by extreme codification," and which require, therefore, "a large investment of time in the study of grammar and rhetoric," as well as schools, with their complements of scholars, for the pursuit of such study (Gumperz 1968:469). These codes serve "as the language of special administrative and priestly classes," and function, at least in part, "to maintain group exclusiveness" (Gumperz 1968:469). When government "remains in the hands of a small ruling group," it is possible, even in the face of increasing mobilization of the population, to maintain considerable language distance between the administrative and sacred codes, on the one hand, and the rest of the code matrix on the other (Gumperz 1968:469). It may be reasonably hypothesized, therefore, that intermediate societies as described by Gumperz offer singularly fertile ground for the emergence of classical diglossia.

While eschewing a rigidly monogenetic stance on the subject, Ferguson (1959:338) himself nonetheless identifies three literacy-related conditions which repeatedly seem to contribute to the emergence of diglossia: (1) the existence in a language of a sizable body of literature which embodies some of the fundamental values of the speech community, (2) the restriction of literacy to a small social elite, and (3) the passage of a considerable period of time, on the order of several centuries, between the emergence of the literary tradition and the establishment of general popular literacy. In this claim resides the germ, hitherto largely ignored, of what Coulmas (1987:122) has appropriately described as "a sociolinguistic theory of writing and written language which accounts for the nexus between literacy, writing system, and diglossia." In Coulmas' own version of the theory, the degree of difference between the written and spoken norms, and therefore the prospect for the emergence of diglossia, is a function of (1) the degree of association between the literary tradition and other great cultural achievements of a religious or artistic nature, (2) the period of time over which the literary tradition flourishes, (3) the extent to which the written language is cultivated by a small caste of scribes and is prevented from adjusting to changes in the spoken language, (4) the literacy rate of the speech community, (5) the acceptance of the written language by the illiterate mass of the population as the only valid manifestation of their language, and (6) the relative fit of writing system and orthography for the language in question (1987:121–22, 1989:13).

    Four principal mechanisms account for the manner in which the development of writing contributes to the linguistic diversity of a speech community and thus may facilitate the subsequent emergence of diglossia. In the first instance, the socio-cultural norms operative in the social contexts in which writing is used often dictate that the grammatical structure of written text be less casual than the grammatical structure of spoken discourse. Second, the different psychopragmatic constraints imposed upon the realization of written and spoken text determine to some degree the relative frequencies of occurrence of certain grammatical forms and structures in the two modalities. Third, to the extent that the opportunity for the acquisition and use of literacy skills is disproportionately allocated across the various segments of a speech community for any significant period, the grammatical features of written or literate text may come to signal membership in those typically more privileged social groups within the community which have access to the occasions on which written or literate text is appropriate. Finally, writing as a medium acts as a fixative agent for linguistic structure. Except for memorized oral text transmitted intact from generation to generation, the structure of oral language is in general much more subject to diachronic change, due to phonetic erosion, than is the structure of written language. To the extent that written language in general, or a particular genre of written language, is not directly influenced by developments in the structure of oral language, then the potential arises for major discrepancies between the two. In sum, writing, "by opening up new stylistic possibilities and by freezing a given linguistic state, . . . leads to potential diglossia in every speech community that becomes literate" (Coulmas 1987:114).

    The development of writing in and of itself, however, is not a sufficient condition for the emergence of diglossia and may not even be a necessary one. As Ferguson himself (1959:337, n. 18) has pointed out, although all clearly documented instances of diglossia occur in literate societies, "it seems at least possible that a somewhat similar situation could exist in a non-literate community where a body of oral literature could play the same role as the body of written literature in the examples cited." In more recent times, the point has frequently been made that ritual or artful genres of expression in oral traditions differ in linguistic form and social function from everyday talk in much the same way as written and other noncasual types of discourse differ from colloquial speech in literate cultures (Akinnaso 1982:8, Chafe 1982:49–50, Feldman 1991:47–48). More than the development of writing as such, it seems that the fundamental prerequisite for the emergence of diglossia is the existence of a body of literature in the sense of "that body of discourses or texts which, within any society, is considered worthy of dissemination, transmission, and preservation in essentially constant form" (Bright 1982:272; cf. also Martin Joos, cited in Voegelin 1960:60, n. 4). The oral literature of ancient India offers a remarkable case in point. The need to preserve the religious effectiveness of the orally composed Vedic hymns by transmission in their exact original form and the desire to preserve the special status and distinctness of the language of the educated classes culminated in the Sanskrit grammar of Panini (c. 500 B.C.), itself in all likelihood an oral composition also (Bright 1982:273, Hock and Pandharipande 1978:21–22).

Beyond the existence of a highly valued body of literature, in Bright's sense of the term, the emergence of classical diglossia appears to be contingent upon a long-term monopoly of a small elite on literacy or, in the absence of literacy, on specialized and highly valued knowledge in the speech community (cf. Coulmas 1989:13, and Ferguson 1959:338). Thus, for example, the differences between classical and colloquial style in written Chinese appear to have arisen as a result of the lengthy accumulation of literary tradition among the literati, the early fixation of the form of writing by the printing press in China, and extremely low literacy rates in the general population (De Francis 1972:8). Similarly, the maintenance of Latin as a prestige language vis-à-vis the emergent Romance vernaculars has been attributed to a "virtual monopoly of knowledge" acquired by the church as a result of the emphasis on clerical literacy, monastic control over manuscript production and reproduction, and the decline in lay literacy between the fourth and the tenth centuries (Parker 1983:336–37). On the other hand, the spread of general literacy as a result of the transition from mercantilism to an industrial society in England has been invoked to account for the absence of any diglossialike register ranges in English (Ure 1982:17).

Just as classical diglossic register repertoires appear often to be sustained by the sharp social stratification of education, and of literacy in particular, their dissolution seems frequently to be preceded by the emergence of "a new class structure which gives increased power to groups previously at the margins of, or below the range of, elite society" (Kahane and Kahane 1979:190; cf. also Sotiropoulos 1982:5, 19), and by the democratization of education and literacy (Kahane and Kahane 1979:191). In the words which Kahane (1986:498) uses to describe the decline of Western prestige languages generally: "The prestige comes in with status and elitism; it goes out under the pressures of popular developments and movements which we may call nativist rebellions." As described by Ferguson (1959:338), the three principal popular developments, all attributes of modernizing societies, which presage the disintegration of a diglossic code matrix are: (1) the spread of literacy beyond the privileged classes, (2) the broadening of communication among different regional and social segments of the community, and (3) the emerging desire for a full-fledged standard national language as an attribute of autonomy or sovereignty.

Examples which support Ferguson's and Kahane and Kahane's analyses are not hard to come by. In the case of Hebrew, it was "the success of the popular-based Maccabaean revolution against radical Hellenism and Jewish aristocratic Hellenizers (after 167 B.C.E.)" and of "the lower- and middle-class based Pharisee (early Rabbinic) movement" that permitted the vernacular variety to make significant inroads against the Biblical variety in Jewish religious literature (Fellman 1977:108). In Europe, the decline in the importance of the clerical orders in secular administration contributed significantly to the weakening of the church's monopoly of knowledge by the fourteenth century and probably reduced barriers to the subsequent introduction of the Romance vernaculars into certain spheres of official language use (Parker 1983:339), just as the growth in urban commercial activity created a new demand for literate individuals to meet growing needs in administration, law, and business (Parker 1983:338). In Japan, the collapse of the shogunate in the 1860s; the subsequent opening of the Japanese ports, which exposed the Japanese people to the influences of Western culture and scientific and technological modernization; and the growing internal pressures for democratic reform may all be seen as having contributed to the rise of a colloquial style of Japanese writing during the Meiji era (Coulmas 1991:134, 139). Likewise, the eventual vernacularization of the Chinese literary language was made possible by its association with the cause of Chinese nationalism, by the replacement of the traditional scholar-bureaucracy of the Qing dynasty with a republican form of government, and, ultimately, by the advent of public education and the abolition of the Confucian civil service examination system in the early 1900s (De Francis 1972:11, Barnes 1982:261–62). In many formerly diglossic Arabic-speaking communities, too, the democratization of education and the growth in the cross-communal exchange of people, goods, messages, and ideas have brought about the modernization of the code matrix (Ibrahim and Jernudd 1986:6; see also Abdulaziz 1986:13–14, Mahmoud 1986:245). Finally, the emergence of a new educated middle class in Greece toward the end of the nineteenth century and, much more recently, the ouster of the military junta in 1974 and its replacement with a civilian democratic government, provided the necessary impetus for the rise of demotic Greek and the eventual disestablishment of *katharevousa* (Kahane and Kahane 1979:190; cf. also Alexiou 1982:159–60, 184–88, Browning 1982:53–57).

The manner in which social developments such as those just discussed influence the linguistic character of a diglossic code matrix is of special relevance here, and three claims, in particular, are likely to withstand the test of closer scrutiny. First, the linguistic distance between the elevated and vernacular registers, or register ranges, is diminished; second, the elevated register survives vestigially in the form of a superstrate influence on the lexicon of the newly emerging standard; and, third, the pragmatics of discourse become more salient, and the requirements of communicative decorum less so, as determinants of linguistic form.

With regard to the first claim, Gumperz (1968:469) has argued that the urbanization of intermediate societies and their mobilization and absorption into national social networks result in structural convergence between the subcodes in their speech repertoires, in some cases reducing the discrepancy between standard and local dialects virtually to the point of extinction. Structural variation between elevated and vernacular codes tends to be restricted to the syntactic, lexical, and phonological levels, and it is rare to find such register differences revealed, for example, in separate sets of inflectional morphemes or function words, as is sometimes the case in intermediate societies (Gumperz 1968:470). Moreover, what formerly may have been categorical differences between high and low varieties may now manifest themselves only as subtle shifts in the statistical frequencies of occurrence of particular linguistic alternants. In Gumperz' (1968:470) own terms: "It almost seems that shallow linguistic contrast in styles is a direct correlate of the fluidity of roles symbolized by the distinction between caste and class."

As to the second claim, Kahane and Kahane (1979:194) have shown that, in the history of Western prestige languages at least, the high-status variety survives the decline of diglossia by means of "a large-scale transfer of terminology characteristic of the culture behind H," most notably in the domains of upper-class civilization, abstractions, and professional technologies. This clearly is how Sotiropoulos (1982:19) assesses the aftermath of Greek diglossia, noting that while "the phonological, morphological, and syntactic structures of the new language prevail" in the end, the one element of the H variety that survives in the new standard is "the lexicon, especially words for abstract notions and professional and scientific terminologies."

Finally, concerning the third claim, Gumperz (1968:470) noted early on that such variation as remains between the subcodes of the code repertoire in highly urbanized societies is explained to a greater degree than previously "by special requirements for technical terminology," signaling, it seems likely, a transition from speech repertoires in which register choice is dictated by the demands of communicative decorum to repertoires in which the dictates of communicative efficacy prevail. The point as it applies to the transition from diglossic to postdiglossic speech repertoires has been stated explicitly by Neustupný (1974:40), who claims that "most of the variation between a Classical and a Modern standard in the case of a premodern diglossia is nonfunctional [i.e., not determined by the pragmatics of the discourse context]" and that it is not, therefore, a matter of chance "that the diglossia, a typical case of non-functional variation, is most often removed at an early stage of modernization." Furthermore, "the number of functional varieties sharply increases with modern development of a language, while the amount of nonfunctional variation . . . gradually decreases."

Recent research on register differentiation in Nukulaelae Tuvaluan (Besnier 1988) and English (Biber 1988) tends to corroborate the distinction drawn earlier in this chapter between sociocultural and psychopragmatic determinants of linguistic variation and provides at least tentative support for the suggestion that the role of psychopragmatic constraints in determining linguistic choice is more salient in socially and technologically advanced societies (in this volume, see also the chapters by Kim and Biber on Korean and by Biber and Hared on Somali.) Setting the details aside, grammatical form in English appears to be determined primarily by the situational potential for interaction between the interlocutors; by the real-time opportunities available for planning, editing, and processing discourse; and by the nature and function of the communicative exchange (involved versus informational production, explicit versus situation-dependent reference, narrative versus nonnarrative; see Biber 1988, chapters 6–7). In Nukulaelae Tuvaluan, on the other hand, grammatical form seems to be determined to a greater extent than in English by the social significance of the communicative event (Besnier 1988:731).

Although it is surely the case that both sociocultural and psychopragmatic determinants of linguistic form operate in every communicative event and in every speech community, it is also highly probable that sociocultural considerations take precedence in some speech communities and in some communicative events, while psychopragmatic considerations take precedence in others. Although undoubtedly an oversimplification, it is tempting to view grammatical variation in English as being organized predominantly according to a principle of communicative efficacy and that in Nukulaelae Tuvaluan according to a principle of communicative decorum. The distinction between these two types of speech community may be correlated with complexity of sociocultural organization and with econotechnical development.

The relevance of this discussion to diglossia lies in the proposition that speech repertoires such as those on Nukulaelae may be considered prediglossic repertoires in the sense that they could eventually evolve into diglossic repertoires given the presence of additional precipitating factors such as those listed by Ferguson (1959) and by Coulmas (1987, 1989), discussed previously. These factors do not appear to be present in the case of Nukulaelae Tuvaluan, and so neither a diagnosis nor a prognosis of diglossia is indicated. On the other hand, the varied speech repertoires of contemporary British English speakers may be considered postdiglossic repertoires in the sense that diglossic repertoires, once they begin to disintegrate under the pressure of various kinds of social change, dissolve into repertoires of this type, although not all such repertoires, English itself being a case in point, necessarily have evolved from a diglossic state.

References

Abdulaziz, M. 1986. "Factors in the Development of Modern Arabic Usage." *International Journal of the Sociology of Language* 62:11–24.

Alexiou, M. 1982. "Diglossia in Greece." In W. Haas, ed., *Standard Languages: Spoken and Written*. Manchester: Manchester University Press. Pp. 156–92.

Akinnaso, F. Niyi 1982. "The Literate Writes and the Nonliterate Chants: Written Language and Ritual Communication in Sociolinguistic Perspective." In William Frawley, ed., *Linguistics and Literacy*. New York: Plenum. Pp. 7–36.

Barnes, D. 1982. "Nationalism and the Mandarin Movement: The First Half-Century." In Robert Cooper, ed., *Language Spread: Studies in Diffusion and Social Change*. Bloomington: Indiana University Press & Washington, DC: Center for Applied Linguistics. Pp. 260–90.

Bartsch, Renate 1989. "A Normtheoretical Approach to Functional and Status Types of

Language." In U. Ammon, ed., *Status and Function of Languages and Language Varieties*. Berlin: Walter de Gruyter. Pp. 197–215.

Bernstein, Basil. 1964. "Elaborated and Restricted Codes: Their Social Origins and Some Consequences." In John Gumperz and Dell Hymes, eds., *The Ethnography of Communication. American Anthropologist* 66(No. 6, Part 2):55–69.

Besnier, Niko. 1988. "The Linguistic Relationships of Spoken and Written Nukulaelae Registers." *Language* 64:707–36.

Biber, Douglas. 1988. *Variation Across Speech and Writing*. Cambridge: Cambridge University Press.

Bright, William. 1982. "Literature: Written and Oral." In Deborah Tannen, ed., *Analyzing Discourse: Text and Talk*. (Georgetown University Round Table on Languages and Linguistics 1981). Washington, DC: Georgetown University Press. Pp. 271–83.

Britto, Francis. 1986. *Diglossia: A Study of the Theory with Application to Tamil*. Washington, DC: Georgetown University Press.

Browning, R. 1982. "Greek Diglossia Yesterday and Today." *International Journal of the Sociology of Language* 35:49–68.

Chafe, Wallace. 1982. "Integration and Involvement in Speaking, Writing, and Oral Literature." In Deborah Tannen, ed., *Spoken and Written Language: Exploring Orality and Literacy*. Norwood, NJ: Ablex. Pp. 35–53.

Coulmas, Florian. 1987. "What Writing Can Do to Language: Some Preliminary Remarks." In S. Battestini, ed., *Developments in Linguistics and Semiotics, Language Teaching and Learning, Communication Across Cultures*. (Georgetown University Round Table on Languages and Linguistics, 1986). Washington, DC: Georgetown University Press. Pp. 107–29.

———. 1989. "Language Adaptation." In Florian Coulmas, ed., *Language Adaptation*. Cambridge: Cambridge University Press. Pp. 1–25.

———. 1991. "Does the Notion of Diglossia Apply to Japanese? Some Thoughts and Some Documentation." In Alan Hudson, ed., *Studies in Diglossia. Southwest Journal of Linguistics* 10:125–42.

De Francis, John. 1972. *Nationalism and Language Reform in China*. New York: Octagon Books.

Ervin-Tripp, Susan. 1964. "An Analysis of the Interaction of Language, Topic, and Listener." In John Gumperz and Dell Hymes, eds., *The Ethnography of Communication. American Anthropologist* 66(No. 6, Part 2):86–102.

———. 1971. "Sociolinguistics." In Joshua Fishman, ed., *Advances in the Sociology of Language*. Vol. 1. The Hague: Mouton. Pp. 15–91.

———. 1972. "On Sociolinguistic Rules: Alternation and Co-occurrence." In John Gumperz and Dell Hymes, eds., *Directions in Sociolinguistics: The Ethnography of Communication*. New York: Holt, Rinehart & Winston. Pp. 213–50.

Fasold, Ralph. 1990. *The Sociolinguistics of Language*. Oxford: Basil Blackwell.

Feldman, C. 1991. "Oral Metalanguage." In David Olson and Nancy Torrance, eds., *Literacy and Orality*. Cambridge: Cambridge University Press. Pp. 47–65.

Fellman, Jack. 1977. "Diglossia: The Hebrew Case." *La Monda Lingvo-Problemo* 6:107–11.

Ferguson, Charles. 1959. "Diglossia." *Word* 15:325–40.

Givón, Talmy. 1979. "From Discourse to Syntax: Grammar as a Processing Strategy." In Talmy Givón, ed., *Syntax and Semantics 12. Discourse and Syntax*. New York: Academic Press. Pp. 81–112.

———. 1991. "Markedness in Grammar: Distributional, Communicative and Cognitive Correlates of Syntactic Structure." *Studies in Language* 15:335–70.

Gumperz, John. 1964. "Linguistic and Social Interaction in Two Communities." In John Gumperz and Dell Hymes, eds., *The Ethnography of Communication. American Anthropologist* 66(No. 6, Part 2):137–53.

———. 1968. "Types of Linguistic Communities." In Joshua Fishman, ed., *Readings in the Sociology of Language*. The Hague: Mouton. Pp. 460–72.

Hock, H., and R. Pandharipande. 1978. "Sanskrit in the Pre-Islamic Sociolinguistic Context of South Asia." *International Journal of the Sociology of Language* 16:11–25.

Ibrahim, Muhammed H., and Björn H. Jernudd. 1986. "Introduction." In *Aspects of Arabic Sociolinguistics. International Journal of the Sociology of Language* 61:5–6.

Irvine, Judith T. 1984. "Formality and Informality in Communicative Events." In J. Baugh & J. Sherzer, eds., *Language in Use: Readings in Sociolinguistics*. Englewood Cliffs, NJ: Prentice-Hall. Pp. 211–28.

Kahane, Henry. 1986. "A Typology of the Prestige Language." *Language* 62:495–508.

Kahane, Henry, and Renée Kahane. 1979. "Decline and Survival of Western Prestige Languages." *Language* 55:183–98.

Kay, Paul. 1977. "Language Evolution and Speech Style." In B. Blount and M. Sanches, eds., *Sociocultural Dimensions of Language Change*. New York: Academic Press. Pp. 21–33.

Labov, William. 1972. *Sociolinguistic Patterns*. Philadelphia: University of Pennsylvania Press.

Li, Charles, and Sandra Thompson. 1982. "The Gulf Between Spoken and Written Language: A Case Study in Chinese." In Deborah Tannen, ed., *Spoken and Written Language: Exploring Orality and Literacy*. Norwood, NJ: Ablex. Pp. 77–88.

Mahmoud, Y. 1986. "Arabic After Diglossia." In Joshua Fishman, Andrée Tabouret-Keller, Michael Clyne, B. Krishnamurti, and M. Abdulaziz, eds., *The Fergusonian Impact: In Honor of Charles A. Ferguson on the Occasion of His 65th Birthday*. Vol. 1. Berlin: Mouton de Gruyter. Pp. 239–51.

Neustupný, J. 1974. "The Modernization of the Japanese System of Communication." *Language in Society* 3:33–50.

Ochs, Elinor. 1979. "Planned and Unplanned Discourse." In Talmy Givón, ed., *Syntax and Semantics 12. Discourse and Syntax*. New York: Academic Press. Pp. 51–80.

Parker, Ian. 1983. "The Rise of the Vernaculars in Early Modern Europe: An Essay in the Political Economy of Language." In Bruce Bain, ed., *The Sociogenesis of Language and Human Conduct*. New York: Plenum. Pp. 323–51.

Pawley, Andrew, and Frances Syder. 1983. "Natural Selection in Syntax: Notes on Adaptive Variation and Change in Vernacular and Literary Grammar." *Journal of Pragmatics* 7:551–79.

Sotiropoulos, Dimitrios. 1982. "The Social Roots of Modern Greek Diglossia." *Language Problems and Language Planning* 6:1–28.

Tannen, Deborah. 1982. "The Oral/Literate Continuum in Discourse." In Deborah Tannen, ed., *Spoken and Written Language: Exploring Orality and Literacy*. Norwood, NJ: Ablex. Pp. 1–16.

Ure, Jean. 1982. "Introduction: Approaches to the Study of Register Range." *International Journal of the Sociology of Language* 35:5–23.

Voegelin, Carl F. 1960. "Casual and Noncasual Utterances Within Unified Structure." In T. Sebeok, ed., *Style in Language*. Cambridge, MA: MIT Press. Pp. 57–68.

13

Register and Social Dialect Variation: An Integrated Approach

Edward Finegan and Douglas Biber

1. Introduction

Although certain patterns of linguistic variation have been found repeatedly in sociolinguistic studies across a range of speech communities, the systematic nature of those patterns is still perplexing and controversial. Despite a few attempts to explain particular aspects of these patterns, no theory to date has adequately integrated them.

In this chapter we describe certain systematic patterns of register variation and social dialect variation, arguing that situational variation underlies social dialect variation for a substantial set of linguistic features. The argument relies on two claims: (1) that the distributional patterns of these features across situations can be motivated functionally and (2) that such features function in comparable ways for all members of a speech community. We present evidence that these patterns of variation across situations are a consequence of the communicative functions served by the features, and that the systematic patterns of variation found across social dialects, along with the parallelism between social dialect and register variation, derive from the functional patterns of register variation and the fact that social groups have differential access to the range of communicative tasks.

This paper has been through several cycles of revision and rewriting; we distributed earlier versions under the titles "Towards an Integrated Theory of Social Dialect and Register Variation" and "Parallel Patterns in Social Dialect and Register Variation: Towards an Integrated Theory." We have received comments on earlier versions from Jenny Cheshire, Nancy Dorian, Sandro Duranti, Charles Ferguson, Nelson Francis, James Gee, Alan Hudson, Dell Hymes, Paul Kay, Anthony Kroch, James and Lesley Milroy, Elinor Ochs, Dennis Preston, John Rickford, Suzanne Romaine, Carol Myers Scotton, Peter Trudgill, Keith Walters, Malcah Yaeger-Dror, and an anonymous reviewer. Probably none of these colleagues would concur in all our interpretations, and several disagree fundamentally with the general thrust of our argument. We are much indebted to them for their thoughtful responses and candid reactions.

We use *register* and *register variation* as cover terms for the full range of language varieties associated with differences in communicative situation (including mode and purpose). Many sociolinguists use the related term *style* to describe the distribution of variable features across different situations of use, as in the studies of Labov in New York City and Trudgill in Norwich. In this context, variation in style has been viewed as relating to the single parameter of formality, defined as the attention paid to speech (cf. Labov 1972, Trudgill 1974), although few now accept that view (cf. Bell 1984, Cheshire 1982, Milroy 1980, Rickford this volume, Traugott and Romaine 1985). In fact, numerous components of speech situations have been identified, each thought to have a potential influence on linguistic form (cf. Hymes 1974, Brown and Fraser 1979, Biber this volume). We thus view register variation as multidimensional, influenced by many factors other than conscious manipulation and attention paid to speech.

1.1. The Sociolinguistic Study of Variation

The quantitative sociolinguistics of the last three decades has discerned three principal kinds of variation in linguistic form: variation associated with constraints in the linguistic environment, variation associated with the social or demographic characteristics of speakers, and variation associated with situations of use. Variation associated with linguistic constraints is exemplified in English by word-final consonant deletion, which occurs more frequently when the consonant does not represent a grammatical morpheme than when it does, as in monomorphemic *list* /lɪst/ versus bimorphemic *kissed* /kɪs+t/. Exemplifying variation associated with social characteristics is the alternation between [ð] and [d] in the English of New York City, where [ð] pronunciations in words like *this* and *there* are more frequent among speakers of higher social status than among those of lower social status (Labov 1972). This same example illustrates variation associated with situations of use: among all Labov's social groups in New York City, frequency of [ð] pronunciations in this same class of words increases with increasing formality of situation.

Since the late 1960s considerable effort has been directed to incorporating such facts about phonological variation, particularly those aspects associated with linguistic constraints, into grammars. Aiming to refine the optional rules characteristic of earlier generative-transformational grammar, sociolinguists formulated variable rules (e.g., Labov 1969a, Sankoff and Labov 1979) and argued for their necessity in grammatical theory (Berdan 1975). For a variety of reasons, however, variable rules have not been incorporated into the paradigms of phonological or syntactic theory (cf. Kay 1978, Kay and McDaniel 1979, 1981, Labov 1972, Sankoff and Labov 1979, Romaine 1982, Fasold 1991; see Fasold 1985 for a historical perspective).[1]

The structural and physiological (acoustic and articulatory) factors constraining linguistic variation will need to be accounted for in theories of grammar and performance, but social dialect and register variation, which are intertwined in a peculiarly sociolinguistic way, must be accounted for by sociolinguistic theories. In particular, an adequate theory of sociolinguistic variation must address the systematic relationship between register variation and social dialect variation.[2]

Sociolinguists have been inclined to assume that the distribution of linguistic features socially and situationally is arbitrary or conventional (Hudson 1980:191, Chambers and Trudgill 1980:73, Petyt 1980:144–45). In contrast, we present evidence here that much register variation reflects the differential communicative constraints and purposes of social situations, and we suggest that the distribution of certain linguistic features across social groups reflects differential opportunities for involvement in particular kinds of speech activities among those groups. It is this differential involvement in the range of situations of use that undergirds the distribution of these variable linguistic features across social groups.

1.2. Descriptive Adequacy in an Integrated Theory

The systematic patterns of register variation and social dialect variation, as well as the parallelism between them, have not gone unnoticed. In particular, with respect to many linguistic features, four patterns are so familiar that they need to be accounted for in any theory of sociolinguistic variation:

A. The same linguistic features serve as markers of both social group and social situation.

B. In these cases, the distribution across social dialects and registers (or "styles") is parallel, with the variants that are more frequent in less formal situations also being more frequent among lower-ranked social groups, and variants that are more frequent in more formal situations being more frequent among higher-ranked groups.

C. For many of these features, the distribution across situations is itself systematic, with more formal, more "literate" situations typically exhibiting a more frequent use of explicit and elaborated variants, and less formal, more "oral" situations exhibiting a more frequent use of economy variants.

D. The distribution of these features across social dialects within a community is systematic, with higher-ranked social groups exhibiting more frequent use of the elaborated and explicit variants and lower-ranked groups exhibiting more frequent use of the economy variants.

Observations A and B are sociolinguistic commonplaces. Indeed, it is this pair of observations that underlies the joint representation of social group variation and stylistic variation in the line graphs familiar since Labov's New York City work (Labov 1966a, 1972). As Labov (1969b:22–23) himself captured the contents of observations A and B:

> It is remarkable that . . . the same variables which are used in style shifting also distinguish cultural or social levels of English. This is so for stable phonological variables such as *th-* and *-ing;* for such incoming prestige forms as *-r;* for the grammatical variables such as pronominal apposition, double negative, or even the use of *ain't.* If we plot the average values of these phonological variables for *both* style and social levels, we find such regular patterns as [Figure 13.1] . . . each group . . . shows regular style shifting in the same direction; al-

though these social groups are very different in one sense, they are all very similar in another sense: they all *use* the variable in the same way. . . . Thus we see that the same linguistic features are used to register style shifting and social stratification—functional varieties *and* cultural levels.

He further noted, "This situation is not unique to English. It is generally the case, even in the languages of Southeast Asia which have extremely complex systems for registering respect." Labov (1969b:23–24) viewed such patterns as "logical" because, as he claimed, "each group models its formal style on the speech behavior of those groups one or two steps above it in the social scale."

Romaine (1980b:228) describes the pattern represented by observations A and B as:

the classic sociolinguistic finding that socially diagnostic variables will exhibit parallel behavior on a stylistic continuum . . . if a feature is found to be more common in the lower classes than in the upper classes, it will also be more common in the less formal than the most formal styles, with each social group occupying a similar position in each continuum.

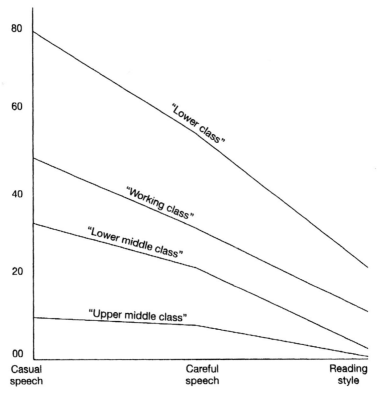

FIGURE 13.1 Class and style stratification of (ing) in *working, living,* etc., for white New York City adults (Labov 1969b:24).

Less often noted by sociolinguists are observations C and D, although functional linguists frequently note C. Individually, the patterns described in C and D have been recognized, but the overall systematic association of more frequent explicit and elaborated forms with higher-ranked social groups has been downplayed, probably as a consequence of the unacceptable implications many have seen in the work of Basil Bernstein when he analyzed similar patterns. It is perhaps antipathy for Bernstein's work that has led some sociolinguists to reject the validity of observation D, at least implicitly.[3]

To date, two major theories have been proposed to account for aspects of these four observations. Kroch (1978) provides a motivated explanation for the systematic patterns across social dialects (observation D), although he does not address the systematic patterns across registers (observation C) and, hence, does not account for the parallel patterns across registers and dialects (observations A and B). Bell (1984) offers a detailed explanation for the parallel patterns of variation across registers and dialects (observations A and B) but does not address the systematic nature of the distribution across registers (observation C) or across dialects (observation D). We return to a discussion of these theories in section 4.

First, in what follows, we propose a view of sociolinguistic variation that addresses the systematic patterns of variation across situations of use (observation C) and the systematic patterns of variation across social groups (observation D); we also address the parallel patterns across these two types of variation (observations A and B). In our view, register variation exhibits its systematic patterns because the distribution of many linguistic features across situations of use is functionally motivated. Social dialect variation in turn exhibits systematic patterns for the same linguistic features because speakers and writers from different social groups have differential access to, and characteristic involvement in, the potential range of spoken and written registers. Thus, in our view, the functional patterns motivating register variation also underlie social dialect variation for these features.

The remainder of this chapter is organized as follows: In section 2 we describe the systematic patterns of register variation and the functional motivations that underlie and constrain them. In section 3 we describe the systematic nature of certain patterns of social dialect variation and their striking similarity across speech communities. In section 4 we examine the competing theories of Kroch and Bell. In section 5 we propose an integrated account to help explain the parallelism between the patterns of social dialect and register variation. Section 6 summarizes and concludes.

2. Patterns of Register Variation

For strategic reasons, grammar and lexis have played second fiddle to phonology in the study of social dialect variation.[4] For quite different reasons, register variation has had the same relation to social dialect variation in sociolinguistics generally (see Biber and Finegan this volume, Cazden 1970, Ferguson this volume, Rickford this volume). It is not that register studies have been neglected; indeed, there have been quite a few studies of registers such as baby talk (Ferguson 1977), sports announcer talk (Ferguson 1983), note taking (Janda 1985), legalese (Crystal and Davy 1969), testament language (Finegan 1982), and numerous others (see Atkinson and Biber this volume). Functional studies describing the use of particular grammatical structures and lexical features across registers are also abundant (see Appendix II in Biber 1988 for references). But despite the precedent of Ferguson's (1959) analysis of diglossia, studies that attempt to address the systematic nature of variation across registers are few, and attempts to integrate situational variation into sociolinguistic theory are scarcer still, despite calls for integrated views by Gumperz (1964), Hymes (1973, 1974), Brown and Fraser (1979), and others (cf. Hudson this volume).

The few attempts to provide a systematic approach to register variation have arisen principally from pidgin and creole studies or studies addressing the characteristics of speech and writing. Mühlhäusler (1986) and Romaine (1988) are recent discussions of pidgins and creoles with useful bibliographies. Chafe and Tannen (1988) provide a thorough review of the literature on variation across spoken and written registers. Biber (1988) shows that many of the conflicting findings on the systematic nature of spoken and written varieties stem from confounding independent dimensions of situational and linguistic variation, and he describes the complexity of the task of identifying the dimensions of variation.

In our analysis here we focus on features of economy and of elaboration, and we regard such features as representing degrees of implicit and explicit communication, respectively. Many variables and optional expressions can be regarded as more or less elaborated (alternatively, more or less compressed or economical). For example, the loss of phonological segments in *that's* (for *that is* or *that has*) produces a compressed variant. Likewise omission of the marker *that* from a relative or complement clause produces a more economical or compressed variant than the same utterance with the marker expressed. The presence of a prepositional phrase, on the other hand, yields a more elaborated noun (or verb) phrase than its absence. This much we think straightforward enough.

We further consider such linguistic economy to be indicative of a greater degree of implicit meaning, with a greater reliance on contextual channels rather than lexicon and syntax. While we make no assumption regarding the actual clarity of the ultimate communication, we simply observe that, in general, compressed expression leaves more meaning implicit than elaborated expression does. As Sinclair (1988:130) puts it, "Compression, by losing distinctions, can give rise to ambiguity. . . . "

From a communicative perspective, use of economy and elaboration features can be related to Grice's maxim to be as brief as possible but as elaborate as necessary. In production terms, Slobin (1979) identifies two competing charges to language that reflect the same concerns: "Be quick and easy" and "Be clear." Finegan (1987) discusses how these two competing forces are associated with opposed ideals of human communication. One ideal would utilize maximal expression in order to achieve a one-to-one correspondence between linguistic expression and semantic content, allowing for no ambiguity. The competing ideal would utilize only minimal expression, with all content represented by the same simple utterance (presumably "uh"). Neither ideal can be attained, of course. The centrifugal ideal fostering elaborated linguistic expression could not be mastered within a lifetime and would require exceedingly explicit (and therefore lengthy) expression for communicating even simple content. The centripetal ideal of extreme linguistic economy would require no time to master and little time to utilize, but its successful decoding, premised on telepathy, would lie beyond human ability—a fact to which all child language acquisition gives eloquent testimony! Between these extremes of unique expression and infinitely ambiguous expression fall all registers (or "styles") of all languages. As Hymes (1973:73) has observed in a sociolinguistic framework, "The cost, as between expressing things easily and concisely, and expressing them with difficulty and at great length, is a real cost, commonly operative, and a constraint on the theoretical potentiality of language in daily life." (Givón 1979 addresses many of these same questions, drawing a contrast between syntactic and pragmatic modes of communication; see also Hudson this volume.)

These competing production mandates interact in important ways with a number of situational characteristics so that the resulting level of linguistic elaboration fits the demands of the communicative situation. For example, to the extent that interlocutors share a communicative context and background information, less elaboration and explicitness of expression will be necessary, and more economy and compression will be tolerable. Biber (1988) discusses the interaction between these production mandates and various situational parameters (e.g., involved versus informational purpose, opportunity for careful production of text) and shows that linguistic features of economy and elaboration function in complementary ways to define continuous parameters of variation associated with situational differences.[5]

Combining the socio-psycholinguistic perspective represented in the work of Slobin with the functional view of register variation represented in that of Biber, we claim that, because of their differing communicative demands, different registers have a functional preference for the clarity mandate or for the ease mandate. In other words, some situations require more explicitness; others tolerate greater economy. For example, conversational situations favor the ease mandate to the extent that interlocutors can rely on shared physical environment and shared background to provide information lacking in the text, whereas situations surrounding writers of academic prose promote the clarity mandate because the degree of shared personal information is relatively little (despite comparable training and general knowledge) and there is no shared physical environment. Naturally, there are situations where the functional forces are in competition—for example, the situation surrounding a person giving a public speech tugs in both directions, with shared physical environment but relatively little shared background information.

We focus here on three situational parameters: (1) opportunity for careful production, (2) purpose of communication, and (3) degree of shared context. These parameters interact in important ways with the production mandates for ease and for clarity, resulting in marked differences in the use of linguistic features representing economy and elaboration.

It would be possible to illustrate these linguistic differences by reference to underlying dimensions of variation, representing basic patterns of linguistic co-occurrence and alternation. To simplify our argument, however, we focus here on seven individual features of economy and elaboration, which are all defining fea-

322 Registers, Social Dialects, and Sociolinguistic Theory

tures of the single most important dimension of variation identified by Biber (1988) and labeled "Involved versus Informational Production."

We present the distributions of four linguistic features representing economy: contractions, *that*-deletions in verb complement clauses, the referential pronoun *it*, and the pro-verb *do*. Contractions (e.g., *can't, it's, they're, I'll*) represent phonological economy. These compressed forms are less explicit than fuller expressions; for example, in speech [ɪts] can represent possessive *its*, or *it is*, or *it has*. *That*-deletion ("She said ∅ he went") represents one measure of syntactic economy and compression. *Do* and *it* represent lexical economy in that they are pro-forms substituting for fuller, semantically more expicit verb phrases and noun phrases.

We analyze three features that function to increase elaboration and explicitness (serving the clarity mandate): prepositional phrases, attributive adjectives, and lexical diversity. Prepositional phrases serve a number of functions that create a more explicit or elaborated nominal or clausal form. Prepositional phrases as postnominal modifiers can be restrictive, specifying the referent of the head noun, or nonrestrictive, adding elaborating information. Prepositional phrases can also modify verbs, specifying additional semantic roles (a function that can also be served by case marking in inflected languages). Attributive adjectives also serve to specify or elaborate the referentiality of noun phrases. Finally, as a measure of lexical diversity, type/token ratio measures the number of distinct lexical items used in a text and thus indexes lexical explicitness.

These features illustrate the complementary relationship between the production mandates: elaboration features, such as prepositional phrases, attributive adjectives, and lexical diversity represent greater clarity, but they also require more effort at production; economy features such as contractions, *that*-deletions, pronoun *it*, and pro-verb *do* represent greater ease but lesser clarity and explicitness. The following sections show that the actual distributions of these features across registers reflect these functional differences.

The frequency counts in the following sections represent the number of occurrences of a feature per one thousand words of text, averaged over the texts in each register. Most texts are taken from the London-Lund corpus of *spoken* English (see Svartvik and Quirk 1980) and the Lancaster-Oslo/Bergen corpus of *written* English (see Johansson, Leech, and Goodluck 1978), and the counts themselves are taken from Biber (1988), who describes the particular corpus used for this study and the algorithms for the feature counts. Seven registers are considered here: four written registers (personal letters, general fiction, press reportage, and academic prose) and three spoken ones (conversation, interviews, and public speeches).[6]

2.1. Opportunity for Careful Production

Academic prose and prepared public speeches are registers that differ primarily with respect to the opportunity for careful production. Both are informational in purpose and addressed to large, noninteractive audiences, but because academic prose is written it can be extensively planned and revised, while the speeches represented in our corpus are produced on-line (although often planned). Given this difference, writers of academic prose have greater opportunity to honor the clarity mandate by

TABLE 13.1   Influence of *Production Circumstances*
on the Distribution of Features in Two Registers

A. Economy Features

	Contractions	That *Deletions*	Pro-verb do	Pronoun it
Public speeches	13.3	1.9	2.4	8.9
Academic prose	0.1	0.4	0.7	5.9

B. Elaboration Features

	Attributive Adjectives	*Prepositional Phrases*	*Type/Token Ratio*
Public speeches	48.9	112.6	49.0
Academic prose	76.9	139.5	50.6

being explicit and elaborated, while speech makers are more likely to be influenced by the ease mandate, resulting in a greater use of economy features. Table 13.1 confirms these functional expectations; all four economy features are more frequent in public speeches than in academic prose, while the three elaboration features are more frequent in academic prose than in public speeches.

2.2. Purpose

Next consider purpose, which has a relatively straightforward functional relationship to the production mandates. Because informational purposes are facilitated by greater elaboration and explicitness of form, informational registers favor the clarity mandate. In contrast, because precise, elaborated expression is generally less crucial for interpersonal, affective purposes, speech activities with such purposes permit greater tolerance for the ease mandate. Conversations and public interviews are comparable speech situations that differ primarily in purpose. Both are produced online, and speaker and hearer can interact directly in both. They differ in that conversation is typically affective and involved (participants are concerned with both interpersonal relationships and particular informational messages), while interviews are primarily informational, with less emphasis on the relationship between participants. Table 13.2 shows that this situational difference corresponds to the predicted linguistic differences. Conversations show a consistently greater use of the economy forms; interviews are consistently more explicit and elaborated in form.

2.3. Degree of Shared Context

Finally, there are many ways in which speech situations can differ in the extent of shared context. At one extreme, interlocutors can share the same physical and temporal surroundings, interact freely, and have a close relationship with extensive shared background—as in a face-to-face conversation between intimates. At the other extreme, participants can be separated by time and space, have no direct interaction, and be unknown to one another (thus having little shared personal background)—as in typical expository prose. In general, the ease mandate is facili-

TABLE 13.2   Influence of *Purpose* on Distribution of Features in Two Registers

A. Economy Features

	Contractions	That *Deletions*	Pro-verb do	Pronoun it
Conversations	46.2	9.6	9.0	20.0
Interviews	25.4	4.3	4.6	11.9

B. Elaboration Features

	Attributive Adjectives	Prepositional Phrases	Type/Token Ratio
Conversations	40.8	85.0	46.1
Interviews	55.3	108.0	48.4

tated by greater shared context, whereas clarity is promoted in situations where participants share less context. Greater shared context permits interlocutors to rely on implicit, contextual meaning to supply information left lexically and syntactically unexpressed; in situations where participants share less context, there is greater need for more elaborated and more specific expression.

Interviews and public speeches are similar registers in many respects, but they differ in the extent of shared context. Both are produced on-line and both are informational in purpose. In an interview, speaker and hearer may know one another personally and often have a good deal of shared information about the subject of the interview; they are also in direct contact so that they can interact in the course of the communication and rely on facial expression and gesture. In contrast, public speakers typically do not know the members of their audience and cannot readily interact with them. These differences in the extent of shared communicative context are reflected in linguistic differences, as shown in Table 13.3. Interviews consistently have more frequent occurrences of the four economy features than public speeches. The picture is not so consistent with the elaboration features, where interviews and speeches are about equally elaborated. The explanation lies in the fact that the communicative demands of interviews result in a functional conflict: the on-line production constraints and the shared context of interviews promote the ease mandate, whereas their informational purpose requires elaborated form and specific

TABLE 13.3   Influence of *Shared Context* on Distribution of Features in Two Registers

A. Economy Features

	Contractions	That *Deletions*	Pro-verb do	Pronoun it
Interviews	25.4	4.3	4.6	11.9
Public speeches	13.3	1.9	2.4	8.9

B. Elaboration Features

	Attributive Adjectives	Prepositional Phrases	Type/Token Ratio
Interviews	55.3	108.0	48.4
Public speeches	48.9	112.6	49.0

content. Public speeches illustrate a similar conflict but one in which the balance tips toward clarity: both the informational purpose and the relatively little shared background favor the clarity mandate, while only the constraints of on-line production promote quick and easy expression.

2.4. Overview of Situational Variation

The three situational parameters we have described (opportunity for careful production, purpose, and degree of shared context) are closely intertwined, and they combine to produce different degrees of preference for one or the other mandate. Table 13.4 gives frequencies of the economy and elaboration features for four written and three spoken registers.

Situationally, academic prose most favors the clarity mandate: it provides extensive opportunity for production, has an extreme informational purpose, and is characterized by little shared context (relative to the other registers). At the other extreme, conversation provides little opportunity for careful production, is most involved in its purpose, and is characterized by the highest degree of shared context (shared space and time, extensive interaction between participants, and, typically, significant shared personal background knowledge). The frequencies of particular features reflect these extremes: academic prose consistently shows the fewest economy forms and the most frequent use of forms representing elaboration and explicit-

TABLE 13.4   Overview of Situational Variation

A. Economy Features

	Contractions	That *Deletions*	Pro-verb do	Pronoun it
Written				
Personal letters	22.2	12.8	4.3	11.0
General fiction	11.2	3.0	3.3	11.5
Press reportage	1.8	2.0	1.3	5.8
Academic prose	0.1	0.4	0.7	5.9
Spoken				
Conversations	46.2	9.6	9.0	20.0
Interviews	25.4	4.3	4.6	11.9
Public speeches	13.3	1.9	2.4	8.9

B. Elaboration Features

	Attributive Adjectives	Prepositional Phrases	Type/Token Ratio
Written			
Personal letters	44.2	72.0	52.5
General fiction	50.7	92.8	52.7
Press reportage	64.5	116.6	55.3
Academic prose	76.9	139.5	50.6
Spoken			
Conversations	40.8	85.0	46.1
Interviews	55.3	108.0	48.4
Public speeches	48.9	112.6	49.0

ness;[7] conversation shows the most frequent economy forms and the least frequent elaboration forms.

The situations surrounding the use of the other registers fall between these extremes, and the frequencies of particular features reflect the competing functional forces. For example, the writer of general fiction gradually constructs a shared contextual background with readers and relies on it in advancing the narrative, thus bit by bit promoting the ease mandate. As a result, the shared background is relatively high in fiction compared to academic prose (as reflected in the significantly higher frequencies of economy features in fiction). However, compared to conversation, fiction has relatively little shared background, no interaction, and considerable opportunity for careful production, resulting in lower frequencies for economy features and higher frequencies for elaboration features. Similarly, interviews are intermediate between conversation and public speeches: they allow for more planning than conversations but less than public speeches, and they rely on shared context less than conversations do but more than speeches. Corresponding to this situational cline, the features for both economy and elaboration features in interviews are intermediate between the frequencies for conversations and public speeches. Thus the extent to which the three situational parameters favor one or the other mandate influences the frequencies of the corresponding features.

The literature on variation demonstrates that the distribution of linguistic features across communicative situations cannot be adequately characterized by reference to a single dimension (such as casual/formal; written/spoken; or attention paid to speech); rather, a multidimensional framework is needed (see Hymes 1974, Biber 1988). It is nevertheless convenient to use the shorthand terms *literate* and *oral* to represent a number of independent dimensions of situational and linguistic variation. In these terms, a variety can be called *literate* to the extent that it has the situational and linguistic characteristics associated with stereotypical writing; a variety can be called *oral* to the extent that it has the situational and linguistic characteristics stereotypically associated with speech. Stereotypically literate varieties such as academic prose arise in circumstances characterized by careful production, informational purposes, and relatively little shared context between interlocutors. Stereotypically oral varieties such as conversation arise in situations characterized by on-line production, involved purposes, shared contexts, and extensive interaction. Naturally, most registers fall between these stereotyped extremes. In this section, we have shown how the linguistic variation among more and less "literate" varieties has direct functional correlates associated with particular communicative demands inhering in their situations.

3. Patterns of Social Dialect Variation

In section 2 we illustrated the systematic patterns of variation across seven registers for seven linguistic features, offering functional explanations for those patterns. In this section we turn to the patterns of social dialect variation that have been reported in dozens of studies during the last three decades. Our discussion draws on communities speaking English, French, Spanish, Portuguese, and Flemish.

Whether identified by researchers as members of social-class groups, socio-economic status groups, or other socially or educationally ranked status groups, socially stratified speakers exhibit systematic patterns of linguistic variation. Although manifested in several ways, such systematic patterns are especially transparent with respect to processes of phonological, syntactic, and lexical compression. In this section *phonological economy* refers to alternative forms of the same lexical item, where one variant is formally abbreviated with respect to the other. Examples would include consonant cluster simplification, postvocalic *r*-deletion, and word-initial *h*-elision. As in section 2, *syntactic compression* refers to alternative structures one of which is linguistically less explicit than the other, as in relative pronoun deletion (*The teacher ⊘ I told you about . . .*). Lexical economy is again gauged by type/token ratio.

3.1. Phonological Variation

The most commonly investigated linguistic variables across social groups are phonological variables, and many studies show that phonological economy is more frequent among lower-ranked social groups. As an example, Wolfram's study of the speech of four groups of Detroit residents illustrates some of these patterns. With respect to word-final consonant cluster reduction, Wolfram (1969:60) found greater economy of expression among lower-ranked groups. In Table 13.5 we illustrate this economy with percentages for the absence of a consonant from clusters belonging to a single morpheme. As in all tables in section 3, roman numeral I represents the highest status group in the comparison, II the next to highest group, and so on; higher numerals represent increasingly lower status. Thus in Table 13.5, I represents upper middle-class (UM) speakers, II lower middle-class (LM) speakers, III upper working-class (UW) speakers, and IV lower working-class (LW) speakers. With respect to postvocalic /r/, Wolfram (1969:110) found a similar pattern, with increasingly more deletion among lower-ranked groups, as shown in Table 13.6. Here again the pattern shows that the speech of lower-ranked social groups exhibits greater phonological economy than that of higher ranked groups in the same community. Representing two forms of phonological economy, these findings exemplify more frequent use of phonologically compressed forms among lower-ranked groups than among higher-ranked groups.

Similar patterns of more phonological economy among lower-ranked social groups have been reported for other speech communities. Kemp and Pupier (1976; cited in Kroch 1978; see also Kemp, Pupier, and Yaeger 1980) report increasing percentages of consonant cluster reduction for three socially ranked groups of French speakers in Montreal, as shown in Table 13.7.[8]

TABLE 13.5   Percentage of Word-Final Consonant
Cluster Reduction in Detroit

I (UM)	II (LM)	III (UW)	IV (LW)
51.0	65.9	79.2	84.2

TABLE 13.6   Percentage of /r/-Deletion in Detroit

I (UM)	II (LM)	III (UW)	IV (LW)
20.8	38.8	61.3	71.7

In another study of Montreal French speakers, deletion of /l/ in a variety of linguistic environments is consistently more frequent among laborers than among professionals, as indicated in the data of Table 13.8, from Sankoff and Cedergren (1971:81).

More frequent loss of /l/ in lower status groups is also reported by Poplack and Walker (1986:188) for French speakers in Ottawa-Hull, where "rates of (*l*)-deletion are a function of social class membership . . . in the expected direction: speakers in the lower socio-economic groups delete (*l*) systematically more in all categories than those in the higher ones." Significantly, Poplack and Walker add, "This effect is solidly corroborated by that of schooling . . . the greater the number of years completed, the lesser the probability of deleting (*l*) . . . ."

Studies of Portuguese-speaking communities in Brazil show the same pattern. According to Kroch (1978:26), Gregory Guy and M. L. Braga, in an unpublished paper, found "a pronounced tendency for the plural morpheme to be deleted from non-initial elements of the noun phrase, often leaving only one marker of plurality per phrase. This articulatory simplification . . . was much more pronounced in 'lower class' than in 'middle class' speakers." In Rio de Janeiro, Scherre (1981) found similar patterns of distribution for the same feature: lower-status speakers exhibited less agreement within nominal plurals than higher-status speakers, as shown in Table 13.9.

Spanish, too, shows the same pattern in various communities. In Panama, Cedergren (unpublished paper; cited in Labov 1972; see also Cedergren 1973) found a consistent pattern of increasingly greater phonological economy in progressively lower-social-status groups, as shown in Table 13.10 for four features.

In Argentine Spanish, prepausal /s/ is variably deleted (Terrell 1981:119). Among six ranked occupational groups, the percentage of deletion increases among lower-ranked groups, as shown in Table 13.11.

Returning to other English-speaking communities, the studies carried out by Labov (1966a, 1972) in New York City and Trudgill (1974) in Norwich (England) exhibit similar patterns, as does the study by Petyt of West Yorkshire. Table 13.12 gives the figures for the deletion of postvocalic /r/ (as in *car* and *beard*) in New York City, and Table 13.13 gives the figures for deletion of word-initial /h/ (as in *happy*) in Norwich (with figures for two situations of use) and in West Yorkshire.

TABLE 13.7   Percentage of Consonant Cluster
Reduction in Montreal French

I (Bourgeois)	II (Intermediate)	III (WC)
82.3	91.1	97.7

TABLE 13.8   Percentage of /l/-Deletion
in Montreal French

	I (Professionals)	II (Laborers)
il (impersonal)	89.8	99.6
ils	75.5	100
il (personal)	71.6	100
elle	29.8	82.0
les (pronoun)	19.2	61.5
la (article)	11.3	44.2
la (pronoun)	13.3	37.5
les (article)	9.1	33.1

TABLE 13.9   Percentage of Marked Agreement
in Nominal Plurals in Brazilian Portuguese

I (Higher Status)	II (Lower Status)
80.0	58.8

TABLE 13.10   Social Stratification of Four
Variables* in Panamanian Spanish

	I	II	III	IV
/r/	1.62	1.88	2.29	2.29
PARA	1.11	1.37	1.39	1.69
ESTA	1.26	1.56	1.62	1.71
S	2.03	2.24	2.31	2.36

*/r/ represents devoicing, fricativization, pharyngealization, and de-
letion of syllable-final /r/, with values ranging from 1 to 6 in the
direction of these processes. PARA represents alternation of the
preposition *para* with *pa*, assigned values of 1 and 2, respectively.
ESTA represents alternation of *esta* with *ta*, assigned values of 1 and
2, respectively. S represents the syllable-final alternation of [s], [h],
and [Ø], assigned values of 1, 2, and 3, respectively.

TABLE 13.11   Percentage of Deletion of Prepausal
/s/ in Argentine Spanish

I	II	III	IV	V	VI
14	16	19	41	63	68

TABLE 13.12   Percentage of Postvocalic
/r/-Deletion in Reading Style in New York City*

I	II	III	IV	V	VI
70	74	78	83	85	96

*Estimated from graph, Labov 1966a:240, 1972:114.[9]

In English-speaking communities in North America and Britain, then, the pattern of variation across socially ranked groups is the same as in the French-, Spanish-, and Portuguese-speaking communities we have cited: phonological economy is more frequent among speakers of lower social status. The observation of this pattern is not unique to us, of course; it has been made before, among others by Kroch (1978:25), who noted that each of several studies he examined "shows distinct social variation and in each case the less prestigious social groups use the articulatorily reduced variants more often than does the most prestigious group."[10] We can say that all the cited studies point in the direction of a consistent and widespread pattern wherein lower-ranked social groups display greater degrees of phonological economy than higher-ranked groups in equivalent situations of use.

3.2. Grammatical Variation

Given the emphasis on phonological variation in sociolinguistic studies, data from other levels of the grammar are not plentiful. There are nevertheless a few studies of grammatical variation, and they generally point in the same direction as the studies of phonological variation: to greater elaboration and more explicit forms among higher-status groups than among lower-status groups.

In Norwich the distribution of third person singular present tense verb forms (*swim/swims*) follows the predicted pattern. Trudgill (1974:62) reports that higher social classes express this morphological marker more frequently than lower-ranked groups in both casual and formal speech as shown in Table 13.14.

For the three morphological markers of plural (*cat/cats*), possessive (*cat/cat's*), and third person singular (*swim/swims*), the pattern among black residents of Detroit is the same as for third person singular present tense verb forms among the white residents of Norwich. Wolfram (1969:136, 141, 143) reports the percentages

TABLE 13.13   Percentage of Deletion of Word-Initial /h/ in Norwich
and West Yorkshire

	I (LM)	II (UW)	III (MW)	IV (LW)
Norwich				
Formal speech	4	24	43	41
Casual speech	14	40	59	61
West Yorkshire*	27	66	88	91

*West Yorkshire percentages estimated from graph, Petyt (1980:166).

for markerless forms among four socially ranked groups given in Table 13.15. The same pattern appears in the zero realization of the copula by the same groups (Wolfram 1969:169), as shown in Table 13.16. Thus Tables 13.14, 13.15, and 13.16 demonstrate that there is more frequent morphological explicitness among higher-ranked social groups than among lower-ranked groups.

As evidence that syntactic explicitness is more frequent among higher-ranked social groups, we cite a study of Philadelphia English by Kroch and Hindle (1982:69). The occurrence of relative clauses in the speech of upper-class adults, lower middle-class college students, and working-class adults shows the same graded pattern we have seen for phonological and morphological variables, as shown in Table 13.17.

In a study of twelve speakers in Ayr (Scotland), Macaulay (1991:64) found that "the middle-class speakers are much more likely than the lower-class speakers to use nonrestrictive relative clauses." Macaulay (1991:65) also found that WH-relative markers were very rare among the lower-class speakers but very common among the middle-class speakers, as shown in Table 13.18. He also reports (1991:68) that deletion of subject markers in relative clauses ("I've a girl $\emptyset$ works in Slough") occur in only 3 percent of the cases among the middle class as compared to 24 percent among the lower class.

In an analysis of data from the Detroit study of Roger Shuy, Walter Wolfram, and William Riley, Williams and Naremore (1969:786–88) examined speech samples from forty fifth-grade and sixth-grade children, randomly selecting black and white students matched by sex and socioeconomic index, with twenty lower-status and twenty higher-status students. They found consistently greater verb elaboration and greater elaboration of subject nominals in the higher-status groups. With respect to adverbial elaboration, the status differences favored the higher-status sample only among blacks. With respect to nominal explicitness measured by the use of relative clauses, the higher-status groups showed about twice as much use as the lower-status groups.

In a study very different from the others we've examined, a higher percentage of *that*-deletion occurred among telephone callers to a radio talk-show than among the higher-status talk-show hosts. Examining occurrences of subordinator *that*-deletion, Kroch and Small (1978:49) divided the occurrences into two groups depending on the matrix verb, as shown in Table 13.19.

In languages other than English, similar patterns of grammatical variation occur. Ashby (1981) found variable deletion of the first element of the discontinuous French negative *ne . . . pas* in the usage of three "informally defined social classes." Table 13.20 reports the percentage of *ne* deleted in speech samples of upper middle-class, middle-class, and lower middle-class speakers. The pattern is the same as in other speech communities.[11]

In another community in France, Diller (1980:70) found that lower-class speakers exhibited 48 percent deletion of *ne* with pronominal subjects, whereas higher-class speakers exhibited only 25 percent *ne*-deletion in the same circumstances. (With nominal subject NPs, neither group exhibited much deletion.)

In a third French-speaking community, Lindenfeld (1969) found in an experimental situation that higher-status (professional) speakers used more relativization (i.e., explicitness) than lower-status (working-class) speakers.

TABLE 13.14   Percentage of Markerless Forms in Norwich

	I (MM)	II (LM)	III (UW)	IV (MW)	V (LW)
Formal speech	0	5	38	64	87
Casual speech	0	29	75	80	97

TABLE 13.15   Percentage of Markerless Forms in Detroit

	I (UM)	II (LM)	III (UW)	IV (LW)
Third person singular present	1.4	9.7	56.9	71.4
Possessive	0.0	5.8	24.9	26.8
Plural	0.5	1.2	4.4	5.8

TABLE 13.16   Percentage of Zero Copula
in Detroit

I (UM)	II (LM)	III (UW)	IV (LW)
4.7	10.9	37.3	56.9

TABLE 13.17   Relative Clauses per 100 Sentences
in Philadelphia

I (UC)	II (LMC)	III (WC)
14	5	3

TABLE 13.18   Percentage of WH-Forms
in Relative Clauses in Ayr

I (MC)	II (LC)
53	10

TABLE 13.19   Percentage of Talk-Show
that-Deletion

	I (Hosts)	II (Callers)
With *think*	79	89
With other verbs	37	60

TABLE 13.20 Percentage of *ne* Deletion
by French Speakers

I (UMC)	II (MC)	III (LMC)
55	53	85

In the Flemish-speaking community of Maaseik, syntactic simplicity was more common among working-class respondents than middle-class respondents, according to Van den Broeck (1977). Among eight residents of the town, in two situations of use, middle-class speakers exhibited greater elaboration by longer T-units than lower-class speakers in both formal and informal situations, as shown in Table 13.21.[12]

While most studies of syntactic variation treat spoken language and have consistent results, the results of the few studies of writing have proved inconclusive.[13]

3.3. Lexical Variation

Too few studies have systematically investigated lexical variety across socioeconomic status groups to allow clear patterns to be identified. Until further research is carried out, our arguments on this topic must remain tentative. Among residents of Ayr, Scotland, Macaulay (1991:113–14) found that middle-class speakers had somewhat greater lexical variety than lower-class speakers. Moreover, of the words that were unique to the middle class, 41 percent were polysyllabic as compared to 27 percent of those unique to the lower class (and compared to only 14 percent for the words common to both groups).[14]

3.4. Discourse Variation

As with lexical variation, little is known about the social distribution of discourse features (but see, e.g., Dines 1980, Macaulay 1991). By way of illustration, we present some of the findings from Coupland's (1983) study of service encounters in a Cardiff (Wales) travel agency. Coupland grouped fifty-one clients into three educational classes (those with college or university education, those who had taken O-level or A-level examinations but had no university experience, and those who had not taken public examinations) and examined their use of four discourse features: transition boundary marking (TBM), explicit purpose identification (EPI), explicit role identification (ERI), and closing transaction marking (CTM). He found

TABLE 13.21 Mean Length of T-Units
in Two Situations in Maaseik

	I (MC)	II (WC)
Formal	9.44	7.01
Informal	7.48	7.28

TABLE 13.22   Index Scores for Explicit
Marking of Four Discourse Variables
by Three Education Groups in Cardiff*

	Education Groups		
Variables	*I*	*II*	*III*
TBM	101	077	065
ERI	100	073	050
CTM	154	129	129
EPI	31	15	14

*I = College/university level; II = O-/A-level; III = No public
examinations (scale for TBM, ERI, CTM: 0–200; for EPI: 0–100).
TBM, transition boundary marking; ERI, explicit role identification;
CTM, closing transaction marking; EPI, explicit purpose
identification.

generally that clients in higher-education groups used explicit markers more frequently than clients belonging to lower groups, as shown in Table 13.22.

3.5. Overview of Dialect Patterns

We have now seen strikingly similar patterns of linguistic variation across socially
ranked groups in a range of speech communities. For the kinds of variable linguistic
features cited and for the kinds of communities studied, there is a consistently
greater degree of phonological and syntactic economy among lower-ranked social
groups than among higher-ranked groups. It is therefore undeniable that a certain
kind of linguistic variation across social groups is systematic and patterned.

We reiterate that the features investigated here are of a particular kind, namely
those that are *variable* within their communities across both social groups and
situations of use, representing degrees of economy or elaboration. We make no
claims concerning linguistic features that are distinctive to a dialect (and thus not
variable). Further, most of the communities hosting the variable features reported in
section 3 are Westernized and urbanized, and it may be that variation in other kinds
of communities will differ in some respects.

There are a few counterexamples to the patterns described above. First, in some
cases less economical variants characterize the speech of lower-ranked groups;
multiple negation in certain American English dialects, *for-to* constructions in
American and Irish English, and resumptive pronouns in English, Spanish, and
Portuguese exemplify this pattern. Second, in a few cases higher-ranked groups
show a preference for variants that are more economical; *r*-deletion in Britain is a
notable example of this type. These patterns are rare relative to the examples cited in
sections 3.1 to 3.4, and for the time being we simply recognize them as counterexamples that need to be handled at some point.

In contrast, the type of pattern described in the eighteen tables of section 3 is not
at all rare, and despite these qualifications, there can be little doubt that these
patterns constitute an important fact that must be accounted for in any adequate
sociolinguistic theory. Some sociolinguists have suggested that, because linguistic
variation across social groups is essentially unpatterned, even experts cannot distin-

guish among the dialects of socially ranked groups (see, e.g., Hudson 1980:181). As illustrated above, however, many patterns of linguistic variation across social groups are remarkably consistent from speech community to speech community. The studies cited in sections 3.1 to 3.4 show that, in equivalent situations of use, higher-ranked social groups repeatedly show greater elaboration of linguistic forms than lower-ranked groups. This generalization holds true for English-speaking groups in the United Kingdom and North America; for French speakers in North America and on the Continent; and for communities speaking Spanish, Portuguese, and Flemish. From this perspective we would hesitate to accept without extensive qualification the claim that variation across social groups is generally unpatterned or that a linguist presented with the grammars of socially ranked groups could not tell which belonged to the higher-status group and which to the lower.

In no sense, of course, should our hesitation suggest that some dialects are better or worse than others, any more than registers are better or worse in absolute terms. For example, the economy that characterizes typical conversation is suited to that register and suffices in that social situation, even though it would prove inadequate to the tasks of, say, academic prose. Likewise the elaboration and explicitness of legalese and academic prose would test the patience of interlocutors sharing physical and social background when conversing on everyday topics: it would be needlessly elaborated and explicit.

In section 2 we showed how the distributional patterns of certain linguistic features across situations of use are functionally motivated. In section 3 we have shown that, at various levels of grammar, patterns of economy and elaboration similar to those that characterize different registers have parallels in the social dialect variation characteristic of different speech communities. It remains now to examine the parallel relationship between these patterns.

While the register variation described in section 2 reflects usage among speakers of Standard English (i.e., usage among a relatively homogeneous social group), there is no reason to doubt that similar patterns hold for other social groups. Such patterns are governed by a combination of production mandates and the communicative demands of particular social situations, both of which operate independently of social group membership. Indeed, although we have not marshalled the evidence in this chapter, considerable systematic stylistic variation has been reported for various socially ranked groups, as the data represented in Tables 13.13 and 13.14 show for English, and those in Table 13.21 show for Flemish. It is precisely such data that are implicated in Romaine's "classic sociolinguistic finding" of parallelism cited earlier. Such data suggest that, for many features, essentially the same patterns of situational variation obtain across social groups. To the extent that variable features are communicatively functional, this is not surprising in the least. What then accounts for the patterns of social dialect variation so characteristic at least of urban Western societies? We address this question in section 5.

4. Two Theories of Sociolinguistic Variation

Before presenting our view of social and register variation, we examine two theories of sociolinguistic variation with respect to the four observations made in section 1.2 and summarized here for convenience.

A. Certain linguistic features serve to mark both social dialect and social situation.
B. Patterns of linguistic variation across situations of use within a speech community and patterns of linguistic variation across socially ranked status groups in that community are parallel.
C. Patterns of linguistic variation across situations of use within a speech community are systematic, with more "literate" situations typically exhibiting a more frequent use of explicit and elaborated variants, and more "oral" situations exhibiting a more frequent use of economy variants.
D. Patterns of linguistic variation across socially ranked status groups within a speech community are similarly systematic, with higher-ranked social groups exhibiting more frequent use of the elaborated and explicit variants and lower-ranked groups exhibiting more frequent use of the economy variants.

Kroch (1978:17–18) offers an "explanatory theory of the mechanisms underlying social dialect variation" (essentially observation D). He expresses his theory as a two-part hypothesis:

> i) "the public prestige dialect of the elite in a stratified community differs from the dialect(s) of the non-elite strata (working class and other) in at least one phonologically systematic way. . . . It characteristically resists normal processes of phonetic conditioning . . . that the speech of non-elite strata regularly undergo";

> ii) "the cause of stratified phonological differentiation within a speech community is to be sought not in purely linguistic factors but in ideology."

According to Kroch (1978:30), "Dominant social groups tend to mark themselves off symbolically as distinct from the groups they dominate and to interpret their symbols of distinctiveness as evidence of superior moral and intellectual qualities." He argues that the reason for the differences between the dialect patterns of socially ranked groups is that the users of the prestige dialect exert energy to distance themselves from nonelite speakers.

Kroch acknowledges that the patterns of variation across different speech communities are strikingly similar, but he does not attempt to explain the patterns themselves. (In his view, the parallelism in the patterns of social and register variation could be coincidental.) Nor does he discuss the fact that every group is capable of distancing itself linguistically from all other groups—from those higher in status as well as from those lower. If distancing were indeed the chief motivation for social dialect differences, as Kroch suggests, the elite classes could accomplish their goals equally well—though more easily—by accelerating the natural processes of phonetic conditioning rather than by inhibiting them. But such patterns of acceleration appear to be extremely rare. Kroch's theory—by his own admission a provocative one[15]—thus does not address observation C, cannot explain the parallel patterns between social and register variation noted in observation B, and does not adequately account for observation D.

Bell (1984) has proposed a basically complementary theory. He enumerates the linguistic, social, and stylistic factors that can be correlated with linguistic variation, noting that "The social axis has been subjected to considerable examination, which convincingly shows that linguistic variation correlates with variation in a speaker's class, gender, social network, and so forth" (p. 145). Taking these established correlations between linguistic form and social group membership as self-explanatory, Bell argues that "Stylistic or intraspeaker variation derives from and mirrors interspeaker variation." In his view, "Style is essentially speakers' response to their audience." His theory is thus a theory of accommodation, building on the linguistic accommodation theory of Giles and his colleagues (see, e.g., Giles and Smith 1979).

Bell's theory offers an explanation for the parallel relationship between register variation and social dialect variation (observation B), but it does not address the internal systematicity of social dialect variation (observation D) or even of register variation (observation C). His theory would work as well for variation in which the degree of consonant cluster simplification *increased* with "formality," instead of *decreasing* (as in all reported cases). In explaining patterns that both do and do not exist, Bell's theory overexplains and therefore essentially leaves unexplained why we find just the patterns that we do and not other conceivable patterns. While it is unquestionably true that speakers accommodate their speech to their interlocutors, Bell's theory takes for granted the existing patterns of social dialect variation and thereby leaves them without an explanation.

5. A Proposal for an Integrated Approach

From a comparison of the patterns of distribution across registers and social dialects, recognizing the need to account for all four distributional observations (A–D), we arrive at conclusions quite different from those of Kroch and Bell. In our view, the evidence suggests that, for the kinds of linguistic features studied here, the patterns of register variation are basic and the patterns of social dialect variation result from differential access among social groups to the communicative situations and activities that promote register variation. This dependence of social dialect variation on register variation explains why the same features so often serve to mark both social group membership and situational context (observation A), producing the "classic" parallel distribution of social and stylistic markers (observation B). Observation C is a natural consequence of the functionality of register variation. That is, the patterns of linguistic variation across situations of use arise from the inherent communicative constraints of those situations. In particular, *all* interlocutors, irrespective of social affiliation, produce more explicit and elaborated expression in "literate" situations—having little direct interaction, little shared context, high informational purposes, and extensive opportunity for careful production. Conversely, all interlocutors produce more economical expression in "oral" situations—having extensive interaction and shared context, low informational purposes, and little opportunity for careful production. Finally, we claim that the systematic social dialect patterns comprising observation D are derivative from these register patterns. The link between observations C and D is that speakers from different social groups have differential access to the range of spoken and written registers in a community; thus speakers from lower social groups tend to use "oral" variants (i.e., more economical variants) more frequently, while speakers from higher social groups, who engage in literate activities more often, tend to use "literate" variants (i.e., more elaborated variants) more frequently.

Sociolinguists have frequently remarked upon the differential access to opportunities for different kinds of speaking and writing activities, as illustrated by the following.

Heath (1986:156), in her analysis of language use by children of different language minority groups:

> The greater the opportunities for experiencing language uses across a variety of contexts, the greater the language repertoire the children . . . will learn.

Van den Broeck (1977:174):

> The more access a person has to various situations, the greater the verbal repertoire he can develop. It is difficult to learn a formal variety if you hardly ever find yourself in a formal context (and if you are not supposed to say much in it anyway).

Hymes (1974:205):

> A salient fact about a speech community, realistically viewed, is the unequal distribution of abilities, on the one hand, and of opportunities for their use, on the other.

Kay (1977:31):

> When a society develops writing and differentiates into social classes, literate persons will usually have more occasion to speak explicitly and will tend to develop a speech style more attuned to explicit, technical, context-independent messages.

It is thus widely accepted that using a language for a greater or lesser range of communicative tasks influences the development of language repertoire; indeed, many think it obvious. Clearly, too, this developmental pattern is not randomly distributed in societies. Rather, in a wide variety of social settings, higher ranked social groups typically use language in broader ranges of communicative situations, thus becoming socialized into more extended repertoires. Lindenfeld (1969:896) found in her working-class French speakers "a very narrow stylistic range" compared to that of her higher-status speakers. Heath (1983:198–99, 218–20, 258–59), in her ethnography of three American communities, shows that middle-class town dwellers experience an extended range of reading and writing situations relative to working-class residents in rural communities. Gumperz (1964:421) makes a similar point about a village in India:

> Stylistic variation seems least pronounced in the speech of those individuals who tend to their own farms. It is greater with those who have outside economic interests or are active in religion and greatest with those who seem to have political ambitions. This suggests that, as in the case of the talking chiefs of Samoa, ability to manipulate argots might be one of the attributes of leadership in

village India. The need for command of diverse styles increases as we go up the scale to the sub-regional and regional speech strata.

The conclusion reached by Heath, Van den Broeck, Hymes, Kay, Gumperz, and others, is similar to one reached by Bernstein (1971): that middle-class speakers, who typically participate in a wider range of communicative roles than working-class speakers, develop a wider range of registers.

The validity of this conclusion is obscured when the scope of analysis is restricted to sociolinguistic interviews and conversational interactions (as has been typical of many sociolinguistic investigations to date).[16] Indeed, as Coupland (1988:55) has observed, the interview setting "is clearly able to capture only a tiny part of that variation in language that may be called 'stylistic' or 'contextual'. . . ." But when fuller ranges of spoken and written language are examined, researchers of diverse theoretical persuasions have noted marked differences in the linguistic repertoires across social groups. We do not endorse the unfortunate interpretations (and misinterpretations) put on Bernstein's work. Still, on the relationship between repertoire range and social ranking, there is general agreement.

Labov (1972:271) has commented "A speaker adapts his language to the immediate context of the speech situation." It should not be surprising that speakers develop speech patterns influenced by the communicative situations in which they typically participate, although the exact processes of socialization into these patterns are little understood. We believe that, for each such variable linguistic feature, the acquired range of variation is influenced by a speaker's characteristic communicative activities. If individuals frequently engage in speech activities requiring (and permitting) relatively explicit expression and relatively specific content, their speech will come to reflect their customary realizations of the features representing those values.

Given, then, the strong tendency for members of particular social groups to engage in communicative activities in characteristic ranges—for example, in various kinds of literacy activities—the typical values ("norms") for variable linguistic features can be expected to pattern themselves after the group's characteristic speech and literacy activities. In particular, because higher-social-status groups have verbal repertoires that more typically include professional, institutional, and other "literate" registers, even their conversational norms will come to reflect more frequent use of literate forms (i.e., exhibiting less economy and more specificity) than those of other status groups.[17]

Social dialect variation, we believe, depends upon register variation,[18] and register variation is largely shaped by communicative constraints inherent in particular situations. Labov (1969b) hits the nail on the head in his observation that "the social situation is the most powerful determinant of verbal behavior."

6. Summary and Conclusion

The principal points of our analysis are the following:

    i. Much register variation within a speech community is systematic, showing a correspondence between elaboration features and more literate varieties on the one hand, and between economy features and more oral varieties on the other.

ii. Much social dialect variation within a speech community is also systematic in the correspondence between elaboration features and higher-ranked social groups on the one hand, and compressed linguistic forms and lower-ranked groups on the other.

iii. The patterns of linguistic variation across situations of use are functionally motivated. The communicative setting of more literate varieties (e.g., extended opportunity for planning, informational purpose, and having little shared context) requires greater explicitness. The converse situational characteristics of oral varieties afford less opportunity for explicitness and tolerate more compressed expression. In contrast, the particular patterns of social group variation have no obvious functional motivation in themselves (aside from identifying social characteristics of speakers).

iv. The patterns of linguistic variation across situations and social groups are parallel. Higher-ranked groups and more literate registers show a greater preference for forms of elaboration.

v. Register variation is basic and characterizes the speech repertoire of all speech communities (see Dorian this volume). The pattern of linguistic variation across social groups is partly derivative of the situational patterns. This follows from the observation that much register variation is directly motivated by functional considerations, while the particular patterns of social group variation cannot be independently motivated.

vi. Social groups have differential access to communicative tasks and activities. In particular, higher-ranked groups have more access to stereotypically literate language activities than lower-ranked groups.

vii. The claim that register variation is basic, coupled with the differential range of register use across social groups, helps account for the parallel distribution of linguistic features across social groups and registers. In particular, each social group apparently develops a linguistic norm, representing a kind of average of its register range, with higher-ranked social groups developing norms closer to literate registers than lower-ranked social groups.

Naturally, we recognize that the distribution of only some linguistic variables across social groups is communicatively motivated; indeed, some features seem to serve principally (even solely) as markers of group identity and to be independent of communicative constraints. Nor do we claim that social groups have no influence on the speech patterns of one another; clearly, people who communicate with one another influence one another's speech patterns (cf. Kroch 1978, Bell 1984). We also think that Milroy (1980) has persuasively argued the importance of social networks on the distribution of certain linguistic variables. Finally, we recognize the need for considerable additional research; for example, to analyze the relation between register variation and other demographic parameters, such as sex differences, and to analyze the role of register variation in historical change.

Our goal here has been to broaden the scope of sociolinguistic inquiry and to show the importance of register variation as one predictor of social dialect variation.

We are not arguing, however, that the framework proposed here can account for the full range of socially motivated linguistic variation. Rather, a truly comprehensive theory of sociolinguistics must account for a much broader range of phenomena.

In New York City, Labov uncovered parallel patterns of social dialect and register variation with phonological variables. Applying the insights of the sociologist Bernard Barber, he ascribed the parallelism between social dialect and register variation (style variation, as he called it) to "the normal workings of society [which] have produced systematic differences between certain institutions or people, and . . . these differentiated forms have been ranked in status or prestige by general agreement" (1966a:64).

We hope we have shown that if the normal workings of people in their efforts to communicate economically and efficaciously within their community could produce systematic linguistic differences among social groups, the patterns of variation that we have examined would be explained. We also hope to have shown, however, that it is not by "general agreement" or by convention in any significant sense of those words that all variable linguistic features are ranked by communities in status and prestige. Rather, the communicative/functional value of many linguistic features underlies their parallel distribution across groups and situations and gives them their communal value. Van den Broeck (1977:175) comments, "Sameness, not difference, may be the starting point from which to understand the patterning of language according to class." Viewing sameness as the uniform communicative constraints exercised on the language of all social groups in equivalent situations of use, we endorse his statement.

Finally, although we hope it goes without saying, we wish to stress that the approach to social dialect and register variation outlined here, even if basically correct, provides only a partial explanation of the facts of variation. Further investigation of other kinds of linguistic features, and the patterns of variation in rural or non-Western societies, is needed to achieve more integrative theories of sociolinguistic variation.

Notes

1. Insofar as the factors conditioning linguistic variation are strictly structural (i.e., are unrelated to situation or social group membership), they are not peculiarly sociolinguistic and can be accommodated within a theory of linguistic performance. Further, insofar as such variation is similar to that described in historical linguistics, its incorporation into theories of grammar is essential to an adequate view of language structure and language change (cf. Weinreich, Labov, and Herzog 1968). Structurally governed variation may have related explanations to the communicative ones we offer for social group and register variation, because structural variation is also governed by communicative constraints (cf. Bickerton 1981, Givón 1979).

2. We do not address linguistic variation that is correlated with linguistic environment; see Fasold's (1985) interesting comments.

3. Romaine (1980a) is exceptional in that her examination of relative clause marking in Scots English focuses on the interplay among systematic complexity, style and register variation, and historical development.

4. For example, the frequency of occurrence of phonological features is typically much greater than of syntactic or lexical features, and it is generally clearer that phonological variants are indeed variants of the same linguistic unit.

5. Brown and Levinson (1987) address some of these matters in terms of politeness and such universals of interaction as "face."

6. Type/token ratio was calculated only on the first four hundred words of a text. For a detailed description of the texts from which the counts are extracted, the algorithms used to identify the variable features automatically, and the procedures used in calculating the frequencies, see Biber (1988).

A total of 255 texts was analyzed, representing approximately 500,000 words of text, distributed as follows:

Register	Number of Texts
Press reportage	44
Academic prose	80
General fiction	29
Personal letters	6
Conversations	44
Interviews	22
Public speeches	30

7. Note, however, that the type/token ratio for academic prose is lower than for the other written genres. The reason is that academic prose, like other types of technical writing, derives part of its exactness from repeated use of a single word with a technically defined meaning. For example, in writing about sound systems, linguists might repeatedly use the words *phoneme* and *phonological;* the stylistic use of alternative expressions is undesirable in discussing technical subjects, since readers might attempt to infer slight differences in meaning.

8. Among these same speakers, Kemp, Pupier, and Yaeger (1980:28) found that those who ranked lower on a linguistic integration index ("the degree to which each individual is integrated into the linguistic market") show a higher degree of compressed forms than higher ranked speakers. "A reading near 1.00 . . . indicates that the speaker occupies a socio-economic position in which a high degree of competence in the legitimized or standard language is required, to wit, lawyer, dean, actor. At the other end of the scale are speakers for whom knowledge of the standard language appears to play little part in their work, for example, manual workers." Though social class is "closely related" to it, the integration index is not an index of social class: "It simply represents aggregate subjective evaluation of the actual role that linguistic practice has in the productive life of each speaker in comparison with the others."

9. In the most formal situations, experimentally simulated by reading lists, the lower middle class exceeds the upper middle class in the degree of fuller expression; Labov (1966b) notes that this pattern of hypercorrection is indicative of historical change in progress and does not reflect a stable sociolinguistic marker.

10. Kroch (1978:27) further reports an "informal pilot survey of eastern Connecticut speech patterns . . . indicat[ing] that working-class casual speech favors some very marked articulatory reductions and assimilations."

11. Note that MC speakers exhibit somewhat less deletion than those of the UMC. Whether this is explainable by reference to class definition or sample size or to features of the linguistic environment such as pronoun versus full NP subject (cf. Diller 1980, discussed later in the chapter) we are unable to judge.

12. Middle-class speakers also exhibited greater subordination and more multiple embeddings than working-class speakers but only in the formal situations. In the informal

situation, working-class and middle-class speakers exhibited essentially the same levels of subordination and embedding. (The working-class respondents exhibited a statistically insignificant higher complexity in the informal situation.)

13. In a review of the literature, Poole (1983:360–70) found "no clear evidence for a strong association between socioeconomic status and written language." Nevertheless, using a rigorous meta-analysis, she found that in eleven of thirteen studies "middle-class subjects performed 0.3 of a standard deviation above the level of lower-class subjects in writing tasks."

14. Macaulay (1991:113) warns that "generalizations about social class differences in vocabulary should be treated with caution." Pending further research, we certainly concur.

15. Kroch (1978:30) concedes that his views should be seen "not as positions to be defended at all costs, but as stimuli to further theoretical reflection in a field that has been, thus far, descriptively oriented."

16. For example, this restricted range of variation is assumed when Preston (1991) argues in support of Bell's (1984:151) Style Axiom, "Variation on the style dimension within the speech of a single speaker derives from and echoes the variation which exists between speakers on the 'social' dimension." That is, the main supporting evidence cited by Preston (1991:33) is that "in a large number of sociolinguistic surveys the range of variability along the dimension associated with style is always smaller than that along the dimension associated with social status." From our perspective, the crucial flaw in this argument relates to the research design: the construct *style* used in these studies has no external validity. That is, *style* has been used to refer to the variation among danger-of-death stories, answers to interview questions, reading passages, and word lists—all within the context of a sociolinguistic interview. It is doubtful that this range of variability corresponds to any real-world construct, and therefore a comparison of the relative extent of variability across these styles and across social dialects has no valid theoretical status. Rather, valid comparisons should be based on the range of variability across the full range of speaking and writing situations in which members of a community participate; only this range represents the actual stylistic repertoire of speakers.

17. Reder (1981) is the only empirical study that we know of investigating the direct influence of literacy practices on speech. (This study was carried out as part of Scribner and Cole's investigation of literacy practices among the Vai in West Africa.) Reder analyzed the use of two linguistic features in Vai: the presence or absence of /l/, and indefinite articles. Similar to the patterns reported in section 2, the more elaborated variants were used more frequently in writing than in speech. More importantly, for both features the norms of literate men *when speaking* were markedly different from the norms of nonliterate men and women; in particular, the spoken norms for literate men were closer to the patterns of use in writing. This systematic shifting in speech practices, resulting from involvement in a wider range of registral activities, is exactly the kind of mechanism that we are positing in our framework.

18. The primacy of register over social dialect is further reflected in the fact that all individuals control multiple registers ("There are no single-style speakers," writes Labov [1969b:19]) but often, perhaps typically, they control only a single social dialect. It is also noteworthy that register variation appears to be more widespread across cultures than social dialect variation, which is highly marked in socially stratified urban communities.

References

Ashby, William J. 1981. "The Loss of the Negative Particle *ne* in French: A Syntactic Change in Progress." *Language* 57:674–87.

Bell, Allan. 1984. "Language Style as Audience Design." *Language in Society* 13:145–204.

Berdan, Robert. 1975. "The Necessity of Variable Rules." In Ralph W. Fasold, ed., *Variation in the Form and Use of Language: A Sociolinguistics Reader.* Washington, DC: Georgetown University Press. Pp. 63–78.

Bernstein, Basil. 1971. *Class, Codes and Control,* Vol. 1. London: Routledge.

Biber, Douglas. 1988. *Variation Across Speech and Writing.* Cambridge: Cambridge University Press.

Bickerton, Derek. 1981. *Roots of Language.* Ann Arbor, MI: Karoma.

Brown, Penelope, and Colin Fraser. 1979. "Speech as a Marker of Situation." In Klaus R. Scherer and Howard Giles, eds., *Social Markers in Speech.* Cambridge: Cambridge University Press. Pp. 33–62.

Brown, Penelope, and Stephen C. Levinson. 1987. *Politeness: Some Universals in Language Usage.* Cambridge: Cambridge University Press.

Cazden, Courtney B. 1970. "The Situation: A Neglected Source of Social Class Differences in Language Use." *Journal of Social Issues* 26(2):35–60. Reprinted in J. B. Pride and Janet Holmes, eds., *Sociolinguistics.* Harmondsworth: Penguin, 1972. Pp. 294–313.

Cedergren, Henrietta C. J. 1973. "The Interplay of Social and Linguistic Factors in Panama." Ph.D. Dissertation, Cornell University.

Chafe, Wallace, and Deborah Tannen. 1988. "The Relation Between Written and Spoken Language." *Annual Review of Anthropology* 16:383–407.

Chambers, J. K., and Peter Trudgill. 1980. *Dialectology.* Cambridge: Cambridge University Press.

Cheshire, Jenny. 1982. *Variation in an English Dialect.* Cambridge: Cambridge University Press.

Coupland, Nikolas. 1980. "Style-Shifting in a Cardiff Work-Setting." *Language in Society* 9:1–12.

———. 1983. "Patterns of Encounter Management: Further Arguments for Discourse Variables." *Language in Society* 12:459–76.

———. 1988. *Dialect in Use: Sociolinguistic Variation in Cardiff English.* Cardiff: University of Wales Press.

Crystal, David, and Derek Davy. 1969. *Investigating English Style.* New York: Longman.

Diller, Anne-Marie. 1980. "Subject NP Structure and Variable Constraints: The Case of *ne* Deletion." In Shuy and Shnukal, eds. Pp. 68–75.

Dines, Elizabeth R. 1980. "Variation in Discourse—'and stuff like that'." *Language in Society* 9:13–33.

Ellis, Jeffrey O., and Jean N. Ure. 1969. "Language Varieties: Register." In A. R. Meetham, ed., *Encyclopaedia of Linguistics, Information and Control.* Oxford: Pergamon. Pp. 251–59.

Fasold, Ralph W. 1985. "Perspectives on Sociolinguistic Variation (review article [of Romaine's *Sociolinguistic Variation in Speech Communities*])." *Language in Society* 14:515–25.

———. 1991. "The Quiet Demise of Variable Rules." *American Speech* 66:3–21.

Ferguson, Charles A. 1959. "Diglossia." *Word* 15:325–40. Reprinted in Giglioli, ed., 1972. Pp. 232–51.

———. 1977. "Baby Talk as a Simplified Register." In Catherine E. Snow and Charles A. Ferguson, eds., *Talking to Children.* Cambridge: Cambridge University Press. Pp. 209–35.

———. 1982. "Simplified Registers and Linguistic Theory." In Loraine K. Obler and Lise Menn, eds., *Exceptional Language and Linguistics.* New York: Academic Press. Pp. 49–66.

————. 1983. "Sports Announcer Talk: Syntactic Aspects of Register Variation." *Language in Society* 12:153–72.

————. 1985. "Editor's Introduction." *Discourse Processes* 8:391–94.

Finegan, Edward. 1982. "Testament Language." In Robert J. Di Pietro, ed., *Linguistics and the Professions*. Norwood, NJ: Ablex. Pp. 113–20.

————. 1987. "On the Linguistic Forms of Prestige." In Phillip Boardman, ed., *The Legacy of Language*. Reno: University of Nevada Press. Pp. 146–69.

Giglioli, Pier Paolo, ed. 1972. *Language and Social Context*. Harmondsworth: Penguin.

Giles, Howard, and P. Smith. 1979. "Accommodation Theory: Optimal Levels of Convergence." In Howard Giles and Robert St. Clair, eds., *Language and Social Psychology*. Oxford: Basil Blackwell. Pp. 45–65.

Givón, Talmy. 1979. "From Discourse to Syntax: Grammar as a Processing Strategy." In Talmy Givón, ed., *Syntax and Semantics 12: Discourse and Syntax*. New York: Academic Press. Pp. 81–112.

Gumperz, John J. 1964. "Speech Variation and the Study of Indian Civilization." In Dell Hymes, ed., *Language in Culture and Society*. New York: Harper and Row. Pp. 416–28.

Gumperz, John J., and Robert Wilson. 1971. "Convergence and Creolization: A Case from the Indo-Aryan/Dravidian Border." In Dell Hymes, ed., *Pidginization and Creolization of Language*. Cambridge: Cambridge University Press. Pp. 151–67.

Halliday, M. A. K. 1968. "The Users and Uses of Language." In Joshua A. Fishman, ed., *The Sociology of Language*. The Hague: Mouton. Pp. 139–69.

Heath, Shirley Brice. 1983. *Ways With Words*. Cambridge: Cambridge University Press.

————. 1986. "Sociocultural Contexts of Language Development." In *Beyond Language: Social and Cultural Factors in Schooling Language Minority Students*. Los Angeles: California State University, Los Angeles (Evaluation, Dissemination and Assessment Center).

Hudson, R. A. 1980. *Sociolinguistics*. Cambridge: Cambridge University Press.

Hymes, Dell. 1973. "Speech and Language: On the Origins and Foundations of Inequality Among Speakers." *Daedalus* 102:59–85. Reprinted in Einar Haugen and Morton Bloomfield, eds., *Language as a Human Problem*. New York: Norton, 1973, 1974. Pp. 45–71.

————. 1974. *Foundations in Sociolinguistics: An Ethnographic Approach*. Philadelphia: University of Pennsylvania Press.

Janda, Richard D. 1985. "Note-Taking English as a Simplified Register." *Discourse Processes* 8:437–54.

Johansson, Stig, Geoffrey N. Leech, and Helen Goodluck. 1978. *Manual of Information to Accompany the Lancaster–Oslo/Bergen Corpus of British English, for Use With Digital Computers*. Oslo: Department of English, University of Oslo.

Kay, Paul. 1977. "Language Evolution and Speech Style." In Ben G. Blount and Mary Sanches, eds., *Sociocultural Dimensions of Language Change*. New York: Academic Press. Pp. 21–33.

————. 1978. "Variable Rules, Community Grammar and Linguistic Change." In Sankoff, ed. Pp. 71–84.

Kay, Paul, and Chad K. McDaniel. 1979. "On the Logic of Variable Rules." *Language in Society* 8:151–87.

————. 1981. "On the Meaning of Variable Rules: Discussion." *Language in Society* 10:251–58.

Kemp, William, Paul Pupier, and Malcah Yaeger. 1980. "A Linguistic and Social Description of Final Consonant Cluster Simplification in Montreal French." In Shuy and Shnukal, eds. Pp. 12–40.

Kroch, Anthony S. 1978. "Toward a Theory of Social Dialect Variation." *Language in Society* 7:17–36.

Kroch, Anthony, and Cathy Small. 1978. "Grammatical Ideology and Its Effect on Speech." In Sankoff, ed. Pp. 45–55.

Kroch, Anthony S., and Donald M. Hindle. 1982. "A Quantitative Study of the Syntax of Speech and Writing." Final report to the National Institute of Education.

Labov, William. 1966a. *The Social Stratification of English in New York City*. Washington, DC: Center for Applied Linguistics.

———. 1966b. "Hypercorrection by the Lower Middle Class as a Factor in Linguistic Change." In William Bright, ed., *Sociolinguistics*. The Hague: Mouton. Pp. 84–113.

———. 1969a. "Contraction, Deletion, and Inherent Variability of the English Copula." *Language*. 45:715–62.

———. 1969b. *The Study of Nonstandard English*. Champaign, IL: National Council of Teachers of English.

———. 1969c. "The Logic of Nonstandard English." *Georgetown Monographs on Language and Linguistics* 22:1–31. Excerpted in Giglioli, ed. Pp. 179–215.

———. 1972. *Sociolinguistic Patterns*. Philadelphia: University of Pennsylvania Press.

Lindenfeld, Jacqueline. 1969. "The Social Conditioning of Syntactic Variation in French." *American Anthropologist* 71:890–98. Reprinted in Joshua A. Fishman, ed., *Advances in the Sociology of Language*, II. The Hague: Mouton, 1972. Pp. 79–90.

Macaulay, Ronald K. S. 1988. "The Rise and Fall of the Vernacular." In Caroline Duncan-Rose and Theo Venneman, eds., *On Language: Rhetorica, Phonologica, Syntactica*. London: Routledge. Pp. 106–13.

———. 1991. *Locating Dialect in Discourse: The Language of Honest Men and Bonnie Lasses in Ayr*. New York: Oxford University Press.

Milroy, Lesley. 1980. *Language and Social Networks*. Oxford: Basil Blackwell.

Mühlhäusler, Peter. 1986. *Pidgin and Creole Linguistics*. Oxford: Basil Blackwell.

Petyt, K. M. 1980. *The Study of Dialect*. London: Andre Deutsch.

Poole, Millicent. 1983. "Socioeconomic Status and Written Language." In M. Martlew, ed., *The Psychology of Written Language*. New York: Wiley. Pp. 335–75.

Poplack, Shana, and Douglas Walker. 1986. "Going Through (*L*) in Canadian French." In David Sankoff, ed., *Diversity and Diachrony*. Amsterdam: Benjamins. Pp. 173–98.

Preston, Dennis R. 1991. "Sorting Out the Variables in Sociolinguistic Theory." *American Speech* 66:33–56.

Reder, Stephen. 1981. "The Written and the Spoken Word: Influence of Vai Literacy on Vai Speech." In Sylvia Scribner and Michael Cole, *The Psychology of Literacy*. Cambridge, MA: Harvard University Press. Pp. 187–99.

Romaine, Suzanne. 1980a. "The Relative Clause Marker in Scots English: Diffusion, Complexity, and Style as Dimensions of Syntactic Change." *Language in Society* 9:221–47.

———. 1980b. "Stylistic Variation and Evaluative Reactions to Speech." *Language and Speech* 23:213–32.

———. 1982. *Sociolinguistic Variation in Speech Communities*. London: Edward Arnold.

———. 1988. *Pidgin and Creole Languages*. London: Longman.

Sankoff, David, ed. 1978. *Linguistic Variation: Models and Methods*. New York: Academic.

Sankoff, David, and Henrietta Cedergren, eds. 1981. *Variation Omnibus*. Edmonton: Linguistic Research.

Sankoff, David, and William Labov. 1979. "On the Uses of Variable Rules." *Language in Society* 8:189–222.

Sankoff, Gillian, and Henrietta Cedergren. 1971. "Some Results of a Sociolinguistic Study of Montreal French." In Regna Darnell, ed., *Linguistic Diversity in Canadian Society.* Edmonton: Linguistic Research. Pp. 61–87.

Scherre, Maria Marta Pereira. 1981. "La Variation de la Regle d'Accord du Nombre dans le Syntagme Nominal en Portugais." In Sankoff and Cedergren, eds. Pp. 125–33.

Shuy, Roger W., and Anna Shnukal, eds. 1980. *Language Use and the Uses of Language.* Washington, DC: Georgetown University Press.

Sinclair, John. 1988. "Compressed English." In Mohsen Ghadessy, ed., *Registers of Written English: Situational Factors and Linguistic Features.* London: Pinter. Pp. 130–36.

Slobin, Dan I. 1979. *Psycholinguistics,* 2nd ed. Glenview, IL: Scott, Foresman.

Svartvik, Jan, and Randolph Quirk. 1980. *A Corpus of English Conversation.* Lund: Gleerup.

Terrell, Tracy. D. 1981. "Diachronic Reconstruction by Dialect Comparison of Variable Constraints." In Sankoff and Cedergren, eds. Pp. 115–24.

Traugott, Elizabeth Closs, and Suzanne Romaine. 1985. "Some Questions for the Definition of 'Style' in Socio-Historical Linguistics." *Folia Linguistica Historica* 6:7–39.

Trudgill, Peter. 1974. *The Social Differentiation of English in Norwich.* Cambridge: Cambridge University Press.

Van den Broeck, Jef. 1977. "Class Differences in Syntactic Complexity in the Flemish Town of Maaseik." *Language in Society* 6:149–81.

Weinreich, Uriel, William Labov, and Marvin Herzog. 1968. "Empirical Foundations for a Theory of Language Change." In Winfred P. Lehmann and Yakov Malkiel, eds., *Directions for Historical Linguistics.* Austin: University of Texas Press. Pp. 87–195.

Williams, Frederick, and Rita C. Naremore. 1969. "Social Class Differences in Children's Syntactic Performance: A Quantitative Analysis of Field Study Data." *Journal of Speech and Hearing Research* 12:778–93.

Wolfram, Walt A. 1969. *A Sociolinguistic Description of Detroit Negro Speech.* Washington, DC: Center for Applied Linguistics.

V

A SURVEY OF
EMPIRICAL REGISTER
STUDIES

14

Register: A Review of Empirical Research

DWIGHT ATKINSON AND DOUGLAS BIBER

1. Introduction

1.1. Rationale

Situationally defined language varieties have been examined from numerous theoretical perspectives, in a wide range of fields including linguistics, anthropology, composition research, folklore, rhetoric, education, sociology, psychology, literature, and communication. These studies adopt such terms as *register, genre, style,* and *text type* to label their primary object of investigation—terms that can themselves be defined in multiple ways. In the present survey, we consider this body of research under the cover term *register,* which is used to refer to any language variety associated with particular situational or use characteristics.

There is need for a broad survey of register research showing the relationships among the multitude of register investigations that have been undertaken. Major approaches to register analysis have included synchronic analysis of particular registers at different linguistic levels (e.g., of phonology, lexicon, syntax, and discourse structure), historical investigations of the evolution of particular registers, and studies taking a variationist approach—delineating linguistic differences across two or more registers. Using these as well as other analytical distinctions, our aims in the present review are (1) to survey a large number of empirical investigations relevant to the analysis of registers, (2) to classify specific register studies according to these analytical criteria, and (3) to show that studies from a number of related subfields share the primary goals of register analysis.

We would like to thank Paul Bruthiaux, Ann Daubney-Davis, Charles Ferguson, Genevieve Patthey-Chavez, and Doreen Wu for their generous assistance and advice.

1.2. Defining Register Studies

In order to delimit our area of inquiry, we first identify four typifying characteristics of register studies:

1. Register studies involve *descriptive analysis of actually occurring discourse.*
2. Register studies aim to characterize *language varieties,* rather than either the linguistic styles of individuals or specific linguistic structures.[1]
3. Register studies present *formal linguistic characterizations of language varieties*—characterizations which obtain at various levels of language.
4. Register studies also analyze *the situational characteristics of language varieties,* and *functional or conventional relationships between form and situation* are posited.

In addition to the "typical" register studies which meet these criteria, and to which the larger part of this review is devoted, various other types of studies are related to register investigation. Such work may provide detailed analysis of situational contexts, describe functional underpinnings of particular linguistic features, or characterize rhetorical functions in text. We briefly review some of these research areas in section 3.

1.3. Categorizing Register Studies

Having located register research in a preliminary way, we provide here a series of analytical distinctions that can be used to categorize register studies:

1. Single-register versus register variation studies
2. Synchronic versus diachronic register studies
3. Analysis of spontaneous versus elicited discourse
4. Quantitative versus qualitative research methodologies
5. Size and type of textual database
6. Level/s of linguistic analysis (e.g., lexical, syntactic, discourse)
7. Mode (speech versus writing)
8. Topical or disciplinary domains
9. Language/s studied

These analytical categories have been used to organize the present review. In particular, items 1 and 2 considered together provide the basic four-way categorization used to section our survey. The other distinctions, where they obtain, provide further organization for the discussion within and across sections.

2. Studies of Single Registers

2.1. Synchronic Analysis of Single Registers

Synchronic single-register analysis is probably the approach most frequently adopted by register researchers and the one most often identified as prototypical register research. The majority of studies in this area (and certainly of those written in English) focus on English-language registers.

An early and precedent-setting example of work in this tradition is Crystal and Davy's *Investigating English Style* (1969). Although they make a point of avoiding the term *register*, Crystal and Davy provide five model analyses of situated language use—in the domains of religion, newspaper reporting, conversation, legal documents, and unscripted radio commentary. In each case, the authors first introduce example-texts that differ from one another according to one or more situational parameters, then comprehensively discuss their linguistic characteristics at the levels of phonology/orthography, lexicon, syntax, and, to a lesser extent, discourse. At the same time, they propose functional motivations for many of the features they discuss.

Other early synchronic single-register studies of note include Mellinkoff's (1963) investigation of the lexis of (mostly written) legal language, Ferguson's (1964) pioneering work on baby talk, and Leech's (1966) treatment of British television and print advertising.

A classic but more recent study is Ferguson's (1983) investigation of radio sportscasting. Ferguson begins by "locating" the sportscasting register at three cross-cutting levels of situational distinctiveness: in terms of time, focusing on events in progress rather than past and finished events; in terms of the nature of the audience, as an unseen, unknown mass-media audience who cannot themselves see the sports event; and in terms of the shared conventional knowledge domains of sportscaster and audience, regarding, for example, game rules, technical terminology, and performance expectations for players. Ferguson then proceeds to describe the register's distinctive lexicosyntactic characteristics—including deletion of sentence-initial elements and copulas, subject-verb inversions, heavy NPs, and the use of special formulas—while investigating the communicative functionality or conventionality of each of these features. (Other studies of sports-related language include Heath and Langman this volume, focusing on the "register of coaching," and Romaine this volume, analyzing written sports reporting in Tok Pisin.)

Numerous other synchronic single-register studies follow approaches similar to those of Crystal and Davy and Ferguson. One major focus of such research has been the description of professional registers. Studies of this type are treated in the following section.

2.1.1. STUDIES OF PROFESSIONAL REGISTERS

Legal language—both spoken and written—has received substantial attention from register analysts. Danet (1980) reviews earlier studies of written legal language, summarizing their findings in regard to characteristic prosody, lexicon, grammar, and clause-level syntax, while Danet (1985) describes the lexical, syntactic, and discourse features of a British legal document known as the Assignment. Finegan (1982) examines the functional grammar and clause-level syntax of wills and their accompanying letters of transmittal. In research focusing on parliamentary acts, Maley (1987) treats their highly formalized syntax, lexicon, and speech-act sequencing, while Hiltunen (1990:chapter 3) provides a comprehensive linguistic description, with a lesser emphasis on the situational correlates of their language. Gustaffson (1984), studying both parliamentary and congressional acts, discusses binomial expressions (e.g., "by or on behalf of") as a distinctive marker of legislative language.

Regarding studies of oral legal registers, Atkinson and Drew (1979) examine the conversation structure of courtroom proceedings, as well as some of their register-marking features. O'Barr (1982) looks at various features of courtroom testimony, including syntactic markers of "powerful" versus "powerless" speech, discourse structure, and management of witness talk. One area of spoken legal language that has received particular attention is the use of questions—an important register marker in courtroom discourse. Thus Harris (1984) treats the syntax and pragmatics of questions in hearings before county magistrates in England, while Lane (1990) describes the syntax, discourse structure, and speech-act sequencing of witness-examination portions of New Zealand criminal trials. Philips (1984) studies question and answer types in American courts. As with much other research on legal language, these latter studies are centrally concerned with the distribution of power in the courtroom.[2]

Spoken and written medical communication has also been extensively analyzed. Studies of the former, however, have typically been either nonstructural investigations of specific speech events or nonlinguistic studies of communicative effectiveness and will not be treated here.[3] Exceptions include Dubois' (1980) qualitative analysis of the functional syntax and discourse structure of biomedical speeches, and Tannen and Wallat's (1982) brief description of three registers used alternatively by a single pediatrician during a patient examination. Research on written medical registers has been undertaken by, among others, Van Naerssen (1985), who studied the lexical, syntactic, and discourse characteristics of hospital discharge summaries; Adams Smith (1984), who examined a wide range of lexical and syntactic markers of stance and "author's comment" in medical journal research articles, case reports, and editorials; and Salager-Meyer et al. (1989), who examined seventeen syntactic variables—also in articles, case reports, and editorials—in order to determine their rhetorical functions. An earlier study by Salager (1983) characterizes the core lexis of medical research articles, reviews, and textbooks, while Dubois (1982) and Salager (1984) describe the medical register–marking feature of compound nominals (e.g., "human blood group B"). Other studies include Dunham (1986), which looks briefly at register-marking punctuation, lexicon, syntax, and discourse structure in medical diagnostic statements. (Cf. Atkinson 1992, discussed in section 2.2.)

Although scientific discourse has received attention from a variety of disciplines, there have been comparatively few attempts to characterize it broadly as a synchronic situational variety or set of varieties. Reichman-Adar (1984) gives a partial description of spoken "technical discourse"—which includes scientific discourse—in terms of the choice of deictic *that,* present progressive tense, and pronominalization options. Lynch's (1985) study of "shop talk" in the neuroscience laboratory may explain why at least *some* types of language spoken by scientists have not been widely treated—Lynch was unable to find features which distinguished shop talk from less situation-specific forms of conversation. Swales

(1990:chapter 7) reviews much of the research on the English scientific research article and contains a useful table of studies on the various functional features of scientific writing. Swales (1981) gives a rhetorico-linguistic description of the highly conventionalized introduction section of research articles, including its over-all four-part discourse structure, thematic information structure, and selected rhetor-ically functional verb tenses and nominals; his data base was a corpus of forty-eight scientific, medical, and social science journal articles. Tarone et al. (1981) treat the functional determinants of passive versus active verb choice in two astrophysics journal papers, while Smith (1985) considers the "interpersonal" functions of a range of grammatical features (e.g., imperatives, modals, passive verbs, and pro-nouns) in four types of scientific writing on recombinant deoxyribonucleic acid (DNA) research. Myers (1991) investigates differences in lexical cohesion across two types of scientific writing, as described in section 2.3.5.[4] (Cf. Bazerman 1984 and Halliday 1988, discussed in section 2.2.)

The language of the media has been widely treated, with news reporting in particular a frequent topic. Thus Geis (1987a) examines verb tenses, deixis, quota-tions, and conversation structure in six American television network newscasts, while Roeh and Nir (1990) look at the ideological uses of pronouns, intensifiers, parallelism, and repetition in four "speech presentation" styles of Israeli Hebrew radio news reports. Greatbatch (1988) delineates the distinctive turn-taking system and conversation structure of BBC news program interviews. In a wide-ranging study, Bell (1991) describes story structure, phonological variation, and selected grammatical features (including speech act verbs, direct and indirect speech, and noun phrases) across a variety of news writing and reporting situations. In a study of non-news media speech, Montgomery (1988) characterizes radio disk jockey talk in terms of its use of interpersonal speech markers—direct address, deictics, inter-rogatives and imperatives, asides and insertions, and speech-act *expressives*. Re-garding print journalism, van Dijk (1988) extensively characterizes the proposition-al and discourse structure of informational news reports, while describing their lexicon and clause-level syntax in less detail. Wallace (1981) discusses a number of the distinctive features of newspaper language but focuses his own investigation on sentence length and frequency of passive verbs. Carter (1988) briefly treats the lexicon of newspaper front pages, and Mardh (1980) examines the grammar and clause-level syntax of front-page headlines. Using systemic-functional methods developed by Halliday (e.g., 1985), but working within the framework of critical discourse analysis (Kress 1991), Kress (1983) analyzes two feature news articles and an editorial in one Australian tabloid, while Fowler (1991) considers markers of ideological stance in newspaper writing, including transitivity relations, clause types, lexical structure, and modality. In a third Halliday-influenced study, Ghadessy (1988a) describes British newspaper sports commentary in terms of the collocational possibilities of various lexicogrammatical items.

Leech (1966) is one of the most complete analyses of media advertising lan-guage, offering separate chapters on clause structure and clause types, verbal groups, nominal groups, lexis, and cohesion. It is surpassed in its coverage of linguistic features, however, by Pandya's (1977) study of Indian and British English press advertising, although Pandya provides much less information on the variety's situational and functional correlates. In other studies of advertising registers, Geis (1982) examines the persuasive lexicon, syntax, and speech acts associated with television advertising, while Schmidt and Kess (1985) use a similar range of features to describe the promotional speech of American television evangelists. Haarmann (1984) investigates the use of register-marking foreign lexis in Japanese mass-media commercials, and Bell (1990), in a related study, shows how the features of other English dialects figure prominently in New Zealand television advertising.[5] (Cf. Bruthiaux this volume for an analysis of the "personal ads" register.)

In regard to the language of business, Merritt (1976) and Ventola (1983) characterize distinctive aspects of service encounters. Merritt focuses on the questions of servers in response to customer questions, as well as the discourse-organizing function of this *adjacency pair,* while Ventola characterizes the overall schematic discourse structure of such transactions. Regarding business writing, Broadhead and Freed (1986) examine proposals written by two management consultants in terms of their T-unit length, frequency of cohesion markers, and syntax, although they are more interested in the writers' composing processes. Zwicky and Zwicky (1980) consider the lexicon, syntax, and discourse structure of American restaurant menus, showing how their language is designed to advertise dishes rather than accurately describe them.

Research on bureaucratic language has been undertaken more often for prescriptive than descriptive ends; much work in this area has been generated by the "plain English" movement (cf. Felker et al. 1980). Charrow (1982) and Redish (1983), for instance, examine the grammar, lexis, and discourse structure of American government forms and regulations in order to make them comprehensible to average users. More purely descriptive studies of "bureaucratese" include Longe (1985) on sentence complexity, complementation types, and NP and VP structure in Nigerian government official letters.

Language use in schools has received an enormous amount of attention, with several studies focusing explicitly on school-related registers.[6] In an early study, Barnes et al. (1969) characterize the speech of British primary and secondary teachers in terms of various question types, technical lexis, and use of "literate" language. Sinclair and Coulthard (1975) and Mehan (1979) describe the pervasive Initiation-Response-Evaluation (IRE) discourse structuring of classroom lessons, while Poole (1990) extends the latter analysis to include a linguistic description of the IRE in the context of the "quiz review" speech event. Lemke (1990) investigates the discourse of high school science teaching in terms of its thematic information structure, talk-management techniques, and overall discourse structure. Cazden (1988:chapter 9) characterizes the "teacher-talk" register in terms of politeness features and control talk, and employs her analysis to account for special language use in two Latino bilingual primary classrooms. Heath (1978) briefly characterizes teacher talk in relation to caregiver registers such as baby talk (discussed below), as well as describing the directive and other speech act functions of teacher discourse. In a series of studies, Michaels (e.g., Michaels 1981, Collins and Michaels 1986) has identified a school-sponsored "literate" style of student narrative performance, which is opposed to a dispreferred style with predominantly oral roots. The former is characterized by such features as "topic-centered" discourse structure, nominal complements, relative clauses, lexical and grammatical parallelism, cohesion markers, and sentence-marking intonation. The main point of this research is to show how the early educational experience of minority children substantially handicaps them. In other work on school registers, Cazden (1988:chapter 10) characterizes the stereotypical register expectations that teachers have for student talk in primary and secondary schools. Patthey (1991) deals with problem-solving expert-novice interactions in an academic computing center, focusing on their overall discourse structure, conversational and topic-marking strategies, and use of various types of repetitions to accomplish learning goals.

Regarding the written registers of schooling, Luke (1988) describes the simplified lexicon (of a total of 159 words), grammar, and story structure of the "Dick and Jane" series of American basal readers, while Taylor (1983) examines lexis, cohesion markers, thematic information structure, and grammatical features in eighteen Australian high school textbooks from six subjects. Martin (1985), who represents a recent tradition of Australian research on school-based language varieties (see note 6), describes selected specimens of expository and persuasive writing in systemic-functional terms, including analysis of lexical density, grammatical metaphor, modality, "private" verbs, and intensification. In other work on school-based or school-sponsored written registers, Purcell-Gates (1988) had kindergarten and primary school students who were frequently read to at home relate two stories, one based on the storyline of a picture book, the other on the subjects' memories of their last birthday party. She found the book-based stories to be representative of a "written-narrative" register, as characterized by markers of textual integration and involvement, decontexualization, and literary style. Biber (1991) used a multidimensional analysis (for which see section 2.3.1) to describe the linguistic characteristics of primary school textbooks and basal readers, as well as juvenile novels and comics. Studies of cohesion-marking features in school-related registers include Fitzgerald and Speigel (1986), DeStefano and Kantor (1988), and Cox et al. (1990); these are described in section 2.3.5.[7]

2.1.2. OTHER SYNCHRONIC SINGLE-REGISTER RESEARCH

The language of religion has also been the focus of synchronic single-register research. Several studies preceded Crystal and Davy's (1969) influential work, including Barr's (1961) in-depth description of the grammar (especially verb-types) and lexis of Biblical English, and Brook's (1965) investigation of the lexis, grammar, and pervasive repetition in the *Book of Common Prayer*. Ferguson (1976) briefly describes the formulaic features—doublets, relative clauses with second person referent, and overall discourse structure—of the "collect" Christian prayer form. Mitchell (1970), Heath (1983:chapter 6), and McGinnis (1986) all characterize distinctive aspects of the African American folk preaching style, including intonation patterns, interactive call-and-response discourse structure, and lexical repetition. In studies of non-English varieties, Forth (1988) describes the formulaic parallelism, repetition, and discourse structure of ritual speeches in the Sumbanese language of Indonesia, while Sherzer (1989) treats the special phonology, morphology, clause structure, lexicon, and metaphor used in three related Cuna speech events—chanting, disease-curing, and puberty rituals.[8]

Simplified registers have a comparatively long history of research dating to Ferguson's (1964) early interest in baby talk, mentioned previously. Of the many studies in this area, just a few can be mentioned. Ferguson (1977) summarizes the findings of research on baby talk across a number of languages—simplified forms in this register include phonological assimilation and reduplication, fewer inflections, substitution of third person for other pronouns, zero copula, and vastly simplified lexicon. Early (1985) reviews approximately forty studies of foreigner talk (i.e., talk *to* foreigners) undertaken in natural, experimental, and classroom settings. The results of these studies are varied, although they tend to agree regarding the presence of slower and more clearly articulated speech, exaggerated stress patterns, and shorter and syntactically simpler utterances, as well as the absence of infrequently occurring words. Studies of foreigner talk include the cross-linguistic classroom investigations of Henzl (1974, 1979), who found characteristic simplification at the levels of lexicon, grammar, and phonology in Czech, German, and English; Clyne's (1977) study of worker talk in an Australian factory setting; and the experimental research program of Long (e.g., 1981a, 1981b).[9] In research on other simplified or formulaic spoken registers, Gibbon (1981, 1985) examines the lexicon, syntax, and discourse structure of talk among international amateur radio operators. Formulaic speech resulting from serious production constraints (e.g., the calling of horse races) is also the subject of a series of studies by Kuiper (Kuiper and Haggo 1984, Kuiper and Tillis 1986, Kuiper and Austin 1990). Finally, T. Murray (1985) focuses on the crucial role of formulaic language in American singles bars. (For a register perspective on simplification in diglossia, see Hudson this volume.)

Researchers studying simplification in written communication include D. Murray (1985, 1988), who looked at syntactic deletion, use of standard and nonstandard abbreviations, discourse structure, and various means of signaling affective and paralinguistic expression in interactive electronic messages and mail. In a related study, Ferrara et al. (1991) elicited electronic messages via a role-play task and found them marked by short sentence length, abbreviated lexicon, and omission of pronouns, articles, and finite copulas; however, these texts contained a mixture of literate and oral language features, indicating the hybrid nature of the register. Janda (1985) examined the simplified lexicon and syntax of note-taking, while Zak and Dudley-Evans (1986) studied syntactic deletions and abbreviation conventions in English business telexes. Bruthiaux (this volume) describes the simplified, conventionalized syntax and lexicon of newspaper "personal advertisements."

Finally, research within the framework of ethnographic speech-event analysis invariably provides detailed situational descriptions of the speech events under analysis. Examples of such synchronic single-register studies include Besnier (1989) on affect-marking and discourse-framing features in Nukulaelae Tuvaluan personal letters; Brown and Herndl (1986) on the use of nominalizations and narrative structure as markers of job security and social role in business writing; Latour and Woolgar (1986:chapters 2, 4) concerning the roles of speaking and writing in fact construction in the scientific laboratory; and Duranti (1983) on ceremonial speech forms in Western Samoa. Several other ethnographic analyses have already been mentioned in this section. Ethnographic speech-event studies that include less linguistic information but provide detailed situational descriptions are briefly reviewed in section 3.3.

2.2. Diachronic Studies of Single Registers

The evolutionary development of specific registers has received much less attention than the synchronic description of single registers. One area in which substantial work of this kind has been done, however, is the study of scientific/academic research writing. For example, Bazerman (1984) investigates the distribution of technical lexis and nominal compounds, noun and verb types, relative clauses, sentence length, and subordinate clause types—as well as the occurrence and relative length of rhetorical text sections—in experimental reports from one American physics journal for the period 1893 to 1980. His findings indicate that certain features became more prominent with the growth of a research community based on a shared theory of (quantum) physics. Atkinson (1992) uses a combination of multidimensional register analysis (for which see section 2.3.1) and rhetorical text analysis to determine that medical research writing has become more referentially explicit, less narrative, and less writer-centered and "involved" over a 250-year period—characteristics partly attributable to the changing relationship between medicine and the nonmedical sciences. Halliday (1988) has provided a close analysis of syntactic development in English physical science writing from the fourteenth century onward. Others who have studied scientific or social science writing from a diachronic perspective include Huckin (1987), Dudley-Evans and Henderson (1990), and Melander (in press).[10]

Other diachronic studies of a single register include Hiltunen (1990), cited previously, which undertakes a textual history of legal English from 635 A.D. to the present. Myers and Cortina (1985), in a diachronic study of the Chicano Spanish press in Milwaukee, Wisconsin, investigate the effects of English on the lexicon and syntax of two newspapers. In a very different kind of diachronic research, Kemper (1987, 1990) examined diaries of turn-of-the-century Americans for evidence of linguistic change across their lifespans. She found clearly increased complexity across age in narrative story structure, and decreased complexity in clause structure and the use of certain cohesion markers.

Register acquisition represents an additional type of diachrony treated in work on single registers. Berkenkotter, Huckin, and Ackerman (1988, 1991) provide a linguistic-rhetorical description of the developing academic writing competence of one student in a graduate rhetoric program. Cross-time studies of childhood register acquisition include Snow et al.'s (1986) work on hospital talk; Andersen's (1990) "apparent-time" study of four-, five-, and six-year-olds' role-playing interactions in the home, doctor's office, and classroom; and Bordeaux and Willbrand's (1987) research, also across apparent time, on acquisition of the discourse rules of telephone conversation. It should also be observed that there are studies treating a single stage of register acquisition: Hoyle (1989) and Pettinari (1988) examine the syntactic and discourse characteristics of, respectively, children sportscasting and surgical residents writing post-operation summaries.

2.3. Synchronic Studies of Register Variation

There is a long tradition of comparative register research in linguistics and related fields. Studies taking this approach have tended to focus on single situational parameters of variation, such as formality, plannedness, or mode. Analysis of register variation involves the comparison of two or more varieties that differ with respect to at least one of these parameters.

2.3.1. COMPARISONS OF SPOKEN AND WRITTEN REGISTERS IN ENGLISH

Variation across spoken versus written language has been intensively investigated.[11] In general, such studies have relied on quantitative methods of analysis and have focused on the differing relative distributions of linguistic features across texts, including lexical features such as type/token ratio, word length, and the frequency of once-occurring words; grammatical features such as frequencies of adjectives, prepositional phrases, and nominalizations; and clause-level syntactic features such as the frequencies of various clause types, T-unit length, and subordination indexes.

Numerous comparisons of spoken and written registers have examined elicited discourse. A relatively early study was done by Drieman (1962), whose subjects talked and wrote about pictures, analyzing features such as lexical variety, long words, and text length. DeVito (1966, 1967) examined published research articles and then interviewed their writers on the same topics, analyzing a wide range of features including lexical diversity, simple sentences, nouns, adjectives, verbs, and adverbs. O'Donnell et al. (1967) collected spoken and written descriptions of films by students in grades three, five, and seven and compared them with respect to T-unit length and frequencies of various syntactic transformations. Gibson et al. (1966), Golub (1969), Blass and Siegman (1975), Harris (1977), Cayer and Sacks (1979), and Price and Graves (1980) likewise focused on lexical, grammatical, and clause-level syntactic characteristics of speech and written compositions elicited from students. In an especially thorough study, Kroch and Hindle (1982) elicited student interviews and compositions across descriptive, narrative, and argumentative tasks. They then compared these varieties to one another as well as to newspaper articles and sociolinguistic interviews. This study also considered some linguistic characteristics not previously investigated, including the distribution of given/new information, referential strategies, and types of relativization.

Research on spoken versus written register variation has also analyzed spontaneously occurring discourse. Blankenship (1962) studied the lectures and published writing of public figures, focusing on complexity features such as sentence length and passive constructions. In a more elaborate study, Blankenship (1974) compared six spoken and written registers with respect to a wide variety of features including word and sentence length, type-token ratio, adjectives, and prepositions. At the opposite extreme in scale, O'Donnell (1974) compared a spoken and a written text from one individual. In a series of studies, Chafe (1982, 1984, 1985; Chafe and Danielewicz 1986) examined dinner table conversations, personal letters, lectures, and academic papers, describing the importance of linguistic markers of "integration/fragmentation" (e.g., nominalizations, participles, and relative clauses versus clause coordination) and "involvement/detachment" (e.g., first person pronouns versus passive constructions). Redeker (1984) has partially replicated some of Chafe's findings in an analysis of elicited spoken and written personal narratives and explanations.

Tannen (1982) collected spontaneous conversational narratives from subjects and then elicited written versions of the same story. She used qualitative research methods to compare the spoken and written versions in terms of such discourse phenomena as the use of repetition, parallelism, and structural elaboration. In a related study, Tannen (1989) presents a detailed qualitative investigation of "literary/involvement" features, including repetition, dialogue, details, and imagery. Although this study concentrates on conversation, it includes drama and literary fiction as standards for comparison. Macaulay (1990) also focuses on spontaneously occurring discourse but combines quantitative with qualitative analysis. She analyzes spoken and written texts collected in the public domain, representing five communicative tasks: narration, description, exposition, instruction, and argumentation.

Other studies examine more specialized kinds of speech and writing and often include analysis of other linguistic characteristics. Burton (1980) juxtaposed drama and natural conversation. Hu (1984) compared passages from *The Great Gatsby* and the screenplay of a movie based on the novel. The latter study also considered some little-examined features—pronominal reference, thematic structure, lexical cohesion, and exclamations. Halpern (1984) compared tape-recorded interviews and written versions of the interviews edited for publication, focusing on such features as discourse structure, tense switching, and pronominal reference. Lakoff (1982) compared the use of persuasive features in written advertising and conversation in terms of lexical, morphological, and syntactic novelty; the absence of subjects; and unusual uses of definite articles.

The multidimensional (MD) approach to register variation was developed by Biber (1986, 1988) for comparative analyses of spoken and written registers in English. This approach uses computerized analysis of text corpora combined with multivariate statistical techniques. In early MD analyses of English, approximately five hundred texts from twenty-three registers were analyzed, including conversations, speeches, broadcasts, letters, press reportage, academic prose, and fiction. Linguistic features analyzed in these studies include lexical characteristics, grammatical features, and clause-level syntax. In MD analysis, registers are compared along multiple *dimensions* of variation, with each dimension representing a group of linguistic features that co-occur frequently in texts.

Biber (1989) uses the MD approach to identify the linguistically well-defined *text types* of English (i.e., text varieties which are maximally similar in terms of their linguistic characteristics). Other MD analyses of English include Biber (1987, 1991, 1992a, b) and Biber and Finegan (1989a, 1992a).

2.3.2. SPOKEN VERSUS WRITTEN REGISTERS IN OTHER LANGUAGES

There have been far fewer comparisons of spoken and written registers in languages other than English. Comparing oral and written stories in the Arawakan language Amuesha, Duff (1973) found differences in discourse organization, explicitness (e.g., the use or omission of temporal markers), and noun phrases. Deibler (1976) compared letters and conversations in Gahuku, a Papua New Guinean language, with respect to such features as contractions, shortened verbs, imperatives, and sentence length. Hurd (1979) described the general characteristics of speech and writing in the Solomon Islands language Nasioi, on the basis of an analysis of repetitions, grammatical reductions, conjunctions, and vocabulary selection in a traditional legend, a personal narrative, and a procedural text.

A relatively detailed description of Japanese spoken versus written narratives is presented by Clancy (1982). This analysis grew out of the "Pear Stories" project, in which subjects watched a short silent film and then described it in speech and writing (see Chafe 1980). The spoken/written differences examined in this study concerned referential choice (full NP, pronoun, or zero), word order, and relative clause types. Tannen (1984b) also used pear story narratives to compare speech and writing in Greek and English. Li and Thompson (1982) compared the characteristics of written Classical Chinese with spoken and written modern Mandarin, focusing on zero anaphora, clause length, and the presence of grammatical morphemes. (Cf. Romaine this volume, which analyzes the development of the sports reporting register in Tok Pisin.)

Spoken and written registers in other languages have also been subjected to multidimensional analysis. Besnier (1988) analyzed the characteristics of seven spoken and written registers in Nukulaelae Tuvaluan (e.g., conversations, political meetings, private-setting speeches, sermons, letters) with respect to three underlying linguistic dimensions of variation ("Attitudinal versus Authoritative Discourse," "Informational versus Interactional Focus," and "Rhetorical Manipulation versus Structural Complexity"). Kim (1990; Kim and Biber this volume) studied the relations among twenty-two spoken and written registers in Korean with respect to six underlying dimensions (e.g., "On-Line Interaction versus Planned Exposition," "Overt versus Implicit Logical Cohesion"). Finally, Biber and Hared (1992a, b, this volume) investigated patterns of variation among twenty-six spoken and written registers in Somali, identifying six basic dimensions of variation (e.g., "Structural Elaboration: Involvement versus Exposition" and "Argumentative versus Reported Presentation of Information").

2.3.3. VARIATION ALONG OTHER SITUATIONAL PARAMETERS—FORMALITY, PLANNEDNESS, AND ELABORATION

Formality is another parameter of variation to which register analysts have given considerable attention. Although this term has been frequently used in register research, there is substantial disagreement over its definition. Irvine (1979) identifies three major uses of *formality* in previous discourse analytic research: (1) to describe linguistic characteristics of discourse (in terms of increased structuring and predictability), (2) to describe characteristics of the social situation, and (3) to refer to a kind of linguistic analysis in which the rules governing discourse are made maximally explicit. An early register study employing the notion of formality is Joos' (1961) discussion of five different *styles,* which he labeled "frozen," "formal," "consultative," "casual," and "intimate." In another early study, Fischer (1958) distinguished among three levels of formality in sociolinguistic interviews. Ervin-Tripp (1972) studied linguistic co-occurrence patterns in formal versus informal styles. Hudson (this volume) compares diglossia to the opposition between formal and informal language.

Finegan (1987, Finegan and Biber 1986) compares registers along a parameter of "prestige," which relates linguistically to both formality and spoken/written register differences. In his investigations of social variation in New York City, Labov (1972) employs a "scale of formality," which he characterizes in terms of "attention paid to speech." Distinguished on this scale are five styles of speech ranging from informal to highly formal: casual, interview, reading passage, word list, and minimal-pair list.

Several studies compare the conversational registers produced by individuals in different situations, in different settings, and with different purposes and topics. For example, Van den Broeck (1977) studied differences in syntactic complexity of speech produced during a structured interview and in casual situations. Hindle (1979) studied vowel shifts in the conversational speech of one individual, in relation to the situational parameters of setting (including goals and formality), addressee (sex differences, familiarity of participants, and power considerations), and key (relating topic and purpose). Coupland (1980) undertook a similar study, analyzing phonological variation in the language of a travel agent. Four discrete situations of language use ("casual," "informal work-related," "client," and "telephone") were identified in this study, and shifts in communicative purpose and role-relations within situations were found to influence phonological variation far more than shifts in discourse topic. Coupland (1983) continues the investigation of language use in the same travel agency, analyzing functional explicitness across situations and social groups. Bell (1984) develops a framework to account for stylistic variation in terms of a speaker's response to her audience or addressee; Bell attempts to explain other aspects of register variation, along parameters such as topic and setting, by reference to their association with addressee types. Rickford and McNair-Knox (this volume) approach register variation from a similar perspective.

Another closely related parameter of variation is the distinction between planned and unplanned discourse described by Ochs (1979), who compared unplanned spoken narratives with planned written narratives on the same topic. Linguistic features analyzed include referent deletion, grammatical encoding of propositional relations, demonstratives, definite articles, and active and passive voice.

Other studies have tested Bernstein's distinction between "restricted" and "elaborated" codes (e.g., Bernstein 1970). These studies typically involve comparisons across social groups as well as registers. Robinson (1965) compared formal and informal letters by middle-class (MC) and working-class (WC) students with respect to the distribution of common linguistic features, including nouns, pronouns, adjectives, prepositions, and various clause types. Rushton and Young (1975) compared imaginative descriptive writing, opinionative discursive writing, and technical explanatory writing of MC and WC students, focusing primarily on their use of complex nominal modifiers, passives, WH subordinators, and deeply embedded clauses. Poole and Field (1976) used factor analysis to compare interviews and written personal essays by MC and WC undergraduates with respect to mean sentence length, subordinate clauses, adjectives, adverbs, passives, and pronouns.

2.3.4. VARIATION ACROSS WRITTEN REGISTERS

Several studies have used multivariate statistical techniques (e.g., factor analysis or discriminant analysis) to analyze the parameters of variation among written registers in English. Probably the earliest of these was Carroll (1960), who identified parameters of variation among 150 texts from nine written registers (e.g., novels, essays, scientific papers, and letters). This study includes variables reflecting subjective ratings of writing style in addition to grammatical characteristics. Related research was undertaken by Marckworth and Baker (1974) on the comparative linguistic characteristics of fiction, government documents, newspapers, and popular and academic prose. Grabe (1987) used a multidimensional analysis to identify parameters of variation across thirteen registers of English expository prose, representing six major use domains—natural science, social science, law, humanities, business reports, and news—and three audience levels—academic, introductory, popular. This study included analysis of cohesion markers as well as lexical and grammatical features. Biber (1987) employed a multidimensional analysis to describe dialect differences between paired samples of nine written registers in British and American English. Connor-Linton (1988) used a multidimensional analysis to contrast two markedly different registers of nuclear discourse. Dubuisson et al. (1989) used multivariate statistical techniques to analyze the patterns of structural complexity among written narratives, informative writing, and argumentative written discourse.[12]

2.3.5. VARIATION WITH REGARD TO PARTICULAR LINGUISTIC CLASSES

Numerous other studies have compared registers with respect to some particular lexical or grammatical class. Much of this research focuses on spoken and written registers, often using the Brown, LOB, or London/Lund corpora of English as its data base.[13] Studies in this category include Tottie (1986), who describes the differing use of adverbials; Coates (1983), Tottie (1985, Tottie and Overgaard 1984), and Hermeren (1986), who analyze the differing patterns of modals; Tottie (1981, 1983, 1991), who discusses the different types and distributions of negation; and Altenberg (1984, 1986), who describes patterns of causal and contrastive linking. In other comparisons of spoken and written registers, Chafe (1986) describes evidentiality markers in English spoken and written registers, and Biber and Finegan (1988, 1989b) analyze spoken and written English registers with respect to the marking of stance.

Several studies have focused on patterns of coordination, subordination, and syntactic complexity. Thompson (1983) compares the discourse functions of detached participial clauses in "depictive" and "nondepictive" written discourse. In two other studies, Thompson examines various types of structural dependency in formal writing, informal writing, and conversation (1984) and compares initial and final purpose clauses in narratives and procedural texts (1985). Beaman (1984) has analyzed the patterns of coordination and subordination in spoken and written narratives based on the "Pear Stories" film, while Kroll (1977) analyzed patterns of coordination and subordination in spoken and written "threat of death" stories by college freshmen. Mair (1990) analyzed the distribution and functions of infinitival complement clauses across the written and spoken registers included in the corpus of the Survey of English Usage. Bäcklund (1984, 1986) focuses on conjunction-headed abbreviated clauses in the registers of the Brown, LOB, and London-Lund corpora.

Biber (1992a) uses confirmatory factor analysis to compare the relative strengths of several models of discourse complexity, identifying a particular five-dimension model as the most adequate with respect to the thirty-three linguistic markers of complexity analyzed. This model is used to highlight a fundamental distinction between the discourse complexity of written and spoken registers: while written registers exhibit many complexity profiles, differing in both degree and type of complexity, spoken registers manifest a single pattern differing only in degree.

Other studies focus on differences in textual information structure across registers, related to the marking of anaphora, text deixis, definiteness, and cohesion. Kurzon (1985) reports on the marking of text deixis in the written registers of the LOB Corpus. Fox (1987a, 1987b) analyzes the marking of anaphora and discourse structure in conversation, written articles, and written narratives. Fraurud (1988) studies pronoun resolution in Swedish short stories, court reports, and technological articles; Fraurud (1990) examines the relationship between definiteness and the processing of noun phrases in Swedish brochures, newspaper articles, textbooks, and debate books. Chafe (1991) analyzes the varying forms of grammatical subjects in conversation, fiction, and news reports.

Other related studies focus on markers of informational organization and prominence: Prince (1978) describes *WH-* and *it*-clefts in speech and writing; Prince (1981) analyzes given and new information types in speech and writing; Green (1982) compares colloquial and literary use of subject-verb inversions; and Collins (1987) details the differing distributions of clefts and pseudo-clefts across the major spoken and written registers in the LOB and London-Lund corpora.

Cohesion patterns within and across registers have also been studied from a functional perspective. Halliday and Hasan (1976) initiated this area of study in their exhaustive analysis of cohesion in English (an appendix illustrates different patterns of cohesion through analysis of passages from a conversation, a novel, a sonnet, a dramatic dialogue, an autobiography, and an informal interview; cf. Halliday and Hasan 1989). Smith and Frawley (1983) analyze the patterns of conjunctive cohesion in the registers of fiction, journalism, religion, and science. Gumperz et al. (1984) describe the different patterns of thematic cohesion in spoken and written discourse. Biber (1992b) analyzes the distribution of features relating to informational prominence and lexical cohesion across nine spoken and written registers, identifying marked differences in their referential strategies. Several studies analyze cohesion and coherence in school-related registers: Fitzgerald and Speigel (1986) describe patterns of cohesion and coherence in children's writing; DeStefano and Kantor (1988) analyze the different patterns of cohesion in conversation and dialogue from children's storybooks; Cox et al. (1990) compare the patterns of cohesion in the writing of good and poor readers. Myers (1991) has described the contrasting patterns of lexical cohesion in scientific journal articles and popularized accounts of the same research.

Grammatical devices for interaction and clarification have also been shown to vary systematically across registers. Philips (1985), for example, analyzes the clarification structures used in judges' spoken versus written statements of constitutional rights to defendants.

2.4. Diachronic Register Variation Studies

There have been far fewer studies dealing with diachronic register variation—that is, the analysis of the relations among two or more registers across time. Several early studies of this type combine literary and linguistic concerns. For example, Vallins (1956), Gordon (1966), and Bennett (1971) trace the linguistic and rhetorical development of literary prose styles in English.

A more strictly linguistic approach is Romaine's (1980, 1982) "socio-historical" linguistics, which is based on analysis of the relative frequency of forms across registers in different historical periods. She illustrates this approach through an analysis of the alternation among relative clause markers in Middle Scots English, considering registers such as verse drama, narrative prose, epistolary prose, and record prose. Kytö and Rissanen (1983), Rissanen (1986), Kytö (1986, 1991), Nevalainen (1986), and Nevalainen and Raumolin-Brunberg (1989) adopt this approach in studying the patterns of historical syntax in early British and American English. Devitt (1989a, b) also uses this approach to analyze the influence of register variation on historical processes of standardization in Scots English and American English. She considers five registers (private records, private correspondence, official correspondence, religious treatises, and public records) and shows how such linguistic features as present participle inflections and relative pronouns were standardized at different rates in different registers. Hared (1992) adopts a similar methodological approach to analyze the historical changes in three Somali press registers over the first seventeen years of their history (1972–1989), associated with the complementary processes of standardization and modernization.

The multidimensional approach has also been used to study diachronic register variation. Biber and Finegan (1989a, 1992a, b) trace the development of English registers from 1650 to the present, with respect to three of the linguistic dimensions identified in Biber (1988). The 1989a study focuses on the development of fiction, essays, and letters, interpreting the observed patterns of change relative to the changing purposes and readership of written texts and to the changing attitudes toward various registers. The 1992a study adds analysis of fictional and dramatic dialogue to the earlier description. The 1992b study uses the framework developed in these previous studies to compare the written styles of particular eighteenth-century authors (e.g., Swift, Addison, and Johnson) across registers.

Biber and Hared (1992b, this volume) also use a multidimensional analysis to study historical change in Somali since the introduction of native-language literacy in 1973. The 1992b study compares the range of register variation found before 1973 (when only spoken registers existed) with that found immediately after 1973 (among spoken *and* written registers). The chapter in the present volume traces the evolution of seven press registers from 1973 to 1989.

3. Other Research Areas Relevant to Register Analysis

Several other types of studies within linguistics and related fields are highly relevant to register research.[14] We have divided these studies into five categories, each of which is treated briefly below: studies of functional grammar and discourse, psycholinguistic studies of discourse structure, ethnographic speech event and speech act analysis, studies of cross-cultural discourse, and rhetorical text studies.

3.1. Studies of Functional Grammar and Discourse

Studies of functional grammar and discourse are important to register analysts in that they help to establish the discourse functions of particular linguistic features. Many of these studies analyze conversational discourse. Such studies include Menn and Boyce (1982) on the functions of different intonation patterns, Givón (1983) on patterns of "topic continuity," and Thavenius (1983) on the use of referential pronouns. Aijmer (1984) analyzes the functions of *sort of* and *kind of,* while Aijmer (1986) analyzes the uses of *actually.* A series of functional studies have been undertaken by Schiffrin: Shiffrin (1981) focuses on tense variation in conversational narratives; Schiffrin (1985a) examines the discourse functions of *well* in conversation; Schiffrin (1985b) focuses on variation in causal sequences; and Schiffrin (1987) is a book-length treatment of conversational discourse markers. Labov (1984) describes the marking of intensity in conversational sociolinguistic interviews. Weiner and Labov (1983) analyze the distribution of agentless passives in sociolinguistic interviews. Hasan (1989) studies topic variation in conversation. Fox and Thompson (1990) show how the choices among structural options for English relative clauses depend on information flow considerations in conversation. Stenström (1986) describes the different uses of *really* in both speech and writing.

Several functional grammar studies undertake analysis of features in other languages. For example, Duranti and Ochs (1979) describe the functions of left-dislocation in Italian conversation; Duranti (1984) describes the functions of subject pronouns in Italian conversations; Biber (1984) describes the discourse functions of focus constructions in Somali folktales; and Clancy (1989) describes the functions of *WH*-questions in Korean conversation.

Other functional studies describe the role of linguistic features in written texts. Brown (1983) describes patterns of topic continuity in fiction. Hiltunen (1984) analyzes the types and functions of clausal embedding in legal English. Jones and Jones (1985) focus on the discourse functions of clefts, extraposed sentences, and rhetorical questions, illustrated with examples from written expository registers. Huckin et al. (1986) for *WH*-deletions and Huckin and Pesante (1988) for existential *there* describe the use of functional features across a wide variety of written registers. Ward (1990) treats the discourse functions of verb-phrase preposing in English, on the basis of examples from newspaper articles and news broadcasts. There are also numerous studies of functional text features in written scientific and technical registers, for example, West (1980) for "*that*-nominal" constructions, Heslot (1982) for verb tense, Weissberg (1984) for structuring of given and new information, Baker (1988) and Myers (1992) for first person personal pronouns, and Myers (1989) for markers of politeness.

3.2. Linguistic and Psycholinguistic Studies of Discourse Structure

Processing-oriented and linguistic analyses of discourse structure describe the text-structural characteristics of various text types. The text-comprehension research program conducted by Meyer (e.g., 1975, 1985), for instance, seeks to describe the propositional and top-level text structure of broad types of expository prose, while Mandler (e.g., 1984, 1987), among others, characterizes the story structure of written and spoken narratives. Notable research by linguist-psycholinguist teams includes van Dijk and Kintsch (e.g., 1983) and Mann and Thompson (1988). Other recent studies of this type include van Dijk (1988, reviewed in section 2.1.1) and Bazerman (1985).

3.3. Ethnographic Speech Event and Speech Act Analysis

Ethnographic speech event and speech act analysis has been undertaken by a wide range of researchers; studies taking these approaches almost always give detailed situational descriptions of specific contexts of language use. Examples include OchsKeenan (1973) on Malagasy oratory; Becker (1979) on the language of Javanese shadow theatre; Knorr-Cetina (1981:chapter 5) on scientific research writing in the context of the laboratory; Heath (1983) on speaking and writing practices in three communities in the American South; Borker (1986) regarding the services of one Scottish religious sect; Freed and Broadhead (1986) on the writing practices of competing management consultant firms; Foster (1989) on the "performance" style of one African American college teacher; and Fishman (1991) on writing in the American Amish community.

3.4. Cross-Cultural Studies of Discourse

Another area of research with consequences for the study of register is cross-cultural discourse studies. This area includes research on oral discourse strategies across cultures and languages in comparable situational settings; for example, Tannen (1984a) discusses cultural differences among Americans in their informal conversational styles, Tannen (1984b) compares narrative styles in Greek and English, and

Yamada (1992) compares language use in Japanese and American business meetings. A second type of cross-cultural discourse study concentrates on comparing particular genres of writing across languages and cultures. Studies in this area, which is commonly termed *contrastive rhetoric* (Kaplan 1966), include Clyne (1987) on German and American social-science writing; Hinds (1980) and Connor (1988) on Japanese and American expository prose and written business correspondence, respectively; Purves (1988) on high school compositions across a variety of cultures; and Lux and Grabe (1991) on editorials in Portuguese and English, and student compositions in Spanish and English. In addition, ethnographic research (e.g., Scollon and Scollon 1981) draws explicit comparisons of language use across cultures.

3.5. Rhetorical Text Studies

A final area of register-related investigation is research into the rhetorical characteristics of specific situational language varieties. Studies, for example, on the rhetoric of specialist/technical prose analyze texts in terms of classical rhetorical categories such as *topoi* (e.g., Miller and Selzer 1985, for engineering reports), or more modern rhetorical features such as analogy and metaphor (e.g., Gross 1990:chapter 2, for scientific research writing) and metadiscourse (Crismore and Farnsworth 1990, for specialist versus popular scientific writing). Bazerman's work (1988:chapter 3) on rhetorical change over time in experimental articles in the *Philosophical Transactions of the Royal Society*—the prototypical modern scientific journal—is an excellent example of a rhetorical study which sets the stage for an accompanying register analysis.

4. Conclusion

In this chapter we have attempted to (1) provide a wide-ranging survey of empirical register studies, (2) classify studies according to a set of analytical criteria, and (3) emphasize the common ground that studies from a wide range of methodological and disciplinary perspectives share. A more general purpose has also motivated us here: to raise the level of awareness among *all* language-in-context researchers— linguists, anthropologists, rhetoricians, educational researchers, sociologists, literary scholars, and those in other fields—to the existence of highly relevant work on registers in a wide range of disciplines.

Notes

1. Also included under this criterion are studies of *register markers* (Ferguson 1983)— features which function, through frequency of occurrence or conventionalized association with specific contexts, as high-profile signals of particular registers (e.g., compound nominal phrases in medical research writing). There is a well-recognized danger in assuming that single linguistic features can function as absolute markers of specific registers, especially

when registers have been widely defined in terms of the *co-occurrence of features* (Ervin-Tripp 1972, Brown and Fraser 1979, Halliday 1988, Biber 1988). Still, there seem to be grounds for claiming that some linguistic features—through conventionalization, frequency of occurrence, or perceptual salience—act as more powerful psycholinguistic cues than others for knowledge of the sort which comprises registral or generic competence (cf., Atkinson 1991).

2. There are several reviews and surveys of legal language. Danet (1980), mentioned previously, is a full review of research on language and the law up to the late 1970s; Levi (1982) also reviews earlier studies. Bhatia (1987) reviews legal language studies with a pedagogical focus. Other reviews include Shuy (1987), Swales (1991), and Maher and Rokosz (1992), although the areas covered by the two latter articles are not limited to legal language. Special journal issues on legal discourse include Danet (1984) and Bhatia and Swales (1982).

3. Studies of this type can be found in Fisher and Todd (1983, 1986); a special issue of *Discourse Processes* (7.2, 1984) on physician-patient communication edited by Frankel; an issue of the *International Journal of the Sociology of Language* (no. 51, 1985) on language use in the health professions, edited by Coleman; and a special issue of *Text* (7.1, 1987) on spoken medical discourse edited by Freeman and Heller. Maher (1986) reviews studies of medical language with a pedagogical focus.

4. Surveys of scientific discourse include the pedagogically oriented review by Van Naerssen and Kaplan (1987). Swales (1990) offers probably the most complete bibliography on the scientific research article available.

5. Geis (1987b) reviews media language, while Todd and O'Donnell (1980) give brief general accounts of media and advertising English along with short lists of relevant sources.

6. Cazden (1988) is a book-length review of classroom discourse studies, while Cazden (1986) is a shorter but useful review. Poole (1991) surveys some of the more recent literature on language and schooling, while Christie (1992) provides partial coverage of the educational language research currently under way in Australia (but not yet widely available in the United States).

7. In the area of school-based composition research, Hillocks (1986:chapter 2) reviews linguistically oriented studies up to the mid-1980s.

8. Samarin (1976) is an edited, register-oriented volume on language and religion, while Fox (1988) is a collection of ethnographies on ritual language use in eastern Indonesia. Webster (1988) gives a useful conceptual overview of the language of religion.

9. Foreigner talk is also the subject of issue 28 (1981) of the *International Journal of the Sociology of Language,* edited by Clyne.

10. Melander's study comes out of an active European tradition of research on *Language for Special Purposes* (LSP). Other studies in this tradition can be found in Pugh and Ulijn (1984). Schröder (1991) is a theory-oriented review and bibliography.

11. Indeed, the more general topic of speech versus writing has been such a productive research area that several survey papers have appeared. Of these, Chafe and Tannen (1987) is probably the most complete, but Rubin (1980), Schafer (1981), Akinnaso (1982), Liggett (1984), and Halliday (1979, 1989) are also useful.

12. Grabe (1990) provides an overview of written register research.

13. The Brown, LOB, and London-Lund corpora are large, computer-based text collections from many registers of English. The Brown Corpus is composed of sixteen major written registers from American English (e.g., press reportage, editorials, biographies, academic prose, general fiction; there are also many subregisters, such as humanities and technical/engineering academic prose). The LOB Corpus represents the same registers as the Brown Corpus for British English. The London-Lund Corpus comprises six major spoken

registers of British English (i.e., face-to-face conversations, telephone conversations, interviews, broadcasts, spontaneous public speeches, prepared speeches). General reference works on these corpora are Francis and Kučera (1982), which presents the distribution of words and grammatical classes across the registers in the Brown Corpus; Johansson and Hofland (1989), which presents the distribution of words and grammatical classes across the registers in the LOB Corpus; and Svartvik (1990), which describes recent research based on the London-Lund Corpus. The bibliographies in Svartvik (1990), the *ICAME Journal* (1986), and Altenberg (1991) provide numerous references to register and functional-linguistic studies based on these text corpora.

14. In this final section, we cover only a few of the areas of language study that are relevant to empirical register research. Examples of other areas include research in computer science on *sublanguages* (Kittredge and Lehrman 1982, Grishman and Kittredge 1986) and linguistically oriented studies of literary style (e.g., Pratt 1977, Leech and Short 1981, Toolan 1990). Studies of *register range* (i.e., attempts to describe the full situational language repertoires of languages or countries) should also be mentioned here—Ellis and Ure (1982) are a valuable source for such studies, which appear to be meant primarily to serve the needs of language planners.

References

Adams Smith, Diane. 1984. "Medical Discourse: Aspects of Author's Comment." *ESP Journal* 3:25–36.

Aijmer, Karin. 1984. "*Sort of* and *kind of* in English Conversation." *Studia Linguistica* 38:118–28.

———. 1986. "Why Is *actually* So Popular in Spoken English?" In Tottie and Bäcklund, eds. Pp. 119–30.

Akinnaso, F. Niyi. 1982. "On the Differences Between Spoken and Written Language." *Language and Speech* 25:97–125.

Altenberg, Bengt. 1984. "Causal Linking in Spoken and Written English." *Studia Linguistica* 38:20–69.

———. 1986. "Contrastive Linking in Spoken and Written English." In Tottie and Bäcklund, eds. Pp. 13–40.

———. 1991. "A Bibliography of Publications Relating to English Language Corpora." In Stig Johannson and Anna-Brita Stenström, eds., *English Computer Corpora: Selected Papers and Research Guide*. Berlin: Mouton. Pp. 355–96.

Andersen, Elaine S. 1990. *Speaking with Style: The Sociolinguistic Skills of Children*. London: Routledge.

Atkinson, Dwight. 1991. "Discourse Analysis and Written Discourse Conventions." *Annual Review of Applied Linguistics* 11:57–76.

———. 1992. "The Evolution of Medical Research Writing from 1735 to 1985: The Case of the Edinburgh Medical Journal." *Applied Linguistics* 13:337–74.

Atkinson, J. Maxwell, and Paul Drew. 1979. *Order in Court: The Organisation of Verbal Interaction in Judicial Settings*. Atlantic Highlands, NJ: Humanities.

Bäcklund, Ingegerd. 1984. *Conjunction-Headed Abbreviated Clauses in English*. Uppsala: Studia Anglistica Upsaliensia.

———. 1986. "Beat Until Stiff: Conjunction-Headed Abbreviated Clauses in Spoken and Written English." In Tottie and Bäcklund, eds. Pp. 41–56.

Baker, Mona. 1988. "Subtechnical Vocabulary and the ESP Teacher: An Analysis of Some Rhetorical Items in Medical Journals." *Reading in a Foreign Language* 4:91–105.

Barnes, Douglas, James Britton, and Mike Torbe. 1969. *Language, the Learner and the School*, 4th ed. Portsmouth, NH: Boynton/Cook-Heinemann.

Barr, James. 1961. *The Semantics of Biblical Language*. London: Oxford University Press.

Bauman, Richard, and Joel Sherzer, eds. 1989. *Explorations in the Ethnography of Speaking*, 2nd ed. Cambridge: Cambridge University Press.

Bazerman, Charles. 1984. "Modern Evolution of the Experimental Report in Physics." *Social Studies of Science* 14:163–96.

———. 1985. "Physicists Reading Physics." *Written Communication* 2:3–23.

———. 1988. *Shaping Written Knowledge: The Genre and Activity of the Experimental Article in Science*. Madison: University of Wisconsin Press.

Beaman, Karen. 1984. "Coordination and Subordination Revisited: Syntactic Complexity in Spoken and Written Narrative Discourse." In Tannen, ed. Pp. 45–80.

Becker, A. L. 1979. "Text-building, Epistemology, and Aesthetics in Javanese Shadow Theatre." In A. L. Becker and Aram A. Yengoyan, eds., *The Imagination of Reality*. Norwood, NJ: Ablex. Pp. 211–43.

Bell, Allan. 1984. "Language Style as Audience Design." *Language in Society* 13:145–204.

———. 1990. "Audience and Referee Design in New Zealand Media Language." In Bell and Holmes, eds. Pp. 165–94.

———. 1991. *The Language of News Media*. Oxford: Blackwell.

Bell, Allan, and Janet Holmes, eds. 1990. *New Zealand Ways of Speaking English*. Clevedon, UK: Multilingual Matters.

Bennett, James R. 1971. *Prose Style: A Historical Approach Through Studies*. San Francisco: Chandler.

Berkenkotter, Carol, Thomas N. Huckin, and John Ackerman. 1988. "Conventions, Conversations, and the Writer: Case Study of a Student in a Rhetoric Ph.D. Program." *Research in the Teaching of English* 22:9–44.

———. 1991. "Social Context and Socially Constructed Texts." In Charles Bazerman and James Paradis, eds., *Textual Dynamics of the Professions*. Madison: University of Wisconsin Press. Pp. 191–215.

Bernstein, Basil. 1970. *Class, Codes, and Control*. Vol. 1. *Theoretical Studies Towards a Sociology of Language*. London: Routledge.

Besnier, Niko. 1988. "The Linguistic Relationships of Spoken and Written Nukulaelae Registers." *Language* 64:707–36.

———. 1989. "Literacy and Feelings: The Encoding of Affect in Nukulaelae Letters." *Text* 9:69–91.

Bhatia, V. K. 1987. "Language of the Law." *Language Teaching* 20:227–34.

Bhatia, V. K., and John M. Swales, eds. 1982. "Special Issues on Legal English." *English for Specific Purposes* (Newsletter), 67 and 68.

Biber, Douglas. 1984. "Pragmatic Roles in Central Somali Narrative Discourse." *Studies in African Linguistics* 15:1–26.

———. 1986. "Spoken and Written Textual Dimensions in English: Resolving the Contradictory Findings." *Language* 62:384–414.

———. 1987. "A Textual Comparison of British and American Writing." *American Speech* 62:99–119.

———. 1988. *Variation Across Speech and Writing*. Cambridge: Cambridge University Press.

———. 1989. "A Typology of English Texts." *Linguistics* 27:3–43.

————. 1991. "Oral and Literate Characteristics of Selected Primary School Reading Materials." *Text* 11:73–96.

————. 1992a. "On the Complexity of Discourse Complexity: A Multidimensional Analysis." *Discourse Processes* 15:133–63.

————. 1992b. "Using Computer-Based Text Corpora to Analyze the Referential Strategies of Spoken and Written Texts." In Jan Svartvik, ed., *Directions in Corpus Linguistics: Proceedings of Nobel Symposium 82.* Berlin: Mouton. Pp. 213–52.

Biber, Douglas, and Edward Finegan. 1988. "Adverbial Stance Types in English." *Discourse Processes* 11:1–34.

————. 1989a. "Drift and the Evolution of English Style: A History of Three Genres." *Language* 65:487–517.

————. 1989b. "Styles of Stance in English: Lexical and Grammatical Marking of Evidentiality and Affect." *Text* 9:93–124. (special issue on "The Pragmatics of Affect," ed. by Elinor Ochs).

————. 1992a. "The Linguistic Evolution of Five Written and Speech-Based English Genres From the 17th to the 20th Centuries." In M. Rissanen, O. Ihalainen, T. Nevalainen, and I. Taavitsainen, eds., *History of Englishes: New Methods and Interpretations in Historical Linguistics.* Berlin: Mouton de Gruyter. Pp. 688–704.

————. 1992b. "Multi-dimensional Analyses of Author's Style: Some Case Studies from the 18th Century." *Research in Humanities Computing.*

Biber, Douglas, and Mohamed Hared. 1992a. "Dimensions of Register Variation in Somali." *Language Variation and Change* 4:41–75.

————. 1992b. "Literacy in Somali: Linguistic Consequences." *Annual Review of Applied Linguistics* 12:260–82.

Blankenship, Jane. 1962. "A Linguistic Analysis of Oral and Written Style." *Quarterly Journal of Speech* 48:419–22.

————. 1974. "The Influence of Mode, Submode, and Speaker Predilection on Style." *Speech Monographs* 41:85–118.

Blass, Thomas, and Aron W. Siegman. 1975. "A Psycholinguistic Comparison of Speech, Dictation, and Writing." *Language and Speech* 18:20–33.

Bordeaux, Marcy Annice, and Mary Louise Willbrand. 1987. "Pragmatic Development in Children's Telephone Discourse." *Discourse Processes* 10:253–66.

Borker, Ruth A. 1986. "'Moved by the Spirit': Constructing Meaning in a Brethren Breaking of Bread Service." *Text* 6:317–37.

Broadhead, Glenn J., and R. C. Freed. 1986. *Variables of Composition: Process and Product in a Business Setting.* Carbondale: Southern Illinois University Press.

Brook, Stella. 1965. *The Language of the Book of Common Prayer.* London: Andre Deutsch.

Brown, Cheryl. 1983. "Topic Continuity in Written English Narrative." In Givón, ed. Pp. 313–41.

Brown, Penelope, and Colin Fraser. 1979. "Speech as a Marker of Situation." In Klaus R. Scherer and Howard Giles, eds., *Social Markers in Speech.* Cambridge: Cambridge University Press. Pp. 33–62.

Brown, Robert L., and Carl G. Herndl. 1986. "An Ethnographic Study of Corporate Writing." In Barbara Couture, ed., *Functional Approaches to Writing: Research Perspectives.* Norwood, NJ: Ablex. Pp. 11–28.

Burton, D. 1980. *Dialogue and Discourse: A Sociolinguistic Approach to Modern Drama, Dialogue and Naturally Occurring Conversation.* London: Routledge.

Carroll, John B. 1960. "Vectors of Prose Style." In Thomas A. Sebeok, ed., *Style in Language.* Cambridge, MA: MIT Press. Pp. 283–92.

Carter, Ronald. 1988. "Front Pages: Lexis, Style, and Newspaper Reports." In Ghadessy, ed. Pp. 8–16.

Cayer, Roger L., and Renée K. Sacks. 1979. "Oral and Written Discourse of Basic Writers: Similarities and Differences." *Research in the Teaching of English* 13:121–28.

Cazden, Courtney B. 1986. "Classroom Discourse." In M. C. Whittrock, ed., *Handbook of Research on Teaching*. New York: Macmillan. Pp. 432–674.

———. 1988. *Classroom Discourse: The Language of Teaching and Learning*. Portsmouth, NH: Heinemann.

Chafe, Wallace L., ed. 1980. *The Pear Stories: Cognitive, Cultural, and Linguistic Aspects of Narrative Production*. Norwood, NJ: Ablex.

———. 1982. "Integration and Involvement in Speaking, Writing, and Oral Literature." In Tannen, ed. Pp. 35–54.

———. 1984. "Speaking, Writing, and Prescriptivism." In Schiffrin, ed. Pp. 95–103.

———. 1985. "Linguistic Differences Produced by Differences Between Speaking and Writing." In Olson et al., eds. Pp. 105–23.

———. 1986. "Evidentiality in English Conversation and Academic Writing." In Wallace L. Chafe and Johanna Nichols, eds., *Evidentiality: The Linguistic Coding of Epistemology*. Norwood, NJ: Ablex. Pp. 261–272.

———. 1991. "Grammatical Subjects in Speaking and Writing." *Text* 11:45–72.

Chafe, Wallace L., and Jane Danielewicz. 1987. "Properties of Spoken and Written Language." In Rosalind Horowitz and S. J. Samuels, eds., *Comprehending Oral and Written Language*. New York: Academic Press. Pp. 83–113.

Chafe, Wallace L., and Deborah Tannen. 1987. "The Relation Between Written and Spoken Language." *Annual Review of Anthropology* 16:383–407.

Charrow, Veda R. 1982. "Language in the Bureaucracy." In Di Pietro, ed. Pp. 173–88.

Christie, Frances. 1992. "Literacy in Australia." *Annual Review of Applied Linguistics* 12:142–55.

Clancy, Patricia M. 1982. "Written and Spoken Style in Japanese Narratives." In Tannen, ed. Pp. 55–76.

———. 1989. "Form and Function in the Acquisition of Korean *Wh*-questions." *Journal of Child Language* 16:323–47.

Clyne, Michael G. 1977. "Multilingualism and Pidginization in Australian Industry." *Ethnic Studies* 1:40–55.

———. ed. 1981. Issue on "Foreigner Talk." *International Journal of the Sociology of Language* 28.

———. 1987. "Cultural Differences in the Organization of Academic Texts." *Journal of Pragmatics* 11:211–47.

Coates, Jennifer. 1983. *The Semantics of the Modal Auxiliaries*. London: Croom Helm.

Coleman, Hywel, ed. 1985. Issue on "Language and Work 2: The Health Professions." *International Journal of the Sociology of Language* 51.

Collins, James, and Sarah Michaels. 1986. "Speaking and Writing: Discourse Strategies and the Acquisition of Literacy." In Jenny Cook-Gumperz, ed., *The Social Construction of Literacy*. Cambridge: Cambridge University Press. Pp. 207–22.

Collins, Peter C. 1987. "Cleft and Pseudo-Cleft Constructions in English Spoken and Written Discourse. *ICAME Journal* 11:5–17.

Connor, Ulla M. 1988. "A Contrastive Study of Persuasive Business Correspondence: American and Japanese." In Sam J. Bruno, ed., *Global Implications for Business Communications: Proceedings of the 15th International Conventions of the Association for Business Communication*. Houston: University of Houston-Clear Lake. Pp. 57–72.

Connor-Linton, Jeff. 1988. "Author's Style and World-View in Nuclear Discourse: A Quantitative Analysis." *Multilingua* 7:95–132.

Connor-Linton, Jeff, Christopher J. Hall, and Mary McGinnis, eds. 1986. *Social and Cognitive Perspectives on Language. (Southern California Occasional Papers in Linguistics 11).* Los Angeles: University of Southern California.

Coupland, Nikolas. 1980. "Style-Shifting in a Cardiff Work-Setting." *Language in Society* 9:1–12.

———. 1983. "Patterns of Encounter Management: Further Arguments for Discourse Variables." *Language in Society* 12:459–76.

Cox, Beverly E., Timothy Shanahan, and Elizabeth Sulzby. 1990. "Good and Poor Elementary Readers' Use of Cohesion in Writing." *Reading Research Quarterly* 25:47–65.

Crismore, Avon, and Rodney Farnsworth. 1990. "Metadiscourse in Popular and Professional Science Discourse." In Walter Nash, ed., *The Writing Scholar: Studies in Academic Discourse.* Newbury Park, CA: Sage. Pp. 118–36.

Crystal, David, and Derek Davy. 1969. *Investigating English Style.* New York: Longman.

Danet, Brenda. 1980. "Language in the Legal Process." *Law and Society Review* 14:445–564.

———, ed. 1984. Special issue on "Legal Discourse." *Text* 4.

———. 1985. "Legal Discourse." In Teun A. van Dijk, ed., *Handbook of Discourse Analysis,* Vol. 1. Orlando, FL: Academic Press. Pp. 273–89.

Deibler, Ellis W., Jr. 1976. "Differences Between Written and Oral Styles in Languages Near Goroka." *Read* 11:77–79.

DeStefano, Johanna S., and Rebecca Kantor. 1988. "Cohesion in Spoken and Written Dialogue: An Investigation of Cultural and Textual Constraints." *Linguistics and Education* 1:105–24.

DeVito, Joseph A. 1966. "Psychogrammatical Actors in Oral and Written Discourse by Skilled Communicators." *Speech Monographs* 33:73–76.

———. 1967. "Levels of Abstraction in Spoken and Written Language." *Journal of Communication* 17:354–61.

Devitt, Amy J. 1989a. *Standardizing Written English: Diffusion in the Case of Scotland, 1520–1659.* Cambridge: Cambridge University Press.

———. 1989b. "Genre as Textual Variable: Some Historical Evidence From Scots and American English." *American Speech* 64:291–303.

Di Pietro, Robert J., ed. 1982. *Linguistics and the Professions.* Norwood, NJ: Ablex.

Drieman, G. H. J. 1962. "Differences Between Written and Spoken Language." *Acta Psychologica* 20:36–57, 78–100.

Dubois, Betty Lou. 1980. "Genre and Structure of Biomedical Speeches." *Forum Linguisticum* 5:140–66.

———. 1982. "The Construction of Noun Phrases in Biomedical Journal Articles." In J. Hoedt et al., eds., *Pragmatics and LSP.* Copenhagen: Copenhagen School of Economics. Pp. 49–67.

Dubuisson, Colette, Louisette Emirkanian, and David Sankoff. 1989. "The Development of Syntactic Complexity in Narrative, Informative and Argumentative Discourse." In R. Fasold and D. Schiffrin, eds., *Language Change and Variation.* Philadelphia: Benjamins. Pp. 333–50.

Dudley-Evans, Tony, and Willie Henderson. 1990. "The Organization of Article Introductions: Evidence of Change in Economics Writing." In Tony Dudley-Evans and Willie Henderson, eds., *The Language of Economics: The Analysis of Economics Discourse. (ELT Documents 134).* London: British Council. Pp. 67–78.

Duff, Martha. 1973. "Contrastive Features of Oral and Written Texts in Amuesha." *Notes on Translation* 50:2–13.

Dunham, George. 1986. "The Role of Syntax in the Sublanguage of Medical Diagnostic Statements." In Ralph Grishman and Richard Kittredge, eds. Pp. 175–94.

Duranti, Alessandro. 1983. "Samoan Speechmaking Across Social Events: One Genre In and Out of a Fono." *Language in Society* 12:1–22.

———. 1984. "The Social Meaning of Subject Pronouns in Italian Conversation." *Text* 4:277–311.

Duranti, Alessandro, and Elinor Ochs. 1979. "Left-Dislocation in Italian Conversation." In Talmy Givón, ed., *Syntax and Semantics, 12: Discourse and Syntax.* New York: Academic Press. Pp. 377–416.

Early, M. M. 1985. *Input and Interaction in Content Classrooms: Foreigner-Talk and Teacher-Talk in Classroom Discourse.* Ph.D. Dissertation, University of California at Los Angeles.

Ellis, Jeffrey, and Jean Ure, eds. 1982. Issue on "Register Range and Change." *International Journal of the Sociology of Language* 35.

Ervin-Tripp, Susan. 1972. "On Sociolinguistic Rules: Alternation and Co-Occurrence." In John J. Gumperz and Dell Hymes, eds., *Directions in Sociolinguistics.* New York: Holt. Pp. 213–50.

Felker, D., F. Pickering, V. Charrow, V. M. Holland, and J. Redish. 1980. *Guidelines for Document Designers.* Washington, DC: American Institute for Research.

Ferguson, Charles A. 1964. "Baby Talk in Six Languages." In John J. Gumperz and Dell Hymes, eds., *The Ethnography of Communication.* Special Issue of *American Anthropologist* 66:103–14.

———. 1976. "The Collect as a Form of Discourse." In Samarin, ed. Pp. 101–9.

———. 1977. "Baby Talk as a Simplified Register." In C. E. Snow and C. A. Ferguson, eds., *Talking to Children.* Cambridge: Cambridge University Press. Pp. 209–35.

———. 1983. "Sports Announcer Talk: Syntactic Aspects of Register Variation." *Language in Society* 12:153–72.

Ferrara, Kathleen, Hans Brunner, and Greg Whittemore. 1991. "Interactive Written Discourse as an Emergent Register." *Written Communication* 8:8–34.

Finegan, Edward. 1982. "Form and Function in Testament Language." In Di Pietro, ed. Pp. 113–20.

———. 1987. "The Linguistic Forms of Prestige." In Phillip Boardman, ed., *The Miracle of Language: Essays in Honor of Charlton Laird.* Reno: University of Nevada Press. Pp. 146–61.

Finegan, Edward, and Douglas Biber. 1986. "Two Dimensions of Linguistic Complexity in English." In Connor-Linton et al., eds. 1986. Pp. 1–24.

Fischer, John. 1958. "Social Influences on the Choice of a Linguistic Variant." *Word* 14:47–56.

Fisher, Sue, and Alexandra Dundas Todd, eds. 1983. *The Social Organization of Doctor-Patient Communication.* Washington DC: Center for Applied Linguistics.

———, eds. 1986. *Discourse and Institutional Authority: Medicine, Education, and the Law.* Norwood, NJ: Ablex.

Fishman, Andrea. 1991. "Because This Is Who We Are: Writing in the Amish Community." In David Barton and Roz Ivanic, eds., *Writing in the Community.* Newbury Park, CA: Sage. Pp. 14–37.

Fitzgerald, J., and D. Speigel. 1986. "Textual Cohesion and Coherence in Children's Writing." *Research in the Teaching of English* 20:263–80.

Forth, Gregory. 1988. "Fashioned Speech, Full Communication: Aspects of Eastern Sumbanese Ritual Language." In James J. Fox, ed. Pp. 129–60.

Foster, Michele. 1989. "'It's Cookin' Now': A Performance Analysis of the Speech Events of a Black Teacher in an Urban Community College." *Language in Society* 18:1–29.

Fowler, Roger. 1991. *Language in the News: Discourse and Ideology in the Press.* London: Routledge.

Fox, Barbara A. 1987a. *Discourse Structure and Anaphora: Written and Conversational English.* Cambridge: Cambridge University Press.

———. 1987b. "Anaphora in Popular Written English Narratives." In Russell S. Tomlin, ed., *Coherence and Grounding in Discourse.* Amsterdam: Benjamins. Pp. 157–74.

Fox, Barbara A., and Sandra A. Thompson. 1990. "A Discourse Explanation of the Grammar of Relative Clauses in English Conversation." *Language* 66:297–316.

Fox, James J., ed. 1988. *To Speak in Pairs: Essays on the Ritual Language of Eastern Indonesia.* Cambridge: Cambridge University Press.

Francis, W. Nelson, and Henry Kučera. 1982. *Frequency Analysis of English Usage: Lexicon and Grammar.* Boston: Houghton Mifflin.

Frankel, Richard, ed. 1984. Special Invited Issue on "Physicians and Patients in Social Interaction: Medical Encounters as a Discourse Process." *Discourse Processes* 7.2.

Fraurud, Kari. 1988. "Pronoun Resolution in Unrestricted Text." *Nordic Journal of Linguistics* 11:47–68.

———. 1990. "Definiteness and the Processing of Noun Phrases in Natural Discourse." *Journal of Semantics* 7:395–433.

Freed, Richard C., and Glenn J. Broadhead. 1986. "Discourse Communities, Sacred Texts, and Institutional Norms." *College Composition and Communication* 38:154–165.

Freeman, Sarah H., and Monica S. Heller, eds. 1987. Special issue on "Medical Discourse." *Text* 7.1.

Geis, Michael L. 1982. *The Language of Television Advertising.* New York: Academic Press.

———. 1987a. *The Language of Politics.* New York: Springer-Verlag.

———. 1987b. "Language and Media." *Annual Review of Applied Linguistics* 12:64–73.

Ghadessy, Mohsen. 1988a. "The Language of Written Sports Commentary: Soccer—a Description." In Ghadessy, ed. Pp. 17–51.

———, ed. 1988b. *Registers of Written English: Situational Factors and Linguistic Features.* London: Pinter.

Gibbon, Dafydd. 1981. "Idiomaticity and Functional Variation: A Case Study of International Amateur Radio Talk." *Language in Society* 10:21–42.

———. 1985. "Context and Variation in Two-Way Radio Discourse." *Discourse Processes* 8:395–419.

Gibson, James W., C. R. Gruner, R. J. Kibler, and F. J. Kelly. 1966. "A Quantitative Examination of Differences and Similarities in Written and Spoken Messages." *Speech Monographs* 33:444–51.

Givón, Talmy, ed. 1983. *Topic Continuity in Discourse.* Philadelphia: Benjamins.

Golub, L. S. 1969. "Linguistic Structures in Students' Oral and Written Discourse." *Research in the Teaching of English* 3:70–85.

Gordon, Ian A. 1966. *The Movement of English Prose.* Bloomington: Indiana University Press.

Grabe, William. 1987. "Contrastive Rhetoric and Text-Type Research." In Ulla Connor and Robert B. Kaplan, eds., *Writing Across Languages: Analysis of L2 Text.* Reading, MA: Addison-Wesley. Pp. 115–37.

———. 1990. "Current Developments in Written Discourse Analysis." *Lenguas Modernas* 17:35–56.

Greatbatch, David. 1988. "A Turn-Taking System for British News Interviews." *Language in Society* 17:401–30.

Green, Georgia M. 1982. "Colloquial and Literary Uses of Inversions." In Tannen, ed. Pp. 119–53.

Grishman, Ralph, and Richard Kittredge, eds. 1986. *Analyzing Language in Restricted Domains: Sublanguage Description and Processing.* Hillsdale, NJ: Lawrence Erlbaum.

Gross, Alan G. 1990. *The Rhetoric of Science.* Cambridge, MA: Harvard University Press.

Gumperz, John J., Hannah Kaltman, and Mary Catherine O'Connor. 1984. "Cohesion in Spoken and Written Discourse." In Tannen, ed. Pp. 3–20.

Gustaffson, Marita. 1984. "The Syntactic Features of Binomial Expressions in Legal English." *Text* 4:123–41.

Haarman, Harald. 1984. "The Role of Ethnocultural Stereotypes and Foreign Languages in Japanese Commercials." *International Journal of the Sociology of Language* 50:101–21.

Halliday, M. A. K. 1979. "Differences Between Spoken and Written Language: Some Implications for Literacy Teaching." In Glenda Page, John Elkins, and Barrie O'Connor, eds., *Communication Through Reading: Proceedings of the 4th Australian Reading Conference,* Vol. 2. Adelaide: Australian Reading Association. Pp. 37–52.

———. 1985. *An Introduction to Functional Grammar.* London: Edward Arnold.

———. 1988. "On the Language of Physical Science." In Ghadessy, ed. Pp. 162–78.

———. 1989. *Spoken and Written Language.* Oxford: Oxford University Press.

Halliday, M. A. K., and Ruqaiya Hasan. 1976. *Cohesion in English.* London: Longman.

———. 1989. *Language Context, and Text: Aspects of Language in a Social-Semiotic Perspective.* Oxford: Oxford University Press.

Halpern, Jeanne W. 1984. "Differences Between Speaking and Writing and Their Implications for Teaching." *College Composition and Communication* 35:345–57.

Hared, Mohamed. 1992. *Modernization and Standardization in Somali Press Writing.* Ph.D. Dissertation, University of Southern California.

Harris, Mary M. 1977. "Oral and Written Syntax Attainment of Second Graders." *Research in the Teaching of English* 11:117–32.

Harris, Sandra. 1984. "Questions as a Mode of Control in Magistrates' Courts." *International Journal of the Sociology of Language* 49:5–27.

Hasan, Ruqaiya. 1989. "Semantic Variation and Sociolinguistics." *Australian Journal of Linguistics* 9:221–75.

Heath, Shirley Brice. 1978. *Teacher Talk: Language in the Classroom.* Washington, DC: Center for Applied Linguistics.

———. 1983. *Ways With Words.* Cambridge: Cambridge University Press.

Henzl, Vera M. 1974. "Linguistic Register of Foreign Language Instruction." *Language Learning* 23:207–22.

———. 1979. "Foreign Talk in the Classroom." *IRAL* 17:159–67.

Hermeren, Lars. 1986. "Modalities in Spoken and Written English: An Inventory of Forms." In Tottie and Bäcklund, eds. Pp. 57–92.

Heslot, J. 1982. "Tense and Other Indexical Markers in the Typology of Scientific Texts in English." In J. Hoedt et al., eds., *Pragmatics and LSP.* Copenhagen: School of Economics. Pp. 83–103.

Hillocks, George. 1986. *Research on Written Composition.* Urbana, IL: ERIC Clearinghouse on Reading and Communication Skills.

Hiltunen, Risto. 1984. "The Type and Structure of Clausal Embedding in Legal English." *Text* 4:107–21.

————. 1990. *Chapters on Legal English: Aspects Past and Present of the Language of the Law. (Annals of the Finnish Academy of Science ser. B 251)*. Helsinki: Finnish Academy of Science.

Hindle, Donald M. 1979. *The Social and Situational Conditioning of Phonetic Variation*. Ph.D. Dissertation, University of Pennsylvania.

Hinds, John. 1980. "Japanese Expository Prose." *Papers in Linguistics* 13:117–58.

Hoyle, Susan M. 1989. "Form and Footing in Boys' Sportscasting." *Text* 9:153–73.

Hu, Zhuang-Lin. 1984. "Differences in Mode." *Journal of Pragmatics* 8:595–606.

Huckin, Thomas N. 1987. "Surprise Value in Scientific Discourse." Paper Presented at College Composition and Communication Conference. Atlanta, GA.

————, Elizabeth H. Curtain, and Debra Graham. 1986. "Prescriptive Linguistics and Plain English: The Case of 'Whiz-Deletions.'" *Visible Language* 20:174–87.

Huckin, Thomas N., and Linda Hutz Pesante. 1988. "Existential There." *Written Communication* 5:368–91.

Hurd, Conrad. 1979. "A Study of Oral Versus Written Nasioi Discourse." *Read* 14:84–86.

Irvine, Judith. 1979. "Formality and Informality in Communicative Events." In John Baugh and Joel Sherzer, eds., *Language in Use: Readings in Sociolinguistics*. Englewood Cliffs, NJ: Prentice-Hall. Pp. 211–28.

Janda, Richard D. 1985. "Note-Taking as a Simplified Register." *Discourse Processes* 8:437–54.

Johansson, Stig, and Knut Hofland. 1989. *Frequency Analysis of English Vocabulary and Grammar, Based on the LOB Corpus*. 2 vols. Oxford: Clarendon.

Jones, Larry B., and Linda K. Jones. 1985. "Discourse Functions of Five English Sentence Types." *Word* 36:1–21.

Joos, Martin. 1961. *The Five Clocks*. New York: Harcourt.

Kaplan, Robert B. 1966. "Cultural Thought Patterns in Intercultural Education." *Language Learning* 16:1–20.

Kemper, Susan. 1987. "Life-Span Changes in Syntactic Complexity." *Journal of Gerontology* 42:323–28.

————. 1990. "Adults' Diaries: Changes Made to Written Narratives Across the Life Span." *Discourse Processes* 31:207–24.

Kim, Yong-Jin. 1990. *Register Variation in Korean: A Corpus-Based Study*. Ph.D. Dissertation. University of Southern California.

Kittredge, Richard, and John Lehrberger, eds. 1982. *Sublanguage: Studies of Language in Restricted Semantic Domains*. Berlin: De Gruyter.

Knorr-Cetina, Karin D. 1981. *The Manufacture of Knowledge*. Oxford: Pergamon.

Kress, Gunther. 1983. "Linguistic and Ideological Transformations in News Reporting." In Howard Davis and Paul Walton, eds., *Language, Image, Media*. London: Basil Blackwell. Pp. 120–38.

————. 1991. "Critical Discourse Analysis." *Annual Review of Applied Linguistics* 11:84–99.

Kroch, Anthony, and Donald M. Hindle. 1982. *A Quantitative Study of the Syntax of Speech and Writing*. (Final Report to the National Institute of Education.)

Kroll, Barbara. 1977. "Ways Communicators Encode Propositions in Spoken and Written English: A Look at Subordination and Coordination." In Elinor O. Keenan and Tina Bennett, eds., *Discourse Across Time and Space. (Southern California Occasional Papers in Linguistics 4)*. Los Angeles: University of Southern California. Pp. 69–108.

Kuiper, Koenraad, and Douglas Haggo. 1984. "Livestock Auctions, Oral Poetry and Ordinary Language." *Language in Society* 13:205–34.

Kuiper, Koenraad, and Frederick Tillis. 1986. "The Chant of the Tobacco Auctioneer." *American Speech* 60:141–49.

Kuiper, Koenraad, and Paddy Austin. 1990. "They're Off and Racing Now: The Speech of the New Zealand Race Caller." In Bell and Holmes, eds. Pp. 195–220.

Kurzon, Dennis. 1985. "Signposts for the Reader: A Corpus-Based Study of Text Deixis." *Text* 5:187–200.

Kytö, Merja. 1986. "On the Use of the Modal Auxiliaries *Can* and *May* in Early American English." In Sankoff, ed. Pp. 123–38.

———. 1991. *Variation and Diachrony, With Early American English in Focus.* Frankfurt: Peter Lang.

———, and Matti Rissanen. 1983. "The Syntactic Study of Early American English: The Variationist at the Mercy of His Corpus?" *Neuphilologische Mitteilungen* 84:470–90.

Labov, William. 1972. *Sociolinguistic Patterns.* Philadelphia: University of Pennsylvania Press.

———. 1984. "Intensity." In Schiffrin, ed. Pp. 43–70.

Lakoff, Robin. 1982. "Persuasive Discourse and Ordinary Conversation, With Examples from Advertising." In Deborah Tannen, ed., *Analyzing Discourse: Text and Talk.* Washington, DC: Georgetown University Press. Pp. 25–42.

Lane, Chris. 1990. "The Sociolinguistics of Questioning in District Court Trials." In Bell and Holmes, eds. Pp. 221–51.

Latour, Bruno, and Steve Woolgar. 1986. *Laboratory Life: The Social Construction of Scientific Facts.* Princeton: Princeton University Press.

Leech, Geoffrey N. 1966. *English in Advertising.* London: Longman.

Leech, Geoffrey N., and Michael H. Short. 1981. *Style in Fiction: A Linguistic Introduction to English Fictional Prose.* London: Longman.

Lemke, Jay L. 1990. *Talking Science: Language, Learning and Values.* Norwood, NJ: Ablex.

Levi, Judith N. 1982. "Linguistics, Language and Law: A Topical Bibliography." Bloomington: Indiana University Linguistics Club.

Li, Charles N., and Sandra A. Thompson. 1982. "The Gulf Between Spoken and Written Language: A Case Study in Chinese." In Tannen, ed. Pp. 77–88.

Liggett, Sarah. 1984. "The Relationship Between Speaking and Writing: An Annotated Bibliography." *College Composition and Communication* 35:334–44.

Long, Michael. 1981a. "Input, Interaction and Second Language Acquisition." *Annals of New York Academy of Sciences* 379:259–78.

———. 1981b. "Questions in Foreigner Talk Discourse." *Language Learning* 31:1–42.

Longe, Victor U. 1985. "Aspects of the Textual Features of Officialese—the Register of Public Administration." *IRAL* 23:301–13.

Luke, Allan. 1988. *Literacy, Textbooks and Ideology.* London: Falmer.

Lux, Paul, and William Grabe. 1991. "Multivariate Approaches to Contrastive Rhetoric." *Lenguas Modernas* 18:133–60.

Lynch, Michael. 1985. *Art and Artifact in Laboratory Science: A Study of Shop Work and Shop Talk in a Research Laboratory.* London: Routledge.

Macaulay, Marcia I. 1990. *Processing Varieties in English: An Examination of Oral and Written Speech Across Genres.* Vancouver: University of British Columbia Press.

Maher, John. 1986. "English for Medical Purposes." *Language Teaching* 19:112–45.

Maher, John, and Denise Rokosz. 1992. "Language Use and the Professions." In William Grabe and Robert B. Kaplan, eds., *Introduction to Applied Linguistics.* Reading, MA: Addison-Wesley. Pp. 231–56.

Mair, Christian. 1990. *Infinitival Complement Clauses in English: A Study of Syntax in Discourse*. Cambridge: Cambridge University Press.

Maley, Yon. 1987. "The Language of Legislation." *Language in Society* 16:25–48.

Mandler, Jean. 1984. *Stories, Scripts, and Scenes: Aspects of Schema Theory*. Hillsdale, NJ: Lawrence Erlbaum.

———. 1987. "On the Psychological Reality of Story Structure." *Discourse Processes* 10:1–29.

Mann, William C., and Sandra A. Thompson. 1988. "Rhetorical Structure Theory: Toward a Functional Theory of Text Organization." *Text* 8:243–81.

Marckworth, Mary L., and William J. Baker. 1974. "A Discriminant Function Analysis of Co-Variation of a Number of Syntactic Devices in Five Prose Genres." *American Journal of Computational Linguistics*, Microfiche 11.

Mardh, Ingrid. 1980. *Headlinese: On the Grammar of English Front Page Headlines*. (*Lund Studies in English 58*). Lund: CWK Gleerup.

Martin, James R. 1985. *Factual Writing: Exploring and Challenging Social Reality*. Oxford: Oxford University Press.

McGinnis, Mary. 1986. "Preachin': A Black Speech Event." In Connor-Linton et al., eds. Pp. 99–124.

Mehan, Hugh. 1979. *Learning Lessons: Social Organization in the Classroom*. Cambridge, MA: Harvard University Press.

Melander, Björn. In press. "Patterns of Content Structure in Swedish LSP Texts." In M. Ehlich and B. Rehbein, eds., *Kommunikation und Institution (Special Issue of LSP Communication/Fachsprachliche Kommunikation)*.

Mellinkoff, David. 1963. *The Language of the Law*. Boston: Little, Brown.

Menn, Lise, and Suzanne Boyce. 1982. "Fundamental Frequency and Discourse Structure." *Language and Speech* 25:341–83.

Merritt, Marilyn. 1976. "On Questions Following Questions in Service Encounters." *Language in Society* 5:315–57.

Meyer, Bonnie J. F. 1975. *The Organization of Prose and Its Effects on Memory*. Amsterdam: North Holland.

———. 1985. "Prose Analysis: Purposes, Procedures, and Problems." In Bruce K. Britton and John B. Black, eds., *Understanding Expository Text: A Theoretical and Practical Handbook for Analyzing Explanatory Text*. Hillsdale, NJ: Lawrence Erlbaum. Pp. 11–64.

Michaels, Sarah. 1981. "Sharing Time: Children's Narrative Styles and Differential Access to Literacy." *Language in Society* 10:423–42.

Miller, Carolyn R., and Jack Selzer. 1985. "Special Topics of Argument in Engineering Reports." In Odell and Goswami, eds. Pp. 309–41.

Mitchell, Henry H. 1970. *Black Preaching*. Philadelphia: JB Lippincott.

Montgomery, Martin. 1988. "D-J Talk." In Nikolas Coupland, ed., *Styles of Discourse*. London: Croom Helm. Pp. 85–104.

Murray, Denise E. 1985. "Composition as Conversation: The Computer Terminal as Medium of Communication." In Odell and Goswami, eds. Pp. 203–27.

———. 1988. "Computer-Mediated Communication: Implications for ESP." *ESP Journal* 7:3–18.

Murray, Thomas E. 1985. "The Language of Singles Bars." *American Speech* 60:17–30.

Myers, Greg. 1989. "The Pragmatics of Politeness in Scientific Articles." *Applied Linguistics* 10:1–35.

———. 1991. "Lexical Cohesion and Specialized Knowledge in Science and Popular Science Texts." *Discourse Processes* 14:1–26.

————. 1992. "'In this Paper we Report . . .': Speech Acts and Scientific Facts." *Journal of Pragmatics* 16:295–313.

Myers, Oliver T., and Rodolfo J. Cortina. 1985. "A Diachronic Study of Chicano Vocabulary." *International Journal of the Sociology of Language* 53:31–41.

Nevalainen, Terttu. 1986. "The Development of Preverbal Only in Early Modern English." In Sankoff, ed. Pp. 111–21.

Nevalainen, Terttu, and Helena Raumolin-Brunberg. 1989. "A Corpus of Early Modern Standard English in a Socio-Historical Perspective." *Neuphilologische Mitteilungen* 90:67–110.

O'Barr, William M. 1982. *Linguistic Evidence: Language, Power, and Strategy in the Courtroom.* New York: Academic Press.

Ochs-Keenan, Elinor. 1973. "A Sliding Sense of Obligatoriness: The Poly-Structure of Malagasy Oratory." *Language in Society* 2:225–43.

Ochs, Elinor. 1979. "Planned and Unplanned Discourse." In Talmy Givón, ed., *Discourse and Syntax.* New York: Academic Press. Pp. 51–80.

Odell, Lee, and Dixie Goswami, eds. 1985. *Writing in Nonacademic Settings.* New York: Guilford.

O'Donnell, Roy C. 1974. "Syntactic Differences Between Speech and Writing." *American Speech* 49:102–10.

O'Donnell, Roy C., W. J. Griffin, and R. C. Norris. 1967. "A Transformational Analysis of Oral and Written Grammatical Structures in the Language of Children in Grades Three, Five, and Seven." *Journal of Educational Research* 61:36–39.

Olson, David R., Nancy Torrance, and Angela Hildyard, eds. 1985. *Literacy, Language, and Learning.* Cambridge: Cambridge University Press.

Pandya, Indubala H. 1977. *English Language in Advertising: A Linguistic Study of Indian Press Advertising.* Delhi: Ajanta Publications.

Patthey, Ghislaine G. 1991. *The Language of Problem Solving in a Computer Lab.* Ph.D. Dissertation. University of Southern California.

Pettinari, Catharine Johnson. 1988. *Task, Talk and Text in the Operating Room: A Study in Medical Discourse.* Norwood, NJ: Ablex.

Philips, Susan U. 1984. "The Social Organization of Questions and Answers in Courtroom Discourse: A Study of Changes of Plea in an Arizona Court." *Text* 4:225–48.

————. 1985. "Strategies of Clarification in Judges' Use of Language: From the Written to the Spoken." *Discourse Processes* 8:421–36.

Poole, Deborah. 1990. "Contextualizing IRE in an Eighth-Grade Quiz Review." *Linguistics and Education* 1:185–211.

————. 1991. "Discourse Analysis in Ethnographic Research." *Annual Review of Applied Linguistics* 11:42–56.

Poole, Millicent E., and T. W. Field. 1976. "A Comparison of Oral and Written Code Elaboration." *Language and Speech* 19:305–11.

Pratt, Mary Louise. 1977. *Toward a Speech Act Theory of Literary Discourse.* Bloomington: Indiana University Press.

Price, Gayle B., and Richard L. Graves. 1980. "Sex Differences in Syntax and Usage in Oral and Written Language." *Research in the Teaching of English* 14:147–53.

Prince, Ellen F. 1978. "A Comparison of Wh-Clefts and It-Clefts in Discourse." *Language* 54:883–906.

————. 1981. "Toward a Taxonomy of Given-New Information." In Peter Cole, ed., *Radical Pragmatics.* New York: Academic Press. Pp. 223–55.

Pugh, A. K., and Jan M. Ulijn, eds. 1984. *Reading for Professional Purposes.* London: Heinemann.

Purcell-Gates, Victoria. 1988. "Lexical and Syntactic Knowledge of Written Narrative Held by Well-Read-To Kindergartners and Second Graders." *Research in the Teaching of English* 22:128–60.

Purves, Alan C., ed. 1988. *Writing Across Languages and Cultures: Issues in Contrastive Rhetoric.* Newbury Park, CA: Sage.

Redeker, Gisela. 1984. "On Differences Between Spoken and Written Language." *Discourse Processes* 7:43–55.

Redish, Janet C. 1983. "The Language of Bureaucracy." In R. W. Bailey and R. M. Fosheim, eds., *Literacy for Life: The Demand for Reading and Writing.* New York: Modern Language Association. Pp. 151–74.

Reichman-Adar, Rachel. 1984. "Technical Discourse: The Present Progressive Tense, the Deictic 'That,' and Pronominalization." *Discourse Processes* 7:337–69.

Rissanen, Matti. 1986. "Variation and the Study of English Historical Syntax." In Sankoff, ed. Pp. 97–109.

Robinson, W. P. 1965. "The Elaborated Code in Working Class Language." *Language and Speech* 8:243–52.

Roeh, Itzhak, and Raphael Nir. 1990. "Speech Presentation in the Israel Radio News: Ideological Constraints and Rhetorical Strategies." *Text* 10:225–44.

Romaine, Suzanne. 1980. "The Relative Clause Marker in Scots English: Diffusion, Complexity, and Style as Dimensions of Syntactic Change." *Language in Society* 9:221–47.

———. 1982. *Socio-Historical Linguistics: Its Status and Methodology.* Cambridge: Cambridge University Press.

Rubin, Andee. 1980. "A Theoretical Taxonomy of the Differences Between Oral and Written Language." In Rand J. Spiro, Bertram C. Bruce, and William F. Brewer, eds., *Theoretical Issues in Reading Comprehension: Perspectives from Cognitive Psychology, Linguistics, Artificial Intelligence, and Education.* Hillsdale, NJ: Lawrence Erlbaum. Pp. 411–38.

Rushton, James, and George Young. 1975. "Context and Complexity in Working Class Language." *Language and Speech* 18:366–87.

Salager, Françoise. 1983. "The Lexis of Fundamental Medical English: Classificatory Framework and Rhetorical Function (a Statistical Approach)." *Reading in a Foreign Language* 1:54–64.

———. 1984. "Compound Nominal Phrases in Scientific-Technical Literature: Proportion and Rationale." In Pugh and Ulijn, eds. Pp. 136–45.

Salager-Meyer, Françoise, Gerard Defives, Cathy Jensen, and Maria De Filipis. 1989. "Principal Component Analysis and Medical English Discourse: An Investigation into Genre Analysis." *System* 17:21–34.

Samarin, William, ed. 1976. *Language in Religious Practice.* Rowley, MA: Newbury House.

Sankoff, David, ed. 1986. *Diversity and Diachrony.* Amsterdam: Benjamins.

Schafer, John C. 1981. "The Linguistic Analysis of Spoken and Written Texts." In Barry M. Kroll and Roberta J. Vann, eds., *Exploring Speaking-Writing Relationships: Connections and Contrasts.* Urbana, IL: National Council of Teachers of English. Pp. 1–31.

Schiffrin, Deborah. 1981. "Tense Variation in Narrative." *Language* 57:45–62.

———, ed. 1984. *Meaning, Form, and Use in Context: Linguistic Applications.* Washington, DC: Georgetown University Press.

———. 1985a. "Conversational Coherence: The Role of *Well.*" *Language* 61:640–67.

———. 1985b. "Multiple Constraints on Discourse Options: A Quantitative Analysis of Causal Sequences." *Discourse Processes* 8:281–303.

———. 1987. *Discourse Markers.* Cambridge: Cambridge University Press.

Schmidt, Rosemarie, and Joseph F. Kess. 1985. "Persuasive Language in the Television Medium." *Journal of Pragmatics* 9:287–308.

Schröder, H. 1991. "Linguistic and Text-Theoretical Research on Language for Specific Purposes." In H. Schröder, ed., *Subject-oriented Texts*. Berlin: Mouton de Gruyter. Pp. 1–48.

Scollon, Ron, and Suzanne B. K. Scollon. 1981. *Narrative, Literacy and Face in Interethnic Communication*. Norwood, NJ: Ablex.

Sherzer, J. 1989. "Namakke, Sunmakke, Hormakke: Three Types of Cuna Speech Event." In Richard Bauman and Joel Sherzer, eds. Pp. 263–82.

Shuy, Roger. 1987. "Language and the Law." *Annual Review of Applied Linguistics* 7:50–63.

Smith, E. L., Jr. 1985. "Functional Types of Scientific Prose." In W. S. Greaves and J. D. Benson, eds., *Systemic Perspectives on Discourse*, Vol. 2. Norwood, NJ: Ablex. Pp. 241–57.

Smith, Raoul, and William J. Frawley. 1983. "Conjunctive Cohesion in Four English Genres." *Text* 3:347–74.

Snow, Catherine E., Fredi Shonkoff, Kathie Lee, and Harry Levin. 1986. "Learning to Play Doctor: Effects of Sex, Age, and Experience in Hospital." *Discourse Processes* 9:461–73.

Stenström, Anna-Brita. 1986. "What Does *Really* Really Do? Strategies in Speech and Writing." In Tottie and Bäcklund, eds. Pp. 149–64.

Svartvik, Jan, ed. 1990. *The London-Lund Corpus of Spoken English: Description and Research. (Lund Studies in English 82)*. Lund: Lund University Press.

Swales, John. 1981. *Aspects of Article Introductions*. (Aston ESP Research Reports 1).

———. 1990. *Genre Analysis: English in Academic and Research Settings*. Cambridge: Cambridge University Press.

———. 1991. "Discourse Analysis in Professional Contexts." *Annual Review of Applied Linguistics* 11:103–14.

Tannen, Deborah. 1982. "Oral and Literate Strategies in Spoken and Written Narratives." *Language* 58:1–21.

———, ed. 1982. *Spoken and Written Language: Exploring Orality and Literacy*. Norwood, NJ: Ablex.

———. 1984a. *Conversational Style: Analyzing Talk Among Friends*. Norwood, NJ: Ablex.

———. 1984b. "Spoken and Written Narrative in English and Greek." In Tannen, ed. Pp. 21–41.

———, ed. 1984c. *Coherence in Spoken and Written Discourse*. Norwood, NJ: Ablex.

———. 1989. *Talking Voices: Repetition, Dialogue, and Imagery in Conversational Discourse*. Cambridge: Cambridge University Press.

Tannen, Deborah, and Cynthia Wallat. 1982. "A Sociolinguistic Analysis of Multiple Demands on Pediatricians in Doctor/Mother Interaction." In Di Pietro, ed. Pp. 39–50.

Tarone, Elaine, Sharon Dwyer, Susan Gillette, and Vincent Icke. 1981. "On the Use of the Passive in Two Astrophysics Journal Papers." *ESP Journal* 1:123–40.

Taylor, Charles V. 1983. "Structure and Theme in Printed School Text." *Text* 3:197–228.

Thavenius, Cecilia. 1983. *Referential Pronouns in English Conversation. (Lund Studies in English 64)*. Lund: CWK Gleerup.

Thompson, Sandra A. 1983. "Grammar and Discourse: The English Detached Participial Clause." In Flora Klein-Andreu, ed., *Discourse Perspectives on Syntax*. New York: Academic Press. Pp. 43–65.

———. 1984. "'Subordination' in Formal and Informal Discourse." In Schiffrin, ed. Pp. 85–94.

———. 1985. "Grammar and Written Discourse: Initial vs. Final Purpose Clauses in English." *Text* 5:55–84.

Todd, Loreto, and W. R. O'Donnell. 1980. *Variety in Contemporary English.* London: George Allen & Unwin.

Toolan, Michael J. 1990. *The Stylistics of Fiction: A Literary-Linguistic Approach.* London: Routledge.

Tottie, Gunnel. 1981. "Negation and Discourse Strategy in Spoken and Written English." In H. Cedergren and D. Sankoff, eds., *Variation Omnibus.* Edmonton, Alberta: Linguistic Research. Pp. 271–84.

———. 1983. *Much Ado About Not and Nothing: A Study of the Variation Between Analytic and Synthetic Negation in Contemporary American English.* Lund: CWK Gleerup.

———. 1985. "The Negation of Epistemic Necessity in Present-Day British and American English." *English World-Wide* 6:87–116.

———. 1986. "The Importance of Being Adverbial: Focusing and Contingency Adverbials in Spoken and Written English." In Tottie and Bäcklund, eds. Pp. 93–118.

———. 1991. *Negation in English Speech and Writing: A Study in Variation.* San Diego: Academic.

Tottie, Gunnel, and Ingegerd Bäcklund, eds. 1986. *English in Speech and Writing: A Symposium. (Studia Anglistica Upsaliensia 60).* Stockholm: Almqvist and Wiksell.

Tottie, Gunnel, and Gerd Övergaard. 1984. "The Author's Would: A Feature of American English." *Studia Linguistica* 38:148–65.

Vallins, G. H. 1956. *The Pattern of English.* London: Andre Deutsch.

Van den Broeck, Jef. 1977. "Class Differences in Syntactic Complexity in the Flemish Town of Maaseik." *Language in Society* 6:149–81.

Van Dijk, Teun A. 1988. *News as Discourse.* Hillsdale, NJ: Lawrence Erlbaum.

Van Dijk, Teun A., and Walter Kintsch. 1983. *Strategies of Discourse Comprehension.* New York: Academic Press.

Van Naerssen, Margaret M. 1985. "Medical Records: One Variation of Physicians' Language." *International Journal of the Sociology of Language* 51:43–73.

Van Naerssen, Margaret M., and Robert B. Kaplan. 1987. "Language and Science." *Annual Review of Applied Linguistics* 7:86–104.

Ventola, Eija. 1983. "Contrasting Schematic Structures in Service Encounters." *Applied Linguistics* 4:243–48.

Wallace, William D. 1981. "How Registers Register: Toward the Analysis of Language Use." *IRAL* 19:267–86.

Ward, Gregory L. 1990. "The Discourse Functions of VP Preposing." *Language* 66:742–63.

Webster, Jonathan. 1988. "The Language of Religion: A Sociolinguistic Perspective." In Ghadessy, ed. Pp. 85–108.

Weiner, E. Judith, and William Labov. 1983. "Constraints on the Agentless Passive." *Journal of Linguistics* 19:29–58.

Weissberg, Robert C. 1984. "Given and New: Paragraph Development Models from Scientific English." *TESOL Quarterly* 18:485–99.

West, G. K. 1980. "That-Nominal Constructions in Traditional Rhetorical Divisions of Scientific Research Papers." *TESOL Quarterly* 14:485–500.

Yamada, Haru. 1992. *American and Japanese Business Discourse: A Comparison of Interactional Styles.* Norwood, NJ: Ablex.

Zak, Helena, and Tony Dudley-Evans. 1986. "Features of Word Omission and Abbreviation in Telexes." *ESP Journal* 5:59–71.

Zwicky, Ann D., and Arnold M. Zwicky. 1980. "America's National Dish: The Style of Restaurant Menus." *American Speech* 55:83–92.

Printed in the United States
39489LVS00002B/322